Eugene O'Neill

VOLUME II

CRITICAL COMPANION TO

Eugene O'Neill

A Literary Reference to His Life and Work

VOLUME II

ROBERT M. DOWLING

Facts On File
An imprint of Infobase Publishing

Critical Companion to Eugene O'Neill:
A Literary Reference to His Life and Work

Facts On File, Inc.
An imprint of Infobase Publishing
132 West 31st Street
New York NY 10001

Library of Congress Cataloging-in-Publication Data
Dowling, Robert M., 1970–
Critical companion to Eugene O'Neill : a literary reference to his life and work /
Robert M. Dowling.
2 v. cm.
Includes bibliographical references and index.
ISBN-13: 978-0-8160-6675-9 (acid-free paper)
ISBN-10: 0-8160-6675-2 (acid-free paper) 1. O'Neill, Eugene, 1888-1953—
Criticism and interpretation—Handbooks, manuals, etc. I. Title.
PS3529.N5Z627266 2009
812'.52—dc22   2008024135

Text design by Erika K. Arroyo
Cover design by Cathy Rincon/Takeshi Takahashi

Printed in the United States of America

VB Hermitage 10 9 8 7 6 5 4 3 2 1

This book is printed on acid-free paper and
contains 30 percent postconsumer recycled content.

This project is dedicated to my mother,
Janet B. Kellock

CONTENTS

PART II

Works S–Z

"The Screenews of War"
(completed, 1916;
first published, 2007)

About the time the PROVINCETOWN PLAYERS first discovered Eugene O'Neill in Provincetown, Massachusetts (summer 1916), the amateur playwright probably revised the plot of his early one-act play *The* MOVIE MAN (1914), a vaudeville sketch about American intervention in the Mexican Revolution (1910–19). Soon after, he rewrote it as a short story entitled "The Screenews of War." This work of fiction was presumed lost or destroyed for decades but was published in 2007 by the journal *Resources for American Literary Study*. O'Neill's WORK DIARY includes a section headed "list of all plays ever written by me, including those I later destroyed, giving where and when they were written" (quoted in Floyd 1981, 388). Under 1916, O'Neill lists "'The Movie Man' (Short Story made from play) House, New London" as the final entry for that year (Floyd 1981, 389). The short story is "The Screenews of War" (the title was changed from "The Movie Man" to "Screenews" on the typescript found at the University of Virginia), and the house is MONTE CRISTO COTTAGE in NEW LONDON, CONNECTICUT, where O'Neill's greatest tragedy, LONG DAY'S JOURNEY INTO NIGHT, takes place.

On the journey back to New York City after his triumphant stay in Provincetown in summer 1916, O'Neill stopped at New London to visit with his parents, MARY ELLEN "ELLA" O'NEILL and JAMES O'NEILL, during which the radical journalist JOHN REED's fiancée LOUISE BRYANT, with whom O'Neill was conducting an affair, made a scandalous appearance as well (Sheaffer 360). As he arrived in New York around October 4 (Gelb 580), O'Neill must have written "Screenews" in New London in late September or early October 1916. A 1960 memo by author and O'Neill friend HAROLD DEPOLO tells a great deal about the story's provenance:

> This manuscript of The Screenews of War, with the last page missing, by Eugene G. O'Neill, was given to me in the spring of 1918 at Provincetown, Massachusetts.

We had gone to Provincetown that season, our first one away from the lake, to be near Gene. It was before he had any financial success whatsoever—just prior to his selling his first long play, BEYOND THE HORIZON—and he and AGNES BOULTON, whom he had recently married, were living on the ten dollars a week given Gene by his father. He told me, when he gave me the story, that he had written it several years before and had submitted it to some of the smooth-paper magazines, but that it had been turned down every time with printed rejection slips. Could I possibly try to sell it for him. Whatever we could get for it would be wonderful. I told him that, at least, I could get him readings "right from the stable," with editors who were good friends of mine and with whom I had been dealing for ywar [sic]. Anyway, I sent it to Henry W. Thomas of Street and Smith and Matthew White of Munsey Company. I didn't, alas, sell it—hanged if I know why—and when I broke the bad news to Gene after the second throwdown he grinned and said "To hell with it. Throw it away if you want."

I didn't. I tossed it into a drawer with some other stuff and it has been traveling about with me, in and out of storage, in and out of attics, ever since. There we are.

In both the play *The Movie Man* and "The Screenews of War," a character named General Pancho Gomez, whom O'Neill identifies as the "Commander-in-Chief of the Constitutionalist Army," resembles the true-to-life Mexican revolutionary and former cattle rustler Pancho Villa, though he also approximates Villa's enemy, the military dictator Victoriano Huerta. In 1913, the year before O'Neill composed *The Movie Man*, Villa led a group of mercenaries against Huerta's brutal regime. At first, he sided with the constitutionalist revolutionary Venustiano Carranza, who was elected president of Mexico after the revolution. O'Neill was probably thinking of Carranza as the sympathetic, highly educated character General Fernandez (Floyd 1985, 77n), as after Huerta was deposed in 1914, the year O'Neill wrote the first draft of *The Movie Man,* Villa turned against his former leader.

General Gomez has signed a contract for money and weapons with the fictional Earth Motion Picture Company that stipulates the general must only stage attacks during the day. This was to ensure that his cameraman Sid Brown could film the attacks in camera-friendly light. Gomez has sworn to execute his former commander and political nemesis General Fernandez, who languishes in a jail cell. The story opens with the movie producer Jack Hill engaged in an intimate conversation with the imprisoned Fernandez. O'Neill describes Fernandez, unlike Gomez, as an American Catholic university graduate who speaks proper English and represents an ethically superior counterpoint to the power-hungry Gomez. Hill promises to help Fernandez escape, an assurance he later repeats to the general's charming daughter Anita. When Gomez arrives to execute Fernandez, Hill threatens to cut off Gomez's funding and promises an American military retaliation (predicated on Hollywood's political influence) if he refuses to delay Fernandez's execution and await proper sunlight for his cameraman. The ruse is meant to hold up the execution until General Amayo, Fernandez's ally, can arrive with troops. At the conclusion, the liberator General Amayo rides in to save Fernandez just before Gomez orders his firing squad to shoot him down. Sid Brown's camera is rolling, and Jack Hill's urge to make a dramatic film overwhelms his desire to save Fernandez; he stops the action of the competing forces, barks orders as if on a Hollywood set, and demand that the generals reenact the scene more dramatically. The typescript's last page is missing.

"The Screenews of War" contains much repetition, stilted dialogue, and unconvincing plot twists, but the story remains important as a rare example of political satire by O'Neill. He undoubtedly wrote the piece to make money, but as with all of O'Neill's work, the story behind "Screenews" also reveals a good deal about the playwright's personal life, the development of his career, and the American scene at the time of its composition (see Dowing, passim). In 1913, the radical journalist John Reed reported as a war correspondent on the Mexican Revolution in a widely circulated series for *Metropolitan Magazine.* In all probability, Reed and O'Neill first met in May 1914 at Polly and Louis Holladay's restaurant, Polly's Café, in GREENWICH VILLAGE. At Polly's, Reed recounted his incredible experience working as a war correspondent for the Mexican Revolution. Reed and O'Neill became close friends in summer 1916 in Provincetown, and O'Neill conducted a love affair with Reed's lover, Louise Bryant, whom Reed married in November that year, dramatized in the film *Reds* [1981] with Jack Nicholson as O'Neill, Warren Beatty as Reed, and Diane Keaton as Bryant.

On O'Neill's first night as a potential playwright for the Provincetown Players, Harry Kemp recalled in an April 1930 *Theatre Magazine* article that O'Neill read "a play that was frightfully bad, trite and full of the most preposterous hokum. It was, as I remember, something about an American movie man who financed a Mexican revolution for the sake of filming its battles. One of the scenes depicted the hero's compelling the commanding generals on both sides—both being in his hire—to wage a battle all over again because it had not been fought the way he liked it!" (96). If the story is accurate, and there is little reason to believe that it is not, "Screenews" importantly contains the first plot idea O'Neill ever read to the Provincetown Players. Scholars have assumed that Kemp was referring to *The Movie Man* since it also takes place during the Mexican Revolution, but "Screenews," not the play, shows the hero "commanding generals on both sides . . . to wage a battle all over again because it had not been fought the way he liked it." Since Kemp's article specifies that it was a play, O'Neill most probably revised his 1914 script using the plot we find in "Screenews," then wrote the short story version. This would explain why O'Neill notes *The Movie Man* in his Work Diary as written at the "Fisherman's Shack" in Provincetown in 1916, rather than in New London in 1914, as the copyright date would have us believe.

O'Neill employs a double entendre with his peculiar title that combines the "screen news," or "newsreels" of the early 20th century, to the "screen use of," or "sensational (ab)use of" geopolitical conflict by Hollywood moguls. At the time of Pancho Villa's insurrection, there was, in fact, a fantastic Hollywood deal brokered between Frank M. Thayer of the Mutual Film Corporation and Villa himself. Villa was offered $25,000 and a percentage of the film's profits to allow cameramen to go along with his band on rebel raids against the loyalist Mexican forces. D. W. Griffith, the famous Hollywood filmmaker, was also involved. Villa accepted, and Thayer sent a film crew to shoot the battles. There were some reports that Villa staged battles during the daytime so the cameramen could film them properly, but there is no evidence for this. It was also reported, probably falsely, that at one stage in the filming Villa shelled a hillside stocked mainly with prisoners from the Mexican army, who were filmed being bombarded by Villa's artillery. Entitled *The Life of Villa*, the film was completed, but ownership issues prevented its release (Gelb 429).

BIBLIOGRAPHY

Bogard, Travis. Foreword to *The Unknown O'Neill: Unpublished and Unfamiliar Writings of Eugene O'Neill*. Edited by Travis Bogard. New Haven, Conn.: Yale University Press, 1988, vii–viii.

DePolo, Harold. Typescript of memo dated 1/30/60. New London: Sheaffer-O'Neill Collection, Connecticut College.

Dowling, Robert M. Introduction to "'The Screenews of War': A Previously Unpublished Short Story by Eugene O'Neill." *Resources for American Literary Study* 31 (2007): 169–198.

Floyd, Virginia. *The Plays of Eugene O'Neill: A New Assessment*. New York: Ungar, 1985.

Floyd, Virginia, ed. *Eugene O'Neill at Work: Newly Released Ideas for His Plays*. New York: Ungar, 1981.

Gelb, Arthur, and Barbara Gelb. *O'Neill: Life with Monte Cristo*. New York: Applause Books, 2000.

Kemp, Harry. "Out of Provincetown: A Memoir of Eugene O'Neill." *Theatre Magazine* 51 (April 1930): 22–23. Reprinted in *Conversations with Eugene O'Neill*, edited by Mark W. Estrin, 95–102. Jackson: University of Mississippi Press, 1990.

O'Neill, Eugene. "'The Screenews of War': A Previously Unpublished Short Story by Eugene O'Neill." Edited with an introduction by Robert M. Dowling. *Resources for American Literary Study* 31 (2007): 169–198.

Richter, Robert A. *Eugene O'Neill and Dat Ole Davil Sea: Maritime Influences in the Life and Works of Eugene O'Neill*. Mystic, Conn.: Mystic Seaport, 2004.

Sheaffer, Louis. *O'Neill: Son and Playwright*. Boston: Little, Brown, 1968.

Servitude: A Play in Three Acts (completed, 1914; first produced, 1960)

Eugene O'Neill completed *Servitude*, his second full-length play, in late summer 1914 in NEW LONDON, CONNECTICUT. At the time, he was embroiled in a relationship with BEATRICE ASHE, one of the most passionate romances of his life; Ashe was a partial model for the independent-minded Mrs. Ethel Frazer in the play. The nascent playwright sent his manuscript to George Tyler, a producer and good friend of JAMES O'NEILL's. Tyler only vouchsafed a perfunctory note containing, in his own words, "the usual customary polite remarks about how Gene undoubtedly showed signs of talent" (quoted in Sheaffer 291). The manuscript was returned two years later unwrapped and unread. O'Neill later claimed the play had been destroyed, but he had copyrighted it at the Library of Congress on September 23, 1914, and it reemerged in the unauthorized *Lost Plays of Eugene O'Neill* (1950). *Servitude* was first produced on April 22, 1960, by Tom Del Vecchio in the Skylark Theatre at New York International Airport (now JFK).

Most critics agree with O'Neill critic Virginia Floyd's estimation that "*Servitude* has no merit whatsoever" (84), and that aside from some disturbing discoveries over O'Neill's view of women's roles in marriage, it would have been better left to decompose slowly in Tyler's filing cabinet. Though *Servitude*'s characters and dialogue are wooden and the ending is overwrought and far-fetched, the play is quite funny at parts and includes signature O'Neillian themes: disillusionment, individualism versus conformity, outer masks and inner selves, and the psychological effects of the marital contract.

Along with DAYS WITHOUT END; AH, WILDERNESS!; and (in a far more complex variation) A TOUCH OF THE POET, this play contends, contrary to the bulk of O'Neill's domestic canon, that one must relinquish individual needs to find love.

SYNOPSIS

Act 1

The novelist and playwright David Roylston's study at about 10 o'clock at night in Tarryville-on-Hudson, New York (in real life Tarrytown or Hastings-on-Hudson). Roylston, a celebrated author, is seated at his desk "puzzling over a problem of construction" for his next play (1:240). Benton, the Roylstons' manservant, appears wearing a livery and warns his master that leaving the house windows open at night might attract burglars. "Never mind," Roylston says, "there's nothing much worth the stealing in this house except ideas and the thieves of ideas are not usually housebreakers" (1:237–238). Benton informs him that Alice Roylston, David's wife, has arrived in New York City with their two children and that they are planning to attend the theater. Bored by the news, Roylston orders Benton not to admit a "young lady in question" with whom he has been having an affair, as she is, presumably like all of the women in his life, "becoming a bore" (1:238). The doorbell rings, and Roylston irritably wonders whether it might be the woman "in question." Benton returns and hands him a card from a new admirer whom he describes as "young and pretty." Roylston's libido is sufficiently ignited, and Benton sends her in (1:239).

Mrs. Ethel Frazer enters dressed in a *"plain black dress such as is worn by the poorer class of working women"* (1:239). She introduces herself as having met Roylston briefly at an artist's ball in New York, a lie he accepts out of hand. Roylston's hopeful guess is that she is an aspiring playwright looking for "advice," a catchword that for him evidently means sex as well. Mrs. Frazer is a great enthusiast of his work, in fact, but rather than harboring literary ambitions, she aspires to emulate Roylston's liberated female characters in her actual life. Eight months before the play's action, she left her husband, George Frazer, after attending Roylston's play *Sacrifice* for the 10th time. The play, along with his muckraking exposé of Wall Street entitled

The Street, "awakened" her to the drudgery of her marriage to a Wall Street stockbroker; so she left her husband to pursue her own dreams, just as Roylston's character Mrs. Harding does in *Sacrifice*. She clarifies that she did not leave for another man, but for "an ideal" she learned from Roylston's writing, "the ideal of self-realization, of the duty of the individual to assert its supremacy and demand the freedom necessary for its development" (1:244). She "demands" the author's reassurance that she has chosen "the right path" (1:249), that her turn to a single life of wage labor was not for nothing.

Congratulating her on her resolve, Roylston sententiously assures Mrs. Frazer that she will "achieve a victory well worth the winning" (1:249). He announces suggestively that she has missed the last train, and, as there is no lodging in the area but a disreputable roadhouse, she must stay the night. Demurring at first, she protests that if she were to stay the night with a married man without his wife present, it might cause a scandal. He assures her that neither he nor his wife care about appearances or convention; in fact, he is given (cruelly, we find out later) to reading her the love letters he receives from adoring fans. After arrogantly likening his wife to a housekeeper, he brushes aside the subject of spousal love. "The family relationship was the most important thing in the world for you at the time [before Mrs. Frazer left her husband]. With me it is purely secondary. My work comes first. As long as my home life gives free scope for my creative faculty I will demand nothing further of it" (1:253).

Mrs. Frazer convinces herself, for the moment, that Roylston would not betray his marital contract. Before retiring to the guest room, she confesses that she had known the train schedule before her arrival and would need to stay the night. In the manner of a detective, she wished to determine firsthand whether Roylston was "a real man with the courage of your convictions or just a theorist" (1:254). After she exits, leaving Roylston in a sexually frustrated funk, he takes up his hat, coat, and cane and storms out of the house.

Act 2

The same setting at nine o'clock the following morning. The Roylstons' elderly gardener arrives to discuss reports of burglaries in the area with Benton. Benton points to Mrs. Frazer's hat and insinuates that Mr. Roylston regularly entertains young devotees alone in the house. Mrs. Frazer comes down, and Benton openly conveys the same message to her. His impudence insults her but also makes her reconsider her inflated view of Roylston's character. Mrs. Alice Roylston arrives home early, and Benton shunts Mrs. Frazer into an adjoining room to hide. Mrs. Roylston enters the study and explains that one of the children, seven-year-old Ruth, took ill the night before, so she caught an early train back to Tarryville for an appointment with their family doctor. The children, Davie and Ruth, ask to play outside, and she relents with the outdated advice to "be sure and stay in the sun" (1:260). She dismisses Benton, who exits reluctantly. A few moments later, Mrs. Frazer steps boldly into the room. At the sight of the interloper, *"Mrs. Roylston grows very pale. Her lips tremble and it seems as if she were shrinking up in her chair, becoming small and pitiful"* (1:260).

Mrs. Roylston accuses her of being the author of love letters she discovered on her husband's desk, all from the same woman, and says she knew he was having an affair. Mrs. Frazer attempts in vain to disabuse her of the notion that she is that woman (1:261). Mrs. Roylston thinks she is lying but unaccountably proceeds to relate her history with Roylston: The son of a wealthy businessman, Roylston married Alice to save her honor. She was his father's stenographer, and when the father discovered they were involved, he fired her out of hand; this moved Roylston to act on her behalf and marry her. He was subsequently disinherited, and Mrs. Roylston labored for years to finance Roylston's incipient writing career. She felt he had married the wrong woman and promised herself that she would grant him a divorce, and thus his freedom, after he achieved success. But when his debut play "made a sensation" (1:266), she was pregnant with their first child and could not uphold her unspoken promise. Nevertheless, for over 11 years, she has been "happy in serving him, happy in the knowledge that I have had my little part in helping him to success, happy to be able to shield and protect him" (1:267). Greatly moved by this

speech, Mrs. Frazer exclaims, "How much you have taught me! Happiness, then, means servitude?" "Love means servitude," Mrs. Roylston responds, "and *my* love is my happiness" (1:268). Still in a fit of jealous rage, she refuses to accept Mrs. Frazer's account.

Roylston enters wearing the same clothes from the previous night. Indifferent to his wife's untimely arrival, Roylston acknowledges the impropriety of Mrs. Frazer's visit and entirely misjudges his wife's reaction to it: "Nothing if not compromising. Married man, married lady—not to each other—lonely country house—stormy night—wife returns home unexpectedly the next morning and—does not believe the worst. . . . My dear Alice, you are really the perfect wife" (1:270). Soon enough, he apprehends his mistake but turns the table by condemning his wife for not believing them and for reading his letters without permission. He announces his plans to leave, and Mrs. Roylston begs for forgiveness, but he heartlessly turns his back on her. Mrs. Frazer then rebukes him for his callousness; Mrs. Roylston turns on her and, just before rushing from the room, shouts, "How dare you intercede for me! Don't you know how I hate you!" (1:272).

Act 3

The same setting, with no time passed. Benton enters the room and expresses the gardener's concern that he noticed a man prowling the grounds the night before. Roylston again dismisses the idea of burglars, but Benton suggests that Mrs. Frazer might be involved in a "badger game" (1:273), or a blackmailing scheme against him. "Go to the devil!" Roylston yells, and Benton exits with a smirk. Roylston voices disbelief over his wife's reaction and sardonically mourns the loss of his illusion that his home life was, as he had referred to it in act 1, "pleasant enough" (1:253). Mrs. Frazer's illusion, too, has been shattered: "[y]ou see nothing beyond yourself. You are so preoccupied with the workings of your own brain that your vision of outside things is clouded. . . . Your cruel vanity has torn off the mask" (1:274–275). She now sees Roylston's theory that it is "the duty of the individual to triumph over environment" as purely selfish, an outlook in which "you see yourself as the only individual in the world" (1:275). Evoking the individualist philosophies of FRIEDRICH NIETZSCHE and GEORGE BERNARD SHAW, she declaims prior thoughts of him as "the superman . . . the creator, the maker of new values" (1:275). In patronizing tones, Roylston surrenders to the "superwoman" (1:276).

Mrs. Frazer denounces him for seducing and then casting aside the young woman with whom he was having the affair; this incites a cynical recitation of the standard breakup letter he writes to all hapless women who fall for his charms: "Our love is forbidden by cruel, man-made laws and it is on your frail shoulders their punishment must fall, etc., ad nauseam. . . . Remember in my heart of hearts, my soul of souls, etc., ad lib, your image will remain, the inspiration of my work; that in spirit all my work will be dedicated to you—and so on ad infinitum" (1:278). He further submits that the woman will forever be in his debt, as when she grows old, her romance with a famous author will be, in the mode of a woman whose lover committed suicide for her, "recompense for a double chin" (1:279). Disgusted by this, Mrs. Frazer recounts Mrs. Roylston's story in every detail, and he is instantaneously moved to remorse. Once she concludes the account, he renounces his past abuses against his wife's loyalty and servitude—"I see, I see! Poor Alice! What a woman she is! . . . Lord, what a cad I've been! What a rotten cad!" (1:284). Mrs. Frazer restates Mrs. Roylston's lesson—"Happiness is servitude." "Of course it is!" he cries out in earnest. "Servitude in love, love in servitude! Logos in Pan, Pan in Logos! That is the great secret—and I never knew!" (1:285). When Mrs. Frazer questions what will happen to his Nietzschean/Shavian superman, Roylston responds, "My love will be a superlove worthy of the superman" (1:286). Mrs. Frazer expresses the same attitude about her own marriage and exultantly vows to return to her husband.

Benton enters, flustered, to announce a new arrival. Seconds later, George Frazer furiously pushes past the manservant and draws a revolver from his pocket. Mrs. Frazer convinces him to put down the weapon, which he does. Roylston swears to Frazer he had no relations with his wife and that once he has heard them out, "this ludicrous melo-

drama will end" (1:287); he exits, affronted, out the back door. Frazer confesses to his wife that he hired a detective to spy on her. Knowing of her adoration for Roylston's work, he surmised she would eventually find her way to Tarryville. The two reunite in a loving embrace as Mrs. Roylston reenters with a traveling bag. The Frazers make their apologies and depart in marital bliss.

Roylston enters, ecstatic to see his wife. He explains the whole episode was a misunderstanding, that he had spent the previous night at the roadhouse. Roylston promises that "the future will be all that the past has not been" (1:291). But he questions how she could have lived a life so far removed from the individualist theories of his writing—so purely selfless and forgiving. She responds with the last line of the play: "That was my happiness." He then kisses her "*reverently*" as the curtain falls (1:291).

COMMENTARY

O'Neill's second full-length play, *Servitude* essentially shows us the flip side of marriage from his first, *BREAD AND BUTTER*: If *Bread and Butter* ends with the suicide of a bitter malcontent who sacrificed his individuality and artistic ambitions in the name of conformity in marriage, *Servitude* seems to contend that only through such sacrifice is the revelation of true love possible. The first shows that if one does not follow their own path in the mode of Nietzschean or Shavian individualism, spiritual and physical death will ensue; the second critiques the same philosophy by submitting that when one does so, their hands become, like David Roylston's, "bloody with the human sacrifices he has made" (1:275). Indeed, O'Neill biographer Louis Sheaffer remarks that *Servitude* is a speculative sequel to HENRIK IBSEN's *A Doll's House*—"what happens to a Nora [Mrs. Frazer] after she has slammed the door" on domestic incarceration (285). And one may add that act 4 of *Bread and Butter,* after John Brown relinquishes his dreams for Maud Steele, is what may befall David Roylston after the "happy ending" of *Servitude* (which closely resembles act 3 of *Bread and Butter*). O'Neill critic Doris Alexander asks how O'Neill could have written *Ah, Wilderness!* and *Days Without End*—both plays that accept the status quo in the name of love—if his social philosophy is that "the only solution . . . for mankind is death." She looks back to *Servitude* for "a clue to this riddle" (quoted in Alexander Cargill 403): All three plays demonstrate the fact that "when [O'Neill] sought love, he could see it only in the context of total acceptance, conformity to the status quo that he despised" (405).

In his transformation scene, Roylston exclaims that "the great secret" to his life, and thus to the play itself, is his blending of "Servitude in love, love in servitude! Logos in Pan, Pan in Logos!" (285). This second line is a quote from another Ibsen play, *Emperor and Galilean*, which O'Neill probably borrowed indirectly from George Bernard Shaw's *The Quintessence of Ibsenism*, a book that made an enormous impact on O'Neill's dramatic vision. But O'Neill uses the line for his own purposes, only partially Ibsen's. Ibsen applies it to strike a note of revelation, while the mystic Maximus explains to the Emperor Julian how to bond his pagan, Dionysian worldview with that of Judeo-Christianity. In O'Neill's *Servitude*, Pan, a fertility god, denotes marital love and family, while *logos*, the meaning of all things through language, is meant to correspond with Roylston's art and philosophy. Kurt Eisen explains Roylston's "motto" this way:

> [If] "logos" denotes language, the word, and "pan" signifies a creative life force (as O'Neill would later incorporate it in the person of Dion Anthony in *The Great God Brown*), then this ideal of marriage as the merging of individual selves becomes the paradigm of a truth beyond words, the truth of love itself. (96)

Travis Bogard contends that the result of this "paradigm of truth" is not as sanguine as Eisen might have it, since "the Roylston's must submerge their individualities by an ultimate act of will which is itself a denial of will. . . . Will, however, is antithetical to happiness" (33, 34). (*Will* here is used as Schopenhauer, Shaw, and Ibsen used it, not as a conscious act of deliberation and choice, but as an unconscious life force against which man must struggle for independence.) The use of the Greek god Pan is greatly complicated in O'Neill's later expressionistic play *The*

GREAT GOD BROWN, in which Dion Anthony's Pan-mask attracts women but prohibits mutual understanding; once Dion's mask is removed, his wife Margaret (quite similar in many respects to Mrs. Roylston) is repulsed by the sight of his inner self—the "masochistic, life-denying spirit of Christianity as represented by St. Anthony" (quoted in Clark 160). O'Neill does not take this concept as far in *Servitude*, even though, again, it is explicitly identified as the play's "great secret."

Shaw's chapter on Ibsen's play in *Quintessence* must have been on O'Neill's mind as he wrote *Servitude*. Even the Roylston children, oddly enough, share a hidden connection with the chapter. In it, Shaw discusses the naïveté of literary critics, or "commentators" as he calls them, who presume authors "intend" meaning, rather than allowing meaning to flow through their work organically. He remarks that had some meddling commentator told Ibsen the "meaning" of his thematic progression from play to play, Ibsen would have "repudiated it with as much disgust as a maiden would feel if any one were brutal enough to give her the physiological *rationale* of her dreams of meeting a fairy prince" (28). Shaw's is an offhanded remark, but when the Roylston children voice their desire to play outside, Ruth says, "I'm going to play I'm the Princess in the play last night." Davie, of course, wants to be the dragon, who was, according to Mrs. Roylston, "very, very wicked." Davie responds (like father like son) "tha's why I wanta be him" (1:260). Significantly, when they leave to go outside, Mrs. Roylston warns them to "be sure and stay in the sun" (1:260). In Greek mythology, if Pan was denied the sun, he turned, as Anthony Dion explains in act 2, scene 3 of *The Great God Brown*, "sensitive and self-conscious and proud and revengeful—and became Prince of Darkness" (2:508), essentially Roylston's character—"very, very wicked." Roylston's profession denies him access to the sun, and O'Neill specifies that he only works at night. Hence Roylston's denial of his Pan-self, denoting his wife and children, turned him into the Prince of Darkness.

From the very first, the Roylston character is portrayed as a pompous ass. There is no question O'Neill meant him to be just that, rather than a wish fulfillment for his own life as many critics suggest. The character is entirely ironic, insofar as he is a celebrated author who promotes feminism, class equality, and independent thinking in his work, while at the same time permitting his wife to sacrifice her life for his, treats his manservant with open disdain, and respects no mind other than his own. As a satirical figure, the Roylston character is the best thing about the play; as a convert to "love is servitude," he is its greatest flaw. Given what we know of Roylston's life up to the action of act 3, the transformation scene is truly impossible to imagine. Over the course of his career, he has shown virtually no respect for women save in his work and considers himself the ultimate authority on his own life and the lives of others. The reversal of this sensibility that O'Neill proposes would take years to come about, if it were feasible at all.

As such, much of the criticism of Roylston's character to date—that he is the embodiment of O'Neill's (all too true) personal longing for artistic solitude and wifely servitude—does not entirely hold up. O'Neill obviously recognizes, in this play and *Days Without End* at least, that the one-sided servitude Mrs. Roylston provides her husband is unfairly balanced and precludes any real expression of love on Roylston's part. Thus, for a Shavian "disquisitory" drama, O'Neill is not only concerned with women in the marriage bond but men as well. The play's final message, take it or leave it (O'Neill opted to leave it), is that, as Travis Bogard writes, "marital happiness lies in the placid acceptance of bondage" (32)—a veritable wed*lock*.

Like so many early O'Neill plays, *Servitude* is a draft of one of his later masterpieces—in this case, *A Touch of the Poet* even more so than *Days Without End* or even WELDED, a full-length play about his marriage to AGNES BOULTON. In *Poet*, Con and Nora Melody play out the Roylstons' conflict to a somewhat more believable, far more tragic, and imminently more satisfying end. Though Con ultimately rejects his British superman self for his IRISH "bogtrotter" self after Nora had slaved in servitude to protect the first for decades, the leveled playing ground in marriage they achieve will furnish the Melodys with inner peace, if not the spiritual ascendance the Roylstons anticipate.

CHARACTERS

Benton David Roylston's discreet but cynical valet. O'Neill describes Benton, who has served David Roylston since Roylston's childhood, as *"fifty-five, clean-shaven, discreetly soft-spoken. One of his eyes is badly crossed giving him a look of sly villainy quite out of keeping with his placid temperament"* (1:237). Benton adds a comic depth to the plot, as he is aware from the outset that his employer ironically abuses women and servants while at the same time working as a celebrated author of feminist, anticapitalist, individualist plays and novels.

Frazer, Ethel A paradigm, more than a fully developed character, of George Bernard Shaw's and the modernist movement's cult of New Womanhood. Mrs. Frazer was inspired to leave her husband, the Wall Street broker George Frazer, by David Roylston's play *Sacrifice* and his exposé *The Street*. "A tall, strikingly beautiful woman about twenty-eight years old" (1:239), Mrs. Frazer visits Roylston's house one night to seek reassurance that she has taken the right step by pursuing personal individuation. The following morning, when Alice Roylston unexpectedly appears at the house and finds Mrs. Frazer in her husband's study, she exposits on the sacrifices she has made for her husband and convinces Mrs. Frazer that "love means servitude" (1:268). Mrs. Frazer then presents this life lesson to Roylston, who accepts it and exchanges that worldview for his previous egoism. O'Neill BIOGRAPHERS Arthur and Barbara Gelb and Louis Sheaffer posit that O'Neill's girlfriend of the time, BEATRICE ASHE, was the likely model for Mrs. Frazer: The Gelbs characterize Ashe as having both "beauty and eagerness to absorb an artist's ideals"; more pointedly, O'Neill "constantly urged Beatrice Ashe not to be governed by her parents but to lead her own life, to be a free independent soul" (444). In fact, like Mrs. Frazer to Roylston, she was more than he bargained for, as she rejected O'Neill on the grounds that she felt he wanted a woman "content to place her own desires and needs after his" (Sheaffer 288).

Frazer, George A Wall Street broker and Alice Frazer's husband. At the end of act 3, Frazer, suffering from a nervous breakdown after Mrs. Frazer left him eight months prior to the play's action, hunts his wife down at Tarryville and accosts David Roylston in his study, where he looks *"haggard and shows plainly the traces of deep-rooted grief and anxiety with their consequent sleepless nights"* (1:286). Frazer draws a revolver with the intention of murdering Roylston, presumably for alienation of affection, but Mrs. Frazer talks him out of it and admits she made a great mistake by leaving him. According to Mrs. Frazer in act 1, her husband "never could see his business in all its hideousness as I came to see it, and I don't think he wore a mask just for my benefit; but you never can tell" (1:243). Nevertheless, by act 3 she has accepted what was previously repugnant to her about her husband and pledged her undying love to him. Unlike most of O'Neill's businessmen characters—Sam Evans from STRANGE INTERLUDE or William Brown from *The Great God Brown,* for instance—O'Neill portrays Frazer as a victim of individualism rather than a destructive harbinger of materialism and conformity.

Roylston, Alice   The long-suffering wife of David Roylston who embodies O'Neill's ideal woman, as he told Agnes Boulton cruelly in the first days of courtship—"mistress, wife, mother, and valet" (quoted in Boulton 63). Mrs. Roylston is *"a pretty woman of thirty or so, with a mass of light curly brown hair, big thoughtful eyes, rosy complexion, tiny hands and feet, and a slight girlish figure"* (1:259). This extreme femininity in her physical description is compounded by a servile attitude toward her husband, David Roylston. Travis Bogard aptly characterizes her as "Patience's monument" (32). Mrs. Roylston was Roylston's father's stenographer before they became involved, and once they did, she was fired. Soon after, Roylston married her, and she spent the next 11 years catering to his needs as an artist. Thinking he had married the wrong woman, Mrs. Roylston planned to grant her husband a divorce once his career got off the ground. When he did write a hit play, she was pregnant with their first child, Davie, and remained in the marriage. She knew he conducted affairs with other women, which tortured her, but she was determined to allow her husband the utmost

freedom, though her life was bound in servitude to him. When she discovers the wayward Mrs. Ethel Frazer in her husband's study, she recounts her history with Roylston and declares her life philosophy that "love means servitude" (1:268). When Mrs. Frazer relays this message to Roylston, he implausibly renounces his past abuse and accepts that life lesson as well.

Roylston, David   A successful playwright and author who, before the play's action, wrote about women's liberation in the mode of Henrik Ibsen yet treated his long-suffering wife's servitude to him and his art as a matter of course. Taken as a whole, his work argues, along with many modernist thinkers of the era—George Bernard Shaw, Friedrich Nietzsche, and Henrik Ibsen, among others—that "it is the duty of the individual to triumph over environment" (1:275). Roylston is clearly an early avatar of the playwright himself, having, as O'Neill did at the time of composition, *"large handsome features, a strong, ironical mouth half-hidden by a black mustache, and keenly-intelligent dark eyes"* (1:237). Though unlike the Poet in FOG or John Brown in *Bread and Butter,* Roylston is not a romantic portrait of artistic nonconformity. Roylston is the son of a wealthy businessman who disinherits him after discovering his son is having a sexual relationship with his stenographer, the future Mrs. Alice Roylston. He marries her out of love and honor but soon tires of her, though she labored for years to finance his artistic career. Along the way, Roylston, an extreme sexist, conducted many affairs with female devotees, always discarding them once they had fallen in love with him. When Mrs. Ethel Frazer comes to visit his home in Tarryville with the intention of conferring with Roylston over her declaration of New Womanhood, she has a confrontation with Mrs. Roylston that ends in her adopting the coda that "love is servitude" (1:267). She then implausibly transforms Roylston from a sexist egotist into a loving husband and father.

Roylston, Davie   Alice and David Roylston's son. Davie is nine years old, and his conception prevented Mrs. Roylston from carrying through with her plan to divorce her husband after financing his career in order to grant him freedom. O'Neill describes Davie as, along with his sister Ruth, "healthy, noisy, delightful" (1:259). Before going outside to play in the beginning of act 2, he informs his mother that he will play the dragon from the show they saw the previous night because, as his mother points out, the dragon was "very, very wicked" (1:260). Boys will be boys. Mrs. Roylston instructs him and his sister to "be sure and stay in the sun" (1:260), a clue that they might be associated with the Pan-god Roylston evokes in his transformation scene; in Greek mythology, if Pan was denied the sun, he turned into a prince of darkness.

Roylston, Ruth   Alice and David Roylston's daughter. O'Neill describes Ruth as, along with her brother Davie, "healthy, noisy, delightful" (1:259). Before going outside to play in the beginning of act 2, she informs her mother that she will play the princess from the show they saw the previous night. Girls will be girls. Mrs. Roylston instructs her and her brother to "be sure and stay in the sun" (1:260), a clue that they might be associated with the Pan-god Roylston evokes in his transformation scene; in Greek mythology, if Pan was denied the sun, he turned into a prince of darkness.

Weson   Alice and David Roylston's loose-lipped gardener. He is *"an old withered man with a drooping gray mustache stained yellow by tobacco juice"* (1:256). The Roylstons' valet Benton shows Weson Ethel Frazer's hat; the valet begins to gossip that she is one of many ladies who have stayed the night without Mrs. Roylston's knowledge, but he thinks better of it since Weson is "an old scandalmonger" (1:257). Weson spots George Frazer's detective wandering the grounds to spy on Mrs. Frazer and mistakenly believes he is a burglar.

BIBLIOGRAPHY

Alexander, Doris M. "Eugene O'Neill as Social Critic." In *O'Neill and His Plays*, edited by Oscar Cargill et al. New York: New York University Press, 1961.

Bogard, Travis. *Contour in Time: The Plays of Eugene O'Neill*. Rev. ed. New York: Oxford University Press, 1988.

Boulton, Agnes. *Part of a Long Story: Eugene O'Neill as a Young Man in Love*. Garden City, N.Y.: Doubleday & Company, 1958.

Clark, Bennett. *Eugene O'Neill: The Man and His Plays*. Rev. ed. New York: Dover, 1947.

Eisen, Kurt. *The Inner Strength of Opposites: O'Neill's Novelistic Drama and the Melodramatic Imagination*. Athens: University of Georgia Press, 1994.

Floyd, Virginia. *The Plays of Eugene O'Neill: A New Assessment*. New York: Ungar, 1985.

Gelb, Arthur, and Barbara Gelb. *O'Neill: Life with Monte Cristo*. New York: Applause Books, 2000.

Shaw, George Bernard. *The Quintessence of Ibsenism*. 1891. Reprint, New York: Dover Publications, 1994.

Sheaffer, Louis. *O'Neill, Son and Playwright*. Boston: Little, Brown, 1968.

Shell Shock: A Play in One Act (completed, 1918; never produced)

O'Neill wrote *Shell Shock* after his move from New York City to Provincetown, Massachusetts, subsequent to the death of his close friend Louis Holladay on January 22, 1918 (Floyd 1981, 11–12n). Alternately titled *Butts, A Smoke*, and *At Jesus' Feet, Shell Shock* is O'Neill's second attempt to dramatize the horrors of World War I. Whereas his first, *The* SNIPER, takes place in Belgium, with Belgian and Prussian characters, *Shell Shock* is set on the home front, in a university club grill. Three veterans meet there—a medic, an infantry lieutenant, and an infantry major—and recount a terrifying incident in which the major gallantly saved the lieutenant's life during a trench battle in FRANCE. Unlike *The Sniper, Shell Shock* was never produced in O'Neill's lifetime.

SYNOPSIS

An oppressively hot September afternoon at *"the grill of the New York club of a large Eastern University"* (1:657). Steam rises from the asphalt outside, but inside the room is cool and still. A waiter stands between two rows of tables, languidly gazing out a back window; another man in a Medical Corps officer's uniform sits reading a newspaper and drinking iced coffee. Footsteps are heard at the entrance, and Herbert Roylston appears in the infantry uniform of a first lieutenant. Roylston, a recent veteran, has eyes of *"a healthy child . . . shadowed by the remembrance of pain, witnessed and not by them to be forgotten"* (1:657). The first man is Robert Wayne, a military psychologist and the former college roommate of Jack Arnold, a war hero who led Roylston's command in Europe. The two men soon recognize each other as having a mutual acquaintance.

Complaining about the heat outside, Roylston blames his weakness on wounds he incurred fighting the "Bosche," or Germans. He relates a war story in which Jack Arnold rescued him from what World War I soldiers called "No Man's Land," the contested space between occupied trenches. The Germans cut off communications between Arnold's company and the rest of their division, forcing them to dig in and wait while a group of wounded men, including Roylston, were slowly dying in No Man's Land. After the third day, Roylston remembers being aroused from his cataleptic state by his own terrifying scream; the scream alerted Jack Arnold, who bore his unconscious body back to the trench amid heavy machine gun and artillery fire. The next thing Roylston remembers is waking up in a hospital bed. It was a sensational act of heroism, and Arnold had achieved "a whole caboodle of such stunts to his credit" (1:664). Wayne is dumbfounded by Roylston's story, as he understood from fragmented reports that the man Arnold retrieved had been killed. Roylston assures him that he came very close to death but eventually pulled through.

Wayne treated victims of shell shock as a medical officer on the European front and since his return has continued with a successful treatment of his own design. A colleague, Doctor Thompson, wrote from the front lines that he had diagnosed Jack Arnold with shell shock and that Arnold, who has recently returned home, will most probably be his newest patient. Arnold had suffered a standard nervous breakdown, Wayne says, though "there was something queer about the case he couldn't get hold of" (1:661). Thompson's missive included an enigmatic postscript that read, "Watch Arnold—

cigarettes!" This was strange, as Wayne remembers Arnold, a former all-star fullback for the Harvard football team, as a nonsmoker. Roylston disabuses him; "he [smoked] over there—a great deal. As I remember him he had one stuck in his mouth all the time." For his part, Roylston is astonished that so courageous a soldier could become mentally unwound and describes Arnold's rescue as "rank suicide. The chances were a thousand to one he would come back alive" (1:662).

Roylston heads off to write some letters. A few moments later, Jack Arnold arrives wearing the uniform of an infantry major. His appearance indicates a great deal of physical and mental suffering; in addition, he has the odd nervous tick of *"raising the fore and middle fingers of his right hand to his lips as though he were smoking an invisible cigarette"* (1:663). The former roommates greet each other affectionately. Wayne notifies Arnold about Thompson's diagnosis, which Arnold rejects outright: "He's a fossilized old woman, your Thompson—fusses like a wet hen about imaginary symptoms" (1:663), he says, all the while performing the unconscious motion of bringing a cigarette to his mouth. Wayne regards Arnold as a patient from this point on. Arnold insists that he is "fit as a fiddle," aside from a torturous "silence" (1:664); when Wayne asks what silence he is referring to, Arnold ignores the question and asks for a cigarette. After only a few puffs, he puts it out and deposits the remainder in his uniform pocket. He then cadges another cigarette, and again after only a few puffs, begins to place the second in his pocket. Guiltily apprehending Wayne's nonplussed expression, Arnold flings the butt to the floor and furiously stamps it out. He explains that cigarettes were hard to come by during the war, and ever since he has had the insufferable habit of "sniping butts" from other smokers and stashing them in case he runs out. "It's natural enough," Wayne responds in the unmistakable voice of a trained psychologist, but Arnold adds, "There's something back of it I can't get at—something that drives me to do it" (1:665). His compulsion is so extreme that immediately after his explanation, he produces a cigarette pack from each pocket and sets them on the table, then calls the waiter for more.

Arnold launches into a graphic account of life on the battlefield—the noise, the death, the pain, the hunger, the exhaustion, and the sensation that "Nothing is fixed or certain. The next moment of your life never attains to the stability of even a probable occurrence." After years of this, the silence of home life is unbearable, "like the old Chinese water torture . . . and then you think—you have to think—about the things you ought to forget—" (1:666). Wayne assures him that he will adapt over time and, tactfully changing the subject, brings up his encounter with Roylston. Arnold adamantly insists Roylston is dead, that it was a corpse he retrieved from No Man's Land. Wayne convinces him that Roylston is very much alive. Strangely agitated by what should be good news, Arnold resumes his smoking fetish, compulsively raising his fingers to his lips. Disregarding his own cigarettes, he extracts one from Wayne's box, lights it, and quickly snuffs it out and stores it in his pocket. Thoughts of Roylston and Château-Thierry inspire a rush of unpleasant memories, but he submits that the worst trial of his three days holed in by the Germans—more than the hunger, the mutilation, the men driven to madness—was that they had run out of cigarettes. "I didn't feel hunger or thirst at all. All I wanted was a smoke—and not a one!" (1:668). Cigarettes seemed the greatest palliative to the horrifying smell of death, a means to forget the reality of what was happening around him. At one point, a "little Italian private" was hit by shrapnel: "A shell fragment came down on his skull—his brains spattered all over—(*shuddering*)—over my face. And all that time not a cigarette—not a damned smoke of any kind—to take your mind off—all that!" (1:669)

"You ought to try and forget those unavoidable horrors, Jack," Wayne advises soothingly. "War has to be what it is—until we make an end to it forever" (1:669). Ignoring this, Arnold continues that though the wounded soldiers trapped in No Man's Land screamed incessantly, he ordered his men to stay put. Wayne reminds him that he went out for Roylston, but Arnold again dismisses this— "No; Roylston was dead. I saw him fall flat on his face" (1:669). To Wayne's consternation, Arnold's recounting of the events becomes ever more

graphic in its gruesome detail, and his monologue concludes once again with the doleful fact that his company had run out of cigarettes. At length, his nightmare fully reveals itself. When replacements finally arrived after the third day, no one had brought cigarettes. In an act of desperation, Arnold charged into No Man's Land after recollecting that Roylston had a whole pack of cigarettes before he left to fight, and his memory of the rescue itself, for which he was honored with glory among the troops and with medals of valor from his superiors, is a "blank" (1:670). Arnold's psychological torment derives from this shameful certainty: He had saved Roylston for a cigarette, nothing more.

Wayne refuses to accept this shameful version of events and pushes Arnold further—he must have seen his wounded comrade stand up, or perhaps he heard screaming. Yes, he remembers the screaming, and in fact, one cry does stand out among the others. The actual memory of what happened that day rushes into his head. "*His face contracts convulsively. He beats his head with his hands, his eyes shut in his effort to visualize the scene. . . . He throws his head back and screams as if in horrible pain*" (1:671). He heard the scream, recognized Roylston's voice, and charged out into No Man's Land to save him. Arnold's self-hatred is over. He is cured. Roylston reenters, and the two veterans embrace. Arnold refuses a celebratory cigarette from his former lieutenant. "Not on your life! Never another! A pipe for mine the rest of my life!" (1:671–672).

COMMENTARY

Shell Shock is an unwieldy war story, one that might have at least proven worthy of an O. Henry short story. O. Henry's stories nearly always ended in what is now called an "O. Henry Twist," a quirky plot contrivance that delighted audiences with a surprise ending in the last few lines of each tale. This would only have been the case, however, if O'Neill had left well enough alone and allowed Arnold to have, in fact, performed the daring rescue simply for a pack of cigarettes. If he had done this, two fairly substantial points might have been made: (1) the limited capability of psychoanalysis to handle the impact of war on man's psyche, and (2) the baser motives behind courageous acts—

as Stephen Crane had done with *The Red Badge of Courage* (1895). As it stands, *Shell Shock* has the dubious distinction of being, as Travis Bogard quips, "possibly the shortest course of psychoanalysis on record" (99).

Louis Sheaffer makes a strong case that although *Shell Shock* is a trivial play in itself, the hero worship Wayne and Roylston feel toward Arnold looks forward to Sam Evans's hero-worship of the World War I veteran Gordon Shaw in STRANGE INTERLUDE. Arnold's character also tentatively suggests O'Neill's skepticism about the perceived moral superiority of overly admired men such as Arnold and Jack Townsend in ABORTION, who notably shares his first name. Unfortunately, once Arnold is disabused of his nightmare, he returns to the one-dimensional paragon of virtuous human perfection Wayne and Roylston had described in the opening scene.

What battle O'Neill had in mind is difficult to determine. The exploit the soldiers describe took place, according to one character, "after Chateau Thierry" (1:658). The well-known Battle of Château-Thierry, however, which thwarted a German offensive on Paris, began on May 31, 1918, and went on until August 11—yet O'Neill copyrighted the play on August 5 and sent the typescript, dated May 5 that year, to the Library of Congress (Floyd 1981, 12n). In an eerie quirk of fate, O'Neill specifies the action of the play as taking place in September 1918, well after the play's composition; but September would be historically accurate in the context of the play if he had, indeed, written it with knowledge of the Battle of Chateau Thierry.

CHARACTERS

Arnold, Jack   A veteran of the infantry in World War I. A war hero and former all-American college football player, Arnold rescued his first lieutenant, Herbert Roylston, after Roylston had been wounded and trapped for three days in No Man's Land. Over the course of the war, Arnold achieved "a whole caboodle of such stunts to his credit" (1:658). His physical description resembles O'Neill in his 20s, with the added tension about his face of a seasoned war veteran: "*He is a tall, broad-shouldered, and sinewy-built man of about thirty with black hair*

and a moustache. The sun tan on his strong-featured, handsome face has been faded to a sickly yellow by illness. . . . His dark eyes have a strained expression of uncertain expectancy as if he were constantly holding himself in check while he waited for a mine to explode" (1:663). Arnold was diagnosed with shell shock in Europe, where he developed an unusual nervous tick that signified an obsession with cigarettes. Robert Wayne, Arnold's college roommate and a military psychologist who specializes in treating shell shock, meets Arnold at a university club in New York. Arnold tells Wayne of the horrors he encountered on the battlefield and confesses that his celebrated rescue of Roylston was motivated by his addiction to cigarettes. Wayne successfully psychoanalyzes Arnold, who ultimately remembers that, upon hearing Roylston scream, he bravely reacted to save him. In the final scene, he exultantly relinquishes smoking, and Wayne pronounces him cured.

Roylston, Herbert   A veteran of the infantry in World War I. According to O'Neill, he is "*Blond and clean-shaven, his rather heavy, good-natured face noticeably bears the marks of a recent convalescence from serious illness. Lines of suffering about the lips contrast with his ever-ready, jovial grin*" (1:657). Roylston, a first lieutenant, was saved in a daring rescue by his superior officer, the war hero Jack Arnold. Roylston recounts the episode to Robert Wayne, a military psychologist who treats victims of shell shock. After three days wounded in No Man's Land, Roylston startled himself awake from a state of delirium by his own scream. Arnold heard the scream, charged into No Man's Land amidst heavy enemy fire and returned him unconscious to the trench. After Wayne successfully treats Arnold, Roylston returns for a reunion with his rescuer.

Wayne, Robert   A member of the Medical Corps during World War I. Wayne is a military psychologist who specializes in curing shell shock. Wayne is "*under medium height, slight and wiry, with a thin, pale face, light brown hair and mustache, and grey eyes peering keenly through tortoise-rimmed spectacles*" (1:657). His friend and former college roommate, Jack Arnold, has been diagnosed with shell shock, and he has been referred to Wayne for treatment.

Wayne explains all this in a conversation with Herbert Roylston, whom Arnold heroically saved after Roylston had been wounded and was trapped for three days in No Man's Land. Arnold enters after Roylston leaves; he has an unusual nervous tick that signifies an obsession with cigarettes. Arnold recounts a blood-curdling battle experience in which his company was trapped for three days and incurred enormous casualties. At first, Arnold admits to having rescued Roylston, whom he believed dead, because the wounded man had cigarettes and the other men had run out. However, after Wayne encourages him to dig deeper into his memory, Arnold recalls that he had been moved to save Roylston after heeding his scream. Over a period of less than 20 minutes, Wayne has cured his patient.

BIBLIOGRAPHY

Bogard, Travis. *Contour in Time: The Plays of Eugene O'Neill.* Rev. ed. New York: Oxford University Press, 1988.

Floyd, Virginia. *The Plays of Eugene O'Neill: A New Assessment.* New York: Ungar, 1985.

Floyd, Virginia, ed. *Eugene O'Neill at Work: Newly Released Ideas for His Plays.* New York: Ungar, 1981.

Sheaffer, Louis. *O'Neill, Son and Playwright.* Boston: Little, Brown, 1968.

Sniper: A Play in One Act, The (completed, 1915; first produced, 1917)

The Sniper is one of two surviving plays by Eugene O'Neill that he wrote for GEORGE PIERCE BAKER's playwriting workshop at Harvard University, the other being The PERSONAL EQUATION. (A one-act farce called *The Dear Doctor,* which must be an ironic title given the spiteful representation of medical DOCTORS throughout his canon, has since been lost.) In contrast to SHELL SHOCK, O'Neill's unwieldy attempt to capture the horror of World War I in a domestic setting, *The Sniper* takes place in war-torn Europe. O'Neill won honorable men-

tion with it for Baker's one-act play competition. The winning three plays were produced by the Harvard Dramatic Club, and he wrote to his "Dear Heart" BEATRICE ASHE that it was just as well he had lost, as "Those amateur butchers on the Dramat. [sic] would murder *The Sniper*" (O'Neill 60). Additionally, the three winners were all women, and O'Neill quipped that "Harvard spirit and taste runs to the sort of clever plays women usually write. (Sorehead!)" (61) But Baker and other critics at Harvard appreciated the play's well-wrought structure, timely subject matter, and dramatic power. O'Neill sent a typescript of the play to his father, the famous actor JAMES O'NEILL, who shopped it around the vaudeville circuit in March 1915. O'Neill told Ashe that the play "has made a big hit with all the people he has had read it," but his father was told that censors would quash the play unless O'Neill "omitted all reference to Prussians, French, Belgians, etc)"; additionally, Holbrook Blinn, a well-known vaudevillian actor, agreed to act in it, but only after the war was over (68).

Unlike *Shell Shock,* a later play but an inferior one, *The Sniper* was, in time, produced on February 16, 1917—just two weeks prior to the day President Woodrow Wilson broke off diplomatic ties with Germany (Gelb 598–599). The PROVINCE-TOWN PLAYERS listed the piece in what they called their "War Bill" at the PLAYWRIGHTS' THEATRE in New York City, with the cast including GEORGE CRAM "JIG" COOK and Ida Rauh.

SYNOPSIS

The interior of a small cottage in the Belgian countryside at sundown on a September evening. The room is in a state of utter destruction. Two large breaches in the back wall look out onto a beautiful vista of hills and fields, and massive cracks in the ceiling expose *"a fantastic fretwork against the sky"* (1:295). The windows are blown out, most of the furniture is upturned or in pieces, the main door is missing, and over the remaining door hangs a black crucifix. The muted sound of cannon fire can be heard in the distance. Rougon, a Belgian peasant of about 65, enters through one of the gaping breaches in the back wall. He bears the body of his son, Charles, who has been killed by the invading

German forces. He cries out, "Charles! My little one!" and lays the body in a cleared space on the floor (1:295). He takes up a functioning chair, puts his head in his hands, and moans in grief *"like a wounded animal"* (1:296).

The village priest appears wearing a black robe and steps through the rubble to comfort Rougon. He heard about Rougon's boy and has come to offer spiritual succor. Predictably, he assures Rougon that his son's death is the "will of God." Rougon rails against the injustice of it and curses the "Prussian" invaders. To make matters worse (and more sentimental than necessary), it was to be Charles's wedding day. Earlier that day, Charles had sent his mother and fiancée to join the Belgian evacuees who were escaping to Brussels. He urged his father to evacuate as well, but Rougon refused to leave. Charles then made his stubborn father promise not to fight. The priest is of the same mind, as someone must harvest the crops or the village will starve. Rougon rejoins that the fields have been trampled by soldiers and pummeled by artillery fire; he bitterly denounces the French as well, their supposed allies, for requisitioning his only two horses. The priest assures him that he will be repaid for his losses—"at a time like this all must bear their share of sacrifice" (1:298).

Rougon recounts hiding in his well that morning where he could view Charles with his regiment in a nearby orchard. They were under attack, and guided by German warplanes—"their devilish flying machines which look like great birds"—the enemy's artillery shelled the regiment, and Charles was killed (1:300). The priest comforts him that Charles was well-loved and died bravely. Rougon swears he would fight if it were not for his wife, but the priest scolds him, "your country has need of you; as much need of you as of her soldiers. . . . It is your duty [to stay alive]" (1:301). Rougon boasts that he may be too old to enlist, but "With my little rifle in there I could pick off more Prussian swine than a whole regiment of youngsters like my Charles" (1:301). The priest makes Rougon vow again not to fight, which he does, and promises to help officiate at Charles's burial the following night. The two kneel beside Charles's body to pray, but the meaningless phrases "Almighty God," "merciful," "Infinite jus-

tice," and so on merely agitate Rougon into another fit of grief-stricken rage (1:302).

A German captain of infantry appears through a breach in the wall. He is a young man, visibly embarrassed by the intrusion. Twirling his moustache, the captain says self-consciously, "I honor the brave dead on whichever side they fall" (1:302). The priest is the only local authority left, and the captain has orders to deliver a warning that any villager caught bearing arms will be shot on sight; in addition, the captain guarantees that the German army will pay reparations for any supplies taken from the village. The priest haughtily agrees to pass along the message. Just as the captain exits the cottage, Rougon, who had been biting his tongue, shouts out to him, "Dog of a Prussian!" (1:303). The priest sharply warns him to stay quiet but the captain had moved out of earshot.

Jean enters after the German has gone. A frightened Belgian peasant boy, Jean was with the evacuation party but has returned with terrible news. The priest coaxes him into telling them what happened. The evacuation party stumbled across a battleground strewn with the bodies of dead soldiers from both sides. They heard gunfire in the distance and rode their horses as fast as possible toward Brussels. Jean incoherently describes the hillsides as having been "covered with white spots like,—like daisies; and they floated 'way up in the air." Rougon calls him an idiot and demands an explanation, which the priest supplies: "It was smoke from the guns you saw, my child" (1:305). Rougon grows more impatient, but the priest implores him to let the boy continue. Artillery shells landed all around them, the boy goes on, and both Margot, Rougon's wife, and Louise, Charles's fiancée, were killed in the assault.

Rougon is devastated. Jean walks to one of the breaches and peers outside. A bugle call blares from the distance. Jean hurries back to alert the men that the Germans are headed their way. Marching soldiers can be heard in the near distance. Rougon purposefully walks to the other room and returns holding his rifle. Heedless of the priest's pleas to lay down his weapon, Rougon positions himself against the breach, aims carefully, and fires. "That for Margot!" He fires again. "That for Louise!" As

Rougon reloads, the captain and four German privates storm the cottage. One soldier disarms Rougon, who then stands proudly against the back wall while another soldier takes hold of the priest. Rougon admits to firing on them and insists the priest is innocent of any wrongdoing. After verifying this, the four soldiers form a firing squad. With Charles's body lying between the Germans and Rougon, the captain fiercely tells Rougon that if he wishes to pray he should do so. Rougon replies: "I want no prayers! . . . To hell with your prayers!" (1:307–308). The priest begs him to "make peace with God," but Rougon spits on the floor and yells back defiantly, "That for your God who allows such things to happen!" (308). Before the priest can finish his benediction, the Germans fire, and Rougon is dead. The captain shrugs, saying, "It is the law," and he departs with his men. At the curtain, Jean is weeping in the corner, while the priest, *"looking down with infinite compassion at the still bodies of father and son,"* intones the final lines: "Alas, the laws of men!" (1:308).

COMMENTARY

The Sniper reveals O'Neill's antipathy toward the contemporaneous world war, but the play is also an early demonstration of his "black Irish" side—that is, we can find the core of the play in Rougon's final rejection of God as a figure of "infinite justice." The narrative arc is well-crafted and bears the unmistakable stamp of Baker's plot-driven influence. Paul D. Voelker, in opposition to Travis Bogard, contends that O'Neill's craftsmanship in this play shows evidence that Baker's influence was a positive one, helping form "a theatrically effective and thematically significant one-act play. It portrays in a convincing manner the last minutes and the catastrophic end of a rounded, dynamic character. It is a great deal more than an 'anecdote'. . . It is, in fact, one of O'Neill's best one-act plays" (1:214). None of the characters but Rougon captures the imagination, however. Rougon's impassioned reactions to the stereotypical village priest, the peasant boy Jean, and the young German captain of infantry are the stuff of O'Neill's more mature writing. There is even a trace of the later EXPRESSIONISM that would solidify O'Neill's

reputation in the 1920s when the priest intones the prayer over Charles's corpse: The only words Rougon hears, and thus also the audience, are basically meaningless religious platitudes (1:302); and the black crucifix on the wall reads as an outdated cliché in the modern world.

The captain's bureaucratic final line—"It is the law" (308)—brings the pathos to a human level while at the same time signifying the inhumanity of machine-like governments and their culpability in the death of God. The captain's dispassionate line looks backward to the first plain clothes man in *The WEB*, who concludes the play by telling the prostitute Rose Thomas's baby, about to be taken into state custody, that he is his mother now. The scene also looks forward to the police captain in *The GREAT GOD BROWN*, who asks the prostitute Cybel in act 4, scene 2 if she knows William A. Brown's name after policemen under his command have shot Brown dead; when she replies, "Man!," he takes up a notebook and asks her to spell it. And much like Anthony Dion's unmasked self in the same play—the "masochistic, life-denying spirit of Christianity as represented by St. Anthony" (quoted in Clark 160)—the village priest's spiritual lessons are ultimately rejected by the modern secular world. As O'Neill critic Paul D. Voelker contends of the play, "it places by implication the ultimate blame upon God himself, the creator of warmongering human nature" (1:213).

Setting the play in the Belgian countryside was a noteworthy choice for the time. Germany's Schlieffen Plan to conquer FRANCE (August 1914) required German troops to pass through Belgium. But Belgium, a neutral country, refused to grant permission, so Germany did so by force. The invasion of that small nation, which was depicted in political cartoons as a child (like a more defiant Jean) barring the path of an imposing German officer, inspired a great deal of sympathy for the Belgians at the outset of World War I and intensified American indignation toward the Germans. In the play, the Belgian villagers are hapless victims of war, and when Rougon asks the priest how the warmongering governments could kill innocent civilians and destroy their homes, the priest sagely replies, "God knows. Our poor country is a lamb among wolves" (1:298).

CHARACTERS

German Captain of Infantry An uncommonly young officer in the German infantry. The captain brings a directive to Rougon and the village priest not to allow the village peasantry to take up arms against the German invading forces. When the captain returns with troops, Rougon opens fire, probably killing two German soldiers. The captain enters the cottage with four privates of the regiment and orders Rougon's execution. Once Rougon is dead, he shrugs dispassionately and tells the priest, "It is the law" (1:308).

Jean A 15-year-old Belgian peasant boy who survived a massacre of many evacuees heading to Brussels. When he appears in the cottage, *"His clothes are mud-stained and ragged and he is trembling with fear"* (1:303). Jean brings news to Rougon and the village priest that Rougon's wife and his son's fiancée have been killed by artillery fire. As O'Neill writes it, Jean's incoherence makes him sound more like a village idiot than a terrified boy. This may have been O'Neill's intention, as Rougon refers to him as a "dolt," a "half-witted calf, and an "idiot" (1:304, 305). After Rougon's execution, the audience can hear Jean, who witnessed it, weeping from fright in the corner of the room.

Rougon A Belgian peasant of about 65 whom O'Neill describes as *"a great hulking old man"* (1:295). Just prior to the action of the play, Rougon's son, an infantryman in the Belgian army, was killed by artillery fire. Soon after Rougon bears his son's corpse into his cottage, the village priest enters to console him. A peasant boy, Jean, follows soon after and announces that Rougon's wife and his son's fiancée have been killed as well. Rougon, the title character, is an expert shot with a rifle. When a group of German soldiers approach his cottage, he opens fire on them in retribution, probably killing two men. The German captain of the infantry orders his execution, and when he is asked if he wishes to pray, he rejects God and dies before the village priest can administer a benediction.

Village Priest The spiritual and secular leader of Rougon's devastated village. The priest is *"old, white-haired, with a kindly, spiritual face"* and wears a black robe (1:296). He means to provide succor to Rougon over the loss of his son and convince him not to arm himself against the invading German forces. But when Rougon hears that his wife and his son's fiancée have been killed as well, he denounces God and swears revenge on the Germans. The priest is ultimately ineffectual as Rougon ignores his pleas, first to disarm, and then, after Rougon is captured by the Germans, to "make your peace with God" (1:308). The priest's rejoinder to the German captain of infantry, who bureaucratically considers Rougon's execution as a matter of law, comprise the final lines of the play—"Alas, the laws of men!" (308).

BIBLIOGRAPHY

Clark, Barrett. *Eugene O'Neill: The Man and His Plays.* Rev. ed. New York: Dover, 1947.

Gelb, Arthur, and Barbara Gelb. *O'Neill: Life with Monte Cristo.* New York: Applause Books, 2000.

O'Neill, Eugene. *Selected Letters of Eugene O'Neill.* Edited by Travis Bogard and Jackson R. Bryer. New Haven, Conn.: Yale University Press, 1988.

Voelker, Paul D. "Eugene O'Neill and George Pierce Baker: A Reconsideration." *American Literature* 49, no. 2 (May 1977): 206–220.

"S.O.S."
(completed, 1918; first published, 1988)

In 1918, *Eugene O'Neill* rewrote his one-act SEA play WARNINGS as a "long short story" entitled "S.O.S." while residing with his second wife, AGNES BOULTON, in Provincetown, Massachusetts. One of three surviving short stories—the other two are "TOMORROW" and "The SCREENEWS OF WAR"— O'Neill probably intended to sell it to the *Saturday Evening Post*, which had been publishing such war stories after the United States entered World War I in April 1917. As Boulton records in her memoir

Part of a Long Story, her husband was bitterly disappointed that his play BEYOND THE HORIZON still lacked a producer (1918; produced 1920), though it would later earn him his first of four PULITZER PRIZEs. Suffering a period of both financial and creative bankruptcy, O'Neill drank a great deal, wrote intermittently and without enthusiasm, and grimly spent his time reading and rereading stories in the *Post*; as Travis Bogard writes, "His desire to write magazine fiction may have had the same motivation that drove his protagonist to sea—the need of money" (332).

The settings of "S.O.S." are significantly divided among O'Neill's three most used settings—New England, New York, and the open SEA. Though *Warnings,* written in 1913, would undoubtedly bring the 1912 *Titanic* disaster to audience's minds, "S.O.S." more directly relates to contemporary events. Rather than having the ship sink after colliding with a derelict (as happens in *Warnings*), a German raider destroys it, and the crew are taken aboard the hostile ship as prisoners. In 1917, after the German government announced a brutal policy of "unrestrained submarine warfare," the United States joined the Allies (Egri 128).

In scene 1 of *Warnings,* the main character James Knapp, a wireless operator on the SS *Empress,* discovers he is going deaf and will not be able to perform his duties at sea. His wife, Mary Knapp, browbeats him into working anyway, as the family is suffering from terrible financial hardship. In scene 2, Knapp does not hear warning calls from another ship that a derelict is ahead; the *Empress* sinks as a result, and overwhelmed with guilt, Knapp commits suicide by shooting himself with a revolver.

The narrative arch in "S.O.S." is similar to *Warnings* insofar as the opening sequence deals with domestic issues as well. In it, O'Neill leads us through his disaffected main character John Lathrop's courtship and marriage to Susannah Darrow, a wealthy spinster who lives in a neighboring village. The two move to New York, but over time Lathrop, who like Knapp cuts an unimpressive figure, feels emasculated by living off his wife's fortune. After a long search, Lathrop finds a job as a ship's wireless operator on the SS *Rio Grande.* The Lathrops live a comfortable life onboard for many voyages, until Susannah loses her money in a real estate crash. Lathrop, like Knapp, loses his hearing but must make one more voyage for the money. Unlike Knapp, it is Lathrop, not his wife, who convinces himself to continue working as DOCTORS "were always making matters worse to keep you coming to them" (O'Neill 351), which is identical to Mary Knapp's argument. Interestingly, the doctor reluctantly admits that there may be some hope, but it might do Lathrop well not to hold on to that hope, since "no hope is preferable to one which is doomed to disappointment" (349). O'Neill inverts this theme of "hopeless hope" in his play *The STRAW* and in his late masterpiece *The ICEMAN COMETH,* in which the hopeless hopes of the patrons of Harry Hope's saloon are life-sustaining illusions that make their lives worth living.

During the trip, Lathrop misses crucial radio warnings that a German raider is cruising their line of passage. Unlike Knapp, Lathrop survives the initial sinking and is captured by the Germans, along with the rest of the crew, and he becomes a prisoner of war. While he is aboard the enemy vessel, the Germans derisively treat Lathrop as a war hero and, to the disgust of his fellow American prisoners, give him free reign of the ship. While he is languishing in a state of utter shame under a German cannon, the Germans fire the weapon, the shock of which causes Lathrop to unaccountably regain his hearing. He then steals into the wireless room, kills the operator, and signals for help—less an act of heroism than an act of desperation to prove to his shipmates that he is no traitor. The Germans find out too late to save themselves, but they execute Lathrop by firing squad, thus making Lathrop, ironically, a martyred war hero.

Both *Warnings* and "S.O.S." are closely based on Joseph Conrad's sea tale "The End of the Tether." As with Conrad's story, O'Neill's protagonists are responsible for their ship's destruction. But unlike what happens with Conrad's Captain Whalley, who becomes blind rather than deaf, the disasters in *Warnings* and "S.O.S." are mainly caused by O'Neill's characters respective moral failings. "Showing the influence of his youthful experiences and his naturalistic leanings," Peter Egri writes of *Warnings,* "O'Neill diminishes Whalley's heroic stature; Knapp manifests only the weakness of Whalley" (127).

Though never published, "S.O.S." is a more satisfactory read than *Warnings,* which was never produced in O'Neill's lifetime. Similar to the character Henry Fleming in Stephen Crane's novel *The Red Badge of Courage,* which O'Neill certainly read, John Lathrop is driven to a heroic deed by base emotions—fear with Henry Fleming, shame with John Lathrop. Rather than have him commit suicide, in "S.O.S." the story of the dauntless wireless operator becomes the stuff of legend. As such, "S.O.S.," which O'Neill probably never submitted for publication, is an incipient treatment of a theme he later developed with ingenious innovation on the stage—"the contrast between appearance and reality" (Egri 127).

BIBLIOGRAPHY

Bogard, Travis, ed. *The Unknown O'Neill: Unpublished and Unfamiliar Writings of Eugene O'Neill.* New Haven, Conn.: Yale University Press, 1988.

Egri, Peter. "The Use of the Short Story in O'Neill's and Chekhov's One-Act Plays." In *Eugene O'Neill: A World View,* edited by Virginia Floyd, 115–144. New York: Frederick Ungar Publishing, 1979.

O'Neill, Eugene. "S.O.S." In *The Unknown O'Neill: Unpublished or Unfinished Writings of Eugene O'Neill.* Edited by Travis Bogard. New Haven, Conn.: Yale University Press, 1988, 333–371.

Strange Interlude (completed, 1927; first produced, 1928)

Strange Interlude, Eugene O'Neill's self-described "woman play," is the most ambitious psychological drama in the O'Neill canon and the dramatist's most popular play of the 1920s. O'Neill first considered the idea in April 1923 after hearing the tale of a young woman whose fiancé was an aviator "formerly of the Lafayette Escadrille," shot down just after the armistice ended World War I (Alexander 1992, 103). The woman turned to alcohol and sexual promiscuity for solace and eventually married

so she might bear a child to ameliorate her loss. O'Neill had just completed WELDED, a barely concealed account of his marital struggles with AGNES BOULTON. His experience writing the play compelled him to explore modern womanhood more fully than ever before. O'Neill's innovative use of inner dialogue, his treatment of the pioneering psychological and literary ideas of the German psychologist Sigmund Freud and Irish novelist James Joyce, and uncompromising look into male/female relationships in the modern era make *Strange Interlude* the crowning achievement of 1920s AMERICAN THEATER.

Strange Interlude was produced by the THEATRE GUILD, at the time the most innovative and important theatrical production company in the United States. In a visit to O'Neill at his home SPITHEAD in Bermuda, Guild producer Lawrence Langner accepted both *Strange Interlude* and MARCO MILLIONS (the latter mainly to contract the former). Expertly directed by Philip Moeller, who had just directed O'Neill's far less successful *Welded, Strange Interlude* opened at the John Golden Theatre on January 30, 1928. Originally meant to be performed over two consecutive nights, the show began at 5:30 in the evening with a dinner break at 8:00 and final curtain at 11:00. Boston and Providence banned the play as a "disgusting spectacle of immorality and advocacy of atheism, of domestic infidelity and the

Glenn Anders, Lynn Fontanne, Tom Powers, and Earle Larimore in *Strange Interlude,* 1928. *(Courtesy of the Yale Collection of American Literature, Beinecke Rare Book and Manuscript Library)*

destruction of unborn human life" (Alexander 1992, 126). Most clergymen, however, recognized the moral and spiritual cost of the characters' actions.

Rarely revived today, *Strange Interlude* enjoyed a 17-month run (1:426 performances) and two equally successful touring company productions. In fact, performances sold out so quickly that for the first few months, in a theater of approximately 900 seats, many audience members chose to stand than miss out on what was reported as nothing less than a cultural phenomenon. O'Neill suspected beforehand it would be, as opposed to the extravagant *Marco Millions*, his and the Guild's "big bacon-bringer." "Myself," he laughed, "I wouldn't stand up 4 1/2 hours to see the original production of the Crucifixion!" (O'Neill 1985, 125). It also became a best-selling book and an MGM feature film starring Clark Gable and Norma Shearer (1932); though he never saw it, O'Neill described the Hollywood FILM ADAPTATION as a "dreadful hash of attempted condensation and idiotic censorship" (quoted in Alexander 1992, 127). *Strange Interlude* won O'Neill, now indisputably the United States's leading playwright, his third PULITZER PRIZE in 1928.

SYNOPSIS

First Part
Act 1
A late afternoon in August 1919 at the Leeds's home in a *"small town in New England"* (2:633). The action takes place in Professor Henry Leeds's library, described as small, comfortable, and stacked from floor to ceiling with antiquated books. Charles "Charlie" Marsden enters; he remarks to the Leedses' maid Mary, who is faintly heard offstage right, that he will await his former professor's return in the library. Just back from serving as an army correspondent in World War I, Marsden is 35, tall, and effeminate-looking, and he exudes a *"quiet charm, a quality of appealing, inquisitive friendliness, always willing to listen, eager to sympathize, to like and be liked."* Marsden's voice *"takes on a monotonous, musing quality,"* and his expression indicates that the lengthy soliloquy to follow takes place in his head, not to be mistaken for spoken dialogue (2:634). Marsden's thoughts exposit on the Leeds family, in particular Professor Leeds's daughter

Nina and the tragedy of Gordon Shaw, an air force pilot and Nina's great love who was shot down in combat two days before the armistice ended the war. Inwardly, Marsden reveals a highly conflicted sexuality that prudishly scorns sex yet desperately yearns for it at the same time.

Professor Leeds enters. A scholar of classical literature, Leeds is 55, undersized, and thin. He appears worried but attempts to hide his anxiety. The men exchange pleasantries and discuss Gordon Shaw's demise. Leeds's thoughts indicate that Nina's obsession over Gordon's untimely death has unbalanced the house's emotional tenor. Leeds openly confesses that ever since the news of Gordon's death, Nina acts as if she hated him. She has been accusing her father of preventing Gordon from marrying her before going to war, thus preventing the consummation of their love and her a child to remember him by. Professor Leeds waffles between self-righteousness and extreme guilt. Nina's accusation is not unwarranted. A man of honor, Gordon Shaw had respected Professor Leeds's appeal.

Nina enters. An athletic-looking, statuesque 20-year-old, Nina acts chillingly distant to both her father and her old friend "Charlie," whom she resents for having survived the war instead of Gordon. Nina announces that she has accepted a post nursing at a sanitarium for wounded veterans. The men try in vain to dissuade her, but she will depart that night. She infuriates her father and shocks Marsden by openly admitting her intentions to "give" herself to wounded soldiers and thus fill the psychological (and implicitly sexual) void Gordon's death left in her: "I must learn to give myself, do you hear—give and give until I can make that gift of myself for a man's happiness without scruple, without fear, without joy except in his joy!" (2:647). "What an animal!," Leeds thinks, "and my daughter! . . . she doesn't get it from me! . . . was her mother like that?" (2:649). Equally revolted, but titillated in spite of himself, Marsden thinks, "who would dream she was so sensual?" Leeds admits he resented Gordon, that he was "glad when he died," but begs her forgiveness (2:649). She forgives him but will go through with her plans nonetheless. Marsden worries about his mother, and Nina escorts him out. Leeds, in anguish over the loss of his daughter, takes up Manilius's *Astronomicon*, and begins reading the Latin text, *"sonorously like a child whistling to keep up his courage in the dark"* (2:652).

Act 2

Same as act 1; around nine o'clock at night in early fall over a year later, 1920. The room appears *"more withdrawn from life than before."* Leeds is dead, and Marsden sits mournfully in a chair at center. He hears a car approaching, and then a man and a woman's voice. Nina enters alone. She has toughened considerably, and though her expression shows a hardened cynicism, she is *"really in a more highly strung, disorganized state than ever"* (2:655). Marsden suspects that while nursing the veterans back to health, she has also been sleeping with them. Her thoughts reveal a sincere grief over her father's death, but she believes all men, including her father, died for her after the news of Gordon's death. She announces that the doctor who ran the veteran's hospital, Gordon's friend Edmund "Ned" Darrell, has joined her. Marsden broods jealously over this news. Nina leaves to escort Darrell to her father's deathbed. Sam Evans, a schoolmate of Gordon's, bashfully and apologetically enters the room. Though 25, Evans appears the archetypical American undergraduate in looks and attire. After some concerned discussion about Nina, Evans admits he has asked her hand in marriage (2:660).

Darrell enters, writes a prescription for Nina, and assertively dispatches Evans to fill it at a local drugstore. Darrell and Marsden size each other up. Darrell is 27, lithely handsome, and self-assured. His first thoughts concern the prudishness of Marsden's novels: "well-written surface . . . no depth, no digging underneath . . . why? . . . he has talent but doesn't dare . . . afraid he'll meet himself somewhere . . . one of those poor devils who spend their lives trying not to discover which sex to belong to!" (2:662). Marsden thinks equally critical thoughts, wondering if Darrell might be a psychoanalyst—"a lot to account for, Herr Freud! . . . . pah, what an easy cure-all . . . sex the philosopher's stone . . . 'O Oedipus, O my king! The world is adopting you!'" (2:662). Darrell frankly discusses Nina's promiscuity at the hospital, thus affirming Marsden's suspicions. He believes Marsden should encourage her mar-

riage to Evans, whose innocent adoration and the prospect of a child might heal her psychologically.

Nina enters. At first distraught over her father's death, she quickly reverts to her former cynical state. Darrell leaves Nina with Marsden. Nina begins expressing a cosmic disillusionment in spoken monologues, which are juxtaposed with Marsden's intermittently angry, shocked, and dismayed inner thoughts. She confesses her promiscuity at the hospital but has difficulty explaining its reasons. What she does know is that she damaged not only herself but also the patients, each of whom "loathed the cruel mockery" of her "gift" (2:672). Nina refers to Marsden unconsciously as "father" (2:673). While he consolingly kisses her hair and pets her affectionately, he counsels her that she must marry Evans regardless of whether she shares his love. Nina falls asleep at his feet. Evans enters, and Marsden informs him that he put in a good word. Evans effusively thanks Marsden and performs *"a joyful, coltish caper."* As Marsden exits and the curtain falls, he cynically responds to Evans's gratitude with a *"bitter laugh"* (2:674).

Act 3

A day in late spring the following year, 1921. The dining room of the Evans ancestral home in upstate New York. Nina and Evans have been married for six months. The light in the room is *"cheerless and sickly."* The room is dilapidated, with an *"ugly table"* at center, *"repulsive brown"* wallpaper, and *"blotches of mildew"* staining the ceiling. Nina, who sits at a table writing a letter to Edmund Darrell, looks *"contented"* and *"prettier [than the last act] in a conventional way"* (2:675). She scolds Darrell for not writing and complains about the "hideous old place" she at first believed haunted. Her thoughts reveal that she is pregnant.

Marsden enters. Nina furtively hides the letter and then admits writing to Darrell. She teases Marsden about his bachelorhood and exits to the kitchen for coffee. Marsden broods over her complacent happiness, wondering if it is for show and suspects she is pregnant. He exits. Evans enters with his mother, radiating *"love and devotion and boyish adoration."* Mrs. Evans has eyes that appear *"grim with the prisoner-pain of a walled-in soul"* (2:680). She openly inquires whether Nina is pregnant, though she inwardly knows it to be true; she discovers her son does not yet know. Evans goes to the kitchen. Mrs. Evans's thoughts indicate that she hopes to convince Nina to have an abortion. Nina returns with a cup of coffee. Mrs. Evans emotionally recounts the "curse on the Evanses" (2:685), a secret kept from her son that his father's side suffers from congenital insanity. First aghast and then infuriated, Nina cruelly admits that she never loved Evans but now she hates him, as she always trusted her husband to be "so healthy and sane" (2:687). Mrs. Evans persuades Nina to stay with her son, terrified that a breakup would doom Sam Evans to the family curse. She then confesses her lifelong dream to have had a child by a healthy man, thus saving her from a life of torment and worry. Nina agrees to an abortion but pitifully mourns the fate of her unborn child.

Act 4
Professor Leeds's study on an early evening the following winter, 1921. The antiquated books now commingle with volumes of *Encyclopaedia Britannica* and contemporary self-help books. Crumpled papers and office supplies litter the room. Evans is seated in the professor's old chair, smoking a pipe in a state of extreme agitation. Disgusted by his inability to write an advertisement for a powdered milk company, he frets over Nina's sickness and wonders what she and his mother discussed the previous spring. Nina enters, her thoughts besieged by mixed feelings for Evans and the death of her unborn child. Up to then, she had purposefully avoided sleeping with Evans; not wanting to get pregnant by him, she elates him by agreeing to sleep with him that night.

Evans informs Nina that Darrell is expected soon. She cheers up at the news and goes upstairs to change. The doorbell rings. Evans exits and reenters with Marsden, who is delivering Nina's outline for Gordon's biography with his suggestions. He believes Nina's prolonged obsession with Gordon in the form of a biography foolish and psychologically harmful. The doorbell rings again. It is Darrell, whose *"manner is more convincingly authoritative, more mature"* (2:701).

Desperately concerned about his mother, who suffers from stomach pain, Marsden asks Darrell's advice; the doctor recklessly diagnoses her with cancer, but he apologizes after Marsden rebukes him. After he recommends a specialist, Marsden leaves with Evans to go to the store. Nina enters, having prettied herself for Darrell's visit. Their flirtations devolve into accusations over Darrell's bachelorhood and Nina's lack of children; he also senses the "Gordon myth strong as ever . . . root of her trouble still" (2:705). Nina admits to her conversation with Mrs. Evans and says that she went through with an abortion. They discuss the possibility of surrogate parenthood in the third person, as if objectively discussing a mutual acquaintance named "Nina" with a medical problem only "Ned" can solve. But her tone becomes imploring, and we follow Darrell's thought process until he finally, exultantly agrees. "I shall be happy for a while!" his inner thoughts shout; Nina also thinks, "I shall be happy!" and adds: "I shall make my husband happy!" (2:713).

Act 5
The Evans sitting room in a home *"of the quantity-production bungalow type"* located in a *"seashore suburb near New York"* (2:714). The room contains the familiar clutter of the professor's study in act 4. Nina sits at center, again pregnant but with *"no impression of the neurotic strain from her now, she seems nerveless and deeply calm"* (2:714). Darrell is the father, and Nina muses over her newfound love for him.

Evans enters, suffering from a *"chronic state of nervous panic and guilty conscience"* (2:716). Now unemployed, he lives off Nina's small inheritance and Darrell's generosity. Nina inwardly considers divorce. "I've sacrificed enough of my life," she thinks indignantly, and "what has he given me?" (2:717). Evans hopes Darrell, who is scheduled to arrive shortly, will bring news from a potential employer and wonders whether Marsden, whose mother has died of stomach cancer (as Darrell first suspected), will also visit. Darrell enters with an *"expression of defensive bitterness and self-resentment about his mouth and eyes"* (2:718). He feels overwhelming guilt over his and Nina's deception but still loves her and is willing to sacrifice his friend's well-being to prolong their affair. He passes the letter from the employer to Evans, who excitedly heads off to prepare for an interview. Once alone,

Darrell and Nina cry out in ecstasy and express their mutual devotion.

The doorbell rings; Darrell guiltily recants his love. Marsden enters *"dressed immaculately in deep mourning"* (2:721) and grief-stricken over his mother's death. While Nina and Darrell try to comfort him, Marsden senses the passion in the room; it ignites his soul for a moment, but then he inwardly denounces Nina and Darrell's betrayal of Evans. Out loud, he condemns his mother's DOCTORS, the specialists Darrell had recommended, as "a pack of God-damned ignorant liars and hypocrites" (2:724). Nina scolds him, and Marsden obediently goes to Evans. Darrell accuses her "romantic imagination" for her belief that she loves him "as you did once before with Gordon Shaw!" (2:725); his jealousy of Gordon delights her strangely. She announces that she will divorce Evans to marry Darrell. Thinking mostly of the potential disruption of his career, he shouts, "I wouldn't marry anyone—no matter what!" (2:726), and then he falls back on his devotion to Evans. She asks whether their own happiness is not worth more than Evans's psychological well-being; *"as if it were forced out of him by an impulse stronger than his will,"* Darrell agrees that it is (2:727).

Evans enters. Nina curtly remarks that she and Darrell plan to have a "long talk" with him and exits (2:727). Evans asks what Nina meant, which sends Darrell into a reverie of guilty inner thoughts. Darrell announces plans to study in Europe and tells Evans that Nina is pregnant. He instructs Evans to wish Nina well, then exits, thinking himself free of her at last. Nina returns to find Darrell gone, while Evans kneels at her feet glorying in her pregnancy. She nearly reveals that the child is Darrell's but, maternally drawn to Evans's boyishness, restrains herself at the last moment. She calls him "Sammy" for the first time (Mrs. Evans's pet name for her son) and revels over the unborn child. "God is a Mother," she thinks exultantly, but she despairs over the loss of her lover (2:732).

Second Part
Act 6
Same as act 5; about eight o'clock in the evening over a year later, 1923. The sitting room now exudes *"a proud air of modest prosperity"* (2:733).

Nina, Evans, and Marsden are each seated—Nina knitting an infant's sweater in a chair at center, Evans at the table reading a newspaper, and Marsden on a sofa with a book while surreptitiously peeking at Nina and Evans. Evans looks *"full and healthy and satisfied"*; Nina appears *"noticeably older, the traces of former suffering are marked on her face, but there is also an expression of present contentment and calm"*; and Marsden also looks older, still suffering from *"deep grief"* over his mother's death (2:733). The child, named Gordon after Gordon Shaw, is napping upstairs. Marsden believes Nina must have chased Darrell away by getting pregnant with Evans's child; he briefly encountered Darrell in Europe and inwardly recalls how terrible the other looked. Evans forecasts an economic boom, and Marsden thinks bitterly that "his kind are inheriting the earth . . . hogging it, cramming it down their tasteless gullets!" (2:735). He suggests out loud that he will invite his sister to live with him. Nina again teases him about his bachelorhood; he cruelly retorts by mentioning his meeting with Darrell in Europe, and she reacts with guilty alarm. Marsden then mentions that a girl was with him, and Nina again shows outward distress. Marsden lies that he too had mistresses in Europe, then changes the subject when she inquires further. Nina suspects Marsden knows the truth about Darrell and makes a mental note to be careful around him. Nina and Evans go up to the baby's room, as Marsden's inner thoughts torment him with self-loathing. Evans returns and makes Marsden an investment proposition. Marsden politely declines. Evans good-naturedly invites Marsden to join him as a silent partner and not worry about a down payment, then goes out for a walk.

The doorbell rings. Marsden unenthusiastically welcomes Darrell into the house. Darrell appears dissipated and exhausted. He announces himself to Nina from downstairs, and Nina responds in frightened tones that she will join them in a moment. Darrell's expression and Nina's temerity convince Marsden that the two are in love. Darrell says he has returned to settle his late father's estate, a conscious excuse to come back to Nina. Nina descends the staircase feeling *"a mixture of love, of triumphant egotism . . . and of fear and uncertainty"*

(2:747). She instantly realizes that Darrell loves her, though Darrell is not as confident about her feelings for him. Marsden announces plans to invest with Evans. Nina thinks to herself, "I couldn't find a better husband than Sam . . . and I couldn't find a better lover than Ned . . . I need them both to be happy" (2:750). They discuss little Gordon, which arouses Marsden's suspicions about the identity of the father. Nina senses this and pleadingly calls out to Marsden. Still unaware of the truth, he reassures her that everything is all right. Once Marsden leaves, Darrell demands that Nina divorce Evans, but Nina resolves to retain him as her lover and Evans her husband. This outrages Darrell, who vows to notify Evans of the truth about the child just as Evans enters from his walk. However, Darrell cannot confess in the face of Evans's innocent good cheer. Marsden returns, and Nina triumphantly announces, "You are my three men!" (2:754). Moments later she reflects on this more deeply: "My three men! . . . I feel their desires converge in me! . . . I am pregnant with the three! . . . husband! . . . lover! . . . father! . . . and the fourth man! . . . little man! . . . he is mine too! . . . that makes it perfect!" Nina kisses Evans as a *"big brother,"* Marsden as *"her father,"* and Darrell *"lovingly on the lips as she would kiss her lover,"* and *"walks quietly out the room"* (2:757).

Act 7

Almost 11 years later, 1934, in the Evans sitting room in their Park Avenue apartment in New York City; again in the early fall. Nina is 35, and though physically healthy, tan, and *"in the full bloom of her womanhood,"* *"her expression is set and masklike."* Gordon, 11, is a precocious child with eyes *"full of a quick-tempered sensitiveness"* and shows early signs of athleticism (2:758). Darrell, who has been back for six months from his hobby at a biological research center in Antigua, looks much older. His features show a chronic sense of aimlessness. It is Gordon's birthday, and the boy's thoughts indicate open hatred of Darrell, as he cannot understand his mother's continued affection for him. Nina has lost all drive for happiness and inwardly voices love for her son and pity for Darrell, though she wants him to leave. Darrell resents Evans, for whose sanity he

and Nina have forfeited their own, and he blames Nina "for the mess [he has] made of life" (2:761). He and Marsden have collected a fortune from Evans's investments. Darrell quips over Evans's self-satisfaction, which enrages Gordon. An argument erupts between the two, and Nina sends her son from the room.

Darrell tolerates Gordon's hatred of him and wonders whether the boy subconsciously realizes that Darrell is his father. He brought a toy boat as a gift but left it in the hallway so Gordon would not be tempted to destroy it, as he has done in the past. Nina convinces Darrell it is time to return to Antigua, and they kiss twice; the second time, Gordon appears in the doorway and witnesses the kiss *"in a passion of jealousy and rage and grief"* (2:766). Nina senses his presence. Pretending he saw nothing, Gordon calls in that Marsden has arrived.

Marsden enters, *"if not happy . . . at least living in comparative peace with himself"* (2:767). Darrell directs a stream of barely couched invective against Marsden, whom he resents for having won over his son's affection. Nina defends Marsden and thinks, "[P]oor Charlie, . . . dear Charlie, what a perfect lover he would make for one's old age! . . . what a perfect lover when one was past passion!" (2:769). She then thinks how all her men, save Gordon, make her "sick" (2:769); she invites Marsden to help with dinner, and they exit together.

Gordon enters from the hallway carrying the toy boat *"in a terrific state of conflicting emotions"* (2:770). He smashes the toy in tears. Darrell and Gordon have it out, and in spite of himself Gordon is won over. Evans appears, and Darrell tells Gordon to hide the broken boat. Now exuding the authoritative air that comes with financial success, Evans hugs Gordon and welcomes Darrell. Darrell suffers from witnessing Evans's father role and excuses himself to prepare for his journey.

Gordon asks Evans why he was named Gordon. Once realizing his mother's love for Gordon Shaw, he inwardly decides to emulate his mythic namesake and thus supplant Darrell. Nina enters from the kitchen. After Gordon behaves in a mean-spirited manner toward her and delights over Darrell's departure, she suspects that he must have seen them kissing. Nina thinks of Darrell affectionately, at which point Gordon jumps from her lap. Shocked with the realization that Gordon can read her thoughts, Nina vows never to think of Darrell in her son's presence. Evans scolds her that Gordon should not be coddled as Marsden had been. "Oh, Mother God," she thinks as the curtain falls, "grant that I may some day tell this fool the truth!" (2:777).

Act 8

Ten years later; late afternoon in early June 1944, on the afterdeck of Evans's motor yacht at anchor on a river near Poughkeepsie. Nina, Darrell, Marsden, Evans, and Gordon's fiancée Madeline Arnold await the start of Gordon's rowing race. Nina's hair matches the white of her boating costume, and her face *"recalls instantly the Nina of Act Four, neurotic, passionately embittered and torn"* (2:778). Darrell appears more like the self-assured, clinically detached physician of act 2. Marsden, whose sister has now died, looks aged beyond his years and miserable. *"Evans is simply Evans"* (2:779). Madeline Arnold calls to mind an emotionally balanced Nina from act 1. Only Evans and Madeline express enthusiasm over the rowing event. Evans remarks that Gordon takes more after his namesake than himself and good-heartedly invites everyone into the cabin for a drink. Nina insists she be left alone with Darrell. In her thoughts, she exposits on how she and Darrell are no longer in love, "the only living life is in the past and future . . . the present is an interlude . . . strange interlude in which we call on past and future to bear witness we are living!" (2:784).

Nina remarks how young and handsome Darrell looks, which he attributes to his work at the biology research center. His research partner, a young biologist named Preston, has supplanted his affections for Gordon, whom he now sarcastically refers to as Nina's "ideal of college hero—like his never-to-be-forgotten namesake!" (2:786). Nina expresses her intense jealousy of Madeline. She wants Darrell to persuade Gordon not to marry her, but he has renounced meddling in any life "that has more than one cell" (2:789). Evans appears. The race is on, and Darrell inquires which crew Gordon fears most. Evans tells him Navy, and disappears back into the cabin. Darrell cheers for Navy. Nina resolves to inform Evans of the truth and convince

Darrell to verify it, thus using the secret to compel Gordon to break off his engagement—that way, she will rid herself of both Evans and Madeline and have Gordon to herself. Darrell reconsiders, still resentful of Evans's happiness, and wonders about the happiness he might have had; in the end, however, he refuses.

Marsden enters, drunk, and cheerily informs them they have no reason to feel guilty. Not unlike the effect of alcohol on the Tyrone men in LONG DAY'S JOURNEY INTO NIGHT, Marsden's drunkenness unleashes candid speech that would have been strictly consigned to his thoughts had he been sober. He announces he will wait for Evans to die and marry Nina and concludes his lengthy monologue by vowing to write a novel about all that has happened. Nina determines now to break off Gordon's engagement by having a conversation with Madeline like the one Mrs. Evans had had with her. Nina tells Madeline the engagement must be called off, but Darrell stops her before she can finish and walks off to watch the race.

Marsden approaches Nina, and she tells him everything. After his initial horror, he forgives her. Nina, who near-consciously thinks of him as her father, forgives him as well. The other characters cheer on Gordon, everyone except Darrell, who shouts, "Come on, Navy!" (2:799). This provokes Evans, but he eventually dismisses the outburst. The race is close, but Gordon's boat pulls ahead in the final sprint. Evans shouts with joy, embraces Nina, and cries, "Our Gordon! The greatest ever!" Nina lashes back, "No!—not yours!—mine!—and Gordon's!" (2:800). Himself still a worshipper of Gordon Shaw's, Evans exultantly agrees, then collapses to the deck. Darrell diagnoses the attack as a stroke and convinces Nina they must take care of him. Marsden guiltily thinks his turn is coming to marry Nina. Madeline, unaware of what has happened, looks out at her exhausted fiancé and thinks as the curtain falls, "your head will lie on my breast . . . soon!" (2:802).

Act 9

A few months later in the same year, 1944; the terrace of the Evans's *"pretentious villa"* on the south shore of Long Island (2:803). Evans is now dead.

Gordon and Madeline can be seen. Gordon is in mourning and resembles the character, if not the physical features, of Evans in act 2. Madeline tenderly consoles him. Gordon resents his mother for having been indifferent to his father during the final days. He also voices concern that Nina and Darrell had had an affair and tells Madeline of the incident in act 7. She convinces him not to blame them if they loved each other. They kiss, and Marsden approaches the veranda carrying freshly picked roses and shears. He contemplates their love, first prudishly, then with acceptance. Marsden announces himself, and at Gordon's request, he heads in to fetch Nina.

Nina and Darrell emerge from the house. Nina appears even older than the last act, and Darrell has lost his healthy looks and self-assured bearing. Gordon tells them his father's will leaves everything to himself and Nina, save half a million dollars to Preston and Darrell's biology station. Darrell resents this, damning Evans for co-opting Preston's goodwill from the grave. Gordon has something else to say, but when Darrell rushes him, he threatens his biological father with a "spanking" (2:811). Darrell continues provoking him, and Gordon slaps him forcefully across the face. Nina cries out that he is hurting his father, which Gordon takes figuratively and begs Darrell's forgiveness. Gordon tells them he is aware of their love for each other and wishes them well in marriage. Deeply moved, Darrell nearly tells him the truth, but Nina prevents this by asking Gordon if he ever thought she was unfaithful. His horrified denial silences Darrell's confession. Gordon leaves, and Darrell halfheartedly asks Nina to marry him for Gordon's sake. Nina kindly refuses. They say goodbye, with Darrell advising Nina to marry Marsden for peace of mind.

Marsden enters. She asks if he wants to marry her, and he says he does. Darrell wishes them well. Gordon passes directly overhead in a seaplane, and Darrell shouts that he is his father; then, *"with a grim fatalism,"* he cries out, "Good-bye, Gordon's son!" (2:816) and exits. Nina tells Marsden that her son had never been fully hers, that not even he could provide her the happiness she has so mercilessly sought throughout her life. Marsden advises her to forget the "Gordons." "There was something

unreal in all that has happened since you first met Gordon Shaw, something extravagant and fantastic, . . . [R]egard it as an interlude." "Strange interlude!" she responds. "Yes, our lives are merely strange dark interludes in the electrical display of God the Father!" (2:817). She again refers to Marsden as her "father" and falls asleep on his shoulder murmuring, "dear old Charlie!" Marsden is at first dejected—"God damn dear old . . . !"—but then reconciles with his identity: "No, God bless dear old Charlie . . . who, passed beyond desire, has all the luck at last! . . ." (2:818). With Nina asleep on his shoulder, Marsden looks about contentedly as the shadows deepen, and the curtain falls.

COMMENTARY

Strange Interlude marks Eugene O'Neill's full maturation as an artist. With groundbreaking stylistic, technical, and thematic devices, the playwright had perfected his stagecraft over the previous two decades, and he would continue to develop those devices in the years to come. The play's first production led most critics to praise it as "the most significant contribution any American has made to the stage" and "the top of O'Neill's career" (quoted in Sheaffer 287, 288). Others, given its length—nine acts, calling to mind both his heroine's name "Nina" and the average length of a pregnancy (Day 84)—and the somewhat disruptive back-and-forth between inner and outer dialogue, lacked some conviction on this point. O'Neill's first notes for *Strange Interlude* appear in 1923, at which point he called it *Godfather*, a word game on one of the play's most resonant themes, "God, the Father" or "the Father God." (These early notes comprised the exonerating evidence to PLAGIARISM brought to the playwright by George Lewys, the penname of Gladys Lewis, in a trial on March 13, 1931.) Later, in his WORK DIARY, O'Neill wrote,

Method—Start with soliloquy—perhaps have the whole play nothing but a thinking aloud (or this entrance for other play—anyway the thinking aloud being more important than the actual talking—speech breaking through thought as a random process of concealment, speech inconsequential or imperfectly expressing the thought behind—all done with the most drastic logic and economy and simplicity of words (Thought perhaps, always naturally expressing itself to us—thinking itself—or being thought by us—always in terms of an adolescent level of vocabulary, as if we thereby eternally tried to educate to mature self-understanding, the child in us.) (in Floyd 1981, 74)

On the page, O'Neill indents inner thoughts to distinguish between speaking and thinking, a method that combines Elizabethan soliloquy with 20th-century psychology. Clearly, O'Neill's asides—alternatively called "spoken thoughts, inner monologues, thought asides, double dialogue, poetry of the unconscious, Freudian chorus, and silences out loud" (Wainscott 234)—recall the psychological theories and "stream of consciousness" concepts one finds in the work of William James, Sigmund Freud, Carl Jung, Alfred Adler, and James Joyce (O'Neill was reading Joyce's novel *Ulysses* [1922] at the time of *Strange Interlude*'s composition [Mandl]). O'Neill wrote one of the play's reviewers that "these same ideas are age-old to the artist and . . . any artist who was a good psychologist and had had a varied and sensitive experience with life and all sorts of people could have written *S.I.* without ever having heard of Freud, Jung, Adler & Co" (O'Neill 1988, 247). But these names, perhaps aside from James, meant little to an average American audience member in 1928, when *Strange Interlude* was considered "a revelation" (Bogard 297). The technique entered the American popular consciousness as well. Groucho Marx of the Marx Brothers, for instance, parodied O'Neill's inner monologues hilariously in the film *Animal Crackers* (1930; screenplay by S. J. Perelman).

At a rehearsal, O'Neill once quipped to Lawrence Langner of the Theatre Guild that "if the actors weren't so dumb, they wouldn't need asides; they'd be able to express the meaning without them" (quoted in Bogard 307)—a sentiment shared by several reviewers. Yet the playwright's experiment goes beyond a simple device to assuage his well-known mistrust of actors, as it exposes the lies people tell to dissemble their true feelings and beliefs to the outside world. Numerous critics explain

O'Neill's thought asides as exposing his characters' Freudian "unconscious" to the audience. However, if this was O'Neill's intent in the final draft, he fails utterly, since the characters appear fully aware of their painful inner struggles. Each character *consciously* responds to his or her own thoughts—no matter how bizarre or abstract—often hiding them with *consciously* "inconsequential" dialogue. That their thoughts are conscious, in fact, mounts the tragic tension and dramatic irony (a form in which the audience knows what some characters do not) over the course of the play and builds as we increasingly realize that our lives, even to our closest intimates, are based on lies. O'Neill himself described *Strange Interlude* as an "attempt at the new masked psychological drama . . . without masks—a successful attempt, perhaps, in so far as [sic] it concerns only surfaces and their immediate subsurfaces, but not where, occasionally, it tries to probe deeper" (O'Neill 1961, 119).

Philip Moeller, the play's first director, interpreted the majority of O'Neill's inner dialogues as "conscious thought" (Wainscott 234). Once this decision was made, another challenge remained: By what technical means might he represent conscious thought on the stage without the audience confusing thought with actual speech? Considering the dilemma on a train ride one day, Moeller clenched his body suddenly when the conductor made an emergency stop. The other passengers froze too. Looking about the car, he had stumbled upon the answer: When one actor delivered an inner monologue, the rest of the players on stage should freeze, a technique he called "arrested motion" or "physical quiet" (Wainscott 235). Though there were many possibilities—for example, spotlighting or voiceovers—this one proved extremely successful.

O'Neill describes nearly all his characters in ways more suitable for a novel than a play. With this in mind, according to Philip Parry, the play is the foremost example of what he calls the "O'Neill paradox"—that "America's foremost dramatist is scarcely a dramatist at all"; indeed, Parry characterized O'Neill's experiment as an "abdication of a dramatist's traditional responsibilities and a decisive move into the territory of the novel" (325). Spoken dialogue comprises less than a third of the script. The remaining two-thirds consist of inner monologues voicing characters' actual thoughts, masked as they are by the superficiality of everyday speech, and STAGE DIRECTIONS so intricate as to make the script read more like a novel than a play. How is an actor, no matter how talented, to interpret this aspect of the Marsden character: *"There is an indefinable feminine quality about him, but it is nothing apparent in either appearance or act"* (2:633); or this description, a less extreme example, of Mrs. Evans: *"the ghost of an old faith and trust in life's goodness, hovers girlishly, fleetingly, about the corners of her mouth and softens into deep sorrow the shadowy grimness of her eyes"* (2:680)?

Dudley Nichols of the *New York World* wrote that "it would seem that [O'Neill] has not only written a great American play but the great American novel as well" (quoted in Sheaffer 288). Dr. Edmund Darrell echoes O'Neill's sentiment about novelists in general when he says, "well-written surface . . . no depth, no digging underneath . . . why? . . . he has talent but doesn't dare . . . afraid he'll meet himself somewhere" (2:662). O'Neill himself responded to the critic Joseph Wood Krutch by writing that on the one hand, he appreciated the comparison to the play as a novel. On the other, novelists as a class "appear to me as mere timid recorders of life, dodging the responsibility of that ruthless selection and deletion and concentration on the essential which is the test of an artist—the forcing of significant form upon experience. No, I think the novelists are worse than the playwrights—they waste more of one's time!" (O'Neill, 1994, 247). Indeed, unlike *The GREAT GOD BROWN*, in which the playwright employed physical masks to demonstrate the outer self-representation of his characters, O'Neill's newest experiment allowed inner monologues and nonrepresentational stage directions to coexist with outer dialogue and thus emphasize—more realistically than the EXPRESSIONISM of *The Great God Brown*—the duality of psychological states and social worlds, inner thoughts and spoken words, reality and lies.

One of several god-searching plays—others include *GOLD* (the money god), *DYNAMO* (the technology god) and *DAYS WITHOUT END* (the Catholic god)—*Strange Interlude* charts Nina Leeds's futile quest for a god figure to live by. Her first conviction is that a just universe would allow God to be found in Woman:

> The mistake began when God was created in a male image. Of course, women would see Him that way, but men should have been gentlemen enough, remembering their mothers, to make God a woman! But God of Gods—the Boss—has always been a man. That makes life so perverted, and death so unnatural. We should have imagined life as created in the birth-pain of God the Mother. Then we would understand why we, Her children, have inherited pain, for we would know that our life's rhythm beats from Her great heart, torn with the agony of love and birth. (2:670; see also 2:732, 789, and 800)

By act 8, however, Nina views "God the Mother" as losing the battle with "God the Father" when Gordon's marriage to Madeline is imminent; and by act 9, she capitulates fully to life being "merely strange dark interludes in the electrical display of God the Father" (2:817). (O'Neill would return to this concept of an "electric" God quite literally in his next play, *Dynamo.*) In the final scene, Nina offers herself up to the paternal Marsden in order to find comfort and protection in old age (if one considers the mid-40s old). Thus, although O'Neill identified *Strange Interlude* as his "woman play"—or his "theatrical allegory of gender," as Bette Mandl has described it (123)—it cannot be regarded as a feminist play by contemporary standards.

Charles Marsden sees Nina as morally corrupted, Edmund Darrell considers her viciously manipulative, and Sam Evans is too simpleminded to take anything seriously. So just what elements of her being are meant to appeal to the audience, or at least offer some understanding of her appeal to the male characters, is a vexed mystery. Barrett Clark describes Nina as "mother, wife, mistress, prostitute, materialist, idealist: in short, the artist's conception of Woman" (174). Apparently O'Neill's "conception of Women" did not include "professional," "intellectual," "partner," or any variation thereof. Even when volunteering as a nurse at the veterans sanatorium, she constructs for herself a "species of inverted brothel" wherein she "gives" her body to wounded soldiers and only succeeds in psychologically damaging both herself and them. As she goes on to effectively destroy the lives of her men, she might be considered another example of O'Neill's "women destroyers," a character type O'Neill borrowed from one of his greatest dramatic influences, AUGUST STRINDBERG. Nina's inner thoughts, as Judith E. Barlow points out, "rarely go beyond the males in her life" (167), and Doris Nelson adds that as she grows old, Nina experiences "physical rather than intellectual changes" (quoted in Barlow 168). Barlow suggests that in general, given the substantial role of PROSTITUTION in the O'Neill canon, "if O'Neill's female characters earn their own living, they are likely to do so on their backs" (166).

O'Neill describes Nina's face as "striking, handsome rather than pretty" (2:642), and thus her whole allure, particularly among her three men, is derived from her attractive shape—an athletic figure she never loses. We get our last glimpse at her physical form in the stage directions of act 8, in which O'Neill emphasizes that although at 45 her hair has gone white and her face has lost its *"charm," "she has kept her beautiful figure"* (2:778). Though her dialogue, internal and external, reveals a tremendously passionate, severely disillusioned, and conscious victim of modernity, Nina's character remains largely instinctual and reactive rather than intellectual and proactive.

Strange Interlude is a far cry from O'Neill's more overtly sexist early play, SERVITUDE. There is no question that Nina Leeds is one of his most fully realized female characters, and her needs supersede those of her men. But in the end, there is little to Nina as a gendered being than her desperate need to procreate in pursuit of self-fulfillment and happiness. Thus, although Nina does require sex as well as a child from Darrell, love emerges as another influence O'Neill has brought to bear on the play—a biological force, which the German philosopher Arthur Schopenhauer believed serves only to "fulfilling the needs of the species" (Alexander 1992, 114).

Travis Bogard argues that because O'Neill's play projects itself 19 years into the future (1944) with so few substantial historical referents, the play demonstrates "O'Neill's tendency to look at life without reference to a society, to tell his story only in terms of personality" (306). But when looked at allegorically, history proves a more rewarding window into Nina's character and the play as a whole than GENDER. Most critics tend to read *Strange Interlude* as a purely psychological experiment and reject the importance of history in the play. Perhaps the most interesting argument on this end is that although the play can be considered a work of science fiction—since it ends in 1944—O'Neill makes little effort to project into the future historically (though one exception might be Gordon Evans owning his own airplane). However, Brenda Murphy has contested powerfully that O'Neill uses Nina as a "central figure in his mythicizing of American culture between the wars" (140) and that her men are the conflicting forces at work in the nation at large—namely, the genteel tradition (Professor Leeds), American "schoolboy ideals" (Gordon Shaw), venture capitalism (Evans), Puritan morality (Marsden), scientific progress (Darrell), and national innocence (Nina's son Gordon).

With this paradigm in mind, Murphy considers *Strange Interlude* "by far the most ambitious of O'Neill's treatments of contemporary American culture." For a time in *Strange Interlude,* Puritanism and science benefit from venture capital's dominance (Darrell and Marsden make a fortune after investing with Evans), but they must ultimately pursue fulfillment in their own ways. "This tenuously balanced system inevitably breaks down . . . as each of the forces proceeds on its own trajectory" (Murphy 144). Puritanism may have won out in the form of Marsden's eventual marriage to Nina, but this union becomes an allegory for a kind of national spiritual atrophy.

Nina's extreme disillusionment corresponds to the general zeitgeist of the country after World War I—the source of modernism's bleak ethos—and thus Nina's quest for happiness is symbolic of the national recovery from its loss of innocence, the death of Gordon Shaw. Additionally, O'Neill's own notion of PHILOSOPHICAL ANARCHISM—whose practitioners rejected the "fixed ideas" of government, myth, and God—appears in act 2 when Darrell remarks on Nina's "fixed idea" about Gordon Shaw (American "schoolboy ideals") and the "Gordon myth" in act 4, and in Nina's conscious attempt after Gordon's death to "believe in any God at any price—a heap of stones, a mud image, a drawing on a wall, a bird, a fish, a snake, a baboon—or even a good man preaching the simple platitudes of truth, those Gospel words we love the sound of but whose meaning we pass on to spooks to live by!" (2:669). What each character strives for in this play is happiness. *Strange Interlude* is thus an account of the psychological pain that comes with our collectively futile pursuit of meaning and happiness, and how the absence of pain only comes with forgiveness.

CHARACTERS

Arnold, Madeline Gordon Evans's fiancée. Madeline is 19, very pretty, and recalls Nina Leeds's athletic figure in act 1. Nina expresses intense jealousy toward Madeline's co-optation of her son Gordon, which echoes Professor Henry Leeds's Freudian jealousy toward Gordon Shaw in act 1. Nina nearly lies that Gordon suffers from the same recessive insanity as her husband Sam Evans, but her lover Dr. Edmund Darrell prevents her from carrying out the deception. In the final act, Madeline convinces her fiancé to forgive his mother for loving Darrell; as a result, Gordon wishes them well in marriage after his father's death, though in the end Nina chooses Marsden. Practical-minded, caring, and lovely, Madeline will be the ideal wife for the inevitably successful Gordon Evans.

Darrell, Doctor Edmund "Ned" Nina Leeds's lover and Gordon Evans's biological father. When first introduced, Darrell is 27, *"short, dark, wiry, his movements rapid and sure, his manner cool and observant, his dark eyes analytical"* (2:661). Darrell was the presiding physician at the sanitarium where Nina worked as a nurse and where she slept with the wounded veterans to fill the void of her fiancé Gordon Shaw's death. He instructs Charles Marsden, Nina's longtime friend, to convince Nina that her salvation lies in marrying Sam Evans, which she does. After being warned of the congenital insanity in her husband's family by her mother-in-law, Mrs. Amos Evans, Nina persuades Darrell to impregnate her so she might have a healthy baby. He accepts, but his guilt over betraying his naive friend Evans

transforms him physically and psychologically into a state of dissipation that only achieves a brief respite after some research work at a biological institute in Antigua with a young scientist named Preston. Preston becomes like a son to Darrell, as his actual son Gordon despises him for having such a close relationship to his mother (in act 7, Gordon witnesses them kissing).

Darrell serves Nina only as a "lover," while Charles Marsden takes the role of her "father," and Evans her "husband." Darrell can also be seen as the force of science in the modern America (personified by Nina), with Marsden as Puritanism and Evans as venture capitalism (see Murphy). Once Evans dies, Gordon gives Darrell and his mother his blessing if they choose to marry, but Nina decides instead to marry Marsden, who will protect her and give her peace in her final years. Darrell is one of the O'Neill canon's few fully developed doctors, who usually appear as Marsden characterizes them—"a pack of God-damned ignorant liars and hypocrites" (2:724). Darrell initially has the ability to restrain his *"intense passion"* by maintaining a calculating, objective view of love *"through his scientific understanding of its real sexual nature"* (2:661), a belief echoed in the works of O'Neill philosophical influence Arthur Schopenhauer (see Alexander 1953). Darrell shares the same first name as O'Neill's deceased older brother, EDMUND BURKE O'NEILL, who died at the age of two before O'Neill was born.

Evans, Mrs. Amos Sam Evans's mother. Mrs. Evans outwardly displays the characteristics of a *"wonderfully made, lifelike doll,"* but *"her big dark eyes are grim with the prisoner-pain of a walled-in soul"* (2:680). She suspects Nina Leeds is pregnant with her grandchild in act 3, and when Nina confirms this, Mrs. Evans reveals the "curse on the Evanses" (2:685)—a recessive insanity gene on her husband's side. They swore never to have children, but one night when the two were drunk, she got pregnant. Mr. Evans succumbed to the illness when Sam was eight; she hid the truth from her son, and her fear of Sam's condition never waned. She persuades Nina to have an abortion and choose a healthy male to father her child; Nina eventually chooses Edmund Darrell.

Evans, Gordon Nina Leeds's son and Dr. Edmund Darrell's biological son, who was raised to believe Sam Evans is his father. Gordon first appears in act 7, when he is 11 years old, *"a fine boy with, even at his age, the figure of an athlete. He looks older than he is. There is a grave expression to his face"* (2:758). Strangely, he resembles neither his mother nor his father. Gordon resents Edmund Darrell's place in his mother's life and witnesses Nina and Darrell kissing, an experience he never forgets. Upon learning he was named for Gordon Shaw, he inwardly determines to emulate Shaw in order to gain his mother's exclusive devotion. Gordon grows up to be more like his namesake, Gordon Shaw, than either his mother or his presumed father Sam Evans. By act 8, he is a star collegiate rower, his future is secure, and he has become engaged to marry a beautiful girl, Madeline Arnold. Dependent on her son for happiness, Nina hates Madeline as an interloper. By act 9, O'Neill describes Gordon as *"extremely handsome after the fashion of the magazine cover American collegian"* (2:803).

Gordon and Darrell confront each other in the final act, and Gordon slaps his biological father for treating him like a child. Nevertheless, Madeline convinces Gordon to accept Nina and Darrell's love for one another, and he consents to their marriage. (Nina decides to marry Marsden for peace of mind.) In the final scene, Gordon and Madeline fly off in Gordon's private airplane. Darrell first shouts up that he is his actual father, then cries out, "Good-bye, Gordon's son!" (2:816). Much like Gordon Shaw, Gordon symbolizes American innocence and "schoolboy ideals." As such, since the businessman Sam Evans claims him as his son, the plot reflects American venture capital co-opting the American innocence as its own (Murphy 141). Gordon also resembles EUGENE O'NEILL, JR., O'Neill's son by KATHLEEN JENKINS, who was raised to believe he was her second husband's son (Alexander 1992, 119).

Evans, Sam Nina Leeds's husband. O'Neill first describes Evans in act 2 as *"above medium height, very blond, with guileless, diffident blue eyes, his figure inclined to immature lumbering outlines"* (2:657).

He is 25 years old but takes pride in his collegiate clothing, manners, and physical attributes. Evans adores Nina Leeds, and after Dr. Edmund Darrell and Charles Marsden convince her to marry him for salvation, he acts as the model husband, if not a lover like Darrell or a father figure like Marsden. Evans's family on his father's side has a recessive insanity gene about which he is unaware, though his mother, Mrs. Amos Evans, informs Nina. "Rather presciently in 1928," writes Brenda Murphy, "O'Neill has Sam suffering from a congenital disease that will destroy him eventually," as venture capital will be by the stock market crash, which would take place the year following its premiere (143). As a result, Nina chooses Darrell to be her child's biological father, and the two keep this secret from Evans to his death by a stroke at the end of the play.

Simpleminded but hardworking, Evans fails at his first attempts to support Nina but soon discovers a propensity for venture capitalism and makes a fortune. He is the most sympathetic businessman in the O'Neill canon with the possible exception of William A. Brown in *The Great God Brown*. His opposite can be found in the destructively acquisitive character Marco Polo of *Marco Millions*. If one considers Nina as metaphorical of the United States between the world wars, Evans represents venture capitalism as a social force while Darrell represents scientific progress and Marsden Puritan morality.

Leeds, Professor Henry Nina Leeds's father and Charles Marsden's former professor. He is 55, thin, balding, and extremely professorial in manner and act. His study, the setting for acts 1, 2, and 4, reveals a great deal about the character: *"The atmosphere of the room is that of a cozy, cultured retreat, sedulously built as a sanctuary where, secure with the culture of the past at his back, a fugitive from reality can view the present safely from a distance, as a superior with condescending disdain, pity, and even amusement"* (2:633). Professor Leeds—symbolically, an "overlay of classical Western culture on American Puritanism" (Murphy 141)—studies ancient literature and the European classics. The English texts he owns come from the period when "s *was still* *like an* f," and the most modern writer he owns is "*probably Thackeray*" (2:633). Leeds's wife died six years before the action of act 1, and his daughter Nina has taken her place as the dominant female presence in the house. When she fell in love with the college hero Gordon Shaw, before the action of the play, Leeds became intensely jealous and convinced Shaw not to marry his daughter until he returned from his tour as a fighter pilot in World War I. Shaw died in combat two days before the armistice, and Nina loathes her father for having interfered before she and Shaw could consummate their relationship and give her Shaw's child. Leeds dies before the action of act 2. In his final lines, he consoles himself by reading from Manilius's *Astronomicon*, which looks forward to Nina's concept of the "electrical display of God the Father" line in act 9. Nina grieves his death, but for her, "when Gordon died, all men died" (2:656).

Leeds, Nina Professor Henry Leeds's daughter, Charles Marsden's friend and later fiancée, Sam Evans's wife, Edmund Darrell's lover, and Gordon Evans's mother. One of the most finely drawn female characters in the O'Neill canon—perhaps bested only by Josie Hogan in A MOON FOR THE MISBEGOTTEN and Mary Tyrone in *Long Day's Journey into Night*—Nina, whom O'Neill describes in an early note as "ultra-neurotic" (quoted in Floyd 1985, 336), is first introduced as "*twenty, tall with broad square shoulders, slim strong hips and long beautifully developed legs. . . . Her face is strikingly handsome rather than pretty, the bone structure prominent,*" with eyes the color of a "*deep greenish blue*" (2:642). Over time, her hair whitens and her face collapses into a figurative mask of despair, but her figure retains its shape. Her physical description strongly calls to mind that of O'Neill's then-estranged wife, AGNES BOULTON (see Alexander 1992, 105). Travis Bogard has also suggested that Nina is O'Neill's first serious attempt to portray his mother, MARY ELLEN "ELLA" O'NEILL, given not only her physical description but also her acute nervousness and ability to dominate the emotions of the men in her life as her avatar Mary Tyrone does in *Long Day's Journey* (301). Biographer Stephen A. Black adds that O'Neill told his wives that he believed

his mother insane before discovering her morphine addiction, and as a result felt that he too would become insane (346). Black also suggests there is an autobiographical aspect to Nina's character, since she loses her mother at 14, as O'Neill symbolically lost his mother upon discovering her morphine addiction; and like Nina, at the time of composition, he too was jumping from one dependency on a member of the opposite sex to another in order to lessen the sense of loss he felt over his mother's death (346–348).

A year before the play's action, Nina lost her fiancé, Gordon Shaw, an aviator who was shot down two days before the armistice that ended World War I. She correctly blames her father for convincing Shaw not to marry her before he left for the war, which in effect left her childless and thus without a living memory of Shaw. To fill the void of emptiness she suffers after Shaw's death, Nina volunteers at a sanatorium for wounded veterans and sleeps with the patients in a perverse attempt to atone for her inability to "give" herself to Shaw (2:647). Nina returns to her father's house after his death and exhibits a remarkable personality change for the worse to those who know her best—her father's friend and former student, Charles Marsden, and Dr. Edmund Darrell, a friend of Shaw's from the war who ran the sanatorium. Hers is a profound disillusionment that borders, to their mind, on the early stages of insanity: "Do you understand me, Charlie? Say lie," she taunts Marsden after a bitter and lengthy monologue. "L-i-i-e! Now say life. L-i-i-f-e! You see! Life is just a long drawn out lie with a sniffling sigh at the end!" (2:668).

Nina agrees to marry Sam Evans, a boyish, adoring young man who would provide her with the love and devotion that may save her. She becomes pregnant, but his mother Mrs. Evans informs her that insanity runs in her late husband's family, and thus in Sam. Nina agrees to have an abortion and chooses Edmund Darrell to father her child. The secret of the boy's true father is withheld from Evans to the end, along with Nina and Darrell's continued affair, to protect Evans from descending into insanity. The child, named Gordon after Nina's dead fiancé, grows up to hate Darrell for stealing his mother's attentions.

Following the death of Gordon Shaw, around whom she constructs an undying myth of perfection, Nina surrounds herself with male figures who separately cannot offer her what she needs, but combined make her perfect man: "My three men! . . . I feel their desires converge in me! . . . I am pregnant with the three! . . . husband! [Sam Evans] . . . lover! [Edmund Darrell] . . . father! [Charles Marsden] . . . and the fourth man! . . . little man! [Gordon Evans] . . . he is mine too! . . . that makes it perfect!" (2:756). Desperately jealous over Gordon's engagement to Madeline Arnold in act 8, Nina almost lies to Madeline that Gordon shares Evans's history of insanity, and she nearly tells Gordon of his true parentage—but Darrell intervenes. When Sam Evans dies of a stroke, she agrees to marry Marsden in order to "be in love with peace together . . . to die in peace!" (2:817).

In the modernist era in which FRIEDRICH NIETZSCHE pronounced that "God is Dead," Nina's desperation for a sense of purpose and happiness makes her long for a "Mother God" who might protect her from the tauntingly egotistical and guilt-inducing "God the Father." Her belief in the "Mother God" sustains her for a time, but by the final act, she accepts "God the Father" as the victor and longs for pity and peace rather than happiness and self-fulfillment. Not only can the men in her life be regarded as embodying the traits of manhood that might make Nina (Woman) happy, but they also offer a reading, as Brenda Murphy has argued, of Nina as a metaphor of the United States between the two world wars. In this interpretation, the men act as the dominant social forces then shaping the nation—Gordon Shaw representing American "schoolboy ideals," Sam Evans venture capitalism, Charles Marsden Puritan morality, Edmund Darrell scientific progress, and her son Gordon American innocence. As no one force can be fully compatible with the others, the nation (Nina) defaults in the end to the protective, if complacent and spiritually bankrupt realm of American Puritanism (Marsden).

Marsden, Charles "Charlie" Professor Henry Leeds's former student and friend, Nina Leeds's friend and future husband, and a writer of well-regarded if innocuous novels of manners. Marsden served as a correspondent in World War I; since his return, he has enjoyed a steady career as an author. O'Neill describes him as "*an Anglicized New England gentleman*" who contains "*an indefinable feminine quality about him, but it is nothing apparent in either appearance or* act" (2:633); he is someone "*always willing to listen, eager to sympathize, to like and be liked*" (2:634). The one constant in Nina Leeds's life, Marsden is alternately revolted and allured by Nina's unconventional sex life. Brenda Murphy characterizes Marsden as embodying "a puritanical rejection of the new sexual freedom being asserted by the artists of O'Neill's generation in the twenties" (143). He is a comfort to Nina in difficult times, so much so that she often unconsciously refers to him as "father," though his judgmental attitude frequently annoys her. In the end, she chooses to live in peace with him rather than in sexual turmoil with Darrell.

Repeatedly characterized by the other characters and his creator in the stage directions as effeminate, Marsden showers his mother with a near-unnatural devotion and never recovers from the devastation he feels after her death. Nina Leeds's final lines in the play sum up Marsden's function as both a purveyor of guilt and a comforting, stable companion: "Thank you, Father—have I been wicked?—you're so good—dear old Charlie!" (2:818).

Most critics consider Marsden the only homosexual in the O'Neill canon. In an early note in his 1925 WORK DIARY, O'Neill unambiguously wrote, "he is bisexual" (quoted in Floyd 1981, 71) and later as "positively gushing about men" (quoted in Floyd 1985, 337). His name probably comes from the combined names of the homosexual artists Charles Demuth and Marsden Hartley, both of whom O'Neill knew in GREENWICH VILLAGE and Provincetown, Massachusetts; and his bisexuality is confirmed in the final script when Dr. Edmund Darrell thinks of him in their initial encounter as "one of those poor devils who spend their lives trying not to discover which sex to belong to!" (2:662). There is no evidence in the text to conclusively demonstrate Marsden prefers men, but the subconscious sense is there: When he first glimpses Darrell, for instance, he thinks to himself, "good looking? . . . more or less . . . attractive to women, I dare say" (2:662). Whatever the case, Marsden is important in the O'Neill canon for being the only representation O'Neill ever provided of either bisexuality or HOMOSEXUALITY, latent or otherwise. Notably, Marsden is a writer like his creator, shares similar physical traits, also attempted to reconcile his relationship with his dying father on his deathbed, and experiences extreme self-loathing for having lost his virginity to a prostitute (Floyd 1985, 337). After Nina, Marsden was O'Neill's favorite character: "I've known many Marsdens on many different levels of life and it has always seemed to me that they've never been done in literature with any sympathy or real insight" (O'Neill, 1988, 247).

Shaw, Gordon Nina Leeds's fiancé before the play's action and Gordon Evans's namesake. Margaret Loftus Ranald finds a possible source for Shaw in the "quintessential Princeton hero" and World War I aviator Hobart Amory Hare Baker (1892–1918), who was also killed at the end of the war (668). An offstage character, the "Gordon myth" pervades the script, and Nina Leeds never recovers from his death. Gordon died in combat as a fighter pilot during World War I. Before going off to war, Nina's father, Professor Henry Leeds, persuaded Gordon not to marry Nina. Nina despises her father for preventing the consummation of their relationship, which would have given her a child to remember Gordon by. No one man can replace her image of her dead fiancé, so Nina surrounds herself with several who together approach her sense of his perfection, but they never fully achieve it. As a result, her father Professor Henry Leeds, her lover Dr. Edmund Darrell, and her future husband and surrogate father figure Charles Marsden all resent Gordon Shaw years after his death. The only men in her life who do not are her husband Sam Evans, who worships Shaw almost as much as Nina, and her son, who vows in adolescence to emulate him in order to win his mother's love. Gordon is remembered by all of the characters, often cynically, as the quintessential college hero; as such, Brenda Murphy reads the offstage character as speaking to the myth of America's "schoolboy ideals" (141).

BIBLIOGRAPHY

Alexander, Doris. *Eugene O'Neill's Creative Struggle: The Decisive Decade, 1924–1933*. University Park: Pennsylvania State University Press, 1992.

———. "*Strange Interlude* and Schopenhauer." *American Literature* 25 (1953): 213–228.

Barlow, Judith. "O'Neill's Female Characters." In *The Cambridge Companion to Eugene O'Neill*, edited by Michael Manheim, 164–177. New York: Cambridge University Press, 1998.

Black, Stephen A. *Eugene O'Neill: Beyond Mourning and Tragedy*. New Haven, Conn.: Yale University Press, 1999.

Bogard, Travis. *Contour in Time: The Plays of Eugene O'Neill*. Rev. ed. New York: Oxford University Press, 1988.

Clark, Barrett H. *Eugene O'Neill: The Man and His Plays*. Rev. ed. New York: Dover, 1947.

Day, Cyrus. "The Iceman and the Bridegroom: Some Observations on the Death of O'Neill's Salesman." In *Twentieth Century Interpretations of The Iceman Cometh*, edited by John Henry Raleigh, 79–86. Englewood Cliffs, N.J.: Prentice Hall, 1968.

Floyd, Virginia. *The Plays of Eugene O'Neill: A New Assessment*. New York: Ungar, 1985.

Floyd, Virginia, ed. *Eugene O'Neill at Work: Newly Released Ideas for His Plays*. New York: Ungar, 1981.

Krutch, Joseph Wood. "Strange Interlude." 1928 review. In *O'Neill and His Plays: Four Decades of Criticism*, edited by Oscar Cargill, N. Bryllion Fagin, and William J. Fisher, 184–186. New York: New York University Press, 1961.

Mandl, Bette. "'Thinking Aloud' in Eugene O'Neill's *Strange Interlude*." *Eugene O'Neill Review* (2004). Available online. URL: http://www.eoneill.com/library/review/26/26d.htm. Accessed September 8, 2007.

Murphy, Brenda. "O'Neill's America: The Strange Interlude between the Wars." In *The Cambridge Companion to Eugene O'Neill*, edited by Michael Manheim, 135–147. New York: Cambridge University Press, 1998.

O'Neill, Eugene. "Memoranda on Masks." In *O'Neill and His Plays: Four Decades of Criticism*, edited by Oscar Cargill, N. Bryllion Fagin, and William J. Fisher, 116–122. New York: New York University Press, 1961.

————. *Selected Letters of Eugene O'Neill*. Edited by Travis Bogard and Jackson R. Bryer. New Haven, Conn.: Yale University Press, 1988.

Parry, Philip. "Eugene O'Neill." In *The Oxford Encyclopedia of American Literature*. Vol 3, edited by Jay Parini. New York: Oxford University Press, 2004.

Ranald, Margaret Loftus. *The Eugene O'Neill Companion*. New York: Greenwood Press, 1984.

Shaeffer, Louis. *O'Neill: Son and Artist*. Boston: Little, Brown, 1973.

Wainscott, Ronald H. *Staging O'Neill: The Experimental Years, 1920–1934*. New Haven, Conn.: Yale University Press, 1988.

Straw: A Play in Three Acts, The (completed, 1919; first produced, 1921)

One of Eugene O'Neill's earliest full-length plays, *The Straw* is second only to LONG DAY'S JOURNEY INTO NIGHT for its autobiographical content. Written in the winter of 1918–19, *The Straw* premiered on November 3, 1921, at the Lyceum Theatre in NEW LONDON, CONNECTICUT, and then moved to the Greenwich Village Theatre on November 10, 1921. "ANNA CHRISTIE," for which O'Neill received his second PULITZER PRIZE, opened that same month. *The Straw* recounts O'Neill's actual experience at the GAYLORD FARM SANATORIUM in Wallingford, Connecticut, from Christmas Eve 1912 to June 3, 1913, after the 24-year-old O'Neill had been diagnosed with tuberculosis, then known as "consumption" or the "Great White Plague." *The Straw* can thus be read as a sequel to O'Neill's greatest tragedy, *Long Day's Journey*, in which his most autobiographical character, Edmund Tyrone, first discovers that he has contracted the killer disease. Other than their names, the only real discrepancy between *The Straw*'s protagonist Stephen Murray and Edmund Tyrone is that Stephen is somewhat older than Edmund—30, O'Neill's age when he created the character.

O'Neill experienced a self-professed intellectual and psychological rebirth during his convalescence at Gaylord. Over a year after his release from the sanatorium, he wrote to its superintendent David Russell Lyman that "if, as they say, it is sweet to visit the place one was born in, then it will be doubly sweet for me to visit the place I was reborn in—for my second birth was the only one which had my full approval" (O'Neill 25). While there, he began reading many of the authors and specific playwrights who would become some of his greatest literary influences—including writers from the Irish Literary Renaissance, JOHN MILLINGTON SYNGE, William Butler Yeats, and Lady Gregory, who all wrote for the ABBEY THEATRE, and the Swedish playwright AUGUST STRINDBERG. He read the *Rubáiyát* of Omar Khayyam, and Francis Thompson's epic poem "The Hound of Heaven" was sent to him later by a strict Irish Catholic nurse at Gaylord in the futile hope that the poem might bring back the young apostate's faith in the church (Gelb 387). Less famously, he conducted a long flirtation with a working-class IRISH-AMERICAN girl named Kitty MacKay, the model for Eileen Carmody in *The Straw*, who died of tuberculosis in 1915.

SYNOPSIS

Act 1, Scene 1

Kitchen of the Carmody home in "*the outskirts of a manufacturing town in Connecticut*" (Waterbury, Connecticut; 1:717) at around eight o'clock on a frigid evening in late February. The room's atmosphere is cheery, a pot simmers on the stove, and "*everything has a clean, neatly-kept appearance*" (1:717). Bill Carmody, a middle-aged Irish widower, sits in a rocking chair near the stove reading a newspaper and smoking a blackened clay pipe. His eight-year-old daughter Mary reads a picture book at a table at center. Carmody roughly chides her for reading, instead of "rompin' and playin'" outside, and he blames her bookishness on his deceased wife's side of the family: "They always was dreamin' their lives out" (1:718).

Carmody rails against raising five children without a wife or mother to support them; this coarse mention of her deceased mother reduces Mary to tears. He orders her to stop as three other children, Nora, Tom, and Billy, enter the house. Nora and Tom are breathless after racing to the house, while

Catherine Mackay (the model for Eileen Carmody) and an unidentified patient at Gaylord Farm *(Courtesy of the Sheaffer-O'Neill Collection, Charles E. Shain Library of Connecticut College)*

Billy, a 14-year-old replica of his father, looks on in adolescent disdain. Carmody sends the youngest ones upstairs and refuses to allow them to visit Eileen, his bedridden 18-year-old daughter, as a doctor is upstairs attending to her illness. As Carmody and Billy argue over the boy's future, Doctor Gaynor enters from the rear door. He gravely hands a prescription to Carmody, who first complains of the price, then begrudgingly sends Billy off to fill it. Doctor Gaynor diagnoses Eileen with pulmonary tuberculosis—"consumption" (1:721). At first terrified, Carmody flies into a rage when Gaynor instructs him to send Eileen to the Hill Farm Sanatorium. Not only will he lose his eldest daughter, who cares for the children in lieu of her mother, but it will cost him seven dollars a week. Disgusted by Carmody's stinginess, Gaynor threatens to inform the Society for the Prevention of Tuberculosis; he makes to leave, but returns from the hall with news that someone is at the door.

Fred Nicholls enters the room. Nicholls, Eileen's intended fiancé, is 23 and exudes the supercilious air of someone above the Carmodys' social status. Carmody goes upstairs to Eileen, leaving the two others to disparage Carmody's parsimony. Gaynor informs Nicholls of Eileen's illness, mentioning she may have infected the children had she kissed or coddled them too closely. Horror-stricken at the thought a kiss might spread the disease, Nicholls tensely bids the doctor goodnight. Gaynor exits, and Carmody reenters. Nicholls first hints of and then outwardly threatens Carmody with the townspeople's wrath if he refuses to deliver Eileen to the sanatorium. Nicholls makes to leave, selfishly hoping to avoid exposure to the contagious disease, but Eileen enters before he can make his escape. Carmody loudly exits to the saloon, and Eileen and Nicholls discuss her condition. She tries to kiss him, but he shrinks away, thus indicating his fear of contagion. Nicholls fumbles an explanation, but she understandingly asks for a kiss on the forehead, gulps back a sob, and says, "I'll have to get used to it, won't I?" (1:731).

Act 1, Scene 2

Nearly eight o'clock at night a week later in the reception room of Hill Farm Sanatorium. The hospital walls are painted white, beds are lined up with the heads of patients *"peeping out from under piles of heavy bedclothes"* (731–732), and a Victrola (a type of phonograph invented in 1905) is *"whining out the last strains of Dvorak's Humoresque"* (1:732). Stephen Murray, a 30-year-old newspaper reporter with literary aspirations whose tubercular symptoms are waning, lounges pensively in a chair by the fireplace with an open book beside him. A beautiful, blond 20-year-old nurse, Miss Howard, stands chatting with Miss Gilpin, a middle-aged nurse with dark hair and *"a strong, intelligent face"* (1:732). The nurses kid Murray about a new female patient who will be arriving soon.

Carmody, Eileen, and Nicholls enter. Carmody is very drunk, and Nicholls looks like *"one who is accomplishing a necessary but disagreeable duty with the best grace possible, but is frightfully eager to get it over and done with"* (1:735). Eileen exits with Miss Gilpin. While Murray pretends to be absorbed in his book, he closely observes the two men. Carmody takes a flagrant swig from his flask, and Nicholls accuses him of being drunk. Carmody good-naturedly makes small talk with Murray, identifying the young patient as "Irish as Paddy's pig" (1:737). When Eileen reenters, he introduces her to him, saying, "He's Irish and he'll put you on to the ropes of the place" (1:737). Nicholls's temper rises, and he and Carmody leave Eileen with vague promises of returning the following week.

Murray's cynicism at first disturbs Eileen, but she quickly warms to him. He exposits on his background, telling her that he has worked on a small-town paper for 10 years, all the while putting off his true calling—fiction writing. Eileen convinces Stephen to begin writing at the sanatorium and promises to help with his typing. She expresses concern about the rules and treatments at the sanatorium, but Stephen eases her mind. Eileen exits to her room, and Miss Howard serves him his "diet" (1:745), milk, teasing him about falling in love with Eileen. He jokingly recites a parody of the *Rubáiyát* of Omar Khayyam: "A glass of milk, and thou / Coughing beside me in the wilderness— / Ah—wilderness were Paradise enow!" Miss Howard calls the parody "old stuff," and Stephen patronizingly calls her a "sly minx"; she exits haughtily (1:746).

Act 2, Scene 1

Four months later on a beautiful Saturday morning in June in the sanatorium's assembly room. A pianola sits on a raised platform, and potted plants, bookshelves, and other niceties line the walls. French windows look out on the gardens outside, and another row of four windows are at right. The din of patients eating breakfast comes from the dining room next door. Doctor Stanton, the sanatorium's chief physician; his assistant Doctor Simms; and Mr. Sloan, a philanthropist, enter the room. Dr. Stanton relates the various stages of the illness

and guidelines for keeping patients at Hill Farm. "We have no time to waste on incurables," he tells Mr. Sloan, and goes on that they need to make room for people they can save (1:749).

Eileen enters, and though she appears to have gained some weight since the last act, she looks *"in a state of nervous depression"* (1:750) and sinks into an armchair. Dr. Sloan weighs the patients every Saturday. Those who gain weight are considered improved; those who have lost it are worsening. Stephen enters close behind. In contrast to Eileen, *"He is the picture of health"* (1:750; the same words were used by the *New London Telegraph* to describe O'Neill on a brief visit to New London from Gaylord [Sheaffer 249]). Stephen announces that he has sold his first story, and the editor has requested more. He kisses her, and she lightly scolds him for his indiscretion, as the sanatorium staff is, according to Dr. Stanton, "strictly anti-Cupid" (1:749). Stephen tells of his dream to move to New York City in order to "live, and meet real people who are doing things" (1:751). Eileen voices her anxiety over the scales; she has lost weight three weeks in a row. Stephen blames her distress on letters from her family and "that slick Aleck, Nicholls, with his cowardly lies" (1:752). Eileen halfheartedly defends her family and Nicholls, but something else evidently bothers her. Stephen pressures her to tell him what it is, but she refuses.

About 40 patients file in from the dining room and separate themselves by gender—women on the left, men on the right. *"They are all distinctly of the wage-earning class"* (1:754). An unnamed woman goads a male patient named Peters into playing a piano rag, which he does. Mrs. Turner, the matron, enters. Dr. Stanton and his assistant wheel in a *"Fairbanks scale on castors"* (1:756), now the center of attention among the patients. The women are called up first. When Eileen's turn comes, she tries to *"assume an air of defiant indifference."* But when the scale's weights make little movement, she realizes despondently that she has lost weight again. Mrs. Turner consults with her; she has lost three pounds and is consigned to bed rest. Meanwhile, *"The great majority have gained"* (1:758). Mrs. Turner attempts to comfort Eileen but notices there is something else on her mind. Eileen again refuses to discuss it and makes up something about her family. Rumor has it that Dr. Stanton will release Stephen if he gains weight. His name is called, they weigh him, and he has gained three pounds. "I'm so glad—you gained—the ones I lost, Stephen," Eileen says, sobbing uncontrollably. (O'Neill wrote in a 1914 letter to his doctor at the sanatorium, David Russell Lyman, that his "weight has varied, but never has fallen over three pounds below what I tipped the scales at when I left the San" [O'Neill 25]). No longer triumphant, Stephen frantically tries to silence her in case Dr. Stanton notices; such behavior is grounds for further restrictions.

Act 2, Scene 2

Midnight the same day on a moonlit crossroads in the midst of a wood near the sanatorium. Eileen stands at center, where the road is thrown into *"white shadowless relief and masses the woods into walls of compact blackness"* (1:764). She hears footsteps and fearfully plunges into the shadows. Stephen appears and softly calls out her name. She had left him a note to meet her before his departure the following morning. Eileen reveals herself, and he scolds her for being out at night in her condition. The clock bell rings 12 from the nearby village. They briefly discuss his plans to visit his sisters, who may love him, he says, but "what's love without a glimmer of understanding—a nuisance! They've never seen the real me and never wanted to" (1:766). Then he plans to move to New York and earn enough money on his writing to travel or move out to the countryside.

Eileen tells Stephen that she wrote a letter to Nicholls and broke off their engagement. Stephen had encouraged the breakup for months, but he equivocates now the step has been taken. She assures him that Nicholls had been hoping to end their engagement as well but felt he could not, given the townspeople's reaction if he did. Stephen continues to speak evasively, and Eileen, crestfallen, bids him goodnight. But she turns back and rushes into his arms, passionately confessing her love for him. They kiss, but she stops to avoid his having a relapse. She also knows that he does not love her, and she forgives him for it. "It's been beautiful," she responds to his apologies, "all of

it—for me!" (1:771). She begs him not to see her in the morning "with people watching"; he agrees and promises to write her often. She cries out again that she loves him and rushes up the road. Stephen calls out her name, then clenches his fists and curses, "Christ!" (1:772).

Act 3

Four months later on a late Sunday afternoon at the end of October. The action takes place in the isolation room of the Hill Farm infirmary and a sleeping porch to its right. The colorful leaves of a New England autumn can be seen through windows and the glass doorway leading out onto the porch. Eileen lies in a bed on the porch. She has grown terribly thin and *"gazes straight before her into the wood with an unseeing stare of apathetic indifference"* (1:773). A door leading to the hallway opens, and Miss Howard, Carmody, Mary, and Carmody's new wife, Maggie Brennan, enter the infirmary. Now sober, Carmody appears visibly uncomfortable in a respectable black suit. Mary has lost her sweet demeanor and glares defiantly at her stepmother. Mrs. Brennan intermittently scolds Mary for her curiosity and henpecks Carmody about not missing the next train. Miss Howard informs them that in a few days Eileen will be transferred to the State Farm sanatorium—a death sentence (1:774).

They go out to Eileen on the porch. Eileen ignores everyone but Mary, whom she takes in her arms. Mary shouts for her to let go, and Eileen sinks back into a state of indifference. Carmody nervously unleashes a stream of news and gossip, then contritely tells her that he and Mrs. Brennan have been married for two weeks. Eileen takes this news dispassionately. He hopes she will accept Mrs. Brennan as her new mother, but Eileen retorts, "No, No!" in an uncharacteristically violent outburst. Mrs. Brennan insists they leave at once. Carmody feels a mixture of rage and anguish and swears to get "dead rotten drunk" that night (1:779). They leave to catch the train.

Miss Howard arrives, serves Eileen her milk diet, and informs her that Stephen Murray has arrived to see her. Stephen comes in a few moments later. Though thin and dissipated, he is dressed in a *"well-*

fitting, expensive" suit (1:781). Miss Howard congratulates him on his literary success and exits. He goes out to the porch, and Eileen gently scolds him for not writing; he stammers out an apology, accusing the New York lifestyle for his inconsistent letter writing. When she asks about his success in the publishing world, he responds dismissively, "It's like everything else, I guess. When you've got it, you find you don't want it" (1:783). She tells him that "everybody" at the sanatorium has read his stories and "thinks they're fine." "Then they must be rotten," he says with a smile (1:784). He summons the courage to mention their last night before he left. She pleads with him not to speak of it. He leaves to visit Dr. Stanton. Incapable of sleep, Eileen begins to cry and call out his name. Miss Gilpin enters the infirmary and informs Stephen that Eileen will be transferred to the State Farm. They talk over her fate, and Miss Gilpin convinces him to persuade Eileen that he loves her, to pay her way to a nicer sanatorium, and to let her die in peace with him by her side. Regardless of his feelings, Stephen compassionately agrees, adding that he must marry her as well.

Stephen returns to the porch and tenderly kisses Eileen. He tells her he has always loved her, proposes, and she blissfully accepts. As she talks about their new life together, tears appear in Stephen's eyes. He realizes suddenly that he does, in fact, love her, and he shouts out, "I love you! I love you!" But then the realization of her impending doom *"confronts him face to face as a menacing reality"* (1:791). She reads his expression correctly—he knows her diagnosis—and cries out in anguish. But he convinces her that Dr. Stanton examined him and diagnosed a fatal relapse. She does not believe him at first, but Miss Gilpin enters, and Stephen induces her to substantiate his lie, which she does reluctantly. Miss Gilpin then asks to speak to him alone, and they move into the infirmary.

Stephen tells Miss Gilpin what happened and that he actually does love Eileen; but then he falls into a chair *"with a groan of despair,"* speaking to no one in particular, "Oh, why did you give me a hopeless hope?" (1:793). Miss Gilpin compassionately responds, "Isn't all life just that—when you think of it? *(her face lighting up with a consoling revela-* tion). But there must be something back of it—some promise of fulfillment,—somehow—somewhere—in the spirit of hope itself" (793–794). He bears up and swears she will survive the disease, then reacts violently to Miss Gilpin's fatalism: "There's always hope somewhere, isn't there? What do you *know*? Can you say you *know* anything?" (1:794). Miss Gilpin rushes off in a strange mixture of laughter and tears, and Stephen returns to Eileen's bedside. He kisses her with genuine passion, and adopting a wistful tone of maternal love, she begins to enumerate how she will uphold the regulations of his illness and of their marital state, as the curtain falls (1:794).

COMMENTARY

At the time of its premiere in 1921, most critics dismissed *The Straw* as an artistic misfire, finding its subject matter depressingly clinical. "We wish Mr. O'Neill would stick to the sea as his background," carped the *New York Sun.* "His salt water dramas never make us seasick, but this play sort of makes us landsick, as it were. . . . This particular sanitarium [sic] may cure a patient when there is the straw of love and hope to cling to, but it is likely to kill the audience" (Playgoer 38). Another reviewer considered it "the most lugubrious and depressing play that could possibly be encountered within theatre walls" (quoted in Wainscott 92). *The Straw* was the first play of O'Neill's to be published, and those who had read the play before seeing it were often less critical than those who attended the production cold; the former generally blamed the director for the lackluster production (Wainscott 91–92). O'Neill himself always considered *The Straw* one of his favorite plays; in a preproduction letter to its director, George C. Tyler, he called it "the best play I have written—better even than Beyond the Horizon" (O'Neill 121). Those familiar with O'Neill's life and work might readily appreciate why. For one thing, it is his most autobiographical play of the period save Exorcism, which gives an account of his suicide attempt at Jimmy "the Priest's" bar in 1912 (destroyed soon after its premiere in 1920). For another, it contains major themes that would reappear with near-obsessive consistency across the entire O'Neill canon.

Eugene O'Neill (the autobiographical character Stephen Murray) at Gaylord Farm *(Courtesy of the Sheaffer-O'Neill Collection, Charles E. Shain Library of Connecticut College)*

In his 1948 profile with Hamilton Basso for the *New Yorker,* the final interview of his career, O'Neill claimed that were it not for his time convalescing at the Gaylord Farm Sanatorium, he might never have become a playwright (Gelb 388). In the same interview, he borrows a line directly from *The Straw* (written 30 years earlier) when he caustically remarks, "When *everybody* likes something, watch out!" (quoted in Sheaffer 383). Stephen Murray, for his part, responds to Eileen that if "everybody" at the sanatorium liked his stories, "they must be rotten" (1:784). These corresponding sentiments, produced 30 years apart, are typical of this play's remarkable foreshadowing of so many of O'Neill's ideas on theater and life that would reappear with startling consistency in plays, interviews, and personal correspondence over the totality of his career. In this way, *The Straw* proves fascinating in O'Neill

studies for what the work portends, the soundings of work to come.

Aside from the obvious parallels between O'Neill's bout with tuberculosis and Stephen Murray's, other more significant autobiographical details figure in the play. Stephen has worked 10 years on a small-town newspaper, as O'Neill had (though not for 10 years), and determines, with encouragement from his fellow patient Eileen Carmody, to pursue fiction writing. As Kurt Eisen notes, this genre choice—fiction rather than drama—is a "suggestive departure from O'Neill's own ambition to write drama" (99). O'Neill's complex STAGE DIRECTIONS and lengthy expositions in dialogue are often taken as evidence of a frustrated fiction writer, and by the time he finished *The Straw,* he had already written four short stories, three of which survive—"TOMORROW," "The SCREENEWS OF WAR," and "S.O.S." ("The Hairy Ape," upon which his play of the same title is based, has been lost.)

First and foremost, we see in Bill Carmody parallels to O'Neill's father, JAMES O'NEILL, whom O'Neill later portrayed as the respectably rich but insufferably penurious Irish-American James Tyrone in *Long Day's Journey into Night.* If we construct a fictional chronology of O'Neill's most autobiographical plays, *The Straw* would come immediately after *Long Day's Journey,* when O'Neill, in the character of Edmund Tyrone, has just been diagnosed with tuberculosis, and well before *A MOON FOR THE MISBEGOTTEN,* by which time Edmund, an offstage character in *A Moon,* is married with children. By this chronology, *Exorcism* would immediately precede *Long Day's Journey.* Unlike James Tyrone, Bill Carmody is a member of the working poor (no doubt a deliberate discrepancy given O'Neill's growing reconciliation with his father by 1918), but he shares Tyrone's distrust of DOCTORS, his complaints over the cost of sending his child to a finer sanatorium as opposed to the State Farm, and his terror of the "Great White Plague" that to his Irish mind heralded certain doom (MARY ELLEN "ELLA" O'NEILL's father died of the disease).

Gaylord Farm, as specified in *The Straw,* cost James O'Neill seven dollars per week. "Seven dollars!" Carmody harps. "Glory be to God, I'll not have a penny saved for me old age—and then it's the poor house!" (1:723). James Tyrone also expresses terror over the "poor house," as Edmund refers to it (3:802) and clutches to a *"hopeless hope"* while discussing Edmund's prognosis with Edmund and his wife Mary Tyrone (3:768). Given that O'Neill wrote *The Straw* only five years after his bout with tuberculosis, his bitterness toward his father's hurtful miserliness, which lies at the tragic core of *Long Day's Journey,* must have been closer to the truth than one might suspect from a man looking back nearly three decades. O'Neill later distinguished between the Tyrone character (his father) and Carmody in the form of Shaughnessy in *Long Day's Journey* and Phil Hogan in *A Moon for the Misbegotten.* O'Neill based both characters on James O'Neill's tenant pig farmer in New London, Connecticut, JOHN "DIRTY" DOLAN. And just as Hogan treats his daughter Josie in *A Moon,* Carmody makes Eileen "a slave," as the Nicholls character describes it; and like Josie, she "defended him" (1:725).

O'Neill composed *The Straw* "in the period of lull before *Beyond the Horizon* was produced" (Bogard), and most critics point out that *The Straw* closely parallels *Beyond the Horizon* thematically and structurally. Both plays deal with unrequited love and both combine elements of REALISM with MELODRAMA. The final scene of *Horizon* also approximates that of *The Straw:* Anthony Mayo, like Miss Gilpin, pleads with Ruth Atkins to tell his brother Robert that she has, indeed, loved him before he dies of pleurisy. But *The Straw* also contains more subtle echoes of future characters and scenarios from O'Neill's experimental period in the 1920s as well as his late masterpieces.

For instance, Virginia Floyd suggests that the relationship between Eileen and Stephen Murray reflects "man's insensitivity to a woman's love," as Kukachin and Marco Polo's relationship does in MARCO MILLIONS; Floyd continues that in the final scene of *The Straw,* O'Neill strikes "a note of embittered romanticism that he was to sound again, notably in WELDED and ALL GOD'S CHILLUN GOT WINGS" (114).When Stephen describes children as "squally little brats.... I don't get them. They're something I can't seem to get acquainted with" (1:743), we see this autobiographical character in

Curtis Jayson of *The FIRST MAN,* who turns against his wife for getting pregnant without his permission, and more clearly in O'Neill's statement to his second wife, AGNES BOULTON, when he told her early on in their relationship, "I don't understand children, they make me uneasy, and I don't know how to act with them" (quoted in Boulton 68).

Furthermore, the near-expressionistic division of male and female patients in the weighing scene of *The Straw* (act 2, scene 1) closely resembles the racial separation in act 1, scenes 1 and 4 of *All God's Chillun Got Wings.* O'Neill's description of Stephen Murray, whose eyes *"can quicken instantly with a concealment mechanism of mocking, careless humor whenever his inner privacy is threatened"* (1:732) is fully borne out in the character Anthony Dion of *The GREAT GOD BROWN,* whose mask comprises *"a fixed forcing of his own face—dark, spiritual, poetic, passionately supersensitive, helplessly unprotected in its childlike, religious faith in life—into the expression of a mocking, reckless, defiant, gaily scoffing and sensual young Pan"* (2:475). Even *The Straw*'s *"pile of round stones"* included in the description of the moonlit woods in act 2, scene 2 calls to mind Brutus Jones's journey through the jungle in *The EMPEROR JONES,* in which his food cache is hidden underneath one of many white stones in the jungle in scene 2. O'Neill returns to this awkward, clandestine love scene in act 4, scene 2 of *AH, WILDERNESS!,* in which Richard Miller (another O'Neill self-portrait) quotes the actual lines from the *Rubáiyát of Omar Khayyam* that *The Straw*'s Stephen Murray parodies—the very lines that give *Ah, Wilderness!* its title.

Long Day's Journey only fleetingly alludes to O'Neill's "hopeless hope" idea, but it exists at the thematic core of *The ICEMAN COMETH.* "Oh, why did you give me a hopeless hope?" Stephen asks no one in particular. Miss Gilpin's response expresses more plainly perhaps than anywhere else the playwright's own lifelong philosophy that "there must be something back of it—some promise of fulfillment,—somehow—somewhere—in the spirit of hope itself" (1:794). In *Iceman,* O'Neill identifies the "pipe dreams," or life-sustaining lies, that each of his characters rely upon to maintain a sense of purpose in a meaningless world, just as Stephen

Murray remarks that not believing the tuberculosis patients are "really sick" bolsters the "pipe dream that keeps us all going" (1:733). *Iceman's* character "Jimmy Tomorrow"—the leader of Harry Hope's saloon's "Tomorrow movement"—is based on O'Neill's friend JAMES FINDLATER BYTH, from whom O'Neill derived the central motif of his short story "Tomorrow." This thematic connection deepens Stephen's admittance of procrastination; becoming a serious writer, he says, was something he had always planned to do "tomorrow—and tomorrow never came. I got in a rut—and stayed put" (1:742).

Eileen Carmody will probably die of the disease (Kitty Mackay, upon whom she is closely based, died two years after O'Neill's release from Gaylord), but the "straw" of the title clearly points to O'Neill's faith in the hopeless hope, the straw of hopefulness that might rescue himself along with all the other "drowning" men and women he met throughout his life. "It is for this reason," Barrett Clark writes of the ending of *The Straw*, "that I have always considered O'Neill at bottom an optimist. He never leaves us feeling that life is not living. If he were as pessimistic as he is often said to be, in the first place he would not have gone to the trouble of trying to prove the futility of existence" (102). O'Neill would later apply his "hopeless hope"—the lie, or pipe dream, that enables us to struggle on—to a play idea entitled "The Last Conquest." Originally titled "More Straw for the Drowning," the hopeless hope culminates at the conclusion of his career as a "universal hope for mankind" (Floyd 171).

CHARACTERS

Brennan, Maggie Bill Carmody's second wife. Mrs. Brennan is a *"tall, stout woman of fifty, lusty and loud-voiced, with a broad, snub-nosed, florid face, a large mouth, the upper lip darkened by a suggestion of mustache, and little round blue eyes, hard and restless with a continual fuming irritation"* (1:773). Bill Carmody hired Mrs. Brennan to act as a surrogate housekeeper and mother to his four remaining children, replacing his eldest daughter Eileen, who was sent away to a sanatorium for tuberculosis patients. Mary Carmody, his youngest daughter, visibly resents Mrs. Brennan, and when she visits Eileen

with Mary and Carmody in act 3, Eileen refuses to acknowledge her as a new "mother" (1:779). This prompts the termagant stepmother to command Carmody to leave his dying daughter and catch the next train home.

Carmody, Bill Eileen Carmody's father. Bill Carmody is a composite character of both O'Neill's father, James O'Neill and John "Dirty" Dolan, James O'Neill's tenant pig farmer in New London, Connecticut. Dolan is also the model for Phil Hogan in *A Moon for the Misbegotten* and the offstage character Shaughnessy in *Long Day's Journey into Night*. O'Neill describes Carmody as *"a man of fifty, heavy-set and round-shouldered, with long muscular arms and swollen-veined, hairy hands. . . . [H]is complexion [is] mottled—red, purple-streaked, and freckled. . . . The expression of his small, blue eyes is one of selfish cunning"* (1:717). A first-generation Irish immigrant, Carmody resembles the popularly caricatured "stage Irish," one that had appeared with fair regularity in O'Neill's early plays, such as Sweeney in *The* ROPE and Paddy in the SS GLENCAIRN plays (Engel 37). Carmody drinks heavily, acts abusively toward his children, and *"adopts a whiny tone"* in the face of authority (1:721). Like James Tyrone in *Long Day's Journey*, he fears the "poor house" perhaps even more than his own child's death to tuberculosis; it takes a threat from Dr. Gaynor to report his negligence to the Society for the Prevention of Tuberculosis for Carmody to consent. A widower, he feels put upon by his four younger children—Mary, Nora, Tom, and Billy—and his low financial state. By act 3, he has married Maggie Brennan, who acted as surrogate housekeeper after Eileen left for the sanatorium. Essentially an unsympathetic miser and brute, Carmody does, in the final scene, express real tenderness toward the dying Eileen, but in the end, he obeys Maggie Brennan's command to leave and vows to get "dead, rotten drunk" (1:779).

Carmody, Billy Bill Carmody's eldest son and Eileen Carmody's brother. *"A fourteen-year-old replica of his father"* (1:719), Billy quit school to go to work against his eldest sister Eileen's wishes. "Aw," he retorts when Carmody second-guesses the decision, "goin' to school didn't do me no good. The teachers was all down on me. I couldn't learn nothin' there" (1:721). "Nor any other place, I'm thinkin,'" Carmody replies (1:721). Carmody rails against his son's inability to earn a raise at work, but by act 3 he has received a raise to seven dollars a week (the exact price of Eileen's stay at the sanatorium). Billy fails to join Carmody, Mary, and Mrs. Brennan to visit his dying sister because he had arranged a date with a girl.

Carmody, Eileen Bill Carmody's daughter. Eileen's character is based on Catherine "Kitty" Mackay, an actual working-class Irish-American young woman with whom O'Neill conducted a flirtation with at the Gaylord Farm Sanatorium. Mackay was also from a large Irish family in Waterbury (10 children including herself), her father was also heartlessly miserly and self-pitying, and she also fell in love with her fellow patient with literary aspirations (Sheaffer 254). O'Neill's portrayal of her exactly describes a surviving photograph of Kitty Mackay at Gaylord: *"Her wavy mass of dark hair is parted in the middle and combed low on her forehead, covering her ears, to a knot at the back of her head. The oval of her face is spoiled by a long, rather heavy, Irish jaw contrasting with the delicacy of her other features,"* and her shape is *"slight and undeveloped"* (1:729). O'Neill kissed Kitty's hand upon his departure from Gaylord and informed her, that she would "find herself some day in one of his plays" (according to biographer Louis Sheaffer 257). Tragically, she never did, as she died of the disease in 1915.

Before her diagnosis, Eileen was training to be a stenographer, like Mrs. Roylston in SERVITUDE and Anna Christophersen in CHRIS CHRISTOPHERSEN (Eisen 99). O'Neill gives the strong impression that the relationship between Eileen and Stephen Murray is ultimately untenable as a result of CLASS differences, and thus his flirtation with Kitty Mackay might be read in a similar light. In addition, Kurt Eisen writes of the character that her "dual function as melodramatic heroine and literary muse is plain enough, but the fact that Stephen cannot return her love even though he considers her absolutely essential to his writing reenacts O'Neill's own

ambivalence toward the sources of his art" (990). Thus, Stephen Murray's revelation that he loves Eileen might be more a statement on the necessity for a female muse and caretaker, a role Eileen and O'Neill's third wife, CARLOTTA MONTEREY O'NEILL, had performed for their respective men. Though Eileen is a stock character for MELODRAMA in many ways, O'Neill complained about casting a very young Helen Hayes to the director George C. Tyler because "the role of 'Eileen' is so tremendous in its requirements that only one of our very best and proved dramatic actresses should be allowed to attempt it" (O'Neill 121).

Dr. Gaynor diagnoses Eileen with tuberculosis in act 1, scene 1, and he instructs her father, Bill Carmody, to send her to the Hill Farm Sanatorium. While there, she becomes estranged from her self-centered family and intended fiancé, Fred Nicholls, who fears catching the disease. On her first day at Hill Farm, Eileen meets Stephen Murray, a small-town reporter who dreams of becoming a serious writer, and falls in love with him. When she breaks her engagement with Nicholls, however, it becomes clear that Stephen does not return her love. Stephen's health improves as rapidly as hers declines. After being discharged from the sanatorium, he goes on to pursue a career in writing, leaving her behind to pine for him and live solely for his letters, which come sporadically. When he returns for a checkup and a visit, Eileen's disease has advanced, and she will be transferred to the State Farm, meaning certain death. Stephen realizes that he does, in fact, love her and, lying to her that he has suffered a relapse, asks for her hand in marriage. She accepts, and in the final scene, she enumerates her future marital duties as the curtain falls.

Carmody, Mary Bill Carmody's youngest daughter and Eileen Carmody's sister. When first introducing Mary in act 1, scene 1, O'Neill describes her as a *"delicate, dark-haired, blue-eyed, quiet little girl about eight years old"* (1:717); but by act 3, after having been hospitalized and her father married, *"the sweetness of her face has disappeared, giving way to a hangdog sullenness, a stubborn silence, with sulky, furtive glances of rebellion directed at her stepmother"* (1:773–774). Eileen's illness evidently frightens

Mary, and when her dying sister embraces her, she screams to be let go, then quietly speaks her last lines, "Eileen—you look so—so funny" (1:776).

Carmody, Nora Eileen Carmody's sister and Bill Carmody's daughter. O'Neill describes Nora as a *"bright, vivacious, red-haired girl of eleven"* (1:719). In act 1, scene 1, she and her younger brother Tom bicker back and forth, which exasperates Carmody, who sends them upstairs. By act 3, Carmody informs Eileen that Nora could not make the trip on account of her parochial school, but she is now "pretty as a picture, and the smartest girl in her school," according to her schoolmaster "Father Fitz" (1:777).

Carmody, Tom Eileen Carmody's brother and Bill Carmody's son. O'Neill describes Tom as a 10-year-old who resembles his sister Nora and is *"a healthy, good-humored youngster with a shock of sandy hair"* (1:719). In act 1, scene 1, he and Nora bicker back and forth, which exasperates Carmody, who sends them upstairs. In act 3, Carmody tells Eileen that Tom is not doing well at school, "always playin' hooky and roamin' the streets" (1:777).

Gaynor, Doctor Eileen Carmody's family doctor in Waterbury, Connecticut. Gaynor is *"a stout, bald middle-aged man, forceful of speech, who in the case of patients of the Carmodys' class dictates rather than advises"* (1:721). In act 1, scene 1, Gaynor diagnoses Eileen Carmody with tuberculosis. When Bill Carmody balks at sending his daughter to the Hill Farm Sanatorium, Gaynor threatens to inform the Society for the Prevention of Tuberculosis, which intimidates Carmody as it is run by powerful local leaders.

Gilpin, Miss Nurse at Hill Farm Sanatorium. Miss Gilpin is a *"a slight, middle-aged woman with black hair, and a strong, intelligent face, its expression of resolute efficiency softened and made kindly by her warm, sympathetic gray eyes"* (1:732). Her character is based closely on O'Neill's nurse Mary A. Clark, with whom he became good friends during his stay at the Gaylord Farm Sanatorium. "As self-consciously Irish as Eugene," write O'Neill BIOGRA-

PHERS Arthur and Barbara Gelb, "Mary Clark shared his view of life as tragic but exhilarating; she could agree with him that the only true hero was one who struggled to triumph over his fate—even knowing the odds were against him" (386). Miss Gilpin articulates O'Neill's lifelong motif of the "hopeless hope" in the final scene, telling Stephen Murray, "Isn't all life just that—when you think of it? (*her face lighting up with a consoling revelation*) But there must be something back of it—some promise of fulfillment,—somehow—somewhere—in the spirit of hope itself" (1:793–794).

Howard, Miss Nurse at Hill Farm Sanatorium. She is *"tall, slender and blond—decidedly pretty and provokingly conscious of it, yet with a certain air of seriousness underlying her apparent frivolity"* (1:732). Miss Howard and Stephen Murray conduct a harmless flirtation in act 1, scene 2. She is a composite portrait of two nurses at Gaylord Farm Sanatorium, Wilhelmina Stamberger and Katherine Murray. The latter was a strict Irish Catholic who sent O'Neill a copy of Francis Thompson's "The Hound of Heaven" after his release. Apparently she wanted the poem to convert the young apostate; though it failed, O'Neill memorized the entire 183 lines of the poem and was known to recite it when drunk at the HELL HOLE in GREENWICH VILLAGE (Gelb 387).

Murray, Stephen Patient at Hill Farm Sanatorium (modeled closely on Gaylord Farm Sanatorium). Stephen looks just like his creator, *"a tall, slender, rather unusual looking fellow with a pale face, sunken under high cheek bones, lined about the eyes and mouth, jaded and worn for one so young"* (1:732). O'Neill's closest self-portrait up to that time, Stephen, who is 30 years old—O'Neill's age at the time of the play's composition—also resembles the Poet in FOG; Robert Mayo in *Beyond the Horizon*; Richard Miller in *Ah, Wilderness!*; and, most famously, Edmund Tyrone in *Long Day's Journey into Night*. Stephen's name is probably a composite of Katherine Murray, a model for the nurse Miss Howard, and Stephen Dedalus, James Joyce's alter ego in *A Portrait of the Artist as a Young Man* and *Ulysses*. O'Neill's description of his character also calls to mind the character Anthony Dion in *The*

Great God Brown, whose cynicism and introversion O'Neill reveals by employing physical masks. He describes Stephen thusly: *"His intelligent, large hazel eyes have a tired, dispirited expression in repose, but can quicken instantly with a concealment mechanism of mocking, careless humor whenever his inner privacy is threatened"* (1:732). If Stephen comes across as callous or self-involved, so much the better for the play's realistic portrait of O'Neill at Gaylord. As Clare O'Rourke, one of the Gaylord nurses, recalled of O'Neill, "He could be gentle and sensitive, but there was also a rough sadistic streak in him" (quoted in Sheaffer 247).

A small-town newspaper reporter, Stephen Murray is a veteran tuberculosis patient at Hill Farm Sanatorium when Eileen Carmody arrives. The two begin a friendship that quickly turns into a flirtation on her first day. Eileen also encourages Stephen to pursue fiction writing, his self-professed calling, and acts as his typist and muse. Thanks to her, he gets his first short story published with a request for more from the editor. Stephen's health steadily improves as Eileen's declines. But when Eileen informs Stephen in a secret meeting in the woods outside the sanatorium that she broke off her engagement to the pretentious Fred Nicholls because she loves him instead, Stephen begins to equivocate on his feelings. After his case arrests and he is discharged from the sanatorium, Stephen moves to New York City to carry out his dreams of becoming a writer, to "live, and meet real people who are doing things" (1:751). He returns to the sanatorium disillusioned by fame and appears incapable of creativity without her. After experiencing a revelation that he does, in fact, love her, he adheres to a "hopeless hope" that she will survive, and that they will get married (1:793).

Nicholls, Fred Eileen Carmody's intended fiancé. O'Neill describes Nicholls as *"a young fellow of twenty-three, stockily built, fair-haired, handsome in a commonplace, conventional mold. His manner is obviously an attempt at suave gentility; he has an easy, taking smile and a ready laugh, but there is a petty, calculating expression in his small, observing, blue eyes"* (1:724). Nicholls has maintained a relationship with Eileen throughout their school years, but he

comes from a higher class than the Carmodys, a fact of which he is snobbishly and openly aware. Once she comes down with tuberculosis, however, he quickly distances himself. She breaks off their engagement after falling in love with Stephen Murray at the sanatorium. She knows that Nicholls wished to break up but would not dare take the step because of social appearances.

Sloan, Mr. A philanthropist. O'Neill describes him in the opening of act 2, scene 1 as *"fifty, short, stout, and well-dressed."* Mr. Sloan is *"one of the successful business men whose endowments have made the Hill Farm possible"* (1:747), and his presence allows Dr. Stanton to explain the sanatorium's rules and regulations.

Stanton, Doctor Chief physician and superintendent of Hill Farm Sanatorium. Dr. Stanton, who speaks with a slight southern accent, *"is a handsome man of forty-five or so with a grave, care-lined, studious face lightened by a kindly, humorous smile. His gray eyes, saddened by the suffering they have witnessed, have the sympathetic quality of real understanding"* (1:747). Based on Dr. David Russell Lyman, O'Neill's physician at the Gaylord Farm Sanatorium, Dr. Stanton's name comes from J. G. Stanton, a popular doctor in New London, Connecticut (Gelb 384). O'Neill and Lyman remained close for many years after his tuberculosis was arrested and O'Neill was released from Gaylord. These letters reveal a great deal of respect and intimacy, and in 1917 O'Neill wrote to him for advice about being relieved from the draft when the United States entered World War I, given that "conditions in the camps and at the front are the worst possible for one susceptible to T.B." "I want to serve my country," O'Neill told him, "but it seems silly to commit suicide for it" (O'Neill 80).

Turner, Mrs. Matron of the Hill Farm Sanatorium. O'Neill describes her as *"a stout, motherly, capable-looking woman with gray hair"* (1:755). Mrs. Turner weighs the patients in act 2, scene 1, and kindly consoles Eileen Carmody when she finds out she has lost weight for the fourth week in a row—a sure sign that her tuberculosis is worsening.

BIBLIOGRAPHY

Bogard, Travis. *Contour in Time: The Plays of Eugene O'Neill.* Rev. ed. New York: Oxford University Press, 1988.

Boulton, Agnes. *Part of a Long Story: Eugene O'Neill as a Young Man in Love.* Garden City, N.Y.: Doubleday & Company, 1958.

Clark, Barrett H. *Eugene O'Neill: The Man and His Plays.* Rev. ed. New York: Dover, 1947.

Eisen, Kurt. *The Inner Strength of Opposites: O'Neill's Novelistic Drama and the Melodramatic Imagination.* Athens: University of Georgia Press, 1994.

Engel, Edwin A. *The Haunted Heroes of Eugene O'Neill.* Cambridge, Mass.: Harvard University Press, 1953.

Floyd, Virginia. *The Plays of Eugene O'Neill: A New Assessment.* New York: Ungar, 1985.

Gelb, Arthur, and Barbara Gelb. *O'Neill: Life with Monte Cristo.* New York: Applause Books, 2000.

O'Neill, Eugene. *Selected Letters of Eugene O'Neill.* Edited by Travis Bogard and Jackson R. Bryer. New Haven, Conn.: Yale University Press, 1988.

Playgoer. "Eugene O'Neill's *The Straw* Is Gruesome Clinical Tale," *Sun* (New York), November 11, 1921. In *The Critical Response to Eugene O'Neill,* edited by John H. Houchin, 37–38. Westport, Conn.: Greenwood Press, 1993.

Sheaffer, Louis. *O'Neill: Son and Playwright.* Boston: Little, Brown, 1968.

Wainscott, Ronald H. *Staging O'Neill: The Experimental Years, 1920–1934.* New Haven, Conn.: Yale University Press, 1988.

Thirst: A Play in One Act
(completed, 1913; first produced, 1916)

Eugene O'Neill wrote *Thirst,* his first of many SEA plays, in fall 1913 at his family's summer home, MONTE CRISTO COTTAGE, in NEW LONDON, CONNECTICUT. The play was published in *"THIRST" AND OTHER ONE-ACT PLAYS* in 1914 by Gorham Press of Boston, a volume underwritten with $450 from O'Neill's father, the popular actor JAMES O'NEILL. The collection, O'Neill's first, also included *The WEB, WARNINGS, FOG,* and *RECKLESSNESS.* The PROVINCETOWN PLAYERS first produced it in August 1916 after the resounding success of *BOUND EAST FOR CARDIFF.* O'Neill himself played the West Indian Mulatto Sailor ("so deeply tanned," O'Neill BIOGRAPHERS Arthur and Barbara Gelb note, "he needed no makeup" [571]), GEORGE CRAM "JIG" COOK played the Gentleman, and LOUISE BRYANT the Dancer. With some reluctance on the part of set designer William Zorach, the group decided on a naturalistic set, rather than a symbolic one, in which the ocean was represented by yards of "sea cloth with someone wriggling around underneath it" (Gelb 573). The critical response was tepid at best, and the stripped-down production at the WHARF THEATRE in Provincetown, Massachusetts, was the last staging of the play O'Neill would see in his lifetime.

All three of O'Neill's first sea plays, starting with *Thirst* and then *Warnings* and *Fog,* take place during or just after a shipwreck, which indicates two possibilities for biographer Louis Sheaffer: (1) "because disaster at sea is so dramatic" and (2) the fact that "from a psychological point of view . . . the ships may be taken as a mother symbol" (271). Sheaffer refers to O'Neill's mother MARY ELLEN "ELLA" O'NEILL's emotionally distancing morphine addiction and O'Neill's time in a Catholic preparatory school as a preadolescent while his parents toured the country (an experience he considered a kind of abandonment). Perhaps historically we may also look to the sinking of the *Titanic* for O'Neill's plot device, as that catastrophe, in which 1,503 people perished at sea, took place in April 1912, the year before *Thirst*'s conception. O'Neill himself had kept watch in the crow's nest of the SS PHILADELPHIA on the same route around the Grand Banks where the thousand-foot transatlantic liner collided with an iceberg (Richter 138). The incident affected the national consciousness nearly as deeply as the terrorist attacks of September 11, 2001, though without the long-lasting geopolitical effects.

SYNOPSIS

The life raft of a shipwrecked transatlantic liner cast away on the open sea and rolling to the rhythm of the waves. The midday sun *"glares down from straight overhead like a great angry eye of God"* (1:31), creating *"writhing, fantastic heat waves"* that come off the white deck. A school of sharks are slowly encircling the craft. Two men and a woman are discovered—a Gentleman, a West Indian Mulatto Sailor, and a Dancer. They are dressed in attire that indicate their stations in life—the Gentleman in dinner clothes, the Dancer in a *"costume of black velvet covered with spangles,"* and the Sailor in a blue uniform, all of which are in tatters. The Sailor stares at the steady rounds of the sharks and sings *"a monotonous negro song"* as the Gentleman licks his cracked, swollen lips with a tongue blackened from thirst, starvation, and the heat. The Dancer, face down and sprawled across the deck, weeps ceaselessly. *"In the eyes of all three,"* O'Neill writes in his STAGE DIRECTIONS, *"the light of a dawning madness is shining"* (1:32).

When the Sailor stops singing, the Dancer complains of the unremitting silence and says that red drops have begun to speckle her field of vision, creating the illusion that it is raining blood. The Gentleman responds that his eyesight was similarly affected, but now everything is tainted by the redness, as if the sea were filled with the blood of dead passengers from the catastrophe. The Gentleman remarks hopelessly that he is desperate for water, and the Sailor (O'Neill uses "negro" in his stage directions, though he specifies the character is "mulatto," or mixed race, in the list of characters) stops singing and asks who has water. The Gentleman accuses him of having stolen the last of the water while he and the Dancer slept. Intolerant of the oppressive silence, the Dancer implores the Sailor to continue singing. He assents, and after a few lines, the other two ask what the words mean. He explains that he is singing to the sharks, that the song contains a charm that will put the sharks off from eating them. The Dancer becomes frightened and the Gentleman assures her that sharks as a species "are all cowards" (1:34).

The Gentleman and the Dancer discuss the mysterious Sailor behind his back. He apparently speaks good English but rarely responds when addressed. According to the Dancer, he sounds as if there were "some impediment in his throat." The Gentleman voices some remorse over accusing him of taking the last of the water, since they are "all in the same pitiful plight" (1:35). As the Sailor is the only one who seems capable of standing, the other two ask him to see if any boats are on the horizon. He complies, laconically reports that he sees nothing, and continues singing. The Gentleman and the Dancer carry on their despairing conversation. The Gentleman informs her that the captain of their sunken vessel, whom the Dancer characterizes as "kind and good-natured," shot himself as the passengers were abandoning the ship. She says if he was guilty of the catastrophe, "he has paid with his life"; but the Gentleman contradicts this, reflecting philosophically that "the dead do not pay" (1:37).

The Gentleman withdraws a small, black object from his coat pocket and laughs at the irony of his discovery. It is the menu for a dinner held in his honor at the United States Club of BUENOS AIRES, listing the contents of a lavish meal—"martini cocktails, soup, sherry, fish," and so on. The Dancer finds the humor ghastly and demands he throw the menu into the ocean, which he does. He remarks how beautiful she looked in her performance back on the passenger ship, and that he overhead an audience member say, "How pretty she is! I wonder if she is married?" (1:38). He laughs darkly at the silly memory—one that reflects reports from *Titanic* survivors that some passengers on board the sinking vessel "seemed to deny their doom by fixating on unimportant details" (Richter 138)—and recounts the last hour of the sinking ship. There was a "horrible dull crash," he says, and then everyone was thrust forward; he stepped into a boat that soon became overcrowded and swamped. A group of survivors on another boat beat him away with oars, and then, swimming for his life, he saw the sharks and "became frenzied with terror" (1:39). He finally found the raft with the Dancer and the Sailor on it and climbed aboard, wild with fright.

The Dancer relates that when the boat began to sink, she ran to her state room and salvaged a diamond necklace worth $5,000. She then scolds him for lying about the sharks, but agrees that given their situation, the sharks are immaterial. The Dancer goes on that as the frantic crowds leapt into the sea and boarded life rafts, someone on deck kissed her, most likely the handsome second mate. The Gentleman agrees, adding that the officer had disregarded his duty to others by ensuring her a place on the raft. The Gentleman questions the Sailor about this, but he responds irritably that he does not know and continues singing. The Gentleman utters a "prayer of protest": "Oh God, God! After twenty years of incessant grind, day after weary day, I started on my first vacation. I was going home. And here I sit dying by slow degrees, desolate and forsaken. Is this the meaning of all my years of labor? Is this the end, oh God?" (1:42).

The Dancer hallucinates that she saw a "green and clean looking" island and can hear a stream trickling down rocks. The Gentleman shakes her and insists no island is ahead. The Sailor uncharacteristically cries out for water. The Gentleman shouts at him that he is responsible, that he emptied the cask behind their backs and deserves to suffer; he then voices his suspicion that the Sailor saved some water in a flask, a possibility that perks up the Dancer. They contemplate killing him for it, but the Gentleman admits he is too weak to overtake the stronger man. We also learn the Sailor is armed with a knife. The Gentleman suggests that the Dancer bribe him with her necklace, a present from an old Duke who wished to marry her. She refuses at first, then realizes her life is at stake and makes the offer. When she touches the Sailor's shoulder, he looks back at her with "*round, animal eyes dull and lusterless*" (1:45–46). She pleads with him, promising that with the money the necklace will bring he will never have to work again; but he again insists that he has no water, pushes her hand away, and the necklace clatters to the deck. Now the Dancer grotesquely spruces herself up and tries to seduce him, offering her body for a drink. He appears tempted at first, but then he firmly maintains that he has none. "Have I humbled myself before this black animal," she screams, "only to be spurned like a wench of the streets. It is too much! You lie, you dirty slave! You have water. You have stolen my share of

the water" (1:48). She lunges at him, demanding water, but he easily shoves her away.

The Sailor goes back to observing the sharks, and the Dancer lies for a time in a heap, but then jumps up in animation. "*All her former weakness seems quite gone. . . . She mutters incoherently to herself. The last string has snapped. She is mad*" (1:49). Now she believes she is in her dressing room. She orders her assistant about and complains of the glare of the footlights. She begins her stage act, and the Sailor turns to watch her. At first, the Gentleman is delighted. "It is as good as a play," he says, and "*bursts into cackling laughter*" (1:49). Dancing "*like some ghastly marionette jerked by invisible wires,*" she tears off the top of her bodice and dances before them half-naked, baring breasts that are "*withered and shrunken by starvation*" (1:50); a "*crimson foam*" appears at the corner of her mouth. The Gentleman goads her on, but she collapses to the floor, dead. The Sailor looks relieved; he begins sharpening his knife on his shoe and singing a "*happy negro melody*" (1:50). Appalled by the idea of cannibalism, the Gentleman heaves her corpse into the sea, and there is a great flurry of activity as the sharks devour her body. In a rage, the Sailor lunges at the Gentleman and stabs him. As the Gentleman falls into the water, he grasps onto the Sailor's jersey and pulls him into shark-infested water after him. "*The waiting fins rush in. The water is lashed into foam*" (1:51). The Sailor's head bobs to the surface in a grimace of terror and pain, but he is swiftly wrenched back down. The sharks disappear, and the "*sun glares down like a great angry eye of God*" (1:51). The heat waves rise from the deck of the raft, and the necklace sparkles in the sunlight.

COMMENTARY

The first of O'Neill's one-act sea plays, *Thirst* was heavily influenced by the fiction writers Joseph Conrad, Stephen Crane, and Jack London, all of whom O'Neill read avidly. All three also wrote in the naturalistic mode of *Thirst* and created a sensation publishing similar sea tales at the turn of the 20th century. As Louis Sheaffer points out, when the critic and playwright Clayton Hamilton visited the O'Neill family home, Monte Cristo Cottage, in summer 1913, there was as yet no American playwright of the sea. "Here, so far as the theater was concerned, was virgin territory, a fertile opportunity for one of Eugene's experience [in the MERCHANT MARINE]" (271). One of history's many ironies is that Jack London died in 1916, the year *Bound East for Cardiff* and *Thirst* premiered in Provincetown, Massachusetts.

All of O'Neill's precursors wrote in the vein of NATURALISM, however, while O'Neill, heavily influenced by the expressionistic Swedish playwright AUGUST STRINDBERG and others, chose a more symbolic narrative. The result was, O'Neill critic Travis Bogard writes, "a somewhat dismaying mixture of both" (30). For example, in contrast to Crane's most famous story, "The Open Boat," which recounts an actual experience Crane had while steaming toward Cuba to report on the Spanish-American War, and which uses all male characters from fairly similar backgrounds, O'Neill diversifies his fictional castaways—a woman Dancer, a white male Gentleman, and a West Indian Mulatto Sailor. As such, the race, CLASS, and GENDER divides that O'Neill imposes add sociological depth to the play—"the raft as microcosm" (Ranald 52)—even if the symbolism is rather heavy-handed. In this way, the play is extremely similar in concept to his one-act sea play *Fog,* which appeared in *"Thirst" and Other One-Act Plays* and had a Business Man, a Poet, and a Polish Peasant Woman (an immigrant), who are also cast adrift after a shipwreck, though *Fog*'s EXPRESSIONISM is far more evident in the final scene.

Racially speaking, the Gentleman and the Dancer construct an unnecessary tension between themselves and the mulatto Sailor, and eventually their dialogue with him is reduced to racial epithets—"nigger," "black dog," "black animal," "dirty slave" (1:40, 46, 48, 48). The Gentleman's racism lies behind his accusations that the Sailor has stolen their cask of water, an infectious assumption that the Dancer soon adopts as well. The only evidence against the Sailor is that he is stronger than they, but his ability to withstand nature's torments is more in line with his profession. It is also in line with a kind of racial romanticism O'Neill subscribed to that other ethnicities are physically and/or morally superior to Anglo-Saxons, a theme we also

find in *The EMPEROR JONES, ALL GOD'S CHILLUN GOT WINGS,* and *A MOON FOR THE MISBEGOTTEN,* among others (Floyd 34). In his stage directions, O'Neill refers to the Gentleman's perspective as a *"mad fixed idea"* (1:44). "Fixed ideas," or socially mandated beliefs, were the bugaboo of the German philosopher Max Stirner, the grandfather of O'Neill's self-professed social philosophy PHILOSOPHICAL ANARCHISM. The idea that the Dancer would overcome her disgust about the Sailor's race and offer him her body demonstrates the extent of her desperation and thus how taboo—in fact illegal in many states—miscegenation (interracial sex) was at the time: "Have I humbled myself before this black animal only to be spurned like a wench of the streets. It is too much!" (1:48).

Hence, the gender issue is as inextricably intertwined with race as with class. This play readily introduces the O'Neillian theme that all women, not just prostitutes, are willing to sell their bodies for economic gain or survival (Ranald 53). With the economics of sex in mind (one telling bit of exposition is that the Dancer dumped the duke but kept the necklace), we can also see that both the Gentleman and the Dancer are class-conscious materialists. While the passenger ship was going down, the Gentleman rushed to his state room to save his wallet and ironically picked up a sumptuous-sounding menu for a dinner in his honor by mistake; the Dancer rushed back to save her $5,000 diamond necklace, given to her by an old duke, that, equally ironically, survives where the others perish. In contrast, the Sailor, Floyd writes, "thought only of saving his sole possession: Life" (1:34).

But in O'Neill's world, death too is a possession to cling to in the face of tragedy. The Gentleman informs us through exposition that the captain committed suicide once he recognized he was to blame for the shipwreck. "If he was guilty," the Dancer says, "he has paid with his life." But the Gentleman responds, "No. He has avoided payment by taking his life. The dead do not pay" (1:37). Louis Sheaffer identifies the same theme in MOURNING BECOMES ELECTRA, in which Lavinia Mannon reveals O'Neill's lifelong struggle with survival guilt, mixed in with a good dose of residual CATHOLICISM, by saying that death is a means of escaping punishment, and thus "living alone here with the dead is a worse act of justice than death or prison" (quoted in Sheaffer 272).

The irony of the necklace's survival, co-opted by nature without mankind's imposition of its arbitrary value (see Marco Polo's explanation for the value of gold in act 2, scene 1 of MARCO MILLIONS), speaks to two naturalistic forces in this play and throughout the O'Neill canon: the "ironic life force," or "ironic fate" concept we find personified in *The Web*, and nature's utter indifference to mankind—a staple of naturalism and particularly resonant in the works of Crane and London. If the symbol of that indifference can be found in the title of *Fog*, the symbol is now, along with the sea and its man-eating associates, the merciless sun glaring *"down from straight overhead like a great angry eye of God"* (1:31). And the irony of all three dying, when one or two could have survived by ignoring the moral laws of mankind and adopting the laws of nature, is robustly captured by the symbol of the diamond necklace, still on the raft *"glittering in the blazing sunshine"* (1:51).

CHARACTERS

Dancer, A   O'Neill describes her as a young blond, striking an *"even more bizarre figure than the man in evening clothes* [the Gentleman], *for she is dressed in a complete short-skirted dancer's costume of black velvet covered with spangles"* (1:31). After days without food or water, she has transformed from a beautiful entertainer to *"a mocking spectre of a dancer"* (1:32). While the ship was sinking before the play's action, the Dancer rushed to her state room and, like the Gentleman with his wallet, salvaged a diamond necklace worth $5,000—an act demonstrating that material objects apparently mean more to her than her own life. The Dancer recalls from the experience that an unknown man kissed her before she found her way to a life raft. The Gentleman agrees with her that it was probably the second mate, who then saved her life by disregarding his duty to the other passengers. Robert Richter argues that this second mate was probably autobiographical, "a combination of wish and reality." O'Neill also was, as the Dancer describes the officer, "tall, handsome, with dark eyes" and "had many liaisons with Dancers and actresses" (141).

When the Gentleman convinces her that the West Indian mulatto Sailor probably stole the remainder of the water, the Dancer first tries to trade it for her necklace, then for her body. Indeed, Louise Bryant, who was then having an affair with O'Neill while she was engaged to his good friend JOHN REED, considered baring her breasts as O'Neill instructs in the stage directions, but the group decided on discretion. All the same, Arthur and Barbara Gelb aptly remark that "it is a wonder, given O'Neill's avowal that Louise's fingernail touch could ignite a prairie fire, that his scenes with her did not incinerate him on the spot" (572). One can only imagine what Reed, though he seemed at ease in his knowledge of the affair, must have been thinking. In the play, the Sailor rejects both the necklace and the offer of the Dancer's body, insisting he has no water. Her race and class consciousness powerfully emerge with his refusal: "Have I humbled myself before this black animal only to be spurned like a wench of the streets. It is too much!" (1:48). After this rant, she flings herself to the floor. When she stands again, she has clearly gone insane, believing she is back in the theater, and dances *"like some ghastly marionette jerked by invisible wires"* (1:50). The Gentleman cheers her on until she literally dances to death. The Sailor suggests they eat her corpse to survive, but the Gentleman, refusing to give up his humanity, throws her body over the side to be devoured by sharks. In the final scene, after the Gentleman and the Sailor unwittingly plunge into the water after her, nothing is left but her diamond necklace—now utterly worthless.

The Dancer is one of many women in the O'Neill canon who either go "mad or completely irrational," including, as the most famous example, Mary Tyrone in LONG DAY'S JOURNEY INTO NIGHT, but also Ella Harris in *All God's Chillun Got Wings*, Deborah Harford in MORE STATELY MANSIONS, and Annie Keeney in ILE (Floyd 37n).

Gentleman, A   "A *middle-aged white man*," the Gentleman is wearing *"what once was an evening dress; but sun and salt water have reduced it to the mere caricature of such a garment"* (1:31). He was a first-class passenger on the ship, and like the

Dancer with her necklace, he demonstrates that material objects mean more to him than his own life by salvaging what he thought was his wallet from his stateroom before abandoning the sinking ship. He recounts the catastrophe in a monologue that O'Neill undoubtedly drew from survivors' accounts of the *Titanic* (Richter 140). The Gentleman had been beaten away from one life raft, as reportedly happened on the *Titanic,* and finally made his way to the raft occupied by the Dancer and the mulatto Sailor.

In the first scene, the Gentleman accuses the Sailor of having stolen the remaining water onboard, with the explicit logic that the Sailor is stronger than the other two, but given O'Neill's inclusion of racial epithets, the implicit logic is the "fixed idea" of racism. The Gentleman convinces the Dancer to try selling the Sailor her diamond necklace for water; when the Sailor insists he has no water, she offers him her body, which he also refuses. The Dancer dies in the throes of a mad hallucination, and the Sailor suggests eating her corpse to survive. The Gentleman's sense of human dignity moves him to toss her body overboard before temptation gets the better of him. The Sailor knifes him, but as the Gentleman falls into the water, he drags the Sailor into the shark-infested waters with him. Human dignity thus leads the Gentleman to his own destruction in the face of nature's indifference.

West Indian Mulatto Sailor, A

Played by Eugene O'Neill at the Provincetown Players' Wharf Theatre premiere in Provincetown, Massachusetts, in August 1916. Arthur and Barbara Gelb note that that summer O'Neill was "so deeply tanned he needed no makeup" (571). Wearing a torn sailor's jersey with "Union Mail Line" stitched across it in red letters (calling to mind O'Neill's favorite sweater, part of his merchant marine uniform with "American Line" stitched across the chest), when the Sailor speaks, *"it is in drawling sing-song tones as is he were troubled by some strange impediment of speech"* (1:31). In the opening scene, the Sailor is discovered singing a *"monotonous negro song"* that the Dancer describes as "more of a dirge than a song" (1:33). "I have heard many songs in many languages in many places I have played," she goes on, "but never a song like that before" (1:33). The life raft is encircled by sharks, and when asked what the words mean, the mulatto responds, "It is a charm. I have been told it is very strong. If I sing long enough they will not eat us" (1:34).

Both the Gentleman and the Dancer believe that the Sailor has stolen the remainder of their water, but he persistently refutes the accusation. Over time, the other two, much weaker than the Sailor, plead to him for water. The Dancer finally attempts to trade her $5,000 diamond necklace for a sip, but the Sailor keeps to his story. When she offers him her body, *"For a second his nostrils dilate—he draws in his breath with a hissing sound—his body grows tense and it seems as if he is about to sweep her into his arms. Then his expression grows apathetic again. He turns to the sharks"* (1:48). This rejection from a mulatto proves too much for the Dancer, who goes insane and dances herself to death. The Sailor expresses relief when she dies, as he realizes that only by eating her will the two men survive. The Gentleman's sense of humanity cannot accept this, and he shoves her corpse into the shark-infested waters. The Sailor draws his knife and stabs the Gentleman, no doubt planning to replace her meat with his, but the Gentleman has just enough strength to drag the Sailor into the water with him.

The mulatto Sailor is one of several AFRICAN AMERICANS in the O'Neill canon who are physically and/or morally superior to their Anglo-Saxon counterparts, including Brutus Jones from *The Emperor Jones* and Jim Harris from *All God's Chillun Got Wings* (Floyd 34).

BIBLIOGRAPHY

Bogard, Travis. *Contour in Time: The Plays of Eugene O'Neill.* Rev. ed. New York: Oxford University Press, 1988.

Floyd, Virginia. *The Plays of Eugene O'Neill: A New Assessment.* New York: Ungar, 1985.

Gelb, Arthur, and Barbara Gelb. *O'Neill: Life with Monte Cristo.* New York: Applause Books, 2000.

Ranald, Margaret Loftus. "From Trial to Triumph (1913–1924): The Early Plays." In *The Cambridge Companion to Eugene O'Neill,* edited by Michael

Manheim, 51–68. New York: Cambridge University Press, 1998.

Richter, Robert A. *Eugene O'Neill and Dat Ole Davil Sea: Maritime Influences in the Life and Works of Eugene O'Neill.* Mystic, Conn.: Mystic Seaport, 2004.

Sheaffer, Louis. *O'Neill: Son and Playwright.* Boston: Little, Brown, 1973.

"Tomorrow" (completed, 1916; first published, 1917)

Eugene O'Neill completed "Tomorrow," the only one of his short stories published in his lifetime (the other two stories that survive are "The SCREENEWS OF WAR" and "S.O.S."), during the legendary summer of 1916 in Provincetown, Massachusetts. O'Neill became an overnight success after the experimental drama group the PROVINCETOWN PLAYERS premiered BOUND EAST FOR CARDIFF and THIRST at the fisherman's wharf in Provincetown. "Tomorrow," unlike the two SEA plays, takes place in New York during what O'Neill refers to autobiographically as his period of "great down-and-outness" ("Tomorrow" 3:947). At the time, 1911–12, he was boarding above JIMMY "THE PRIEST'S" saloon, an all-night waterfront dive near South Street in lower Manhattan.

In autumn 1916, O'Neill moved into a flat at 38 Washington Square, a few paces from the apartment of LOUISE BRYANT (with whom he had conducted an affair in the summer that same year) and her fiancé, the radical journalist JOHN REED. Reed sent the manuscript of "Tomorrow" to Carl Hovey, an editor at the magazine *Metropolitan*, where he worked as a correspondent. Hovey responded with kind encouragement but still rejected the piece. On October 11, he wrote Reed, "I've read O'Neill's story 'Tomorrow,' . . . and agree with you that he can write. This thing is genuine and makes a real man live before you. . . . But my judgment is that it would not interest the majority of people who take things as they come. There is a lack of either plot or a situation with suspense enough to carry the

reader beyond the first pages. . . . With all its fine sincerity and effectiveness, there is a kind of overemphasis and sense of repetition which makes the story drag" (quoted in Sheaffer 360).

Louise Bryant then recommended the piece to Waldo Frank, one of the most influential critics of the time and the editor of *Seven Arts*, a highly regarded though short-lived avant-garde journal for the arts. Frank praised the story to O'Neill as a "fine document . . . and I believe that we shall buy it provided that you can correct what seemed to us a few minor imperfections. . . . When you have made the changes will you send the manuscript back to us so that we can ship you a check for $50" (quoted in Sheaffer 382). It was published that summer, June 1917, and Frank soon after accepted IN THE ZONE, a one-act play from the SS GLENCAIRN series. The magazine disappointingly folded as a result of its antiwar sentiments before the play could appear.

In 1944, O'Neill sent a manuscript version of "Tomorrow" to the famous literary critic Mark Van Doren to be auctioned off for the war effort. In the accompanying letter, he remarked, "As a short story—well, let's not go into that, but I though it was pretty devastating stuff at the time, and so evidently did Van Wyck Brooks, Waldo Frank, etc., although I doubt if they were as overwhelmed by its hideous beauty as I was" (1994, 553).

Nevertheless, "Tomorrow" has immense importance as the seed for the idea of the "hopeless hope" O'Neill takes up decades later in his late masterpiece *The ICEMAN COMETH*.

SYNOPSIS

Tommy the Priest's all-night saloon and flophouse near South Street in lower Manhattan, early March 1912. The autobiographical narrator, Art, describes the period as "back in my sailor days, in the winter of my great down-and-outness" (O'Neill "Tomorrow" 1988, 3:947). Art has been rooming at Tommy the Priest's for six months after working as an able seaman. He lives on a small monthly allowance from his family, which he routinely disposes of in two days of drinking; "indifferent to things in general," Art scoffs openly at ambition (3:947). But the story is about his roommate Jimmy Anderson, a "gentleman-ranker" like the narrator and, according to Anderson, a former war correspondent in the Boer War in South Africa (1899–1902). Their room overlooks a courtyard and is decorated only with Anderson's "dyspeptic geranium plant," which never blossoms and symbolizes to Art the "everlasting futility" and "irritating inefficiency" of Anderson's life (3:948).

On the first night, Art moodily takes up one of Anderson's books from his small library of "impossible poetry and incredible prose, written by unknown authors and published by firms one had never heard of" (3:948). He is distracted by the "inmate" next door, a retired telegrapher know to the men as "the Lunger," who suffers from terminal tuberculosis. Art yells at him to silence his hacking cough and exhibits a suicidal predisposition by consciously not opening his window to disperse the germs. "What did I care? I had failed—or rather I had never cared enough about it all to want to succeed" (3:950). The oil lamp is low on fuel, and Art irritably blames his roommate Anderson for not returning with oil as he had promised. Anderson enters with the oil, and Art yells at him for nearly leaving him in the dark. Anderson is wearing a clean shirt and collar and appears uncharacteristically sober. He cautions Art to temper his drinking habits. Art writes this off as the hounding of a "respectable nuisance" (3:951). Anderson reminds him that he is the best friend Art has, and Art apologizes for the "full-sized grouch" he has on that night (3:951). Anderson's temperance lecture continues, however, only arriving in fragments to Art's consciousness—"Wasted youth—your education—ability—a shame—lost opportunity—drink—some nice girl" (3:952). Art reflects that "some of the things he was saying were true; and truth—that kind of truth—should be seen and not heard" (3:953).

Anderson recounts his life story, an irritating habit of his since the regulars at the bar are all well-versed in the details. Though Art doubts its verity, Anderson never contradicts the facts as he presents them. He then tells him that a friend of his, Edwards, had been promoted to an editorship at a daily newspaper and has promised Anderson a position; he begins the following day. Art is skeptical, recalling that all of Anderson's schemes are predicated on starting "tomorrow." Anderson also claims to have received a letter, which he promptly lost, from his 86-year-old aunt in Scotland; she reports that her illness has taken a turn for the worse and hopes he will visit. Art plies Anderson for the price of a drink, but his application for "financial aid" is unnecessary (3:957), as the door bangs open to reveal a stoker named Lyons and a deep-water sailor named Paddy Mehan. Just disembarked in New York, they have hunted down Art and Anderson to share their pay on a bender. Still in the reform frame of mind, Anderson excuses himself, and the other three head down to the bar. As the friends depart, Art wishes Anderson good luck on his first day at the job "tomorrow." That evening is filled with "songs of the sea and yarns about ships punctuated by rounds of drinks" (3:958).

After sleeping through a hangover the following day, Art awakes to find Anderson "very elated, full of the dignity of labor, tremendously conscious of his position in life, provokingly solicitous concerning [Art's] welfare" (3:959). Anderson vanishes for days after, presumably working, while Art continues the bender with Lyons and Paddy. But over time, Anderson arrives back at Tommy's, despondent and withdrawn. Art asks what happened, and Anderson demands to be left alone. The next morning, Art discovers that although he had heard Anderson pacing the room the previous night, his bed is still made and "had the suggestion of a shroud about it—a shroud symbolically woven for one whose life had been threadbare and full of holes" (3:961). Art spends the following day with Lyons and Paddy "lounging on one of the benches" at Battery Park. Anderson returns to Tommy's after midnight that night, looking "incredibly haggard and pale" (3:962) with a blank stare. He downs a full glass of whiskey and miserably admits that he lost his job at the paper. "What I wrote was rot. I couldn't get any news. No initiative—no imagination—no character—no courage! All gone. Nothing left—not even cleverness, no memory even! . . . I'm done—burnt out—wasted! It's time to dump the garbage. Nothing here [tapping his head]" (3:963).

Anderson blames his wife Alice for his irreversible self-destruction, recounting an incident in

South Africa in which he was called back to his home in Cape Town and found Alice *"flagrante delictu"* (sic) with a staff officer (3:964). He had never told the men what happened in Cape Town, but always ended his tales with, "and then—something happened" (3:965). Art, generally a cynic, is sincerely moved by the story: "He was in a mood for truth. So this was the something which happened! Here was real tragedy" (3:965). According to Anderson, Alice is "too cute" to allow him a divorce, as she is waiting for the aunt's money. Anderson goes up to bed, and Art drifts off into a drunken half sleep. He and the other "rounders" at the bar are awakened by a "sharp cracking smash in the back yard" (3:965). Anderson comes down with tears in his eyes and informs them his geranium had fallen from the window sill. He then bursts into real tears, crying for a full 15 minutes, and exits with the excuse that he is going back to sleep.

The barroom erupts with concerned chatter and "then it happened—a swish, a sickish thud as of a heavy rock dropping into thick mud" (3:966). The men rush to the yard outside to find Anderson's body shattered on the flagstones in a black pool of blood. "The sky was pale with the light of dawn," the story concludes. "Tomorrow had come" (3:967).

COMMENTARY

"Tomorrow" probably takes place in the year 1912, the same year as *The Iceman Cometh* and LONG DAY'S JOURNEY INTO NIGHT. A year earlier, in April 1911, O'Neill returned from BUENOS AIRES, ARGENTINA, on the SS IKALA and boarded at Jimmy the Priest's, the basis for "Tommy the Priest's" in the story. But O'Neill served on the SS PHILADELPHIA in August 1911, and as Art worked with the character Lyons on the *Philadelphia* in the story, and he had boarded at Tommy the Priest's for six months, that would bring us close to March 1912, rather than 1911. O'Neill had attempted suicide the previous January, either on New Years Eve 1911 or a couple of weeks after that (Alexander 23). A kind of subconscious arrogance on O'Neill's part comes through in this tale, as not only does the character Art often act maliciously toward his fellow down-and-outers, but if we accept that the story takes

place in 1912, he appears to be a kind of trendsetter for suicidal tendencies as well. O'Neill settled there after working in the MERCHANT MARINE and lived in a seemingly unending state of drunkenness and unemployment. Like his narrator, Art, O'Neill was 23 years old at the time and lived off a monthly allowance from his father, which he drank up within a couple of days; he then lived for the rest of the month off the kindness of his barroom friends. O'Neill later described life at Jimmy the Priest's this way: "One couldn't go any lower. . . . Gorky's *Night's Lodging* was an ice cream parlor in comparison" (quoted in Gelb 294).

After receiving Waldo Frank's letter accepting the story for publication in *Seven Arts*, O'Neill responded promptly with his revisions in a parcel dated March 31, 1917. In it, he apologized for not having a typist available, as he was then in Provincetown and unprofessionally sent the manuscript with the corrections and omissions marked in pencil. He made the corrections with "a view to eliminating the imperfections" Frank had mentioned in his letter (O'Neill *Selected Letters* 1988, 78). One of these was to eliminate the postscript, which was wise. The first draft ends with Art stopping by a theatrical booking agency where Anderson received his mail. O'Neill describes a "fat little Jew" who hands Art a letter addressed to Anderson from the lawyer of the aunt's estate; it announces that she had passed away and left 20,000 pounds to her nephew. Both the anti-Semitism and the ironic O. Henry twist—punctuated with the final line, in which Art looks up at the sky and cries out, "You ironic, cruel demon! . . . but I couldn't help smiling" (O'Neill "Tomorrow" 1988, 331n)—are well dispensed with.

However, some of the "over-emphasis and sense of repetition" that, as Carl Hovey originally pointed out, "makes the story drag," remains in the final draft, while some quite interesting, revealing, and well-written passages were deleted. One instance of over-emphasis is the geranium on the window sill that never blossomed, a fine touch but not when O'Neill unsubtly identifies it as a "symbol of Jimmy's everlasting futility" (3:948); another is when Anderson's bedclothes appear to Art as a foreshadow, "a shroud symbolically woven for one whose life had been threadbare and full of holes" (3:961). In addition, though O'Neill omits in the final draft a number of references to the word *tomorrow* as it relates thematically to Anderson's life, the word is used so many times in the published version that about half way through it is difficult to take the theme as seriously as it deserves. Nevertheless, after Frank's "imperfections" were removed, "Tomorrow" became a more satisfying read, and it proves an enormously useful tool for understanding the development of O'Neill's vision over the course of his literary career.

O'Neill admitted that many of the "imperfections" Waldo Frank alluded to in his acceptance letter came from an artistic "obsession" of his, "in which the story-teller was to hog most of the limelight—a sort of Conrad's Marlow" (O'Neill *Selected Letters* 1988, 78). The reference to Joseph Conrad, one of O'Neill's strongest influences, should be taken as more than a passing analogy. As Travis Bogard has written, O'Neill probably borrowed much of the psychological tension of Anderson's "disease of hope" from Conrad's story of the same title, "Tomorrow" (1903; dramatized in the play *One Day More* in 1926). In Conrad's version, a sea captain awaits the return of his sailor son on land and obsesses over his son's return—always expected "tomorrow." When his son finally does return, the father refuses to relinquish his perpetual sense of anticipation and rejects him (Bogard 93).

Most important for O'Neill scholars, "Tomorrow" stands as O'Neill's first treatment of the controlling idea of his late masterpiece *The Iceman Cometh*. Indeed, O'Neill's first title for *Iceman* was "Tomorrow," though he changed it a day later (Gelb 334). The story's central theme, embedded in the title, is one that O'Neill would revisit time and again in his work—namely, the "hopeless hope" idea of the life-sustaining pipe dream, which he writes about in his 1919 play *The* STRAW. *Iceman* also takes place in a New York dive, but Harry Hope's saloon is modeled after the Golden Swan, rather than Jimmie "the Priest's"; known to regulars as the HELL HOLE, the Golden Swan was O'Neill's favorite haunt from his GREENWICH VILLAGE years.

Eugene O'Neill based James "Jimmy" Anderson closely on JAMES FINDLATER BYTH, O'Neill's actual roommate above JIMMY "THE PRIEST'S" saloon, who worked for a time as JAMES O'NEILL's press agent; Byth also claimed to have worked as a correspondent during the Boer War (1899–1902), though this has been difficult for scholars to verify. A confirmed alcoholic, Byth (née Bythe, a.k.a. Findlater-Byth) was also the model for Jimmy in O'Neill's 1919 one-act play EXORCISM (destroyed), and James "Jimmy Tomorrow" Cameron in *The Iceman Cometh*.

O'Neill BIOGRAPHERS Arthur and Barbara Gelb write of the story, "When Byth/Anderson can no longer lie to himself about the job he will find tomorrow, the job that will give him back his self-respect, his hopeless hope is shattered and there is nothing left but suicide" (336). Though the majority of O'Neill's barroom characters in *Iceman* return to blissful ignorance after Theodore "Hickey" Hickman temporarily snaps them out of their respective stupors, the two characters that do not return are Larry Slade and Don Parritt. The latter, like Jimmy Anderson—who significantly returns in *Iceman* as "Jimmy Tomorrow"—jumps to his death from a room above the bar and lands with a "muffled, crunching thud" (710).

On June 8, 1913, the *New York Times* reported that "James Findlater Byth, 46 years old, for many years connected with newspaper and theatrical work, died yesterday at the New York Hospital of injuries sustained last week when he fell from the window of his house at 252 Fulton Street [the address of Jimmy the Priest's]" (quoted in Alexander 22). O'Neill assumed it was a suicide, but Doris Alexander contends that if Byth really wanted to end his life, he might have chosen a better way than jumping from a third-floor window. Either way, Byth was a tragic figure who, like Jimmy Anderson, drank heavily and refused to take full advantage of his intellectual abilities.

No matter the "depths" Byth reached, according to O'Neill, he was "always my friend—at least always when he had had several jolts of liquor—saw a turn in the road tomorrow. He was going to get himself together and get back to work. Well, he did get a job and got fired. Then he realized that his tomorrow never would come. He solved everything by jumping to his death from the bedroom of Jimmy's" (quoted in Alexander 23). Though Byth's death by suicide is questionable (he may have simply fallen drunk out the window; see Alexander 22), the conclusion O'Neill reached early in life remained at least as late as his composition of *The Iceman Cometh*: Once stripped of any pipe dream, no matter how apocryphal, life's great disappointments become intolerable.

CHARACTERS

Anderson, James A former war correspondent and Art's roommate at Tommy the Priest's all-night saloon and flophouse. The character is based on James Findlater Byth, the former press agent for O'Neill's father JAMES O'NEILL; he later appears under the new name James Cameron, or "Jimmy Tomorrow," in *The Iceman Cometh*. Arthur and Barbara Gelb describe the actual Jimmy, in stark contrast to the fictional character, as "incontestably brilliant, witty, wondrously resourceful and entirely persuasive—if often drunk" (235). O'Neill roomed with Byth at Jimmy the Priest's, upon which Tommy's is based, in 1911 and 1912; and like Anderson from the story, at one time Byth worked as a war correspondent in the Boer War. O'Neill describes Anderson's face as having "the squat nose, the wistful eyes, the fleshy cheeks hanging down like dewlaps on either side of his weak mouth with its pale, thick lips" (318), in similar terms as his character "Jimmy Tomorrow" in *Iceman*, who had "folds of flesh hanging from each side of his mouth" (quoted in Gelb 335). Jimmy Anderson's temperance lectures might also remind audiences of Theodore "Hickey" Hickman's speeches in *Iceman* (Gelb 336).

Anderson boasts that he was raised in an "old manor house" on his family's estate in Scotland, one still owned by his dying aunt. He claims that when his aunt passes away, he will treat his friends in the barroom to a "rare blowout" (319). Art and the others do not fully believe the story, but Art adds that since the men like him, "a fairy tale like that is no great matter to hold against a man" (319). Anderson also claims to have graduated with honors from Edinburgh University in Scotland, after

which he took a position in a European news service that eventually sent him to cover the Boer War in South Africa. This last is the only claim of Anderson's Art was able to verify. But after catching his wife "*flagrante delictu*" (sic) (3:964–965) with a staff officer, Anderson grew dissipated and listless, devoting himself to drink and eventually winding up at Tommy the Priest's.

Then a ray of hope appears—his friend, Edwards, has just been promoted to an editorship at a daily newspaper and offers him a position. Once on the job, however, it rapidly becomes clear that Anderson's former skills as a journalist have been obliterated by 10 years of dissipation. Sulking over this revelation, Anderson confesses to the men at the bar about his wife Alice's infidelity, which he blames for his condition. The combination of losses, and the loss of his "dream of tomorrows" (314), as Art describes it ("dope-dream" in the original version; 314n), compels him to leap to his death from the window of his room. O'Neill's unpublished first draft contains a postscript in which we find out in an ironic twist that Anderson's aunt was, in fact, rich and had passed away, leaving the bulk of her fortune to him—20,000 pounds.

Art Narrator, former sailor in the merchant marine, and James Cameron's roommate at Tommy the Priest's all-night saloon and flophouse. Art is named after O'Neill's friend from NEW LONDON, CONNECTICUT, Arthur McGinley. As autobiographical a figure as Edmund Tyrone in *Long Day's Journey into Night*, O'Neill's early self-portrait deepens our understanding of that character, as well as O'Neill himself. The story also takes place just months before the summer day described in *Long Day's Journey*. The story's autobiographical elements are clearer in the omitted passages, in which Art refers to "a play in seven acts about the feast of Belshazzar & the fall of Babylon," which O'Neill had written in GEORGE PIERCE BAKER's playwriting workshop at Harvard University (though the script has not survived). Also, in the postscript, he switches to the third person and writes, "There isn't much more to tell.... I don't expect you to believe it. It's really too good to be true. You know that I write plays and you'll lay it to my sense of the dramatic" (330n). Art's tone in the story differs markedly from Edmund's, however. Rather than the rather boyish, if hyper-intellectual, Edmund, Art comes across as a bully toward his friend James Anderson. Like Anderson, he is a serious alcoholic, though only 23 years old. Art lives hand-to-mouth at Tommy the Priest's, surviving only on a small allowance provided by his family and the "financial aid" of his fellow rounders at Tommy's. O'Neill himself attempted suicide at Jimmy's and reveals a subtle claim that he may have contracted his own tuberculosis, recalled in *Long Day's Journey*, as a result of his fellow boarder "the Lunger's" illness, against which he does not properly protect himself in the story.

"Lunger, The"   Retired telegrapher who occupies the room next to Art and James Cameron's at Tommy the Priest's. "The Lunger" suffers from tuberculosis and, according to the narrator Art, dies soon after the story's action. He is based on a fellow boarder at Jimmy the Priest's saloon, where O'Neill lodged between trips while sailing in the merchant marine; he was a retired telegrapher whom the men at the bar nicknamed "the Lunger" (a disparaging term of the period for someone suffering from tuberculosis). He also appears as James Knapp in O'Neill's one-act play WARNINGS and short story "S.O.S." "The Lunger" did die of tuberculosis, but not before unsuccessfully attempting to teach O'Neill the International Code of Signals for wireless communication.

Lyons   Stoker on a steam liner, regular at Tommy the Priest's, and friend of Art and James Cameron. Lyons is based on O'Neill's friend DRISCOLL, upon whom the character of that name in the SS *Glencairn* series is also based, along with Robert "Yank" Smith from *The* HAIRY APE. Like the actual Driscoll had done with O'Neill, Lyons had served on the SS *Philadelphia* with Art.

Mehan, Paddy   An "old deep-water sailor" (3:957), a regular at Tommy the Priest's, and a friend of Art and James Cameron. Paddy is more fully developed in the character Paddy in *The Hairy Ape*.

BIBLIOGRAPHY

Alexander, Doris. *Eugene O'Neill's Last Plays: Separating Art from Autobiography.* Athens: University of Georgia Press, 2005.

Bogard, Travis. *Contour in Time: The Plays of Eugene O'Neill.* Rev. ed. New York: Oxford University Press, 1988.

Gelb, Arthur, and Barbara Gelb. *O'Neill: Life with Monte Cristo.* New York: Applause Books, 2000.

Gramm, Julie M. "'Tomorrow': From Whence the Iceman Cometh." *Eugene O'Neill Review* 15, no. 1 (1991): 78–92.

O'Neill, Eugene. *Selected Letters of Eugene O'Neill.* Edited by Travis Bogard and Jackson R. Bryer. New Haven, Conn.: Yale University Press, 1988.

———. "Tomorrow." In *The Unknown O'Neill: Unpublished or Unfinished Writings of Eugene O'Neill.* Edited by Travis Bogard. New Haven, Conn.: Yale University Press, 1988, 313–331.

Wilkins, Frederick C. "Editor's Foreword: Something Old, Something Borrowed." *Eugene O'Neill Newsletter* 7, no. 3 (Winter 1983). Available online. URL: http://www.eoneill.com/library/newsletter/vii_3/vii-3a.htm. Accessed October 22, 2007.

Touch of the Poet, A
(completed, 1942; first produced, 1957)

Eugene O'Neill first conceived *A Touch of the Poet*—working title, *Hair of the Dog*—in 1935, and he finished a first draft on March 18, 1936; however, he held off reworking it until its final revision in 1942, shortly after the United States entered World War II. American involvement in the conflict powerfully affected O'Neill's work routine, so much so that he wrote to the Irish playwright Sean O'Casey: "All I've done since Pearl Harbor is to rewrite one of the plays in my Cycle. *A Touch of the Poet*—an Irish play, incidentally, although located in New England in 1828" (quoted in Shaughnessy 162). A finely written and engaging play, *A Touch of the Poet* is also notable for being the only completed

Al Hirschfeld's caricature of, from left to right, Eric Portman as Cornelius "Con" Melody, Betty Field as Deborah Harford, Helen Hayes as Nora Melody, and Kim Stanley as Sara Melody in the 1958 production of *A Touch of the Poet*. (Courtesy of the estate of Al Hirschfeld)

play from O'Neill's planned historical cycle of 11 full-length plays, A TALE OF POSSESSORS, SELF-DIS-POSSESSED. O'Neill had abandoned the cycle to write his masterpieces *The* ICEMAN COMETH and LONG DAY'S JOURNEY INTO NIGHT before a neurological tremor in his hands put an end to his writing career. Along with *A Touch of the Poet*, he partially completed its sequel, MORE STATELY MANSIONS. Truly one of O'Neill's greatest works and the second to last full-length play he ever wrote, the last being A MOON FOR THE MISBEGOTTEN, A *Touch of the Poet* was never produced in his lifetime, though O'Neill offered it to the ailing THEATRE GUILD in 1946. It was first produced on March 29, 1957, at the Royal Dramatic Theatre in Stockholm, and

later at the Helen Hayes Theatre in New York City on October 2, 1958, to largely appreciative reviews. In the *Nation* magazine, novelist Gore Vidal aptly described the play as "at once so human and so gently wise" (236).

SYNOPSIS

Act 1

A tavern on the outskirts of Boston at nine in the morning on July 27, 1828. The tavern is a once-thriving stagecoach rest stop long ago fallen into disrepair. Bartender Mickey Maloy, a young Irishman of 26, is reading a newspaper at one of two tables arranged in the foreground. Jamie Cregan enters. Cregan, a middle-aged Irishman with a saber scar on one cheek, looks visibly hung over. Both men speak in strong Irish brogues. Maloy offers Cregan a drink on the house to put an end to the "blacksmith at work" on Cregan's head. Cregan inquires whether the tavern keeper, Cornelius "Con" Melody, has "been down yet for his morning's morning," his whiskey to cure his hangover (3:184). He has not. Cregan, Melody's distant cousin, had served under him as a corporal in the British army, and they reunited for the first time the night before. Melody had wounded Cregan's pride by offering free drinks to all but Cregan, since Melody only extends credit to "gentlemen." Cregan fears he might have sought retribution by telling tales of Melody's lurid past once the tavern keeper retired for the night.

Maloy confirms this and relates what he learned: Con Melody, who bogusly dresses and acts like a member of the British aristocracy, is actually the son of a "shebeen keeper," or unlicensed pub owner. An Irish peasant who treacherously made it rich off his own class, Con's father Ned Melody sent his son to a Dublin school to be educated in the style of the landed gentry. Once there, his classmates ridiculed him for his pretenses, and Melody challenged and killed one of these antagonists in a duel. Cregan, who fought under Melody's command in Spain, assures Mickey Maloy that for all of the man's boasting over "fightin' and women, and gamblin' or any kind of craziness," the tales are probably true. "There nivir was a madder devil" (3:186). Melody also told Maloy that he was pressured into marrying his wife Nora Melody by local priests, who scolded him for impregnating her before marriage. Since then, Maloy says, Melody has despised priests. Cregan insists that this was a lie: "He may like to blame it on [the priests] but it's little Con Melody cared what they said." Melody fell in love with Nora, Cregan continues, but her father was an Irish peasant on his family's estate, "as poor, as poor," and Melody always considered her beneath him in social position (3:187). He joined the British army, leaving his wife and daughter Sara alone, and served honorably on the side of the British against the French as a major in the Peninsular War (1808–14). Soon after, however, Melody, an insufferable womanizer, seduced

a Spanish nobleman's wife and killed his rival in another duel. As a result, the army forced him to resign, and having squandered his father's estate on PROSTITUTES and whiskey, Melody emigrated with his family to the United States to make his fortune and avoid further scandal.

Cregan hears Sara approaching from the hallway at stage right, and he retreats to the bar. Sara enters from the kitchen, asks Maloy for the bar book, and sits to settle the business accounts. Maloy quips that "if it's profits you're looking for, you won't find them," since Melody rarely, if ever, charges his clientele for drinks (3:188). Sara ignores him, but he continues on, this time about Simon Harford, a wealthy young Yankee whom Sara has been nursing back to health. Sara is evidently enamored with the young man. Maloy teases that she became stuck up as a result of Harford's affections. He informs her that a Yankee woman visited the tavern and appeared to be looking for Harford, though she never mentioned him by name and looked too young to be his mother. This upsets Sara, who is obviously in love. She recognizes that class barriers might keep them apart and that his parents would in no way approve of their union.

Nora Melody appears in the doorway. Nora is 41 but looks much older after years of unrelieved toil due to her husband's laziness; she suffers from rheumatism but fears DOCTORS, particularly the affordable ones, as "they bring death with them" (3:191). This prompts Sara to complain about their finances—the tavern is mortgaged to the hilt; they have no credit left at the store; and Melody gives away free drink, hires a bartender to do his work for him (Maloy), and squanders what funds they do have to keep an extravagant thoroughbred mare. But unlike her daughter, Nora respectfully accepts her husband's ignoble facade and defends his right to keep the thoroughbred, "his greatest pride" (3:191) because the horse helps preserve some of his former glory.

The local priest, Father Flynn, counseled her to put an end to Melody's sneering attitude toward the local IRISH AMERICANS and his open disdain for Andrew Jackson, the presidential hopeful who would grant the working-class Irish some political clout; he warned her that it might lead to trouble with the Irish townspeople. Sara berates Nora for slaving over Melody. "You'd leave him today, if you had any pride!" (3:192). She resents her father for being duped into buying the tavern on false advice that a railroad was to be built nearby. Believing more in the American Dream than in her father, she proclaims that "this is a country where you can rise as high as you like, and no one but the fools who envy you care what you rose from, once you've the money and the power goes with it" (3:194).

Con Melody sluggishly makes his entrance. Melody is 45, well-built, barrel-chested, and dressed in the well-tailored clothing of a British aristocrat. Some details about his appearance, however, smack of the stereotypical Irish peasant—his arms are hairy and too long for his body, which has a *bull-like, impervious strength, a tough peasant vitality* (3:197); like Cregan, Melody is terribly hungover, a fact made evident by his shaky hands, pallid face, unsteady gait, and bloodshot eyes. He civilly wishes Sara good morning, to which Sara replies with impolite curtness, a tone that typifies their repartee until the final scene of the play. Sara exits to change into her "Sunday best" with the excuse that she must persuade the shopkeeper Neilan to extend them more credit, but she actually does so to impress Harford. Melody takes up the newspaper; his hands shake terribly, and he openly resents Nora's guilt-inducing presence. "Well? I know what you're thinking! Why haven't you the courage to say it for once? By God, I'd have more respect for you! I hate the damned meek of this earth!" (3:199). He accuses her of encouraging his ALCOHOLISM as well, since his addiction is the "one point of superiority you can lay claim to, isn't it?. . . But, in God's name, who am I to reproach anyone with anything? Why don't you tell me to examine my own conduct?" (3:199, 201–202).

Melody looks at the date on the newspaper and realizes that it is the 19th anniversary of the Battle of Talavera (July 27, 1809), at which he had been publicly commended by the duke of Wellington (at the time, Lieutenant General Sir Arthur Wellesley) for bravery on the battlefield. Nora promises to arrange a commemorative dinner, as she does every year. Melody's guest list includes Jamie Cregan, Patch Riley, Paddy O'Dowd, and Dan Roche—all local Irish boozers and parasites of the bar. Some

political discussion follows as Melody continues reading his paper. He rails against Jackson but still predicts the radical Democrat's victory and asserts that the United States will "drive the English from the face of the earth." Nora adds that the Irish might be freed as well, a notion Melody dismisses— "Ireland? What benefit would freedom be to her unless she could be freed from the Irish?" (3:201).

Nora heads to the kitchen to prepare Melody's breakfast. Now on his third whiskey, Melody grows perceptibly more confident and vain. He stands erect before the large mirror and pompously recites lines from the romantic poet Lord Byron's "Childe Harold." Theatrically repeating the line, "Among them, but not of them" (3:203), Melody reflects on his struggle to maintain dignity in his poor financial state and social exile. Sara interrupts his reverie—"I hope you saw something in the mirror you could admire!" (3:203). Ignoring the insult, Melody applauds her potential union with Simon Harford, remarking, as Nora did, that although "he is a bit on the sober side for one so young . . . there is a romantic touch of the poet behind his Yankee phlegm" (3:205). He informs her that he made "enquiries" about Harford's family and found them an appropriate match in station. He also tells her that he will negotiate her "settlement," though clearly a dowry is impossible for him. Sara, who considers her father a poseur and a liar, cries out in anguish. "Father! Will you never let yourself wake up—not even when you're sober, or nearly? Is it stark mad you've gone, so you can't tell what's dead and a lie, and what's the living truth?" (3:207).

In the final scene, Roche, O'Dowd, and Riley pile into the tavern in the mode of vaudevillian farce. Roche loudly praises Andrew Jackson. Melody roars for quiet, and Sara exits out the front door. When Nora appears with breakfast, Melody apologizes for not being hungry and joins the men in the bar. The curtain falls with Nora sobbing alone over a plate of cooling eggs and bacon (3:209).

Act 2

Same as act 1, about half hour later. Con Melody enters the dining room from the bar, calling for silence to recall the Battle of Talavera in noble solitude. A couple of whiskeys more (and still no breakfast), Melody sits at a table and strikes his usual pose of the romantic Byronic hero, one he cannot maintain without an audience; his hauteur soon collapses into *"hopelessness and defeat bringing a trace of real tragedy in his ruined, handsome face"* (3:210). Sara returns from her humiliating errand at Neilan's, but she apprehends the "real tragedy" in his look and shows genuine concern. Melody is startled to see her but regains his composure and pompously reminds her that today is the anniversary of Talavera. Sara responds sardonically, "a great day for the spongers and a bad day for this inn!" (3:210), and she scolds him for making her mother prepare the feast (3:211). She pointedly informs her father that she was reduced to begging for credit and that Neilan the shopkeeper only consented out of pity for her mother.

Nora enters with milk for Simon Harford. Hearing they gained more credit, she praises Neilan for his kindness. Melody explodes with resentment, then accuses the women of carrying on like "scheming peasants" by entrapping the Yankee visitor into wedlock beneath his station. After Sara calls him a liar, he responds harshly that if acting the ministering angel will not accomplish her goal, there is "always one last trick to get him through his honor" (3:212). This is an insult to both women: Sara for being louche enough to consider sex with Harford in order to blackmail him into marriage; and, if backhandedly, Nora for having victimized *him* in precisely the same way. Sara storms out, only partially understanding the insinuation. Nora excuses Melody by admitting that Sara provoked him. Melody and Nora discuss the benefits of Sara's marriage to Harford, though money does not appear to be of much concern. Nora approves of the young man, having remarked to Sara in act 1 that "young Master Harford has a touch av the poet in him . . . the same as your father" (3:195). Melody approves as well, though when Nora reports he is too shy to kiss Sara's hand, he jibes, "When it comes to making love the Yankees are clumsy, fish-blooded louts. They lack savoir-faire. They have no romantic fire! They know nothing of women" (3:213; an ironic foreshadow of his disastrous seduction attempt that soon follows).

Melody heads into the bar, and Sara appears with news that Harford at last found the courage to kiss her. Sara's hard tongue against her father is softened for a time. She and Nora both exit to prepare Melody's uniform, which he ceremoniously wears each year for the anniversary of Talavera. Melody reenters the dining room, again striking his pose before the mirror and reciting the same lines from Byron. Deborah Harford, Simon Harford's mother, quietly intrudes upon Melody's narcissistic ritual. Caught in the act again, Melody initially lashes out in a fury, but seeing the attractive Yankee "lady," he adopts a gallant, welcoming attitude. She inquires whether he is "the innkeeper, Melody," and Melody responds, "I am *Major* Cornelius Melody, one time of His Majesty's Seventh Dragoons" (3:217). What follows is a pitiful, though not at first unsuccessful, attempt at seduction on Melody's part. He flatters Deborah with a charming flow of "blarney," bemoans the sad state of his business, and impresses her by telling of his role in the Battle of Talavera. He bends down to kiss her. Drawn to him in spite of herself, she then smells whiskey on his breath: "Pah! You reek of whiskey! You are drunk, sir! You are insolent and disgusting! I do not wonder your inn enjoys such meager patronage, if you regale all your guests of my sex with this absurd performance!" (3:218). Nora and Sara enter from the doorway and instantly comprehend what has happened. Sara suspects this must be the woman Maloy had warned her of in act 1. Deborah substantiates this by introducing herself as Simon Harford's mother and asks to see her son. *This is a bombshell for Melody* (3:218). Sarah accompanies Deborah, who now treats Melody icily, to Simon's room. When Melody regains his composure, shame once again turns to rage. He vows to apologize like a gentleman and prove his valorous past, which he assumes she has now taken for drunken lies. Donning his uniform, he exits, making Nora pledge to stall Deborah until he can return in uniform.

Sara reenters, having left Deborah alone at her son's bedside, but she stood outside the door and eavesdropped on the ensuing conversation. She reports that someone sent Henry Harford, Simon's father, an unsigned letter informing him of his son's whereabouts. Convinced Deborah hates her and resentful of her condescension, Sara unconsciously sides with her father: "Maybe she liked it, for all her pretenses," she says (3:221). In spite of her disdain for her father's pose, Sara hopes Deborah will remain long enough to see her father in uniform, but she takes it back in an instant: "Och! I'm as crazy as he is. As if she hadn't the brains to see through him" (3:222). Sara asks her mother to remove herself to the kitchen so she might confront Deborah about her future with Simon. Nora obeys, worried she might fail to stall Deborah until Melody's return.

Deborah reenters, again gracious, but with a persistent, amused smile and an ironically distant attitude toward Sara. Deborah vouchsafes a series of short monologues pertaining to the illustrious history of the Harford family, who fought in both the American and French Revolutions, and she characterizes Harford men throughout history as "great dreamers" who stop at nothing to attain their dreams or ever "part with them even when they deny them" (3:223, 225). She admits they would approve of Sara for her ambition and ends with an odd exposition on the sublime effects of tramping alone through the woods to find her son, having never left her cultivated garden in years. Deborah departs and Nora reappears, guilt-ridden that she failed to keep Deborah at the tavern until her husband's return. Sara relates Deborah's strange communication, understanding there was supposed to be some meaning to it but not comprehending what it was. She is convinced Deborah asked Harford to delay marrying Sara and assumes she will concoct a plan to prevent the union.

Melody opens the door slowly for dramatic effect, and Nora flees to avoid her husband's wrath. Sara is prepared to do battle, but appears reluctantly impressed by the striking figure of her father in military regalia: "Oh, Father, why can't you ever be the thing you can seem to be?" (3:228). He admits to having "put his foot in it" with Deborah Harford, but accuses the Yankee lady of mistaking gallantry for licentiousness: "It must be their damned Puritan background. They can't help seeing sin hiding under every bush" (3:229). He suggests that she probably was not as scandalized

as she made out. Sara, in another weak moment, agrees with him—"I'll wager she wasn't for all her airs." Again adopting a sneering tone, however, she fearlessly informs her father that it was she who let Deborah leave before Melody could "make bad worse by trying to fascinate her with your beautiful uniform" (3:229).

Melody affects an attitude of relief, and Sara exits. Melody stands holding the top of a chair and crushes it with a brute strength brought on by shame-fuelled passion. Cregan enters and praises Melody's uniform and fine figure, instantly cheering up his old superior. As the curtain falls, the comrades toast each other's valor at the Battle of Talavera (3:230–231).

Act 3

Around eight o'clock that evening. The dining room, lit dimly with candlelight, appears filthier than before, more cramped and dilapidated. Cregan and Melody are seated at the center table, with Melody at the head. Consigned to their own table, Riley, O'Dowd, and Roche are at left. The men have finished eating, and all five are in various stages of drunkenness. Melody is the most intoxicated, but *"holding his liquor like a gentleman"* (3:232), he reenacts the Battle of Talavera on the table with silverware and shakers to indicate troop movements and positions. To the other men's delight, Riley has brought his Irish pipes; he plays "Baltiorum" and sings a bawdy Irish ditty that includes innuendo about a priest's sexual misconduct with a young woman, Biddy O'Rafferty. Melody tells him to play the tune again when his wife returns, since she still holds to her benighted Old World devotion to priests.

Sara waits on the men in disgust, sarcastically adopting the brogue of an Irish peasant servant when addressing her father. In retaliation, Melody tells the men that he need not apologize for the quality of the wine, if the service is unsatisfactory. The stinging truth of the "spongers" at the table comes out when O'Dowd and Roche hold a conversation behind Melody's back: They consider him a fraud and curse him for fighting on the side of the British. Both agree, however, that they are grateful for his foolishness, since it comes with free whiskey.

Melody recites a few lines from Byron, *"quietly, with a bitter eloquence"* (3:235), while the men stare at him incomprehensively. The lines pertain to existential loneliness, and Melody contemptuously remarks that it is just as well they do not understand. He asks Riley to play "Modideroo," an Irish hunting song, again to the other men's delight. The song sends Melody into a rapturous monologue about fox hunting in his youth; the memories significantly wash away his aristocratic front, and a *"strong lilt of brogue"* enters his voice (3:236). Sara must clear the table and asks in feigned politeness if the "gintlemen" could retire to the bar and let her finish. Melody dismisses his companions, but says he wishes to speak to Sara in private.

Sara senses danger, knowing through experience that at this stage of drunkenness, her father can be horribly cruel. She intends to leave, but he startles her into staying by mentioning a meeting that took place between him and Simon Harford that afternoon, in which they discussed marriage as a means to preserve Sara's reputation. Simon told Melody that Deborah Harford wanted Sara and him to prolong their engagement for a year to ensure their love was strong enough for marriage. Sara suspected as much. Melody continues that they discussed a "settlement," or dowry, for Sara; he also mentions that Henry Harford should come up with a figure for Simon's allowance. She mentions the possibility that Harford's father might not approve of their union at all, but Melody refuses to acknowledge this. After reminding her that she was born in a castle, he turns the table and concludes that it is he, not Henry Harford, who will not consent to their marriage. "Such a marriage would be a tragic misalliance for him—and God knows," he adds cruelly, "I know the sordid tragedy of such a union" (3:242). Melody suggests, cutting ever deeper, that she marry Mickey Maloy instead. "He's a healthy animal. He can give you a raft of peasant brats to squeal and fight with the pigs on the mud floor of your hovel" (3:243). In the end, he suggests that if she tricked Harford into making her pregnant, this would force Henry Harford's consent. Sara threatens to follow his advice if all else fails, but Melody contemptuously dismisses her and heads for the bar. Sara exits in quiet despair.

Melody, contrite and begging forgiveness for his drunken malice, calls Sara back. But she has gone, and standing before the mirror, he quotes Byron to consol himself (3:244).

The Harford family attorney, Nicholas Gadsby, enters. He has been dispatched by Henry Harford to bribe Melody into breaking off the engagement between Sara and Simon Harford. The dialogue commences with a series of comic miscommunications. When Gadsby first introduces himself as an attorney, Melody responds, "Attorney, eh? The devil take all your tribe, say I" (3:245). Gadsby is unprepared for such effrontery from a common tavern keeper. They insult each other further, until Gadsby clarifies that he is in the employ of Henry Harford, instantly transforming Melody's attitude to one of respect and hospitality. Gadsby then informs him that Henry Harford is prepared to pay $3,000 if Melody breaks the engagement between their children and leaves the region. "There is such a difference in station," he says, "The idea is preposterous" (3:247). Melody cocks his fist back in a fury, but Sara, who has been listening in, jumps between them. Anticipating a fight, Cregan, O'Dowd, Riley, and Roche pile in from the bar. Physically subdued but fuming, Melody orders the men to expel the lawyer and "kick it down to the crossroads" (3:248). They gleefully obey.

Melody swears revenge on Henry Harford, decides to challenge him to a duel, and forbids Sara from marrying Simon. Inwardly proud of her father's defense of her honor, Sara nevertheless vows to go ahead with the union. Melody threatens to kill her if she does—"You filthy peasant slut! You whore! I'll see you dead first—! By the living God, I'll kill you myself!" (3:250). Cregan rescues Sara by coaxing Melody to go to the Harfords. Melody agrees, and he and Cregan, who will be his witness, head off for the Harford estate. Nora is worried but also proud of her husband and confident he will prevail. "What chance will this auld stick av a Yankee have against him?" (3:252). Sara, adamant that her dreams not be destroyed, declares that she "can play at the game of gentleman's honor too!" and heads upstairs to carry out the "trick" her father suggested (3:252). Unaware of her daughter's intentions, Nora remains in the dining room to wait out the night.

Act 4

Around midnight the same night. One candle barely illuminates the room, intensifying the cramped effect from the previous act. Mickey Maloy enters from the bar to cheer Nora up. He offers her whiskey, and she accepts. Maloy flatters her integrity and good looks, assuring her that Melody has the support of the men in the bar. "If they do hate Con Melody, he's Irish, and they hate the Yanks worse" (3:254–255), he says, then moves to his post behind the bar. Sara returns, looking dreamy and contented. *"All the bitterness and defiance have disappeared from her face"* (3:255). Glad for the company, Nora openly criticizes Melody for the first time: "His pride, indade! What is it but a lie? What's in his veins, God pity him, but the blood of thievin' auld Ned Melody who kept a dirty shebeen?" (3:256). Appalled at her own betrayal, Nora renounces her words, as she has never before questioned her husband's facade. Bemoaning the "mortal sin" she and Melody had committed before marriage, Nora vows to confess to a priest that night. Knowing full well her mother would not go through with it, Sara prods her along until Nora admits she cannot.   .

Nora senses the change in her daughter, who confesses proudly that she and Harford made love and that now he will commit to marriage out of honor. But before they consummated their love, Sara reflects, "I knew nothing of love, or the pride a woman can take in giving everything—the pride in her own love! I was only an ignorant, silly girl boasting, but I'm a woman now, Mother, and I know" (3:261). Nora strongly disapproves, but her anguish over Melody's well-being supersedes her shock at her daughter's indiscretion. "All I hope now," Sara says, "is that whatever happened wakes him from his lies and mad dreams so he'll have to face the truth of himself in that mirror" (3:263).

Cregan quietly enters the tavern, not wanting to alert the men in the barroom of their arrival. His face is bruised and bloodied, and he supports Melody, also badly injured. Melody suffered a severe blow to the head and stares blankly at his wife and daughter without recognition. When they arrived at the Harfords' mansion, a band of servants stopped them at the door. Cregan and Melody had the upper hand in the ensuing fight, but then the police arrived. Melody and Cregan fought well, but the police got the better of them with clubs. "Arrah, the dirthy cowards!" Nora responds with disgust. "Always takin' sides with the rich Yanks against the poor Irish!" (3:266). Dazed by his head injury, Melody rants wildly over his abysmal conduct, past and present, and the "pale Yankee bitch" (Deborah Harford), who watched the Donnybrook from an upstairs window. According to Cregan, Melody has been raving like this, battling his conflicting selves, since the fight broke off—"speakin' av the pigs and his father one minute, and his pride and honor and his mare the next" (3:267). After the brawl, the police locked them up, but Harford had them released, afraid of a scandal if the escapade was reported in the newspaper. Melody charges up the stairs to his bedroom in a semicatatonic state, followed close behind by Nora. Nora returns terror-stricken and orders Cregan to follow her husband, who has run to the barn with his dueling pistols.

A pistol shot is heard over the commotion from the bar. Horror-stricken, Nora believes her husband has shot himself. Cregan and Melody enter. Cregan is disgusted with Melody, who has shot the mare; after depositing him in the dining room, he exits the bar. Sara falls into a laughing fit over the killed mare; Nora tries to quiet her, but Melody, now lucid, silences his wife *"in the broadest brogue, his voice coarse and harsh"* (3:272): "Lave Sara laugh. Sure, who could blame her? I'm roarin' meself inside me. It's the damnedest joke a man ivir played on himself since time began" (3:272). Sara and Nora stare at him in stunned silence. Sara believes he is playacting, as he always has, and Nora that he has gone insane. Neither is correct. Melody killed the mare to kill the major in him. His peasant Irish son of a "shebeen keeper" self has overcome his aristocratic veneer. The "damnedest joke" he refers to is that the major had planned to kill both the horse and himself; but by killing the mare, he destroyed the major in the process, so there was no use bothering to go through with the suicide.

The major reappears in his voice one last time. Choking with grief, he describes the look of forgiveness in the mare's eyes before the life went out of them. "Begorra," Melody says, "if that wasn't the mad Major's ghost speakin'!" (3:273). Sara begs him to stop. The major was the one playing the charade, Melody coldly responds, and he plans to live the rest of his days as a common Irish tavern keeper—his legitimate birthright. Melody stands mockingly in front of the mirror and recites the lines from "Childe Harold" in a deep brogue. Sara's formerly unconscious slips of pride in her father come out in this final scene—she beseeches the major to return, even offering, incredibly, to renounce her love for Harford in return. Melody slaps her viciously, warning her not to persist in "tryin' to raise the dead" (3:279). For her part, Nora appears overjoyed by the transformation. Melody pledges his love to her, kisses her on the lips and hair, and promises to fire Maloy and take his place behind the bar. Nora rejects this, and Melody agrees that his inclinations lean more to whiskey than work.

Melody joins the men in the bar to a roar of welcoming cheers. As Nora and Sara talk over the transformation, he is heard shouting in the back room, "Here's to our next President, Andy Jackson!" (3:280). Sara reconciles herself to Melody's new persona—"He's beaten at last and he wants to stay beaten" (3:279)—but tearfully mourns the major. Nora, who will "play any game he likes and give him love in it" (3:280), tenderly scolds her daughter in the last line, "Shame on you to cry when you have love. What would the young lad think of you?" (3:281).

COMMENTARY

A Touch of the Poet incorporates the full scope of O'Neill's mature themes: the destructive effects of vanished pipe dreams, the spiritual bankruptcy that ensues in the mad pursuit of the American dream, the sacrifice of the individual soul for wealth and social position, the ethnic clash between Irish Americans and New England Yankees, generational conflicts, the mask of pretense hiding the authentic self within, and the more terrifying possibility that no authentic self exists behind the masks we present to the outer world. *A Touch of the Poet* is also concerned, like its more esteemed predecessor *The Iceman Cometh*, with the sustaining power of pipe dreams. In a *Time* magazine review for the

1978 revival of *A Touch of the Poet*, starring JASON ROBARDS as Cornelius "Con" Melody, critic T. E. Kalem sums up "the fierce tension at the heart of [O'Neill's] dramatic imagination" we find in this play as the theme that "a life of illusions is unpardonable but that life without illusions is unbearable" (236).

In *A Touch of the Poet*, as literary historian Joel Pfister perceptively argues about much of O'Neill's work, "the social, the ideological, and the psychological [are not] distinct categories but [are] categories complexly intertwined" (184). Socially, "Major" Melody wishes to be accepted by upperclass New England Yankees; ideologically, he wishes to disenfranchise the uneducated "rabble," who are ironically his only companions; psychologically, Melody is a conflicted soul, the son of an Irish "shebeen" keeper and the proud, formally educated military officer. Con Melody is thus a tormented soul, a man who lived life as his creator had, "among them, but not of them." Melody's self-pitying remarks also reflect Mary Tyrone's on the present as past in *Long Day's Journey into Night*: In the end, as an Irish immigrant in America in 1828, he can offer no future for his daughter Sara, as he is "finished—no future but the past" (3:213).

Does the death of Melody's illusion in the form of the major, then, represent a symbolic death or a triumphant rebirth? There is no clear answer in the play. On the one hand, particularly when placed side by side with *The Iceman Cometh*, we can only see the loss of Con Melody's illusion as a form of death in life, as the men in *Iceman*'s bar had until Hickey's arrest and the resumption of pipe dreams in the bar. Melody dies only a few years after the action of *A Touch of the Poet*, as we learn from the play's unfinished sequel *More Stately Mansions*, in which Jamie Cregan importantly remarks, "He could have drunk a keg a day and lived for twenty years yet, if the pride and spirit wasn't killed inside him ever since the night that he tried to challenge that Yankee coward Harford to a duel and him and me got beat by the police and arrested" (quoted in Porter 249n). On the other hand, *A Touch of the Poet* is a more unmistakably historical play than *The Iceman Cometh* (in which O'Neill makes clear that the men at the bar must sustain their pipe dreams to survive psychologically), as O'Neill tackles the larger American dream in equal proportion to individual pipe dreams.

Edward Shaughnessy finds the central theme of O'Neill's planned historical cycle of 11 plays, *A Tale of Possessors Self-Dispossessed*, embedded in Con Melody's remarks about the potential marriage between Sara and Simon Harford, which importantly echo James Tyrone's sentiments in *Long Day's Journey into Night* (a character based on O'Neill's father, JAMES O'NEILL): "Although there is no more honorable calling than that of poet and philosopher, which his son has chosen to pursue, there is no decent living to be gained by its practice" (241). Shaughnessy contends that "such hypocrisy posing as both courtly wisdom and good business was to be the key to his analysis of American greed in the cycle of plays" (166). In the end, Melody has shrugged off his arrogant posturing, reasserted his Irish birthright, revealed his love for his "shanty Irish" wife, allied himself with the "downtrodden," and found a sense of belonging he so desperately sought over the course of his life. "Be God, *I'm* alive and in the crowd and they *can* deem me one av such," he declares in the final scene. "I'll be among thim and av thim, too—and make up for the lonely dog's life the Major led me" (3:278). If *A Touch of the Poet* can be considered a tragedy, it is Sara Melody, not her father, who suffers most from his final defeat.

O'Neill told his son, EUGENE O'NEILL, JR., that "the one thing that explains more than anything about me is the fact that I'm Irish"; he also said, seemingly contradicting this statement, that "the battle of moral forces in the New England scene is what I feel closest to as an artist" (quoted in Floyd 537). *A Touch of the Poet* reconciles these two assertions more starkly than any other play in the canon. O'Neill had designed his *Tale of Possessors* cycle to chart the development of a New England family, the Harfords, from 1775 to 1930, as an allegory of American history as a whole. In his words, he wished to mete out "the development of psychological characterization in relation to changing times—what the railroads, what the panics did to change people's lives" (quoted in Pfister 182). As such, *A Touch of the Poet* importantly takes place

in 1828, the same year Andrew Jackson defeated the incumbent presidential candidate John Quincy Adams in his bid for president of the United States. This political race was culturally significant as well, in that Jackson was the son of a poor Irishman while Adams was a member of one of the most prominent families in Massachusetts. Significantly, the play's central external conflict is that of the early Irish immigrants' larger bid to accomplish the American dream in the established realm of New England.

For a historical setting, Gore Vidal wrote in his review of the 1958 American premiere, "1828 is just right: Andrew Jackson; the rise of the democrats; the fall of J.Q. Adams and with him that oligarchical, gentlemanly society which began the nation. All this is symbolically right, and pleasing" (235). Edward Shaughnessy has called Con Melody's psychologically significant recitation of lines from the romantic British poet Lord Byron's "Childe Herald" historically "stunning in its anti-Jacksonian sentiment" (163):

> I have not loved the World, nor the World me;
> I have not flattered its rank breath, nor bowed
> To its idolatries a patient knee
> Nor coined my cheek to smile,—nor cried
>   aloud
> In worship of an echo: in the crowd
> They could not deem me one of such—I stood
> Among them, but not of them . . . (3:203)

Once in the United States, Melody is an archetypal "in-between" character, caught between the Yankee New Englanders whose station in life he covets, but against whose rejection of him he rebels, and the Boston Irish he outwardly disdains and who reciprocally despise him for his pretensions. Though the four scenes in which Melody absurdly recites lines from Byron's poem in front of his mirror mainly serve to ridicule his pretentiousness, they also highlight the tragic reality of his position—"among them, but not of them." And if O'Neill employs mealtimes in *Long Day's Journey* as a structural device to chart the course of the day moving toward night, as Laurin Porter has suggested, in *A Touch of the Poet*, time is marked by "the four mirror scenes, which measure not only time but also Con's increasingly desperate and finally futile efforts to maintain his dignity by clinging to his Byronic pose" (Porter 243). In the first scene, Melody's performance is interrupted by his scornful daughter; in the second, by the Yankee interloper Deborah Harford; in the third, by Henry Harford's lawyer Nicholas Gadsby; and, finally, he himself stands before the mirror, his own peasant Irish persona sarcastically reciting the poem in "mocking brogue, guffawing contemptuously afterwards" (Porter 243–244). These mirror episodes thus represent the "inexorable and irreversible" nature of time that drives the Melody and Harford families onward and downward (Porter 244).

"The mirror," Joel Pfister adds, "reassures Con that by controlling how he sees himself, he may have some measure of control over how others perceive him" (183). *A Touch of the Poet* can in this way be defined as a "social drama" in that it charts the particular course of a person attempting to elevate his social status through manipulation and wile. In such social dramas, Edward Shaughnessy writes, "As long as there exists a capacity for guilt, the protagonist remains human, no matter how hateful he has become to himself or others" (164). Melody's mask drops in several scenes, though never while another character bears witness, until his final transformation. Most poignantly, after Con and Sara's confrontation in act 3, Con cries out his daughter's name and weakly apologizes for his brutal verbal assault.

O'Neill's use of vernacular in *A Touch of the Poet* is highly significant. Until the moment when Con's nostalgia for fox hunting early in act 3 coaxes out his Irish brogue, it is unclear whether, in fact, he had ever spoken in brogue, though his father had been a "shebeen" (an illegal Irish bar) keeper in the Old World. True, Melody's college classmates jeered at his pretentiousness, but we still have no indication what his persona might have been before his education. We discover this persona in the dramatic transformation scene of act 4. Con Melody hides his peasant brogue to gain access to New England society as O'Neill's father, James O'Neill, had done to gain full access to the American stage. Nora's ethnic cohesion, typical for first-generation immigrants, is reflected in the

fact that she only speaks in brogue, along with her acceptance of Con's drinking habits and her superstitious belief that only a confession to a priest will thwart the family curse. Sara speaks intermittently in an Irish brogue and in cultivated American English, thereby demonstrating her logical melding of the two cultural traditions, her acculturation as a second-generation Irish immigrant into the New World. But by *More Stately Mansions*, which treats her marriage to Simon Harford, she has fully assimilated as the wife of a New England Yankee.

Melody is thus caught between the love of his wife, the unpretentious daughter of ignorant peasants, and the social ambitions of his daughter Sara. Edward Shaughnessy has rightly characterized Nora as having a virtue "so great . . . that O'Neill ran the risk of implausibility in creating her" (165). Nora will "play any game he likes and give him love in it" (3:280), while Sara "rivals Con in her pride" (Shaughnessy 164), desperately wishing that her father's aristocratic facade were true. In act 2, when Deborah Harford appears and informs Sara about her walk through the woods, she insinuates that Sara is analogous to Harford's "dream" of living in the uncultivated wilderness (the Irish working class), one that Harford will probably reject for the more stable, familiar environs of cultivation (the New England upper class). In addition, Deborah's viewing of Melody's defeat in act 4 has the same effect on Melody as Mildred Douglas's witnessing Robert "Yank" Smith's rant in the stokehold in *The Hairy Ape*—it destroys each character's delusional sense of pride.

Michael Manheim argues that *A Touch of the Poet* can be read as a study of O'Neill's father, James O'Neill, a fellow "actor, father, and proud Irishman" (145) that O'Neill dramatized in the character James Tyrone in *Long Day's Journey*. And like James Tyrone, Con Melody also "uses illusions about his glorious past [for O'Neill, being a promising Shakespearean actor; for Melody, a military god] to obscure his humble, shanty Irish origins." Both men attempt to bolster their pride through material means, and both had children who thought they should "know better" (Manheim 146). Parallels also exist between Con Melody and Theodore "Hickey" Hickman from *The Iceman Cometh*. Con

Melody loathes his wife for her unconditional love, knowing deep down that he is undeserving of it, a theme that stretches in the O'Neill canon as far back as one of O'Neill's earliest one-act plays, ABORTION; but unlike Hickey, Con Melody openly admits his resentment. In terms of stagecraft, O'Neill reduces the tavern room's size and comfort level over the course of the play to evoke desperation and ensnarement in a domestic hell, a staging device he employed in BEYOND THE HORIZON, ALL GOD'S CHILLUN GOT WINGS, and *Long Day's Journey into Night,* among others.

From O'Neill's early work, a more historical comparison might be made with the AFRICAN-AMERICAN character Brutus Jones from the experimental play *The* EMPEROR JONES. Similar to Con Melody, Jones embellishes his enormous ego with a Napoleonic-era military uniform and surrounds himself with the trappings of high aristocracy, represented in *The Emperor Jones* by Jones's royal court and in *A Touch of the Poet* by Melody's thoroughbred horse. And like Melody, Jones has a working-class companion—for Melody, Jamie Cregan and, to some extent, Nora; for Jones, a cockney confidence man named Smithers. Each acts as sounding board and counterpoint to the central figure's overblown sense of self-worth and entitlement. Both protagonists also construct an illusory world around themselves modeled on the very classes of people who had oppressed their own groups—the British aristocracy and the white colonizers of African nations, respectively. And both times, finally, the hidden victimized identities refuse to remain trapped behind the masks of the victimizing oppressors. Although many critics assume that Con Melody, again, has destroyed himself by destroying his image, from a historical point of view, the misbegotten Irish race to some extent prevails.

Throughout his adult life, O'Neill felt that the United States had become so obsessed with material wealth that it forfeited spiritual joy and personal fulfillment in the process. The external, socially charged conflict between the Irish and the "Yanks" is a preoccupation O'Neill would further develop in his last full-length play, *A Moon for the Misbegotten.* Among the Melody family, the conflict revolves around Melody and his daughter, both of whom share equally the dream of "belonging" to

New England Yankee culture. For the first-generation Irish immigrant Con Melody, this is an unachievable pipe dream. Sara, in fact, does marry into a wealthy Yankee family, the Harfords, as we see in the play's sequel, *More Stately Mansions.* But she does so at enormous cost to her spiritual well-being. In the final scene of *A Touch of the Poet,* Con Melody's pipe dream has vanished; what remains is a defeated self, though one that has found a sense of belonging, however short-lived, and one no longer obsessed with monetary gain or social station.

A Touch of the Poet brings in several stock plot devices and characters from Irish folklore—including the Irish peasant girl trickster overcoming poverty through sexual wiles (Manheim 150) and "the great Irish victory," as Edmund Tyrone calls the Shaughnessy/Harker incident in *Long Day's Journey into Night* (3:726), over the wealthy Anglo-Saxon property owner. Nevertheless, the play can only be considered a tragedy. But whose tragedy? Probably not Melody's, as that character simply replaces one role with a less pretentious if more complacent one; and Nora, for all of her suffering, ultimately gains a great deal by her husband's transformation. Sara surely is the most tragic figure, as she has lost the most psychologically and spiritually, if not financially. By the end of the play, Sara has been stripped of any illusion her father's facade had unconsciously afforded her. Like her creator, she recognizes just how dependent on her father's illusions she had become and, again like O'Neill, how devastating the feeling of loss becomes once those illusions are taken away. One of the stronger and more resourceful female characters in the O'Neill canon, however, Sara will forcefully, but with equal futility, take on her father's dream in the play's sequel, *More Stately Mansions.*

CHARACTERS

Cregan, Jamie Formerly a corporal in the Seventh Dragoons under Cornelius "Con" Melody during the Peninsular War (1808–14), now a loafing alcoholic Irish immigrant who heard his major was in Massachusetts and came to visit him the night before the play's action. Cregan, who reappears in *More Stately Mansions,* is a middle-aged alcoholic with a saber scar across his cheek. He provides exposition on Melody's past and verifies that regardless of his self-promoting ways, most of Melody's boasts are in fact true. Cregan accompanies Melody on his avenging mission to fight a duel with Henry Harford. He brings Melody home safely, if severely injured, back to the tavern after the donnybrook. Aside from Melody's wife, Nora Melody, Cregan is the only character in the play who accepts, if on his own terms, Melody's aristocratic pose.

Gadsby, Nicholas   The Harford family attorney. Even more than Deborah Harford, Gadsby is the quintessential New England Yankee. His demeanor is stuffy, cold, and matter-of-fact, and like T. Stedman Harder from *A Moon for the Misbegotten*, he is entirely unprepared to do verbal or physical battle with the Irish. Also like the scene with Harder in *Moon*, the verbal sparring between Melody and Gadsby is hilariously written. Of course, the Irish in both plays win hands down. Gadsby is sent by Henry Harford to pay Cornelius "Con" Melody $3,000 to prevent the engagement between his son, Simon Harford, and Melody's daughter, Sara Melody. Outraged by the dishonorable suggestion, Melody attacks the attorney. Sara saves Gadsby from Melody's wrath, but Melody then orders Dan Roche, Paddy O'Dowd, and Patch Riley to throw him out and "kick it down to the crossroads," which they do (3:248). Gadsby probably went on to warn the Harford household that Melody was preparing an assault, which would explain how the servants were prepared to battle Melody and his friend Jamie Cregan when they arrived, and that the police had already been called.

Harford, Deborah   Simon Harford's mother. Deborah, who reappears in *More Stately Mansions*, is a youthful 41-year-old woman with a pale complexion and delicate, angular Anglo-Saxon features. She resembles Mary Tyrone from *Long Day's Journey into Night* in that "*About her whole personality is a curious atmosphere of deliberate detachment, the studied aloofness of an ironically amused spectator*" (3:216). But if Mary Tyrone's detachment derives from morphine, Deborah's is a more sophisticated, New England Yankee hauteur. She wears a simple white dress, always a sign of foreboding in O'Neill's

women characters. Other examples include Ruth Atkins from *Beyond the Horizon*, Mildred Douglas from *The Hairy Ape*, and Margaret Anthony from *The Great God Brown*. Deborah is symbolically similar to Mildred Douglas insofar as her destructive effect on Cornelius "Con" Melody's hyperinflated ego. Following the visit to her son at Melody's tavern, and Melody's drunken attempt to seduce her, Deborah's husband, Henry Harford, offers to pay off Melody to put an end to their children's engagement. Deborah, for her part, wishes her son to stall the marriage for one year, at which time he can make a more informed decision about their betrothal. Sara Melody, Con Melody's daughter, hates her for this and believes, perhaps unfairly, that the bitter feeling is mutual. Melody then seeks to defend his family's honor by challenging Henry Harford to a duel. What ensues, however, is a stereotypical Irish brawl between the intoxicated Melody with his friend Jamie Cregan and the Harford's servants. Melody apprehends Deborah observing the scene from a window above, and his bogus aristocratic pride irretrievably collapses.

Harford, Simon   Sara Melody's offstage lover in *A Touch of the Poet* and husband in *More Stately Mansions*. Harford is a philosophically enlightened youth with "a touch of the poet," as both Cornelius "Con" Melody and Nora Melody approvingly observe. Born into wealth and position, Simon rejects his family's materialism and, for a time, lived the life of an ascetic in the woods on Con Melody's land. Sara reports that regardless of his high station, Simon, an aspiring poet and political philosopher, is dedicated to living a hermit's Thoreauvian life in which he can "support himself simply, and feel one with Nature" (3:195). He is a Harvard University graduate who could certainly take up his father's place in his giant trading firm, but in the play he shares O'Neill's belief that people, in Sara's words, should not "be greedy to own money and land and get the best of each other but will be content with little and live in peace and freedom together" (3:195). Over the action of the play, Sara successfully seduces the shy Harford. At first, he is too shy even to kiss her, but by the last scene they have slept together and are engaged to be married, and Sara—far more materialistic than she lets on—has seemingly persuaded Harford to accept a partnership in a friend's cotton mill.

Maloy, Mickey   Cornelius "Con" Melody's bartender. Maloy is a good-humored foil to the domestic tensions that erupt between Melody, his wife Nora, and his daughter Sara. Maloy is 26, with a face, like Jamie Cregan's, that O'Neill describes in his STAGE DIRECTIONS as *"obviously Irish."* Maloy has *"a sturdy physique and an amiable, cunning face, his mouth usually set in a half-leering grin"* (3:183). Maloy respects Nora Melody, telling Cregan that "a sweeter woman never lived" (3:187). At one point, he even flirts with her while she awaits Melody's return from the Harford estate: "Sure, it's be the joy av me life to have a mother like you to fight for me—or, better still, a wife like you" (3:255).

Melody, Cornelius "Con"   Nora Melody's husband and Sara Melody's father. Con Melody, an Irishman who puts on the airs of a British aristocrat, was in fact the son of a swindling Irish "shebeen keeper," or unlicensed publican, who made his fortune, as we find out from his longtime friend and fellow soldier Jamie Cregan, by "moneylendin' and squeezin' tenants and every manner of trick" (3:185). Melody's mother died giving birth to him, and his father sent him away to Dublin for secondary school and college, determined that his son be raised in the mode of the British aristocracy. At college, Melody's classmates were apprised of his low upbringing and chided him for his pretense— his "con"—and he once killed such an offender in a duel. He married Nora Melody, an Irishwoman from the peasant class, presumably because she became pregnant with their daughter, Sara, and the local priests subsequently cajoled him into marriage. Soon after, he joined the British army and fought in Spain and Portugal during the Peninsular War (1808–14) against the French, during which he was eventually promoted to major. Melody was forced to resign his commission after cuckolding a Spanish nobleman and then killing him in a duel. Once relieved of duty, and having squandered the lion's share of his father's estate on prostitutes and whiskey, Melody emigrated with his wife and daughter to the United States, ostensibly to make

his fortune but more probably to escape further scandal. Once in Massachusetts, he bought a tavern on a plot of land that promised to serve the railroads, but the railroads were never built through that area, and the tavern, an unprofitable venture, fell into disrepair.

Con Melody wears a British officer's uniform and histrionically quotes poetry while bemoaning the treachery of those around him. Years of acting the part of the landed gentry are shattered when Henry Harford offers him a bribe to put an end to any idea of marriage between Sara and his son Simon Harford. When Melody attacks the Harford estate to challenge Harford to a duel (a tradition past its day), a rowdy donnybrook takes place between himself, accompanied by his chosen witness Jamie Cregan, and the Harford servants. Ultimately the police arrive, overpower him, and lock him up. None of this might have had the dramatic psychological effect it did on Melody if Deborah Harford, Simon's mother, had not witnessed the savage affair from an upstairs window. Just as in *The Hairy Ape*, when the upper-class Mildred Douglas destroyed the fireman Robert "Yank" Smith's inflated ego by calling him a "filthy beast" in the steamship stokehold—presumably his domain—so too does Deborah Harford destroy Melody's pretense by her "sneering" viewing of the brawl. In the final scene, Melody has stripped away his aristocratic self and taken the role of the Irish peasant son of a shebeen keeper. By killing the thoroughbred mare that drained the family's resources, he has symbolically killed the major as well. Sara remarks of the metamorphosis, "He's beaten at last and he wants to stay beaten" (3:279).

Melody, Nora   Cornelius "Con" Melody's wife and Sara Melody's mother. She is 40, but years of toil under Con Melody's slavish demands have eradicated any youthful beauty she might have retained. Of Irish peasant stock, with none of her husband's pretension, Nora still clings to her Old World respect for priests. As such, she is in a continuous state of torment over the sin she and Melody committed before marriage—conceiving their daughter Sara. She wishes to confess her sin but feels that doing so would be a betrayal of her husband, who despises priests and blames them for forcing him into a marriage below his station. Nora also suffers from rheumatism but feels, like so many O'Neill characters—notably Robert Mayo in *Beyond the Horizon* and James Tyrone, Jr., and Edmund Tyrone in *Long Day's Journey into Night,* that doctors cause more harm than good—"They bring death with them"—particularly the ones the Melodys could afford (3:191). The character is mainly an ideal, an uncomplicated Old World peasant willing to sacrifice all for her daughter and husband's well-being. Throughout the play, she defends her husband's right to keep up appearances of a high social station, but after his transformation into a "low" Irish peasant, she supports him in that role as well. Her simplicity makes her highly sympathetic, even exceptionally so for an O'Neill character. "Nora Melody is drawn," Travis Bogard notes, "with the most complete, uncomplex affection of any character in the O'Neill canon. She has found in her total acceptance of her husband a way to resolve all the conflicts of love and hate that beset O'Neill's characters, generally. She is without a mask, humble in her devotion" (400).

Melody, Sara Cornelius "Con" Melody's and Nora Melody's daughter, whose conception out of wedlock forced the couple into marriage. Sara, who reappears in *More Stately Mansions,* is a good-looking 20-year-old who intermittently speaks in Irish brogue and cultured English. Though the action of the play takes place in 1828, Sara is a prototype of turn-of-the-20th century "New Womanhood": "I'll love where it'll gain me freedom and not put me in slavery for life" (3:193). She is also, as Joel Pfister characterizes her, "the outspoken feminist-capitalist in the play" (184). When she and her mother Nora Melody discuss a possible union between her and the upper-class New England Yankee Simon Harford, Sara's condition is that, unlike her mother, she'll "not let love make me any man's slave. I want to love him just enough so I can marry him without cheating him or myself" (3:196).

Over the course of the play, Sara plots to secure Harford's hand in marriage, which she eventually

does by sleeping with him. Virginia Floyd notes that "Sara possesses the same promiscuous spirit that caused her father's downfall, only in her it facilitates her rise in the world" (446); Laurin Porter adds that Sara's "mixture of peasant and aristocratic features embodies the inner tension of Con Melody, suspended between the worlds of innkeeper and military hero" (242). Her spoken desire to marry Simon vacillates between moving up the social ladder (achieving the American dream) and satisfying her passionate love for the young man—but her avaricious side intensifies sharply in *More Stately Mansions.* She is like her father: "She too wants a place in the world," Edward Shaughnessy writes, "and she intends to get it" (164).

Con Melody's transformation in the final scene has the most destructive effects on Sara, as Nora is willing to accept any role her husband chooses to adopt. Sara, on the other hand, remains dependent on the illusion of grandeur her father had concocted. With Melody's decision, in Sara's words, "to stay beaten" (279), her illusions disappear with his, making her, in Michael Manheim's words, "the conniving Irish wench she fears she really is" (147). The problem lies deeper, since she cannot even claim that identity, as she has never presented herself that way, and thus could not play the role convincingly. Throughout the play, Sara's image of herself alternates between that of the educated, ambitious New Englander in love and the scheming daughter of a shanty Irish publican. Tragically, by the end of A *Touch of the Poet* at least, she is both and neither, and her father's defeat serves only to exacerbate this identity crisis.

O'Dowd, Paddy An Irish "sponger" who drinks for free at Cornelius "Con" Melody's tavern, possibly the lowest specimen. Unlike Patch Riley, who can play music, and Dan Roche, who demonstrates some limited political awareness, O'Dowd's manner, as O'Neill writes in the stage directions, *"is oily and fawning, that of a born sponger and parasite"* (207).

Riley, Patch An elderly Irish piper and tenor who provides the music for Cornelius "Con" Melody's dinner commemorating the anniversary of the Battle of Talavera. He is one of the crowd of "spongers," if perhaps the least offensive one to Melody and his daughter, Sara Melody. In his first scene, he flatters Sara with rather formulaic Irish "blarney": "Sure it's you, God bless you, looks like a fairy princess as beautiful as a rose in the mornin' dew" (3:208), and he offers to play her a tune. Sara rejects the idea coldly at first, but then she thanks him tenderly for the offer.

Roche, Dan   An Irish "sponger" who drinks for free at Cornelius "Con" Melody's tavern. O'Neill describes him as *"middle-aged, squat, bowlegged, with a potbelly and short arms lumpy with muscle"* (3:207). When he first appears, he offends Melody and establishes one of the main themes of the play by shouting above the ruckus of the other spongers what he had told his boss that day: "And I says, it's Andy Jackson will put you in your place, and all the slave-drivin' Yankee skinflints like you! Take your damned job, I says, . . ." (3:207–208) Roche seems to be the most political of the group. During Melody's dinner celebrating his victory in the Battle of Talavera, he curses Melody behind his back for having fought on the side of the British (3:235).

BIBLIOGRAPHY

Bogard, Travis. *Contour in Time: The Plays of Eugene O'Neill.* Rev. ed. New York: Oxford University Press, 1988.

Floyd, Virginia. *The Plays of Eugene O'Neill: A New Assessment.* New York: Ungar, 1985.

Kalem, T. E. "Theatre: Dream Addict." *Time* (January 9, 1978). Reprinted in *The Critical Response to Eugene O'Neill,* edited by John H. Houchin, 236–238. Westport, Conn.: Greenwood Press, 1993.

Manheim, Michael. "Remnants of a Cycle: *A Touch of the Poet* and *More Stately Mansions.*" In *Eugene O'Neill,* edited by Harold Bloom, 145–164. New York: Chelsea House Publishers, 1987.

Pfister, Joel. *Staging Depth: Eugene O'Neill and the Politics of Psychological Discourse.* Chapel Hill: University of North Carolina Press, 1995.

Porter, Laurin. "*A Touch of the Poet*: Memory and the Creative Imagination." *The Critical Response to Eugene O'Neill,* edited by John H. Houchin, 238–250. Westport, Conn.: Greenwood Press, 1993.

Shaughnessy, Edward L. *Down the Nights and Down the Days: Eugene O'Neill's Catholic Sensibility.* Notre Dame, Ind.: University of Notre Dame Press, 2000.

Vidal, Gore. "Theatre." *Nation* (October 25, 1958). Reprinted in *The Critical Response to Eugene O'Neill,* edited by John H. Houchin, 234–236. Westport, Conn.: Greenwood Press, 1993.

Warnings: A Play in One Act (completed, 1913; never produced)

Eugene O'Neill probably completed *Warnings* in December 1913, and the one-act play in two scenes appeared a year later in *"THIRST" AND OTHER ONE-ACT PLAYS,* his first published volume that also includes *The WEB, THIRST, FOG,* and *RECKLESSNESS.* During the previous fall, 1913, O'Neill boarded with the Rippin family of NEW LONDON, CONNECTICUT, and scene 1 is notable in that O'Neill convincingly portrays the children (one of whom is named Dolly after a Rippin child; Black 149) and the mother, Mary Knapp. *Warnings* is also the first domestic drama O'Neill wrote, a genre that would culminate in his full-length masterpiece LONG DAY'S JOURNEY INTO NIGHT. Indeed, O'Neill named his main characters James and Mary after his parents JAMES O'NEILL and MARY ELLEN "ELLA" O'NEILL, and the eldest child, an offstage character who lives away from the family, is named after his older brother JAMES O'NEILL, JR. (Jamie). Scene 2 takes place on an ocean liner on its way back from South America. O'Neill had served in the MERCHANT MARINE just two years before, and the seaman's language O'Neill includes throughout scene 2 demonstrates an intimate knowledge of maritime life (Richter 143). As such, the play merges the opposing worlds foremost on the young playwright's mind—home and SEA. O'Neill later revised *Warnings* in 1918 as a lengthy short story entitled "S.O.S.," first published in Travis Bogard's collection *The Unknown O'Neill* (1988).

SYNOPSIS

Scene 1

James and Mary Knapp's dining room in their apartment in Bronx, New York. O'Neill rather contemptuously describes the room as containing all the trappings of lowbrow working-class culture, with *"impossible green"* wallpaper and worn rugs of the same color, *"several gaudy Sunday-supplement pictures in cheap gilt frames,"* a *"gilt cage in which a canary chirps sleepily,"* and a framed "Home Sweet Home" motto hanging above the mantelpiece (1:77). Mary Knapp, a 40-year-old woman beaten down by the struggle of bearing and raising five children under conditions of extreme poverty, sits at a table with her two daughters, Lizzie and Sue. Sue, an eight-year-old, is being coached on writing by her older sister Lizzie, who is 11. Lizzie superciliously corrects Sue and impatiently snatches away her pencil to demonstrate how to write a proper letter *g*, which brings Sue to tears (1:78). Mary boxes Lizzie on the ear and scolds her in exasperation. Defeated by further bickering and whining, however, she bribes the children with candy to behave.

When the clock strikes 8:30, Mary orders the children to bed. She warns them not to wake up the baby, who is asleep behind a heavy green curtain; the girls slink off reluctantly, and Mary breaths a sigh of relief. Charles and Dolly Knapp, 15 and 14 respectively, bang on the locked door, loudly entreating entrance. Mary's momentary respite is over. She unlocks the door and demands they quiet down so as not to wake up the baby. The teenagers are in a high state of excitement, both jockeying to tell on the other. Dolly informs her mother that she saw Charlie buying an ice cream soda for a neighborhood girl at the local drug store; Charlie, in his turn, tells her that he witnessed Dolly flirting with a German saloon keeper's son in a dark hallway. Charlie threatens to beat up the German boy and teach his sister a lesson as well if she keeps up the flirtation, but Mary cracks him on the side of the head, warning him never to lay a hand on his sister.

She scolds both of them and bemoans the vulgar behavior of "young folks nowadays" (1:81). Changing the subject, Charlie mentions that his father, James Knapp, appears to be losing his hearing. Mary insists that he "has a bad cold and his head is all stopped up" and complains that he is wasting five dollars by consulting an ear specialist (1:82). We learn through exposition that James is a wireless operator on a steamship, and his salary is too low to provide for the family without Mary taking in washing and some meager help from her eldest child, Jim. She admits, however, that he has not been acting himself since his last voyage, speculating that "it must be that South American climate that's affectin' him" (1:82). We also find out that it is his last night home, as the ship embarks the following day.

James Knapp enters the apartment dolefully. Mary offers him a seat, remarking with concern that he looks exhausted. Clearly preoccupied by terrible news, James assures her he is only "thinking about how I've got to sail tomorrow on that long, lonesome trip, and how I won't see any of you for three months" (1:83–84). Charlie tries to cheer him, but James cannot hear him and asks his son to talk louder. Charlie then shouts, "Cheer up!" and wakes the baby (1:84). After a stern reproach, Mary goes through a heavy green curtain to soothe the child back to sleep. Charlie seizes the opportunity to implore his father for a new suit, as he has outgrown the threadbare one he has on. Guilt-ridden over his desperate financial situation, James promises to buy him one after he returns. James then begins to sob, and Charlie comforts him. The father kindly sends his son off to bed with assurances that he feels a little ill and that is all.

Mary returns and complains about Charlie "always prowlin' around the streets" (1:85). James responds that it is perfectly healthy for a boy of his age, and that he has enough to worry about without dwelling on their teenagers misbehaving. Seething with resentment, Mary chides him that his worries on the open sea, eating "the best food" and talking "to the pretty women in the First Class," are petty compared to "cookin', scrubbin', takin' care of the children, puttin' off the grocer and the butcher, doin' washin' and savin' every penny" (1:86). Her husband tries to calm her, but he breaks down and announces the news from the ear specialist: He could become stone deaf at any time. Mary shrugs off the diagnosis, insisting that DOCTORS always "scare you so you'll keep comin' to see him" (1:86). She then inquires whether he has informed the ship's captain of his condition. When he responds that he has not, she argues that no one will be the wiser. He rejoins that she does not understand "the responsibility of a man in my job," but she declares that the doctor is a liar, and his hearing is fine. At length, she successfully bullies him into putting duty to family first. *"Writhing under the lash of her scorn,"* James *"is tortured beyond endurance at her last reproaches"* and unwillingly consents to go (1:88). He vows, however, it will be his last voyage.

Scene 2

About 11 o'clock at night in a section of the SS *Empress*, "abaft of," or behind, the bridge of the steamer. *"The background is a tropic sky blazing with stars"* (1:89). Officers' cabins with lighted portholes are at left, a life raft is situated at right, and the wireless room is at center. James Knapp is bent over the wireless instrument, as if desperately trying to hear a message; *"every time he taps on the key the snarl of the wireless sounds above the confused babble of frightened voices that rises from the promenade deck"* (1:88). The *Empress* has struck a derelict, and the ship is listing badly. Captain Hardwick enters and demands to know if Knapp has heard any reply to their call for help. Knapp, who sees the captain but cannot understand what he is saying, only repeats, "I haven't heard a thing yet, sir" (1:89). The captain is certain another ship, the *Verdari*, is somewhere nearby and should be responding. Mason, the first officer, enters and informs the captain that the bulkhead is buckling, and the ship will sink within the hour. Hardwick voices concern that Knapp appears "scared to death" because they have received no response to the calls (1:90). He adds that Knapp had been acting strangely the whole voyage, uncharacteristically refusing to talk with anyone. They step back over to the wireless room, and Hardwick asks if the machine is operating correctly. When Knapp responds, again, that

he has not heard anything, Mason concludes that Knapp cannot hear properly. Hardwick snatches off Knapp's headgear and demands an answer. Knapp looks up at the captain and, only just then realizing that he has lost his hearing, piteously and incoherently explains, "I wanted to give up the job this time but she wouldn't let me. She said I wanted them to starve—and Charlie asked me for a suit. . . . I thought it would be all right—just this trip. I'm not a bad man, Captain" (1:91).

Hardwick orders Mason to retrieve Dick Whitney, an experienced wireless operator onboard who is recovering from tropical fever. Whitney arrives, takes Knapp's place at the machine, and informs the captain that not only had the *Verdari* been responding to their radio calls, but they also sent out warnings the previous day to steer them away from the derelict's position. In a rage, the captain threatens to pummel Knapp, but Mason calmly stands between them. Recovering himself, the captain orders Whitney to write out the situation and show the paper to Knapp. He then orders the life rafts to be lowered, motions for Knapp to follow, and exits. Knapp sits *"staring at the paper in his hand with wild eyes and pale, twitching features."* "God! It's my fault then! It's my fault!" he cries. Looking astern, he sees the boats being lowered and now understands the ship will go down on account of his negligence. Knapp frantically takes a revolver from the desk drawer, points it to his head, cries out, "She *is* lost!" He pulls the trigger. Whitney rushes into the room to retrieve Knapp. Glancing down at the body in horror, he exclaims "Good God!" Leaving Knapp's body to go down with the ship, he makes a break for the waiting life rafts astern (1:94).

COMMENTARY

Based on the plot of the British novelist Joseph Conrad's sea tale "The End of the Tether," in which a captain sinks his vessel after losing his sight, *Warnings* delineates the tragic course of events after a ship's wireless operator discovers he is going deaf. As with Conrad's story, the ship sinks because of the sailor's impairment, and the character commits suicide out of extreme guilt. Historically, like its predecessor *Thirst*, *Warnings* calls to mind the sinking of the *Titanic* in 1912, just one year prior to its composition. One tragic irony of the *Titanic* disaster was that the steamer *Californian* was within 20 miles of *Titanic* when it sank, but the *Californian* did not hear the sinking ship's call for help, as they had no wireless operator on duty. After the tragedy, in which 1,503 people died, legislation was passed that stipulated all vessels must have a radio operator on duty at all times (Richter 142).

O'Neill juxtaposes two sinking ships in *Warnings*: Figuratively speaking, the Knapp family in scene 1 is sinking under the combined weight of dire financial stress and too many mouths to feed, while in scene 2 the *Empress* is actually sinking as a result of James Knapp's physical disability and temperamental weakness. Both his wife and the crew of the *Empress* hold Knapp directly responsible for their plights. "In retrospect," Stephen A. Black writes, "it is clear that what interested Eugene in the story was the web of circumstance that leads inexorably from marital misery to shipwreck" (149). As such, *Warnings*, like two other early plays, BEFORE BREAKFAST and BREAD AND BUTTER, ends with a man nagged by his wife into suicide (either by the razor or the gun), revealing yet another glimpse of O'Neill's dismal view of the marital state; and like his later play *The FIRST MAN*, children are portrayed here mainly as psychological and economic burdens. *Warnings*, then, provides an early view into O'Neill's lasting take on domesticity: "the children whine, the wife nags, the husband feels guilty" (Black 149).

Unfortunately, in terms of the work's artistry and O'Neill's developing ties with the deterministic elements of literary NATURALISM, in which lives are destroyed through no real fault of the characters, Knapp *is* responsible, as his wife's accusations that the doctor is lying holds little water; and if Knapp had simply informed Captain Hardwick that he lost his hearing, no harm would have been done. On the other hand, clearly O'Neill means Knapp's economic circumstances have coerced him into moral peril, and the wife's abusive interpretation of Knapp's sense of responsibility—his caring more, to her mind, about his duty to the ship than to their family—might have been more feasible with a less-certain diagnosis from the ear specialist. As it stands, Knapp is portrayed as more of a pushover than a victim of external forces. There is also a genre-bending aspect to the play. Peter Egri argues that "the fact that the action turns around a chance event" makes the play read more as a short story than a play (127), and ultimately O'Neill did in 1918 rewrite it as a short story entitled "S.O.S."

Some autobiographical elements exist in the play as well, but they are more elusive than some other of O'Neill's large body of autobiographical writing. Though Travis Bogard insists that "the embittered mother and the father viewed as a failure bear no resemblance to the two older Tyrones [from *Long Day's Journey into Night*]," Black, Virginia Floyd, and Arthur and Barbara Gelb all read an early avatar of Mary Tyrone/Ella O'Neill in Mary Knapp's scornful response to both her husband's condition and the doctor's diagnosis. As Floyd points out, in *Long Day's Journey*, Mary Tyrone uses the identical line of her earlier avatar when she deludes herself that Edmund, who has been diagnosed with tuberculosis, just "has a bad cold" (Floyd 48). She too, like Mary Knapp, believes the doctor is a quack. And as the events that take place in *Long Day's Journey* happened the year before O'Neill wrote *Warnings*, Floyd goes on that "Ella O'Neill's lamentations about [Eugene's] sickness would still be fresh in his memory" (49n). In terms of James O'Neill, Black submits that "the play takes the father's side in the O'Neill family MELODRAMA that arose from the father's never being able to quit his tedious, urgent work because poverty had so haunted him." In addition, reading the play from James O'Neill's perspective, Knapp performs "that prime Victorian virtue, duty" (149).

CHARACTERS

Hardwick, Captain The captain of the SS *Empress*. Hardwick is a *"stocky man of about fifty dressed in a simple blue uniform"* (1:89). He is a compassionate leader, though prone to violence. Upon finding that his ship might have been saved from collision if his wireless operator James Knapp had confessed that he had gone deaf, Hardwick directs Knapp's replacement, Whitney, to write a message to Knapp indicating his responsibility. Upon reading the missive, Knapp commits suicide.

Knapp, Charles James and Mary Knapp's son. Charles, or "Charlie," is a *"gawky, skinny youth of fifteen"* (1:80) who arrives home in the middle of scene 1 with his sister Dolly after cavorting with neighborhood teenagers. Upon their entrance, Dolly tattles on Charlie for buying an ice-cream soda for a redheaded girl from the block with money his father gave him. Charlie informs his mother that Dolly was flirting with a German saloon keeper's son in a dark hallway. In his turn, he threatens to "punch [the German saloon-keeper's son] in the eye" for compromising his sister, and also warns that he'll slap her if she gets "too fresh." At this Mary Knapp jumps from her seat and gives him *"a crack over the ear with her open hand"* (1:81). At first, we see Charlie as just one more burden on Mrs. Knapp. When his father returns from the ear specialist, however, Charles asks him for a new suit. Comprehending his father's sorrow over being too poor to oblige, he switches from self-centered teenager to loving, understanding son (1:85).

Knapp, Dolly James and Mary Knapp's daughter. Dolly is a pretty, dark-haired 14-year-old-girl. She arrives home in the middle of scene 1 with her brother Charles after cavorting with other neighborhood teenagers. Upon their entrance, she informs her mother that she saw Charlie buying an ice-cream soda for a redheaded girl from the block with a quarter their father gave him. In his turn, he says that Dolly was flirting with a German saloon keeper's son in a dark alley. Dolly represents a new generation of young women, and Mary significantly responds to the news of her indiscretion: "Don't you let me hear of you bein' in any dark hallways with young men again or I'll take you over my knee, so I will. The idea of such a thing! I can't understand you at all. I never was allowed out alone with anyone,—not even with your father, before I was engaged to be married to him. I don't know what's come over you young folks nowadays" (1:81). Dolly is named for one of the girls in the Rippin family of New London, Connecticut, with whom O'Neill boarded in fall 1913 when writing the play.

Knapp, James A wireless operator on the SS *Empress* and Mary Knapp's husband. Arthur and Barbara Gelb find a model for Knapp's charac-

ter in a boarder at JIMMY "THE PRIEST'S" saloon, where O'Neill lodged between trips as a merchant mariner. This was a retired telegrapher nicknamed "the Lunger" (a disparaging term of the period for someone suffering from tuberculosis), who appears under that name in O'Neill's short story "TOMORROW." Indeed, "the Lunger" died of the disease, but not before unsuccessfully attempting to teach O'Neill the International Code of Signals for wireless communication. O'Neill describes Knapp as *"a slight, stoop-shouldered, thin-faced man of about fifty,"* whose expression *"must be unusually depressed"* (1:83). One of the reasons for his depression is that he has just been informed by his doctor that he is going deaf. Although his wife Mary grants James moments of tenderness, she fiercely cajoles her husband into operating the wireless machine onboard the *Empress*, regardless of his pending disability, in order to keep the family finances (if not the ship) afloat.

In scene 2, Knapp is completely deaf and cannot perform his duty. The SS *Verdari* had been sending warnings of a derelict ship ahead, but Knapp could not hear them. When his disability is discovered, the captain informs him that his negligence is responsible for the *Empress* having hit the derelict. Overwhelmed with guilt in the final scene, Knapp commits suicide. Caught in a web of desperate poverty, Knapp is an intensely moral man without the willpower to carry through his convictions, a fact compounded by the helplessness he feels as an indigent husband and father of five.

Knapp, Lizzie James and Mary Knapp's daughter. Lizzie is 11 years old with blond, curly hair like her sister Sue. She opens scene 1 with a snippy line to her eight-year-old sister Sue about how to properly write the letter g. The squabbling that ensues is quelled by Mary Knapp bribing with candy what O'Neill sarcastically calls her *"two good little girls"* in the STAGE DIRECTIONS; then she sends them off to bed with a great sign of relief (1:79). Both Lizzie and Sue are meant to highlight the relentlessness of child rearing.

Knapp, Mary James Knapp's wife. Mary is *"a pale, thin, peevish-looking woman of about forty, made* *prematurely old by the thousand worries of a penny-pinching existence"* (1:77). Mary's character is a rather confusing mixture of affectionate and caring mother and wife—a side of her character O'Neill probably modeled after Helen Rippin, with whose family he resided in fall 1913—and dispassionate shrew in the mode of Mrs. Rowland of *Before Breakfast*. Mrs. Rowland, like Mary Knapp, badgers her husband into eventual suicide. In the opening scene, the audience might initially respond sympathetically to Mary's hardships, but in her monologue at the end of scene 1, in which she badgers her husband into going to sea deaf for the sake of their family, she comes across despicably. *Warnings* is the first of many O'Neill plays in which the wife, Mary Knapp in this case, precipitates her husband's death, whether by suicide or some other desperate action.

Knapp, Sue James and Mary Knapp's daughter. Sue is eight years old with blond, curly hair like her sister Lizzie. In the opening scene, she quarrels with her sister over how to properly write the letter *g*, and when Lizzie snatches the pencil from her hands to demonstrate, Sue cries, exasperating her mother into boxing Lizzie on the ear. After Mary bribes her to behave with candy, she calms down instantly and is soon after sent off to bed. Both Lizzie and Sue are meant to highlight the relentlessness of child rearing.

Mason First officer of the SS *Empress*. Mason is a *"tall, clean-shaven, middle-aged man in uniform"* (1:89) who acts as Captain Hardwick's confidante and voice of reason. He is the first to comprehend that James Knapp, their wireless operator, has gone deaf. When Hardwick threatens to pummel Knapp for losing his ship, Mason steps in between and defuses the situation.

Whitney, Dick A passenger aboard the SS *Empress* and an experienced wireless operator. Whitney, who is recovering from a bout of tropical fever, is *"a thin, sallow-faced young fellow of about twenty-five, wearing a light sack suit"* (1:92). Captain Hardwick orders him up to the wireless room to replace James Knapp after they discover Knapp has

gone deaf. After a few moments at the instrument, Whitney informs the officers that the SS *Verdari* had been sending radio warnings to the *Empress* about a derelict ship in their path. Whitney discovers Knapp's body after Knapp shoots himself. His is the last line of the play—"Good God!" (1:94)—and he rushes out to the life rafts as the ship sinks with Knapp's body onboard.

BIBLIOGRAPHY

Black, Stephen A. *Eugene O'Neill: Beyond Mourning and Tragedy*. New Haven, Conn.: Yale University Press, 1999.

Bogard, Travis. *Contour in Time: The Plays of Eugene O'Neill*. Rev. ed. New York: Oxford University Press, 1988.

Egri, Peter. "The Use of the Short Story in O'Neill's and Chekhov's One-Act Plays." In *Eugene O'Neill: A World View*, edited by Virginia Floyd, 115–144. New York: Frederick Ungar Publishing Co., 1979.

Floyd, Virginia. *The Plays of Eugene O'Neill: A New Assessment*. New York: Ungar, 1985.

Gelb, Arthur, and Barbara Gelb. *O'Neill: Life with Monte Cristo*. New York: Applause Books, 2000.

Ranald, Margaret Loftus. "From Trial to Triumph (1913–1924): The Early Plays." In *The Cambridge Companion to Eugene O'Neill*, edited by Michael Manheim, 51–68. New York: Cambridge University Press, 1998.

Richter, Robert A. *Eugene O'Neill and Dat Ole Davil Sea: Maritime Influences in the Life and Works of Eugene O'Neill*. Mystic, Conn.: Mystic Seaport, 2004.

Web: A Play in One Act, The
(completed, 1913; first produced, 1982)

First produced as late as November 4, 1982, at Playhouse 46 in New York City, *The Web* is one of Eugene O'Neill's least-famous plays. It was never produced in the playwright's lifetime and has received little critical attention since its first publication in *"THIRST" AND OTHER ONE-ACT PLAYS* in

1914. O'Neill claimed, at one point, that *The Web* was his first play, though he admitted that *A WIFE FOR A LIFE* (later published posthumously in *The Lost Plays of Eugene O'Neill*), was in fact his first, though in his mind "it was nothing" (O'Neil 21n). A melodramatic thriller influenced by literary NATURALISM, *The Web* is an exposition on the plight of the urban streetwalker. O'Neill included 14 PROSTITUTES directly in seven of his published plays and as offstage characters in five more (Gelb 126). His most famous use of the prostitute heroine, "ANNA CHRISTIE," brashly featured a retired prostitute in the title role. Prostitutes and their pimps were urban types O'Neill knew well from months of carousing at JIMMY "THE PRIEST'S," the HELL HOLE, the Bradley Street brothels of NEW LONDON, CONNECTICUT, and the waterfront dives of BUENOS AIRES, ARGENTINA, and Liverpool, England. As such, in *The Web*, as Arthur and Barbara Gelb write of the play, "it is possible to discern Eugene's first shaky steps toward exposing social injustice and hypocrisy . . . even though he seems at times more intent on showing off his familiarity with New York's seamy street life than in revealing the social iniquity that caused prostitution" (Gelb 398).

SYNOPSIS

A Lower East Side rooming house in which a prostitute, Rose Thomas, and her illegitimate child live in squalor. Rose's face is *"that of a person in an advanced stage of consumption—deathly pale with hollows under her eyes, which are wild and feverish."* Like most victims of advanced tuberculosis, Rose coughs loudly and often. Informed by personal experience, O'Neill describes her symptom as *"a harsh, hacking cough that shakes her whole body"* (1:15). Rose's opening line sets the play's scandalous tone: As she listens to the rain fall outside her open window, she tosses a cigarette aside and darkly pronounces, with a touch of sarcastic hilarity, "Gawd! What a night!" (1:15).

Steve, Rose's "cadet" (early New York slang for pimp) enters the room *"showing on his face the effects of drink and drugs"* (1;16). She pleads for a night off and money to see a doctor, whereupon Steve lashes out by reminding her of the limits of his services and the demands of hers: "D'yuh think I'm a simp

to be gittin' yuh protection and keepin' the bulls from runnin' yuh in when all yuh do is to stick at home and play dead?" (1:17). The baby is an aggravation to Steve, as she takes up room on the bed, cries incessantly, and requires repeated feedings that distract Rose from her job. Steve insists she send the baby to an orphanage. The victim throughout the play, with no agency or poise, Rose threatens to kill herself if he takes her baby away. "Dat's what they all say," he rejoins, and threatens not only to remove the child, but turn Rose in to the police and relegate her to "the Island," or Blackwell's Island (now Roosevelt Island), a notorious prison on the East River (1:19).

Tim Moran, a recently escaped convict and yeggman (yegg—a safecracker), overhears the quarrel through the tenement's thin walls and breaks his cover to chase the villain out. After he assures Rose, unfoundedly, that Steve "won't bother yuh no more," the two engage in impassioned accounts of their wretched lives. Tim first suggests that Rose find a respectable job, but she has already tried her hand at housekeeping, a job from which she was fired when a dinner guest recognized her and exposed her identity (1:21–22). (O'Neill, apparently to stress the determinism of her situation, ignores the historical reality that many prostitutes at the time "supplemented their jobs with part-time PROSTITUTION or hooked for a short period, rather than devoting their lives to it" [Johnson 89]).

Tim next suggests that Rose take what money he has and flee to the restorative atmosphere of the countryside. Steve appears in the window; he is hiding on the fire escape with a gun, building up his nerve as the two embrace and pledge their mutual loyalty. In due course, Steve shoots Tim dead, flings the gun into the room, and disappears down the fire escape. At the sound of the gunshot, three policemen storm the front door and find Rose wailing mournfully over Tim's body. She is arrested for murder, and the child will be taken into custody. The officers briefly interrogate her, but Rose has lost her grip on reality, and her eyes stare blankly ahead *"like the eyes of a blind woman"* (1:27). The first plainclothes policeman moves to take her into custody, and she cries out to God why he hates her so. As she is led down the stairway, Rose lets out a *"hollow cough"* that appears to wake up the baby. "Maamaaaa!" she cries. The first plainclothes policeman picks her up lovingly, cuddles her in his lap, and says, "Mama's gone. I'm your Mama now."

COMMENTARY

O'Neill's first attempt at dialect writing, *The Web* is also his first dramatic exploration into the urban underworld, an obsession that culminates in his late masterpiece, *The ICEMAN COMETH*. Though hackneyed dialogue sours the impact of the play—with lines like "take yer hand away from that gat or I'll fill yuh full of holes" (1:19–20)—the conversation between Rose and Tim reveals two unhappy victims of social circumstance, the destructive, impregnable "web" of the title that ultimately leads to Tim's death and Rose's imprisonment. GREENWICH VILLAGE, New York's bohemian center where O'Neill spent much of his young adult life, hosted an established prostitution ring at the turn of the 20th century, but it was also a neighborhood that accommodated respectable writers and artists, including the doyens of Victorian fiction, Edith Wharton, William Dean Howells, and Henry James. As one New York real estate agent lamented in 1887, the Village "is occupied by some very respectable residences and apartment houses, but I fear they will be driven away if the evil [prostitution] . . . is not soon suppressed" (quoted in Gilfoyle 213). But by the time O'Neill resided there, less than 20 years later, the "evil" had, in fact, flourished. Indeed, rampant prostitution carried on throughout the city (far more visibly, in fact, than today) until approximately 1920, notably the same year *"Anna Christie"* was produced and won O'Neill his second PULITZER PRIZE (Johnson 88).

O'Neill inserts a device in *The Web's* final scene that smacks of his later EXPRESSIONISM, one perhaps more interesting to read than it might be on stage: He depicts Rose's catatonic state as a face-off between herself and an unidentified, otherworldly presence, *"something in the room which none of the others can see—perhaps the personification of the ironic life force that has crushed her"* (1:28). O'Neill presents the "ironic life force" to fully realize the play's naturalism, a dramatic form that, along with

providing realistic settings, true-to-life dialogue, and believable dramatic action, presents the belief that we are all controlled deterministically by forces beyond our control and often our comprehension. Three main threads of O'Neill's web—the "respectable" homeowners that temporarily employ Rose, the pimp, and the cop—conspire to prevent her from ever reforming.

Originally entitled *The Cough,* the play was written just after O'Neill's release from GAYLORD FARM SANATORIUM, the health resort where he convalesced from a bout of tuberculosis. O'Neill critic Travis Bogard argues that the working title speaks to the author's desire that Rose's affliction "should be taken as symbolic of all the social evil for which there is no possible cure" (20). In one of the play's more poignant STAGE DIRECTIONS, while the officers accompany Rose down the stairwell, making way through a cluster of spectating lodgers, Rose lets out a final *"hollow cough"* (1:28). "'The Web' is melodrama at its worst, with all its outworn technique connoted by the name," theater critic Isaac Goldberg wrote in 1922; but he agreed that "already there appears, in the sound of Rose's coughing as she is led away by the officers, O'Neill's predilection for the potency of pure sound upon the stage" (235). A powerful piece of dramatic punctuation, the cough emphasizes the significance of the disease as a theme, as his subtitle suggests. Importantly, moral reformers at the time, as one 19th-century journalist phrased it, considered "the physical and moral . . . closely allied. The habit of living in squalor and filth engenders vice, and vice, on the other hand, finds a congenial home in the midst of physical impurities" (quoted in Smith-Rosenberg 183). Hence prostitution, and the kind of activities O'Neill engaged in as a youth before contracting tuberculosis, was firmly associated with biological contagion, a perspective that led reformers to consider prostitutes more as infectious influences than as victims of their social environment. True compassion for the downtrodden, O'Neill suggests in the Irish figure of Tim Moran, only comes from within the ranks of the downtrodden themselves.

Once Rose is gone, the child cries out "Maamaaaa!" (in an excessively dramatic touch on the part of the playwright), to which the officer gently responds, "Mama's gone. I'm your Mama now" (1:28). Hence, as O'Neill critic Judith E. Barlow argues, "the 'web' in which Rose is caught is clearly patriarchal; she earns her living pleasing men, gives her money to a man, and ultimately is replaced by a policeman. . . . At its worst, prostitution prevents women from fulfilling their primary role: motherhood" (Barlow 166). But the symbolic web—one in which, like an insect caught in a spider's web, the more you struggle, the more entangled you become—reaches out across the private sector to Progressive reform movements as well, the majority of which were supported by women. At one point during Tim and Rose's brief tryst, Rose explains the hypocrisy of the reform movement:

> They—all the good people—they got me where I am and they're goin' to keep me there. Reform? Take it from me it can't be done. . . . That's the trouble with all of us girls. Most all of us ud like to come back but we just can't and that's all there is to it. We can't work out of this life because we don't know how to work. We was never taught how. (1:22)

Here O'Neill castigates the central contradiction of Progressive-era reform and strict Victorian morality: On the one hand, prostitution is a social "evil" that must be annihilated through reform; on the other, prostitutes are social parasites that, vampire-like, feed on the sins of otherwise "good people." Earlier plays with prostitute heroines, such as GEORGE BERNARD SHAW's *Mrs. Warren's Profession* (1905) and Eugene Walter's *The Easiest Way* (1911), were also repressed in the United States before the end of World War I (Johnson 88). That Rose is the victim of this play, and reformers the victimizers, might constitute the reason that, as late as 1913, O'Neill could never find a producer for his thriller. But the melodramatic plot might also provide an explanation for his paradoxical assessment of *The Web* in a letter accompanying the manuscript to the literary critic Mark Van Doren over 30 years after he wrote it: "To be sure the pages were in order I had to read *The Web* again, and I want to tell you . . . that if ever a man felt he was enduring hardship in the line of duty, I was

certainly that gent! I love it but I sure don't like it!" (O'Neill 553).

CHARACTERS

First Plain Clothes Man   Notably the first policeman in the O'Neill canon to utter the final, ironic lines of his play—"I'm your Mama now" (1:28)—others being DESIRE UNDER THE ELMS and *The GREAT GOD BROWN*.

Moran, Tim   A good-guy criminal on the lam. Tim is caught up in a web of crime like Rose Thomas, the tubercular prostitute he temporarily saves from her abusive pimp. As a youth, Tim was unfairly arrested for stealing and spent his childhood in a reform school. Once released, he turned to stealing to survive. In and out of prison his whole life, Tim learned how to be a yeggman, or safe cracker while incarcerated. He broke out of prison two weeks prior to the play's action. For a week, he lived next to Rose and Steve, Rose's abusive pimp. After overhearing Steve's cruelty once too often, Tim breaks into their apartment and chases the craven Steve from the room. Tim and Rose commiserate over the "webs" of fate that have entangled them into lives of thievery and prostitution, respectively. Once Tim discovers Rose has tuberculosis, he offers to give her the money he stole on a recent burglary so she can leave the city for the fresh air of the countryside. But Tim informs her that the police may be wise to his location. He must leave but promises that when it is safe, he will return and they can start a new life together. Steve then reappears, entering from the fire escape, and murders Tim, extinguishing Rose's last hope for a normal life. When the police enter the apartment to investigate, they find Rose with the gun Steve left behind and arrest her for the murder. Like so many O'Neillian characters, it appears that Tim is better off dead than left a victim, like Rose, of *the ironic life force* that has crushed them both (1:28).

Thomas, Rose   A tubercular prostitute with an illegitimate child and a live-in "cadet," or pimp, named Steve. Rose is only 22, but she looks 30, and her garish clothing, overdone makeup, and cheap costume jewelry signal her profession straightaway. Her maternal kindness demonstrates O'Neill's lifelong sympathy for, and fascination with, prostitutes. "What a life! Poor kid!" she groans after kissing her daughter touchingly on the forehead (1:15). Rose's life is redeemed by the love of a good-guy fugitive, Tim Moran, who intervenes during a squabble between Rose and Steve and promises to help her in any way he can. In the final scene, Steve reenters the apartment from the fire escape, shoots Tim, throws the murder weapon into the apartment, and flees the scene. Thus, when the police arrive to investigate, Rose is arrested for Tim's murder, and her child will be taken by the authorities. Just before being taken off to Blackwell Island, a notorious prison, Rose has a vision, or notion, that there is *"something in the room which none of the others can see—perhaps the personification of the ironic life force that has crushed her"* (1:28).

Steve   Rose Thomas's "cadet," or pimp. Steve is an alcoholic, opium-smoking gambling addict, and although he too is a member of the dispossessed, we see none of the sympathy O'Neill feels for Rose, aside perhaps from the fact that he had grown up in an orphanage, which signals that his criminality may be institutional. Steve speaks in New York gangster slang and has no pity on the hooker or her child. After Tim Moran, a fugitive "yeggman" with whom Rose swiftly falls in love, chases him from the apartment Steve and Rose share, Steve returns with a handgun and murders the far more sympathetic Tim. By throwing the gun into the apartment after Tim's death, he sets Rose up to be arrested for murder. Unlike the well-rounded, more realistic criminals O'Neill would later create, Steve is a one-dimensional stock villain character in the tradition of MELODRAMA.

BIBLIOGRAPHY

Barlow, Judith E. "O'Neill's Female Characters." In *The Cambridge Companion to Eugene O'Neill*, edited by Michael Manheim, 164–177. New York: Cambridge University Press, 1998.

Bogard, Travis. *Centour in Time: The Plays of Eugene O'Neill.* Rev. ed. New York: Oxford University Press, 1988.

Gelb, Arthur, and Barbara Gelb. *O'Neill: Life with Monte Cristo.* New York: Applause Books, 2000.

Gilfoyle, Timothy J. *City of Eros: New York City, Prostitution, and the Commercialization of Sex, 1790–1920.* New York: W.W. Norton & Company, 1992.

Goldberg, Isaac. "At the Beginning of a Career." In *O'Neill and His Plays: Four Decades of Criticism,* edited by Oscar Cargill, N. Bryllion Fagin, and William J. Fisher, 234–243. New York: New York University Press, 1961.

Johnson, Katie N. "'Anna Christie': The Repentant Courtesan, Made Respectable." *Eugene O'Neill Review* 26 (2004): 87–104.

O'Neill, Eugene. *Selected Letters of Eugene O'Neill.* Edited by Travis Bogard and Jackson R. Bryer. New Haven, Conn.: Yale University Press, 1988.

Welded: A Play in Three Acts (completed, 1923; first produced, 1924)

Known at the time of production as Eugene O'Neill's "I love you, I hate you" play, *Welded* is a stylistically ambitious and glaringly autobiographical treatment of love and hate in marriage. Finished in February 1923, five years into O'Neill's marriage with AGNES BOULTON, *Welded* premiered at the PROVINCETOWN PLAYHOUSE on March 17, 1924, and lasted a meager 24 performances. Though the play was probably overshadowed by the controversy hanging over the upcoming production of ALL GOD'S CHILLUN GOT WINGS the following May, *Welded* is the first play produced by what the press called "the TRIUMVIRATE," an experimental theater group that included O'Neill as playwright, KENNETH MACGOWAN as producer, and ROBERT EDMOND JONES as set designer. It has long been regarded as yet another poorly written exposé of the marital bond by America's otherwise most innovative playwright—the others being BREAD AND BUTTER, SERVITUDE, BEFORE BREAKFAST, and The FIRST MAN.

The reviews were generally abysmal, citing the play's overly repetitive and stridently written dialogue. During one performance Doris Keane, who starred in the play, overheard an audience member grumble, "if that fellow says [I love you] again, I'll throw a chair at him" (quoted in Sheaffer 1973, 132); other audience members laughed out loud at the "attitudinizing" happening onstage (Lewisohn 165), a humiliating fact that was partially the actors' faults but more so the script's. For a time O'Neill defended the play's quality on all sides, though he finally accepted the fact that it was a "flat failure" (quoted in Floyd) and wished he had destroyed it. In 1981, the great O'Neill director JOSÉ QUINTERO, chief architect of the EUGENE O'NEILL RENAISSANCE, revived the play if not its reputation. Staged over 50 years after its premiere, that production too, an "unwarranted exhumation" according to one critic, provoked "unintentional laughter" (quoted in McDonough 247).

SYNOPSIS

A winter night in a Manhattan studio apartment with a stairway leading up to a balcony. Eleanor Cape is discovered reclining on a chaise longue; she is encircled by light, and the rest of the room is dark. She lifts up a letter from a table and reads it through rapturously, kisses it, then replaces it on the table. A door beneath the balcony opens, and Michael Cape enters. His form is also illuminated by a circle of light. *"These two circles of light,"* O'Neill writes in the STAGE DIRECTIONS, *"like auras of egoism, emphasize and intensify Eleanor and Michael throughout the play"* (2:235). Michael softly puts down his suitcase, hat, and overcoat; Eleanor, lost in a sentimental reverie, does not hear him but *"suddenly becomes aware of some presence in the room and turns boldly to face it"* (2:235). They speak each other's names and embrace passionately. Eleanor had not expected Michael for a few days, but as a playwright who has sought solitude in the countryside, he finished the last act of his new play and was able to return early.

Michael and Eleanor express a shared pain over their few weeks apart. But when Eleanor teases that he might have rushed the final act out of desperation to see her, he replies, "No. I wouldn't. I couldn't. You know that" (2:236). Stung by the slight, she quickly recovers and eagerly asks him to read his new manuscript. A celebrated actress, Eleanor will play the starring role, as she has done for all his plays since the start of their relationship. Michael refuses to read the play, however, and voices his desire to make "this night as our own. Let's forget the actress and playwright" (2:237). But it is a brief truce, and their conversation soon descends into bickering over the extent of their marital discord; it then turns to a painful, if brief, rehashing of the jealousy they feel over their previous relationships. Michael reminds Eleanor of the "new faith" they intended their marriage to engender, which she sarcastically refers to as the "Grand Ideal" of a "relentless idealist" (2:238). But he reiterates the conditions of the ideal: "Not for us the ordinary family rite, you'll remember! We swore to have a true sacrament—or nothing! Our marriage must be a consummation demanding and combining the best in each of us! Hard, difficult, guarded from the commonplace, kept sacred as the outward form of our inner harmony!" (2:239).

Eleanor then strikes at the heart of their differences: The ideal they vowed to uphold is one in which too much is expected of her. "I can neither take more nor give more—and you blame me! (*She smiles tenderly*) And then we fight!" (2:239). Momentarily reconciled, they kiss, and he muses that their bodies split into separate cells a hundred million years ago, that their cells have yearned to reunite ever since, and this reunion is the product of their marriage. His words send her into an erotic swoon. They start upstairs to bed, but then hear a knock at the door. From the top of the balcony, Michael at first pleads with and then commands Eleanor to ignore the visitor and come to bed; but when another knock comes, *"She gives a sort of gasp of relief"* (2:240). The knocking gets louder and more forceful. Eleanor is caught between her desire to open the door and Michael's insistence she join him. She chooses the door. Michael rushes down from the balcony to stop her, but it is too late.

Michael's producer and their close friend, John, enters genially. After some niceties, John sees that Michael is not very welcoming, so he perfunctorily congratulates his friend on what he assures him will be their latest triumph; he then exits as gracefully as he came in. Michael demands to know why Eleanor ignored his appeal. She apologizes and takes his hand to lead him to bed. But he rejects her "sacrifice" of sex (2:243). Then O'Neill's instructions, looking forward to the interior monologues of STRANGE INTERLUDE, specify the two sit in chairs placed side by side, facing the audience, and "*stare straight ahead and remain motionless. They speak, ostensibly to the other, but showing by their tone it is a thinking aloud to oneself, and neither appears to hear what the other has said*" (2:243). "There's always some knock at the door," he complains, "some reminder of life outside which calls you away from me." She says in her turn, "I feel a cruel presence in you paralyzing me, creeping over my body, possessing it so it's no longer my body" (2:243). He accuses her of taking his every action and word as a personal assault on her individuality. For her part, she resents the fact that he forbids her to enjoy "easy, casual associations" with other people, since he takes it as a violation of their overbearing marital "ideal" (2:244). They turn and face each other. Michael insinuates she is having an affair with John. We find through scant exposition that John, in fact, once asked her to marry him, but she had refused. They agree for the moment to "forget the past" and "talk of something else" (2:247).

The conversation turns to work. Michael relates how the isolation of the countryside in winter enables him to write: "No summer fools about. Solitude and work. I was happy—that is, as happy as I ever can be without you" (2:247). "Thanks for that afterthought," she replies bitterly, "but do you expect me to believe it? When you're working I might die and you'd never know it" (2:247). They then switch to the subject of professional jealousy. Michael insists he was more famous than she before they met, and Eleanor gives John, not Michael, most of the credit for their success. He attacks her again about the nature of her relationship with John, as well as the other lovers she has had. This fact, that he cannot accept her sexual history, goads her into chastising his work: "Now I know why the women in your plays are so wooden! You ought to thank me for breathing life into them!" (2:249). He escalates the argument, and she abruptly confesses that she and John were

having an affair while Michael was gone. It is a lie deliberately designed to hurt him, but he believes her, and "*with a snarl of fury like an animal's he seizes her about the throat with both hands*" (2:250). As he forces her to her knees, she stares at him with intense hatred. Michael releases her, swearing he will destroy the love inside him and storms out of the studio. She repents at first but then cries, "Go! Go! I'm glad! I hate you. I'm free! I'll go—" (2:251). Fetching her hat and coat from upstairs, she rushes out the door.

Act 2, Scene 1

John's library, with a framed portrait of Eleanor reverently positioned on the wall. John is sitting on the edge of his couch; his arms and head hang down sullenly, indicating loneliness and heartbreak. The doorbell rings, and he answers grudgingly. Discovering Eleanor at the threshold, "*pale, distraught, and desperate*," John's face reveals a "*confused mixture of alarm, tenderness, perplexity, passionate hope*" (2:252). Eleanor's expression transforms into one of rage and hatred, but she hastily gains control of her feelings, and her face turns "*mask-like and determined*" (2:252). Eleanor asks John if he still loves her—he does. She claims that her love for Michael is dead, and that they may now freely pursue each other. But her masklike expression reemerges each time John attempts to make a passionate connection. Indeed, when he kisses her, she conveys outright revulsion. He likens the experience to kissing a "corpse" and urges her to go to the guestroom to rest. She struggles to do so, but "*some invisible barrier . . . bars her way*" (2:255). Trying again, she halts at the bottom of the stairs and runs back to John, hysterically claiming she saw Michael at the top of the staircase.

John tells her she does not love him, though she tries to convince herself to, and that she hates Michael. When John offers her a place to stay indefinitely, she realizes her need to return home. John knows the only reason she came was in an act of revenge against her husband, and he accuses her of using his love for her own ends, including one fact Michael had suspected all along: "Twice now you've treated my love with the most humiliating contempt—Once when you were willing to endure it as the price of a career—again tonight, when you try to give yourself to me out of hate for him!" (2:258). He realizes, however, that she would have too much control over him if they consummated a relationship. Eleanor slowly gains a revelation about her marriage and exclaims, "My love for him is my own, not his! That he can never possess! It's *my* own!" (2:258). John tells her to freshen up and goes to get his car as the curtain falls.

Act 2, Scene 2

A prostitute's bedroom. The soft glow of a street lamp comes through a torn window shade, and the walls are decorated with an *"ugly wall paper, dirty, stained, criss-crossed with match-strokes"* (2:259). The door opens, and the hall light reveals the darkened silhouette of a young prostitute, with Michael looming behind her. The prostitute enters and invites Michael, standing stupidly in the doorway, into the flat. She complains of fatigue and good-naturedly asks what his trouble is, reminding him that on the street he was "full enough of bull" (2:260) and that he had grabbed her crazily and kissed her in public in front of a group of cheering onlookers. She asks if he wants to stay the night, an offer he accepts wondering where else she thought he might go. "Home," she replies. "That's where most of 'em goes—afterwards" (2:261). He laughs sardonically and responds that hell is his home.

In elevated philosophical language the prostitute does not understand, Michael explains that his visit to her is a "symbol of release," and she accuses him of having been either drinking that evening or "dopin' up on coke" (2:261). He continues with a stream of invective: "You're my salvation! You have the power—and the right—to murder love! You can satisfy hate!" (2:262). These words, and plenty more besides, make the prostitute alternately nervous and insulted; he, in kind, fluctuates his speech between abject apology and backhanded disparagement. "Do you know what you are? You're a symbol. . . . You're love revenging itself upon itself! You're the suicide of love—of my love—of all the love since the world began!" (2:263). In time the prostitute gets the picture and tells him to go back to his wife. "You love her, don't you? Well, then! There's no use buckin' that game." He finally

takes it too far, saying, "You—you make life despicable." "You just don't like me," she shouts, tossing his money at him and ordering him out. "Take your lousy coin and beat it!" (2:265). He begs on his knees for forgiveness, which she eventually grants. He convinces her to keep the money and asks if she loves her pimp though he beats her. She responds that she does. He thanks her for teaching him her lesson of life and love—that one must, in her words, "loin to like it" (2:267). She looks after him uncomprehendingly as he departs, muttering, "Say—" as the curtain falls (2:267).

Act 3

Back in the studio. Eleanor is facing the doorway where Michael stands rigidly. Neither of them speak. *"For a long, tense moment they remain fixed, staring into each other's eyes with apprehensive questioning"* (2:268). After this pause, they voice each other's name with soulful contrition. He shuts the door and joins her back at the two chairs facing the audience, just as they had in act 1. They look at each other, then away, seeming to have lost the respective understanding reached moments before. They talk back and forth tentatively about the mutual lessons they learned that night, but carefully avoid specific details. Eleanor finally admits she went to John's house. This news hurts Michael terribly, though he responds with restraint (2:270). She tells him she lied about the affair with John, but not about the fact that she had offered herself to him to advance her career. He admits in his turn that he went to a prostitute. Eleanor tenderly suggests that the only way they can survive is by accepting their love, while at the same time "releasing each other" (2:273). "It will give you peace for your work," she argues, but he calls this "nonsense." He finally agrees, though: "Then go now—if you're strong enough" (2:274). Eleanor hastily picks up her coat and heads to the door, but she remains immobile for another long moment; she then knocks on the door and enigmatically utters, "No. Never again 'come out.'" Turning to Michael with a strange smile, she says, "It opens inward, Michael" (2:274) and comes back into the room.

They stare into each other's eyes and appear to fully comprehend their love: *"It is as if now* by a sudden flash from within they recognized them-selves, shorn of all the ides, attitudes, cheating gestures which constitute the vanity of personality" (2:275). Then, with a *"low cry as if she were awakening to maternity,"* she speaks his name, and he responds with hers. They have learned to embrace both love and conflict in matrimony. "And we'll tor-ture and tear, and clutch for each other's souls!" Michael pronounces. [F]ight—fail and hate again ... but!—fail *with pride*—with joy!" (2:275). He repeats his belief that they have been seeking each other over time immemorial and cries out, "I love you! Forgive me all I've ever done, and all I'll ever do" (2:276). "No," she responds, "forgive me—my child, you!" (2:276). After both acknowledge that after this tormenting night, their love will be "deeper and more beautiful" (2:276), she ascends the staircase and beckons to him with arms out-stretched. As he moves toward her, she stretches her arms out wider, forming her body into a cross. He does the same, and the two meet on the stair-case, together forming *"one cross"* (2:276), enwrap, and kiss passionately.

COMMENTARY

An overwrought story of a couple tormented by conflicting expectations of love and matrimony, *Welded* is still important for providing, in Agnes Boulton's words, a "carbon copy" of O'Neill's marriage to her (quoted in Sheaffer 102)—and there is much to substantiate this claim—as well as demonstrating his desire, if not yet his mastered ability, to bring a new level of experimentation to AMERICAN THEATER. *Welded* was, importantly, the first play of O'Neill's new theatrical produc-tion group called "the Triumvirate." This partner-ship with critic Kenneth Macgowan (upon whom the character John is loosely based) and designer Robert Edmond Jones was intent on introduc-ing European-style theater to the United States, with a strong emphasis on the style of AUGUST STRINDBERG, whose play *The Dance of Death* is commonly compared to *Welded* (critic GEORGE JEAN NATHAN referred to the play as "third-rate Strindberg" [quoted in Floyd 249]). O'Neill called the new form "behind life" drama, which, along with super-naturalism, was a conscious rebel-

lion against the action-driven MELODRAMA of his father's day, but also the stark NATURALISM of plays like his own *"ANNA CHRISTIE,"* for which he had recently received his second PULITZER PRIZE. "Behind life" projects characters' inner selves onto the stage, a technique culminating in the inner monologues of *Strange Interlude.* Therefore, what O'Neill intended *Welded* to accomplish dramatur-gically is rather more impressive and exciting than its end result.

O'Neill plainly stated his purpose in an interview with Louis Kantor of the *New York Times,* in which he uncharacteristically laid much of the blame for the play's resounding failure on his shoulders (dur-ing its short-lived run he blamed the actors' inabil-ity to pause correctly):

> The principal reason why my *Welded* was mis-understood by some was that I erred when I conceived the dialogue against a naturalis-tic setting. My notion was to have a man and woman, lovers and married, enact their spiri-tual struggle to possess one the other. I wanted to give the impression of the world shut out, just of two human beings struggling to break through an inner darkness.... But the sets which I described in my stage directions were so "natural" that they inevitably conjured up all the unimportant paraphernalia of daily liv-ing, daily existence, to stand between the life of my characters and the lives in the audience. (quoted in Estrin 49)

In addition, O'Neill was experimenting with something another NOBEL PRIZE–winning play-wright, Harold Pinter, eventually mastered—the dramatic pause (now known as the "Pinter pause"). O'Neill critic Travis Bogard points out that O'Neill indicates 12 long pauses in two pages of the script alone. The dialogue, then, "pitched so high that it seems to have been written more with exclama-tion marks than with words," as O'Neill biogra-pher Louis Sheaffer characterized it (102), should be taken as rather incidental impressions that together make a whole picture of the inner life of this marriage—the cognitive dissonance that arises when extreme feelings of love and hate battle for supremacy—rather than the way spouses actually talk to one another. Who among us would pronounce to their lover (let alone their spouse), "I've become you! You've become me! One heart! One blood! Ours!" (2:240)? (It must be said that there is one person who does—O'Neill often sounds this way in his love letters.) This is why, though he later wished he had destroyed the play, along with GOLD and *The* FOUNTAIN, he initially thought highly of it and blamed its failure on the actors for not understanding that in act 3 in particular, "what was actually spoken should have served to a great extent just to punctuate the meaningful pauses" (quoted in Bogard 187). The pauses in the script are one thing, but how does the actor who plays John convey, as O'Neill instructs him in the stage directions, "*a joy that is incongruously savage*" (2:252) or Eleanor respond to Michael's revelations "*exalted by his exultation rather than by his words*" (2:275)? There are flashes of O'Neill's genius throughout, however. Michael Cape's monologue accusing Eleanor of "fighting against" him like he was her "worst enemy" in act 1, for instance, is worthy of the intensely probing monologues of LONG DAY'S JOURNEY INTO NIGHT.

O'Neill's use of lighting is another important experimental device. He often applied lighting and circles of light to underscore isolation, individuality, and the irrelevance of the outer material world as compared to the inner spiritual one. But he never used them as a surrogate to dialogue the way he does in *Welded*. The two spotlights, or "follow spots," that encircle the Capes like "*auras of egoism*" (2:235; a nod to Max Stirner's "egoism" concept that developed into O'Neill's social philosophy PHILOSOPHICAL ANARCHISM) are meant to emphasize each character's individualism and thus treat visually as well as in dialogue Michael's desire to merge the two circles of light into one. When that happens, it symbolizes both a spiritual as well as physical "welding."

Neither Agnes Boulton nor O'Neill were easy to live with, and O'Neill wrote *Welded* during a particularly bad period in their marriage, one that led him to drink alcohol while working. O'Neill famously remarked on mixing alcohol with work that "I don't think anything worth reading was ever written by anyone who was drunk or even half-drunk when he wrote it" (quoted in Clark 61). In the 1910s and 1920s, his habit was to abstain completely from drink when working on a play and then go on a bender. But in the case of *Welded*, he made an unfortunate exception (Sheaffer 107). This speaks more to O'Neill's fragile state of mind than to worries over drunken blather in the dialogue, though that would explain a lot. O'Neill also lashed out viciously against his wife during the winter of 1922–23, cutting up all his photographs of her, kicking a hole in the center of a coveted portrait of her father by the famous American painter Thomas Eakins, and unjustly accusing her of having affairs with other men.

Michael Cape's revelation in the final scene shows that he has developed from harboring an unreasonable expectation of a perfect union between him and Eleanor to an acceptance that love and strife go hand in hand, particularly when dealing with two such passionate and creative individualists. In his 1927 breakup letter to Agnes Boulton, O'Neill wrote that the fine things of their relationship had been irreparably punctured by "moments of a very horrible hate [that have become] more and more apparent, a poisonous bitterness and resentment, a cruel desire to wound, rage and frustration and revenge. This has killed our chance for happiness together. There have been too many insults to pride and self-respect, too many torturing scenes that one may forgive but which something in one cannot forget" (O"Neill 271). *Welded* is a composite portrait of these "torturing scenes." In the play if not in life, O'Neill accepts them as the stuff of true love.

The cornerstone of the play's message on love and life, though admittedly vague, is the prostitute's injunction that one must "loin to like it" (2:267). O'Neill probably derived this from the chapter "On Child and Marriage" in FRIEDRICH NIETZSCHE's *Thus Spake Zarathustra*, a book he read obsessively through the 1910s and 1920s. In this chapter, the "overman" Zarathustra preaches to his audience that love is a "torch that should light up higher paths for you. Over and beyond yourselves you shall love one day. Thus *learn* first to love.

And for that you had to drain the bitter cup of your love. Bitterness lies in the cup of even the best love: thus it arouses longing for the overman . . ." (71). (O'Neill probably took *Welded*'s working title, *Made in Heaven,* from this chapter as well, as in it Nietzsche sneers at the expression [70].) Michael Cape's pronouncements at the end of the play indicate that O'Neill came to grips with the old chestnut that no marriage is perfect, but he takes it a step further by adding an almost sado-masochistic twist: "And we'll torture and tear, and clutch for each other's souls!—fight—fail and hate again—. . . but!—fail *with pride*—with joy!" (2:275; Sheaffer 101).

O'Neill inscribed Boulton's copy of the play with a line from act 3: "I love you! Forgive me all I've ever done, all I'll ever do" (quoted in Floyd 133). But the acceptance of intermittent marital discord did not overcome the continual transgressions both of them were guilty of enacting. As Ludwig Lewisohn said when he disparaged O'Neill's play in his review in *The Nation,* "union must have rapture; it must also have peace" (164).

CHARACTERS

Cape, Eleanor Michael Cape's wife and a successful actress. Eleanor is plainly based on O'Neill's second wife, Agnes Boulton: "*Her figure is tall. Her face, with its high, prominent cheek-bones, lacks harmony. It is dominated by passionate, blue-gray eyes, restrained by a high forehead from which the mass of her dark brown hair is combed straight back. The first impression of her whole personality is one of charm, partly innate, partly imposed by years of self-discipline*" (2:235). Eleanor shares virtually none of the qualities of wives in O'Neill's previous marriage plays. As opposed to the conventional Maud Steele from *Bread and Butter,* the nagging Mrs. Rowland from *Before Breakfast,* the fawning Ruth Roylston from *Servitude,* or the destructive Ruth Atkins from BEYOND THE HORIZON, Eleanor is an individualist, more closely in the mode of Nina Leeds in *Strange Interlude,* who is very much in love with her husband but refuses to conform to his impossibly high standards of marriage. However, as literary critic Judith E. Barlow

points out, it is symbolically significant that Eleanor "only performs roles written by her husband," and in a rage Michael calls her "actress" as an epithet; thus, "given O'Neill's often harsh comments about the acting profession, it's not hard to detect his own feelings in Michael Cape's distinction between the writer's creativity and the thespian's rote mimicry" (Barlow 165). Similarly, Agnes Boulton wrote popular stories for pulp magazines and never attempted the kind of "literary" work her husband considered true art.

Eleanor first met Michael when she acted in an early play of his. After they married, she devoted her career exclusively to his plays. That she "acts" emerges intermittently in the stage directions, specifically in act 2, scene 1, when she appears to don a protective mask. Eleanor loves her husband intensely, but after having made a pact with him for their marriage to be a "true sacrament—or nothing" (2:239), she finds his possessiveness a spiritually crushing force. Eleanor enjoys "easy, casual associations" (2:244) with friends and coworkers like their producer John, but Michael finds these outside interferences destructive to the "inner harmony" of their marriage (2:239). After a particularly brutal fight with Michael at the end of act 1, Eleanor goes to her friend John, who is in love with her, and attempts to initiate an affair as revenge against her jealous husband. She fails, however, and by the final scene of act 3, she and Michael have reconciled themselves to the fact that a sacramental marriage like theirs involves severe conflicts as well as passionate love.

Cape, Michael Eleanor Cape's husband and a successful playwright. Michael, whose surname is taken from O'Neill's British publisher Jonathan Cape, is the most autobiographical character O'Neill ever created, with the exception of Edmund Tyrone of *Long Day's Journey into Night.* Previous avatars of himself, such as John Brown in *Bread and Butter,* the Poet in FOG, and Tom Perkins in *The* PERSONAL EQUATION, were all given different vocations from O'Neill's—a painter, a poet, and a revolutionary, respectively. But Michael is a playwright like his creator, is 35 years old, and has been married for five years, all of which describes O'Neill at the time of the play's composition. More important, O'Neill's description of the character in his stage directions, a striking physical and psychological self-portrait, demonstrates an extraordinary display of self-knowledge that deserves to be quoted at length:

> His unusual face is a harrowed battlefield of super-sensitiveness, the features at war with one another—the forehead of a thinker, the eyes of a dreamer, the nose and mouth of a sensualist. One feels a powerful imagination tinged with somber sadness—a driving force which can be sympathetic and cruel at the same time. There is something tortured about him—a passionate tension, a self-protecting, arrogant defiance of life and his own weakness, a deep need for love as a faith in which to relax. (2:235)

Michael Cape has been married to his actress wife Eleanor for five years, and they apparently have no children (by this time, O'Neill's and Agnes Boulton's son, SHANE RUDRAIGHE O'NEILL, was four years old). Michael and Eleanor met when she played a role in an early production of his, and a professional jealousy between them intensified over the years. In addition, Michael's needs in marriage are greatly at odds with his wife's. When first married, they made a pact to avoid the pettiness of "commonplace" relationships (2:239), a kind of death in Michael's eyes as well as in those of O'Neill's self-professed "literary idol" Friedrich Nietzsche. As such, the couple "swore to have a true sacrament—or nothing" (2:239). The only way Michael can conceive of accomplishing this is by refusing to allow the outer world to interfere with their "inner harmony" (2:239). Eleanor, on the other hand, though she agreed with Michael in theory, considers the relationship "paralyzing" (2:243) and, though not nearly as literal as Ruth Roylston's wifely role in *Servitude*, enslaving. As O'Neill critic Virginia Floyd says of Michael's character, "What [he] asks, indeed expects, of his wife is much more than any woman, particularly an independent, creative one like Eleanor, can give. He wants nothing short of perfection in marriage" (2:250). Michael

is also intensely jealous of their mutual friend and his producer, John. In act 1, when their argument explodes into real hatred, Michael exits to seek out a prostitute to kill his love, and Eleanor goes to John for the same reason. They both fail, however, and return to their studio in act 3, reconciling themselves to the fact that with great love comes equally great strife.

John Michael and Eleanor Cape's friend and producer. O'Neill describes John, loosely based on fellow Triumvirate member Kenneth Macgowan, as *"not handsome but his personality compels affection. . . . He has no nerves. His voice is low and calming"* (2:241). John has produced many of Michael's plays, and Eleanor gives him credit for making their careers. John had asked Eleanor to marry him before the Capes became involved, but she refused. She did, however, take advantage of his passion to advance her career. In the middle of act 1, John interrupts Michael and Eleanor at midnight, just as they are heading off to bed, and though Michael demands that Eleanor not open the door, she does so anyway, as she was feeling stifled by Michael's demand for unity in their relationship. She then visits John's apartment in act 2, scene 1, after a fight in large part triggered by Michael's jealousy over John's attentions toward her. During the argument, she lies that she and John were having an affair. John still loves her, and though he wants to consummate a relationship with her, his love is not reciprocated. He realizes she is simply after revenge, and that her personality would overwhelm him if they were to marry.

Woman, A A prostitute. She is 26 years old, and O'Neill describes her face as *"rouged, powdered, penciled . . . broad and stupid. Her small eyes have a glazed look. Yet she is not ugly—rather pretty for her bovine, stolid type"* (2:260). The critic Ludwig Lewisohn remarked in his review of the first production that the prostitute "is the only character [in the play] who talks like a human being" (164). Michael found her on the street just after the action of act 1, and she brings him back to her shabby apartment, the setting of act 2, scene 2. Judith E. Barlow notes that she is a particularly "disturbing" example of O'Neill's tendency to romanticize PROSTITUTION, given that she smiles when she tells Michael her pimp might beat her "just for the fun of it" (quoted in Barlow 167). It perplexes her when Michael cruelly voices his belief that she is symbol of all "the tortures man inflicts on woman" and at the same time "the revenge of woman" (2:263). But when he bluntly says that she makes life "despicable," she strikes back in her defense and orders him out. Michael sincerely apologizes and tells her that her coda of life—you "loin to like it"—has made him join her "church" (2:267). O'Neill biographer Louis Sheaffer argues that she is a "preliminary sketch for the idealized prostitute [Cybel] in *The* GREAT GOD BROWN" (103).

BIBLIOGRAPHY

Barlow, Judith. "O'Neill's Female Characters." In *The Cambridge Companion to Eugene O'Neill*, edited by Michael Manheim, 164–177. New York: Cambridge University Press, 1998.

Bogard, Travis. *Contour in Time: The Plays of Eugene O'Neill*. Rev. ed. New York: Oxford University Press, 1988.

Clark, Barrett H. *Eugene O'Neill: The Man and His Plays*. Rev. ed. New York: Dover, 1947.

Estrin, Mark W., ed. *Conversations with Eugene O'Neill*. Jackson: University of Mississippi Press, 1990.

Floyd, Virginia. *The Plays of Eugene O'Neill: A New Assessment*. New York: Ungar, 1985.

Lewisohn, Ludwig. "Welded." Review (1922). In *O'Neill and His Plays: Four Decades of Criticism*, edited by Oscar Cargill, N. Bryllion Fagin, and William J. Fisher, 163–165. New York: New York University Press, 1961.

McDonough, Edwin J. *Quintero Directs O'Neill*. Pennington, N.J.: Cappella Books, 1991.

Nietzsche, Friedrich. *Thus Spake Zarathustra*. Translated and with a preface by Walter Kaufmann, 1883–92. Reprint, New York: Penguin Books, 1978.

O'Neill, Eugene. *Selected Letters of Eugene O'Neill*. Edited by Travis Bogard and Jackson R. Bryer. New York: Limelight Editions, 1994.

Sheaffer, Louis. *O'Neill: Son and Artist*. Boston: Little, Brown, 1973.

Where the Cross Is Made: A Play in One Act (completed, 1918; first produced, 1918)

Eugene O'Neill wrote *Where The Cross Is Made*, the last one-act SEA play he would ever write, in summer 1918 while he was working on the full-length CHRIS CHRISTOPHERSEN. The play is a revision of the final act of his full-length play GOLD, which he completed in 1920. For their 1918–19 season, the PROVINCETOWN PLAYERS had solicited a play by the most talked-about young playwright in New York City (a growing celebrity they nurtured), and he came through with *Where the Cross Is Made*. O'Neill had just moved to Provincetown, Massachusetts, with his second wife, AGNES BOULTON, and Agnes was then struggling over an idea for a short story with the working title "The Captain's Walk." O'Neill read it with great interest but felt there was no "dramatic dialogue" or sufficient action. Though Boulton tried to explain it was intended to be "a story of atmosphere and obsession," he took the project on as his own (Boulton 191). The first production at the PLAYWRIGHTS' THEATRE on November 22, 1918, created a bitter dispute between O'Neill and the Players (discussed in the commentary below).

SYNOPSIS

A moonlit night in fall 1900; the upper room of Captain Isaiah Bartlett's house on the California coastline. The room perfectly resembles a sea captain's cabin, with portholes, lantern, cot, floating ship's compass, and so on. Moonlight illuminates the room "*like tired dust in circular patches upon the floor and table*" (1:695), and the pounding of waves from the shore below is barely audible. In the rear, a door leads downstairs. Nat Bartlett, a young man of 30 whose right arm has been amputated, cautiously comes through the door. Seeing the room empty, he signals to Doctor Higgins, a psychiatrist from a local mental asylum, that it is safe to enter. Nat has brought Higgins up to Captain Bartlett's simulacrum of sea life to make known the depth of his father's madness. He explains that Captain Bartlett's roof has been specially designed to resemble a poop deck, fitted out with a wheel, compass, binnacle light, companionway, and bridge to "keep watch" (1:697). At first Doctor Higgins disclaims the notion that such eccentricity is proof of madness; rather, he muses confidently that "it's very natural—and interesting—this whim of his" (1:696). Nat goes on that his father has never left the cabin or the "poop deck" above in three years. "Understand," he says to the doctor, "that I want you to get all the facts—just that, facts!—and for that light is necessary. Without that—they become dreams up here—dreams, Doctor" (1:696). Nat lights a lantern, assuring the doctor his father will not take notice; during his nightly reveries, the captain's attention is wholly focused on the sea.

Nat informs Higgins that his father is keeping a lookout for his schooner *Mary Allen*, named for his deceased wife and reportedly destroyed at sea by a hurricane three years before. By way of Nat's exposition, we learn that Captain Bartlett's last voyage was seven years ago, when he and a group of six men survived a shipwreck in the Indian Ocean. All other hands had "gone to the sharks" (1:698). The seven castaways made their way in an open boat to a desert island, but only four survived—the captain, his mate Silas Horne, his boatswain (pronounced "bo'sun") Cates, and a Hawaiian harpooner named Jimmy Kanaka. Only speculation remains concerning the other two—either they died of exposure or went mad and drowned themselves, or perhaps they were killed and cannibalized by the survivors. "So much for the facts, Doctor," Nat concludes this portion of his father's story. "They leave off there and the dreams begin" (1:699).

Captain Bartlett and the three survivors met with Nat after their return. Swearing him to secrecy, they claimed that on the island, they discovered the hulk of a Malay war prau, a nimble Malayan-style sailboat, long before abandoned by pirates to rot on the shore. In it they found two treasure chests filled with "diamonds, emeralds, gold ornaments—innumerable, of course. Why limit the stuff of dreams?" (1:699). The captain and his crew buried the treasure and drew a map indicating its hidden position "where the cross is made" (1:700). Captain Bartlett sent the *Mary Allen* to retrieve the treasure and, heedless of the report of its destruction, has been

waiting ever since. Though anxious to join the expedition, Bartlett stayed behind to care for his dying wife. Nat actually believed the story until his father went mad following the death of Mary Allen. He was given a "sample" of the treasure in the form of a jewel-studded bracelet, which upon inspection was assessed as nothing but "paste and brass—Malay ornaments" (1:701). Captain Bartlett had mortgaged the house to pay for the *Mary Allen*'s voyage, and now the banker is ready to foreclose. Nat says he and his sister will be evicted and so believes his father must be committed. Now convinced the captain is mad, Doctor Higgins departs with assurances to return shortly with orderlies in case his new patient puts up a struggle.

Sue Bartlett, Nat's sister and Captain Bartlett's daughter, enters wearing a bathrobe and slippers. She was awakened by the sound of the two men and is astonished to hear the visitor was a doctor from the asylum. Nat implores her to believe that institutionalizing their father is the most sensible course of action. The banker, he gradually reveals, has offered him $2,000 for the house; he has also offered him a position as the house's caretaker once the captain is sent away. The neighbors have grown frightened of the captain's ritual on the roof, and there are rumors of ghosts, which has also lowered the property value. Sue insists that accepting this "blood money" would be an unconscionable betrayal of their father (1:704); but to her consternation, Nat confesses the deal has already been made, and he plans to take the opportunity to write a book and thus write his way out of the "dream" his father imposed on him (1:705). Nat's reasoning deepens, as he admits that he too continues to believe in the treasure, though he knows it is madness. For this reason as well, Nat wants to be rid of his father: "He made me doubt my own brain and give lie to my eyes—when hope was dead—when I knew it was all a dream—I couldn't kill it! . . . . I do hate him! He's stolen my brain! I've got to free myself, can't you see, from him—and his madness" (2:705). He then ceremoniously sets the map on fire as a sign of approaching freedom from what he repeatedly refers to as "the dream."

They hear Captain Bartlett shout out "sail-ho" from the poop deck above (1:706). Bartlett comes down in sailor's garb, a blue double-breasted coat and rubber boots, and moves threateningly toward his son. He accuses him of preparing to send him to an asylum. Visibly terrified, Nat fatuously denies the charge and insists, truthfully, that he still believes in the treasure. The captain maintains his son is a Judas, then scornfully commands him to look out the porthole. In his eyes, the *Mary Allen* has landed at last. Nat peers out into the night and tremulously acknowledges that he sees the red and green lights on the masthead signaling the ship's identity. The two men rush to the companionway and holler joyfully, "Mary Allen, ahoy!" (1:708). Sue then looks out the porthole for herself and sees nothing. When Nat comes down, she desperately tries to drive out the illusion, but he admonishes her as a "blind fool" (1:708). The captain descends soon after, and the two watch as their dream crew lands on the beach and approaches the house. At that point, "*a dense green glow floods slowly in rhythmic waves like a liquid into the room—as of great depths of the sea faintly penetrated by light*" (1:709). Sue attempts to calm the increasingly unwound Nat as he cries out in hysterics, presumably responding to the green glow, that she must save him from drowning. Bartlett announces the crew is at the door with the chests of treasure, and the "*paddling of bare feet sounds from the floor below*" (1:709). The figures of Silas Horne, Cates, and Jimmy Kanaka enter wearing rotted clothing, and their flesh appears to be in a ghoulish state of decomposition. "*Their bodies sway limply, nervelessly, rhythmically, as if to the pulse of long swells of the deep sea*" (1:710).

Sue begs her father and brother to acknowledge no one is there. But Captain Bartlett orders his men up the companionway, announcing they will not share the wealth with his Judas son. Horne hands over a piece of paper to the captain (the ship's copy of the map), and Bartlett scoffs, "That's right—for him—that's right!" (1:710); they ascend the staircase to the companionway, shutting the slide door behind them. Nat bangs on the door, but he cannot force it open. Doctor Higgins enters, and the green glow instantaneously vanishes. Higgins easily opens the slide and ascends to the companionway. He calls down for Nat to lend him a hand, which he does, and the

two reenter bearing the captain's limp body. Higgins checks his pulse and pronounces him dead of heart failure. Nat had seen Horne hand his father the map; he wrenches the phantom paper free from the tightly clenched hands of the corpse and rushes to the table, frantically spreading it before him. "The map of the island! Look! It isn't lost for me after all! There's still a chance—*my* chance!" Sue covers her face in despair and cries for Nat to "Come away" (1:712).

COMMENTARY

Immediately after the opening night of *Where the Cross Is Made*, the actor Hutch Collins, who played the role of Captain Bartlett, and Ida Rauh, who directed and played Sue, both did their best to convince O'Neill that the ghosts who appear in the final scene should be imaginary instead of using actual actors. Ghosts, they argued, do not tread on floorboards, and they feared the audience would find the discrepancy more comical than terrifying. O'Neill refused to sanction the alteration, however, on the basis that "this play presumes that everybody is mad but the girl. . . . I want to see whether it's possible to make an audience go mad too" (quoted in Bogard 103). In this way, the play relates to his earlier one-act play BEFORE BREAKFAST, which O'Neill intended as an experiment to "apply a more than normal pressure on the spectators' sensibilities so as to discover how much the audience could bear" (Bogard 103). As such, the final scene of *Where the Cross Is Made* is designed to allow spectators entrance into the mind of one suffering from psychosis—here a rather blunt if dramatically engaging form of early EXPRESSIONISM that O'Neill would rarify only two years later in the masterful escape sequence of *The EMPEROR JONES*. And like *The Emperor Jones*, O'Neill does not, as Virginia Floyd contends, rely "entirely on the supernatural for his conclusion" as he does in his earlier one-act sea play FOG (163). They are not supernatural since they are figments of the Bartlett men's imagination, so the ghost scene is better understood as an incipient mode of expressionism. Nevertheless, in the later expansion, *Gold*, O"Neill did rewrite the scene by making Captain Bartlett mistake his daughter Sue's ascending footsteps for the crew of the *Mary Allen*.

O'Neill wrote somewhat disparagingly of the play to critic GEORGE JEAN NATHAN: "Where did you ever get the idea that I really valued *Where the Cross Is Made*? It was great fun to write, theatrically very thrilling, an amusing experiment in treating the audience as insane—that is all it means or ever meant to me" (quoted in Clark 89). Louis Sheaffer, however, established a seemingly minor but brilliant connection between the name of Captain Bartlett's schooner, the *Mary Allen*, and the name of O'Neill's mother, MARY ELLEN "ELLA" O'NEILL, which makes it difficult for scholars to believe that theatrical thrill-seeking was "all" the play meant to him. Ella O'Neill was a morphine addict for more than two decades, and through that time, O'Neill, his brother JAMES O'NEILL, JR. (Jamie), and his father JAMES O'NEILL all suffered terribly from her drug-induced isolation and longed for her true self to return. O'Neill, then, "indulging in private symbolism," according to Sheaffer, "apparently had in mind the tragic situation in his own family: all the years the O'Neill men had hoped that their wife and mother would return to them from the depths" (430–431).

What is more, O'Neill employs the words *fact(s)* and *dream(s)* in his dialogue exactly 13 times each over the course of the play. Perhaps unintentional, the symmetry nevertheless, along with the superstitious significance of the number, underscores O'Neill's theme that the distinction between "fact" and "dream" is hazy at best, or perhaps even best not be looked into too closely. At one point, Nat submits that the captain "knows" the truth about his ship, but refuses to "believe" it (1:697), a distinction meant to correspond with the reiterated notion of "facts"—the family's dissolution—and "dreams"—the mother's escapism in drugs. Nat Bartlett's balancing act between the two becomes all the more significant, symbolizing O'Neill's own desperate torment following the revelation in his adolescence of his mother's addiction. In short, like his creator, Nat attempts to free himself of his demons by writing about them.

By the time of this production, Ella O'Neill had kicked her morphine habit and was still very much alive. Louis Sheaffer points out that it is important to remember (particularly among skeptical readers of this interpretation) that in *Gold*, the expanded version of the play, O'Neill changed the name of the ship to the *Sarah Allen* as his mother "might have guessed what was on her son's mind"; the new name, Sarah, now brings to mind O'Neill's childhood nanny Sarah Sandy (Sheaffer 431), a strong influence on his development in childhood. Though, again, Sheaffer's remark appears to be offhanded, it demonstrates just how powerfully O'Neill's despair over his mother's addiction affected him and traces a straight thematic line to his late masterpiece *LONG DAY'S JOURNEY INTO NIGHT*, against which all of his "hopeless hopes" must be reckoned. In addition, as Travis Bogard points out, the play has a great deal in common with the other two one-act plays O'Neill wrote in 1918, *The ROPE* and *The DREAMY KID*, insofar as the three together present "the germinal idea of the hope that holds men to life, of the lie of the pipe dream that, however, [sic] meaningless, nurtures the dispossessed" (106); this coalesces, though Bogard does not announce it, in *The ICEMAN COMETH*—by which time, pipe dreams in O'Neill's mind maintained a kind of sanity in the face of spiritual dispossession, rather than destroying it.

The idea of the plan did, as mentioned in the introduction, originate from Agnes Boulton, O'Neill's second wife, who just after their marriage showed him the sketch of a short story she called "The Captain's Walk":

> Old Captain Curtis. . . . He cannot let go, in spite of his age, his uselessness. The sight and sound of the sea awake in him a passionate longing for something more tangible. His lost ship on which his thoughts dwell becomes the symbol of all this. . . . He's so used to his watch that he wakes up every morning at four o'clock and can't sleep. After prowling for a while through the silent house he always winds up by going up to the walk and keeping watch there for the boat that does not return. (Boulton 163)

Nat articulates the treasure as the "more tangible" pipe dream most unmistakably when he tells his sister, "*He* [Captain Bartlett] taught me to wait and hope with him—wait and hope—day after day. He made me doubt my brain and give the lie to my eyes—when hope was dead—when I knew it was all a dream—I couldn't kill it!" (1:705). In this we might obtain an explanation for the title as well, as throughout his life O'Neill perceived in the figure of Christ on the cross a false idol (with the bizarre exception of DAYS WITHOUT END), and in the play he symbolically equates the pirate's treasure, which in Robert Louis Stevenson's *Treasure Island* is legendarily marked on the map with an "X," with the madness-inducing "pipe dream" of a spiritual savior for mankind.

CHARACTERS

Bartlett, Captain Isaiah A former whaling captain and Nat and Sue Bartlett's father. Physically, Captain Bartlett closely resembles his son, though his *"face is more stern and formidable, his form more robust, erect, and muscular"* (1:706), and his head hoary from years of tragedy and insanity. Bartlett speaks in a heavy accent redolent of the hardened sailor. Seven years before the play's action, Bartlett returned from a fateful voyage that was meant to last two years but kept him away for four. He and six of his crewmen escaped a shipwreck, and after seven days in an open boat, they found themselves stranded on a desert island in the Indian Ocean. A group of Malayan canoeists finally discovered them, but by that time only four survivors remained: the captain, his mate Silas Horne, his boatswain (pronounced "bo'sun") Cates, and the harpooner Jimmy Kanaka. Once they returned to California, they met with Bartlett's son, Nat, and told him that while on the island, they discovered a Malayan war prau filled with "diamonds, emeralds, gold ornaments" (1:699). The captain mortgaged his house to outfit a schooner he christened the *Mary Allen* after his wife, but before setting sail, his wife took ill, and he was compelled to stay behind.

Years later, after being driven to madness by his wife's death, Bartlett received news that the ship had been destroyed in a hurricane. He refused to believe it, however, and for three years he never left his upper room—bizarrely styled as a captain's cabin on a whaler—except to keep watch at night for the *Mary Allen* from a makeshift poop deck on the roof of his house. His son Nat's plan to commit him to a local asylum appears to trigger a hallu-cination that the *Mary Allen* has returned at last. Nat, though he claims to understand the treasure story as nothing but a "dream," is still under the spell of his father's hopeless hope. Once Captain Bartlett slips into his psychotic hallucination, the son shares the same delusion. They believe they see the ghostly forms of the three surviving crewmen bearing the chests of treasure into their home. When the ghosts arrive, Bartlett orders them up to the poop deck and thus away from his son, whom he considers a traitor. Soon after, he dies of heart failure. Captain Bartlett shares some traits with Abraham Bentley from O'Neill's earlier one-act play *The* ROPE and, for his Ahab-like obsessions, Captain David Keeney of ILE.

Bartlett, Nat Captain Isaiah Bartlett's son and Sue Bartlett's brother. Nat Bartlett is 30 but appears much older, and he lost his arm after being compelled by his father to quit school and go to sea. Captain Bartlett returned from a four-year voyage with a tale about finding hidden pirate's treasure on a desert island in the Indian Ocean. He mortgaged his house to send the *Mary Allen*, a schooner named for his deceased wife, with the surviving members of his crew and has not left his upper rooms for three years—always searching the horizon for the ship that has since been reported destroyed in a hurricane. Nat has accepted an offer from the banker who brokered the mortgage of his father's house: He is to commit Captain Bartlett to an insane asylum, as his father's bizarre behavior has devalued the property by spooking the neighbors. In return, Nat will be paid $2,000 and can stay on at the house as its caretaker. He offers to share the money with his sister, Sue, but she rejects it outright as a bribe to sell out their father. But Nat insists the deal is more than a bribe; rather, it is a way out of the nightmare in which his father has entrapped him: "He made me doubt my own brain and give lie to my eyes—when hope was dead—when I knew it was all a dream—I couldn't kill it! . . . I do hate him! He's stolen my brain! I've got to free myself, can't you see, from him—and his madness" (1:705).

Nat brings the asylum's doctor to witness the captain's behavior; the doctor, after concurring that he is insane, leaves with the promise to return with orderlies to take him away. Although Nat consciously understands his father's treasure story is a "dream," we find out in the final sequence that he still believes in it. When the two share a hallucination that the ship has, indeed, arrived—a hallucination orchestrated by his deranged father's imagination—Nat is turned away by the captain as a traitor for attempting to institutionalize him. In the end, the captain dies of heart failure, and Nat is left poring over the phantom treasure map—evidently he has fully lost his mind by the final scene. The dream will survive within him, much as Willy Loman's delusions of grandeur will be carried on by his son Happy in Arthur Miller's *Death of a Salesman* (1949). As such, since the tension of the plot consists of Nat's mental state—will he stay sane like his sister or fall into his father's delirium?—the dream of the treasure appears to be the only life-sustaining force justifying his existence. Only slightly resembling O'Neill physically, Nat does have an autobiographical component insofar as he is attempting to free himself from his demons by writing about them, he has served as a sailor, and the torment of the hopeless hope has left him vulnerable to a severe mental imbalance.

Bartlett, Sue Captain Isaiah Bartlett's daughter and Nat Bartlett's sister. O'Neill describes Sue as *"a tall, slender woman of twenty-five, with a pale, sad face framed in a mass of dark red hair"* (1:702). O'Neill specifies that her hair is her only colorful attribute, as the rest of her features are pale, dark, or gray. Sue is the only completely sane member of the Bartlett family, and she dotes on both her deranged father, whom she supplies with food during his domestic exile, and her psychologically borderline brother. Three years earlier, her father bought a vessel by financing their house to search out pirate's treasure that he had buried on a desert island after he and three other crew members survived a shipwreck. When Sue discovers Nat has agreed to sell their house for money and a caretaking position on the condition that the captain be institutionalized, she reproaches him for profiting from their father's tragic condition. When the two Bartlett men share a psychotic episode in which

they believe the crew of the captain's vessel has returned with treasure, she pleads with them to come back to reality. The captain dies of heart failure during this episode. In the final scene, it is painfully clear to Sue that Nat is now irretrievably lost in the insanity of his father's "dream."

Higgins, Doctor A doctor from the local insane asylum. A *"slight, medium-sized professional-looking man of about thirty-five"* (1:695), Higgins is summoned by Nat Bartlett to inspect Captain Isaiah Bartlett's eccentric ways and pronounce him insane. After inspecting the captain's quarters, which are decorated exactly as a captain's cabin on a ship, and hearing the story of the captain's "dream" of pirate treasure, Higgins is convinced that the man is, in fact, deranged. When he returns to the house to collect the captain, he finds him dead of heart failure, and Nat, who has had a shaky hold on reality himself, has gone completely insane.

BIBLIOGRAPHY

Bogard, Travis. *Contour in Time: The Plays of Eugene O'Neill*. Rev. ed. New York: Oxford University Press, 1988.

Boulton, Agnes. *Part of a Long Story: Eugene O'Neill as a Young Man in Love*. Garden City, N.Y.: Doubleday & Company, 1958.

Clark, Barrett H. *Eugene O'Neill: The Man and His Plays*. Rev. ed. New York: Dover, 1947.

Floyd, Virginia. *The Plays of Eugene O'Neill: A New Assessment*. New York: Ungar, 1985.

Sheaffer, Louis. *O'Neill: Son and Playwright*. Boston: Little, Brown, 1968.

Wife for a Life: A Play in One Act, A (completed, 1913; first produced, 1959)

A confluence of tragic, almost sensational events led up to the first play Eugene O'Neill ever wrote, *A Wife for a Life*. First, O'Neill fled his hasty marriage with KATHLEEN JENKINS and his newborn child EUGENE O'NEILL, JR., by sailing to Honduras as a gold prospector in 1909, a miserable experience reflected in this vaudeville skit involving Arizona gold miners. The next year, with no fortune to show, O'Neill moved into a flophouse above JIMMY "THE PRIEST'S" bar on Manhattan's East Side waterfront. O'Neill's roommate at Jimmy's JAMES FINDLATER BYTH, saved his friend's life in 1912 when O'Neill attempted suicide at their room above the bar; Byth committed suicide himself on June 6, 1913. The disturbing news of Byth's death (they had known each other since 1907) undoubtedly sparked the idea for O'Neill's first play, though his high regard for Byth and the tragedy of his suicide provided much material for his plays throughout his career, most resonantly in his barroom masterpiece *The* ICEMAN COMETH. Arthur and Barbara Gelb and Travis Bogard attribute O'Neill's experience touring on the vaudeville circuit with his father in early 1912 as an inspiration as well (Gelb 395, Bogard 9).

A Wife for a Life was never produced in O'Neill's lifetime (though JAMES O'NEILL agreed to appear as the Older Man if it ever got to the production stage) and was not published until 1950 in the unauthorized *Lost Plays of Eugene O'Neill* or produced until October 27, 1959, at the Key Theatre in New York City.

SYNOPSIS

A night on *"the edge of the Arizona desert"* (1:3) with a *"black and sinister"* butte thrown into relief in the background by the sparkling night sky. A character identified only as the Older Man sits by a campfire awaiting the return of his mining partner, Jack (John Sloan), who is away assessing their claim. A fellow miner named Old Pete enters the campsite and delivers an unsigned telegram from New York meant for Jack—it simply reads, "I am waiting. Come" (1:4). The first correspondence Jack received in their five years as partners, from "South Africa to Alaska," the puzzling note saddens the Older Man: "He's about all I got now and I'd hate to see him leave just when we've struck it rich" (1:4). Five years before, Jack had saved the Older Man's life in the Transvaal—a region in northern South Africa where gold was discovered in 1886, a discovery that fueled the Boer War (1899–1902)—

by rescuing him from drowning in an African river. Ever since, the Older Man stood steadfastly loyal to his partner and savior.

Jack, a younger man in his early 30s, returns to the camp exalted. Their claim has struck more gold than either miner had ever encountered—"five dollars a pan"—and he remarks that one of them will have to head east to manage the profits. The Older Man scoffs at the idea of living a respectable existence in the "effete East" (1:6), submitting that he "never could get along with civilization and (*laughing*) civilization never cared much for me" (1:5). Inquiring what the draw to head east is for Jack, the Older Man teases out some disturbing news. Jack innocently confesses that there is an "angel" awaiting his return to New York, to which the Older Man imparts a misogynist piece of miner wisdom (one that O'Neill demonstrably shared): "They're all angels—at first. The only trouble is their angelic attributes lack staying qualities" (1:6). She had been married years before, Jack continues, to an alcoholic mining engineer who treated her cruelly, and perhaps fortuitously for her rarely spent time at home. Two facts convince the Older Man that Jack's angel is, in fact, his own wife: Jack wants to name their claim "Yvette," the Older Man's wife's first name, and Jack informs him that their romance began in a mining town called San Sebastien, near the Ecuadorian border of Peru, where the Older Man left her five years before. Jack describes Yvette, the daughter of French peasants, as "a lily growing in a field of rank weeds" (1:7), a description that recalls fellow naturalist Stephen Crane's portrayal of his Bowery heroine Maggie Johnson in *Maggie: A Girl of the Streets* (1893) as having "blossomed in a mud puddle" (24).

But when Jack confessed his love to her, she replied, "'I know you love me and I—I love you; but you must go away and we must never see each other again. I am his wife and I must keep my pledge'" (1:7). Yvette loathed her husband throughout their marriage, yet her sense of spousal duty compelled her to stall until she could legally consider him deceased, at which point—the day of the play's action—she promised to send for Jack. This astonishes the Older Man, who jumps to his feet, accuses Jack of lying and nearly draws his pistol. But he subdues his anger and blames his outburst on nerves. He is now deeply conflicted as to whether to hand over the telegram from Yvette, hide the truth and keep his partner by his side, or shoot him dead for revenge. On the one hand, along with being the only true friend he has, Jack risked his own life to save his. On the other, he had sworn vengeance on the young man who robbed his wife's affections—for in his own way, the Older Man truly loved Yvette. In the end, he decides to favor his male companion over his estranged wife, and he gives Jack the telegram. In the final scene, the Older Man exposits in a scene of burdensome asides: "So I have found him after all these years and I cannot even hate him. What tricks Fate plays with us . . . the only two beings I have ever loved. And I—must keep wandering on. I cannot be the ghost at their feast" (1:10). Upon Jack's departure, the Older Man, "(. . . *smiling with a whimsical sadness softly quotes.:*) Greater love hath no man than this that he giveth his wife for his friend" (1:11).

COMMENTARY

A *Wife for a Life* is an "ironic fable" of the O. Henry variety (Bogard 13). O'Neill's title implies an exchange, and the audience must decide whether the "life" in question is relinquished or retrieved, Jack's or the Older Man's. Given that the play is meant for a vaudeville audience, it is fair to assume that O'Neill meant the exchange to signify the Older Man repaying his debt to Jack by handing over his wife without a struggle; however, given O'Neill's own abandonment of Jenkins and his son, it is equally fair to assume that the Older Man's misogyny suggests that he might be gaining a life in the bargain. The Older Man paraphrases Christ's commandment in John—"Greater love hath no man than this, that a man lay down his life for his friends" (15:12–13)—another version of which Jamie Tyrone (James "Jamie" O'Neill, Jr.) in LONG DAY'S JOURNEY INTO NIGHT recites when pronouncing his love for his brother Edmund (Eugene): "Greater love hath no man than this that he saveth his brother from himself" (3:821).

O'Neill never considered the vaudeville skit as a part of his repertoire. In a letter to Mark Van Doren pertaining to his one-act play The WEB, he wrote, "To be scrupulously exact, for the record, 'The Web' is *not* the first thing I wrote *for the stage*. I had some time before dashed off in one night a ten minute Vaudeville skit, afterwards destroyed. But this was not a play. In fact, my friends in Vaudeville crudely asserted it was not a Vaudeville skit, either! It was nothing. And 'The Web' *is* the first *play* I ever wrote" (quoted in Floyd 21n). Regardless of O'Neill's justifiable dismissal of the play as "nothing," it is true, as Travis Bogard has argued, that "the sketch contains many of the elements which O'Neill was later to infuse with theatrical power" (9): the use of background setting to create a psychological mise-en-scène; the love/hate relationship between the Older Man and Jack; the use of soliloquy to exposit characterization and a sense of personal history; and, quite incredibly, his narrowing the focus of the final scene onto a lit circle—the campfire—which closely resembles the halo of light surrounding Mary Tyrone in the final scene of his late masterpiece, *Long Day's Journey Into Night* (Bogard 11–14).

CHARACTERS

Jack, the Younger Man (John Sloan) In contrast to his withered mining partner the Older Man, Jack is in his early 30s and is in love with the Older Man's wife, Yvette. Neither man knows they love the same woman, though they worked and traveled together for five years, until the play's action. The Older Man discovers the truth, but he decides to let Jack form a relationship with his wife out of loyalty and love for his partner. Jack's poetic speech, his dreams of adventures abroad, and his fortune-hunting sensibility, all look forward to O'Neill's self-portraits in FOG, BEYOND THE HORIZON, AH, WILDERNESS!, and *Long Day's Journey into Night*, among others, though Jack is far less-developed and too materialistic to make any direct connections.

Older Man, The The Older Man, for five years the mining partner of Jack, the Younger Man, is a middle-aged miner weary from years of toil mining in South Africa, South America, and the American West. Though his garments suggest the unkempt "*wear and tear*" of a typical miner's costume, his temperament reflects that of O'Neill's recently deceased companion, James Findlater Byth, who had served as a war correspondent in the Boer War in 1911: *"Withal his air and speech are those of an educated man whose native refinement has clung to him in spite of many hard knocks"* (1:3). Before they partnered up, Jack had conducted an affair with the Older Man's wife, though the Older Man was unaware of this and had sworn revenge on the man, John Sloan (Jack), who had cuckolded him. The Older Man's love for Jack moves him to allow his wife to legally consider him dead so she can pursue a relationship with Jack.

Old Pete   Character in the play *A Wife for a Life.* Old Pete, an unsuccessful miner who drinks what little he earns, enters the Older Man's campsite and passes on a telegram, which is addressed to Jack, the Younger Man.

BIBLIOGRAPHY

Bogard, Travis. *Contour in Time: The Plays of Eugene O'Neill.* Rev. ed. New York: Oxford University Press, 1988.

Crane, Stephen. *Maggie: A Girl of the Streets.* In *Crane: Prose and Poetry.* Edited by J. C. Levenson. New York: Library of America, 1984, 5–78.

Floyd, Virginia. *The Plays of Eugene O'Neill: A New Assessment.* New York: Ungar, 1985.

Gelb, Arthur, and Barbara Gelb. *O'Neill: Life with Monte Cristo.* New York: Applause Books, 2000.

PART III

Related People, Places, and Topics

A

Abbey Theatre   In 1926, Eugene O'Neill recalled seeing Ireland's Abbey Theatre in New York during its first United States tour in 1911, witnessing how vastly different the Abbey was from the commercial, melodramatic theater of his father, the actor JAMES O'NEILL: "[The Abbey] first opened my eyes to the existence of a real theater, as opposed to the unreal—and to me then—hateful theater of my father, in whose atmosphere I had been brought up" (quoted in Shaughnessey 36). This is an astonishing revelation in regard to O'Neill's development as a dramatist since in 1911 he was in the throes of his self-destructive behavior and still years away from contemplating a playwriting career.

The Abbey Theatre was opened in December 1904 in Dublin, Ireland, by the Irish National Theatre Society, which became the National Theatre Society, Limited, in 1905. The theater's founding directors were playwrights William Butler Yeats, Lady Augusta Gregory, and JOHN MILLINGTON SYNGE. With Yeats as the driving force, the company was dedicated to reimaging Ireland, which was entirely a British colony until 1922, through noncommercial, nonpopular, independent theater. Popular theater in 19th-century Ireland primarily imitated British MELODRAMA, and it often portrayed the Irish stereotypically as colonized comic buffoons. The Abbey, simply stated, worked to undermine the popular theater's images that debased Ireland and, in its place, critically portray an ideal of Ireland or Ireland's true realities as defined by its playwrights. Yeats, who would receive the NOBEL PRIZE IN LIT-

ERATURE in 1924, believed he could use the Abbey Theatre to transform Ireland into a perceived great culture, as Shakespeare had done for Britain with the Globe Theatre. Consequently, the early Abbey was a theater focused on promoting ideas, directly opposing the commercial theater, which strove to only dazzle and entertain. As a result, the Abbey was not an actors' theater that promoted star actors; instead, it was a playwrights' theater.

To support a playwrights' theater, the early Abbey fostered its own acting style, one that was restrained in movement, which enhanced the playwright's words and did not upstage them and the ideas they portrayed. O'Neill viewed the Abbey style to be very lifelike, and it became his "standard of the art" (Black 116). O'Neill noted of the 1911 Abbey players, "As a boy I saw so much of the old, ranting, artificial, romantic stage stuff that I always had a sort of contempt for the theater. It was seeing the Irish players for the first time that gave me a glimpse of my opportunity" (quoted in Sheaffer 205). He was able to see his opportunity as a dramatist through an acting style such as the Abbey's and through plays like those the Abbey brought to America in 1911.

The Abbey Theatre's 1911 appearance in New York exposed O'Neill to its important playwrights—Synge, Yeats, Gregory, Lennox Robinson, T. C. Murray; even GEORGE BERNARD SHAW was represented during the 1911 tour. The plays the Abbey performed in New York focused on everyday people, regardless of CLASS, which would have appealed to O'Neill, who had hated the heroic counts, such as his father's *Count of Monte Cristo*. Murray's play *Birthright*, for example, with its rural family characters must have spoken directly to O'Neill of his own family experiences as Murray portrays two brothers, "each of whom is favored by one of the parents" (Shaughnessy 35). Yet it is Synge who specifically has the most significant presence of the Abbey dramatists throughout O'Neill's plays, from O'Neill's earliest to his late great masterworks. Synge's plays of the 1911 tour gave O'Neill precedents for plays peopled with boasters and dreamers and plays set with the sea and in barroom settings.

Of course, O'Neill was not the only American moved by the Abbey Theatre's 1911 tour. SUSAN GLASPELL and her husband GEORGE CRAM "JIG" COOK were prominent organizers of the PROVINCETOWN PLAYERS, the first group to produce an O'Neill play (in 1916). She recalled: "Quite possibly there would have been no Provincetown Players had there not been Irish Players. What [Jig] saw done for Irish life he wanted for American life—no stage conventions in the way of projecting with the humility of true feeling" (quoted in Harrington 42). Likewise, one can say that without the Abbey Theatre's 1911 tour, Eugene O'Neill might never have turned to playwriting, and as the early Abbey Theatre moved Ireland away from melodrama, O'Neill's plays did the same for America, portraying an American identity of immigrants seeking and dreaming of fitting in.

Being a theater from Ireland, the Abbey in 1911 perhaps initially attracted O'Neill by fermenting conscious thought of his IRISH heritage outside the anti-Irish prejudice so often encountered during his childhood summers in NEW LONDON, CONNECTICUT. The Abbey may also have instilled in O'Neill an early pride in that heritage, divorced from the problems of his childhood. Such cultural attractions helped lead him to the ideas and possibilities instilled in him by a serious and noncommercial theater. While the Abbey helped nudge the young O'Neill toward playwriting, it also provided an older O'Neill with a "great" sense of pleasure when Yeats, still an Abbey director, wrote to him during the 1930s for permission to stage his play DAYS WITHOUT END (Black 387). In fact, the Abbey Theatre's April 1934 production of *Days*

Without End may well have been the only successful contemporary staging of the play. While O'Neill is undoubtedly an American playwright, he also owes something to the Irish playwriting tradition in the plays put on by the early Abbey Theatre, heightening awareness of his Irish heritage.

Bibliography

Black, Stephen A. *Eugene O'Neill: Beyond Mourning and Tragedy.* New Haven, Conn.: Yale University Press, 1999.

Harrington, John P. "The Abbey in America: The Real Thing." In *Irish Theatre on Tour,* edited by Nicholas Grene and Christopher Morash, 35–50. Dublin: Carysfort Press, 2005.

Shaughnessy, Edward. *Eugene O'Neill in Ireland: The Critical Response.* Westport, Conn.: Greenwood Press, 1988.

Sheaffer, Louis. *O'Neill: Son and Playwright.* New York: Cooper Square Press, 2002.

Nelson O'Ceallaigh Ritschel

African Americans   In the African-American protagonist's image and cause, Eugene O'Neill found a dramatic basis for a universal concern. What he described was the traumatic emergence of a race from the indignity of social inequality toward a nobler degree of human self-esteem. Between 1914 and 1924, O'Neill wrote five "Negro plays," of varying complexity and success.

It is well known that O'Neill's nascent playwriting—the SS GLENCAIRN plays—began with his inspiration from the SEA. But it should be noted that those plays also manifest his interest in the African-American sensibility in both mythic and urban terms. His early play THIRST (1914)—which was published in his first collection of plays, *"THIRST" AND OTHER ONE-ACT PLAYS*—opens with three shipwrecked persons on a raft trying to ensure their individual chances of survival. The Gentleman is a smug and well-to-do white man, the Dancer is a white woman of loose morals, and the Sailor is a mulatto black man; in the original production, the Sailor was played by O'Neill himself. The Gentleman and the Dancer believe the sailor to be in possession of water, they seek to acquire it, they compromise their own positions and priorities and fail to overcome their distrust of the black man. Finally, all three end up in the dark SEA as food for the hungry sharks that have been circling them, achieving equality and peace only in death.

In *The MOON OF THE CARIBBEES* (1918) O'Neill attempts to "achieve a higher plane of bigger, finer values," as he wrote to Barrett Clark in a letter (Clark 83). The sea is the hero responding to the world of humanity with sadness or laughter. But at the basis of the life that is portrayed in the play, there prevails a primordial Negro keening that persists throughout the play like a voice of conscience and ancient sorrow. On the surface of things, this cry is sublimated by the gaiety of alcohol and sex solicited by the Negresses who are welcomed by the sailors for their evening pleasure. But the play begins and ends with the Negro voice from the horizon, interrupted in between by the singular shriek of a knifed sailor. The atmosphere projects with compelling emphasis O'Neill's idea of the "impelling forces behind life" (Clark 83) that he always wanted to portray symbolically on the stage and would do so in the course of his career as a playwright.

O'Neill was part of a group of white playwrights in the early decades of the 20th century who foresaw the dynamic and immediate potential of the indigenous African-American hero in a modern stage setting. Edward Sheldon's *Salvation Nell*, Ridgley Torrence's *Granny Maumee* and *Simon the Cyrenian*, Paul Green's *In Abraham's Bosom*, and O'Neill's own Negro plays—all attained global standards of theatrical excellence. O'Neill also incorporated in his plays the interest in the Negro-primitive subject that Herman Melville (*Moby-Dick*), Joseph Conrad (*Heart of Darkness, Nigger of the Narcissus*), Jack London (*Call of the Wild*), and Mark Twain (*Huckleberry Finn*) pursued in their novels against an ocean/river/frontier setting. But O'Neill's experimentation with the African-American hero brings him close to the frontier of the modern city, the edge of nowhere, inhabited by the alienated or underground man, the hipster who has engaged the attention of other 20th-century white writers such as Norman Mailer ("The White Negro") and Jean-Paul Sartre ("Black Orpheus").

O'Neill's first play with an African-American protagonist was *The DREAMY KID* (1918)—with echoes of Torrance's *Granny Maumee*—which embodied the stereotypical figure of the fugitive black man running from the reach of the law and having finally to face himself. The play served as the basis for his brilliant expressionistic work *The EMPEROR JONES* (1920), portraying another, more flamboyant fugitive, a black despot who believes he can only be killed by a silver bullet and is ironically taken at his own word in his final hour by his own race. *Jones* provided the opportunity to introduce, one after the other, two great African-American actors, CHARLES S. GILPIN and PAUL ROBESON. Both of them contributed significantly to the immortality of O'Neill's Negro play. "Not only the literate American drama but the American drama came of age with the play" (Bogard 134).

O'Neill was very keen to view the African-American individual in the larger perspective of the American historical chronicle that he wished to dramatize in his 11-play cycle, *A TALE OF POSSESSORS SELF-DISPOSSESSED*. To him, the African American's story was particularly interesting not just because it focused on a forced, deterministic transference of a race from another continent to American soil in the evil interests of slavery. It was also identified with the Emersonian quest of self-reliance in a New World that was tragically compelled to resolve its economic and political conflicts through a civil war based on the slavery question in a dialectical paradox. O'Neill conceptualizes his ideas of the passion of the African-American figure in his unpublished play *Bantu Boy* in his WORK DIARY in 1935.

While living in GREENWICH VILLAGE, O'Neill formed a close affinity with the black community as indicated in his Work Diary's initial notes for *ALL GOD'S CHILLUN GOT WINGS*: "Play of Johnny T—base play on his experience as I have seen it intimately" (Floyd 176). Between 1927 and 1934, he worked intermittently on his ideas for *Bantu Boy*. He discussed the plan in his correspondence with Joe Smith, the black gambler he associated with in his HELL HOLE days and a man who was the model for Joe Mott, the gambler in *The ICEMAN COMETH* in 1939. In *Bantu Boy*, O'Neill wished to constitute a "Negro play of the Negro's whole experience in modern times, especially with regard to America" (Floyd 175). The story covers the entire range from the moment of the royal protagonist's enslavement, transportation by ship, conversion to Christianity, and recruitment as a soldier in the Negro regiment during the Civil War; then his subsequent return to his homeland, Africa, to fight in the Zulu War, during which he dies a martyr after prophesying a great freedom for the black people. O'Neill's proposed drama of the African-American hero Bantu Boy corresponds somewhat with that of Alex Haley's *Roots: The Saga of an American Family* (1976), in which Haley finds his hero, Kunta Kinte, while searching for his genealogical origins.

Bibliography

Alexander, Doris. "The Missing Half of Hughie." *Drama Review* (1967) 125.

Bogard, Travis. *Contour in Time: The Plays of Eugene O'Neill.* New York: Oxford University Press, 197.

Bradley, Gerald. "Goodbye Mr. Bones: The Emergence of Negro Themes and Characters in American Drama." *Drama Critique* 2 (September 1964).

Clark, Barrett H. *Eugene O'Neill: The Man and His Plays.* New York: Robert McBride, 1929.

Floyd, Virginia, ed. *Eugene O'Neill at Work: Newly Released Ideas for Plays.* New York: Ungar, 1981.

Isaacs, Edith. *The Negro in American Theatre.* New York: Theatre Arts, 1947.

Lawson, Hilda J. "The Negro in American Drama." Ph.D. diss., University of Illinois. (Microfilm University, 139).

Mailer, Norman. "The White Negro: Superficial Reflections on the Hipster." *Dissent* 3, no. 4 (Summer 1956): 276–293.

Majumdar, Rupendra Guha. *The Paradox of Heroism in Modern American Drama.* Brussels: Peter Lang, 2003, 214–228.

McCombie, J., trans. "Black Orpheus." *The Massachusetts Review* 6 (Autumn 1964).

Mitchell, Loften. *Black Drama: The Story of the American Negro in the Theatre.* New York: Hawthorne, 1967.

Rupendra Majumdar

alcoholism   Use and misuse of alcohol is central to the lives of Eugene O'Neill's characters, from his earliest plays to his last. O'Neill's own alcohol abuse, which continued from his adolescence into his late 30s, contributed to a suicide attempt and a bout with tuberculosis in 1912, while ultimately shaping the language and subjects of many of his dramas. As a young man, O'Neill regularly frequented saloons, where he encountered models for many of his characters, "drinking with them and studying them when drink brought their mental and spiritual guards down," as Harry Kemp stated in a 1930 article on O'Neill (98). Alcoholic characters populated O'Neill's plays from the beginning of his playwriting life and on through his most autobiographical works written near the end.

Among O'Neill's early plays, the PULITZER PRIZE–winning "ANNA CHRISTIE" (1921), set in "Johnny-the-Priest's" saloon, a wharfside bar in New York City, is a fictional amalgam of several such "dives" O'Neill knew in his youth (including JIMMY "THE PRIEST'S" and the aptly named HELL HOLE) and referenced throughout his dramatic works. The title character, a prostitute, arrives at the saloon to meet the father she has not seen since childhood. Observed by Marthy Owen, an old barfly, Anna exhibits spiritual and physical exhaustion. "Gimme a whiskey—ginger ale on the side. And don't be stingy, baby," she demands of the barman (1:968). O'Neill uses liquor in this play and other early works as both an escape and a release from the sufferings and disappointments of life. When Anna's seaman father Chris Christopherson and her prospective lover Mat Burke learn the truth of her profession, they descend into alcoholic stupors before achieving *"resignation and relief"* (1:1,025), and in the end Chris ruminates that life is "Fog, fog, all bloody time. You can't see where you vas going, no. Only dat ole davil, sea—she knows!" (1:1,027). When alcohol is present in O'Neill's other pre-1930s plays, it is the means of escape from emotional pain and undesirable reality, a respite from loss, disillusionment, and the confusions of life.

In O'Neill's only comedy, *AH, WILDERNESS!* (1933), alcoholic escapism is more lightly treated through a gentle mocking of adolescent angst.

Sixteen-year-old Richard Miller, O'Neill's nostalgic reinvention of himself as a teenage radical, is driven to drink by his first romantic disappointment. Picked up by a "swift baby" at the notorious Pleasant Beach House saloon in his small Connecticut hometown in 1906, Richard overindulges in gin rickeys and returns home to shock his stunned parents, spouting lines from HENRIK IBSEN's *Hedda Gabler,* an example of the "scandalous" literature his mother finds secreted in Richard's closet. Presenting Richard's puppy-love heartbreak and resultant abortive bender as a coming-of-age ritual, O'Neill tempers the comedy with sadder ramifications of alcohol abuse as exemplified by Sid Davis, Richard's ne'er-do-well uncle. Sid loses a job and the love of a good woman to compulsive drunkenness, and his wasted life is set in counterpoint to Richard's promising future. Guided by caring parents, Richard swears off alcohol while the disillusionments of the modernist era are still unknown to him, except in the pages of his radical literature.

The genially reminiscent flavor of *Ah, Wilderness!* only hints at the grim portraits of alcoholism in O'Neill's subsequent plays written between 1939 and 1943. For these, the playwright drew on darker memories of his own alcoholism (a periodic alcoholic, he kept this compulsion mostly in check after 1926) and that of those he observed during his dissolute youth. Particularly instructive was the slow alcoholic descent of his older brother, JAMES O'NEILL, JR. (Jamie), a hopeless alcoholic who died in 1923 unable to break free of his addiction. O'Neill dramatized (and forgave) his brother's sad end in his last play, A MOON FOR THE MISBEGOTTEN (1943), in which Jamie Tyrone's alcoholism is the only escape from spiritual emptiness and guilt brought on by his alcoholic behavior. O'Neill found another model in his father, the celebrated 19th-century romantic actor JAMES O'NEILL, a heavy social drinker who prided himself on never performing under the influence. The senior O'Neill, a cultural drinker, considered that his Irish heritage gave him a strong tolerance for alcohol. O'Neill's mother, MARY ELLEN "ELLA" O'NEILL, struggled for much of her adult life with another addiction, morphine, which in its way also contributed to her son's understanding of the deep psychological and physical struggles inherent in any addiction. The family's tragedies continued into another generation as O'Neill's two sons, EUGENE O'NEILL, JR. (alcohol) and SHANE RUDRAIGHE O'NEILL (drugs), both committed suicide (in 1950 and 1977, respectively) as their addictions overwhelmed them. These events occurred after O'Neill's playwriting life ended, and in Shane's case after O'Neill himself had died, although recurrent themes of the sins of the father being visited on sons (intended as a guiding notion of his planned cycle of plays, A TALE OF POSSESSORS SELF-DISPOSSESSED) is inherent in his work.

In *A Moon for the Misbegotten,* as well as LONG DAY'S JOURNEY INTO NIGHT (1939), The ICEMAN COMETH (1939), and HUGHIE (1941), alcohol figures more prominently and more organically than in most of O'Neill's earlier works. The one-act *Hughie,* which features no onstage drinking, shows its effect all too clearly when Erie Smith, the play's central character, returns to his seedy hotel in the aftermath of a week-long bender brought on by the death of his only "pal," a night clerk named Hughie. The other three of these late O'Neill plays delve more deeply into the alcoholic psyche, and O'Neill transforms the metaphor of alcohol in complex ways. For example, most of the characters in *The Iceman Cometh* are habitual drunks in virtual residence at Harry Hope's saloon, where alcohol allows them to retain their diverse individual illusions of a brighter tomorrow. These "pipe dreams," as named by Theodore Hickman, the play's catalytic figure, must be shed so that each individual may face the truth behind the illusion. Yet when stripped of their fantasies of a better life, none are liberated, as Hickey insists they will be, and all sink into a despairing listlessness as an existential abyss opens before them. Alcohol no longer relieves their emotional pain and Hickey comes to realize, as he faces his own harrowing reality, that illusions—"pipe dreams"—are life-giving. Alcohol thus becomes a balm permitting the characters to go on in the face of the hopelessness of existence.

Some scholars suggest that alcoholic imagery in O'Neill's late plays provides a means of depicting the conflicted natures of his characters. The dichotomy between a public mask worn as a defense and one that is deeply hidden expose often contradictory and unconscious feelings and desires more fully in these characters than O'Neill is able to accomplish in his early plays, in which literal masks or spoken asides are obvious means of revealing inner thoughts. In making Freudian distinctions between the public masks adopted by his characters as a defense and the unconscious longings of their hidden inner lives, O'Neill employed literal masks in the classically inspired The GREAT GOD BROWN (1923) and spoken asides in STRANGE INTERLUDE (1928) to reveal these otherwise inexpressible emotions. He addressed the use of masks in a 1932 issue of American Spectator, stressing that "One's outer life passes in solitude haunted by the masks of others; one's inner life passes in a solitude hounded by the masks of oneself." O'Neill abandoned such overt theatrical devices for the sparse realism evident in his last plays, using alcohol to

distinguish the conflicts between the public mask and the private self.

Through alcohol, O'Neill shapes confessional monologues in which the drinker separates truth from delusions even when unaware that such a revelation is taking place. In this regard, alcohol becomes a truth serum in O'Neill's late plays. For example, in Long Day's Journey into Night, Jamie Tyrone insists he can speak truth only when drunk ("'in vino veritas' stuff," as he puts it), while the character's famous actor father sees alcohol merely as a means of escaping his troubles ("a good man's failing," as he puts it) (3:799). Other scholars argue that alcohol reveals merely a superficial change in O'Neill's characters; their underlying personality, or the core truth of their being, remains unaltered by drink. In The Iceman Cometh, the truth behind the "pipe dreams" of the play's multiple characters is revealed when each sobers up (or alcohol has failed to submerge reality), and each retreats back to an alcoholic state in order to recover the "saving lies" that O'Neill insists are the only means of surviving life's disappointments and inevitable losses.

Jason Robards, Jr., as James Tyrone (based on James O'Neill, Jr.), with Bradford Dillman as Edmund (O'Neill) in José Quintero's 1956 production of Long Day's Journey into Night. Photo by Gjon Mili (Courtesy of the Sheaffer-O'Neill Collection, Charles E. Shain Library of Connecticut College)

Bibliography

Black, Stephen A. Eugene O'Neill: Beyond Mourning and Tragedy. New Haven, Conn.: Yale University Press, 1999.

Bloom, Steven F. "Drinking and Drunkenness in The Iceman Cometh: A Response to Mary McCarthy." Eugene O'Neill Review 9, no. 1 (Spring 1985): 3–12.

Dardis, Tom. The Thirsty Muse: Alcohol and the American Writer. New York: Houghton Mifflin, 1991.

Grecco, Stephen R. "High Hopes: Eugene O'Neill and Alcohol." Yale French Studies 50 (1974): 142–149.

Kemp, Harry. "Out of Provincetown: A Memoir of Eugene O'Neill." Theatre Magazine 51 (April 1930): 22–23. Reprinted in Conversations with Eugene O'Neill, edited by Mark W. Estrin, 95–102. Jackson: University Press of Mississippi, 1990.

Leonard, Linda Schierse. Witness to the Fire: Creativity and the Veil of Addiction. Boston: Shambhala, 2001.

O'Neill, Eugene. "Memoranda on Masks." American Spectator (December 1932). Reprinted in O'Neill and His Plays: Four Decades of Criticism, edited by

Oscar Cargill, N. Bryllion Fagin, and William J. Fisher, 116–122. New York: New York University Press, 1961.

Tornqvist, Egil. *Eugene O'Neill: A Playwright's Theatre.* Jefferson, N.C.: McFarland, 2004.

Weegmann, Martin. "Eugene O'Neill's *Hughie* and the Grandiose Addict." *Psychodynamic Practice* 9, no. 1 (February 1, 2002): 21–32.

James Fisher

American theater/American drama   Eugene O'Neill made transformational contributions to the American theater not only in playwriting but also in all aspects of production and presentation—scenic and lighting design, directing, and to some extent acting. By focusing on the thematic and personal issues in the plays, one can overlook the fact that he was a complete man of the theater, the practical theater, and had a wide knowledge and understanding of the craft and the rules of the backstage. His work and creative contributions in all areas of the theater during the first half of the 20th century gave the American theater a stature and presence that made it an international force.

How O'Neill accomplished this transformation, or as Louis Scheaffer, one of O'Neill's major biographers said, how he "helped the American theater come of age" (481) requires a close look at the American theater of the 19th century. In an interview that O'Neill gave in 1946 to Kyle Crichton of *Colliers* magazine during rehearsals of the New York production of The ICEMAN COMETH, he told Crichton, "There's no secret about my father and me. Whatever he wanted I would not touch with a 10 foot pole" (190). Although his father, the famous actor JAMES O'NEILL, had made an enormous success in and significant money from the MELODRAMA *The Count of Monte Cristo,* what James O'Neill had really "wanted" was a more distinguished career performing Shakespeare and other classical plays in order to challenge his talent and burnish his reputation. This was all well within the context and framework of the 19th-century American theater. It was in this theatrical surround, this world, that James O'Neill's success and ambitions were situated, and this was what Eugene O'Neill set himself

against. This was the world that he would not touch with a 10-foot pole.

What was the theatrical world of James O'Neill like? What did James O'Neill encounter as he made his way through the 19th-century theatrical landscape before his son Eugene irrevocably altered that landscape? What did its management, playhouses, actors, and dramatic offerings look like? By 1880, there were approximately 5,000 playhouses supplied by more than 250 companies with actors and stars drawn from no less than 5,000 profession players (Wilson 106). This is a world Eugene O'Neill also knew well because he toured with his father until he was seven years old, and James O'Neill and *The Count of Monte Cristo* missed few of those theaters. Eugene O'Neill subsequently remembered the hotels, which were often part of the depot in those days, and the thrilling sight of the switch engines and the fast freights going through (Crichton 190). He saw his father perform countless times, and when he was older, he went to other plays of the day through "professional courtesies." If one was connected with the theater, he or she could go to any box office, and ask for "courtesies" (Crichton 191). Later in life, O'Neill said that when he went to the theater, he could see all of the machinery of producing a play. "I know everything that every one is doing from the electricians to the stage hands. I was practically brought UP in the wings," he told one interviewer. "Usually a child has regular fixed home," he said, "but you might say I started in as a trouper. . . . I knew only actors and the stage. My mother nursed me in the wings and dressing rooms" (quoted in Gelb 2000, 123).

The theater during the years of James O'Neill's ascendancy was controlled for the most part by commercial syndicates from which only exceptionally popular performers might escape to claim their artistic and financial independence. James O'Neill did manage to break loose from the syndicate, as did William Gillette and Joe Jefferson, who played Rip Van Winkle for 40 years. But even if stars escaped from the syndicates' management, the plays were still melodramatic and plot-heavy. Melodramas of all kinds were on stage, Sherlock Holmes, for example, as well as dozens of farces and sentimental comedies, and romantic costume plays such as *The Count of Monte Cristo, Way Down East, The Foolish Virgin, The Squaw Man* (1905), and *Her Great Match*, are examples of what was being produced. Of course, there was always a Shakespearean play or two on the boards. These productions would be given a Broadway run and then sent out onto the road to play "in every village, hamlet, and town that boasted a playhouse—and most of them did" (Wilson 189).

Playhouses were much as they had been since the 18th century, and in the United States there were thousands of them, and promoters continued to build them rapidly. Traditional features included the picture-frame stage with tiers of boxes and galleries facing it in a horseshoe curve, a lower or orchestra floor, inadequate lobbies, and poorly ventilated dressing rooms (Wilson 188).

Backstage, one could view close up, as O'Neill did, the complex scenic system of the day. In the older downtown theaters there were wings and shutters, painted to give a generic view of woods, a city street, a castle, a mountain, or whatever the play required. Paint rooms either in the theaters themselves or in outside shops provided the painted backdrops, shutters, and wings that gave the play its setting. The wings were pulled on and off by stagehands using ropes and winches, and backdrops were flown from the fly gallery to effect a scenic change. The famous Shakespearean actor Edwin Booth's theater, which sent Booth into bankruptcy, was built in the mid-1800s and had one of the first fly galleries in New York. It was in Booth's theater, under new management after Booth's bankruptcy, where in 1882 James O'Neill opened in *The Count of Monte Cristo* (Matlaw 99). The set included a fully rigged ship, wedding festivities, and the ocean scene where the count makes his escape. Backstage was a bewildering assortment of lights, ropes, riggings, and heavy canvases, and there were traps. Arthur and Barbara Gelb report that O'Neill once told a friend that he knew "more about a trap door than any son of a bitch in the theater" (Gelb 568).

This early immersion in the wings gave O'Neill such an acute sense of what would and would not work backstage that when he began to write, he drew ground plans for his plays—diagrams of the placement of scenic objects on the stage floor. The

Gelbs commented: "The intimate knowledge of stagecraft and actorcraft he acquired from association with his father's companies made him acutely conscious of everything from the proper placing of doors to the timing of costume changes" (Gelb 2000, 568).

These stages and settings provided the performance venue for several styles of acting. There were the remnants of the heroic school; the emotional, overwrought pyrotechnics of Fanny Davenport; the sweet Victorian charms of Maude Adams; and the romantic school that James O'Neill epitomized. Much of the acting was physical, mechanical, and routine. Because of the long runs, which had become the important moneymakers, the acting was centered on technical competence and "external technique" an acting style utilizing an overt, sometimes, florid physicality as compared to an internal emotional approach of the kind that Stanislowski's teaching embodied. There were some attempts at what might be termed "realistic" acting, but these were not the rule nor the preferred style (Wilson 179–180). Actors' voices had to be strong and resonant in these microphone-free playhouses. O'Neill said that his father was "a strong, cello-voiced man who quoted Shakespeare like a deacon quotes the Bible" (quoted in Crichton 190).

There were no directors, as we understand that position today, one that requires artistic oversight, conceptual creation, communication with the actors, and some understanding of a script's physical production. Rehearsals were not the ensemble-based sessions that are now standard preparation technique. In James O'Neill's time, the star of the piece would not give anything like the performance he or she was to perform in front of an audience. Usually a performer would strike a pose and declaim the speech. How they moved or gestured was up to them, and the audience came expecting not an ensemble piece but a star's turn. Eugene O'Neill remembered his father's performance as he watched him from the wings ripping the sack in which he had been thrown into a canvas ocean: "I can still see my father dripping with salt and sawdust, climbing on a stool behind the swinging profile of dashing waves. It was then that the calcium light in the gallery played on his long beard and tattered clothes, as with arms outstretched he declared that the world was his" (quoted in Woolf 117). A James O'Neill's specialty in *The Count of Monte Cristo* was his descent down a wide staircase during the Grand Fete. George Tyler, James's manager, spoke admiringly of "the royal grace with which James O'Neill could walk down a staircase" (Matlaw 99). The female critic for the *Chicago Daily News* loved James's performances: "He could make love better than any man of his time and his airy grace, manliness and lovely voice ... made him unique" (quoted in Matlaw 104).

Eugene did not see his father's performance in such a positive light: "My early experience with the theater through my father really made me revolt against it. As a boy I saw so much of the old, ranting, artificial, romantic stage stuff that I always had a sort of contempt for the theater" (quoted in Merrill 39). This contempt might have been deepened by firsthand experience. Eugene acted for a brief period in early spring, 1912, with his father on a final tour on the Orpheum circuit in a tabloid version of *The Count of Monte Cristo*, as he recalled in an interview: "He [James O'Neill] offered me one of the smaller parts and for a season we traveled all over the country, appearing twice a day, between a trained-horse act and a group of flying acrobats" (quoted in Woolf 118). At another time, he explained: "I had known the theater pretty intimately, because of my father's connection with it. But, with me, to know it had not been to love it! I had always been repelled by its artificiality, its slavish clinging to old traditions. Yet, when I began to write, it was for the theater. And my knowledge of it helped me, because I knew what I wanted to avoid doing" (quoted in Mullett 32).

One of the things O'Neill wanted to avoid was the formulaic arrangement in which an author would build up a thesis for two or three acts and then in the last act proceed to knock over what he had constructed. The syndicate managers felt they knew what the public would accept, and the plays had to conform to those ideas (Woolf 120). Even a well-regarded play like William Vaughn Moody's *The Great Divide* ultimately failed, O'Neill believed, by following that formula. "It was an artificial age," he said, "an age ashamed of its own feelings, and the theater reflected its thoughts. Virtue always triumphed and vice always got its just deserts. It accepted nothing half-way; a man was either a hero or a villain, and a woman was either virtuous or vile" (quoted in Woolf 117).

This formula was what O'Neill sought to change in his plays: "If a person is to get at the meaning of life he must learn to like the facts about himself—ugly as they may seem to his sentimental vanity—before he can lay hold of the truth behind the facts; and the truth is never ugly. Why not give the public a chance to see how the other fellow lives? Give it an insight into the underdog's existence, a momentary glimpse of his burdens, his sufferings, and his handicaps" (quoted in Gelb 272).

Thus, O'Neill's insight into how a theater might be able to reveal a wholly different world occurred when he saw two performances that opened his eyes to the possibility of another kind of theater. HENRIK IBSEN's *Hedda Gabler* came to New York in 1907, with the great Moscow Art Theatre actress Alla Nazimova playing Hedda Gabler. He saw that production 10 times and said later that the "experience discovered an entire new world of the drama for me. It gave me my first conception of a modern theater where truth might live" (quoted in Gelb 2000, 226). Three and a half years later, O'Neill attended all of the plays brought to New York City by the ABBEY THEATRE, beginning with the opening at the Maxine Elliott Theatre on November 20, 1911. "It was seeing the Irish Players that gave me a glimpse of my opportunity. I went to see everything they did. I thought then ... that they demonstrated the possibilities of naturalistic acting better than any other company" (quoted in Gelb 172).

Other influences were at work to create change in O'Neill. He read AUGUST STRINDBERG and Anton Chekhov, and there were social and artistic shifts in American culture. There was talk of "the new woman," "the new psychology," and the "new art" introduced by the Armory Show, an exhibit of Modernist European painting that attracted a great deal of attention in the press. But the Abbey

The budding playwright Eugene O'Neill at his desk, circa 1914 *(Courtesy of the Sheaffer-O'Neill Collection, Charles E. Shain Library of Connnecticut College)*

and Nazimova performances left a deep impression on him. Ibsen's and JOHN MILLINGTON SYNGE's truthfulness in playwriting, the creation of a new seriousness and style in acting, and the depth of performance that could be reached in a repertory system, as demonstrated by the Moscow Art Theatre and the Abbey Players, gave him an insight into another kind of performance, another kind of theatrical system, free of the dictates of management and box office that produced shallow and untruthful plays with artificial scenery.

It is the stuff of O'Neill legend that by the time he got to Provincetown, Massachusetts, he had written several plays that were strong enough to be staged, and just five years after he had seen the Abbey Players in New York, almost to the day, his play BOUND EAST FOR CARDIFF was produced by the PROVINCETOWN PLAYERS. He had found his artistic

life, but just as important, he had been given the opportunity to create a theater, different from the commercial mainstream theater, that could produce plays in significantly different ways—where the scenery and style of playing and the managerial business could be organized so as to enhance the play itself, and where the play is put in its rightful setting rather then surrounding it with false backdrops and bombastic acting.

Because of his background in the old production style, he understood that

> The hope of developing a real spirituality, a real understanding and co-operation between all concerned in the production of plays in this country lies in the development of a repertoire theater where actors may be assured of experience and permanency. If actors are to work for a play in the same spirit that animated the Moscow Art Players, where the same player will give the biggest or the least part the same amount of study and enthusiasm, they must be retained throughout the year; they must feel that they are a part of the whole group. The Provincetown group was organized with that idea in mind. (quoted in Sweeney 59)

O'Neill also stated: "Amusement is important. Do not underestimate it, but culture is also significant. I believe the theater as a cultural influence dates from the WASHINGTON SQUARE PLAYERS in 1914 and the Provincetown Players in 1916. These groups helped make it possible to present serious drama" (quoted in Neuberger 154).

After the Provincetown Players dissolved, and a new TRIUMVIRATE was formed in 1923, consisting of O'Neill, KENNETH MACGOWAN, and the designer ROBERT EDMOND JONES, O'Neill wrote to Macgowan: "All I ask is that we be able to work together. . . . And all I ask in addition is new actors, new directors, and a new theater . . ." to start clean, clear of old people and old conditions, and do our stuff. In fact, I don't believe in much of anything in the theater but this dream. It is this theater I'm writing for" (O'Neill 133).

One example of the kind of working and aesthetic process that O'Neill set in motion with the Triumvirate is exemplified in DESIRE UNDER THE ELMS. *Desire* was produced in 1924 at the GREENWICH VILLAGE Theatre, and O'Neill took care in all aspects to create the kind of physical production that would give life to his play. As previously noted, O'Neill made ground plans for all of his plays as he was writing them. In the case of *Desire under the Elms*, he also made a sketch of the house in which the action is set and included in the sketch the elms which he wanted to hang over the house to give it its melancholy aura. Such a sketch may not look radical to modern eyes, but given the system of wings and drops still in force in the uptown theaters, and around the country, this was a unique set. For the play to work, the scenes of tension and distress between the three principals, Abbie, Eben, and Ephraim, must be lived out in the rooms of that confining house. Infanticide, adultery, and sexual desire are made both more understandable and more intense in that kind of restrictive environment. Robert Edmond Jones directed (the director was now becoming a force in the American theater) and also designed the set where the upstairs bedroom wall separating Eben and Abbie seems to tremble from their lust.

In his early working notes, O'Neill wrote, "the front wall of each of the four rooms must be in a separate removable section so that the interior may be shown separately or in any desired combination" (quoted in Wainscott 164). The set that Jones designed accomplished that direction. The house provided such a strong dramatic statement that it became known as "Bobby's house," but he had worked off O'Neill sketch, and O'Neill was always uncomfortable that Jones had all of the accolades for the design. The critics praised the "extreme ingenuity" of the shifting device of the moveable walls, and they also praised the naturalistic fabric of the dialogue achieved with a "rare skill and beauty" (in Wainscott 166). O'Neill always took a great interest in the casting of his plays, but he was never fully happy with most of the performances. In *Desire*, however, Walter Huston, who was cast as Ephraim, gave one of the few performances in his plays that O'Neill admired (Mullett 32).

Thus, in this one play, we see O'Neill challenging the designers and actors, helping to create the role of director with Robert Edmond Jones, and writing a play that did not have a happy ending—

that did not, as O'Neill said, "knock over" in the last act what had been constructed in the first; a play that was not driven by plot but by character, and one that dared to be a tragic drama not a melodrama. All of this was accomplished because he understood that his plays needed to have a new kind of production ethic and mechanism in order to be fully realized (O'Neill 37). O'Neill wrote to Macgowan that he wanted this new theater to be "mysterious, daring, beautiful and amusing . . . done by actors, authors, designers—that the purpose of this theatre is to give imagination and talent a new chance for such development . . . that they can't see anywhere else. . . . It seems to me this is the one and only reason for this theatre" (O'Neill 45). In short, it seems touchingly clear that O'Neill's great imagination saw a new kind of theater devoted to an entirely different kind of production aesthetic, and this was the theater he not only wrote for but helped to create.

In his later years, O'Neill had a more jaded sensibility. He could still see the mechanics of production, but he always went to rehearsals of his plays, and one of the most touching remembrances of O'Neill is by Theresa Helburn, a founder of the THEATRE GUILD, who wrote in 1936:

> . . . he sits quiet and impassive in the front row, hour after hour, and to every question from actor or director he responds without a second's hesitation and with complete assurance. Here is one playwright who has spent so much time on the preparation of his script, has built his structure so carefully from its foundation, that he knows the right position of every brick from every angle. . . . People have called O'Neill stubborn in rehearsal but it is the stubbornness of inner conviction, a most valuable quality in a medium so easily the prey of contrived effects and emotional tricks as the theatre. And it is a not impractical conviction; it is founded on long experience and an expert sense of "theatre"—the rightful heritage perhaps of an actor's son. (Helburn 149)

Because O'Neill understood the stage, he was able to create a production context, first in the Provincetown Players and then in the reformed theater Triumvirate. Malcolm Cowley wrote in 1936: "He developed a new technique for each of his plays. O'Neill of all the thousands who write for our stage, is the only one who belongs not to his country alone, but to the world" (Cowley 80). O'Neill not only transformed American drama; he helped to lead changes in the world theater, earning an international reputation well before his late great plays were to be written.

Bibliography

Cowley, Malcolm. "Eugene O'Neill: Writer of Synthetic Drama." In *Conversations with Eugene O'Neill,* edited by Mark W. Estrin, 75–80. Jackson and London: University Press of Mississippi, 1990.

Crichton, Kyle. "Mr. O'Neill and the Iceman." In *Conversations with Eugene O'Neill,* edited by Mark W. Estrin, 188–202. Jackson and London: University Press of Mississippi, 1990.

Gelb, Arthur, and Barbara Gelb. *O'Neill.* New York: Harper, 1974.

———. *O'Neill: Life with Monte Cristo.* New York: Applause Books, 2000.

Helburn, Theresa. "O'Neill: An Impression." In *Conversations with Eugene O'Neill,* edited by Mark W. Estrin, 148–151. Jackson and London: University Press of Mississippi, 1990.

Matlaw, Myron. "James O'Neill's Launching of *Monte Cristo.*" In *When They Weren't Doing Shakespeare,* edited by Judith L. Fisher and Stephen Watt, 88–105. Athens: University of Georgia Press, 1989.

Merrill, Flora. "Fierce Oaths and Blushing Complexes Find No Place in Eugene O'Neill's Talk." In *Conversations with Eugene O'Neill,* edited by Mark W. Estrin, 70–74. Jackson and London: University Press of Mississippi, 1990.

Mullett, Mary B. "The Extraordinary Story of Eugene O'Neill." In *Conversations with Eugene O'Neill,* edited by Mark W. Estrin, 26–37. Jackson and London: University Press of Mississippi, 1990.

Neuberger, Richard L. "O'Neill Turns West to New Horizons." In *Conversations with Eugene O'Neill,* edited by Mark W. Estrin, 152–157. Jackson and London: University Press of Mississippi, 1990.

O'Neill, Eugene. "To Kenneth Macgowan." (Letters, summer 1923 and September 1923). In *The Theatre We Worked For,* edited by Jackson R. Bryer, 37, 45. New Haven, Conn.: Yale University Press, 1982.

Sheaffer, Louis. *O'Neill: Son and Playwright.* New York: Paragon, 1968.

Sweeney, Charles P. "Back to the Source of Plays." In *Conversations with Eugene O'Neill,* edited by Mark W. Estrin, 56–59. Jackson and London: University Press of Mississippi, 1990.

Wainscott, Ronald, H. *Staging O'Neill: The Experimental Years, 1920–1934.* New Haven, Conn.: Yale University Press, 1988.

Wilson, Garff, B. *A History of American Acting.* Bloomington: Indiana University Press, 1966.

Woolf, S. J. "Eugene O'Neill Returns after Twelve Years." In *Conversations with Eugene O'Neill,* edited by Mark W. Estrin, 167–173. Jackson and London: University Press of Mississippi, 1990.

Linda L. Herr

anarchism The word *anarchy* comes from the ancient Greek word *anarchos* and means "without a ruler." While rulers, quite understandably, claim that the end of rule will inevitably lead to chaos and turmoil, anarchists maintain that rule is unnecessary for the preservation of order. Rather than a descent into British philosopher Thomas Hobbes's doomsday warning of a war of all against all, a society without government suggests to anarchists the very possibility for creative and peaceful human relations. The French political philosopher Pierre-Joseph Proudhon (1809–65), the first to positively identify his theory as that of anarchism, neatly summed up the anarchist position in his famous slogan: "Anarchy is Order."

For anarchists, the regulatory and supervisory mechanisms of the state are especially suited to producing docile and dependent subjects. Through institutions such as courts and prisons, but also social work, authorities extend the practices of ruling from control over bodies to influence over minds. Moral regulation provides a subtle means for nurturing repression and conformity. It results in relations of dependence rather than self-determination as the external practices of the state increasingly come to be viewed as the only legitimate mechanisms for solving disputes or addressing social needs. For anarchists, the "rule of law" administered through institutions of the state is not the guarantor of freedom but, rather, freedom's enemy, closing off alternative avenues for human interaction, creativity, and community while corralling more and more people within its own bounds.

A distinction is sometimes drawn between "individualist," or "philosophical," anarchism, with its emphasis on individual liberty and personal transformation, and "communist" anarchism, with its emphasis on equality and collective mobilization for broad social change. PHILOSOPHICAL ANARCHISM places greater emphasis on individual freedom to act unfettered by the constraints of social mores and norms. Philosophical anarchism also differs from social anarchism in its distrust of social organization, including the mass organizing for radical or revolutionary social change preferred by socialists and social anarchists.

Perhaps the founding document of philosophical anarchism is *The Ego and Its Own: The Case of the Individual Against Authority* (1844) by Max Stirner (Johan Caspar Schmidt, 1806–56), a colleague and critic of Karl Marx. Stirner, whose nom de plume means "Max the Highbrow," studied under G. W. F. Hegel at Berlin University, becoming one of *Die Freien* (the Free Ones), the so-called Young Hegelians who sought to make Hegel's philosophical works suitable for the real world of politics.

So seriously did Marx view Stirner's philosophy of radical individual liberty that he devoted a full two-thirds of his bulky text *The German Ideology* (1845) to a condemnation of Stirner. For Marx, Stirner failed to grasp the significance of socioeconomic justice in the free development of the individual. This criticism would later be raised against philosophical anarchists by social anarchists and socialists alike.

Philosophical anarchists understand anarchism not as a revolutionary establishment of something new, a leap into the unknown, or as a break with the present; rather, they regard it as the realization of antiauthoritarian practices of mutual aid and solidarity that are already present in society but which have been overshadowed by state authority. Anarchism is the extension of spheres of freedom until they make up the majority of social life. Starting from this perspective, contemporary anarchists seek to develop nonauthoritarian and nonhierarchical relations in the here and now of everyday life.

While Eugene O'Neill initially showed some sympathy for social anarchist movements and looked favorably on the writings of prominent social anarchist EMMA GOLDMAN, his primary personal commitment was to philosophical anarchism, which remained the greatest ideological influence on his thinking. Perhaps the strongest direct influence on O'Neill's anarchist perspective was BENJAMIN R. TUCKER, the editor of the important anarchist journal *Liberty*. Tucker was himself influenced by Stirner, being the first to publish an English-language version of Stirner's work. O'Neill was introduced to Tucker as an 18-year-old and spent much time at Tucker's Unique Book Shop in New York City.

O'Neill was persuaded to abandon socialism for anarchism by his friends TERRY CARLIN and Hutchins Hapgood. O'Neill studied at the Ferrer Center in

Benjamin R. Tucker *(Courtesy of the Sheaffer-O'Neill Collection, Charles E. Shain Library of Connecticut College)*

New York City, an alternative school organized and frequented by numerous anarchists, in 1915. That year he also served an apprenticeship at the anarchist magazine *Revolt* published by HIPPOLYTE HAVEL.

Opponents of anarchism typically respond to it by claiming that it rests upon a naive view of "human nature." The best response to such criticisms is simply to point to the diversity of anarchist views on the question of human nature. There is little commonality between Stirner's self-interested "egoist" and Peter Kropotkin's altruistic upholder of mutual aid. Indeed, the diversity of anarchist views regarding "the individual" and its relation to "the community" may be upheld as testimony to the creativity and respect for pluralism that have sustained anarchism against enormous odds. Anarchists simply stress the capacity of humans to change themselves and the conditions in which they find themselves. Social relations, freely entered and based on tolerance, mutual aid, and sympathy, are expected to discourage the emergence of disputes and aid resolution where they do occur. There are no guarantees for anarchists, and the emphasis is always on potential.

Bibliography

Alexander, Doris. *Eugene O'Neill's Last Plays: Separating Art from Autobiography*. Athens: University of Georgia Press, 2005.

Diggins, John Patrick. *Eugene O'Neill's America: Desire under Democracy*. Chicago: University of Chicago Press, 2007.

Dowling, Robert M. "On Eugene O'Neill's 'Philosophical Anarchism." *Eugene O'Neill Review* 29 (Spring 2007): 50–72.

Marshall, Peter. *Demanding the Impossible: A History of Anarchism*. London: Fontana, 1993.

J. Shantz

Ashe, Beatrice Frances (1894–1974)   Letters (scores of them), poems, and pictures sent by Eugene O'Neill to "Bea" Ashe and housed in the New York Public Library's Berg Collection, as well as Louis Sheaffer's interviews and correspondence with the latter (much of it included in *O'Neill: Son and Playwright*) furnish what is known of the O'Neill-Ashe romance, which began in early summer 1914,

ignited, and fizzled two years later. While the amiable Miss Ashe was not the first to capture the budding playwright's affections (O'Neill had been married to and divorced from KATHLEEN JENKINS by the time he met Bea, and he had been enamored of Maibelle Scott as well), letters to his "Bumble Bee" indicate that he was besotted. A photo of Bea and O'Neill, taken at Ocean Beach, in the summer of 1914, suggests that, at least in youth, the lady was alluring and willowy—an assumption supported by Maibelle Scott's comment that the young Bea was "breathtaking in a bathing suit" (Gelb 1973, 267).

Born in Norwich, Connecticut, December 2, 1894, Bea was a nubile 19, when the 26-year-old O'Neill espied her, though she was unready for the intense relationship that her suitor was to demand of her. In interviews and correspondence, principally 1959–65, with Louis Sheaffer, Bea Maher, as she was by then, shared reminiscences of her romance with O'Neill—his need for her to commit to him (physically, even if that meant marriage) and her conflicting/incompatible aspiration of pursuing a career in music. At 19 she was the soloist soprano at the Groton Congregational Church, where she was a member. Following after her as she warbled was the smitten future playwright, his devotion further evidenced by his rising, uncharacteristically, at 5 A.M. to join her on morning walks.

When in fall 1914 O'Neill—who had by then proclaimed he would be "a writer or nothing"—left NEW LONDON, CONNECTICUT, to study under GEORGE PIERCE BAKER at Harvard, the romance continued unabated. In letters chronicling his love for her, O'Neill writes of his desire to lie with his head on her breast, his wish to lie in her arms, and his dreams of their nights together. He envisions buying her two gifts—a long sable coat and a black silk bathing suit—and he asks her repeatedly to send him one of her orange stockings so that he can sleep with it at night. She did, and he did. In his outpourings, O'Neill presaged the dichotomous impulses later found in his canon—what Doris Falk has referred to as "tragic tension." As he avowed his profane desire for Bea, he cloaked his unbridled lust in sacred diction—for example, their hammock is "blessed," and O'Neill apostrophizes to God frequently to make her his.

In spring 1915, the romance waned, Ashe seeing O'Neill for the last time in late summer/early fall 1916 at Connecticut College, where she was taking music courses. Two years later, in 1918, she married James Maher, then a naval lieutenant who would rise to vice admiral. Still, the influence of Bea Ashe on the successful playwright was to linger—in his affections (in 1948 he asked Ice Casey his old New London friend for a picture of Bea as Mimi in *La Bohème*) and in his writing—the girl with whom he had shared his dream of becoming a playwright (BEFORE BREAKFAST, the new-lost *Belschezzar*, and *The* SNIPER) might still be glimpsed in AH, WILDERNESS!'s Muriel McComber. While

Beatrice Ashe and Eugene O'Neill in 1914 *(Courtesy of the Sheaffer-O'Neill Collection, Charles E. Shain Library of Connecticut College)*

Maibelle Scott is generally accepted as the model for Muriel, the relationship between Bea Ashe and O'Neill, as revealed in his letters to her, reverberates in Richard and Muriel's innocent love.

When she died in New London on January 20, 1974, Bea Ashe had outlived her husband (by seven years) and her onetime suitor by two decades. But in O'Neill's POETRY ("Upon Our Beach," "Rondeau to her Nose," "Just a Little Love, a Little Kiss," "'Full Many a Cup of This Forbidden Wine,'" "A Song of Moods"—over a dozen such poems) and in his letters, and to some degree in the character of Muriel McComber, Bea Ashe survives.

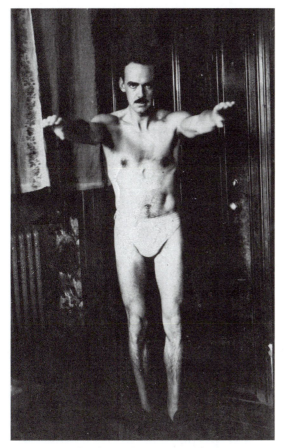

Eugene O'Neill in his underwear around 1914. An unconventional gift to his girlfriend Beatrice Ashe. *(Courtesy of the Yale Collection of American Literature, Beinecke Rare Book and Manuscript Library)*

Bibliography

Falk, Doris V. *Eugene O'Neill and the Tragic Tension.* New Brunswick, N.J.: Rutgers University Press, 1958.

Gelb, Arthur, and Barbara Gelb. *O'Neill.* Enlarged ed. New York: Harper and Row, 1973.

———. *O'Neill: Life with Monte Cristo.* New York: Applause Books, 2000.

O'Neill, Eugene. Letters to Beatrice Ashe [79 extant]. Eugene O'Neill Papers, Henry W. and Albert A. Berg Collection, New York Public Library.

————. *Selected Letters of Eugene O'Neill.* Edited by
Travis Bogard and Jackson R. Bryer. New Haven,
Conn.: Yale University Press, 1988.

Sheaffer, Louis. *Eugene O'Neill: Son and Playwright.*
Boston: Little, Brown, 1968.

————. Notes, correspondence and interviews, Louis
Sheaffer–Eugene O'Neill Collection, Charles E.
Shain Library, Connecticut College, New London.

Smith, Madeline C., and Richard Eaton. "And Thou
Bee-side Me . . . Beatrice Ashe and Eugene O'Neill."
Philological Papers 44 (1998): 80–85.

Madeline C. Smith

Atkinson, Brooks (1894–1984) A *New York
Times* theater critic, author, editor, Dartmouth
English instructor, PULITZER PRIZE–winning journalist, and war correspondent, Brooks Atkinson met
Eugene O'Neill on September 22, 1927. While the
two had known of each other for some time, this
lunch meeting, orchestrated by Manuel Komroff,
a fellow writer and journalist, was their first social
interaction. After this meeting, Atkinson wrote
of O'Neill in his journal, "I like him immensely
for his ability to see all these minor forces [of the
theatre] in true perspective. Although he is gentle and sympathetic, I am sure he would trample
down anything in his path. He is not to be denied"
(quoted in Sheaffer 266). Atkinson quickly became
O'Neill's trusted reader and confidant.

Notably, the two corresponded through 1930
as O'Neill finalized the manuscript of MOURNING
BECOMES ELECTRA. With Atkinson's encouragement
and criticism, O'Neill evaluated and put the finishing
touches on his trilogy. As O'Neill's health and popularity with the American public declined, Atkinson
proved his devotion to his friend by writing in the
Times (August 19, 1951), "In originality, size and passion [the O'Neill canon] is the finest dramatic literature we have. Only an improvident theater, like the
one we have, would neglect work of such a power
and magnitude" (quoted in Sheaffer 663).

Throughout his career, Brooks Atkinson was a
prominent, reasoned voice of criticism on Broadway.
According to O'Neill, Atkinson was a critic "whose

opinions I respect, and whose right to criticize the
drama I admit" (O'Neill 392). Atkinson's esteem
for O'Neill was neither developed nor illustrated
through unqualified glowing reviews—which Atkinson did not produce—but out of honest, shrewd
criticism and his ability to recognize and admire the
depth of O'Neill's plays. Atkinson's marked insight
into O'Neill's plays may be attributed to the candor that characterized the relationship between the
two. In his book *Broadway* (1970), Atkinson says of
O'Neill that he "not only began the modern American drama; to a large extent he sustained it by writing powerful plays in several styles . . . the Broadway
theater began to have cultural significance when he
became part of it" (195).

In addition to his diverse and thriving writing
career, Atkinson served as an original member and
the first president of the New York Drama Critics' Circle. The Circle first met in 1935 with the
intention to create an alternative dramatic honor
to the Pulitzer Prize. To this day, a committee of
New York theater critics continues to recognize the
year's outstanding drama with the Critics' Circle
Award. O'Neill's The ICEMAN COMETH was the
1947 runner-up for "Best American Play" behind
Arthur Miller's *All My Sons,* and in 1957 O'Neill
won the Critics' Circle "Best American Play" award
for his masterpiece LONG DAY'S JOURNEY INTO
NIGHT. Atkinson served on both of these com-
mittees. In November 1980, Atkinson celebrated
his 86th birthday with the Theater Committee for
Eugene O'Neill, which presented him with a medal
in recognition of his contributions to the greater
understanding and appreciation of O'Neill's works.

Bibliography

Atkinson, Brooks. *Broadway.* New York: Macmillan
Company, 1970.

O'Neill, Eugene. *Selected Letters of Eugene O'Neill.*
Edited by Travis Bogard and Jackson R. Bryer. New
Haven, Conn.: Yale University Press, 1988.

Sheaffer, Louis. *O'Neill Son and Playwright.* New York:
Paragon House, 1968.

Shawna Lesseur-Blas

B

Baker, George Pierce (1866–1935) Eclipsed now by the prodigious achievements of his many protégés, George Pierce Baker was in his day an esteemed and erudite, if unlikely, academic. Upon graduating Phi Beta Kappa from Harvard University in 1887, Baker declared he had no interest in or talent for teaching, finding journalism or editing more consistent with his creative bent (Kinnc 32). Nonetheless, in 1888 he accepted, rather by default, an instructorship at his alma mater, where he would remain for 36 years before moving on to another eight years at Yale.

No creative genius, though he had tried his hand at POETRY and plays, Baker had the Midas touch for inspiring others. Among the many gifted students who took his English 47 class were, besides Eugene O'Neill: Philip Barry, Thomas Wolfe, Sidney Howard, Edward Sheldon, Lee Simonson, Heywood Broun, Theresa Helburn, Robert Benchley, Van Wyck Brooks, KENNETH MACGOWAN, S. N. Behrman, John Mason Brown, and ROBERT EDMOND JONES. So influential was Baker that Wolfe, for better or worse, modeled his character Professor James Hatcher in *Of Time and the River* on him.

Born in Providence, Rhode Island, on April 4, 1866, the only son of physician George Pierce Baker, a devoted student of Oliver Wendell Holmes, and his wife Lucy Cady Baker, the future academician evinced an interest in theater early on. His mother, who before her marriage made hats for Edwin Booth, Charlotte Cushman, and other "stars," imparted her love of the stage to her son. A model theater given to the boy, which Baker used to entertain his friends, helped foster his lifelong passion for the genre, as did his undergraduate participation in college theatricals. These formative experiences would pave the way for his innovative playwriting course and give rise to his impressive dramatic arts library.

In 1895, early in his teaching career, Baker, then a rhetoric instructor, published the first of three editions of *The Principles of Argumentation,* but he subsequently turned from undergraduate to graduate teaching; the 1907 publication of *The Development of Shakespeare a Dramatist,* followed by his 1919 *Dramatic Technique,* signaled and affirmed the direction his career would take. Working to exhaustion, Baker was prolific in his scholarship. The scope of his work—books, parts of books, plays, editions, compilations, pamphlets, poetry, published letters, addresses, periodical articles, and newspaper articles—was vast (for a complete list, see Kinne, Appendix 1). Summers and sabbaticals were spent researching theater in England and on the Continent as well as establishing important contacts (William Butler Yeats, Gordon Craig). During the academic term, Baker immersed himself in all things dramatic. He established the Mermaid Club (a society of HENRIK IBSEN enthusiasts, including George Santayana), contributed to college productions, and developed, first at Radcliffe, the drama/playwriting class known at Harvard as English 47.

Here the paths of Baker and O'Neill crossed, the playwright-to-be having announced in his letter of application dated July 16, 1914, his desire to be "an artist or nothing" (quoted in Sheaffer 293). O'Neill's confiding "All my life I have been closely connected with the dramatic profession" (quoted in Kinne 193) may have resonated with Baker, for O'Neill was admitted as a special student in fall 1914. By the time O'Neill entered Harvard, he had written 16 plays, 13 of which survive (Voelker 1). Students taking Baker's course were required to produce a play adapted from a short story, an original one-act play, and an original full-length play. While at Harvard, O'Neill wrote *The PERSONAL EQUATION, The Dear Doctor, Belshazzar, The SNIPER,* and *A Knock at the Door,* but he generated little of substance.

After O'Neill's first year at Harvard, Baker encouraged his student to return, but O'Neill absented himself. Thereafter, the mentor and his student would periodically renew contact. On May 9, 1919, O'Neill wrote to Baker telling him that a copy of his one-acts would be forthcoming. The book, O'Neill explained was a "small token of remembrance of all I owe to my year under your guidance" (Kinne 206); this was *The Moon of the Caribbees and Six Other Plays of the Sea.*

It was due in part to Baker's endorsement that Yale University would confer the D.Litt. degree on O'Neill in 1926. Baker wrote in the *Yale Review:* "Eugene O'Neill today is the best known in other countries of all our dramatists. Vienna, Prague, Dresden, Berlin, Paris, London, Rome—all capitals of Europe have seen his finest plays" (quoted in Majumdar 12).

After decades at Harvard, Baker wearied of the institution's perceived lack of support for his passion. When in 1924 he was offered a chance to head Yale's newly conceived Department of Theatre and to direct its attendant facility, Baker accepted. Thanks to a million dollar endowment from EDWARD S. HARKNESS, Yale would have, as Baker proclaimed, "the first University Theatre in the history of Universities" (Kinne 261). But Baker's health, precarious as a boy, was failing him. At Yale, he oversaw the development of the Department of Theatre and watched enrollment in the program swell before his retirement in 1933. On January 6, 1935, he died, leaving his wife, Christina Hopkinson Baker, and four sons.

O'Neill acknowledged Baker's influence when, on January 20, 1935, the playwright wrote to the bereaved Mrs. Baker that her husband had given him "the greatest gift one human being can give another—the courage to believe in his work and go on" (quoted in Majumdar 13).

Baker material is housed in various COLLECTIONS—catalogued at Yale's Beinecke, Rare Book and Manuscript Library, at Connecticut College, and at Harvard University. A special collection exists at Yale, in the Library Shelving Facility, which contains eight linear feet or 17 boxes of Baker papers.

Bibliography

Baker, George Pierce. *Dramatic Technique.* Boston: Houghton Mifflin, 1919.

Bogard, Travis. *Contour in Time: The. Plays of Eugene O'Neill.* New York: Oxford University Press, 1972.

Gelb, Arthur, and Barbara Gelb. *O'Neill: Life with Monte Cristo.* New York: Applause Books, 2000.

Kinne, Wisner Payne. *George. Pierce Baker and the American Theatre.* Cambridge, Mass.: Harvard University Press, 1954.

Majumdar, Rupendra Guha. "O'Neill's Precursors." *Laconics* 1 (2006). Available online. URL: http://www.eoneill.com/library/laconics/l/Id.htm. Accessed May 31, 2008.

"Prof G. P. Baker, Play Expert, Dies," *New York Times,* January 7, 1935, 17.

Ranald, Margaret Loftus. *The Eugene O'Neill Companion.* Westport, Conn.: Greenwood Press, 1984.

Sheaffer, Louis. *O'Neill: Son and Playwright.* Boston: Little, Brown, 1968.

———. "O'Neill and George Pierce Baker." *Eugene O'Neill Newsletter* 1, no. 2 (1977): 1–2.

Voelker, Paul D. "Eugene O'Neill and George Pierce Baker: A Reconsideration." *American Literature* 49 (1977): 206–220.

———. "Success and Frustration at Harvard: Eugene O'Neill's Relationship with George Pierce Baker (1914–15)." In *Eugene O'Neill and the Emergence of*

American Drama, edited by Marc Maufort, 15–29. Amsterdam: Rodopi, 1989.

Madeline Smith

Barrett House   In one way, Eugene O'Neill was the quintessential actor's child: He was born in a hotel room and he died in one. O'Neill came into the world on October 16, 1888, in the Barrett House, an eight-story family hotel on the northeast corner of Broadway and 43rd Street that had opened five years earlier. At the time, O'Neill's father JAMES O'NEILL was touring in his landmark though ultimately numbing role as *The Count of Monte Cristo,* but he returned to New York for his son's birth. Eugene Gladstone O'Neill was born on the third floor, and in subsequent years, he often pointed out this location to friends. In the late 19th century, the area around the Barrett House was known as Longacre Square (it would be

The Barrett House, O'Neill's birthplace. O'Neill acknowledged to the friend who sent this image to him as a present that the man leaning against the lamppost clearly "had a bun on." *(Courtesy of the Sheaffer-O'Neill Collection, Charles E. Shain Library of Connecticut College)*

renamed Times Square in 1904) and was a hub for the carriage-building trade. The clock in the tower atop the Barrett House also became a familiar and renowned sight.

The hotel was named after the Barrett brothers, well-known hotel managers at that time. In 1900, the adjacent Cadillac Hotel, a fairly new 12-story lodging, took over the Barrett House, changing its name to the Cadillac as well. When management again changed hands in 1910, the Cadillac became known as the Hotel Wallick—again, named for the brothers who ran it. However, when the Wallicks retired five years later, the Cadillac name was restored and retained until the hotel was razed in 1940, an event that greatly disappointed O'Neill. Five years before he died, O'Neill received a picture of the original Barrett House, a gift he treasured.

On October 16, 1957, O'Neill's birthplace was commemorated with a bronze plaque on the site of the Barrett House, attached to a pillar in front of the London Character Shoes Store that then occupied the space. It read:

> Eugene O'Neill
> Foremost American playwright
> was born in the
> Barrett House on this site
> October 16, 1888

The plaque was donated by JOSÉ QUINTERO, Leigh Connell, and Theodore Mann, whose sponsorship of on- and off-Broadway productions of LONG DAY'S JOURNEY INTO NIGHT and *The Ice-Man Cometh* helped to spark the EUGENE O'NEILL RENAISSANCE. Attendees at the ceremony included JASON ROBARDS, Geraldine Page, James Earl Jones, COLLEEN DEWHURST, and TENNESSEE WILLIAMS. However, during the store's renovation in 1961, the plaque disappeared, generating wide public protests.

Bibliography

"Cadillac Hotel to Be Torn Down," *New York Times,* March 19, 1940, 25.

Gelb, Arthur. "O'Neill's Birthplace Is Marked by Plaque at Times Square Site," *New York Times,* October 17, 1957, 35.

"Times Sq. Edifice Linked to History," *New York Times*, March 1935, RE1–2.

Karen Charmaine Blansfield

Bermuda See SPITHEAD.

biographers O'Neill's first biographer was, in a way, himself. Even before he received the advice of the critic Clayton Hamilton in 1914 to write about his experiences at sea, O'Neill was writing from his own life, and most of his plays can be read as reflections on his life (Sheaffer 1968, 271). Some would even say that he was his own best biographer, given a steady stream of profoundly self-reflective writing throughout his career, culminating in LONG DAY'S JOURNEY INTO NIGHT. This was the point of view taken by the recent documentary film on O'Neill (2006), coauthored by Ric Burns and Arthur and Barbara Gelb, but the connection between autobiography and biography in that work is as problematic as ever.

Barrett H. Clark wrote the first book that might be called a biography of O'Neill, though much of it consists of brief critical analyses of the plays. First published in 1926, Clark's study was revised in four subsequent editions, the last in 1947, and constituted the most thorough study of O'Neill's life during his lifetime. Clark reports that O'Neill resisted his writing such a book, questioning whether it was "necessary to be so darned personal." Finally, O'Neill gave Clark permission to gather his life story from others and offered to fill in the gaps. Clark produced an early version of the enduring myth that O'Neill had a questing soul, severely tested by years at sea, leading to a ruggedly individualistic artist, one who cultivated solitude and communion with none but the sea. Little mention was made of O'Neill's marriages and children and prosperity. When O'Neill read Clark's manuscript, he found the story to be "legend," adding: "It really isn't true. It isn't I. And the truth would make such a much more interesting—and incredible!—legend. That is what makes me melancholy. But I see no hope for this except someday to shame the devil myself, if ever I can muster the requisite interest—and

nerve—simultaneously!" (Sheaffer 1973, 191–192). That day would come.

In 1948, Hamilton Basso published a three-part profile of O'Neill in the *New Yorker*, which is based on interviews with the playwright, who was nearly 60 and had written no new play for five years. Basso's profile is therefore skewed to the later part of O'Neill's career and the sadness of his decline. Croswell Bowen, who had written a magazine profile of O'Neill at the time of *The ICEMAN COMETH* opening (1946), had subsequently cultivated a friendship with O'Neill's son SHANE RUDRAIGE O'NEILL, with the goal of writing a major biography of the playwright. O'Neill's death in 1953 opened the door to professional biographers, and Bowen was first to come forward, with *Curse of the Misbegotten* in 1957, a book that took up, in its title, a word that haunted O'Neill's late, autobiographical plays. On behalf of Shane, who received a "with the assistance of" credit on the title page, Bowen portrayed the tragic "curse" on the O'Neill family. In the early pages, he drew heavily on material O'Neill himself provided in *Long Day's Journey into Night* to show the patterns of self-pity and retribution, greed and compensation, within which the O'Neill family was held. In the later pages, he paid close attention to the impact of O'Neill on his children, wives, and former friends, while devoting relatively little space to O'Neill's place in theater history.

The next book to emerge was AGNES BOULTON's 1958 memoir of the first two years of her marriage to O'Neill, *Part of a Long Story*, which critics dismissed as novelistic and filled with errors but which remains the most intimate portrait of O'Neill in existence. CARLOTTA MONTEREY O'NEILL's diaries (1928–43) might have rivaled or surpassed Boulton's book as an "inside" look at O'Neill's life during the years of their marriage, but her evident redacting of the volumes makes them a problematic source.

Louis Sheaffer had been drama critic for the *Brooklyn Eagle* and then was press agent for the Circle in the Square revival of *Iceman* in 1955. Early in 1956, he declared an interest in writing a biographical-critical study of O'Neill. At just about the same moment, Arthur and Barbara Gelb set a similar goal. Sheaffer said from the first that he had no interest in producing a hasty volume, and he set out on a project of interviewing anybody and everybody who had anything to do with O'Neill. However, when approaching his subjects, he kept hearing stories of how aggressively his rivals, especially the Gelbs, were approaching the research. Arthur Gelb was then in the early stages of a long career with the *New York Times*, and he and Barbara, daughter of the playwright S. N. Behrman, could open many doors Sheaffer could not. Above all, they elicited the cooperation of Carlotta, and she gave them many hours of interviews, as well as access to materials that others had not seen. Their book came out in 1962, less than a decade after O'Neill's death, and the reviews were excellent. It presents a heroic view of O'Neill as a man who overcame his problematic upbringing and single-handedly revolutionized the AMERICAN THEATER. In many ways, it remains the most readable O'Neill biography, though it contains factual errors and lapses and lacks critical perspective on many of the plays. It also frustrates the researcher by providing no citations. They have partially remedied that problem in recent years with an extensively revised version of the first part of their biography in 2000, and they have plans to come forward with a revision of the remainder of their biography.

Sheaffer, meanwhile, made good progress with Agnes Boulton and others who were not aligned with Carlotta; he also eventually elicited Carlotta's cooperation. A slow-and-steady approach led to his two prize-winning volumes of "definitive" biography, which appeared in 1968 and 1973; he was awarded the PULITZER PRIZE for the second volume. Sheaffer inexhaustibly pursued leads, spending countless hours interviewing hundreds of people, digging in archives, and traveling to the key sites in O'Neill's life. His volumes are strong on reportage and historical documentation but limited in critical sophistication and rarely challenge the usual opinions.

Doris Alexander also set to work on O'Neill in the years following his death, initially as an academic and later as an independent scholar. Her three volumes of critical biography (1962, 1992, and 2005) sharply challenge received ideas about O'Neill and offer a portrait that, if not entirely consistent from volume to volume, at least constantly

provokes new questions about how O'Neill's life relates to his plays. Another revision of O'Neill's life story can be found between the lines of Travis Bogard's *Contour in Time* (1972), which is a critical overview but based on a profound reading of the plays as reflectors of O'Neill's creative self-consciousness. Unlike Sheaffer and the Gelbs, Bogard and Alexander are willing and able to address the existing scholarly discourse on O'Neill. The work of using the best of critical research to illuminate the biography of O'Neill has been carried on by many, notably Michael Manheim, Virginia Floyd, Normand Berlin, Egil Törnqvist, and Zander Brietzke.

The most recent biography of O'Neill is by Stephen A. Black (1999), who brings a psychoanalyst's as well as a literary scholar's training to his reading of O'Neill's career. In his view, O'Neill's plays represent an ultimately successful self-analysis, in which he moves beyond an incomplete phase of mourning for his parents and brother JAMES O'NEILL, JR., who died around the time he came to prominence as a writer, to a fully tragic vision in the late plays. For Black, as for most of the biographers discussed above, *Long Day's Journey* is the alpha and the omega, and therefore Eugene O'Neill himself still dominates the world of O'Neill biography.

Bibliography

Alexander, Doris. *Eugene O'Neill's Creative Struggle: The Decisive Decade, 1924–1933*. University Park: Pennsylvania State University Press, 1992.

———. *Eugene O'Neill's Last Plays: Separating Art from Autobiography*. Athens: University of Georgia Press, 2005.

———. *The Tempering of Eugene O'Neill*. New York: Harcourt, Brace & World, 1962.

Basso, Hamilton. "The Tragic Sense." *New Yorker* (February 28, 1948): 24–34, (March 6, 1948): 24–34, (March 13, 1948): 24–37.

Black, Stephen A. *Eugene O'Neill: Beyond Mourning and Tragedy*. New Haven, Conn.: Yale University Press, 1999.

Bogard, Travis. *Contour in Time: The Plays of Eugene O'Neill*. New York: Oxford University Press, 1972.

Boulton, Agnes. *Part of a Long Story: Eugene O'Neill as a Young Man in Love.* New York: Doubleday & Company, 1958.

Bowen, Croswell, with the assistance of Shane O'Neill. *The Curse of the Misbegotten: A Tale of the House of O'Neill.* New York: McGraw-Hill, 1959.

Burns, Ric, Arthur Gelb, and Barbara Gelb. *Eugene O'Neill: A Documentary Film.* PBS: *American Experience.* Premiered March 27, 2006.

Clark, Barrett H. *Eugene O'Neill: The Man and His Plays.* New York: Dover Publications, 1947.

Gelb, Arthur, and Barbara Gelb. *O'Neill.* New York: Harper & Brothers, 1962.

———. *O'Neill.* Enlarged ed. New York: Harper & Row, 1973.

———. *O'Neill: Life with Monte Cristo.* New York: Applause Books, 2000.

Sheaffer, Louis. *O'Neill: Son and Artist.* Boston: Little, Brown, 1973.

———. *O'Neill: Son and Playwright.* Boston: Little, Brown, 1968.

William Davies King

Boulton, Agnes Ruby (1892–1968) Agnes Boulton was the second wife of Eugene O'Neill, mother of two of his children, a fellow writer and occasional collaborator, model for several of his characters, and author of the most intimate and extensive portrayal of him in a memoir. Born in London on September 19, 1892 (contrary to earlier reports of 1893), she spent her early years in Philadelphia, where her father, Edward W. Boulton, was a painter (a student of Thomas Eakins and first president of the Art Students League). Her mother, born Cecil Maud Williams, had been a model for Eakins and set an example for her four daughters as a free-thinking woman with a taste for literature and the arts. She was also a convert to CATHOLICISM.

Boulton went to school at the Convent of the Holy Child, also the Philadelphia School of Industrial Arts, but by 1903 her family had moved to West Point Pleasant, New Jersey. In her memoir, she says she began publishing short stories by the age of 17. Over the next decade, she published at least 45 short stories, novelettes, and dramatic sketches in magazines ranging from *Breezy Stories*

Shane, Agnes, Oona, and Eugene O'Neill in Bermuda, 1922 *(Courtesy of the Sheaffer-O'Neill Collection, Charles E. Shain Library of Connecticut College)*

to the *Smart Set*, earning a regular modest income. These pieces show a remarkable range in tone and style and occasionally reflect aspects of her life, but they do not pretend to be anything more than literary diversions.

Mystery surrounds Boulton's reported marriage to a British newspaper man named James Burton, whom she met while visiting her maternal grandmother in England. He was said to have died in Belgium, leaving her pregnant; the child, Barbara Burton, was born in 1915. The following year, Agnes Boulton Burton was the subject of a newspaper story describing her as a "fiction writer" who had taken up dairy farming in Cornwall Bridge, Connecticut. Title to that farm had been signed over to her by Courtland Young, the publisher of two of the magazines in which she regularly published her stories, raising questions about his involvement in her life.

Having found farm life difficult, Boulton left her daughter with her parents and went to GREENWICH VILLAGE late in November 1917, seeking factory work to complement and extend her labors as a writer. While looking for her friend Christine Ell, she met O'Neill in the back room of the Golden Swan saloon, known as the HELL HOLE. At the end of the very first evening they ever spent together, he reportedly said, "I want to spend every night of my life from now on with *you*. I mean this. *Every night of my life*" (Boulton 1958, 21). Some have suggested that O'Neill might have drunkenly confused Boulton with LOUISE BRYANT, wife of JOHN REED, with whom he had previously had an affair and who she resembled.

Turmoil surrounded the first few weeks of their relationship, during which O'Neill was coming to terms with his ambivalence toward the PROVINCE-TOWN PLAYERS and succumbing to his alcoholic compulsion, but by January 1918 he had persuaded Boulton to flee with him to Provincetown, Massachusetts. They spent the winter writing, living in Francis' Flats, and were married on April 12, 1918. Several of Boulton's stories from this period reflect O'Neill's presence in her life, including characters based on him. Some show her attempt at a higher literary style to match his. During the first year of their marriage, her income as a writer more than matched what he was getting as an allowance from his father and from a few sales to commercial publishers.

O'Neill dedicated BEYOND THE HORIZON, which he had completed that first winter, to Boulton, and she often referred to it as "our" play. Its depiction of matrimony as a trap matches the view found in many of Boulton's stories. Not coincidentally, both took a strong interest in the works of AUGUST STRINDBERG—O'Neill in the plays and Boulton in the stories. Evidence that the O'Neill-Boulton marriage itself had a Strindbergian element can be found in O'Neill's WELDED (1923) but also in Boulton's story "The Hater of Mediocrity" (*Smart Set*, July 1920). The farm in DESIRE UNDER THE ELMS might reflect the dairy farm Boulton had eventually sold to pay debts, but it is also visible in the stories Boulton sought to publish in the late 1920s, in a volume to be called *New England Women*.

The couple spent the winter of early 1919 in Boulton's West Point Pleasant house, where O'Neill allegedly, in a fit of anger, destroyed a portrait that Eakins had made of her father. Boulton considered the playwright SUSAN GLASPELL a personal friend, but otherwise she kept her distance from the Prov-

incetown Playhouse circle, indeed from the theater in general, preferring literary associates.

A year and a half after their marriage, and contrary to O'Neill's wishes, on October 30, 1919, Boulton gave birth to SHANE RUDRAIGHE O'NEILL in Provincetown. The presence of a child irrevocably changed the nature of their romantic "solitude," and soon there was a housekeeper, Mrs. Clark, to help with the work. They lived primarily at the life-saving station at PEAKED HILL BAR, near Provincetown, until 1923, when they moved to BROOK FARM in Ridgefield, Connecticut. During these years, Boulton learned to cope with O'Neill's drinking, realizing how destructive it was to his creativity, as well as to their happiness, but evidently she became a heavy drinker herself during these years. There are well-attested reports of O'Neill's physical abuse of her in the early 1920s.

Boulton's literary production dwindled in the early years of the marriage. She readily gave her scenario "The Captain's Walk" to O'Neill for him to adapt

Agnes Boulton *(Courtesy of the Nickolas Muray Photo Archives, LLC)*

into WHERE THE CROSS IS MADE and later GOLD. In exchange, he gave her his incomplete script of NOW I ASK YOU, with the idea that she should finish it as her own work, but she hardly touched it. In 1923 or 1924, he gave her his 1917 or 1918 scenario of "The Reckoning," which she adapted as a play entitled *The Guilty One*. Richard Madden was able to persuade William A. Brady to option the script for Broadway production, but O'Neill subsequently discouraged further dealings with Brady. In 1925, Boulton also completed an original full-length play, *Little Hope*, which Madden circulated among producers, with no result. She gave birth to OONA O'NEILL in Bermuda on May 14, 1925.

O'Neill's struggle with drinking came to a head in 1925, leading him to consult with Dr. Gilbert V. Hamilton, a psychiatrist who was just then embarking on a study of marriage. Boulton also met with Hamilton concerning how to handle O'Neill's ALCOHOLISM, and both she and O'Neill participated in Hamilton's survey of married couples, *A Research in Marriage* (1929); the survey was also reported in a popular book, coauthored by KENNETH MACGOWAN, *What Is Wrong with Marriage?* (1929).

O'Neill blamed Boulton for encouraging a lively social circle around their homes in Connecticut and Bermuda (see SPITHEAD), and also for her continuing to drink, at a time when he was trying to remain temperate. At Belgrade Lakes, Maine, in early fall 1926, they met with Carlotta Monterey, later CARLOTTA MONTEREY O'NEILL, through Elizabeth Marbury, an associate of O'Neill's agent, Richard Madden. In the following weeks, in New York, O'Neill had a brief affair with Monterey, but upon returning to Boulton in Bermuda, he admitted his lapse and pledged his continuing loyalty to her. However, he continued to correspond with Monterey in secret.

Boulton was preoccupied with the two children and occasional visits from her daughter Barbara who was living with her parents at the time and O'Neill's son EUGENE O'NEILL, JR., as well as with the project of renovating SPITHEAD, the new family home in Bermuda. Her father died in spring 1927, and she came to Connecticut to deal with family matters. Her letters to O'Neill indicate her

unchanging devotion to him, despite his recent unfaithfulness. He, too, seemed to have recommitted himself to the marriage, but when he journeyed to New York early in the summer, he resumed his relationship with Monterey.

Back in Bermuda, the hot summer of 1927 was increasingly unproductive for O'Neill, and the marriage bore much of the resulting stress. Finally, in late August, Boulton urged him to go to New York, see friends, and recover his sense of purpose. The night before he left, they made love on a steamer chair on the front porch. However, in New York, his discontent with the marriage grew rapidly. After Carlotta Monterey returned from a trip to Europe, they resumed their relationship. He kept putting off the date of his return to Bermuda, and when he came home, he seemed to have already severed his ties to Boulton.

Returning to New York in December to prepare for the production of STRANGE INTERLUDE and MARCO MILLIONS, O'Neill allied himself irrevocably to Monterey. Boulton came to New York, perhaps in an effort to salvage the marriage, and they made love one final time in her hotel room, but in February 1929, O'Neill sailed with Monterey to Europe, and the marriage was at an end.

A protracted period of negotiation over the divorce eventually led to extreme rancor, with O'Neill using the mystery of Boulton's previous marriage as a lever to force her to accept unfavorable terms. Even those terms he and Monterey came to resent as grossly unfair. Indeed, he felt it was outrageous for her to ask for any support at all.

In summer 1928, Boulton began a relationship with a newspaper writer, James Delaney, which continued for a decade, though without marriage. He helped her create a stable home in New Jersey in which to raise Barbara, Shane, and Oona. In March 1929, she finally acquiesced to the pressure being put on her by O'Neill and his attorney and traveled to Reno to establish residency; the divorce was granted on July 2. She received $6,000–$10,000 per year, as well as money for the children's expenses and Spithead. However, it turned out that she could not afford to live so far from her extended family or at that level of society, so the house was rented through most of the 1930s and fell into disrepair. For the rest of her life, Boulton was constantly pressed for cash, but the only work she undertook was her own writing.

In the early 1940s, Boulton moved the family to Los Angeles and encouraged, or did not stand in the way of, Oona's pursuit of a career in acting and eventual marriage to Charlie Chaplin. Boulton had returned to writing stories at the time of the divorce and later venturing into screenwriting, but she enjoyed little success until 1944, when she published a novel, *The Road Is Before Us,* to good reviews. She renegotiated the terms of the divorce settlement in 1947, accepting a lump sum payment, and married Morris "Mack" Kaufman, a writer and fisherman, whom she divorced around 1960.

Through the late 1940s and 1950s, living mainly in West Point Pleasant, Boulton continued writing, though drinking took more and more of a toll on her work and health. Shane lived nearby, and she saw him through his legal troubles and kept in close contact with his children. She saw much less of Oona, who was busy with her large family, visiting her in Switzerland only once or twice.

One of the terms of the divorce had dictated that Boulton not write about O'Neill in any way or use the name O'Neill in conjunction with her writing. After his death in 1953, BIOGRAPHERS and other writers came to her as a source of information on O'Neill. She assisted some (notably Louis Sheaffer, who became a friend) and rebuffed others, but it turned out that she herself was nearly the first to publish a book looking back at O'Neill's life. *Part of a Long Story* (1958) recounts the story of their meeting, their first year in Provincetown, O'Neill's rejection of the advances of Louise Bryant, his interactions with his brother Jamie (JAMES O'NEILL, JR.), their winter in West Point Pleasant, his bad behavior under the influence of alcohol, and finally the birth of Shane.

Critics found the book readable but puzzling as a source on O'Neill. So little attention was paid to his triumphs as a dramatist, so much to his failures as a husband, and so much to her self-realization as a woman. The book seemed novelistic, romantic, and skewed to a world overwhelmed by such plays as LONG DAY'S JOURNEY INTO NIGHT. Sales were disappointing. Boulton intended to follow this account of the first two years of their marriage with a sequel in two parts, the first to recount the deaths of JAMES O'NEILL, MARY ELLEN "ELLA" O'NEILL, and Jamie, and the second to tell of the demise of the marriage, 1923–28. She had not completed this volume at the time of her death on November 25, 1968.

Bibliography

Some of the information in this piece comes from archival research (at Yale, Connecticut College, Harvard, Princeton, Boston University, and other places) for my book *Another Part of a Long Story: Literary Traces of Eugene O'Neill and Agnes Boulton,* which is currently being prepared for publication. Other sources are as follows:

Alexander, Doris. *Eugene O'Neill's Creative Struggle: The Decisive Decade, 1924–1933.* University Park: Pennsylvania State University Press, 1992.

———. *Eugene O'Neill's Last Plays: Separating Art from Autobiography.* Athens: University of Georgia Press, 2005.

———. *The Tempering of Eugene O'Neill.* New York: Harcourt, Brace & World, 1962.

Bogard, Travis, ed. *The Unknown O'Neill: Unpublished or Unfamiliar Writings of Eugene O'Neill.* New Haven, Conn.: Yale University Press, 1988.

Boulton, Agnes. "The Hater of Mediocrity." *The Smart Set* 62, no. 3 (July 1920): 119–124.

———. *Part of a Long Story.* New York: Doubleday, 1958).

———. *The Road Is Before Us.* Philadelphia: J. B. Lippincott, 1944).

Gelb, Arthur, and Barbara Gelb. *O'Neill.* New York: Harper & Brothers, 1962.

Greeley-Smith, Nixola. "'No Money in Milk Cows' Says Woman Dairy Farmer Who's Made a Brave Fight," *Evening World,* October 7, 1916.

Hamilton, Gilbert V. *A Research on Marriage.* New York: Albert & Charles Boni, 1929.

Hamilton, Gilbert V., and Kenneth Macgowan. *What Is Wrong with Marriage.* New York: Albert & Charles Boni, 1929.

King, William Davies, ed. *"A Wind Is Rising": The Correspondence of Agnes Boulton and Eugene O'Neill.* Madison, N.J.: Fairleigh Dickinson University Press, 2000.

Ranald, Margaret Loftus. *The Eugene O'Neill Companion.* Westport, Conn.: Greenwood Press, 1984.

Scovell, Jane. *Oona: Living in the Shadows.* New York: Warner Books, 1998.

Sheaffer, Louis. *O'Neill: Son and Artist.* Boston: Little, Brown, 1973.

———. *O'Neill: Son and Playwright.* Boston: Little, Brown, 1968.

William Davies King

Brook Farm   Brook Farm, the estate in Ridgefield, Connecticut, that Eugene O'Neill and AGNES BOULTON bought in 1922, signified the epitome of gracious living in wealthy suburbs. With its circular driveway, generous rooms, and fine details, the 12-room mansion would have surely appealed to O'Neill's mother, MARY ELLEN "ELLA" O'NEILL, who had always wanted a more impressive place than the O'Neill family home, MONTE CRISTO COTTAGE in NEW LONDON, CONNECTICUT. Brook Farm was bought as an investment as well as a winter home, wrote O'Neill to Mary Heaton Vorse (O'Neill 174), but it was far more expensive to furnish and maintain than they expected. Croswell Bowen writes that with Brook Farm, O'Neill was realizing an ambition to own and live in a gracious homestead "where an O'Neill family could acquire happy memories" (Bowen 144). But even though Eugene could tell SUSAN GLASPELL in 1924 that "there is wonderful peace in these woods and hills" (O'Neill 186), he was never content there, and the family occupied it for only two winters and parts of two others, between 1922 and 1926, always renting it out for the summer. Initially attracted to the bucolic New England setting—31 acres of woods and meadow, a lawn dotted with mature elms and maples, an orchard and two ponds—O'Neill came to feel hemmed in by the wooded landscape. And there were no expansive, invigorating rooftop vistas as at PEAKED HILL BAR, the converted life-saving station near Provincetown, Massachusetts, that the O'Neills acquired as a summer home in 1919.

Ironically, the grand Connecticut estate, with its service wing and elaborate grounds requiring a gardener, typified the living arrangements favored by rich financiers and captains of industry, a class against whom O'Neill had railed vehemently in the past and would attack again in the future. Agnes's sister, Margery Colman, spent much time at Brook Farm, years later expressing to Louis Sheaffer her insight that "Gene" liked the place for what it "showed," not for what it "gave" (quoted in Sheaffer Papers). The playwright's rising artistic status, lately boosted by the success of *The HAIRY APE* and "*ANNA CHRISTIE,*" seemed to require a bricks-and-mortar parallel in the form of an impressive house, and Agnes diligently oversaw its costly redecoration into a comfortable, conventionally luxurious residence.

But the O'Neills were not conventional people, and the estate was a mismatch from the start. The family, which then included young SHANE RUDRAIGHE O'NEILL and his nanny, Mrs. Fifine Clark, was often in crisis, and O'Neill's drinking binges, symptomatic of deep-seated psychological problems, made matters worse. He had wanted to live close to New York, but the many difficulties with productions (including a dearth of royalties in 1924) and a failed effort to revive the PROVINCETOWN PLAYERS weighed heavily on their proximity. Increasingly bothered by the cold New England winters and worried about ALCOHOLISM (which had killed his brother, JAMES O'NEILL, JR. [Jamie] in 1923) O'Neill and Agnes decided to make a fresh start by abandoning Brook Farm for a more congenial physical and emotional climate away from New York. Renting a villa in Bermuda for the winter of 1924–25, they returned a year later and soon bought SPITHEAD, an 18th-century house on Hamilton Harbor that would become the third residence they had owned in seven years of marriage.

Bibliography
Black, Stephen A. *Eugene O'Neill: Beyond Mourning and Tragedy.* New Haven, Conn.: Yale University Press, 1999.

Bowen, Croswell. *The Curse of the Misbegotten: A Tale of the House of O'Neill.* New York: McGraw-Hill, 1959.

Sheaffer, Louis. *O'Neill, Son and Artist.* Boston: Little, Brown, 1973.

Sheaffer-O'Neill Collection. Department of Special Collections and Archives, Charles E. Shain Library, Connecticut College, New London.

Brian Rogers

Bryant, Louise (Anna Louise Mohan) (1885–1936)   In one of his last known letters to Louise Bryant, Eugene O'Neill declared, "It is more than probable that you have burned yourself so deep into my soul that the wound will never heal and I stand condemned to love you forever. . . . Neither your love nor mine was of the stuff this little breath of life can blow away" (quoted in Roazen 38–39). Though O'Neill and Bryant would never meet again—he would marry AGNES BOULTON a few months later—there is evidence that Bryant's influence on O'Neill was as profound and enduring as the playwright predicted.

Louise Bryant was born Anna Louise Mohan in San Francisco, California, on December 5, 1885. She was the third child of Louisa Flick and Hugh Mohan, a minor politician and journalist who moved the family to Reno before disappearing when Louise was four. She never used the name Anna and took her last name from her stepfather Sheridan Bryant, a Nevada freight train conductor who raised the Mohan children as his own.

Bryant spent several idyllic childhood years with her grandfather in a remote Nevada mining camp, where she lived an adventurous outdoor life and befriended immigrant workers while having little contact with other children. She attended high school in Wadsworth, Nevada. When the family moved to Oregon in 1906, she enrolled at the University of Oregon, where she studied history and earned a reputation as a freethinking iconoclast.

Louise moved to Portland in 1909 and briefly taught school before landing a job as society editor and commercial artist for the *Portland Spectator*. She married Paul Trullinger, a successful dentist and political liberal who accepted Louise's nonconformity, in November 1909. The Trullingers kept up an active social life among Portland's young professionals, but Louise's rebellion against bourgeois complacency went deeper than her husband's. She immersed herself in radical politics, raising subscriptions for the MASSES and sending essays and poems to anarchist Alexander Berkman's San Francisco–based *Blast*.

Bryant met JOHN REED, a poet, journalist, and later communist revolutionary who was already a celebrity for his daring coverage of the Mexican Revolution, while he was visiting his family in Portland in 1915. In January 1916, Louise left her hus-

Louise Bryant in Provincetown, Massachusetts *(Courtesy of the Sheaffer-O'Neill Collection, Charles E. Shain Library of Connecticut College)*

band permanently to live with Reed in GREENWICH VILLAGE. In New York, Bryant began writing for the *Masses*, developing her journalistic skills and finding her political voice.

When Eugene O'Neill met Bryant in Provincetown, Massachusetts, in 1916, she was an aspiring writer, a member of the original PROVINCETOWN PLAYERS, and the lover of O'Neill's great friend Reed. The emerging playwright was immediately taken with Louise, but it was Bryant who initiated their sexual liaison, addressing a poem to O'Neill that began, "Dark eyes, you stir my soul ineffably" (quoted in Dearborn 53). O'Neill was still involved with BEATRICE ASHE and reluctant to betray Reed, but his guilt was assuaged by Bryant's professed belief in free love and her insistence that because of Reed's kidney ailment, she and Jack lived together like brother and sister. The affair that followed—initially carried on behind Reed's back but later with his full knowledge—was the most intense romantic involvement O'Neill experienced during his early career as a dramatist. "When that girl touches me with the tip of her little finger," O'Neill confided to TERRY CARLIN, "it's like a flame" (quoted in Gardner 36). Their relationship was enacted in the 1981 film *Reds*, starring Warren Beatty as Reed, Diane Keaton as Bryant, and Jack Nicholson as O'Neill.

Before and after their affair began, Bryant and O'Neill worked together professionally in significant ways. Bryant's play *The Game*, which some critics have viewed as an influence on O'Neill's early dramatic efforts, was performed on the same bill as O'Neill's debut play, BOUND EAST FOR CARDIFF. Louise also played the role of the seductive dancer alongside O'Neill's mulatto sailor in THIRST, the second O'Neill play ever performed. She later helped O'Neill publish his story "TOMORROW" in Waldo Frank's *The Seven Arts*.

In fall 1916, Reed and Bryant were secretly married just before Reed traveled to Baltimore to undergo a serious kidney operation. While he was recuperating, O'Neill and Bryant lived together in Reed's flat on Washington Square. In December, Bryant became ill from what may have been a botched abortion; Greenwich Village rumor had it that the father was O'Neill (Dearborn 61). Bryant bitterly disappointed

Louise Bryant on the beach at Provincetown, Massachusetts. Bryant sent this as a gift to John Reed, who was covering the 1916 Democratic convention in Chicago. Signed "This is to remind you of 'The Drinks' and all the nice months after the Connection. Please, Honey, take good care of yourself out there." At the time, she and O'Neill were having an affair. *(Courtesy of the Harvard College Library Theatre Collection)*

O'Neill when she left for Europe to begin her career as a foreign correspondent in 1917, covering the war in France. Immediately after returning, she and Reed obtained press credentials and sailed for Russia in time to cover the Bolshevik takeover. Bryant's *Six Red Months in Russia* is her vivid account of the October Revolution. After the book's publication in 1919, Bryant went on a national speaking tour, criticizing U.S. imperialism and calling on Americans to overcome fears of socialism.

Bryant's relationship with O'Neill effectively ended in early 1918, when she returned from Russia several weeks ahead of Reed, and although O'Neill was already living with AGNES BOULTON, she made a determined effort to win back her lover. O'Neill was still powerfully attracted to Louise, but Agnes managed to hold him; he had by this time had enough of free love and instead chose the support and relative peace that Agnes provided.

The inner conflict caused by O'Neill's infatuation with Bryant was artistically productive. O'Neill would have had his relationship with Bryant in mind, for example, when he wrote both BEYOND THE HORIZON, a play in which two brothers are in love with the same woman, and STRANGE INTERLUDE, in which a married woman takes obvious pleasure in her hold over several men. Nina Leeds, the central female character in *Strange Interlude*, is the vital and alluring focus of male admirers whose complex desires converge in her. Nina's wish to preserve the memory of her war-hero lover Gordon Shaw by writing his biography resembles Louise Bryant's devotion to the memory of John Reed, whose death from typhus in 1920 prompted identical desires in Bryant. Like Bryant, Nina struggles to overcome her grief for a romantic idealist loved by many whose death has cast a pall on her subsequent relationships. Arguably, *Strange Interlude* not only underscores O'Neill's admiration of Reed and continued fascination with Bryant; it also indicates his desire to explore the painful nuances of the love triangle that preoccupied him psychologically during his early career and afterward.

Three years after Reed's death, Bryant, now a leading correspondent for the Hearst newspaper chain, married the wealthy diplomat William C. Bullitt, formerly an assistant secretary of state in Woodrow Wilson's administration. Bullitt's discovery of Bryant's lesbian affair with English sculptor Gwen Le Gallienne led to a bitter divorce in 1930, with Bryant denied access to her only child.

From 1926 onward, Bryant's health declined rapidly due to Dercum's disease, a rare disorder whose disfiguring effects resemble elephantiasis, causing terrible pain, fatigue, and mental confusion. Previously a nondrinker, Louise increasingly sought refuge from her symptoms in alcohol. She died alone in Paris on January 6, 1936. At that time, she had been negotiating for the transfer of her personal papers to Harvard researchers who were interested in writing a biography of John Reed but not in interviewing his once-famous widow.

Recent treatments of Bryant's career, including Mary Dearborn's 1996 biography, have argued that Louise Bryant has been unjustly marginalized by the gender bias of historians, and that a rekindled appreciation for her life is overdue. O'Neill himself may have anticipated Dearborn's argument. In one of his first interviews after winning the NOBEL PRIZE IN LITERATURE in 1936, the year of Bryant's death, O'Neill directed the conversation toward the Provincetown summer of 1916, recalling how the Playwrights' Theatre had made his "serious drama" possible. Though he did not mention Bryant by name, he would surely have been thinking of her as he referred to the "theatrical pioneers" who were "responsible for the reception" of his early drama (Neuberger 23). In the Provincetown period and afterward, Louise Bryant was a daring, rebellious, and romantic figure. Her strong personality, along with her beliefs about art, literature, GENDER, and politics, seem to have held O'Neill's long-term interest and appealed to him in complex ways. She was an important member of the generation of leftist idealists who stimulated O'Neill's thinking as a young playwright and to some extent enabled his rise to fame.

Bibliography

Bryant, Louise. *Six Red Months in Russia*. London: William Heinemann, 1919.

Dearborn, Mary V. *Queen of Bohemia: The Life of Louise Bryant*. Boston and New York: Houghton Mifflin, 1996.

Gardner, Virginia. *"Friend and Lover": The Life of Louise Bryant*. New York: Horizon Press, 1982.

Neuberger, Richard L. "O'Neill Turns West toward New Horizons," *New York Times*, November 22, 1936.

Reds, 194 min., Paramount Pictures, Hollywood, 1981. Paramount DVD re-release, 2006.

Roazen, Paul. "Eugene O'Neill and Louise Bryant: New Documents." *Eugene O'Neill Review* 27 (2005): 29–40.

Patrick Chura

Buenos Aires, Argentina   Eugene O'Neill arrived in Buenos Aires from Boston on August 3, 1910. His voyage aboard the square rigger the CHARLES RACINE took 57 days. Even though he had been a passenger aboard the *Racine*, he arrived in Buenos Aires like most sailors do, having experienced the isolation and deprivation of a long period at SEA.

At that time, the seafaring community considered Buenos Aires the most popular South American Atlantic port due to the services and activities available in the city's waterfront district. Like other medium- and large-sized ports, Buenos Aires had a thriving sailortown, which contained boarding houses, brothels, bars, shipping agents, chandlers, and seamen's aid societies that all provided services for sailors. Some of the establishments were more reputable than others. Buenos Aires was not a safe place for sailors and other transients, who were preyed upon by the city's disreputable elements. For example, Tommy Moore, a shipping agent, was known for shanghaing sailors for captains in search of crew (Richter 53). In addition to the bars and brothels to entertain sailors, the waterfront district of Barracas, a suburb of Buenos Aires, was a popular destination due to the theaters that showed pornographic films made in France and Spain. O'Neill makes reference to Tommy Moore and the films in Barracas in his one-act play BOUND EAST FOR CARDIFF.

Upon his arrival in August 1910, O'Neill spent a few nights aboard the *Charles Racine* and other nights at the Continental Hotel. But once the ship had off-loaded its cargo and secured another one, it departed Buenos Aires, and O'Neill was on his own. He eventually moved from the Continental Hotel to a less expensive boardinghouse and took on a few jobs, which included helping to unload lumber for the British square rigger *Timandra*, tracing plans for an electrical supply firm, sorting raw cowhides at

A view of the waterfront at Buenos Aires, Argentina *(Courtesy of the Peabody Essex Museum)*

the Swift Packing House and breaking up old sewing machines for the Singer Sewing Machine Company. O'Neill did not stay at any of these jobs for very long; the jobs themselves were either short in duration, too boring, or in the case of sorting hides too vile, the smell being almost unbearable.

O'Neill frequented many of the bars in Buenos Aires's sailortown, in particular the Sailor's Opera. One of the attractions of the Sailor's Opera was the all-female ensemble who wore short skirts with no underwear and played stringless violins. The music was provided by a piano player hidden behind a curtain (Sheaffer 173). Patronized by men of many nationalities, the Sailor's Opera was described by O'Neill as a "madhouse." The patrons themselves added to the entertainment with stories, songs, and debates over the prowess of their ships. In the midst of all the activity, boys distributed cards to advertise the numerous brothels in the district (Sheaffer

174). It was at the Sailor's Opera that O'Neill met "Smitty," an English nobleman who had fallen on hard times. O'Neill recalled Smitty when he wrote his short story "TOMORROW" and his one-act play *IN THE ZONE.*

As his money began to run out, O'Neill left the boardinghouse and lived on the beach, sleeping on benches at the Paseo Colon and spending what little money he had on alcohol. After seven months in Buenos Aires, falling into a deep depression and hitting rock bottom, he pulled himself together and signed aboard the tramp steamer SS *IKALA* for a passage to New York City.

O'Neill's recollections of Buenos Aires stayed with him throughout his life, and he made many references to the city, the people he met, and the establishments he frequented in his plays, including *Bound East for Cardiff, In the Zone,* and *BEYOND THE HORIZON.*

Bibliography

Hugill, Stan. *Sailortown*. London: Routledge & Kegan
    Paul, 1967.

Richter, Robert A. *Eugene O'Neill and Dat Ole Davil Sea:
    Maritime Influences in the Life and Works of Eugene
    O'Neill.* Mystic, Conn.: Mystic Seaport, 2004.

Sheaffer, Louis. *O'Neill, Son and Playwright*. Boston:
    Little, Brown, 1968.

Robert A. Richter

Byth, James Findlater (James Findlater Bythe, James Findlater-Byth) (1866–1913)

James Findlater Byth was Eugene O'Neill's roommate above JIMMY "THE PRIEST'S" saloon, JAMES O'NEILL's press agent, and a former Boer War (1899–1902) correspondent. Byth (née Bythe and also know as Findlater-Byth) was the model for James "Jimmy" Anderson in O'Neill's short story "TOMORROW," the drunken roommate Jimmy in the 1919 one-act play *EXORCISM* (destroyed), and James "Jimmy Tomorrow" Cameron in *The ICEMAN COMETH*. O'Neill describes the Byth character in "Tomorrow" as living in a "dream of tomorrows" (3:948), while Larry Slade in *Iceman* calls him "the leader of our Tomorrow Movement" (3:584). Byth also informs the character Ted Nelson, the young playwright in *BREAD AND BUTTER*, who remarks, "I'm always going to start that play—tomorrow. . . . They ought to write on my tombstone: The deceased at last met one thing he couldn't put off till tomorrow" (1:151). Echoes of Byth additionally appear in the aspiring fiction writer Stephen Murray in *The STRAW*, who describes his latent passion for writing serious work by saying, "I was always going to—tomorrow—and tomorrow never came. I got in a rut—and stayed put" (1:742).

Although information about Byth's background is scarce, the finest source is Richard M. Little's feature article on Byth and James O'Neill entitled "Haunted by the Ghosts of Monte Cristo," which appeared in the *Chicago Record Herald* on February 9, 1908 (Alexander 2005, 179). Byth was born James Findlater Bythe to the upholsterer George Bythe in a working-class section of Cornwall, England, called Church Town on March 19, 1866 (Gelb 234). He emigrated to the United States some time in 1893 to work as a journalist and theatrical agent. Byth claimed to have graduated with honors from Edinburgh University in Scotland, though the veracity of much of his claims, as O'Neill BIOGRAPHERS Arthur and Barbara Gelb submit, "seemed immaterial, for he was incontestably brilliant, witty, often wondrously resourceful and entirely persuasive—if often drunk" (235).

Byth claimed to have served as a war correspondent in the Boer War, though there has been some controversy about the truth of this. Because Little lists him as having reported for the famous news agency Reuters, O'Neill biographer Louis Sheaffer checked the records and found no one by that name listed in the Reuters manifests. He therefore concludes that Byth—a "fraud, an innocent harmless one, yet still a fraud" (quoted in Alexander 2005, 25)—must have derived his information from friends of his who fought in the war and thereafter worked in the Great Boer War Spectacle that toured, among other places, to the 1904 St. Louis World Fair and New York City (Sheaffer 130). Two of these men, whom O'Neill met through Byth, appear as the characters Piet "The General" Wetjoen and Cecil "The Captain" Lewis (with whom James Cameron shares a table) in *The Iceman Cometh*. Doris Alexander argues, however, that Byth would have been insane to have worked for Reuters during the war, as he also claimed to have marched with the Boers, who would have killed any reporter they found working for the pro-British, pro-imperialist news service (26). Because O'Neill never mentions Reuters in his recollections of Byth, in neither fiction, drama, conversation, nor letters, Alexander concludes that Byth could only have worked for a "continental agency." In addition, she points out that in the short story "Tomorrow," O'Neill discusses the story of Jimmy Anderson/James Byth's wife's being caught "*flagrante delictu*" [sic] in his home in Cape Town. But O'Neill, recognizing his mistake, as "Pretoria, not Cape Town, was headquarters for the Boers," made James Cameron/James Byth in *Iceman* work for "some English paper" so the Cape Town story might still be included (27).

While Byth was working for the publicity firm Liebler and Company, he was hired as James O'Neill's press agent, or "advance man," in September 1907. By the following year, he and the young Eugene O'Neill had become fast drinking buddies. O'Neill was so entranced by Byth's stories of South Africa and the Boers that he signed onto a MERCHANT MARINE steamer shipping mules from BUENOS AIRES, ARGENTINA, to Durban, South Africa, but unfortunately he did not have the £100 fee required to disembark the ship.

Byth and O'Neill shared a room at Jimmy "the Priest's" from late 1911 to 1912, paying three dollars a month in rent. Byth and a man named Major Adams found O'Neill half dead in Byth and O'Neill's room on either New Year's Eve 1911 or sometime in the first two weeks of January 1912. O'Neill had attempted suicide by overdosing on the barbiturate Veronal, a harrowing experience he recounted in *Exorcism*. On June 6, 1913, Byth fell out his bedroom window to the pavement below. O'Neill always believed it was a suicide, but Doris Alexander convincingly argues that if Byth truly wished to end his own life, why would he choose a three-story building with a half-attic "in a city full of accessible ten- and fifteen-story windows" (22)? In addition, on June 8, 1913, the *New York Times* reported of his death: "James Findlater Byth, 46 years old, for many years connected with newspaper and theatrical work, died yesterday at the New York Hospital of injuries sustained last week when he fell from the window of his house at 252 Fulton Street [the address of Jimmy 'the Priest's]'" (quoted in Alexander 22). O'Neill probably heard the news soon after,

as it occurred only a few days following his June 3 release from GAYLORD FARM SANATORIUM, and he always remained "convinced that Jimmy's death had been a suicide" (Alexander 23). Nevertheless, it is Don Parritt, not "Jimmy Tomorrow," who commits suicide in *Iceman*, which leads Alexander to believe it was "as if some part of O'Neill knew what his conscious mind did not know: that the only suicide at Jimmy the Priest's had been his own abortive one, and the real Jimmy had never lost his faith in a glorious tomorrow" (28).

Bibliography

Alexander, Doris. *Eugene O'Neill's Last Plays: Separating Art from Autobiography*. Athens: University of Georgia Press, 2005.

———. *The Tempering of Eugene O'Neill*. New York: Harcourt, Brace, and World, 1962.

Black, Stephen A. *Eugene O'Neill: Beyond Mourning and Tragedy*. New Haven, Conn.: Yale University Press, 1999.

Gelb, Arthur, and Barbara Gelb. *O'Neill: Life with Monte Cristo*. New York: Applause Books, 2000.

O'Neill, Eugene. "Tomorrow." In *The Unknown O'Neill: Unpublished or Unfinished Writings of Eugene O'Neill*. Edited by Travis Bogard. New Haven, Conn.: Yale University Press, 1988, 313–331.

Sheaffer, Louis. *O'Neill: Son and Playwright*. Boston: Little, Brown, 1968.

C

Calms of Capricorn, The See TALE OF POSSESS-ORS, SELF-DISPOSSESSED, A.

Carlin, Terry (1855–1934) Terry Carlin was perhaps the closest of Eugene O'Neill's anarchist friends. Carlin is one of the numerous ephemeral characters who turn up in the history of ANARCHISM: people who led adventurous lives and made their marks through action and through the friendship they nurtured but who left little written record or formal trace for history. Thus little is known of the particulars of Carlin's life, and he is remembered almost solely for his influence on O'Neill and his connection with important anarchist initiatives such as the PROVINCETOWN PLAYERS and the Ferrer Center alternative school. IRISH by background, Carlin spent many years in Chicago, where he worked in various trades before taking up a bohemian life on the road. Quitting work as a tanner, Carlin became a hobo, drifting from town to town and relying on the generosity of friends such as O'Neill, Theodore Dreiser, and the anarchist EMMA GOLDMAN for sustenance.

Carlin, like O'Neill, had been protégé of individualist anarchist BENJAMIN TUCKER during the early decades of the 20th century. Both spent considerable time at Tucker's Unique Book Store in New York City. Carlin lived for a time at the Ferrer Center, the radical free school with which O'Neill was also involved. A long-time anarchist, Carlin had been secretary of the Liberty Group in Chicago.

Carlin, like Tucker, was an advocate of PHILOSOPHICAL ANARCHISM, which stressed individual liberty and self-transformation rather than the revolutionary collectivism of anarchist communism, an emphasis that he encouraged in O'Neill. Carlin was also an enthusiast of Eastern religion and his friends considered him to be something of a mystic. Carlin urged O'Neill to read *The Path of the Light*, and the playwright carved a passage from the text ("Before the soul can fly, its wings must be washed in the blood of the heart!") on the ceiling of their rooming house in Provincetown.

O'Neill and Carlin spent much time on the road together and squatted in derelict tenements in New York City for housing during at least one winter together. They traveled together to Provincetown in 1916, and a chance encounter between Carlin, who mentioned that O'Neill had a "trunk full of plays," and his old friend SUSAN GLASPELL led to the Provincetown putting on O'Neill's play BOUND EAST FOR CARDIFF. The success of the play's run led to a long association between O'Neill and the Provincetown Players.

A hard-drinker with noted skills as an orator and a certain ragged charm, Carlin provided O'Neill with the inspiration for the character of Larry Slade, the "old foolosopher" who spent his days and nights in Harry Hope's Saloon in The ICEMAN COMETH. Carlin also provided O'Neill with the story that would form a crucial part of the plot in *Iceman*. This story involved the McNamara dynamite plot and the subsequent infiltration of Emma Goldman's periodical

Terry Carlin in Provincetown, Massachusetts *(Courtesy of the Sheaffer-O'Neill Collection, Charles E. Shain Library of Connecticut College)*

Mother Earth by the police. Carlin told O'Neill of the police pursuit of anarchists for their supposed involvement in an explosion at the *Los Angeles Times* over that newspaper's antiunion reporting. In order to crack anarchist circles the inspector in charge of the case, Detective William J. Burns, who was much hated by anarchists, offered payment to Donald Vose, the son of an anarchist, who happily betrayed David Caplan and Matthew Schmidt, the two anarchists connected to the bombing who had long eluded the law. Vose gained access to the two men while accompanying Carlin, who was in no way involved in the betrayal, on a visit to Emma Goldman's home. Vose is represented as Don Parritt in *Iceman*, a "stool-pigeon" who informed on his own mother. In *Iceman*, Larry Slade (Carlin) proclaims in disgust: "May his soul rot in hell" (3:579). Perhaps exacting that symbolic justice, O'Neill has the Parritt character kill himself out of guilt for his actions, a fate that did not befall Vose, who was well-rewarded for his betrayal. The event devastated Goldman, who wrote a public denunciation of Vose in *Mother Earth*.

A friend of Hutchins Hapgood while in Chicago, Carlin also served as the hero in Hapgood's

1909 novel, *An Anarchist Woman*. Carlin died in obscurity in New York City of pneumonia in 1934.

Bibliography

Diggins, John Patrick. *Eugene O'Neill's America: Desire under Democracy.* Chicago: University of Chicago Press, 2007.

Frazer, Winifred. *E. G. and E.G.O.: Emma Goldman and The Iceman Cometh.* Gainesville: University of Florida Press, 1974.

———. "O'Neill's Stately Mansions: A Visitor's Reminiscences." *The Eugene O'Neill Newsletter* 8, no. 3 (Winter 1984).

Goldman, Emma. *Living My Life.* New York: Alfred A. Knopf, 1931.

J. Shantz

Casa Genolta   See SEA ISLAND, GEORGIA.

Catholicism   In the last act of LONG DAY'S JOURNEY INTO NIGHT, James Tyrone, Sr., in yet another round of endless verbal sparring, implores his son Edmund not to start with his "damned atheist morbidness" (3:807). Edmund's apostasy was also Eugene O'Neill's. Several years prior to writing *Long Day's Journey*, O'Neill forfeited his Catholicism and the teachings of Thomas Aquinas, adopting instead the ideas of Sigmund Freud, Carl Jung, and FRIEDRICH NIETZSCHE. After the age of 14, he never again sought God within the confines of the Catholic Church—that is, he never practiced his religion, but to a degree, O'Neill remained uneasy about Catholicism. His "liberation" from his faith resulted in an artistic life marked by repeated attempts to find God and to know man. Rather than consider his public disavowals of any belief in, or return to Catholicism, one needs examine the subjects of his plays to understand O'Neill's longing for belief. After he wrote DAYS WITHOUT END (his most "Catholic" play), O'Neill insisted that he had not returned to Catholicism, but he added: "I would be a liar if I didn't admit that, for the sake of my soul's peace, I have often wished I could" (O'Neill 433).

Both of O'Neill's parents were "cradle Catholics"—those baptized into the faith from infancy—and believers who took their obligations to

Catholicism seriously, baptizing both sons (O'Neill's occurred on November 1, 1888, at the Church of the Holy Innocents in Manhattan). His parents sent their sons to Catholic grammar and preparatory schools, and they promoted immersion in the faith. O'Neill's father JAMES O'NEILL attended mass every Sunday and established a reputation as a model Catholic; his mother, MARY ELLEN "ELLA" O'NEILL, though suffering from an addiction to morphine, was known for her piety.

For Edward Shaughnessy, the O'Neills' Catholicism was formed in the crucible of the post-famine IRISH Catholicism of the 19th century, a time when the Catholic Church served as the repository of IRISH AMERICAN identity—an instrument of ethnic survival and a guarantor of personal salvation. At the same time that the faith of Ireland burned brightly in the O'Neill household, the O'Neill sons probably followed the pattern of other children of immigrant parents, becoming less attached to their religion while becoming practitioners of a more secular American faith—a quasi-Christian faith in God with more generic ethical principles, as reflected in the U.S. Constitution.

At the age of seven, Eugene was sent to board with the Sisters of Charity at St. Aloysius; he was drilled in the catechism and served at early mass. He also suffered intense feelings of abandonment (Alexander 24). In fall 1900, he enrolled as a day student at the De La Salle Institute run by the Christian Brothers in Manhattan. During this time period, as his mother's sickness became more apparent and his prayers for her recovery went unheeded, O'Neill apparently became increasingly disillusioned; he decided he could no longer believe in the faith of his ancestors. In 1902, he persuaded his father to send him to the secular Betts Academy.

In summer 1903, after witnessing a demonstration of his mother's addiction to morphine, complicated by the guilty realization that her addiction was probably caused by his own birth, O'Neill made a final break with Catholicism, refusing to attend church with his family. He was looking for a way out of the torture of his own life's history and found that he could better tolerate the addiction, guilt, war between fathers and sons and husbands and wives, and the unspoken love of his family through

the philosophy of Friedrich Nietzsche. He wrote to a friend, "*Zarathustra* . . . has influenced me more than any book I've ever read. I ran into it . . . when I was eighteen and I've always possessed a copy since then and every year or so I re-read it and am never disappointed" (O'Neill 245–246).

O'Neill became the consummate rebel, in flight from family and religion. He embarked on a course of self-destruction—20 years of restlessness, in which his estrangement blossomed into a philosophy of life that assumed God had little to do with the affairs of men, palliated by ALCOHOLISM, womanizing, and wandering. He began to forge associations with a group of intellectuals based in GREENWICH VILLAGE and later in Provincetown, Massachusetts. Included in this same circle was DOROTHY DAY (now a candidate for sainthood in the Catholic Church), who later espoused a Christian-socialist philosophy of charity, poverty, and service to the poor. O'Neill and Day were close companions for a period of six months.

Ironically, O'Neill's recitation to Dorothy Day—from memory—of the lengthy poem "The Hound of Heaven" by the Catholic fin de siècle mystical poet Francis Thompson presaged Day's ultimate adoption of Catholicism. The poem describes Thompson's futile attempt to flee from God: "I fled Him, down the nights and down the days/I fled Him down the arches of the years/I fled Him, down the labyrinthine ways/Of my own mind; and in the midst of tears/I hid from Him (Thompson 88). Soon after O'Neill recited the poem, Dorothy Day and O'Neill parted company; she continued along a downward path—impregnated and abandoned by a hard-drinking journalist after agreeing to an abortion and then marrying on the rebound and divorcing. Dorothy Day finally surrendered to the "Hound of Heaven" and joined the Catholic Church in 1927. She never stopped praying for Eugene O'Neill, who had opened her eyes with the Thompson poem. In her autobiography. *From Union Square to Rome*, Day wrote that the idea of pursuit fascinated her—the inevitableness of it. Inevitably, she felt she would have to pause in the mad rush of living to remember her beginning and her end.

Day ultimately found meaning within the Catholic Church. O'Neill continued his search and abated his restlessness through his writing, which reflects a complex moral sensibility and includes notions of sin, guilt, and punishment—unsurprisingly, since, as Edward Shaughnessy points out, O'Neill's moral sensibility was deeply imprinted on his psychology by his culture, resulting in a moral sense that defies facile interpretations.

O'Neill's plays ultimately are the keys that unlock his complicated relationship to Catholicism. Like James Joyce, another artist apostate, Catholicism fed the source of both artists' metaphoric imaginations. For his part, O'Neill's treatment of religion is always pessimistic: In the face of the cosmos, man remains finite. Yet there remains in O'Neill's work a certain tension between despair and a desire to believe which he identifies as the sickness of modern society—"the death of the old God and the failure of Science and Materialism to give any satisfying new One for the surviving primitive religious instinct to find a meaning for life in, and to comfort its fears of death with" (O'Neill 311).

As an agnostic in search of redemption, O'Neill never stopped looking for a substitute for religion, but he became unsparing in his critiques of various substitutes for religion. In *The HAIRY APE*, Yank is man "struggling for his place in creation" and is sadly rejected by society, never finding his place (Quinn 369). In *DESIRE UNDER THE ELMS*, O'Neill scrutinizes the failed strain of American Puritanism—here, more emblematic of an enormous emphasis on prosperity, rather than on religious or moral scruples. The play is notable for its redemptive quality, if redemption be seen in terms of an act of suffering accepted in good grace: The lovers sin and want to pay for their sin; their willingness to do so reflects the Catholic belief in the "efficacy of suffering"—a notion that suffering is a means to holiness and leads to redemption. Suffering atones for the temporal effects of sin. As these two embrace their punishment, one comes to the conclusion that they have redeemed themselves.

Among O'Neill's strongest "search" plays are *The GREAT GOD BROWN* and *Days Without End*. As he confided in a letter to CARLOTTA MONTEREY O'NEILL: "Yes, one might very well sum up the meaning of *Brown* as my search for God in this life"

(O'Neill 288). In *The Great God Brown*, O'Neill denounces the destructive capability of materialism as a possible faith for modern man (a theme he explores further in *DYNAMO*). Here, salvation cannot be found in a world in which one must wear armor in order to touch or be touched. Dion Anthony scorns man as an "infant blubbering in the dark;" he mocks man's "Fixation on old Mama Christianity!" (2:484). Dion's conflict can be distilled: The peace that God used to offer has now become unrecognizable and trivialized into a notion God equals love: "All the world loves a lover, God loves us all and we love Him! Love is a word—a shameless ragged ghost of a word—begging at all doors for life at any price!" (1:481). As the characters in the play mask and unmask themselves, they fail to find any genuine, sustaining human relationship.

The peace that God offers looms large in *Days Without End*, a work O'Neill dubbed his "miracle play." Most critics saw little that was miraculous in the play and focused more on its weak script, speculating that O'Neill did little to veil his desire to return to the Catholic Church. O'Neill, of course, disavowed any such intention. Yet the play is his most explicitly Catholic work: Roughly three-quarters of it is spent examining the spiritual struggle of apostate John Loving, adulterer; at the end, Loving, remorseful for causing his wife's critical illness, turns to the church and makes a leap toward faith.

Throughout his corpus, including his early one-act plays, *The EMPEROR JONES*, and *Desire under the Elms*, O'Neill punishes sinners. During a final rehearsal for *The ICEMAN COMETH*, he said: "In all my plays sin is punished and redemption takes place" (quoted in Shaughnessy 149). In *Iceman*, Hickey is punished for murdering his wife, yet here, as well as in *Long Day's Journey into Night*, *A MOON FOR THE MISBEGOTTEN*, and *HUGHIE*, punishment for a sin committed is not the issue. Rather, we are left with the understanding that one's guilt can be alleviated, and absolution can be received—through confession.

At the end of his life, O'Neill never sought absolution; his final confession was never heard, and he never sought readmittance to the Catholic Church. When Dorothy Day heard that O'Neill was sick, she asked his friend, Richard Cushing (then a bishop, later a cardinal), to send a priest to see him. Father Vincent Mackey tried to do so, but O'Neill's wife, CARLOTTA MONTEREY O'NEILL, refused to admit him to the dying man's room. At his own request, O'Neill was buried privately and without ceremony at Forest Hills Cemetery in Boston, rather than in the family plot in St. Mary's Cemetery at NEW LONDON, CONNECTICUT.

After O'Neill's death, Dorothy Day wrote: "I would be sinning against hope, faith, and charity if I did not believe that my prayers, and whoever else is praying for the soul of Gene, are heard" (quoted in Shaughnessy 188).

Bibliography

Alexander, Doris. *The Tempering of Eugene O'Neill*. New York: Harcourt, Brace & World, 1962.

Bogard, Travis. *Contour in Time: The Plays of Eugene O'Neill*. Rev. ed. New York: Oxford University Press, 1988.

Gelb, Arthur, and Barbara Gelb. *O'Neill: Life with Monte Cristo*. New York: Applause Books, 2000.

Miller, William D. *Dorothy Day: A Biography*. New York: Harper & Row, 1982.

O'Neill, Eugene. *Selected Letters of Eugene O'Neill*. Edited by Traview Bogard and Jackson R. Bryer. New Haven, Conn.: Yale University Press, 1988.

Quinn, Arthur Hobson. "Eugene O'Neill, Poet and Mystic." *Scribner's Magazine* (December 1926): 369–381.

Shaughnessy, Edward L. *Down the Nights and Down the Days: Eugene O'Neill's Catholic Sensibility*. Notre Dame, Ind.: University of Notre Dame Press,1966.

Sheaffer, Louis. *O'Neill: Son and Playwright*. Boston: Little, Brown, 1968.

Thompson, Francis. *The Complete Poetical Works of Francis Thompson*. New York: Modern Library, 1918.

Eileen Herrmann

censorship/free speech   The act of censoring or banning controversial plays began with the dawn of drama. In America, a proclivity toward censorship commenced in the 17th century when Puritan authorities condemned the stage as a den of idleness and iniquity. Over time, as theater became a dominant entertainment in the United States, censorious forces sharpened their focus to specific content, most particularly challenges to traditional values, racial issues, various human behaviors (especially "accepted" or "deviant" sexuality), and vulgar language. In the mid-19th century, the conflicted views of an audiences were revealed by musical and burlesque performances featuring scantily clad women that seemed to simultaneously titillate and outrage audiences. While limited nudity (or its illusion) and risqué subject matter were generally accepted in light entertainments in New York, on the "road," the vast network of theaters across the country presenting touring productions created complex issues of what was acceptable and what was not in any particular state or town. The legitimate drama encountered even more complex difficulties as it increasingly confronted traditionally taboo subjects in the late 19th century.

After 1880, the focus of censorship shifted toward the increasingly realistic content of modernist plays, with frequent closings (and arrests) associated with the earliest American productions of social-problem dramas by HENRIK IBSEN and GEORGE BERNARD SHAW. Among U.S. playwrights, James A. Herne's *Margaret Fleming* (1890), written in the Ibsenite mode, was not permitted performances in New York or Boston due to its depiction of marital infidelity. In 1905, Arnold Daly produced Shaw's *Mrs. Warren's Profession*, which had been written in the early 1890s as an exploration of the social hypocrisy of prostitution, and he was arrested along with the leading lady, Mary Shaw. American plays running afoul of authorities prior to World War I include Clyde Fitch's *Sapho* (1900), which led to a similar arrest for its star, Olga Nethersole, and George Scarborough's *The Lure* (1913), among others.

After World War I, motion pictures drew many playgoers away from live theater as postwar perceptions of new freedom and enlightenment prompted playwrights and playgoers to demand a theater more truly reflective of modern concerns. In this environment, both the censorious and their targets encountered significant challenges. Eugene O'Neill, who emerged as the dominant American dramatist of that era, found controversy with several of his plays in the 1920s, as did several of his colleagues. Edwin Justus Mayer's *The Firebrand* (1924), Sidney

Howard's PULITZER PRIZE–winning *They Knew What They Wanted* (1924), and Maxwell Anderson and Laurence Stallings's *What Price Glory* (1924), among the most critically acclaimed plays of the period, were all either forced to make revisions or were closed in New York and elsewhere. Mae West appeared in her own play, the blatantly named *Sex* (1926), and was arrested on indecency charges; her next, *The Drag* (1927), featuring homosexual characters, closed before reaching New York. These and other challenging plays led to enactment of the Wales Padlock Law (1927), which allowed city officials to close any theater violating public decency, although it was rarely enforced since determining the boundaries of those standards proved to be difficult.

Among O'Neill's plays, *The HAIRY APE* (1922), DESIRE UNDER THE ELMS (1924), and his Pulitzer Prize–winning STRANGE INTERLUDE (1928) met with resistance over their sexual content (and film adaptations of these and other O'Neill plays suffered significant cuts and changes due to film censorship), with incest (and infanticide) featured in *Desire under the Elms* and an amoral woman as the protagonist of *Strange Interlude*. Other O'Neill works, including the Pulitzer Prize–winning "ANNA CHRISTIE" (1921), with its prostitute heroine, and his seafaring one-acts rife with strong language and various controversial topics, also disturbed some critics and audience members. None, however, met with the controversy that greeted O'Neill's ALL GOD'S CHILLUN GOT WINGS (1924), which depicted an interracial relationship. Public outrage filled editorial pages of newspapers, particularly regarding a scene in which Ella, the central white character played by Mary Blair, kisses the hand of her black husband Jim, played by PAUL ROBESON. When the controversy began, ludicrous suggestions were made for appeasing the outraged voices, including replacing Robeson with a white actor in blackface to avoid offending predominantly white middle-class audiences. Such suggestions were firmly rejected by O'Neill, who threatened to withdraw the play if any changes were made. A photograph of Blair appeared in newspapers across the country provocatively declaring: "White Actress to Kiss Negro's Hand." Veteran playwright Augustus Thomas described the casting of Robeson and the

kiss as unnecessary concessions to reality, and Brigadier General Edward Underwood of the Salvation Army publicly stated that "it is my opinion that the production of this play should be prevented, if the charges of its being objectionable are sustained." John Sumner, secretary of the Society for the Suppression of Vice, insisted that "From my information the play is at least a tactless thing, and if it does nothing more than lead to race antagonisms the police powers of the city should be used to prevent its presentation. Such a play might easily lead to racial riots or disorder, and if there is any such possibility, police powers should be exercised." One newspaper wrote that most protests centered on the hand-kissing business, and that an equal number of blacks and whites had written protesting letters. O'Neill himself received hate mail about *All God's Chillun Got Wings*, including public threats from the Ku Klux Klan, and he was forced to endure several months of police protection.

As the media debate raged, O'Neill himself finally issued a statement defending *All God's Chillun*: "Finally, and plainly, all we ask is a square deal. A play is written to be experienced through the theatre, and only on its merits in a theatre can a final judgment be passed on it with justice. We demand this hearing. We shall play it before our audience, and abide by their verdict in the fullest confidence that the play, produced as it should be, can give no offence to any rational American of whatever creed or race." His frustration, and the intensity of the reaction to the play, is most vividly uncovered in a letter written to a friend: "It seemed for a time there as if all the feeble-witted both in and out of the K.K.K. were hurling newspaper bricks in my direction—not to speak of the anonymous letters which ranged from those of infuriated Irish Catholics who threatened to pull my ears off as a disgrace to their race and religion, to those of equally infuriated Nordic Kluxers who knew that I had Negro blood, or else was a Jewish pervert masquerading under a Christian name in order to do subversive propaganda for the Pope! This sounds like burlesque, but the letters were more so."

Four days before *All God's Chillun Got Wings* opened, O'Neill responded to a reporter's question about whether or not the play promoted interracial marriage. He replied, "I am never the advocate of anything in any play—except humanity toward humanity. I am a dramatist. To me every human being is a special case, with his or her own special set of values. True, often those values are just a variant of values shared in common by a great group of people. But it is the manner in which those values have acted on the individual and his reactions to them which makes him a special case." *All God's Chillun Got Wings* finally opened on May 15, 1924, at New York's Provincetown Playhouse, although the first scene involving several children had to be omitted because the Society for the Prevention of Cruelty to Children successfully brought a court action to stop their involvement in the production. The play's director, JAMES LIGHT, appeared onstage to explain the problem to the audience, who concurred with his suggestion that he read the missing scene. Riot police were stationed outside the theater, but no significant incident occurred. Critics, caught up in the furor, generally condemned the play; for example, Percy Hammond wrote that it is "A bit overdone and breathless, it is a vehement exposition of a marriage between a stupid negro and a stupid white woman. If it is possible for you to get an emotion out of that situation, here is your opportunity."

Even in his reclusive later years, O'Neill could be relied on to protest attempts to censor works of art and literature, running afoul of the censorious who protested the language (particularly the use of the word *whore*) in The ICEMAN COMETH (1939) during its 1946 Broadway premiere, and who objected to his last play, A MOON FOR THE MISBEGOTTEN (1943). In late summer 1947, the play was on its pre-Broadway tryout tour, and following its second performance in Detroit, the local sheriff abruptly closed the theater, charging its management with endangering public decency, ostensibly because the words *mother* and *whore* were used in the same sentence. The production folded in Detroit, and it was 25 years before *A Moon for the Misbegotten* attained Broadway success and critical approval.

O'Neill once stated, "Censorship of anything, at any time, in any place, on whatever pretense, has always been and will always be the last resort of the boob and the bigot," a view that undoubtedly was shaped by his own experiences.

Bibliography

Frank, Glenda. "Tempest in Black and White: The 1924 Premiere of Eugene O'Neill's *All God's Chillun Got Wings*," *Resources for American Literary Studies* 26, no. 1 (2000): 75–89.

Houchin, John H. *Censorship of the American Theatre in the Twentieth Century.* Cambridge: Cambridge University Press, 1997.

———. "Eugene O'Neill's 'Woman Play' in Boston." *Eugene O'Neill Review* 22, nos. 1–2 (Spring–Fall 1998): 48–62.

Laufe, Abe. *The Wicked Stage: A History of Theatre Censorship and Harassment in the United States.* New York: F. Ungar, 1978.

Parkes, Adam. *Modernism and the Theatre of Censorship.* Oxford: Oxford University Press, 2002.

Sova, Dawn B. *Banned Plays: Censorship Histories of 125 Stage Dramas.* New York: Facts On File, 2004.

Wilmer, Steve E. "Censorship and Ideology: Eugene O'Neill (*The Hairy Ape*)." *Cycnos* 9 (1992): 53–60.

James Fisher

Charles Racine   In Eugene O'Neill's most autobiographical play, LONG DAY'S JOURNEY INTO NIGHT, Edmund Tyrone tells his father of some of his experiences at SEA, wistfully recalling memories of the time "when I was on the Squarehead square rigger, bound for Buenos Aires" (3:811). O'Neill is drawing on his own memories from when he sailed aboard the Norwegian bark *Charles Racine* from Boston to BUENOS AIRES, ARGENTINA. He went aboard the *Charles Racine* in June 1910 at the age of 21, and the voyage became one of the most memorable experiences of his lifetime.

The *Charles Racine* was an unusual vessel for its time, an era that was dominated by steam-powered ships. The *Racine* was launched in 1892 under the command of Captain Gustav Waage, who had convinced the Sigval Bergesen Line of Norway to build a square-rigged sailing vessel, while all of the company's other vessels were steamers. Waage, who continued to command the *Racine* beyond O'Neill's voyage, had the reputation of bringing his cargoes to port on schedule and with little damage, which was a difficult task for a vessel that depended on the wind as its only means of propulsion. When O'Neill joined the *Racine*, the ship was engaged in the

SS *Charles Racine* *(Courtesy of the Peabody Essex Museum)*

lumber trade between Boston and Buenos Aires. It was one of the few remaining trades that was viable for square riggers. There was a high demand for lumber in Buenos Aires due to an economic boom and New England had the natural resource.

The *Racine* probably caught O'Neill's eye in Boston harbor because it was one of the few square-riggers in a harbor dominated by steamers. He boarded the *Racine* as a paying passenger; his father, JAMES O'NEILL, who paid for the passage, thought the voyage to Buenos Aires would be good for his son. At the time, James was also receiving a great deal of bad publicity because Eugene was estranged from his wife, KATHLEEN JENKINS, and his newborn son, EUGENE O'NEILL, JR.

As a passenger, O'Neill was not required to do any work onboard, but it is more than likely that he undertook some shipboard tasks. He certainly observed the ship's workings and gained a significant understanding of life aboard a square-rigger. He came to understand the hierarchy of the crew and their trust, dependence, and reliance on each other. He lived a sailor's life; eating their food, singing chanteys to aid their work, and trading stories during the dogwatch. His experiences would have been reminiscent of the great age of sail and the era of the clipper ships in the middle of the 19th century. This particular voyage aboard the *Racine* was unique for all involved. A more typical voyage would have lasted approximately 40 days; O'Neill's lasted 57 days. During the voyage, the ship experienced beautiful sailing weather and record speeds, which was then followed by a period of no wind and being becalmed. The ship encountered three storms including a hurricane, during which the ship lost some of its deck cargo and one sail.

This was O'Neill's only voyage on a square-rigger, but he experienced all the extremes of square-rigged sailing. He drew on those experiences again and again while writing his plays; most notably BEYOND THE HORIZON, *The* HAIRY APE, MOURNING BECOMES ELECTRA, and his unfinished work *The Calms of Capricorn* (part of the planned cycle A TALE OF POSSESSORS SELF-DISPOSSESSED).

Bibliography

Bunting, W. H. *Portrait of a Port: Boston 1852–1914.* Cambridge, Mass.: Belknap Press of Harvard University Press, 1971.

Richter, Robert A. *Eugene O'Neill and Dat Ole Davil Sea: Maritime Influences in the Life and Works of Eugene O'Neill.* Mystic, Conn.: Mystic Seaport, 2004.

Sheaffer, Louis. *O'Neill: Son and Playwright.* Boston: Little, Brown, 1968.

Villiers, Alan. *The Way of a Ship.* New York: Charles Scribner's Sons, 1953.

Robert A. Richter

class   In the Oscar-winning 1981 film *Reds,* a revealing conversation takes place between a young Eugene O'Neill, played by Jack Nicholson, and LOUISE BRYANT, played by Dianne Keaton. It is late 1919, and Bryant has returned from Russia, where she has witnessed the Bolshevik Revolution with her husband, the communist activist JOHN REED. Reed has traveled back to Petrograd, and in his absence Bryant visits O'Neill in his apartment, apparently seeking to renew the love affair that had begun three years earlier. The conversation turns immediately to events in Russia, whereupon Bryant speaks excitedly about social revolution and her work for the communist cause. O'Neill, skeptical of Bryant's revolutionary doctrines and motives, mockingly quells Bryant's enthusiasm:

> You and Jack have a lot of middle-class dreams for two radicals. Jack dreams that he can hustle the American working man, whose one dream is to be rich enough not to have to work, into a revolution led by *his* party. And you dream that if you discuss the revolution with a man before you go to bed with him, it'll be missionary work rather than sex. I'm sorry to see you and Jack so serious about your sports. (Beatty and Griffiths)

This speech, though fictional, indicates much about Eugene O'Neill's attitudes toward issues of social reform and social class. In keeping with terms voiced often in O'Neill's drama, the scorching rebuke of Bryant accurately conveys the playwright's cynicism toward sweeping solutions to social problems, suggests the great suspicion O'Neill felt toward the proponents of such reform efforts, and expresses a trenchant insistence on class identification as a determining feature of human behavior.

Explorations of the class-based realities of American life abound in O'Neill's drama. One of the first plays he ever finished—a one-act entitled *ABORTION,* composed in 1913–14—presents a leisure-class college sports hero who commits suicide when his affair with a working-class girl threatens to become known. Jack Townsend, a "swell college guy" (O'Neill 1964, 160) and captain of the baseball team at an eastern university, is engaged to a woman of his own class, but he takes up with Nellie Murray, a "sweet, lovely" (154) working-girl stenographer who becomes pregnant with Jack's child. A secret abortion is arranged by Jack and paid for by his wealthy father. With his wedding date only three months away, Jack decides to "break off once and for all" (154) with Nellie. But on the day of his greatest college baseball victory, with Jack's family and fiancée on campus to celebrate, Nellie's brother Joe, a machinist stricken with tuberculosis, appears at Jack's dorm room to confront him with the news that his sister is dead from the abortion. "Yuh think yuh c'n get away with that stuff and then marry some goil of your own kind," Joe asserts, threatening Jack with a pistol (161). In the ensuing physical struggle, the athletic hero easily disarms the "narrow-chested" (144) machinist, but Joe gets back at Jack by fleeing to summon the police and make the affair public. As a victory parade in Jack's honor approaches outside his dorm window, he uses the gun he had wrestled from Joe to take his own life.

To the play's upper-class main character, the dalliance with Nellie had seemed "a pleasant game" (156) with consequences no more dire than a lapse of "taste" in associating with a woman socially beneath him. Jack discovers, however, that class barriers cannot be transgressed with impunity, and that the laws of society, though they are in Jack's own estimation "unnatural and monstrously distorted" (154), still force us to conform or pay dearly. The working-class Joe's indictment, "Your kind … treat us like servants" (161), along with the mutual ruin that results from Jack's deviation from social norms, shows that O'Neill began his career as a dramatist with a complex appreciation of the inescapable destructive effects of class barriers in American society.

A more comprehensive attack on the inequities of the capitalist system is contained in the 1925 play MARCO MILLIONS, which is set in 13th-century Venice but whose main character is a thinly veiled parody of the 20th-century American business-man. Spiritually vapid, tactless, and materialistic, the Venetian merchant Marco Polo is nevertheless "born with success in [his] pocket" (O'Neill, 1988, 2:399). He rises to become mayor of Yang-Chau, a city whose operations under the utilitarian dictator are a microcosmic version of big business's rule in the United States. As a representative of the domi-nant class, Marco ruthlessly maximizes profits, abol-ishes taxes on the wealthy, and institutes laws that shift economic burdens from rich to poor. Though a petition signed by a half million citizens charges him with "gross abuse of power," Marco dismisses the majority opinion as that of "a mere handful of radicals" (2:425). Holder of the "highest rank" (2:421) in a land bereft of political liberty and built on the incessant labor of "millions of contended slaves" (2:460), Marco blissfully pursues economic efficiency and the unconstrained satisfaction of crass appetites. But the American plutocrat's rise to the apex of the class system is accompanied by a telling spiritual emptiness. Within the play, Kublai Khan aptly characterizes the successful capitalist and "flesh and blood product" (2:413) of Western civilization: "He has not even an immortal soul, he has only an acquisitive instinct" (2:420).

While O'Neill exposed the soulless materi-alism of the upper classes, he also explored the effects of the class system through the perspective of exploited workers at the bottom of the eco-nomic structure. Years before he became known as a playwright, O'Neill forged a personal iden-tification with the working class that shaped his social views while providing him with a store of literary material that would carry him well into his career. During his excursions as a seaman in the MERCHANT MARINE from 1909 to 1911, he lived in forecastles, scrubbed decks, climbed riggings, spliced rope, ate hardtack, and befriended sailors who became the models for characters in several of his career-launching SEA plays. In the British port of Southampton, the future playwright explored waterfront dives and witnessed the great General Strike of 1911, until then, the worst labor scare in Britain's history, during which he heard strike talk and sympathized with the workers. On his return voyage aboard the SS PHILADELPHIA, O'Neill was proud to be promoted to "able seaman," receiving an American Line uniform jersey and a certificate that showed his "A-B" rating.

Considering his apprenticeship at sea, it is not surprising that the first O'Neill play ever produced depicted the lonely lives of destitute sailors and brought lower-class life and workers' language to the American stage. Critics have viewed BOUND EAST FOR CARDIFF as a turning point in AMERICAN THEATER history. The play's merits stem from its plausible treatment of tragic emotions under lower-class conditions and its accurate rendering of work-ing-class dialects. As O'Neill's friend Harry Kemp recalled after the play's first reading, "we heard the actual speech of men who go to sea; we shared the reality of their lives; we felt the motion and windy, wave-beaten urge of a ship" (96). SUSAN GLASPELL's observation that "The sea has been good to Eugene O'Neill. It was there for his opening" (254) asserts the central importance of the sailor's world—the locus of the author's personal encounter with the lower classes—among O'Neill's distinguishing artistic innovations.

Recent critics have described how the subject matter of O'Neill's early SS GLENCAIRN plays satisfied the psychic need for self-validation of a middle- and upper-class audience who had already become "fas-cinated by exhibits of 'exotic' workers" (Pfister 109). While some of his early success was certainly predi-cated on the role of playwright as sympathetic "tour guide" into the lower classes, O'Neill certainly did not rest on this formula. In The HAIRY APE, first produced in 1922, contact between classes intended to result in mutual understanding is presented as a violent con-frontation producing suffering and alienation on both sides of the class divide. The apex of the play's action is a harrowing encounter between Mildred Douglas, a self-absorbed social worker on a slumming expedi-tion, and Yank, a powerful, hairy-chested, coal-black-ened engine room stoker. The play's meaning derives from the confusion that occurs in Yank's sense of self as a result of the intrusion of Mildred into the stoke-hold, a confusion that epitomizes both the magnitude of barriers between classes and the potential harm of attempting to subvert or deny them.

The play's opening scene presents life in the cramped, hellish stokehole, where "the ceiling crushes down on the men's heads" (2:121), and the attitudes of the stooping workers suggest beasts in a cage. As the action begins, Yank has achieved a method of coping within the capitalist system, a position more fulfilling than Mildred's empty posing as a sincere social reformer. Yank is the authority among the stokers and refers to the stokehold as his "home"; he represents to the workers "the very last word in what they are" (2:124). Self-aggrandizing, arrogant, and given to outbursts of rage, he exults in his ability to cause the ship to move, giving him a form of control over his environment. The enabling construct of Yank's sense of well-being is a belief that he is superior to the upper classes: "We're better men dan dey are," he asserts. "Dem boids don't amount to nothin" (2:125).

Scene 2 introduces and describes Mildred Douglas, a bored do-gooder who has been playing at social work, experiencing the "morbid thrills of social service" (131) on New York's Lower East Side, and who is attempting to use her influence as the daughter of a steel magnate to arrange a tour of the ship's stokehold and "discover how the other half lives" (2:131). Mildred is on her way to England on a journey her aunt refers to as a "slumming international" (2:131). The conversation between the two women on the promenade deck conveys strongly derisive views of Mildred and indirectly of the general motives of the female settlement-house workers who were conspicuous in the play's early 20th-century setting. Effectively foreshadowing the psychological transaction between Mildred and Yank, the aunt scornfully states, "How they must have hated you, by the way, the poor that you made so much poorer in their eyes" (2:131). Conflict thus arises from the aunt's perception that the type of social work practiced by Mildred is actually a form of predation on the lower classes.

The play's crucial moment is the brief but intense scene 3 confrontation in the stokehold between Mildred and Yank, during which Yank "feels himself insulted in some unknown fashion in the very heart of his pride" (2:137). In general terms, the effect on Yank is twofold: "It makes him painfully aware of his social inferiority and suddenly conscious of his inadequacies as a human being" (Floyd 241). Overall, *The Hairy Ape* presents a heavily ironic view of the concept of social progress, as Yank the worker becomes alienated, imprisoned and destroyed by the very processes that were originally intended to help him, personified by the social worker Mildred in the stokehold.

On the whole, O'Neill's drama is strongly pessimistic about possibilities for reforming or transcending the limiting realities of class difference in American society. Equally contemptuous of radical fervor and vapid materialism, equally suspicious of reformers and adherents to the acquisitive status quo, O'Neill laid bare the deficiencies of capitalism but rejected both individualistic and systemic solutions to its problems. In *The Hairy Ape,* O'Neill defined labor class existence in a way that insists on its stark alienation while viewing that alienation as not mitigated but enhanced by upper-class intrusions. In *Marco Millions,* O'Neill focused primarily on the soul of the materialist, portraying the repulsive side of American business and exposing the spiritual alienation at the other end of the economic spectrum.

Insights about the long-term evolution of O'Neill's social outlook are contained in one of his final plays, LONG DAY'S JOURNEY INTO NIGHT. In this extremely autobiographical work, Edmund Tyrone clearly espouses the social theories of the young Eugene O'Neill, while Edmund's father James Tyrone just as persuasively expresses the conclusions reached by the mature playwright. Like O'Neill in 1912, Edmund has recently returned from a slumming adventure at sea, where he has damaged his health while apparently forming a rudimentary socialist class consciousness. Early in the play, Edmund interprets the anecdote of an Irish farmer who allows his pigs to wallow in an ice pond belonging to a Standard Oil millionaire as a parable of class conflict. In Edmund's view, the farmer's "glorious victory" has been in outwitting a "king of America," proving that he is "no slave" (O'Neill 1956, 23–24). For a working-class sympathizer like Edmund, the flavor of hog in the millionaire's ice water is "an appropriate touch" (25).

Edmund's father James Tyrone, however, dismisses these comments as "damned socialist anarchist sentiments" (25). The class-based disagreement between father and son resurfaces in act 4, when Edmund extols the socially productive effects of his experience in poverty, claiming that it has enabled him to relate more sympathetically to his father:

> God, Papa, ever since I went to sea and was on my own, and found out what hard work and little pay was, and what it felt like to be broke, and starve . . . I've tried to be fair to you because I knew what you'd been up against as a kid. (109)

Tyrone realizes, however, that his own childhood had been essentially different from Edmund's adventures—"There was no damned romance in our poverty" (109)—and asserts that there is no way Edmund can understand its actual consequences:

> You said you realized what I'd been up against as a boy. The hell you do! . . . You've had food, clothing. Oh, I know you had a fling of hard work with your back and hands, a bit of being homeless and penniless in a foreign land . . . But it was a game . . . It was play. (110)

While Edmund expresses nostalgia for his self-imposed ordeal and pride in its effects, Tyrone views Edmund's temporary hardship as "a game of romance and adventure" (146–147). In other words, Tyrone's childhood in authentic poverty enables him to discern the pretense of his son's voluntary privation. The tension is heightened by the Tyrone family's growing awareness of Edmund's "ruined health," which Tyrone directly attributes to the "mad life" Edmund has led "ever since he was fired from college" (33)—a life centered around experiences in the lower classes. The drama unfolds on the very day the family learns of Edmund's tuberculosis, the physical price of the young man's slumming excursion before the mast, the "stunt" of "working his way all over the maps as a sailor" (35).

O'Neill often claimed that his "real start as a dramatist" came when he "got out of an academy and among men, on the sea" (quoted in Downes 10). This seems accurate, for his sailor's experience was clearly the catalyst to his early dramatic success. But O'Neill's work also bespeaks his consciousness

of a daunting complexity in class relations that far surpasses the simplistic formula of worker portrayal that had originally helped him make his name in the theater. There is a qualitative difference, for example, between the act of escorting a middle-class audience into the forecastle to experience the pathos of a common sailor's death in *Bound East for Cardiff*, and escorting an audience into the stoke-hold for the harrowing encounter between Mildred Douglas and the "hairy ape"—as much as there is between O'Neill's early reliance on sailing experience for artistic authority and the more realistic questioning of such authority later expressed in *Long Day's Journey*. Looking at the presentation of class as a self-defining concept in O'Neill's plays from his earliest efforts through *Long Day's Journey into Night* makes it easier to understand why O'Neill ultimately gave the condemnatory last word on possibilities for cross-class empathy to Edmund's father James Tyrone. Tyrone's skepticism indicates that O'Neill understood the impermeable nature of class barriers, acknowledged the ways that social class determined identity, and realized that the "game of romance and adventure" often played by reformers, radicals, and revolutionaries could involve consequences more harmful than Edmund's tuberculosis, on both sides of the class divide.

Bibliography

Alexander, Doris. "O'Neill as Social Critic." In *O'Neill and His Plays,* edited by Oscar Cargill, N. Bryllion Fagin, and William J. Fisher, 390–407. New York: New York University Press, 1961.

Beatty, Warren, and Trevor Griffiths. *Reds* (screenplay). Hollywood: Paramount Pictures, 1981.

Chura, Patrick. "Vital Contact: Eugene O'Neill and the Working Class." *Twentieth Century Literature* 49, no. 4 (Winter 2003): 520–546.

Downes, Olin. "Playwright Finds His Inspiration on Lonely Sand Dunes by the Sea." In *Conversations with Eugene O'Neill*, edited by Mark Estrin, Jackson: University of Mississippi Press, 1990.

Egan, Leona Rust. *Provincetown as a Stage*. Orleans, Mass.: Parnassus, 1994.

Floyd, Virginia. *The Plays of Eugene O'Neill: A New Assessment*. New York: Ungar, 1985.

Glaspell, Susan. *The Road to the Temple*. New York: Stokes, 1941.

Kemp, Harry. "Out of Provincetown: A Memoir of Eugene O'Neill." In *Conversations with Eugene O'Neill*, edited by Mark Estrin, 95–102. Jackson: University Press of Mississippi, 1990.

O'Neill, Eugene. *Abortion*. In *Ten Lost Plays*. New York: Random House, 1964, 139–165.

———. *The Hairy Ape* and *Marco Millions*. In *The Complete Plays*, vol. 2. Edited by Travis Bogard. New York: Library of America, 1988, 119–165 and 379–467.

———. *A Long Day's Journey into Night*. New Haven, Conn.: Yale University Press, 1956.

Pfister, Joel. Staging *Depth: Eugene O'Neill and the Politics of Social Discourse*. Chapel Hill: University of North Carolina Press, 1995.

Patrick Chura

collections   The geographical distribution of major Eugene O'Neill research collections across the United States in some ways reflects the vicissitudes of O'Neill's restless life and troubled personal relationships; it also presents a challenge to researchers hoping to conduct a thorough, on-site study of his life and work. In recent years, O'Neill research has been facilitated by www.eoneill.com, an Internet site devoted to the study of Eugene O'Neill, which provides a gateway to many of the collections in research libraries and to online reference and media resources. Created in 1998 by Dr. Harley Hammerman, a St. Louis anesthesiologist and major collector of O'Neilliana, the site promotes the study and teaching of O'Neill's work and is useful to novices as well as to academic literary critics. Hammerman also has provided digitized access to his own fine collection of first editions, manuscripts, letters, and photographs.

The state of Connecticut, where O'Neill spent many of his formative years, is home to two major collections. The papers of Eugene O'Neill and his third wife, CARLOTTA MONTEREY O'NEILL, reside at Yale University's Beinecke Manuscript and Rare Books Collection. The literary papers, early manuscripts, rare books, and other material at Yale make this the most important O'Neill repository. The Beinecke also acquired the papers of other major figures in the O'Neill story, those of his second wife, AGNES BOULTON, and of his son EUGENE O'NEILL, JR., who at one time was a professor of classics at Yale. In nearby NEW LONDON, CONNECTICUT, the Sheaffer-O'Neill Collection, the large archive of the life and work of Eugene O'Neill formed by biographer Louis Sheaffer's research on his two-volume work *O'Neill: Son and Playwright* (1968) and *O'Neill: Son and Artist* (1973), is in the Special Collections of the Charles E. Shain Library at Connecticut College. The success of Sheaffer's biography derives in large part from the detailed picture of O'Neill that emerged from 20 years of exhaustive research. His interviews and investigations in New London provide special insights into O'Neill's early life when the family summered in MONTE CRISTO COTTAGE, the setting for LONG DAY'S JOURNEY INTO NIGHT. The extensive photograph collection and the files pertaining to the PROVINCETOWN PLAYERS and the THEATRE GUILD are of particular interest to researchers. Recently, Connecticut College's O'Neill resources have been augmented by the gift of the research papers of Doris Alexander, author of three books about O'Neill's life and work: *The Tempering of Eugene O'Neill* (1962), *Eugene O'Neill's Creative Struggle* (1992), and *Eugene O'Neill's Last Plays* (2005).

To examine the papers of O'Neill's other major BIOGRAPHERS, Arthur and Barbara Gelb, researchers must travel to the Harry Ransom Humanities Research Center at the University of Texas at Austin. The papers in the Gelb Collection were generated by the research for their biography, *O'Neill*, published in 1962 and in an enlarged edition in 1973. Although some of the material is restricted, much is available to researchers as well as manuscript and published versions of their book. The Performing Arts Collection, also at the University of Texas, contains other interesting O'Neill material. The mecca for O'Neill scholars on the West Coast is the playwright's home at TAO HOUSE in Danville, California, where the Eugene O'Neill Foundation maintains a large research collection, including the papers of O'Neill critic Sophus Winthur. In Massachusetts, where O'Neill studied with GEORGE PIERCE BAKER at Harvard University and spent his final years, the Harvard Theatre Collection in the Houghton Library houses the correspondence between Agnes Boulton and O'Neill; typescripts, some with autograph revisions, of several plays; as well as papers and correspondence relating to the Provincetown Players.

Other O'Neill collections scattered around the United States include the manuscripts of early plays in the Firestone Library of Princeton University in New Jersey, where he spent a short period as an undergraduate. The Clifton Waller Barrett Library of American Literature at the University of Virginia has many original O'Neill letters to his second wife, to his son SHANE RUDRAIGHE O'NEILL, and to his friend Harold DePOLO, as well as the typescript of an early O'Neill story, "The SCREENEWS OF WAR." The highlight of the O'Neill Papers in the Berg Collection of the New York Public Library is the manuscripts, letters, poems, and snapshots dating from 1914 to 1916 that were acquired from BEATRICE ASHE Maher, O'Neill's New London girlfriend, and there is other important material from the archives of the American Play Company as well. Also in O'Neill's native city is the Theatre Collection of the Museum of the City of New York including autograph manuscripts of his early plays, his father JAMES O'NEILL's prompt script for *The Count of Monte Cristo,* and other personal items given by the playwright and his wife Carlotta.

Major Eugene O'Neill Research Collections in American Libraries:

eOneill.com: An Electronic Eugene O'Neill Archive. Available online. URL: http://www.eoneill.com/.

Eugene O'Neill Foundation, Tao House, Research Library. Books, letters, photographs, records, Carlotta's diary. Danville, California. Web site: http://www.eugeneoneill.org/.

Gelb, Arthur and Barbara. Papers. Harry Ransom Humanities Center, University of Texas at Austin.

Harvard Theatre Collection. Houghton Library, Harvard University.

O'Neill, Eugene. Papers. Beinecke Rare Books and Manuscript Library, Yale University, New Haven, Connecticut.

O'Neill, Eugene. Papers. Clifton Waller Barrett Library of American Literature, Special Collections Department, University of Virginia Library, Charlottesville, Virginia.

O'Neill, Eugene. Papers. Theater Collection, the Museum of the City of New York.

O'Neill, Eugene. Plays. Department of Rare Books and Special Collections, Princeton University Library.

O'Neill, Eugene (Gladstone). Papers. Henry W. and Albert A. Berg Collection of English and American Literature, New York Public Library.

Sheaffer-O'Neill Collection. Department of Special Collections and Archives, Charles E. Shain Library, Connecticut College, New London.

Laurie Deredita

Commins, Saxe (Saxe Comminsky) (1892–1958)
In titling her memoir *What Is an Editor?: Saxe Commins at Work,* Dorothy Commins made clear that her husband's passion was not for fixing wayward teeth—as per his dentist's training—but for correcting and improving errant manuscripts. Though he graduated from dental school at the University of Pennsylvania in 1918, Commins was so smitten with skillful writing that he abandoned dentistry altogether to devote himself to literature and editing. Self-effacing and precise by nature, he once identified himself to an ingenue at a book launch as "in the cleaning and repairing business" (quoted in Commins 1978, 99).

Born Saxe Comminsky on January 13, 1892, Commins was one of six children born to Russian immigrants in Rochester, New York; his father was a tinsmith, and his mother was a sister to the anarchist EMMA GOLDMAN. He met Eugene O'Neill through journalist JACK REED. At the time, the dentist was visiting his sister Stella and her husband, actor-sculptor Teddy (Edward) Ballantine, in GREENWICH VILLAGE. It was through these same family connections that Commins was introduced to others of the PROVINCETOWN PLAYERS circle, his sister and brother-in-law being members. By summer 1916, the relationship between Commins and the playwright had blossomed into friendship, the former becoming a welcomed guest of O'Neill and his then-wife AGNES BOULTON at PEAKED HILL BAR in Massachusetts and later at SPITHEAD in Bermuda.

Soon after Commins married concert pianist Dorothy Berliner in 1927, he abandoned his thriving dental practice in Rochester, and in 1928 the pair set sail for England, then FRANCE, where Commins visited the playwright and Agnes's successor, CARLOTTA MONTEREY O'NEILL (though not yet the third Mrs. O'Neill), at Cap d'Ail. Immersing himself in the Parisian literary circle of American expatriates Gertrude Stein, T. S. Eliot, Ezra Pound, Hart Crane, Ernest Hemingway, Sherwood Anderson, and notable Europeans, including James Joyce (Ranald 134), Commins functioned as literary emissary between O'Neill and his agent, Richard Madden. Having O'Neill's trust and Carlotta's imprimatur, Commins was recommended for employment to the publisher Horace Liveright. However, when offered a job, he declined, realizing that the firm was on anything but terra firma financially. He instead accepted a job at Covici-Friede Publishers, leaving within the year (1931) to replace Manuel Komroff at Liveright's, then under Arthur Pell's more stable management.

At the house that published his friend's plays, Commins was tasked early on with seeing MOURNING BECOMES ELECTRA (1931) through production. But here and elsewhere, he was much more than just O'Neill's editor. While in Paris, he had typed for O'Neill the manuscript of DYNAMO (Commins 1986, 35); at home he had researched material with which O'Neill armed himself against Georges Lewys's PLAGIARISM suit; at Liveright's, he safeguarded the playwright's royalties as insolvency loomed and finally descended on the firm; and later, at TAO HOUSE, he retyped LONG DAY'S JOURNEY INTO NIGHT. When Pell's efforts to salvage Liveright, Inc., failed, Commins moved with O'Neill to Random House (1933), where the editor remained for the rest of his career. Its president Bennett Cerf and his partner Donald Klopfer praised Commins as "almost more important to us than O'Neill" and "our prize acquisition of the two" (quoted in Sheaffer, 1973, 417).

At Random House, Commins edited O'Neill's output (DAYS WITHOUT END, AH, WILDERNESS!, The ICEMAN COMETH, A MOON FOR THE MISBEGOTTEN), as well as the work of other literary luminaries, including S. N. Behrman, Sinclair Lewis, William Carlos Williams, Theodore (Dr. Seuss) Geisel, James Michener, W. H. Auden, Irwin Shaw, Budd Schulberg, and most notably William Faulkner, with whom Commins enjoyed a warm friendship. Among Commins's numerous and noteworthy contributions to Random House was his directorship of the Modern Library series.

Wherever O'Neill wandered—to Bermuda (in 1924); France (1928); SEA ISLAND, GEORGIA (1931); and Danville, California (1937)—Commins visited him, but changes were just "beyond the horizon." When Carlotta and O'Neill, the latter then in ill health, returned to the East Coast in 1945, Saxe and Dorothy Commins became unwilling witnesses to the growing hostilities between the ailing playwright and his unstable wife. As Saxe sought to aid his friend, a vindictive Carlotta worked to dismantle a friendship that had lasted for decades. In a series of regrettable incidents, Carlotta accused O'Neill's trusted friend of conspiring to kidnap her husband, of ruining plays entrusted to him, and of stealing manuscripts. Sparing neither ethnic epithet nor religious slur in her attacks, Carlotta succeeded in separating her husband from the man he had called his "brother" (Sheaffer 1973, 655).

Barred from attending O'Neill's funeral, the deeply wounded Commins continued on as editor in chief at Random House until 1955. Having suffered a heart attack that year, he underwent surgery in 1957, recovered, relapsed, and died on July 17, 1958. He left a wife and two children: a son, named Eugene in honor of his friend, and a daughter, Frances Ellen Bennett.

The good opinion and respect of those he worked with were Commins's legacy. Even the restrained W. H. Auden had only praise for his editor: "Efficiency of mind and goodness of heart are rarely combined in equal measure, but in Saxe they were" (quoted in Commins 1978, xv).

Bibliography

Cerf, Bennett. At Random: The Reminiscences of Bennett Cerf. New York: Random House, 1977.

Commins, Dorothy. What Is an Editor?: Saxe Commins at Work. Chicago: University of Chicago Press, 1978.

Commins, Dorothy, ed. "Love and Admiration and Respect": The O'Neill-Commins Correspondence. Durham, N.C.: Duke University Press, 1986.

Commins, Dorothy Berliner, Frank W. Rounds, and Tracy Angas. Reminiscences of Dorothy Berliner. New York: Columbia University Archives, 1962.

Gelb, Arthur, and Barbara Gelb. O'Neill. New York: Harper & Row, 1962.

King, William Davies, ed. *"A Wind Is Rising": The Correspondence of Agnes Boulton and Eugene O'Neill.* Madison, N.J.: Farleigh Dickinson University Press, 2000.

Louis Sheaffer–Eugene O'Neill Special Collection. Department of Special Collections, Charles E. Shain Library, Connecticut College, New London.

O'Neill, Eugene. *Selected Letters of Eugene O'Neill.* Edited by Travis Bogard and Jackson R. Bryer. New Haven, Conn.: Yale University Press, 1988.

Ranald, Margaret Loftus. *The Eugene O'Neill Companion.* Westport, Conn.: Greenwood Press, 1982.

"Saxe Commins, 66, Book Editor Dies," *New York Times,* July 18, 1958, 21.

Saxe Commins Collection. Rare Book and Special Collections, Firestone Library, Princeton University.

Shea, Laura. "O'Neill, the Theatre Guild, and *A Moon for the Misbegotten.*" *Eugene O'Neill Review* 27 (2005): 76–97.

Sheaffer, Louis. *O'Neill: Son and Artist.* Boston: Little, Brown, 1973.

———. *O'Neill: Son and Playwright.* Boston: Little, Brown, 1968.

Madeline Smith

Cook, George Cram "Jig" (1873–1924) A writer, director, professor, and Greek scholar, George Cram Cook—his friends called him "Jig"—was a key figure in the development of AMERICAN THEATER early in the 20th century. Along with his wife SUSAN GLASPELL, Cook helped found two important small theater groups: in 1914, the WASHINGTON SQUARE PLAYERS, which would transform into the THEATRE GUILD; and the following year, the PROVINCETOWN PLAYERS, later renamed the EXPERIMENTAL THEATRE, INC.

Born in Iowa on October 7, 1873, Cook attended the University of Iowa, Harvard, and the University of Heidelberg. After his studies, he returned to Iowa to run a truck farm, a profession that reflected his love of nature and working with his hands, ideals incorporated into his later theatrical work. Cook taught English literature at the University of Iowa from 1895 to 1899 and at Stanford University in 1902. His own writing began with poetry, expanding to novels, plays, and criticism. He became a regular contributor to the *Friday Literary Review,* a supplement to the *Chicago Evening Post* edited by Floyd Dell, with whom he became close friends.

In his seven years with the Provincetown Players, Cook nurtured nearly 50 authors—most notably Eugene O'Neill—and helped produce over 100 plays. He aimed to foster theater as a communal endeavor in keeping with the Athenian ideals he nourished all his life. In his vision, theater should be motivated not by commercial interests but by a group spirit as a kind of Dionysian ritual. He encouraged a native American drama and sought a truly American playwright, finding his model in O'Neill, whose worldwide fame Cook predicted.

Ironically, it was O'Neill's growing prominence that eventually helped drive a wedge between the two men. As O'Neill grew more successful, Cook grew increasingly jealous, due partly to his own failure as a playwright and partly to O'Neill's need to move beyond small, experimental theater, the very kind that Cook sought to keep pure. Cook also grew increasingly dictatorial in his position as the driving force behind the Provincetown Players. His fervent commitment to his idea of theater was evident in 1920, when he insisted on building an expensive plaster sky dome over the company's small New York stage for the production of O'Neill's The EMPEROR JONES.

That production spelled the end of the Provincetown Players, for its great success propelled it uptown and marked the company's shift toward profit, a move that permanently disillusioned Cook. Unwilling to accept popular success, he emigrated to Greece with Glaspell in 1922, answering a lifelong yearning to re-create the classical idealism of Athenian philosophers and thinkers. He died there two years later, on January 14, 1924, and was buried at Delphi, his grave adorned with a stone from the Temple of Apollo.

Bibliography

Glaspell, Susan. *The Road to the Temple: A Biography of George Cram Cook.* Jefferson, N.C.: McFarland, 2005.

Sarlós, Robert Karoly. *Jig Cook and the Provincetown Players.* Boston: University of Massachusetts Press, 1982.

Karen Charmaine Blansfield

D

Darwinism   While Eugene O'Neill may not have cited Charles Darwin (1809–82) as a direct influence on his work, there is no doubt that theories of origin were central to the playwright's worldview, shaped as it was by the various movements and philosophies of European modernism. The writings of FRIEDRICH NIETZSCHE, the plays and theories of AUGUST STRINDBERG, and avant-garde movements such as NATURALISM and EXPRESSIONISM all, to a greater or lesser degree, called upon the materialist precepts of Darwinism to revolutionize a theater governed by bourgeois ideologies such as capitalism and Christianity, targets against which O'Neill himself regularly took aim.

The theory of evolution by natural selection had a deep and lasting effect on both the content and form of modern drama. Playwrights such as HENRIK IBSEN and GEORGE BERNARD SHAW, whose writings were understood as a form of social protest, explored issues of heredity and biological determinism in plays where the ability to adapt to changing environments—natural or cultural—meant either survival or extinction. O'Neill's connection to Darwinism reflected not only a philosophical interest in ancient and modern theories of descent but an intuitive understanding of the complex relationship between evolutionism and theater that first became apparent in the mid- to late 19th century, concurrent with the controversial publications of Darwin's work.

Darwinism entered American public discourse with a vengeance in the 1920s, just as O'Neill was began to enjoy consistent success as a playwright.

Ongoing debates pitting evolutionary theory against creationism became common in the early 20th century; these disputes were dramatized in plays and films and featured on radio programs across the country. In O'Neill's *The HAIRY APE* (1921), the uncultivated stoker Yank spends time in a New York jail and is solicited by a fellow prisoner to join the INDUSTRIAL WORKERS OF THE WORLD (IWW). The inmate proceeds to read from a newspaper editorial written by a prominent senator, condemning the "Wobblies" as "that devil's brew" of men who

> . . . would tear down society, put the lowest scum in the seats of the mighty, turn Almighty God's revealed plan for the world topsy-turvy, and make of our sweet and lovely civilization a shambles, a desolation where man, God's masterpiece, would soon degenerate back to the ape! (2:153)

O'Neill's invented editorial was written with the rhetorical vehemence common to orators such as William B. Riley, author of the anti-Darwinist tract *Menace of Modernism* (1917), and William Jennings Bryan, who would later become the lead prosecutor in the Scopes "monkey trial" in 1925. In the above passage, O'Neill highlights the complex interrelations of science, religion, capitalism, and mass media that allowed the reactionary views of social Darwinism to take root in American culture.

While most audiences would be familiar with the politics surrounding the evolution/creation controversy, they may not have recognized the

Scene 8 of Eugene O'Neill's *The Hairy Ape* (Plymouth Theatre, New York, 1922), in which Yank (Louis Wolheim) frees the gorilla from its cage and offers a handshake. Photo copyright the estate of James Abbe/ Kathryn Abbe *(Courtesy of the Yale Collection of American Literature, Beinecke Rare Book and Manuscript Library)*

deeper engagement with Darwinism that surfaced in O'Neill's earliest plays, written between 1914 and 1921. Commencing with the SEA plays, O'Neill begins to examine racist fears of "degeneration" by likening various characters to their primate ancestors. In *The MOON OF THE CARIBBEES* (1917), he introduces the discourse of species as a corollary to other, more established themes. The first use of the "hairy ape" epithet is found in this play, alongside a comparison of the Caribbean women aboard the tramp steamer GLENCAIRN to "bloody organ-grinder's monkey[s]" (8). This trajectory continued in *The EMPEROR JONES* (1920), wherein O'Neill directly engaged with race and species as they were elaborated under imperialism. When the AFRICAN AMERICAN Brutus Jones is hunted by the "Native Chief" Lem, who is described by O'Neill as *"an ape-faced old savage of the extreme African*

type" (1:1,060), animal instinct becomes the key to adaptation and survival, successfully undermining rationality as the central differentiating quality of humanity. In these plays and others, the powerful trope of animality threatens to realign long-standing kinship models based on race, CLASS, ethnicity, and GENDER with a new term: *species.*

O'Neill once again addressed the social implications of evolutionary theory in *The FIRST MAN* (1921), an aptly titled (though commercially unsuccessful) drama about the familial entanglements of a married anthropologist setting out on a scientific expedition to prove man's origins. The protagonist's interest in man's evolutionary family eventually inhibits his ability to accept the prospect of his own present-day biological family, casting issues of descent and inheritance into overlapping—and seemingly incompatible—realms. As the early critic Richard Dana Skinner observed, "O'Neill [found] himself for the first time under the mental and emotional cloud of late nineteenth-century science and the spiritual chaos it produced" (105).

While that chaos is certainly evident in O'Neill's later work, *The Hairy Ape* contains his most explicit statement on Darwinism and American culture. In scene 1, the STAGE DIRECTIONS tell us that the stokers working on the transatlantic liner *"should resemble those pictures in which the appearance of Neanderthal man is guessed at. All are hairy-chested, with long arms of tremendous power, and low, receding brows above their small, fierce, resentful eyes"* (2:121). The simian qualities assigned to characters in the earlier plays are now in full force; even the *"wizened Irishman,"* Paddy, has become *"extremely monkey-like, with all the sad, patient pathos of that animal in his small eyes"* (2:123). By scene 3, the stokers are *"outlined in silhouette in the crouching, inhuman attitudes of chained gorillas"* (2:135), drawing an explicit link to Darwin's theory of descent from apes and its connection to abolitionist movements in the Anglo-American world.

These stage directions foreshadow the play's final scene, set in *"the monkey house at the zoo"* (2:160), where Yank's feelings of kinship with a caged gorilla result in the animal's freedom (see accompanying illustration). In the end, Yank, crushed by the enraged gorilla, finds himself on display in the shattered cage, where he valiantly performs his own spectacular demise. This sacrificial substitution moves O'Neill's critique of humanism out of the realm of metaphor and into an evolutionary paradigm that revolves around performative interventions in the discourse of species—a direct response to the social, political, and existential revolution engendered by Darwinism. If Yank was, according to an interview with the playwright in 1922, "really yourself, and myself. . . . He is *every* human being" (Mullett 35), then American drama had begun to reflect an understanding of human identity as a series of transformations played out across the vast scale of evolutionary time rather than the static, discreet forms springing from divine creation. O'Neill understood evolution not just as a scientific principle but as a radical theory of history, admitting with typical pessimism in a letter to Theresa Helburn, executive director of the THEATRE GUILD, "We are all a bit sick of answers that don't answer. *The Hairy Ape* at least, faces the simple truth that, being what we are, and with any significant spiritual change for the better in us probably ten thousand years away, there just is no answer" (O'Neill 1999, 484–485).

Bibliography

Goodall, Jane R. *Performance and Evolution in the Age of Darwin: Out of the Natural Order.* London and New York: Routledge, 2002.

Mullett, Mary B. "The Extraordinary Story of Eugene O'Neill." In *Conversations with Eugene O'Neill,* edited by Mark W. Estrin, 26–37. Jackson: University Press of Mississippi, 1990.

O'Neill, Eugene. *Early Plays.* New York: Penguin Books, 2001.

———. *Selected Letters of Eugene O'Neill.* Edited by Travis Bogard and Jackson R. Bryer. New York: Limelight Editions, 1994.

Russett, Cynthia Eagle. *Darwin in America: The Intellectual Response, 1865–1912.* San Francisco: W. H. Freeman and Company, 1976.

Sheehan, Paul. *Modernism, Narrative and Humanism.* Cambridge: Cambridge University Press, 2002.

Skinner, Richard Dana. *Eugene O'Neill: A Poet's Quest.* New York: Longmans, Green, and Co., 1935.

Erika Rundle

Day, Dorothy (1897–1980)   Dorothy Day never wanted to be called a "saint"; such appellations meant nothing to her, while good works meant everything. Her life was characterized by the Bible's Sermon on the Mount; her work in the slums of New York's Lower East Side led to the founding of the Catholic Worker Movement and the *Catholic Worker* newspaper in 1933, in the midst of the Great Depression, in order to implement a radical renewal of CATHOLICISM and the social order. She took her brand of Christianity into the streets, promoting a nonviolent response to social injustice and aligning herself with the marginalized. She practiced voluntary poverty, and lived a life of fidelity to the Scripture.

Born on November 8, 1897, in Brooklyn, Dorothy Day came to be defined by radical Christianity after her conversion to Roman Catholicism at age 30. Yet neither parent—neither John Day (a tepid Congregationalist), nor Grace Satterlee Day (an occasional Episcopalian)—attended church; indeed, both felt uncomfortable with religion, believing that talking about religion was baring your soul. John Day's universe was horseracing and journalism. "Mother Grace," who suffered several miscarriages and endured blinding headaches, was a central figure in Dorothy's semiautobiographical novel *The Eleventh Virgin* (1924), in which Dorothy describes her as heroic in her ability to face daily life. Dorothy had three brothers, two of whom

Dorothy Day, center, at an antiwar rally *(Courtesy of the Dorothy Day Catholic Workers Collection, Raynor Memorial Library, Marquette University)*

became reputable journalists; She was closest to her sister Della, with whom she maintained a life-long relationship, and to her younger brother, John, Jr., to whom she dedicated her book *From Union Square to Rome* (1978).

The intellectual and spiritual bonds Dorothy Day later came to forge between social activism and Christianity were marginally present in a childhood in which she exhibited nascent religious feelings: Neighbors passed along a book to read on the life of Saint Pelagia, to whom she occasionally prayed. She joined the Episcopal Church at age 12, but left it within two years. She retained her belief in God, continued to read the New Testament regularly, but felt it was no longer necessary to attend Church. Always a great reader (she began reading at age four), her secular reading is telling: Her favorite authors included Thomas De Quincey, Upton Sinclair, Jack London, Fyador Dostoyevsky, the work of the anarchists Peter Crooking and Vera Figner, dime novels describing the struggles in the labor movement in Chicago, and the Bible.

The family moved several times, from Brooklyn to the San Francisco Bay area (they survived the great 1906 San Francisco earthquake), to Chicago, and then back to New York. In *The Long Loneliness,* Dorothy Day referred to her "childhood as a happy time," though typical of the houses she lived in were of the tenement house variety, where she found herself unable to bring friends home—such visits were considered impositions on her father's privacy (27). Introspective and lonely as a teenager, she endured a distant, unaffectionate father and dismal family Sunday dinners at which all ate together in gloomy silence. In between moments taking care of her brother John, she took long walks through the slum districts of New York, eyeing the slatternly women and unkempt children. She says of these teenage years that "she wanted to do something toward making a "new earth wherein justice dwelled" (Miller 26).

Dorothy Day never overlooked the plight of the poor or the suffering immigrants, and she attributed her commitment to "radical" causes to those she met living within the Italian, Russian, and Jewish community of New York's East Side in the 1920s; she moved there after spending two list-less years studying at the University of Illinois at Urbana. At university, she had felt unloved and unlovely, closed out everything except the Socialist Club, which she joined because she saw the world's injustices. At age 18, she began her career as a journalist writing for the socialist paper the *Call,* remarkable for its lack of a philosophically consistent position on socialism. She spent time with another reporter, Mike Gold, and she (perhaps also Gold) interviewed Leon Trotsky, then in New York (January–March 1917), writing for the Russian socialist paper *Novy Mir.* From early 1917 to June 1918, she and Mike Gold (later the dean of U.S. proletarian literature) were close companions, if not "engaged." At this point in her life, as she describes herself in *The Eleventh Virgin,* she was "sexless and unemotional" (quoted in Miller 68). She took a second job with the Anti-Conscription League.

Day's life as a young working woman in New York was unconventional. Devoted to social causes, she wrote passionately about women's rights, free love, and birth control; as a journalist, she covered strikes, peace meetings, and food riots. Sometimes referred to as a "red-headed Irish Communist," she was never a card-carrying socialist or communist. But she did fall in love, at an early age, with the masses, and fought—both before and after her conversion to Catholicism—for progressive and radical causes. In November 1917, she marched with the suffragettes on Washington, D.C., was one of 40 women arrested in front of the White House; in prison, they went on a hunger strike and were eventually released through a presidential order; she avidly supported the Russian Revolution; she endured physical punishment—during an antiwar rally, for example, a policeman cracked two of her ribs; she became a card-carrying member of the INDUSTRIAL WORKERS OF THE WORLD and was arrested with the "Wobblies"; while marching for integration, she was shot at; and she was arrested in Fresno, California, in 1973 with Caesar Chavez's United Farm Workers (UFW) Union.

Day's meeting Charles Wood, then drama critic for *The MASSES,* edited by Max Eastman (a protégé of John Dewey), led to her third job with that paper—first as a reporter and then as assistant editor. *The Masses,* under Easton, took a turn to the left and featured writers such as JACK REED, Randolph Bourne, and Upton Sinclair, and poets Vachel Lindsay, Amy Lowell, and Louis Untermeyer. Floyd Dell, oracle of the "new" morality was managing editor and romantically interested in Dorothy. Whether Dell intended to seduce her or not is unclear, but she took him up on his suggestion that they share an apartment on McDougal Street, above the Provincetown Playhouse on loan to *The Masses.* As a result, she came to know members of the PROVINCETOWN PLAYERS. *The Masses'* people would gather at Mabel Dodge's, contributing member of the Provincetown Players and lover of Jack Reed. In the evening, as historian Daniel Aaron corroborates an account by the bohemian doyen Mabel Dodge, they would all gather in "insouciant disarray around the floor," "happily subverting the social order by word and deed" (quoted in Miller 77). The outsider Dorothy Day shared the sentiments of these other outsiders, denizens of GREENWICH VILLAGE, though in later years, she denied being a Greenwich Village habitué and also put down what she considered irresponsible talk about her preconversion life.

Nonetheless from 1917 to 1918, most of Day's friends had some association with the Players and with Greenwich Village, and she became a central figure in the bohemian drama of Village life and one of the regulars at Jimmy Wallace's saloon, the Golden Swan, also known as the HELL HOLE, at Sixth Avenue and Fourth Street. There, Malcolm Cowley says in *Exiles Return,* "the gangsters [the "Hudson Dusters"] admired Dorothy Day because she could drink them under the table; but they felt more at home with Eugene O'Neill who listened to their troubles and never criticized" (69). Day was never an alcoholic, but she was admired for her ability to drink several shots of whiskey and remain sober.

For her part, Dorothy was enough irritated by Cowley's remark about her drinking to type out a response in a short essay, "Told in Context," in which she mentions her Greenwich Village association with Eugene O'Neill. She was introduced to O'Neill by Mike Gold at the Provincetown Playhouse, where Gold's play was in rehearsal.

She began to hang around the Playhouse—either because she harbored hopes of acting, or because she was attracted to O'Neill. At the time, O'Neill was suffering from a failed relationship with LOUISE BRYANT; Day may have felt she could take Bryant's place. AGNES BOULTON, in *Part of a Long Story,* recounts her impressions of Dorothy Day and Day's intimate manner with O'Neill (79–82). While Boulton and O'Neill would eventually become involved, there was a prior time when it was Dorothy Day who whiled away the nights with O'Neill at the Hell Hole and at taverns on the East Side. Day would put the shaking, exhausted O'Neill to bed in her apartment and, according to her, turn O'Neill aside when he volunteered to help her surrender her virginity. Her actions during this time period are reminiscent of Josie Hogan's in O'Neill's *A MOON FOR THE MISBEGOTTEN;* Day may very well have been one of those on whom O'Neill drew for his characterization,

Dorothy Day had a real, important, and abiding interest in O'Neill; she could never forget his presence in her life; his work, which she so admired; or his alcoholic recitation of Francis Thompson's "The Hound of Heaven." O'Neill could recite the entire poem from memory; she believed it "one of those poems that awakens the soul, recalls to it the fact that God is its destiny" (Day 1978, 90). In the end, one can only speculate on why she and O'Neill did not become a couple: Was it more true that while Day's spirit may have touched O'Neill's genius, she did not love the man as Agnes Boulton did? Or did she not have the brand of feminine appeal that would keep O'Neill focused?

Day's relationships with men were always complicated—beginning at age 15 when she experienced intense feelings of physical longing for Armand Hand, a married man with a child. She endured a tortuous relationship with the journalist Lionel Moise, city editor of the *Chicago Post,* during which she attempted suicide and, at his urging, aborted their child; Moise deserted her. Just months after the abortion, in 1920, she married Barkeley Tobey, a wealthy man twice her age; they soon divorced. She found a modicum of domestic peace in a common-law relationship with Forster Batterham, with whom she lived in her beach house on Staten Island; that relationship produced a daughter, Tamar. Forster was a reluctant father, and that relationship ended when Dorothy insisted that Tamar be baptized in the Catholic faith.

With the birth of her daughter, a period of spiritual awakening began. Dorothy was floating between two worlds, and the direction her life would take was as yet unclear. She needed answers to the problems of existence—what lay behind the curtain of time. To the embarrassment of her atheist friends, after her daughter was baptized, she too was received into the Catholic faith in December 1927 at Our Lady Help of Christians' Parish on Staten Island.

After her failed relationships and her conversion, Day began to see her life's purpose when Peter Maurin, having read some of her articles, tracked her down. According to Dorothy, Maurin was a "genius, saint, agitator, writer, lecturer, poor man and shabby tramp, all in one" (Miller 228). Beginning with the pacifist newspaper the *Catholic Worker,* the pair founded the Catholic Worker Movement in 1933; the newspaper's first issue debuted with 2,500 copies. Day hawked the paper in Union Square for a penny a copy (still the price) to passersby.

Maurin, and then Dorothy Day, espoused a philosophy of "personalism," as expressed by writers Emmanuel Mounier and Nicholas Berdyaev, who emphasized the tremendous dignity of the human person, together with a profound understanding of each person's vocation in freedom and personal responsibility. Personalists and Catholic Workers challenged the priority of economics and consumerism in daily life—the bourgeois spirit—and insisted on the primacy of spirituality and generosity in living out one's faith. Acting on their belief in personalism, Day and Maurin established "houses of hospitality" in the slums of New York City, and then a series of farms for the poor to live together communally. The movement spread to other cities in the United States, Canada, and the United Kingdom. Today there are nearly 200 Catholic Worker communities committed to nonviolence; voluntary poverty; prayer; and hospitality for the homeless, exiled, hungry, and forsaken. Catholic Workers are opposed to injustice, war, racism, and violence; and

their communities are located in the United States, Australia, the United Kingdom, Canada, Germany, the Netherlands, the Republic of Ireland, Mexico, New Zealand, and Sweden.

What finally accounts for Dorothy Day's dramatic turn to Christianity, and her remarkable concern for the poor? The twin poles of her thinking were communism and Christianity. Her concern for the poor made her turn to communism for answers: Christians in her mind had lost sight of the communal aspect of Christianity. For their part, communists failed to see Christ in the worker. The two were connected, but it was working with the communists that caused Day to turn to God (Day 1978, 12).

After her conversion and until she died on November 29, 1980, at Maryhouse (a Catholic Worker house for women in New York), Day continued to live among the poor, ministering to the forgotten. In 1971, she was awarded the Pacem In Terris award, named after a 1936 encyclical, as well as the Courage of Conscience award on September 6, 1992. She is buried in Resurrection Cemetery on Staten Island. The Vatican is currently evaluating her case for beatification and canonization as a saint of the Roman Catholic Church. In the meantime, she has been named "Servant of God."

Bibliography

Boulton, Agnes. *Part of a Long Story.* London: Peter Davies, 1958.

Coles, Robert. *Dorothy Day: A Radical Devotion.* New York: Perseus Book Group, 1987.

Cowley, Malcolm. *Exiles Return.* New York: Penguin, 1934.

Day, Dorothy. *The Eleventh Virgin.* New York: Albert & Charles Boni, 1924.

———. *From Union Square to Rome.* New York: Maryknoll, 1978.

———. *House of Hospitality.* New York: Sheed & Ward, 1939.

———. *Loaves and Fishes.* San Francisco: Harper & Row, 1983.

———. *The Long Loneliness: The Autobiography of Dorothy Day.* New York: Harper & Brothers, 1952.

———. *On Pilgrimmage.* New York: Catholic Worker Books, 1948.

———. *On Pilgrimmage: The Sixties.* New York: Curtis Books, 1972.

Dorothy Day: Don't Call Me a Saint, 57 min., One Lucky Day Productions, 2006.

Ellis, Mark. *Peter Maurin: Prophet in the Twentieth Century.* New York: Paulist Press, 1981.

Ellsberg, Robert. *Dorothy Day: Selected Writings.* Maryknoll, N.Y.: Orbis Books, 1992.

Entertaining Angels: The Dorothy Day Story, 112 min., Paulist Pictures, 1996.

Forest, Jim. *Love Is the Measure: A Biography of Dorothy Day.* New York: Paulist Press, 1986.

Merriman, Brigid O'Shea. *Searching for Christ: The Spirituality of Dorothy Day.* Notre Dame, Ind.: University of Notre Dame, 1994.

Miller, William D. *Dorothy Day: A Biography.* San Francisco: Harper & Row, 1982.

O'Connor, June. *The Moral Vision of Dorothy Day: A Feminist Perspective.* New York: Crossroads, 1991.

Zwick, Mark, and Louise Zwick. *The Catholic Worker Movement.* New York: Paulist Press, 2005.

Eileen Herrmann

Harold DePolo *(Courtesy of the Sheaffer-O'Neill Collection, Charles E. Shain Library of Connecticut College)*

DePolo, Harold Urisarri (1889–1960) Eugene O'Neill's friend from 1915 to 1931, Harold DePolo wrote, drank, fought, fished, and womanized—not necessarily in that order—and thereby had much in common with the playwright in the half decade their friendship was at its zenith. Born in New York on October 16, 1889, the son of Latin/South American parents (Gerald DePolo of Havana and Elvira Urisarri of Bogotá), DePolo could number among his friends and acquaintances Provincetown artists and literati GEORGE CRAM "JIG" COOK, SUSAN GLASPELL, Wilbur Daniel Steele, and Harry Kemp; poets Orrick Johns and Edna St. Vincent Millay; and fiction writer Donn Byrne. Through his father-in-law (DePolo had married Helen Cooper, the daughter of Frederic Taber Cooper, critic for *The Bookman* and professor at Columbia and New York Universities), DePolo met other intellectuals and celebrities (Albert Einstein notably) and was himself if not an A-list writer at least prolific (to meet one deadline, he claimed to have produced 6,000 words overnight).

DePolo appreciated books, reading philosophy, history, and literature; he knew their value and had an impressive personal library, as his letter-lists to Denver bookseller Don Bloch indicate. Author of more than 3,000 detective and western stories and several novelettes, he published stories under several noms de plume (including Philip Space and Kenneth Christie) in pulp fiction magazines (*Breezy Stories, Snappy Stories,* and *Black Mask*) and others (*Smart Set*). His tales were predictable in theme (often infidelity), in length (five to seven pages), and in plot (an expected twist at the end). Slick and without literary pretensions, the stories nonetheless evidenced DePolo's stylistic improvisation—a personal narrative, a revenge tale, an interior monologue—despite the predictable subject matter. As the stories sold or did not sell, so the DePolos enjoyed periodic prosperity or not: a summer rental in Culver Lake, New Jersey; trips to Barbados or Bermuda; a maid to do their bidding; an extravagant winter ($4,000) in Darien, Connecticut; summers in Maine. Foster Batterham,

DOROTHY DAY's lover and friend, by turns, of the DePolos, explained that at the root of DePolo's affection for O'Neill was his realization that the playwright possessed the talent that the hack writer respected and coveted but ultimately lacked.

While one might expect collaboration or literary exchange/influence between the writer friends, such seems not to have been the case. Rather, the relationship between O'Neill and DePolo, whom his friend referred to affectionately as "the mad muff hound of Madrid" (Smith and Erban 86), stemmed, it appears, largely from a mutual fondness for rowdiness, pranks and jokes, and, of course, the ubiquitous alcohol (see ALCOHOLISM). Shared experiences (O'Neill was with DePolo in 1917 when the pair was arrested for allegedly spying for the Germans, and the O'Neills and DePolos often vacationed together), the playwright's amusement at his friend's antics, and DePolo's corresponding admiration for O'Neill's talent seem to have been the glue in the relationship. However, as O'Neill's marriage to AGNES BOULTON disintegrated in 1927 and with the advent of his third wife-to-be, CARLOTTA MONTEREY O'NEILL, he saw O'Neill the last time in 1931, but felt by then that the old connection had been broken. Depolo, who foresaw the inevitable, said he "let it [the friendship] ride" (Sheaffer, n. pag.).

On April 27, 1960, the once peripatetic DePolo, who had lived with Helen, according to his wife's calculations, in more than 40 places since their marriage (to escape bill collectors, Agnes Boulton said), died, by then part of Old Lyme, Connecticut's establishment. Bequeathed to the generations were his thousands of amusing, if insubstantial, tales.

Bibliography

Smith, Madeline C., and Richard Eaton. "Harold DePolo: Pulp Fiction's Dark Horse." *Eugene O'Neill Review* 20, nos. 1 and 2 (Spring–Fall 1996): 80–87.

Sheaffer, Louis. Interview with Helen DePolo, April 1959. Sheaffer-O'Neill Collection. Shain Library, Connecticut College, New London.

Madeline C. Smith

Dewhurst, Colleen (1924–1991)   During the latter half of the 20th century, Colleen Dewhurst was one of the leading actresses off and on Broadway. She also had a minor film career and enjoyed more success on television, particularly in her later life, playing actress Candice Bergen's mother in a successful television series, *Murphy Brown,* and the role of Marilla Cuthbert in a series based on the beloved *Anne of Green Gables* books by Canadian author Lucy Maud Montgomery. During her lifetime, Dewhurst received two Tony Awards, two Obie Awards, and four Emmy Awards and also served as the elected president of Actors Equity from 1985 to the time of her death on August 22, 1991.

Colleen Dewhurst was born June 3, 1924, in Montreal, Canada. Her parents emigrated from their native Canada to the United States and lived in various towns in Wisconsin and in the Bronx, New York. Dewhurst attended Milwaukee Downer College, where she was cast in small acting roles in the school's plays. She left college at the end of her sophomore year to attend the American Academy of Dramatic Arts in New York City, where she met JASON ROBARDS, JR., the actor who would become her lifelong friend and her most celebrated O'Neill acting partner. After graduation, she honed her craft doing several years of summer stock and eventually settled in New York City, where she lived with her first husband, the actor James Vickery. During the early 1950s she excelled in the burgeoning Off-Broadway movement and earned the unofficial title of "Queen of Off-Broadway."

Colleen Dewhurst's reputation as the greatest O'Neill actress of her generation evolved gradually during the course of her 40-year acting career. It was Dewhurst's acting teacher, the famous Group Theatre founder Harold Clurman, who cast her in her first professional role in a play by Eugene O'Neill. Dewhurst played the minor part of a neighbor in Clurman's 1952 Broadway production of O'Neill's DESIRE UNDER THE ELMS. She had wanted to play Abbie Putnam, but in the early 1950s she was still an unknown, untried actress.

By 1956, Dewhurst's career was blossoming, and the acclaimed director JOSÉ QUINTERO cast her in Edwin Justin Mayer's play *Children of Darkness* at his theater, the Off-Broadway Circle in the Square. Dewhurst's ability in that production to be an able foil to the formidable George C. Scott (later her husband, 1960–65 and 1967–72) brought Quintero to cast her in A MOON FOR THE MISBEGOTTEN. Dewhurst played Josie Hogan, the compassionate and motherly would-be lover of Richard Kiley's spiritually desolate James Tyrone. This 1958 production, which was produced at the Spoleto Festival in Italy, marked the first time Dewhurst played Josie and also the first time Dewhurst was directed by José Quintero in a play by Eugene O'Neill. In 1963, it was Dewhurst who asked Quintero to direct her at the Circle in the Square in O'Neill's *Desire under the Elms*. Dewhurst's performance as Abbie Putnam, the role she had once wanted to play for Harold Clurman, showcased for the New York critics her superior abilities to act in an O'Neill production. Their rave reviews acknowledged what a lioness of an acting talent she was and expressed unabashed admiration for her poetic delivery of O'Neill's awkwardly crafted but idiomatic phrasing.

The remainder of Dewhurst's stage O'Neill performances took place on Broadway. José Quintero directed her as Sara Harford in MORE STATELY MANSIONS in 1967, as Josie Hogan in *A Moon for the Misbegotten* in 1973 (Tony Award, best actress), and as Mary Tyrone in LONG DAY'S JOURNEY INTO NIGHT in 1988. Theodore Mann directed her as Christine Mannon in MOURNING BECOMES ELECTRA in 1972 (Tony nominee, best actress), and Arvin Brown directed her as Essie Miller in AH, WILDERNESS! In 1988, the latter production played in repertory with the Quintero-directed production of *Long Day's Journey into Night* as part of the centenary celebrations honoring Eugene O'Neill's 100th birthday.

Reviews of Dewhurst's acting performance repeatedly noted her most distinctive qualities as being that she was "strong," "sensuous," and like an "Earth Mother." No matter what female O'Neill character Dewhurst inhabited, she exuded an emotionally titanic stage persona. Dewhurst was one of a handful of actresses in her generation considered to have the physical and psychological stamina required to play the morphine-addicted matriarch Mary Tyrone, a female character who makes demands on the actress portraying her, similar to the demands made on an actor attempting to perform a credible King Lear.

Despite the fact that it was her performances in Eugene O'Neill's plays that became the identifiable center of her acting career, the acclaim Dewhurst received for these productions became, for her, both an honor and a burden. This was because the vast majority of the O'Neill female characters she undertook were either murderous Medea-like predators or the doomed victims of their tragic destinies. Her publicly known passionate love life and her reputation for being willful did nothing to dispel her onstage image. However, because she was a tigress when it came to protecting her children or a beloved social cause, she had lasting and devoted professional friends and fans.

The same devotees knew that Dewhurst had a charmingly playful and childlike side. She relished a humorous story or a good joke. The 5'8" actress had a voluptuous fulsome figure, one that suited the width of her acting range. She sought to temper her healthy appetite for good food and liquor with incessant smoking. The latter habit contributed in part to her distinctive throaty voice, which was easily recognizable onstage and off because of her deliciously robust, hearty laugh. Because she had difficulty reconciling herself to all of the facets of her personality, in private Dewhurst sometimes rued the inevitable probability that her obituary would associate her most with the larger-than-life women she portrayed so believably in the plays of Eugene O'Neill. One glaring clue useful to reconciling Dewhurst's many facets is her statement that what she identified with most in Mary Tyrone was the impulse driving the character's morphine addiction. In order to portray the character believably, Dewhurst researched the drug's effect. Through a friend who had been given morphine after a painful operation, Dewhurst found the insight she needed to reconcile Mary's seemingly irreconcilable behavior and remarks. The insight came to Dewhurst when her friend explained to the actress that once the drug was injected, "you never want to come back" (quoted in Garvey, 1988).

During the last 10 years of her life, Dewhurst agreed to write her autobiography, with the stipulation that the book would be one informative about the theater and not be about scandal and gossip. Dewhurst's publisher Scribner reluctantly consented, despite knowing that Dewhurst's offstage life, one that was often as dramatic as her onstage performances, might sell more books. Because of her untimely death on August 22, 1991, the book was left unfinished. Tom Viola, a writer and AIDS activist friend of Dewhurst's who was also a frequent visitor to her Salem, New York, retreat nicknamed "the farm," opted to complete the highly articulate, richly informative, and carefully sanitized skeleton of an autobiography that Dewhurst managed to leave in draft form. Viola devised a method of remaining true to Dewhurst's initial restrained and logical vision for her text while managing to find a way to illuminate the actress's bohemian, free-spirited persona: He invited Dewhurst's adult children Alex and Campbell and select professional colleagues and friends to submit their recollections and observations of situations alluded to in the manuscript but left undeveloped or unfinished. Viola inserted these additional personal contributions within Dewhurst's original manuscript to complete unfinished chapters or episodes.

The result was the best of possibilities, a seemingly subjective autobiography and a more realistic and insightful biography. Dewhurst's original work remained intact, but the additional articles and essays served to describe the emotionally turbulent, unconventional human side of Dewhurst, facets of her identity that defined her multidimensional personality and made her Eugene O'Neill's Everywoman. The written observations of Dewhurst's friends and colleagues served to illuminate why she had the reputation of being a "force of nature," a reality of her identity she fought even in her memoirs, but a truth of her being that thrust her forward toward her destiny with O'Neill.

In his mother's autobiography, Dewhurst's actor son Campbell Scott honestly sketches the chaotic, disorganized, but loving home environment that Dewhurst forged. Scott provides intimate, telling, descriptions of their family life, revealing sides of Dewhurst's identify that echo the endearingly befuddled, sometimes overwhelmed Essie Miller of O'Neill's *Ah, Wilderness!*

Colleen Dewhurst's death at the age of 67 from ovarian cancer shocked the theater, film, and television communities. It seemed impossible that

Colleen Dewhurst, as Josie Hogan, holds Jason Robards, as James Tyrone, in *A Moon for the Misbegotten*. *(Courtesy of the Sheaffer-O'Neill Collection, Charles E. Shain Library of Connecticut College)*

this indomitable woman could be overpowered by death. It was later disclosed that after being diagnosed with cancer, she refused all medical intervention and instead turned to the homeopathic beliefs of the Christian Science religion she had always practiced. In making the choice to decline medical help or generate attention through sympathy, she succumbed to the side of her that was so like Josie Hogan, the O'Neill character with whom she became most identified. As did Josie with James Tyrone, Dewhurst devoted her life to taking under her wing and mothering every cause and disenfranchised individual who touched her heart. And like Josie as she spoke the prayer-like words that concluded *A Moon for the Misbegotten*—"May you have your wish and die in your sleep soon, Jim, darling. May you rest forever in forgiveness and peace" (3:946)—within Colleen Dewhurst's quiet passing, it seemed as if her deepest wish had at last been fulfilled.

Bibliography

Dewhurst, Colleen, and Campbell Scott. 1988. Interview by Sheila Hickey, Garvey. Yale University, New Haven, Conn.

Garvey, Sheila Hickey. *Not for Profit: A History of New York's Circle in the Square Theatre.* Ann Arbor, Mich.: University Microfilms International, 1985.

Viola, Tom. *Colleen Dewhurst: Her Autobiography.* New York: Scribner, 1997.

Sheila Hickey Garvey

doctors   In a 1973 article about Eugene O'Neill's wife CARLOTTA MONTEREY O'NEILL, biographer Barbara Gelb commented on the playwright's hypochondriac behavior. As Gelb put it, O'Neill "collected doctors the way a hunter collects animal pelts" (Gelb 1973). Yet with the exception of Doctor Ned Darrell in STRANGE INTERLUDE, there are no major physician characters in O'Neill's major plays. In a few plays, physicians have speaking roles but primarily only to deliver a diagnosis. Ironically, the physicians who provide the greatest impact in O'Neill's works, most notably LONG DAY'S JOURNEY INTO NIGHT, are only referred to through offstage action.

As noted by many BIOGRAPHERS, O'Neill's difficult birth led to the prescription of morphine for MARY ELLEN "ELLA" O'NEILL, resulting in her 25-year addiction (Gelb 1987, 58). This familial experience with medical care, as depicted in *Long Day's Journey*, certainly must have clouded the playwright's view of the profession. But at age 25, O'Neill contracted tuberculosis and spent six months at Connecticut's GAYLORD FARM SANATORIUM under the care of Dr. David Lyman. In a later letter to Lyman, O'Neill stated that he had been "reborn" under the care of the medical staff (O'Neill 24). Reading O'Neill's plays reveals a contrast between general practitioners or family doctors, who are distrusted and denounced as quacks and charlatans, and specialists, who deliver an expert diagnosis that often presages the dramatic theme.

A one-act comedy entitled *The Dear Doctor* that O'Neill wrote during college has, unfortunately, been lost. But in another early play, *The PERSONAL EQUATION*, the generic character "the Doctor" offers the line "there is always hope" a precursor to "the hopeless hope" theme in many O'Neill plays (Bogard 56). In WARNINGS, an "ear specialist" correctly diagnoses that James Knapp, a marine wireless operator, may experience instantaneous deafness. But Knapp's wife convinces him that the doctor is lying and he must return to work. When the doctor's "warnings" prove true, Knapp's deafness imperils his shipmates and he commits suicide. Conversely, in the one-act SHELL SHOCK, an army doctor implausibly cures a veteran suffering from what we now term post-traumatic stress disorder by talking the patient through his battlefield experience.

In the one-act ABORTION, the college sports hero Jack Townsend confesses to his father that an affair with a townie girl has led to the illegal procedure. After receiving a grudging absolution from his father, Townsend is confronted by the girl's brother, who reveals that his sister has died. The brother refers to the abortionist as a "dirty skunk of a doctor" and later states "yuh send her to a faker of a doctor to be killed" (1:216). The brother also states that the doctor paid him "blood money" to keep quiet (1:218). As in *Long Day's Journey into Night*, the accusations against the doctor are less a condemnation of the medical profession and more a vehicle to shame the main character.

The doctors in the one-act WHERE THE CROSS IS MADE and the three-act version of the same plot, GOLD, merely allow one character to describe the deteriorating mental state of the central character.

The contrast between distrust of the generalist and reliance on the specialist is apparent in BEYOND THE HORIZON. After years of failure running the family farm, Robert Mayo is emaciated and near death, but like so many of O'Neill's ill characters, he scorns the advice of the "country quack." When brother Andrew returns from Argentina and brings Dr. Fawcett, "a specialist," the obvious diagnosis is that Robert will die. Nevertheless, Dr. Fawcett states that Robert could be saved by "a miracle;" thus allowing for the devastating "hopeless hope" anticlimax.

The general practitioner and the specialist are more critical to the action of *The Straw*, an autobiographical depiction of O'Neill's six months

Dr. David R. Lyman, second from right, behind Mrs. Florence R. Burgess, at Gaylord Farm *(Courtesy of the Sheaffer-O'Neill Collection, Charles E. Shain Library of Connecticut College)*

recovering from tuberculosis. A love story develops out of the medical condition when Eileen Carmody and Stephen Murray meet at Hill Farm Sanatorium. Because of this, physicians determine whether the two characters will meet and stay together or separate. Here the small-town generalist, Dr. Gaynor, actually has the meatier role than the sanatorium specialist, Dr. Stanton. Realizing that Eileen requires immediate care, Gaynor must cajole and threaten her cheap, selfish father in order to commit her to the sanatorium. If *The Straw* is a precursor to *Long Day's Journey*, and Bill Carmody is a more dissolute James Tyrone, then Dr. Gaynor will later become Doc Hardy, the Tyrone's family doctor. Gaynor's condemnation of Carmody's reluctance to pay for his daughter's care is presented in harsh terms similar to Jamie Tyrone's denunciation of his father James. In his brief scene with Eileen's father and her fiancé, Dr. Gaynor displays empa-

thy, anger, and a realistic language nearer to that of O'Neill's later plays.

Conversely, the director of the sanatorium, Dr. Stanton, serves as a stage device to explain the current medical practice for treating tuberculosis. Stanton's decisions concerning which patients are well enough to be discharged and which patients need more critical care are crucial to the conflict and climactic moments in this play. Yet Stanton only robotically calls each patient to be weighed. Considering O'Neill's lifelong friendship with Dr. David Lyman, director of the Gaylord Farm Sanatorium (in 1917, O'Neill wrote a letter to Lyman concerning medical deferment from the draft), the depiction of Dr. Stanton is surprisingly flat and unsuitable.

For *Strange Interlude*, O'Neill describes Dr. Edmund Darrell as *"cool and observant, his dark eyes analytical"* (2:661). Darrell is the antithesis to passion, and he considers himself "immune to love through his scientific understanding of its real sexual nature" (2:661). Initially, Dr. Darrell's goal is to cure Nina Leeds of the psychological ills that have troubled her since the death of her lover, Gordon Shaw. But Darrell's "prescription," that she wed the young Sam Evans and raise a family, backfires when Nina learns that the Evans family has a history of insanity. Nina persuades Darrell to become the father of her child by couching her argument in terms of a doctor caring for a patient. Darrell responds to this argument with initial confusion, but he analyzes the situation and begins speaking, as O'Neill directs, *"in his ultra-professional manner—like an automaton of a doctor"* (2:709).

Nina and Darrell cannot keep their "experiment" on a scientific level, and they become lovers. Ashamed of meddling in the lives of his "patients," Darrell abandons his medical career and becomes a biologist. Only at crucial moments does Darrell rely on his medical skills. When Nina moves to break up her son's engagement, Darrell steps in "as a doctor," instructing the fiancé to dismiss Nina's "queer delusions." Moments later, Sam Evans collapses from a stroke, but Darrell hesitates in response. At the urging of other characters ("Dr. Darrell—a patient!"), Ned reverts to his *"strictly professional manner"* (2:801). Throughout *Strange Interlude*, Dr. Darrell is conflicted in his attempts to be an unemotional medical professional and his desire for love in the arms of Nina Leeds.

The two physicians paramount in the O'Neill canon are only referred to through the dialogue in *Long Day's Journey into Night*. One is the "ignorant quack of a cheap hotel doctor" who prescribed the morphine for Mary Tyrone (3:765). This doctor is not only the source of Mary's addiction, but also the touchstone for James Tyrone's flaw—his stinginess. The hotel doctor is mentioned by Jamie, Mary, and Edmund as a rebuke to the father's attempts to deny culpability in the collapse of his family. Edmund's accusation that James hired the cheapest doctors to care for Mary leads to the father explaining his regrets to the son and the son attempting to describe his existential views to the father. In essence, the "hotel quack" is the impetus for most of the Tyrones' mutual recrimination.

The other physician influencing the Tyrones is Doc Hardy, who diagnoses Edmund's tuberculosis and prescribes the sanatorium. Early in the play, Jamie rants that Hardy is a "cheap quack" (3:757). Further, Mary initially refuses to accept the diagnosis and practically accuses Hardy of malpractice in his treatment of her addiction. Jamie accuses James Tyrone of once again skimping on medical care by pressuring Hardy to refer Edmund to a "cheap" sanatorium. Eventually, both Mary and Jamie rail against the practice of all doctors. But Edmund defends Hardy and accuses his mother of blaming the doctors for her weakness. From the view of James and Edmund, Doc Hardy is a well-meaning family physician, especially since he "called in a specialist" to confirm his diagnosis. As such, the physicians of *Long Day's Journey* depict the origins of the playwright's own conflicted view of physicians.

In some of his final letters, O'Neill railed against the treatment of Carlotta Monterey's allergies as a "quack's racket," then praised the specialist who treated his broken arm and the neurologists treating his tremors (O'Neill 581–582). In life and in his writing, O'Neill could not resolve his view of the medical profession.

Bibliography

Bogard, Travis. *Contour in Time: The Plays of Eugene O'Neill.* Rev. ed. New York: Oxford University Press, 1988.

Gelb, Arthur, and Barbara Gelb. *O'Neill.* New York: Perennial Library/Harper, 1987.

Gelb, Barbara. "To O'Neill, She Was Wife, Mistress, Mother, Nurse," *New York Times,* October 21, 1973. Available online. URL: http://www.eoneill.com/library/on/gelbs/times10.21.1973.htm. Accessed December 12, 2007.

O'Neill, Eugene. *Selected Letters of Eugene O'Neill.* Edited by Travis Bogard and Jackson R. Bryer. New Haven, Conn.: Yale University Press, 1988.

John Curry

Dolan, John "Dirty" (1866–1923)   Though Eugene O'Neill asserted that the important thing about him was his Irishness, he was never able to separate his Irish characters from that stock figure of the theater the stage Irishman. Maybe the characterization was valid. Or maybe the real IRISH AMERICANS were role-playing—playing to outsiders what the outsiders were expecting. Michael Manheim sees elements of the stage figure in early O'Neill—in Paddy and Driscoll of the SEA PLAYS (192); we see him also in Mickey Malloy and Jamie Cregan, even Con Melody, in A TOUCH OF THE POET—he is "stage leprechaun," "incorrigible meddler," "practical joker," "descendant of the clever servants in earlier drama . . . [who] love humiliating the rich and the proud" (192). He himself is rich in his ancestry and proud (he would be a king in Ireland if he had his rights).

We meet O'Neill's Irishman as Shaughnessy in LONG DAY'S JOURNEY INTO NIGHT and, at his fullest development, as Hogan in A MOON FOR THE MISBEGOTTEN. Long Day's Journey, as an anecdote, contains the bare outlines of the story of the pig farmer and the Standard Oil millionaire and his ice pond. But A Moon for the Misbegotten gives a full-fleshed story with full-fleshed characters. We have the pig farmer, his son (briefly, with references to two other sons), his daughter Josie (who should be, but is not, a beauty), his landlord (Jim), the Standard Oil millionaire, and his chauffeur. For the first conflict, there is the expected tension (though in part playful) between the tenant farmer and his landlord. For the second and subordinate conflict, there is the pig farmer and his rich (how un-American) neighbor who apes the English and (how even more un-American) has a chauffeur with him.

The constant in the two conflicts is the pig farmer. And O'Neill did not have to turn to the stage tradition for his character: He had him right in his sights in the NEW LONDON of his youth—John Dolan. In his notes for 1941–42, O'Neill even called the as-yet-unnamed Misbegotten the "Dolan play."

John "Dirty" Dolan was a pig farmer who rented his land from JAMES O'NEILL and later from JAMES O'NEILL, JR. (Jamie), and still later from Eugene. The farm bordered on the land of Edward C. Hammond whose neighbor on the other side was Edward S. Harkness the Standard Oil millionaire (see HARKNESS, EDWARD S., AND HAMMOND, EDWARD C.) And on Hammond's land was the ice pond (Smith 164).

Dolan was born in Ireland in 1866, emigrated to the United States in 1882, and came to Connecticut early. He would have been in his late 40s in 1912, the time of Long Day's Journey, and in his late 50s at the time of Misbegotten's 1923 (Hogan's age in Misbegotten is given as 55). As an adult in middle age, Dolan was short (about 5 feet 4 inches tall), stocky, "built like a barrel," "with arms like tree trunks, very strong," "big and dirty feet." In Misbegotten, Hogan is two inches taller but otherwise the description fits, though O'Neill adds stumpy legs and big (though not noted as dirty) feet. A failure in life generally—but good at growing things like vegetables (he is listed as a gardener in the 1900 U.S. census)—Dolan loved to drink, spoke with a "strong brogue," was intelligent and likeable but "ornery," and could be "stubborn and nasty." Though he had a family—actually two families since he married twice—there are no particular parallels with the Hogan family. (All quotes from Sheaffer.)

James O'Neill, Sr., was a regular at St. Joseph's church in New London. If not necessarily religious, Dolan attended church (or at least his wives' funeral masses) at (for his first wife) St. Mary's Star of the Sea and (for his second) St. Joseph's. As a youth, Dolan was a coachman. In the 1890s, James O'Neill hired coaches for his family outings. In 1911, Dolan is listed as a "driver" of hire cars. MARY ELLEN "ELLA" O'NEILL did her riding around town in hire cars (though Long Day's Journey leaves us with the impression the car and chauffeur were full-time). In so many ways, then, Hogan and Dolan make connections by matching up with each other and with the stage tradition. The firmest connection, however, is that Dolan was not only the tenant of James O'Neill and eventually of Eugene, but of Jamie O'Neill during the time when the play takes place.

A nonconnection worth noting is that Jamie was, around the time of the setting for Misbegotten (September 1923), in sanatoriums in Norwich, Connecticut, and Paterson, New Jersey, "a physical and mental wreck, almost blind" (Ranald 572), so that eventually, on November 8, 1923, he died of chronic ALCOHOLISM—in the same year that John Dolan died.

Bibliography

Floyd, Virginia. *The Plays of Eugene O'Neill: A New Assessment.* New York: Ungar, 1985, 566–582.

Manheim, Michael. *Eugene O'Neill's New Language of Kinship.* Syracuse, N.Y.: Syracuse University Press, 1982, 191–208.

Ranald, Margaret Loftus. *The Eugene O'Neill Companion.* Westport, Conn.: Greenwood Press, 1985.

Sheaffer, Louis. Notes in the Louis Sheaffer-Eugene O'Neill Collection. Department of Special Collections and Archives, Charles E. Shain Library, Connecticut College, New London.

Smith, Madeline C., and Richard Eaton. "The Truth about Hogan," *Eugene O'Neill Review* 18, nos. 1–2 (Spring–Fall 1994): 163–170.

U.S. Bureau of the Census. Censuses for 1900 and 1920. Washington, D.C., 1900, 1920.

Richard Eaton

Driscoll (unknown–unknown)   Eugene O'Neill's friendship with Driscoll, a stoker with the American Line, developed while they were in Southampton, England. However. according to O'Neill, the two first met at JIMMY "THE PRIEST'S," a sailor's bar and flophouse in lower Manhattan. In an interview with Mary B. Mullett that appeared in *American Magazine* in 1922, O'Neill said: "I shouldn't have known the stokers if I hadn't happened to scrape an acquaintance with one of our own furnace-room gang at Jimmy the Priest's. His name was Driscoll, and he was a Liverpool Irishman. It seems that years ago some IRISH families settled in Liverpool. Most of them followed the sea, and they were a hard lot. To sailors all over the world, a 'Liverpool Irishman' is the synonym for a tough customer" (Mullett 31).

When O'Neill and Driscoll met in Southampton, O'Neill had been an ordinary seaman aboard the American Line's SS NEW YORK and Driscoll was a stoker aboard the sister ship SS PHILADELPHIA. Under normal circumstances at the time, stokers and seamen did not fraternize due to the high level of animosity and the shipboard CLASS distinction between the two groups. But while they were in Southampton, dock laborers and transportation workers went on strike; the action was later referred to as the Great Labor Strike of 1911, and stokers and seamen joined together in solidarity to support the striking workers. At the strike's conclusion, both Driscoll and O'Neill returned to New York as shipmates aboard the *Philadelphia.*

O'Neill was incorrect about Driscoll being a "Liverpool Irishman." Driscoll was actually born in Ireland and had become an American citizen (Sheaffer 196). Not much is known about Driscoll's history; even his first name is a mystery—shipping records only list him as J. Driscoll. In any event, O'Neill revered Driscoll, and in a 1924 interview with Louis Kalonyme of the *New York Times,* the playwright described his former shipmate as "a giant of a man, and absurdly strong. He thought a whole lot of himself, was a determined individualist. He was very proud of his strength, his capacity for grueling work. It seemed to give him mental poise to be able to dominate the stokehole, do more work that any of his mates" (Kalonyme 67).

Upon their arrival back in New York City in August 1911, O'Neill and Driscoll returned to Jimmy the Priest's. It was not long before Driscoll returned to SEA, and O'Neill gave up his life as a sailor. There is no evidence that the two men ever crossed paths again, but Driscoll remained a strong presence in O'Neill's life and work. Occasionally O'Neill would return to lower Manhattan and revisit some of his old haunts. On one of these visits, he learned that Driscoll had committed suicide a few months earlier. Driscoll had been serving aboard the American Line's SS *St. Louis.* The captain reported that on August 12, 1915, Driscoll had jumped overboard and was dead by the time he was picked up by one of the ship's boats (Sheaffer 335). Driscoll was 37 at the time of his death (Gelb 690). In her interview, Mullett asked O'Neill why Driscoll had committed suicide. O'Neill responded: "That's what I asked *myself.* 'Why?' It was the *why* of Driscoll's suicide that gave me the germ of the idea for my play, *The* HAIRY APE" (Mullett 31).

In *The Hairy Ape,* through the character Yank, O'Neill tries to come to terms with why someone so strong and confident would commit suicide. Yank, who is based on Driscoll, is unable to fit into society and finally finds peace and acceptance in death. O'Neill wrote *The Hairy Ape* in 1921 in a very short period of time. The play evolved out of thoughts and characters that had been ruminating in his mind for a number of years.

Driscoll was the inspiration for other characters in a number of plays. He first appeared in the one-act play BOUND EAST FOR CARDIFF, which was written in 1914, prior to Driscoll's death. The characters Yank and Driscoll were based on O'Neill's former shipmate. The original version of *Bound East for Cardiff* was called *Children of the Sea,* and it was slightly longer. When O'Neill reworked the play in preparation for the 1916 production in Provincetown, Massachusetts, he eliminated a conversation between Yank and Driscoll about the mysterious disappearance of a hard-driving officer aboard ship. He might have cut the story in order to protect his friend Driscoll, believing that it was an actual experience of Driscoll's and that Driscoll had caused the officer's disappearance (Richter 147–149). Driscoll also appears under his own name in the one-act plays IN THE ZONE, The LONG VOYAGE HOME, and The MOON OF THE CARIBBEES, all written in 1917. The four one-act plays are referred to as the SS GLENCAIRN plays because they deal with the crew of the fictitious ship SS *Glencairn.*

Driscoll served as the inspiration for Lyons in O'Neill's short story, "TOMORROW." In the story, O'Neill recalls the first time he met Driscoll when Art says: "I had made a trip as a sailor on the Phila- delphia when he [Lyons] was in the stokehold, and we had become friends through a chance adventure together ashore in Southampton—which is another story" (O'Neill 957). O'Neill also modeled the stoker Mat Burke in "ANNA CHRISTIE" after his friend and shipmate.

Bibliography

Gelb, Arthur, and Barbara Gelb. *O'Neill: Life With Monte Cristo.* New York: Applause Books, 2000.

Kalonyme, Louis [Louis Kantor]. "O'Neill Lifts Curtain on His Early Days." In *Conversations with Eugene O'Neill,* edited by Mark W. Estrin, 64–69. Jackson and London: University Press of Mississippi, 1990.

Mullett, Mary B. "The Extraordinary Story of Eugene O'Neill." In *Conversations with Eugene O'Neill,* edited by Mark W. Estrin, 26–37. Jackson and London: University Press of Mississippi, 1990.

O'Neill, Eugene. "Tomorrow." In *Complete Plays.* Vol. 3. Edited by Travis Bogard. New York: Library of America, 1988, 947–967.

Richter, Robert A. *Eugene O'Neill and Dat Ole Davil Sea: Maritime Influences in the Life and Works of Eugene O'Neill.* Mystic, Conn.: Mystic Seaport, 2004.

Sheaffer, Louis. *O'Neill: Son and Playwright.* Boston: Little, Brown, 1968.

Robert A. Richter

E

East Asian thought Eugene O'Neill wrote the majority of his final plays while living at TAO HOUSE, a residence in Danville, California, that faced east and was adorned with Chinese artifacts collected by his wife, CARLOTTA MONTEREY O'NEILL (Robinson 170). As the name of this dwelling implies, O'Neill had developed a profound affinity for East Asian thought over the course of his life, particularly in regard to Taoism. While living in Danville, O'Neill had several volumes of Taoist literature in his possession, including Dwight Goddard's *Lao-tzu's Tao and Wu Wei* as well as James Legge's *The Texts of Taoism* (Robinson 23–24). Various elements of this philosophical system are noticeably "infused into the ideas, characterization, style and structure" of his late plays, which are characterized by "ambiguity and identity of contraries" (Haiping 29, 31). Ignoring, for the moment, the metaphysical and mystical implications of Taoism, the word *tao* may refer to a "philosopher's formulation of the 'best' way . . . to guide our behavior in social contexts" (Tanaka 194). Upon examining the facets of Eastern philosophy in *The* ICEMAN COMETH, HUGHIE, and LONG DAY'S JOURNEY INTO NIGHT, one may construct an understanding of O'Neill's own *tao* in relation to Taoism itself and Eastern philosophy in general.

The influence of Eastern philosophy in *The Iceman Cometh* begins with the origin of Larry Slade, the resident "foolosopher" of Harry Hope's bar (3:570). This character is based on TERRY CARLIN, a mystic O'Neill knew from the HELL HOLE who often engaged him in discussions regarding Buddhism and Hinduism (Robinson 12, 17). In the play, Larry represents the leader of a motley crew of derelicts who desire nothing more than to loaf around in Harry Hope's bar getting drunk and sharing stories of their past glories and pipe dreams of tomorrow. Each espouses an intention to reclaim what they lost, although it is apparent that none will take the initiative of their own accord. However, their apathy is not necessarily regarded as a negativity; as Larry observes, "they manage to get drunk, by hook or crook, and keep their pipe dreams, and that's all they ask of life" (3:584). The passivity of these characters corresponds with the Taoist concept *wu-wei*, the principle of sage nonaction or nonstriving (Robinson 171). Adherence to this principle, according to the respective *taos* of Lao Tzu and Chuang Tzu, is the best *way* to live one's life.

The human dregs who occupy Harry Hope's saloon "live in a state resembling the Taoist golden age" (Robinson 171). Their lethargy, which produces "a beautiful calm in the atmosphere" (3:577), emulates Chuang Tzu's belief that by taking no action, "one is at peace . . . and when one is at peace . . . no worry or sorrow can affect him" (Chuang Tzu 208, Robinson 171). Larry observes their ability to hold onto their pipe dreams while doing nothing about them as the quality that makes them the most contented men he has ever known. Hickey, on the other hand, emphasizes the necessity that the men abandon their pipe dreams. He is driven by a desire to provide his comrades with the inner peace they have already achieved, but succeeds only in disrupting their harmony by doing so.

Hickey announces that his goal is to make each of these loafers "contented with what he is, and quit battling himself, and find peace for the rest of his life" (3:629). Contrary to Taoist teachings, his method of accomplishing this involves provoking each of these men to a state of action, urging them to make efforts toward achieving their professed goals. What results is a series of intense altercations between the characters to the point where some go so far as to draw weapons against each other. The denouement presents a return to blissful apathy for these dregs, with the exceptions of Larry and Hickey, who are faced with the reality of their disillusionment in regard to their perceived serenity.

In Taoism, dichotomies such as illusion and reality are not viewed as polar opposites but rather as complementary forces that sustain one another. Such a relationship is noticeably present in the lives of the characters in *Iceman*, especially in those of Larry and Hickey. In his book *Eugene O'Neill and Oriental Thought: A Divided Vision* (1982), James A. Robinson points out that the illusions of their pipe dreams provide the foundation for their existence; as Larry says early in the first act, "the lie of a pipe dream is what gives life to the whole misbegotten mad lot of us" (3:569–570, Robinson 172). By drawing this parallel between illusion and reality, O'Neill "alludes to the doctrine of *māyā*," which holds that "our worldly existence involves a cosmic deception" (Robinson 172). Larry and Hickey both claim to have transcended the illusions of pipe dreams and thereby achieved inner harmony. Come the end, however, as Larry discovers he is really afraid of death and Hickey realizes that hatred, rather than compassion, was his true motive for killing his wife, it is apparent that "illusion provides the foundation of their peace" (172).

There are some scholars who argue that Western religious themes are more prevalent in *Iceman*. For instance, in his essay "The Iceman and the Bridegroom," Cyrus Day relates this play to DaVinci's painting *The Last Supper*, making Hickey an anti-Christ figure and Parritt "a suicidal Judas figure" (quoted in Bogard). Travis Bogard points out sev-eral problems with this argument, emphasizing the seating arrangement. He explains that Hope and Hickey both sit at opposite ends of the tables, rather than in the center, which Larry and Parritt occupy. This proposed connection between *Iceman* and *The Last Supper* is tenuous at best and not nearly as relevant as the Eastern themes that permeate this play and several others. In fact, Frederick Carpenter, in his essay "Eugene O'Neill, the Orient, and American Transcendentalism," emphasizes Orientalism as "the most important and distinctive aspect of his art" (quoted in Haiping 28).

In a letter to Carpenter, O'Neill indicates his deep regard for the teachings of the Taoists, telling him, "The mysticism of [Lao Tzu] and [Chuang Tzu] probably interested me more than any other Oriental writing" (quoted in Haiping 28). Despite this professed predilection for Taoism, it is certain that O'Neill was attracted to Buddhist philosophy as well. After all, several of his plays embody the essence of the first two of the Four Noble Truths, which hold that all of life is suffering and that suffering is caused by desire.

This interest reveals itself in *Hughie*, in which O'Neill makes a direct reference to a central concept in Buddhism, nirvana, which he describes as "the Big Night of Nights" (3:838). The word *nirvana* may be translated as "extinguishment" (i.e., of desire and/or karma). By achieving nirvana, the ultimate goal in Buddhist practice, one is liberated from samsara, the cosmic wheel of suffering in which the cycle of life, death, and rebirth are experienced. The characters in this play—Erie, Hughes, and the absent Hughie—are essentially personifications of these phases of samsara. To begin with, Erie is referred to as "awake and alive" (3:846); he reveals himself as one who is quite familiar with the sensual pleasures of life through his grandiose tales of gambling and debauchery. On the other hand, Hughes is described as responding to Erie "in the vague tone of a corpse" (3:837). He is genuinely detached from life, his consciousness gravitating toward the rhythm of the sounds of the night that "vaguely [remind] him of death" (3:846). Based on these characteristics, it may be argued that Erie and Hughes are symbolic of the realms of life and death, respectively.

The only character who is actually dead ironically represents rebirth. Hughie, as described by Erie, possessed a childlike innocence and naïveté when he was alive. Like Hughes, he worked as a night clerk in the same dilapidated hotel and was not prone to indulging in sensual pleasures, although he was always thrilled when Erie had provided him with a tall tale of his excursions and gambling victories. Hughie's innocence is apparent when Erie reminisces of the time when he brought the clerk to the racetrack: Hughie did not need to gamble for excitement, he was delighted enough just to see the horses, which he thought were "the most beautiful things in the world" (3:840). Finally, Hughie's character is metaphorically reborn through Hughes, who by the end of the play ceases to remain disconnected and displays a Hughie-like enthusiasm for Erie's tales about Arnold Rothstein; he even indulges in a friendly game of craps with Erie.

In his article "Taoism in O'Neill's Tao House Plays," Liu Haiping addresses the interplay of life and death in the structure of *Hughie*, relating it to the wisdom of Chuang Tzu. As previously indicated, aspects of existence that are generally viewed as opposites such as life and death are, for Taoists, complementary rather than contrary forces: "When there is life there is death, and when there is death there is life . . . the 'this' is also the 'that'. The 'that' is also the 'this'. . . . When 'this' and 'that' have no opposites, there is the very axis of *Tao*" (Chuang Tzu 183, Haiping 30–31).

Haiping observes that *Hughie* begins with a mournful quality that is brought to life with Erie's arrival. His lively conversation regresses into one of death while reminiscing about Hughie, to the point where the play recedes into silence as both men contemplate death. Finally, the end of the play returns to a scene of liveliness. The sounds in the street reflect this structure, alternating between silence and sound as the garbage men and el trains pass in the night. The notion that life and death sustain and give rise to one another is represented through the play's rhythmic structure, to the point where "the dividing line between life and death blurs and fades away" (Haiping 32). By structuring the play as he does, O'Neill indicates his confi-

Eugene O'Neill at Tao House *(Courtesy of the Sheaffer-O'Neill Collection, Charles E. Shain Library of Connecticut College)*

dence in the wisdom of Chuang Tzu and its relation to "his own mystical intuitions about reality," which are characterized by ambiguity and interconnectedness (Haiping 28).

The interpenetration of dichotomies observed by Chuang Tzu are also present in the interpersonal relationships of O'Neill's characters, which are not strictly definable in terms of love and hate but rather an ambiguous blend of the two. Whereas Parrit claims to love his mother, he later confesses it was his hatred of her that caused him to betray her. Likewise, Hickey comes to the realization that he killed his wife not out of love and compassion, as he originally professes, but rather out of a deep-rooted hatred toward her. Furthermore, Jamie Tyrone confesses his hatred for his brother Edmund in *Long Day's Journey into Night* because it was Edmund's being born that started their mother

Mary on morphine. Of course, it is his love for Edmund that allows Jamie to reveal his hatred.

In *Long Day's Journey,* O'Neill's most autobiographical play, there is evidence to suggest that his exploration of Eastern philosophy was perhaps an attempt to reconcile a crisis of faith in regard to CATHOLICISM. Such implications are present in his treatment of Mary Tyrone, the representative figure of his mother, MARY ELLEN "ELLA" O'NEILL. While reminiscing about her time in the convent, Mary mentions the prayer she had offered to the Virgin Mary to bring her peace, recalling, "I knew she heard my prayer and would always love me and see no harm ever came to me so long as I never lost my faith in her" (3:828). Of course, the harm she and her family endure as a result of her drug addiction is painfully apparent. O'Neill might have perceived her addiction, at least partially, as a failure of her faith. This plausible perception would certainly have contributed to a certain skepticism about the Catholic Church and perhaps Christianity in general, therefore causing him to seek salvation elsewhere.

O'Neill own mystical intimations and experiences certainly contributed to this exploration as well. Toward the end of *Long Day's Journey,* Edmund recounts a transcendent experience he had while on "the Squarehead square rigger, bound for BUENOS AIRES" (3:811). This passage is undoubtedly inspired from the time O'Neill spent aboard the CHARLES RACINE as a young man, a ship that was also destined for Buenos Aires. The notion of transcendence is a pivotal component of Eastern schools of thought such as Buddhism and Taoism, qualified in terms of enlightenment or unification with the Tao. In each, the essence of the experience relates to the realization of oneness with the universe and the diminishment of the illusion of *māyā* and ego. Through Edmund, O'Neill describes his own mystical experience, which corresponds with the intimations of the Eastern mystics:

> For a moment I lost myself—actually lost my life. I was set free! I dissolved in the sea, became white sails and flying spray, became beauty and rhythm, became moonlight and the ship and the high dim-starred sky! I belonged, without past

or future, within peace and unity and a wild joy, within something greater than my own life, or the life of Man, to Life itself. (3:811–812)

Edmund depicts other similar experiences, describing the essence of them as being "like the veil of things as they seem drawn back by an unseen hand. For a second you see—and seeing the secret, are the secret. For a second there is meaning!" (3:812). As James A. Robinson points out, O'Neill reveals a belief here that "significance lies only in the moments of mystical ecstasy; all else is illusion, a veil corresponding to the Vedantic *māyā* that conceals the oneness of man and universe" (174). However, in doing so, O'Neill also expresses a certain level of exasperation with such experiences, which are essentially temporary. Immediately following these experiences, he relates, "the hand lets the veil fall and you are alone, lost in the fog again, and you stumble on toward nowhere, for no good reason" (3:812).

In response to his father James Tyrone's approbation of his poetic expressions, Edmund explains, "I couldn't touch what I tried to tell you just now. I just stammered" (3:812). The statement that follows soon after resonates with the implications present in Lao Tzu's opening statement of "Tao Te Ching": "The *Tao* that can be told of is not the eternal *Tao*" (Lao Tzu 139). The underlying insinuation here is that the Tao (often translated as Way, alluding to the way or nature of the universe) is a perfect concept and cannot be adequately articulated since language itself is inherently imperfect. Lao Tzu would almost certainly agree with Edmund's assessment that "stammering is the native eloquence of us fog people [mystics]" (3:812–813), for despite his initial revelation, Lao Tzu paradoxically proceeds to eloquently stammer on about the Tao, attempting to put the ineffable into explicit terms.

Long Day's Journey also presents a criticism of the principle of nonaction (*wu-wei*) as the best means to achieve harmony. One finds this in O'Neill's portrayal of Jamie. Similar to the human dregs who occupy Harry Hope's saloon in *Iceman,* Jamie desires nothing more than to loaf around in bars; he has no "loftier dream than whores and whiskey" (3:795). However, there is no evidence to suggest that by leading this lifestyle, Jamie has achieved inner peace. In fact, his confession to Edmund in act 4 reveals the exact opposite, that he is tormented by his laziness, which causes him to attempt to sabotage his brother's life. Like his parents, Jamie considers himself a failure, telling Edmund that he poisoned his mind on purpose, that he never wanted Edmund to succeed and therefore tried to make him "look even worse by comparison" (3:820). While the practice of *wu-wei* may offer the possibility of inner peace, it also has the potential to bring about inner turmoil as well. O'Neill may not have disagreed with the principle of *wu-wei* as a means to achieve harmony, though he may have considered it to be unreliable and unrealistic in a competitive, materialistic society.

For O'Neill, the teachings of Eastern mystics were significant sources of intrigue, as evinced by his subtle infusions of their concepts in these later works, as well as the environment in which he wrote them. At the same time, it cannot be said that he found absolute solace in the wisdom provided by these writings. Regardless of the fact that he may have returned to Catholicism for a short time, one must consider that for his characters, the inner peace that they achieve, or rather perceive, is anything but absolute. For Hickey and Larry in *Iceman,* their perceived harmony is superficial and discovered to be based on illusion. For Edmund in *Long Day's Journey,* tranquility and enlightenment are temporary; for Jamie, they are nonexistent. Although confident in the wisdom professed by Eastern sages, aspects of which he expresses having personally experienced, O'Neill's feelings regarding the actual application of their ideas to Western life are uncertain.

As impressed as O'Neill was with the ideologies of Chuang Tzu, Lao Tzu, and other Eastern philosophers, his final consideration of them might be adequately exemplified by the words of Father Baird in DAYS WITHOUT END, who asserts that Eastern thought is "not for the Western soul" (3:122). Perhaps he perceived a latent paradox involved in a Westerner's embracing of Eastern ideals. The very attempt to live in accordance with Eastern ideals in a Western world would defy its very pre-

scriptions; such action is contrary to the principle of *wu-wei,* for in *trying* to do so, one strives against one's nature and environment. What can be said conclusively is that O'Neill's treatment of the subject, his *tao* if you will, emulates the paradoxical nature of Eastern thought itself, as it is a seemingly simultaneous acceptance and rejection.

Bibliography
Bogard, Travis. "The Door and the Mirror: The Iceman Cometh." In *Contour in Time: The Plays of Eugene O'Neill.* Rev. ed. New York: Oxford University Press, 1988. Available online. URL: http://www.eoneill.com/library/contour/mirror/iceman.htm. Accessed July 8, 2007.
Chuang Tzu. "The Chuang Tzu." In *A Source Book in Chinese Philosophy,* edited and translated by Wing-Tsit Chan, 177–210. Princeton, N.J.: Princeton University Press, 1963.
Haiping, Liu. "Taoism in O'Neill's Tao House Plays." *Eugene O'Neill Newsletter* 12, no. 2 (1988): 28–33.
Lao Tzu. "Tao Te Ching." In *A Source Book in Chinese Philosophy.* Compiled and translated by Wing-Tsit Chan. Princeton, N.J.: Princeton University Press, 1963, 139–176.
Robinson, James A. *Eugene O'Neill and Oriental Thought: A Divided Vision.* Carbondale: Southern Illinois University Press, 1982.
Tanaka, Koji. "The Limit of Language in Daoism." *Asian Philosophy* 14, no. 2 (July 2004): 191–205.

Troy Sheffield

Eugene O'Neill renaissance During a 1988 Eugene O'Neill Centenary gala held at Broadway's Circle in the Square Theatre, the actress COLLEEN DEWHURST reflected on her understanding of Eugene O'Neill's significance by saying, "He [O'Neill] brought to the stage parents locked in hopeless generational conflict with their children, children haunted by Oedipal guilt, self-punishing adulterous lovers, jealous siblings, murderous wives and suicidal husbands. He wrote about self-delusion, deep alcoholism, naked lust . . . the very fabric of all our daily lives" (quoted in Rothstein). It is ironic that in 1953, as the NOBEL PRIZE–winning playwright lay dying, he believed that he had been erased historically as being America's greatest play-wright, surpassed in esteem by the new generation of writers, such as Arthur Miller and TENNESSEE WILLIAMS.

O'Neill's choice to write plays in the form of GREEK TRAGEDY had a purposeful thrust, one that used an ancient convention to contemplate God's role, if any, in man's ultimate fate. His lifelong musing on this philosophical issue reflected his own tendency to despair. Yet O'Neill himself might have at last felt faith, or he might have at least been awed by the extent of the forces motivating the fulfillment of his destiny. In 1956, only three years after his death, O'Neill's reputation was restored.

Upon O'Neill's death, his third wife, CARLOTTA MONTEREY O'NEILL, became the executrix of his estate. Since the tepid response to the opening of The ICEMAN COMETH in 1946, followed by the premature out-of-town closing of A MOON FOR THE MISBEGOTTEN in 1947, she had been declining all New York offers to produce plays O'Neill wrote after 1934. But, because of the Off-Broadway Circle in the Square's good reputation for reviving undervalued plays, O'Neill's widow responded positively when a request came from that tiny, 199-seat theater to produce The Iceman Cometh, directed by a very promising new talent, the Panamanian American JOSÉ QUINTERO. Mrs. O'Neill agreed, saying that she was pleased at the choice largely because Iceman had been one of her husband's "last failures" (Library of the Performing Arts). She was thrilled when ultimately Quintero staged a revival of Iceman that was met with rapturous reviews upon its opening on May 18, 1956. In the New York Times, BROOKS ATKINSON, who was the most important critic of the era, described the production as seeming "not like something written, but like something that is happening" (Atkinson).

During the process of bringing Iceman to the stage, the beautiful and regal 68-year-old widow became deeply impressed by the 32-year-old Quintero because his ability to bring Iceman to its full potential had caused O'Neill's play to become a newly acknowledged masterpiece. In doing so, he had proven to Mrs. O'Neill his ability to make the impossible possible. Quintero was a tall, handsome, charming young man whose Spanish accent and

Latin warmth entranced her. Ironically, his homosexuality often caused him to refer to himself as a "failed Catholic" (Quintero 1986). But the influences of the religion he was steeped in from his childhood were indelible and consequently he felt a bond with O'Neill through the spiritual agonies that permeated the playwright's body of work. Quintero told Mrs. O'Neill that his response to The Iceman Cometh was so wrenching that he had come to believe that "the ceiling of Harry Hope's crummy bum-inhabited bar was that of the Sistine Chapel" (Quintero 1974, 151). Mrs. O'Neill was captivated by this insight. She came to believe that Quintero's talents were almost mystically purging and redeeming O'Neill's final years, which had been enveloped by mental anguish and spiritual torment. Mrs. O'Neill viewed her husband as a "black Irishman," an idea of him dating back to the era when Spanish settlements existed in Ireland. She came to believe that Quintero shared this Irish/Spanish heritage with O'Neill and that, in some mystical way, he had become the vessel through which her husband's plays could best be evoked.

Mrs. O'Neill then, entrusted Quintero and the Circle in the Square with her greatest treasure, the rights to produce O'Neill's sequestered masterwork LONG DAY'S JOURNEY INTO NIGHT. With Carlotta O'Neill's blessing, Quintero cast JASON ROBARDS as James Tyrone, Jr., the prototype of O'Neill's real-life alcoholic and playboy brother, because of his recent success playing Theodore Hickman in the Iceman revival. When the production opened on Broadway on November 7, 1956, the critics deemed it "a magnificent achievement which restores Broadway theatre to its rightful estate as literature and art" ("O'Neill's 'Journey'"). The production won that year's Tony Award and achieved a record-breaking two-year run. Long Day's Journey into Night also garnered O'Neill a posthumous fourth PULITZER PRIZE.

The time for yet another artist's destiny had also emerged. Actor Jason Robards was ecstatic when he learned that the Circle in the Square was going to produce The Iceman Cometh. The 36-year-old Robards had seen the THEATRE GUILD's 1946 production and had strong feelings about the play's central character Theodore Hickman, a salesman called Hickey, whom O'Neill described as "about fifty, a little under medium height, with a stout, roly-poly figure" (3:607). Robards, who had acted previously for Quintero, requested and was granted an audition. Although Robards was some 15 years younger than Hickey, scrawny in physique and in all ways physically unsuited to play the part, he gave an audition that Quintero later remembered as one that "illuminated the decadence of the role. He [Jason] was such a different type than O'Neill called for. I didn't realize it until then that it's inside where the reality lies. You can always pad" (Quintero, 1986). The director immediately cast Robards, who gave such a memorable, shame-ridden rendition of the murderous Hickey that his performance earned him a reputation as the actor who could make guilt seem palpable.

When, six months later, Robards achieved equally resplendent reviews in Long Day's Journey into Night, Carlotta O'Neill affirmed that at last the ideal O'Neill actor had arrived. She gave Robards a first-edition copy of Long Day's Journey into Night inscribing it: "To Jason Jamie Robards" (Black et al. 153–157). Mrs. O'Neill's gift to Quintero was as symbolically telling: She asked him to wear her wedding ring during the production's rehearsals. After its momentous opening, she gave the critically acclaimed "genius" of the AMERICAN THEATER carte blanche to direct any O'Neill play he wanted.

Quintero's next O'Neill production was in 1958 at the Spoleto Festival in Italy. He cast the womanly, full-figured, and ferociously passionate actress Colleen Dewhurst to play O'Neill's iconic Madonna/whore mother-earth figure Josie Hogan in A Moon for the Misbegotten. In 1963, for a Circle in the Square revival of O'Neill's DESIRE UNDER THE ELMS, Quintero again cast Dewhurst, this time as Abbie Putnam, opposite her real-life husband, George C. Scott. The extraordinarily talented actor portrayed Cabot, the play's antagonist, a hardened and indomitable 80-year-old New England farmer.

Quintero's non-naturalistic staging on the Circle's intimate thrust stage was a clever contrast to the famous 1924 Broadway version of Desire. In the original production, set designer ROBERT EDMOND JONES had used lush, sensual branches that he allowed to loom over the production's farmhouse. These served to represent extensions of the full

and bosomy elm trees O'Neill had envisioned as surrounding the star-crossed farm and its ill-fated inhabitants. Quintero solved the problem of his production's outdoor landscape by keeping it as one unseen by the audience except when evoked through the imagination of the actors. This choice to create an abstract setting served to focus the production's intended emphasis on Dewhurst and Scott's titanic and almost operatic renditions of Abbie and Cabot.

The New York theater critics treated Dewhurst's and Scott's potent characterizations as a benchmark event. Reviewers from the major local newspapers, including Walter Kerr, Norman Nadel, and Richard Watts, uncharacteristically united to celebrate the production by agreeing to allow sections of their reviews to be reprinted in the magazine Firstnite. Critic Howard Taubman's selection read like a King's proclamation, one that insisted that it be, "Resolved: That [Dewhurst and Scott's] performances in Eugene O'Neill's 'Desire Under the Elms" at Circle-in-The-Square be cited as evidence of their uncommon artistry, and reason enough for this city to clutch the Scott's affectionately and selfishly to its municipal bosom" (Library of the Performing Arts, Nadel, 8).

At the time of her acclaimed performance in Desire under the Elms, Dewhurst was a highly regarded actress lovingly known within the theater community as "the Queen of Off Broadway" because of her many successes in small but pivotal New York venues. However, her memorable performances in two of O'Neill's great women's roles demonstrated first to Quintero and then to the world that she was the quintessence of O'Neillian womanhood. From the time of her New York success portraying Abbie in Desire under the Elms until her untimely death in 1991, Colleen Dewhurst was regarded as the supreme O'Neill actress.

Throughout their careers, Jason Robards and Colleen Dewhurst enjoyed stage, film, and television acclaim. Yet both performers were inevitably drawn back to the stage to perform O'Neill. In 1964, under Quintero's direction and with Carlotta O'Neill's blessing, Robards created the gambler Erie Smith in the world premiere of O'Neill's one-act play HUGHIE. This was one of several plays in O'Neill's canon that Robards and Quintero revived together, including a 1985 production of *The Iceman Cometh*, this time on Broadway, and a second Broadway version of *Long Day's Journey into Night* in 1988.

Dewhurst's next O'Neill performance after *Desire under the Elms* was in a controversial 1967 Broadway and world-premiere production of O'Neill's unfinished play MORE STATELY MANSIONS, directed by José Quintero. Some critics questioned the production's validity because the play was based on a manuscript that O'Neill had ordered his wife Carlotta to destroy just prior to his death. It was unexpectedly discovered by curator Donald Gallop years after O'Neill's death in the archives the O'Neill's had donated to Yale University. Delighted, Carlotta O'Neill permitted Quintero and Gallop to adapt the play for the American stage in a 1967 production that Quintero directed on Broadway. Although there was some objection to Mrs. O'Neill's decision to ignore her husband's wishes and then tamper with his draft, the playwright's widow was adamant that a production of the play was essential since destiny had once again intervened on behalf of her husband's artistic legacy. The play was Colleen Dewhurst's good fortune, too: Her performance of Sara Melody earned her glowing reviews, ones that far surpassed her female costar, the glamorous internationally renowned movie actress Ingrid Bergman.

In 1970, Carlotta Monterey O'Neill died, having helped to transform her husband's failures into his greatest successes. By the time of her passing, Mrs. O'Neill had also ensured that any remaining plays he had written that had not been produced, or had not been previously performed on Broadway, were staged. These included productions of STRANGE INTERLUDE and MARCO MILLIONS directed by José Quintero and A TOUCH OF THE POET directed by Harold Clurman with Helen Hayes (1958), as well as the Broadway premiere of *A Moon for the Misbegotten* directed by Carmen Capalbo with Wendy Hiller and Franchot Tone (1957). The latter two productions were not of the caliber of those Quintero directed, but both were respectfully received and enhanced O'Neill's status in world theater.

In 1972, five years after her success in *More Stately Mansions*, Dewhurst agreed to play the Clytemnes-tra-like Christine Mannon in O'Neill's MOURNING BECOMES ELECTRA, which Theodore Mann directed to christen the newly opened Circle in the Square Theatre on Broadway. Dewhurst's portrayal of the desperate and emotionally abandoned Christine, a performance reviewer Martin Gottfried deemed "monumentally convincing," earned her another of her many Tony Award nominations.

In 1973, an artistic breakthrough occurred that gave further distinction to O'Neill's literary canon. This happened when Quintero, Robards, and Dewhurst united for a Broadway revival of *A Moon for the Misbegotten*. Newspapers reported how similar the artists' offstage lives were to Eugene O'Neill's life and those of his characters. For Robards and Quintero, this meant publicly revealing their struggles with acute ALCOHOLISM as they described the ways they used the agonies and imminent alcoholic death of the play's central character, Jamie Tyrone, to begin their own process of achieving sober lives. For Dewhurst, this public scrutiny meant revealing how playing Josie Hogan gave the recently divorced actress the vehicle through which she could forgive the painful transgressions and eventual abandonment of her former husband, George C. Scott. Robards's and Dewhurst's expertly crafted, emotionally wrenching performances played to sold-out audiences for over a year, earned numerous Tony awards, and crushed any remaining perceptions of O'Neill as a commercially unviable playwright. Filmed for television, Dewhurst's and Robards's legendary performances as Josie and James as directed by Quintero were preserved for future generations.

Robards, Dewhurst, and Quintero continued their O'Neill odyssey together during the 1988 O'Neill Centenary, when they reunited for repertory revivals of *AH, WILDERNESS!* and *Long Day's Journey into Night*. The productions took place in New Haven, Connecticut, and then moved briefly to Broadway. Both plays were produced by Yale University at the Long Wharf Theatre to honor Eugene O'Neill's 100th birthday. The plays, one O'Neill's idealized version of family life and the other its tragic opposite, were performed on the same set, modified slightly by designer Ben Edwards to suit each play's specifications. The productions became a capstone to Dewhurst's, Robards's, and Quintero's O'Neill careers. The productions also became the trio's last fully staged O'Neill endeavor: Colleen Dewhurst died in 1991, age of 67; José Quintero died in 1999, age 74; and Jason Robards died in 2000, age 78.

Prior to 1956, many great actors and actresses performed O'Neill's characters on stage and in film, among them Greta Garbo, Alla Nazimova, Paul Robeson, Alfred Lunt, and Lynn Fontanne. Since the 1956 Eugene O'Neill renaissance, many great performers have attempted to emulate Jason Robards's and Colleen Dewhurst's O'Neill achievements, among them Kevin Spacey, Glenda Jackson, Al Pacino, Vanessa Redgrave, Gabriel Byrne, and Brian Dennehy. When judged on the basis of the variety of roles they have portrayed or by their artistic acclamation, none have equaled or surpassed Robards's and Dewhurst's O'Neill triumphs. Similarly, no other theatrical director has surpassed Quintero's achievement of staging so many of O'Neill's plays in different venues so successfully. Equally important was Quintero's unique ability to intuitively cast and resplendently stage O'Neill's plays.

Bibliography

Atkinson, Brooks. "O'Neill Tragedy Revived," *New York Times,* May 9, 1956. Available online. URL: http://www.eoniell.com/artifoets/reviews/ic2_times.htm. Accessed June 4, 2007.

Black, Stephen A., Zander Brietzke, Jackson R. Bryer, and Sheila Hickey Garvey, eds. *Jason Robards Remembered, Essays and Recollections.* Jefferson, N.C.: McFarland and Company, 2002, 153–157.

Gottfried, Martin. "'Mourning Becomes Electra,'" *Women's Wear Daily New York Theater Critics Reviews,* November 12, 1972.

Mann, Theodore. Transcript for "O'Neill," Channel 13 television. New York. Library of the Performing Arts, Lincoln Center, 1986.

———. *Theatre Arts,* April 1959, n.p.

———. Norman Nadel. Reprinted in *Firstnite,* January 21, 1963, p. 8.

"O'Neill's 'Journey' Takes High, Exciting Road," *Cue* November 17, 1956.

Quintero, José. *If You Don't Dance They Beat You.* Boston: Little, Brown, 1974.

———. 1986. Interview by Sheila Hickey Garvey. "Eugene O'Neill: The Later Years" conference, Suffolk University, Boston, May 31, 1986.

Robards, Jason. Interview by Sheila Hickey Garvey. John F. Kennedy Center for the Performing Arts, Washington, D.C., August 12, 1985.

Rothstein, Mervyn. "Everybody Attends O'Neill Party," *New York Times,* October 18, 1988. Available online as "O'Neill Lauded in His Own Words." URL: http://tinyurlicom/6326yo. Accessed January 5, 2008.

Sheila Hickey Garvey

Eugene O'Neill Review The *Eugene O'Neill Review* is an annual, scholarly journal devoted to the life, times, and contemporaries of America's only NOBEL PRIZE–winning playwright. Suffolk University in Boston, Massachusetts, publishes the *Review,* a member of the Council of Editors of Learned Journals (CELJ), in cooperation with the EUGENE O'NEILL SOCIETY, whose members receive a copy as a benefit.

Dr. Frederick C. Wilkins, professor of English at Suffolk University, founded the journal in 1977, first as a newsletter to summarize sizable and "far-flung" essays published in other sources, and to announce forthcoming productions and books and review previous ones for the community of O'Neill scholars and enthusiasts. A panel discussion at the Modern Language Association (MLA) convention in San Francisco in 1975, "The Enduring O'Neill: Which Plays Will Survive?," featuring such notable scholars as John Henry Raleigh, Doris Falk, Virginia Floyd, Esther Jackson, and Wilkins, spurred thinking that led to the creation of the *Eugene O'Neill Newsletter.* The *Newsletter* morphed into the *Review* in 1989 with volume 13 of the publication and a vow to continue with the same original intent: to present the best possible forum for sharing facts, opinions, and questions about O'Neill. Still, the new format gave rise to lengthier individual articles and essays, in addition to the traditional attention paid to performances and book reviews. Initially, two issues were planned and published for each academic year, spring and fall, but starting with volume 17 (1993), each subsequent issue combined spring and fall as one.

The *Eugene O'Neill Review*, taking into account its early form as the *Newsletter*, published its 30th anniversary volume in 2008. The journal has appeared each spring since 2004, and a rotating editorial board performs peer review on all articles under the editorship of Zander Brietzke. The board currently favors long essays of 8,000 words or more but considers material of any length, including letters, and reviews of about 800 words. Submissions should adhere to MLA style (in-text citations, endnotes, works cited). For more information, prospective contributors should contact the managing editor at Suffolk University, Department of English, 41 Temple Street, Boston, MA 02114-4280. Tel: 617-573-8271. The journal's Web site is: www.suffolk.edu/college/3461.html.

Zander Brietzke

Eugene O'Neill Society   The Eugene O'Neill Society is a nonprofit international association formed in 1978 to promote the study of the life and works of the man many consider to be the United States's greatest playwright, Eugene O'Neill, and the drama and theater for which his work was in large part the instigator and the model. Eugene O'Neill was awarded four PULITZER PRIZES and is the only American playwright to have received the NOBEL PRIZE IN LITERATURE. Because of the significance of O'Neill's impact on the theater and because of his stature and importance as an American intellectual and artist, the society's members unite in the exploration of O'Neill's life and works by means of historical and critical writing; creating artistic performances on stage, film, television, radio, and recordings; amassing historical documentation; advocating the preservation of important historic sites associated with O'Neill's life and work; and promoting publications relating to O'Neill. The subjects of study include not only Eugene O'Neill and his works but also all aspects of AMERICAN THEATER and world theater. For these purposes, members of the society select times and appropriate occasions to hold international conventions, meet at theatrical performances of his works, and gather at historic sites related to the O'Neill legacy while also fostering panels, discussions, and literary works generated specifically to further understanding of O'Neill as an artist, innovator, and world figure. Society members include theater professionals (directors, actors, designers, producers, dramaturges), academics (teachers, students, administrators), collection curators, and all those directly and tangentially concerned with preserving Eugene O'Neill's heritage.

Each conference hosted by the Eugene O'Neill Society draws leaders in their respective fields who share widely diverse perspectives on topics relating to O'Neill. Since the range of O'Neill's work was so all-encompassing, society members are particularly notable for their willingness to entertain a wide range of interpretations of Eugene O'Neill's life and work. Membership in the society is not limited or restrained by any particular ideology or artistic vision.

In addition to the conferences already noted, the Eugene O'Neill Society has been associated with several other notable O'Neill-related conferences held with the society's support and participation. Three such conferences of particular importance occurred in Nanjing, China; Tokyo, Japan; and Han-sur-Lesse, Belgium, in 1988 at the time of the centenary of Eugene O'Neill's birth. Other related O'Neill events sponsored by the Eugene O'Neill Society have included celebrations of the actor JASON ROBARDS's O'Neill performances; panels with guests including O'Neill actresses Ingrid Bergman, COLLEEN DEWHURST, Ruby Dee, and Geraldine Fitzgerald; and celebrations of other major O'Neillians' work at O'Neill's homes at TAO HOUSE in Danville, California; MONTE CRISTO COTTAGE in NEW LONDON, CONNECTICUT; SPITHEAD in Bermuda; and Le Plessis in Tours, FRANCE.

The Eugene O'Neill Medallion is given to distinguished O'Neillians who have dedicated significant portions of their careers to furthering knowledge and appreciation of O'Neill. The medallion was first awarded at the 1995 Boston International Conference of the Eugene O'Neill Society. Award recipients have included actors Jason Robards and Geraldine Fitzgerald; directors JOSÉ QUINTERO, Arvin Brown, and Theodore Mann; author/scholar Travis Bogard; scholar Normand Berlin; scholar and curator Donald Gallop; scholar and society "father" Jordan Miller; scholar and *Eugene O'Neill Review* founding editor Fred Wilkins; O'Neill biographers Arthur and Barbara Gelb; and producer Paul Libin.

The Eugene O'Neill Newsletter was first published in 1977. Initially the "newsletter" served multiple purposes both as a medium for exchanging information among Society members and as a publication devoted to scholarly writings on O'Neill topics. *The Eugene O'Neill Newsletter's* first editor was Frederick C. Wilkins, Ph.D. (professor emeritus, Suffolk University, Boston, Massachusetts), a distinguished scholar who was also a primary founder of the Eugene O'Neill Society. In 1989, Professor Wilkins spearheaded the expansion of the newsletter into the EUGENE O'NEILL REVIEW, which took on the larger role of publishing peer-reviewed scholarship. As the journal's editor, Dr. Wilkins maintains the mission of the *Eugene O'Neill Review* as being a journal "devoted to the life, works, influence, and significance of the eponymous playwright." The *Eugene O'Neill Review* is published once a year by Suffolk University in cooperation with the Eugene O'Neill Society, whose members receive copies as a membership benefit. *The Eugene O'Neill Newsletter* was retained and renamed the *Eugene O'Neill Society Newsletter*. It continues informing society members of current events and newsworthy items. The *Eugene O'Neill Society Newsletter* is available on the Internet at eugeneoneillsociety.org.

In December 2001, at the time of Jason Robards's death, the board of directors of the Eugene O'Neill Society elected to honor the great O'Neill actor in a book. The result was *Jason Robards Remembered*, edited by Stephen A. Black, Zander Brietzke, Jackson R. Bryer, and Sheila Hickey Garvey. It contains a series of tributes, recollections, and essays written by Robards's colleagues, friends and admirers.

The board of directors of the Eugene O'Neill Society meets annually in conjunction with the national convention of the Modern Language Association (MLA) or the American Literature Association (ALA), or during the annual festivals at either Monte Cristo Cottage or Tao House. A scholarly and/or performance-related panel sponsored by the society takes place yearly at the above locations. The Eugene O'Neill Society also sponsors similar events and panels at the ALA's annual meeting. In addition, members of the Eugene O'Neill Society represent the organization when participating in the many events and activities inspired by O'Neill's abundant legacy.

Sheila Hickey Garvey

Eugene O'Neill Theater Center Located in Waterford, Connecticut, the Eugene O'Neill Theater Center was founded in 1964 by George C. White on the site of the Hammond Estate, which was immortalized by Eugene O'Neill in both poems and plays, particularly in A MOON FOR THE MISBEGOTTEN. Taking its name from Eugene O'Neill, America's only NOBEL PRIZE–winning playwright, the Eugene O'Neill Theater Center's mission is based on theatrical ideals initiated by O'Neill and aims to improve AMERICAN THEATER by providing a developmental center for unique new theatrical voices. In furthering this mission, the center is home to six distinct programs: the O'Neill Playwrights Conference; the O'Neill Music Theater Conference; the Puppetry Conference; the National Theater Institute; the Critics Institute; and MONTE CRISTO COTTAGE, O'Neill's childhood home located in neighboring NEW LONDON, CONNECTICUT.

At the O'Neill Theater Center, writers and directors, puppeteers and singers, students and audiences alike take their first steps in exploring, revising, and understanding their work and the potential of the theater they help create. During its history, work first performed at the center has gone on to regional theaters, Broadway, movies, and television. Students and professionals who have honed their skills at the center can be seen in these venues every day across the country. Staff and alumni from the center have won every major award in theater arts. The Eugene O'Neill Theater Center itself is the winner of a special Tony Award, the National Opera Award, the Jujamcyn Award of Theater Excellence, and the Arts and Business Council Encore Award. The 700 plays and musicals developed and premiered at the center include such notable works as John Guare's *The House of Blue Leaves*; Brian Crawley and Jeanine Tesori's

Violet; Wendy Wasserstein's *Uncommon Women and Others*; August Wilson's *Ma Rainey's Black Bottom*, *Fences* and *The Piano Lesson*; Lee Blessing's *A Walk in the Woods*; *Nine* by Arthur Kopit, Mario Fratti, and Maury Yeston; and *Avenue Q* by Rober Lopez, Jeff Marx, and Jeff Whitty.

Monte Cristo Cottage, in association with the O'Neill Center, provides scholars, artists, and designers the chance to examine aspects of O'Neill's life and two of his greatest works: Long Day's Journey into Night and Ah, Wilderness!. Monte Cristo Cottage is preserved as it was when the O'Neill family spent their summers there and provides a thought-provoking glimpse into the world O'Neill remembered in his plays.

David White

Experimental Theatre, Inc. The Experimental Theatre, Inc. (ETI) was a producing organization formed in 1923 under the direction of Kenneth Macgowan, Robert Edmond Jones, and Eugene O'Neill, sometimes referred to as "the Triumvirate," after the disintegration of the Provincetown Players in 1922. The ETI produced its first season in 1923–24 at the Provincetown Playhouse on Macdougal Street in Greenwich Village and, beginning in the following year, produced plays at both the Provincetown Playhouse and the Greenwich Village Theatre. Although Macgowan became the overall director and Jones the major artistic force in direction and design, O'Neill was the prime mover in establishing the ETI, to ensure that an experimental stage, without the commercial motives that defined the Broadway theater in the 1920s, would continue to be available to him and to other playwrights. Also central to the theater were Eleanor Fitzgerald, who served as its business manager, director James Light, and scenic designer Cleon Throckmorton.

Unlike the Provincetown Players, the ETI produced a mixture of experimental plays by contemporary playwrights and older plays that were reimagined through new approaches to production. The theater's mission is reflected in the productions mounted in its first season: *The Spook Sonata* by August Strindberg; *George Dandin* by

Molière, *Fashion, or, Life in New York* by Anna Cora Mowatt; and two new productions by O'Neill, *The Ancient Mariner*, an adaptation of Samuel Taylor Coleridge's poem, and All God's Chillun Got Wings. The season's successes show the theater's versatility. *Fashion*, Mowatt's 1845 comedy of manners about New York's nouveaux riches, became a hit that drew fashionable Manhattan theatergoers because of Jones's extraordinary design and direction, while *All God's Chillun*'s modernist treatment of a marriage between a black man and a white woman, including an onstage kiss, provided both social and artistic controversy.

In the next five years, the ETI continued to produce plays by contemporary playwrights that were controversial because of their experimental esthetics or edgy subject matter. Among these were Edmund Wilson's *The Crime in the Whistler Room*; Stark Young's *The Saint*; Paul Green's *In Abraham's Bosom*; Thomas Dickinson's *Winter Bound*; and e.e. cummings's *Him*; as well as O'Neill's Desire under the Elms, The Fountain, Welded, The Great God Brown, the SS Glencairn series, and a celebrated revival of *The Emperor Jones* with Paul Robeson. At the same time, the ETI was presenting the New York audience with innovative productions of such classics as William Congreve's *Love for Love*, Strindberg's *A Dream Play*, and Mrs. Henry Wood's *East Lynne*.

The ETI was dedicated to the concept of "total theater" that was advocated by Edward Gordon Craig and Max Reinhardt, who are strong influences on Jones and Macgowan. Macgowan made this clear in a program note early in the theater's life, writing that the ETI was "dedicated to the art of the whole theater and not to the art of the playwright alone" (Macgowan 1924–25, 4), as the Provincetown Players professed to be. This meant that each production was conceived as a total work of art in which set design, costume design, lighting, and the actors' physical direction were considered as much elements in the play as the dialogue and the actors' interpretation of it.

One distinctive feature of the theater's productions was its experimentation with the use of the mask, a theatrical device that was used in several innovative ways to dramatize the modernist representation of subjectivity, one of O'Neill's major preoccupations during the 1920s. Macgowan wrote his study *Masks and Demons*, which looks at the origins of the mask in various cultures, in 1923, and both O'Neill and Light wrote articles about the use of the mask. O'Neill clarified his thinking about masks in a series of articles for the *American Spectator* in 1932 and 1933. His idea that "one's outer life passes in a solitude haunted by the masks of others; one's inner life passes in a solitude hounded by the masks of oneself" (O'Neill 117) was central to the ETI productions of *The Ancient Mariner*, *All God's Chillun*, *The Great God Brown*, and a production of LAZARUS LAUGHED that was planned for the ETI but never mounted because there was not enough money for the epic undertaking. Looking back on the ETI experiments, O'Neill wrote that he considered the use of masks in these productions uniformly successful, and that he would like to see productions of his other plays using masks as well.

The ETI lasted for six and a half seasons; its last production was Thomas Dickinson's *Winter Bound*, an edgy psychological study that hinted at lesbian desire. In spring 1929, the board decided to move out of the Provincetown Playhouse and relocate uptown to the Garrick Theatre. This turned out to be a fatal decision, as its two fall productions, Mike Gold's *Fiesta* and *Winter Bound*, were financial failures, and many subscriptions that had been promised in the spring evaporated with the stock market crash of 1929.

Bibliography

Bryer, Jackson, ed. *"The Theatre We Worked For": The Letters of Eugene O'Neill to Kenneth Macgowan.* New Haven, Conn.: Yale University Press, 1982.

Macgowan, Kenneth. "More Tosh," *Provincetown Playbill*, season 1924–25, no. 1: 4.

———. *The Theatre of Tomorrow.* New York: Boni & Liveright, 1921.

Macgowan, Kenneth, and Herman Rosse. *Masks and Demons.* New York: Harcourt Brace, 1923.

Macgowan, Kenneth, and Robert Edmond Jones. *Continental Stagecraft.* New York: Harcourt Brace, 1922.

Murphy, Brenda. *The Provincetown Players and the Culture of Modernity.* Cambridge: Cambridge University Press, 2005.

O'Neill, Eugene. "Memoranda on Masks," *American Spectator* (November 1932); "Second Thoughts," *American Spectator* (December 1932); "A Dramatist's Notebook" *American Spectator* (January 1933). In *O'Neill and His Plays: Four Decades of Criticism*, edited by Oscar Cargill, N. Bryllion Fagin, and William J. Fisher, 116–122. New York: New York University Press, 1961.

Brenda Murphy

expressionism Expressionism, a German-born arts movement of the early 20th century, can be broadly characterized by its characters' violent emotional states, its grotesque exaggerations of the outer world, and the distorted psychological fantasies of the characters and/or playwrights through whom we glimpse that world. Expressionism was first conceived as a revolt against traditional NATURALISM, which expressionists viewed as uninspiring and politically, psychologically, and artistically restrictive. Like O'Neill, early expressionists were strongly influenced by the Swedish dramatist AUGUST STRINDBERG. Expressionism was originally conceived by art theorist Kasimir Edschmid and dramatist Georg Kaiser as a youth movement for idealists revolting against the fatalism of the naturalists, neoromanticists, and impressionists of the previous generation; as such, the modern themes of alienation and disillusionment that followed World War I at first contradicted the spiritual uplift founding expressionists called for (Hartnoll 303). However, in the 1920s and 1930s, playwrights such as Bertolt Brecht in Germany and Eugene O'Neill in the United States created a novel form of dramatic expressionism that merged the new idealism with modernistic cynicism.

Expressionism marks a deliberate break from the naturalism of the previous generation—or, as O'Neill wrote, "'REALISM,' if you prefer (I would to God some genius were gigantic enough to define clearly the separateness of these terms once and for all!)" (quoted in Clark 130)—but O'Neill, like the avant-garde German playwright Frank Wedekind, incorporated the two by combining realism's and naturalism's use of dialect, their sociological aspect, and their commonplace character types (the two forms, though distinct, share all of these) with the nightmarish visions of expressionistic theater. "The old 'naturalism,'" O'Neill wrote critically, "represents our fathers' daring aspirations toward self-recognition by holding the family kodak up to ill-nature" (quoted in Clark 130).

But O'Neill's experimental plays through the 1920s never fully revolt against the old naturalism of his fathers. As Travis Bogard wrote much later about *The* HAIRY APE, "O'Neill had written a play which appeared to be in a new mode but which was not so startling as to alienate audiences trained in realistic theater, and they responded to the play's thesis which, like the shape of the folk play, was to become an American dramatic 'myth,' the play of social protest" (249). Theater critic KENNETH MACGOWAN considered expressionism "anti-realistic" (quoted in Bogard 232), in that the form consciously rebelled against the old mimesis of naturalism and adapted the techniques of romanticism to "penetrate toward psychological and spiritual truths"; he also maintained that expressionistic theater required an especially close partnership between playwright, designer, and director, "since the playwright has to depend on color and form and a more presentational acting style than was customary" (Bogard 232).

O'Neill's particular style of expressionism—as we see in such plays as *The* EMPEROR JONES, *The Hairy Ape, The* GREAT GOD BROWN, and most successfully, MOURNING BECOMES ELECTRA—became the hallmark of the so-called American style of theater, which gained international recognition in the post–World War II era with the early works of TENNESSEE WILLIAMS and Arthur Miller. In a 1924 conversation with *New York Times* critic Louis Kantor, O'Neill defended expressionist drama by stating bluntly: "The naturalistic play is really less natural than a romantic or an expressionistic play. . . . I don't think it is the aim of the dramatist to be 'true to life,' but to be true to himself, to his vision, which may be of life treated as a fairy tale, or as a dream. Conceive of life as a huge mass of clay and the dramatist scooping up some of it, creating certain forms with his imagination and art, and then calling in his fellows and saying to them, 'Here you are as godlike beings'" (quoted in Kantor 48).

Bibliography

Bogard, Travis. *Contour in Time: The Plays of Eugene O'Neill.* Rev. ed. New York: Oxford University Press, 1988.

Clark, Barrett H. *Eugene O'Neill: The Man and His Plays.* Rev. ed. New York: Dover, 1947.

Hartnoll, Phyllis, ed. *The Oxford Companion to the Theatre.* 3rd ed. London: Oxford University Press, 1967.

Kantor, Louis. "O'Neill Defends His Play of Negro." In *Conversations with Eugene O'Neill,* edited by Mark W. Estrin, 44–49. Jackson: University of Mississippi Press, 1990.

F

film adaptations Like many American playwrights of the first half of the 20th century, Eugene O'Neill had little good to say about Hollywood and its products. Unlike most of these artists, however, he remained financially stable enough to avoid a stint working for the film studios. During his long career, O'Neill accepted no screenwriting contracts, played no creative role in a completed film adapted from his plays, and avoided most movies made from his work. He was certainly happy to sell the screen rights to his plays, but he wanted no involvement with the moviemaking process. For this reason, he usually took his money up front rather than entering into profit-sharing deals with the studios. The films made from O'Neill's work vary in merit, but the content and production histories of several of them are worth examining for what they reveal about the relationship between high culture and mass culture, between the stage and the screen, and between art and commerce.

In its infancy, the film industry was considered the shady cousin of the legitimate stage (itself still regarded with suspicion by many members of the late 19th-century gentility). To gain respectability, and to increase profits, cinema in the new century quickly set its sights on theaters' audiences and creative personnel. In order to attract these people, many filmmakers believed, movies needed to tell stories and become more like plays. The strategy succeeded in that it brought an audience of middle-class women to the movies, yet it often resulted in lackluster products. Innovators such as D. W. Griffith, Georges Méliès, and Sergei Eisenstein were developing uniquely cinematic idioms—in editing techniques, for example—within this new emphasis on narrative forms, but the work of most early directors was filled with stationary cameras, awkward sets, and scenery-chewing actors. The majority of scenes were taken in one continuous shot and with one setup. The scenes were then joined together to tell a simple story. But the effect was as though each scene had been acted on a theater stage and photographed by a camera deposited in the auditorium far enough away from the stage so that the margins of the frame coincided with the stage proscenium. The view was purely frontal, and the movement of the figures was restricted to a horizontal plane.

In the years since, such films, especially when they are adapted from a dramatic work for the theater, have been dismissed as "stagey"; while other adaptations have been praised for "opening up" the play beyond the parameters of the stage set. But John Orlandello, author of a book-length study of cinema versions of O'Neill, believes it is a mistake "to insist on a single model of effectiveness in adapting stage works to the screen" (14). Two of the better films derived from O'Neill's work, The LONG VOYAGE HOME (1940) and LONG DAY'S JOURNEY INTO NIGHT (1962), Orlandello argues, succeed for very different reasons: The former can be said to "open up" the source material; the latter sticks closer to the play.

There is no argument that stage and screen are different media. How they differ is up for debate. Critics such as Susan Sontag have theorized that the dramatic stage is restricted to a continuous use of space and has a fixed point of view, barriers that do not exist for film. It may also be argued that plays rely on words, and films depend on images. The order of the words that combine to form the new word *screenplay* seem to bear this out. The screenplay is not meant to exist on its own, not even to the extent that a dramatic work for the theater, by O'Neill for instance, might come alive on the page. The mediocre businessman William Shakespeare may not have realized that he was the great playwright Shakespeare, but to this day there is still no *Hamlet* of screenplays. The Hollywood script is a written invitation to make visual art, not a literary artwork in its own right.

But this is not to say that film is an inferior, more down-market form. Many "stagey" adaptations are said to fail because they try to remain faithful to the "superior" source material, without taking full advantage of film's own qualities. But it is important to note that film and theater have similarities as well. For example, the theater director and the film director both manipulate aspects of the mise-en-scène to create dramatic intensity. They make choices in costuming, setting, lighting, and the actors' behavior. While it is a myth that film acting calls for less "emoting" than theater acting, the fact that the camera can be positioned from a variety of distances might call for a stronger interplay between restraint and emphasis.

This was a lesson learned by actors like O'Neill's father, JAMES O'NEILL, an early target of the film industry's effort to poach theater people. The elder O'Neill starred in a 1912 silent version of *The Count of Monte Cristo*, doing it for the money. Around the same time, Eugene also tried to sell out, if only a little, writing filmplays to make some quick money (Sheaffer 1968, 222–224, 311). None were sold, and in the 1914 satiric play *The MOVIE MAN*, which concerns a money-grubbing filmmaker who manipulates a war so he can film it, O'Neill marketed his disdain for Hollywood. Later in his career, he would take a stab at adapting *The EMPEROR JONES* and *DESIRE UNDER THE ELMS* (see

FILM TREATMENTS), versions that attracted no buyers, but O'Neill's BIOGRAPHERS depict him as having little creative interest in the movie business. Asked in the 1930s to respond, by collect telegram billed by the word, to a $100,000 screenwriting offer from Howard Hughes, he wrote: "No. No. No. No. No. No. No. No. No. No. No. No. No. No. No. No. No. No. O'Neill" (quoted in Murray 26).

But a lucrative market still remained for O'Neill. If he could not sell originals, he could surely make money off the work he had already done. The studios were clamoring for what were known in the industry as "pre-sold" properties. Films adapted from novels, plays, and short stories had a built-in audience of those who had enjoyed the originals and a larger potential audience of those who recognized the title of the source material. Most authors, like O'Neill himself, were happy to sell the screen rights to their work, and equally happy to disown what had been done to them. Novels and plays and short stories carried the outward signature of one name only, so most of the praise or blame for these products was directed at the author. But adaptation allowed for scapegoats. If the adaptation was successful, the author of the source material could claim all the credit. If not, the blame was on Hollywood.

The first film adapted from an O'Neill play was a 1923 silent version of the PULITZER PRIZE–winning *ANNA CHRISTIE*, produced by Thomas H. Ince and starring Blanche Sweet. Burton Cooper writes that its success "probably derives from its silence. John Griffith Wray, the director, had to find visual means of conveying the notions inherent in the dialogue. Significantly, O'Neill approved of the additions" (75). The film and the playwright each borrowed a little of each other's cultural capital: The movie made O'Neill's name more famous, and O'Neill's name made the film more prestigious. It received good reviews and did well at the box office.

The 1930 remake of *Anna Christie*, starring Greta Garbo, a Swedish actress in her first sound role, was more than a "literary" production. It was a defining moment in movie history. MGM, the most glamorous studio in the most glamorous industry, advertised the film with the tag line "Garbo Talks!" and ticket buyers formed long lines to hear what she

George Marion and Pauline Lord (as Chris Christopherson and Anna Christie) in the film adaptation of *"Anna Christie."* (Copyright the estate of James Abbe/Kathryn Abbe)

would say. The audience had to wait until the film was well underway before Anna gives her order: "Give me a whiskey. Ginger ale on the side. And don't be stingy, baby." Not in the audience was Eugene O'Neill. He never saw this version, complaining it would be "all to the Garbo and very little of the O'Neill" (quoted in Shaeffer 1973, 104).

He was right. The film is definitely "all to the Garbo." The marketing of stars was vital to Hollywood sound cinema, and MGM had carefully chosen the property with which to introduce their biggest star in her speaking debut. Greta Garbo's Scandinavian accent and deep, world-weary voice made *Anna Christie* an ideal vehicle with which to launch her "talkies" career, but at first the actress had been uncomfortable with taking the role, claiming it was derogatory to Swedes. Irving Thalberg, MGM's head of production and the industry's boy genius, had to convince her it would be a good career move.

Anna Christie is Garbo's movie. Adapted for the screen by the director Clarence Brown and writer Frances Marion, O'Neill's play is cleaned up for mass consumption. Anna's early career as a prostitute is only hinted at in the film, the love plot is made more central, and Anna's character becomes less hard-boiled as the result of both. The role of Marthy, played by Marion's friend Marie Dressler as a broad comic foil, is expanded. The settings stick close to the play, with most of the action taking place in the bar or on the boat. Scenes shot to "open up" the play feel forced. An amusement park sequence shot in Coney Island (though in the play, the scene takes place in Boston), which advances the romance in the third act, is too schmaltzy for even a bowdlerized version. Garbo's beautiful face receives many close-ups, but much of the mise-en-scène is short on actor movement, perhaps due to the fact that sound recording was relatively new and too much blocking might have put the characters out of microphone range.

Sound also makes for problems in the 1932 MGM adaptation of STRANGE INTERLUDE, but for a different reason. The play, which won O'Neill his third Pulitzer, used asides to depict the secret thoughts of its characters; the film, which capitalized on the prize in its marketing campaign, uses voiceovers. But because the Production Code—Hollywood's industrywide effort to censor itself in-house, lest the government get involved—forbade the play's frank soliloquies on the existence of a female God, the perils of capitalism, the bummer of male sexual dysfunction, and the joys of female orgasms, there is really no reason for the innocuous musings we hear onscreen to be unspoken. Kurt Eisen writes: "Though the 'thought-aside' narrative device is retained by means of post-synchronous dubbing, the characters' thoughts have been so cleansed of anything provocative or subversive that the whole point of distinguishing their secret thoughts from their audible speech is mostly lost" (124). This time, Thalberg's hunches were wrong. Onstage and on the page, the play is a chronicle of Nina Leeds's sexual history; on film, it is a romance without chemistry starring two of MGM's biggest names: Clark Gable as an intellectual and Thalberg's swanky wife Norma Shearer as a closet libertine.

Orlandello writes: "The austerity of O'Neill's tragic vision, the often titanic scale of the plays, and the frequently incendiary nature of the themes of his works would seem to make them unlikely choices for film adaptation" (13). It is certainly true in the case of *Strange Interlude*. The stage version is said to sometimes run close to eight demanding hours; the film version is under two hours. Despite this abridgement, the film still feels twice as long as it is; many bits of dialogue are followed by the speaker's "true" thoughts. The movie is all talk, no action—which makes for bad cinema. Furthermore, the rhythm and poetry of O'Neill's dialogue, effective as it can be onstage, often sounds over-the-top within the more intimate medium of film. These spoken "thought balloons," accompanied by close-ups of the actor's faces, feel even comical at times. What starts out as an interest-

ing device becomes tiresome by the third or fourth scene. We know the secret of Nina's son Gordon Evans's father (Edmund Darrell—how can we not with their voiceovers always reminding us?), so there's no real drama to the story, and all of the playwright's psychosexual, philosophical musings, the most interesting part of the play, have been expunged. Not surprisingly, O'Neill is said to have hated the film.

If *Strange Interlude* turned a play's attempt at psychological REALISM into a mundane film experiment, United Artists's 1933 movie adaptation of *The Emperor Jones,* written by Dubose Heyward and directed by Dudley Murphy, transforms an expressionistic play into a linear, realistic plot. During the Hollywood studio era, a script's main requirement was pace: Obviously, a movie needed to move. Story was more important than character, and that

Paul Robeson and Dudley Digges in the 1933 film adaptation of *The Emperor Jones (Courtesy of the Sheaffer-O'Neill Collection, Charles E. Shain Library of Connecticut College)*

story avoided digression at all costs. Hollywood was reliant on characters with clear motives and narrative objectives.

The film version of *The Emperor Jones* stands as an example of what can get lost when screenwriting formulas like these are applied too strictly in adapting the source material. The movie begins with Jones as a railway porter who gets into trouble and loses control, scenes only suggested in the source text. PAUL ROBESON is a commanding screen presence in the title role of an alpha male corrupted by power, a man who commits the same type of injustices on his subjects that the dominant American society has committed on him. But the tight, expressionistic jungle scenes that fuel O'Neill's play as Brutus flees his pursuers, his mind bouncing nightmarishly between the present and the past, are reduced to a chase sequence at the tail end of the film. The bulk of the narrative is given up to establishing Jones's "motivation," and what should be what screenwriters call "backstory" becomes the story. By the end credits, O'Neill's expressionistic commentary on race and power has been muted in favor of a linear plot of decline, complete with a couple of female characters written in to provide romantic interest.

The film made from his work that the playwright is said to have liked best contains no love plot and not much dialogue. *The* LONG VOYAGE HOME, made in 1940, is about men who live on ships, one of whom is played by John Wayne. Adapted by O'Neill's friend Dudley Nichols from four O'Neill one-set plays (BOUND EAST FOR CARDIFF, IN THE ZONE, THE MOON OF THE CARIBBEES, and *The Long Voyage Home*), it is a story of alienation, longing, and the whims of fate. These themes are conveyed visually, cinematically rather than through words, and O'Neill is said to have admired the parts with no talking most. In fact, the first five minutes of the movie, which depict the crew of the SS GLEN-CAIRN looking toward shore, contain no dialogue. Directed by John Ford and shot by cinematographer Gregg Toland, the film makes use of technological advances in camera lenses to give the shots rich depth of field. Toland told an interviewer: "*The Long Voyage Home* was a mood picture. Storywise, it was a series of compositions of the mood of the

men aboard the ship. It was a story of what men felt rather than what they did" (quoted in Sipple 11). The film is proof that cinema allows characters to speak without saying anything. In a letter to his daughter OONA O'NEILL, Eugene O'Neill called the film "an exceptional picture with no obvious Hollywood hokum or sentimental love bilge in it" (O'Neill 513). However, this truce with the movies would not last long. Oona's child-bride marriage to the movie comedian Charlie Chaplin, a move O'Neill would never forgive her for, gave him still another reason to dislike Hollywood.

Along with *The Long Voyage Home,* the other cinematic candidate for the most successful O'Neill adaptation is Sidney Lumet's 1962 version of *Long Day's Journey into Night.* But the critical praise for Lumet's film is not unanimous. Burton Cooper, who believes most adapters are too in awe of O'Neill's literary genius and are too reluctant to deviate from his words and scenes, deems it "far too reverentially developed . . . one keeps expecting the curtain to fall every so often" (79). Critics who like *Long Day's Journey into Night* usually like it for being faithful to the play, but that is the same reason those who do not like it, such as Cooper, do not like it. To a certain extent, the movie is "stagey"—aside from a brief exterior opening and a scene in the garage, it takes place almost entirely within one claustrophobic room. Donald Costello, who calls the film "the best movie ever made from an American play" has meticulously traced the numerous differences between the two works, maintaining that Lumet's alterations were necessary in order to retain the spirit of the original. Costello writes: "The paradox of any successful adaptation is that in moving from one medium to another it must be changed so as to be kept the same" (78).

Because films can be circulated far, wide, and (maybe) forever, cinema allows plays and performers to reach a wider audience than the theater ever could. Even flawed adaptations, Cooper believes, "provide a useful record of O'Neill, a means by which we can hear his language spoken, see his scenes acted out" (73). If nothing else, Lumet's picture captures some fine actors doing some fine acting. Well paced and building to a powerhouse climax, the film makes

Katharine Hepburn as Mary Tyrone (based on O'Neill's mother, Mary "Ella" Quinlan O'Neill) in *Long Day's Journey into Night* (Photo by Dennis Stock)

for good drama, without falling into the mawkish, lower register of MELODRAMA that can spoil many O'Neill productions. JASON ROBARDS, the primary interpreter of O'Neill's work onstage, gives an emotional performance as the bitter, self-hating Jamie Tyrone, and the stately Ralph Richardson, cast when Spencer Tracy demanded too much money, does a good job depicting the pain and regret beneath the patriarch's boastful theatricality. But it is Katharine Hepburn's character Mary Tyrone—or, perhaps, the movie star Hepburn herself—that is clearly the focus of the film. Kurt Eisen believes that Mary provides "a mirror of the Tyrone men's guilt and disappointment. Frequent high angle shots further underscore Mary's isolation from the men, drawing the viewer into a posture of surveillance much like that of which Mary accuses her husbands and sons" (129). Hepburn's famous mannerisms, often parodied, seem apt for her characterization of a high-strung woman on the edge. The play's focus is on father/son relationships, but the film's focus, because of Hepburn's star turn, is on Mary and her relationship with her younger son, Edmund Tyrone.

Other O'Neill adaptations, such as 1935's AH, WILDERNESS!, a gentle comedy made into a sappy movie, sold many tickets but were not well reviewed. Still others, such as 1944's *The* HAIRY APE (now believed lost) starring William Ben-

dix and 1947's MOURNING BECOMES ELECTRA, were considered failures on all fronts, and O'Neill shunned them. In fairness, it is worth mentioning that, according to his biographers, O'Neill hated most of the staged versions of his plays as well. It's a simple fact of translation that any interpreter needs to make choices. It would have been impossible for all these choices to correspond with the playwright's Platonic ideal of the production.

O'Neill said he didn't like his work "distorted" by film (Sheaffer 1973, 104), but fidelity often ends in failure as well. A glaring example is the 1958 flop *Desire under the Elms*. The female lead character was rewritten from an American woman to an Italian woman so that Sophia Loren could make her Hollywood dramatic debut as star of the picture, but that is the least of the film's problems. With its allegorical characters, imagistic dialogue, and narrative that walks a tightrope between EXPRESSIONISM and NATURALISM, the movie is faithful to the play, and that is its undoing. A more successful "close" interpretation was the 1973 version of *The* ICEMAN COMETH, directed by John Frankenheimer and produced under the auspices of the ill-fated American Film Theatre organization, which hoped to bring filmed theater to the masses. The movie received generally good reviews for being faithful to the original, despite some critics' misgivings about casting tough-guy actor Lee Marvin in the lead role. According to Orlandello, "This film, like Lumet's version of *Long Day's Journey into Night*, demonstrates that cinematic resources can be employed within confined physical space to focus and intensify the thematic and experiential core of the original work" (160). In the final analysis, however, it is always a tough balancing act to make the play and the film adaptation feel the same—yet different—especially when the reputation of the author of the source material, recipient of the NOBEL PRIZE IN LITERATURE and four PULITZER PRIZES, casts such a large, imposing shadow over the filmmaking process.

Films Discussed

Ah, Wilderness!, directed by Clarence Brown, 98 min., MGM, 1935.

Anna Christie directed by John Griffith Wray, 96 min., Associated First National Pictures, 1923.

Anna Christie, directed by Clarence Brown, 89 min., MGM, 1930.

Desire under the Elms, directed by Delbert Mann, 111 min., Don Hartman Productions, 1958.

The Emperor Jones, directed by Dudley Murphy, 72 min., John Krimsky and Gifford Cochran, Inc., 1933.

The Hairy Ape, directed by Alfred Santell, 92 min., Mayfair Productions, 1944.

The Iceman Cometh, directed by John Frankenheimer, 239 min., 20th Century Fox, 1973.

Long Day's Journey into Night, directed by Sidney Lumet, 174 min. (134 min. edited), Republic Pictures, 1962.

The Long Voyage Home, directed by John Ford, 105 min., Argosy Pictures, 1940.

Mourning Becomes Electra, directed by Dudley Nichols, 173 min., RKO, 1947.

Strange Interlude, directed by Robert Z. Leonard, 109 min., MGM, 1932.

Bibliography

Cooper, Burton. "Some Problems in Adapting O'Neill for Film." In *Eugene O'Neill's Century: Centennial Views on America's Foremost Tragic Dramatist,* edited by Richard F. Moorton, 73–86. New York: Greenwood Press, 1991.

Costello, Donald. "Sidney Lumet's *Long Day's Journey into Night.*" *Literature Film Quarterly* 22 (1994): 78–92.

Eisen, Kurt. "O'Neill on Screen." In *The Cambridge Companion to Eugene O'Neill,* edited by Michael Manheim, 116–134. Cambridge: Cambridge University Press, 1998.

Murray, Edward. *The Cinematic Imagination.* New York: Ungar, 1972.

O'Neill, Eugene. *Selected Letters of Eugene O'Neill.* Edited by Travis Bogard and Jackson R. Bryer. New York: Limelight Editions, 1994.

Orlandello, John. *O'Neill on Film.* Rutherford, N.J.: Fairleigh Dickinson University Press, 1982.

Sheaffer, Louis. *O'Neill: Son and Artist.* Boston: Little, Brown, 1973.

———. *O'Neill: Son and Playwright.* Boston: Little, Brown, 1968.

Sipple, William. "From Stage to Screen: *The Long Voyage Home* and *Long Day's Journey into Night.*" *Eugene O'Neill Newsletter* 7 (Spring 1983): 10–14.

Tom Cerasulo

film treatments On November 6, 1926, O'Neill wrote in his WORK DIARY: "Worked on film scenario I have got interested in for *The* HAIRY APE (finished it) good stuff but they'll never do it." The following day, he wrote: "Worked on film scenario for *DESIRE UNDER THE ELMS* (all day + night + finished it)." Prior to this, O'Neill generally had dismissed films made in Hollywood, which he called "the City of Dreadful Nonsense" (quoted in Bowen 288). However, in 1914 he saw the silent Italian film *Cabiria,* which he thought was "simply stupendous" and which gave him "a much fairer opinion of the artistic value of the movies" (O'Neill 29). Then in 1921 he saw a German film, *The Cabinet of Dr. Caligari,* which led him to believe "that there could be a genuine original art form developed along that line" (quoted in Helburn 277). That same year, he wrote to the journalist Ralph Block: "Indeed I am interested in what you say of planning for a new latitude in screen expression. I saw *Caligari* and it sure opened my eyes to wonderful possibilities I had never dreamed of before" (1988, 156).

Within a year after seeing *Caligari,* O'Neill began to plan his own film of *The Emperor Jones* "along Expressionistic lines," with the idea of making "a startling new film in a startling new way" (1988, 164–165). However, nothing came of this project. He later would recall having begun "to be quite intrigued by the old silent films—so much so that I made treatments of *The Hairy Ape* and *Desire under the Elms* (which, of course, no one would do!)—and then came the Talkies and I gave up" (1988, 428). According to O'Neill, he wrote the film treatment of *The Hairy Ape* to submit to producer Jesse Lasky as a vehicle for German screen star Emil Jannings, who wanted to do a film of the play (444).

The Hairy Ape

O'Neill's 10-page film treatment of *The Hairy Ape* begins with a description of Yank. It states that the character feels that he "belongs," that "it is he and his kind who make the ship . . . and the world move." This is followed by a description of Mildred Douglas. The reader is told that she "is not 'all bad,'" that she "longs to be able to feel some genuine emotion" and "wants to 'belong.'" As in the play, O'Neill describes her on the ship, reclining in a deck chair, and juxtaposes it with Yank in the forecastle below deck. He then cuts back to Mildred, asking to be taken below, where she sees Yank's "brutal, elemental, physical passion" and faints.

Unlike in the play, where Mildred does not appear again after her encounter with Yank, in the film treatment she is a recurring character. Obsessed with Yank, she manages to see him again by boarding the same ship, this time to New York, where she encounters him on Fifth Avenue. As he attempts to insult her, he is stopped by the police, and she watches "with intense admiration for his struggle" as he battles them. In prison, "He suddenly realizes all his proud boast of being Steel is all wrong. Now it is the daughter of the Steel King who has put him in a steel cage." When he is freed from jail at Mildred's behest, he manages to climb onto the roof of the train that she is taking to the family's steelworks in Douglas, Pennsylvania, accompanied by her father and an English nobleman who bores her but whom her father hopes she will marry. "She seems to feel the presence of Yank on the roof of the car. His eyes are before her." At the steelworks, Yank gets a job working with the blast furnaces. When he tries to blow up part of them, he only succeeds in knocking down a portion of a wall. "Immediately a horde of workmen come and the wall is built up again." O'Neill would later describe this as "an expressionistic touch" (1988, 445).

Yank's eyes haunt Mildred, and "she becomes as violent against society as Yank," asking her father for money and throwing it into the fire. Seeing Yank one night, she approaches him, at which point he throws her over his shoulder and climbs a ladder to the brim of one of the furnaces. (This is reminiscent of the capture of the young woman by the somnambulist in *Caligari*.) He raises her above his head, as if to fling her into the furnace. (Its "flaming, egg-shaped funnels spouting fire" recall *Cabiria*'s voracious Temple of Moloch with its "throat of flame.") He then sees in her eyes that she desires him. Petrified, he lets her down, and she kisses him. He returns her kiss but then, frightened, pushes her from him. She orders away the crowd below, "as if they were her slaves. Cringing and awed they move off into a wider circle of faces with blackbrimmed eyes, staring at the two, reflecting the light, a background of eyes." When Yank cowers before her, she "laughs disdainfully and pats his head as if he were a dog, Then she yawns again with boredom." She slaps him and calls him a poor Hairy Ape. Yank wanders off, envisioning her eyes full of triumph. Mildred returns to the party, where she agrees to marry the nobleman. Laughing sardonically, she beats her chest in imitation of Yank.

The film treatment's conclusion matches that of the play: Yank ends up at a zoo where he befriends a gorilla who crushes him. However, the film treatment concludes with his again seeing Mildred's eyes "fixed on him with triumphant contempt. He covers his own eyes and dies."

O'Neill told Robert Sisk, who in 1935 expressed interest in filming the play, that the "idea in the screen story was to build up the attraction—repulsion, hate-lust thing between Yank and Mildred, to make her even more of a bitch" (1988, 446). One cannot help but suspect that this was done in part to make the project more commercially appealing. However, it also accentuates the fact that Yank and Mildred are not dissimilar—a point which the film treatment makes clear by describing their mutual need to "belong." O'Neill offered Sisk

A suggestion which is not in the script. Why not start Yank's boyhood and horrible homelife (a hint of which is in the play, you'll remember) in the slums of the same steel town where Mildred's Steel King Father has his estate—some link between them of attraction—repulsion as children or adolescent—so that in the end you complete a cycle which is, in a way, fated from the beginning. (1994, 446)

Desire under the Elms

In the 13-page film treatment of *Desire under the Elms*, O'Neill changes the principal female character from the play's Abbie, a 35-year-old New England woman, to Stephanie, "a Hungarian immigrant girl." This possibly was done to make her more of a mysterious outsider. O'Neill describes her in the treatment as a "queer foreign woman" and says that she goads Eben at one point "to a frenzy for her own queer gratification in his passion." He spends the first part of the treatment describing her childhood, which is somewhat different from what the character tells us about herself in the play. In that script, she says she was an orphan who had to work in others' homes and who later married a drunk and had a baby, both of whom died; in the treatment, O'Neill describes her growing up in a wretched hut and trying to save enough money to marry a handsome man who only wants her dowry and who rejects her when she spends the money on her father's medical care. When the village priest gives her ship fare to America, "She takes an oath that, in this new land . . . she will own her own land and her own home, and she will revenge on men the injury her fiancé has done to her love and pride."

Arriving in Boston (her mother having died on ship during the voyage), Stephanie works as a chambermaid in a cheap hotel, where the male guests try to seduce her, then is lured by an old man who hires her to work on his farm in New England but who mistreats her. When Cabot, who lives nearby (and whose first name is "Ephraim" in the play and "Ephriam" in the treatment), sees her, he immediately falls in love and asks her to become his employee. Unlike in the play, where Abbie arrives as Cabot's wife just before his two sons leave for the California gold rush, here she arrives as the housekeeper, and his two sons also fall in love with her, while she "deliberately, calculatingly encourages" each of the three men. The sons decide to go to California, each hoping to make some easy money from the gold rush to pay off the mortgage on the house and convince her to marry him. While there, they dream of her and end up killing each other in a fight over gold.

As in the play, Eben, Cabot's stepson from his second marriage, at first resists his stepfather's new wife but eventually falls in love with her. In the play, she marries Cabot, has a son who Cabot thinks is his (but who really is Eben's), then kills the child to prove to Eben that she was not using him to conceive a son to whom Cabot would leave the farm. In the film treatment, she marries Cabot but has no child. (O'Neill may have been concerned that infanticide would not be considered a proper subject for the screen.) She tries to get Eben to murder Cabot (he ends up accidentally killing him) and then, remorseful, joins Eben when he insists on being punished. As a last gesture of self-renunciation, she tears up the deed to the house. "Then, hand in hand, they walk off with the Sheriff behind them and only the farm and the land remain, ownerless now, free and triumphant."

Copies of O'Neill's film treatments are part of the Louis Sheaffer–Eugene O'Neill Collection. Department of Special Collections, Charles E. Shain Library, Connecticut College, New London.

Bibliography
Bowen, Croswell, with the assistance of Shane O'Neill. *The Curse of the Misbegotten.* New York: McGraw-Hill, 1959.

Helburn, Theresa. *A Wayward Quest.* Boston: Little, Brown, 1960.

O'Neill, Eugene. *Selected Letters of Eugene O'Neill.* Edited by Travis Bogard and Jackson R. Bryer. New Haven, Conn., and London: Yale University Press, 1988.

———. *Work Diary, 1924–1943.* Vol. 1. *Preliminary Edition.* Transcribed by Donald Gallup. New Haven, Conn.: Yale University Library, 1981.

John Hagan

France Ten days after the triumphant premiere of STRANGE INTERLUDE on January 30, 1928, Eugene O'Neill and Carlotta Monterey (later CARLOTTA MONTEREY O'NEILL) sailed for Europe to escape the private turmoil and public curiosity generated by his collapsed marriage to AGNES BOULTON. It turned out to be a three-year sojourn, during which the pair occupied three luxurious dwellings, each grander than the last, as well as a favorite hotel for their numerous visits to Paris. Deliberately vague as to their whereabouts during the months while O'Neill's divorce was pending, they first settled into a villa in Guéthary, France, on the Côte Basque near the Spanish frontier, but it did not live up to expectations and they stayed only a few months while Eugene struggled with DYNAMO, ultimately one of his least successful plays. They then embarked on an extraordinary three-month voyage to the Far East that thoroughly tested their relationship but ended in exhausted reconciliation at another rented villa, this time on the Côte d'Azur.

However, the Riviera did not offer the quiet environment O'Neill needed to write, and after a few months they abandoned it in favor of the grandest residence they would ever occupy: the Château du Plessis (or, erroneously, Le Plessis) in the Loire region near Tours. Signing a three-year lease, Carlotta immediately set about making it into a writing sanctuary and Eugene, putting the failure of *Dynamo* behind him, turned to MOURNING BECOMES ELECTRA, his long-gestating "trilogy of the damned." Electricity and plumbing were upgraded, a pool built, servants hired, a Bugatti roadster purchased. O'Neill wrote to Joseph Wood Krutch, "We have a really beautiful place, out of the track of tourists . . . a home with all sorts of room, grand old furniture . . . privacy and peace to the Nth degree! . . .I feel as if I'd at last come home—the sort of home I've always craved" (Gelb, 693). Eugene and Carlotta were married in Paris in July 1929, a month after moving into their stately mansion.

It was an intensely productive year and a half, and when at last O'Neill sent the script of *Electra* to the THEATRE GUILD in April 1931, after months of arduous rewriting during protracted periods of rain and dampness fully as gloomy as the play itself, he discovered that the novelty of expatriate life had evaporated. Louis Sheaffer relates that he was plagued by "a feeling of not really belonging, of having no affinity with the land or the people, of being rootless and growthless" (Sheaffer 364). Homesickness and psychological isolation were amplified by bouts of illness, and when the Theatre Guild agreed to produce the new play, the O'Neills promptly broke their lease and returned to New York with Blemie, their beloved pedigree Dalmatian.

The interlude at the chateau ended abruptly, but for a critical, transitional period it had, under Carlotta's supervision, provided O'Neill with the quiet setting he needed to concentrate on his modern retelling of the ancient Oresteia. Indeed, *Mourning Becomes Electra* marks a seminal turning point in O'Neill's public career and hitherto disordered personal life, articulated by Travis Bogard in the *Selected Letters*: "Finally . . . author and man became integrated in a firm marital relationship and the writing of a great work of theatrical art."

Bibliography

Black, Stephen A. *Eugene O'Neill: Beyond Mourning and Tragedy.* New Haven, Conn.: Yale University Press, 1999.

Bowen, Croswell. *The Curse of the Misbegotten.* New York: McGraw-Hill, 1959.

Gelb, Arthur, and Barbara Gelb. *O'Neill.* Enlarged ed. New York: Harper & Row, 1973.

O'Neill, Eugene. *Selected Letters of Eugene O'Neill.* Edited by Travis Bogard and Jackson R. Bryer. New Haven, Conn.: Yale University Press, 1988.

Sheaffer, Louis. *O'Neill: Son and Artist.* Boston: Little, Brown, 1973.

Brian Rogers

G

Gaylord Farm Sanatorium In autumn 1912, it was discovered that Eugene O'Neill had contracted tuberculosis, a common cause of death before the discovery of antibiotics. He was initially nursed at home; then his father JAMES O'NEILL decided to have him treated at a public (and relatively inexpensive) sanatorium in Shelton, Connecticut. It was quickly deemed unsatisfactory, and Eugene was admitted to the private Gaylord Farm Sanatorium in Wallingford, Connecticut, checking in on Christmas Eve 1912 and responding so well to treatment that he was discharged after five months. Gaylord was a pivotal experience in Eugene O'Neill's life: During the months of enforced rest and steady recuperation under the eyes of caring doctors and nurses, he realized that he wanted to be a playwright. From that moment forward, he was motivated by something he had never before experienced, an overriding purpose in life, and he began to make up for lost time. With a questing mind roaming across the fertile ground of his extraordinary experiences and the writings of AUGUST STRINDBERG, FRIEDRICH NIETZSCHE, and others, he prepared to forge the sprawling canon that ultimately would include several masterpieces and reshape the American theater. One of those masterpieces, LONG DAY'S JOURNEY INTO NIGHT, is generally regarded as the finest work for the stage by an American playwright.

Before arriving at Gaylord's doorstep, O'Neill had spent years at boarding schools; flunked out of Princeton University; fathered a child with his first wife, KATHLEEN JENKINS (and abandoned them); prospected for gold in Honduras; and spent several months at sea and in BUENOS AIRES, ARGENTINA, as a sailor and longshoreman, often homeless and drunk. Back in New York City, he lived for a time at JIMMY "THE PRIEST'S"flophouse and bar, drowning his aimlessness and spiritual homelessness in drink, even attempting to take his life in January 1912 with an overdose of sleeping pills. He was rescued by friends, and his father took him to the family home in NEW LONDON, CONNECTICUT, where he was given a job reporting for the *New London Telegraph* (also contributing POETRY to a column), only to fall ill shortly before his 24th birthday.

As it happened, O'Neill's tuberculosis was mild, and his experience at Gaylord was fortuitously happy and productive. Not only was he restored to physical health, the regimen of attentive mothering care, nutritious meals, sleep-filled nights, and book-filled days fostered the introspection that enabled him to discover and begin to articulate his calling in life. He later came to understand that the five months at Gaylord had allowed him to actually think about his life for the first time, as Louis Sheaffer asserts in *Son and Playwright,* in the fittingly titled chapter "Birth of a Playwright." "It was at Gaylord," O'Neill later said, "that my mind got the chance to establish itself, to digest and valuate the impressions of many past years in which one experience had crowded on another with never a second's reflection" (quoted in Sheaffer 252).

Gaylord Farm Sanatorium *(Courtesy of the Sheaffer-O'Neill Collection, Charles E. Shain Library of Connecticut College)*

Returning to New London in summer 1913, O'Neill began writing plays. Gaylord had taught him how to become "a creator rather than a destroyer," observe Arthur and Barbara Gelb, who also relate that in the last interview O'Neill ever gave, in 1948, 35 years after he was discharged from Gaylord, "he was still eager to stress that if he had not been forced to look hard at himself in the sanatorium, he might not have become a playwright (Gelb 388)." On another level, the significance of the Gaylord experience is revealed in the fourth act of *Long Day's Journey into Night* (written just a few years before the 1948 interview), where it sparks an explosive exchange between James Tyrone and Edmund (the Eugene figure) on the subject of James's miserliness, an exchange Stephen Black characterizes as Edmund/Eugene's harshest criticism of his father in the harrowing autobiographical play (Black 131). Among O'Neill's early plays, the heroine of *The* WEB, written in summer 1913, is afflicted with tuberculosis, as is the hero of BEYOND THE HORIZON (1918), while *The* STRAW (1919) is based directly on his hospitalization, the central character being a version of himself, the others drawn from influential Gaylord figures.

Bibliography

Black, Stephen A. *Eugene O'Neill—Beyond Mourning and Tragedy.* New Haven, Conn.: Yale University Press, 1999.

Gelb, Arthur, and Barbara Gelb. *O'Neill: Life with Monte Cristo.* New York and London: Applause Books, 2000.

Sheaffer, Louis. *O'Neill: Son and Playwright.* Boston: Little, Brown, 1968.

Brian Rogers

gender Like most male playwrights, Eugene O'Neill peopled his dramas primarily with men; a rough count reveals that they outnumber women by about two to one in his plays. This statistic is somewhat misleading because unseen women—alive or dead—are important throughout the O'Neill canon, beginning with A WIFE FOR A LIFE (1913) and ending with A MOON FOR THE MISBEGOTTEN (1943), a play haunted by the ghost of Jim Tyrone's mother. Despite their importance, however, these invisible women remain voiceless and faceless, an unsettling reflection of the female position in a patriarchal culture. It is also true that in many other ways O'Neill hewed to the traditional beliefs of early 20th-century American society, the CATHOLICISM in which he was raised, and even the literary and theatrical clichés of his day—especially when it comes to female characters. While independent women do occasionally appear, notably in the unfinished late cycle A TALE OF POSSESSORS SELF-DISPOSSESSED, accomplished career women are rare in O'Neill's stage world. Far more common are devoted if inevitably flawed wives, maternal females seeking to protect their needy men, and whores whose coarse exteriors hide tender hearts.

Still, O'Neill would not be the great dramatist he is had he not gone well beyond the stock figures this list suggests. His elaboration of these female archetypes is frequently original and often brilliantly theatrical: Few roles in the modern American canon are as coveted by actresses as Nina Leeds in STRANGE INTERLUDE (1927), Christine and Lavinia Mannon in MOURNING BECOMES ELECTRA (1931), Josie Hogan in A MOON FOR THE MISBEGOTTEN, and especially Mary Tyrone in LONG DAY'S JOURNEY INTO NIGHT (1941). Moreover, the playwright's troubled male protagonists are among the most complex and sympathetic on the American stage. Largely eschewing (even mocking) the stoic heroes so dear to the hearts of novelists from James Fenimore Cooper to Ernest Hemingway, O'Neill gives us men with "a touch of the poet" who seek understanding and nurturance rather than conquest.

The inhabitants of O'Neill's early plays, not surprisingly, often lack nuance and depth. Women occasionally appear as victims, like the betrayed streetwalker in The WEB (1913) and the beleaguered Mrs. Keeney in ILE (1917), but more commonly take the guise of the Strindbergian nag from the plays of AUGUST STRINDBERG. Mary Knapp in WARNINGS (1913), Maud Steele in BREAD AND BUTTER (1914), and Mrs. Rowland in BEFORE BREAKFAST (1916) are all directly or indirectly responsible for their husbands' suicides. Only marginally more sympathetic is Ruth Mayo in BEYOND THE HORIZON (1918), whose selfishness and lack of insight contribute to the deaths of both her husband and her daughter. These plays reflect the venerable myth that domesticity kills the male of the species, even when he eagerly pursues such a life.

On the flip side of the coin are the sailors of the SEA plays, who engage in grueling physical labor far from female influence. Yet O'Neill's sympathies lie not with the hard-drinking Cocky and Davis but with the dying Yank and his devoted friend Driscoll in BOUND EAST FOR CARDIFF (1914) and the lovelorn Smitty of IN THE ZONE (1917). The world of the ship is their fate but not—so they claim—their choice. One of the few O'Neill heroes defined by his brawn rather than his brain or sensitivity, the title character of The HAIRY APE (1921) is less man than simian and dies in an ape's embrace.

As his theatrical mastery deepens, O'Neill's female characters grow more complex, but they are rarely artists, adventurers, careerists, or dreamers—unless the dream is of love. The only "profession" practiced by large numbers of O'Neill's women is PROSTITUTION, a business that depends on men. Teachers Hattie Harris in ALL GOD'S CHILLUN GOT WINGS (1923) and Lily Miller in AH, WILDERNESS! (1933) are, like actress Eleanor Cape in WELDED (1923), anomalies in O'Neill's world. More typical is DESIRE UNDER THE ELMS's Abbie Putnam (1924), who sacrifices her baby and perhaps her own life to her longing for her stepson. Throughout the O'Neill canon, as Doris Nelson notes, his heroines define themselves primarily or wholly in terms of "their relationships to the men in their lives" (3) or less commonly their offspring.

Most of O'Neill's male characters do have careers, but unless they are artists, they are rarely deeply invested in their work. In fact, men who are committed to their professions often earn the playwright's scorn. From the cowardly Businessman in FOG (1914) to the buffoonish T. Stedman Harder in A Moon for the Misbegotten, the entrepreneur fares badly in O'Neill's plays. Few other male American writers have so completely rejected both the capitalist world and the notion that masculinity is defined by one's bank account. Nor does he admire warriors. Mourning Become Electra's General Ezra Mannon comes from a long line of soldiers whose battlefield accomplishments reflect their hatred of life rather than their patriotism. The alcoholic Boer War veterans in The ICEMAN COMETH were apparently distinguished primarily for their spinelessness and larceny. Unlike so many of his writing brethren, O'Neill does not valorize the football star, the cowboy, the soldier, the sexual athlete, the hunter, or the gangster. The typical O'Neill protagonist wants to merge with the natural world rather than to dominate it—a vision that most closely allies him with Henry David Thoreau. And despite the preponderance of men in his plays, O'Neill only occasionally celebrates male bonding—most notably in some of the sea plays, HUGHIE (1941), *The Iceman Cometh* (1939), and sporadically in *Long Day's Journey into Night*. The central interactions in O'Neill's dramas are overwhelmingly between men and women.

Two major plays from his "middle period" go far toward delineating O'Neill's vision of male-female relationships. Nina, the protagonist of the nine-act epic *Strange Interlude*, defines herself wholly in terms of the males in her life. In her famous "My three men" soliloquy about her husband, lover, and old friend, Nina muses that "I feel their desires converge in me! . . . to form one complete beautiful male desire which I absorb . . . and am whole . . . they dissolve in me, their life is my life" (2:756). It is *their* desire, not hers, that she experiences. In *Mourning Becomes Electra*, Christine Mannon and her daughter Lavinia are stronger than their male counterparts, and Lavinia is the only character to achieve heroic status. Nevertheless, *Electra* revolves around the jealous feud between the two for the affections of a series of men—a battle that leaves the stage strewn with dead bodies. And as Susan Harris Smith observes, "Lavinia attains classically tragic stature only when she sacrifices the 'natural' and 'female' aspects of herself to the Mannon furies, the bastions of the political and patriarchal norm" (45).

The brooding trees that frame the farmhouse in *Desire under the Elms* symbolize a fertile female principle that O'Neill returned to in *Strange Interlude*. The "Blessed Islands" sought by the Mannons are associated with the natural world of childbirth, trees, water, and flowers. Orin Mannon proclaims to his mother that the tropical isle he visited "was you" (2:972). Orin's literalized Mother Nature is an oedipal vision grounded in male desire, an image of Eden. This womblike existence is what most O'Neill men seek, yet it is not entirely benign: The

STAGE DIRECTIONS for *Desire under the Elms* suggest that "maternity" can be "sinister" (2:318).

As Orin Mannon's account of the Blessed Islands reveals, O'Neill's sensitive, often damaged heroes seek women who will nurture them, protect them from a frightening world, and forgive any and all transgressions—including the "sin" of being born human and fallible. The number of women in the O'Neill canon who regard their husbands or lovers with maternal solicitude encompasses such diverse figures as the earth-mother whore Cybel in *The GREAT GOD BROWN* (1925) and 19-year-old Madeline Arnold, who develops *"a distinct maternal older feeling"* toward her fiancé at the end of *Strange Interlude* (2:803). "My son." "my boy," "my poor little boy," or "my child" are terms uttered, at various times, by Hazel Niles in *Mourning Becomes Electra*, Abbie Putnam in *Desire under the Elms*, Miriam in *LAZARUS LAUGHED* (1926), Nina Leeds in *Strange Interlude*, and Eleanor Cape in *Welded* (1923). In none of these cases are they referring to children. Margaret in *The Great God Brown* considers her husband the eldest of her sons, an attitude she shares with Sara Harford in MORE STATELY MANSIONS.

The typical O'Neill hero that these women nurture is, in scholar Martha Gilman Bower's words, a "solitary, artistic, sensitive, poetic idealist" (11). The gentle, romantic Robert Mayo in *Beyond the Horizon* is destroyed by difficult domestic responsibilities. Dion Anthony, the protagonist of *The Great God Brown*, writes poetry, sings, plays a musical instrument, and paints—all accomplishments of the perfect Victorian woman. *Iceman*'s Larry Slade is older than the typical O'Neill hero, yet he shares with him a concern for others, pity, and a willingness to sacrifice his own psychic comfort to help someone else. Indeed, he closely resembles that most gentle of male religious figures, Christ. Edmund Tyrone's lyric "sea speech" in *Long Day's Journey* testifies to his perceptiveness and vulnerability rather than his physical prowess. Whether or not these characters are "strangely softened" self-portraits, as Travis Bogard persuasively argues (439), they are far from the virile figures favored by writers as ostensibly different from each other as Ernest Hemingway and TENNESSEE WILLIAMS.

Taken together, O'Neill's three late masterpieces—*The Iceman Cometh, Long Day's Journey into*

Night, and *A Moon for the Misbegotten*—reflect and expand on his earlier presentations of gender. Despite being set in a dilapidated saloon and peopled with aging drunks, *Iceman* presents O'Neill's most affirmative picture of male bonding as the down-and-out men protect each others' pipe dreams. Conversely, the salient fact about the major female characters in *Iceman* (and the one-act *Hughie*, written shortly afterward) is their absence. There are no onstage females in *Iceman* except for the three streetwalkers. That "damned bitch" Evelyn Hickman, "that nagging bitch" Bessie Hope, and that "damned old bitch" Rosa Parritt are seen only through the eyes of the men whose lives they have helped ruin. By trying to mold their husbands, lovers, or sons into what they think a man should be, these invisible women have destroyed both themselves and those they ostensibly love. Evelyn's devotion and Bessie's ambition may be admirable, but it is for the *men* in Harry Hope's bar—however sodden—that O'Neill seeks our understanding and empathy.

Mary Tyrone of *Long Day's Journey* is O'Neill's most fully realized female character, a figure whose torment exposes the limitations and paradoxes imposed on women in a world shaped around male desires. Haunted by a series of tragedies—a dead baby, one son an alcoholic and another suffering from consumption—she yearns for the simple life and female companionship she knew as a student in a convent. Like most O'Neill men, the Tyrones look to her to provide compassion, forgiveness, and self-sacrifice, but she seeks only a drug-induced oblivion. In this most autobiographical of his dramas, O'Neill simultaneously understands Mary's maternal failures and blames her for them. By the end of *Journey*, she, too, is marked by absence, kept offstage for most of the long final act while the men exchange stories of recrimination and disappointment. James Tyrone bemoans the great career he might have had. Not surprisingly, the villain is money, or rather Tyrone's decision to favor financial success over artistic achievement. Edmund is the archetypal O'Neill poet, uncomfortable in this family as well as his own skin. Seriously ill and determinedly pessimistic, he futilely tries to protect his warring kin from each other. All three Tyrone men lament Mary's abandonment of them, but it is Jamie most of all who cannot live without the unconditional love he believes Mary should continue to provide. Physically stronger but emotionally weaker than his brother, he has replaced his mother's breast with a bottle of bourbon.

O'Neill's last completed drama, *A Moon for the Misbegotten* continues Jamie's story. Here called Jim, the character is a pitiful wreck mourning the death of his beloved Mary and seeking only a comforting bosom on which to lay his head as he reveals his sins. Josie Hogan, the oversized farm woman he chooses as confessor, pretends to be promiscuous but admits her innocence when she realizes that sexual love is not what Jim wants or needs. Even though she is a virgin, Josie (who has raised three brothers) combines all of the maternal, feminine virtues that the male characters have been seeking throughout the O'Neill canon. The long pietà pose that opens act 4 links Josie with the Virgin Mary and echoes a series of similar tableaux in O'Neill's earlier plays: Abbie holding Eben in the last scene of *Desire under the Elms*, Cybel comforting a dying Billy in *The Great God Brown*, Sara cradling Simon in the epilogue to *More Stately Mansions*. This is a fitting final image for O'Neill's canon: Josie cannot save Jim, but she can bring him a measure of peace.

The dynamics of gender in O'Neill's plays are, of course, far from simple. For the most part, his female characters are perceived from a masculine perspective that demands from them such traditional "virtues" as all-encompassing love and self-abnegation. Josie Hogan is one of only a few women in the O'Neill canon who live up to the expectations the male characters place on them. All too often, the women's failures lead to tragic consequences. Still, many of O'Neill's female characters defy easy categorization *because* of their very human flaws, and even his myriad Madonnas and whores frequently transcend the cultural and theatrical clichés he inherited.

Although they deviate more sharply from societal norms, O'Neill also employed recurring male character types. He rejects the popular myth of masculine stoicism; he has no use for industrial titans or macho poseurs. Instead, he focuses on lost, anguished men trying to find their place in a hostile universe. Since so many of his male characters seem to be on an oedipal quest for maternal mates, they rarely view women as dangerous snares or sexual prey. And even when the female characters are confined to minor or offstage roles, O'Neill refuses to romanticize a world without women.

Bibliography

Barlow, Judith E. "O'Neill's Female Characters." In *The Cambridge Companion to Eugene O'Neill*, edited by Michael Manheim, 164–177. Cambridge and New York: Cambridge University Press, 1998.

Bogard, Travis. *Contour in Time: The Plays of Eugene O'Neill.* Rev. ed. New York: Oxford University Press, 1988.

Bower, Martha Gilman. *Eugene O'Neill's Unfinished Threnody and Process of Invention in Four Cycle Plays.* Lewiston, N.Y.: Edwin Mellen Press, 1992.

Glover, Christopher S. "Female Characters in (and Not in) Eugene O'Neill's *The Iceman Cometh*: Tracing Twentieth-Century Feminist Response into a New Era." *Eugene O'Neill Review* 25, nos. 1–2 (Spring–Fall 2001): 12–23.

Hall, Ann C. *"A Kind of Alaska": Women in the Plays of O'Neill, Pinter, and Shepard.* Carbondale: Southern Illinois University Press, 1993.

Mandl, Bette, ed. Special Issue: "O'Neill and Gender." *Eugene O'Neill Review* 19, nos. 1–2 (Spring–Fall 1995).

Manheim, Michael. *Eugene O'Neill's New Language of Kinship.* Syracuse, N.Y.: Syracuse University Press, 1982.

Nelson, Doris. "O'Neill's Women." *Eugene O'Neill Newsletter* 6, no. 2 (Summer–Fall 1982): 3–7.

Schlueter, June, ed. *Feminist Rereadings of Modern American Drama.* Rutherford, N.J.: Fairleigh Dickinson University Press, 1989.

Smith, Susan Harris. "Inscribing the Body: Lavinia Mannon as the Site of Struggle." *Eugene O'Neill Review* 19, nos. 1–2 (Spring–Fall 1995): 45–54.

Judith Barlow

Gilpin, Charles S. (1878–1930) Charles Sidney Gilpin was born on November 20, 1878, in Richmond, Virginia. Before starring in the 1920 premiere of Eugene O'Neill's *The EMPEROR JONES*, a part that made its leading man an overnight sensation, Gilpin had led a vagabond existence. Along with acting, he worked a string of low-paying trades, including barber, printer, elevator operator, janitor, minstrel performer, boxing trainer, and, like the title character of *The Emperor Jones* Brutus Jones, Pullman porter (Johnson 185). Indeed, for the strong correspondences between Gilpin and Brutus Jones, the actor—equally burly, arrogant, overbearing, and as practiced at the art of survival as his fictional counterpart—was the ideal casting choice.

Gilpin's performance was so powerful, in fact, that the Drama League listed him as one of 10 actors who had done the most for the AMERICAN THEATER for the year 1920. The league's tradition was to invite the chosen few to their annual dinner in order to formally honor their achievements. A public outcry ensued over inviting a black man, however, and the league promptly, if contritely, revoked Gilpin's invitation. In spite of his personal dislike for Gilpin, O'Neill was disgusted by the league's pandering to their racist membership, and he and his

Charles S. Gilpin as Brutus Jones in O'Neill *The Emperor Jones,* product of the Provincetown Player's. Playwrights' Theatre, November 1, 1920 *(Courtesy of the Yale Collection of American Literature, Beinecke Rare Book and Manuscript Library)*

producer KENNETH MACGOWAN swiftly petitioned the remaining nine actors to turn down their invitations, which they all did. Gilpin's invitation was soon reinstated, and in spite of the upheaval, by all accounts, the event was a magnificent success. Just a decade later, James Weldon Johnson wrote that the Gilpin affair already had "an archaic character. It is doubtful if a similar incident today [1930] could provide such a degree of asininity" (184).

The AFRICAN-AMERICAN singer and actor PAUL ROBESON replaced Gilpin in the 1923 revival, and to this day, Robeson is more closely associated with the Brutus Jones role than any other actor. But most critics, including O'Neill himself, maintain that Gilpin surpassed Robeson's ability to capture Jones's tormented psyche and translate it for a theater audience. O'Neill, who never liked Gilpin offstage, admitted much later that "as I look back now on all my work, I can honestly say there was only one character who carried out every notion of a character I had in mind. That actor was Charles Gilpin as the Pullman porter in *The Emperor Jones*" (quoted in Gelb 236). Edged out of the production for his personal indiscretions, his habit of replacing racially charged dialogue with euphemisms, and his growing ALCOHOLISM, Gilpin returned, penniless and blacklisted from theatrical work, to his former post as an elevator operator in 1921. He died on May 6, 1930, in Eldridge Park, New Jersey, and now lies in an unmarked grave in Woodlawn Cemetery.

Bibliography

Gelb, Arthur, and Barbara Gelb. *O'Neill: Life with Monte Cristo.* New York: Applause Books, 2000.
Johnson, James Weldon. *Black Manhattan.* 1930. Reprint, New York: Da Capo Press, 1991.

Glaspell, Susan (1882–1948) Born in Davenport, Iowa, Susan Glaspell is one of the most prominent and prolific women writers of the early 20th century, as well as a pioneer for feminist causes. She and her husband GEORGE CRAM "JIG" COOK, also a Davenport native, founded the PROVINCE-TOWN PLAYERS in 1915, for which Glaspell wrote nearly a dozen plays. Glaspell's practical outlook helped offset Cook's volatile personality and most certainly helped keep the Players intact for seven

Susan Glaspell *(Courtesy of the New York Public Library, Berg Collection)*

years. The couple is also credited with discovering Eugene O'Neill, with whom Glaspell forged a close personal and professional relationship.

As a writer, Glaspell addressed the entrapment of women in a patriarchal society at a time when such a topic was fashionable. Her distinctive dramatic innovations include offstage central characters as well as the use of silence onstage and of the European tradition of EXPRESSIONISM. Although Glaspell considered herself primarily a novelist, her renown rests chiefly on her plays. Her signature work is *Trifles*, a dramatized version of her short story "A Jury of Her Peers," which was based on a murder story she covered for the *Daily News*. In 1931, she won the PULITZER PRIZE for a lesser-known play, *Alison's House*, loosely patterned on the life of Emily Dickinson, making Glaspell the second woman to earn the prestigious award for drama. (The first was Zona Gale a decade earlier.) In the course of her life, Glaspell wrote well over a dozen plays, 10 novels, and more than 50 short stories and essays, as well as a biography of her husband that some critics have regarded as over-reverential.

In 1922, Glaspell and Cook left for Greece, disillusioned with the commercial turn that the Provincetown Players had taken with their successful production of O'Neill's *The EMPEROR JONES*. She remained there until her husband died in 1924, whereupon she returned to Provincetown and quickly became involved with a writer 17 years younger, Norman Matson. The relationship lasted seven years.

In the 1930s, Glaspell had the opportunity to carry on the kind of work she and Cook had aimed for with the Provincetown Players. From 1936 to 1938, she served with the Federal Theatre Project, a program of the Works Progress Administration, as director of the Midwest Play Bureau in Chicago, encouraging and producing new American plays. After leaving this position, Glaspell returned to Provincetown, where she spent the remainder of her life. Although recognized for her achievements while she was alive, Glaspell was relegated to anonymity after her death until the late 20th century, when scholarly studies began to reassert her importance.

Bibliography

Ben-Zvi, Linda. *Susan Glaspell: Her Life and Times.* New York: Oxford University Press, 2005.

Ozieblo, Bárbara. *Susan Glaspell: A Critical Biography.* Chapel Hill: University of North Carolina Press, 2000.

Susan Glaspell Society, The. Web site. Available online. URL: http://academic.shu.edu/glaspell/. Updated March 9, 2008.

Waterman, Arthur E. *Susan Glaspell.* New York: Twayne, 1966.

Karen Charmaine Blansfield

Glencairn, SS   Like his marginal, nascent collection of verse, the quartet of O'Neill's SS *Glencairn* plays—The MOON OF THE CARIBBEES, BOUND EAST FOR CARDIFF, The LONG VOYAGE HOME, and IN THE ZONE—possesses the germinal quality of his work on the stage between the two world wars. With the Atlantic Ocean as the main setting, these one-act plays open windows to a primal journey of self-discovery, a yearning for the healing touch of the Earth Mother's compassion beyond man's legacy of pain.

In 1919, Boni and Liveright were the first publishers to print these plays of a relatively unknown but ambitious American playwright; it was titled *The Moon of the Caribbees and Six Other Plays of the Sea,* the remaining plays being ILE, The ROPE, and WHERE THE CROSS IS MADE. The sequence of the four *Glencairn* plays was not established by O'Neill himself and was altered at times, with *In the Zone* usually being placed last because of its chronological position during World War I.

John Ford's 1940 FILM ADAPTATION of the entire quartet of plays, under the title *The Long Voyage Home,* shifted the setting to World War II.

O'Neill's vision of the SEA and of seafarers connected with it was based on literary as well as personal experience and was embodied in his plays from the beginning to the end of his career. The ship SS *Glencairn* itself was modeled on the SS IKALA, a tramp freighter in the British merchant navy that had recruited O'Neill as a sailor in 1911. The *Ikala* provided the multicultural setting for the development of his characters—Smitty, Driscoll, Yank, Davis, Cocky, Paul, Bella, Susie, Violet, and Pearl—created from traits of people he had known during his voyages.

A predominant influence had on O'Neill was the title role that his famous actor-father JAMES O'NEILL had played in Alexander Dumas's *The Count of Monte Cristo.* The poignant story was about the wronged Edmond Dantès, who rises from the sea, literally and metaphorically, a free man, master of the world that had once exploited him. Samuel Taylor Coleridge's *The Rime of the Ancient Mariner* was also an important source that O'Neill dramatized in the confessional terms of the hypnotic and sinister power that the sea exercised on those connected with it (see ANCIENT MARINER, THE), as were the novels of Herman Melville (*Moby Dick*) and Joseph Conrad (*Heart of Darkness, Nostromo, The Nigger of the Narcissus*).

In *The Moon of the Caribbees,* O'Neill provided the symbolic framework for the primordial pain of creation and death in the persistent Negro keening floating into the ears of the bored inmates of the SS *Glencairn.* This mythic context is projected with dramatic innocence through the young Negresses who come aboard the ship with their wares of alcohol and sex. Discovered in their unsanctioned operation by the second mate, they are sent back to their home in the misty, but not before a jolt is delivered to the status quo. O'Neill dramatically relates the two dimensions, the mundane and the mythic, in the climactic moment of the mysterious knifing of Paddy:

DRISCOLL—(*quickly—in a low voice*) Who knoifed him?

YANK—(*stupidly*) I didn't see it. How do I know? Cocky I'll bet. (1:542)

The abstract pain implicit in the distinct Negro keening thus becomes acutely realized in one body and mind aboard the ship; significantly, O'Neill leaves the perpetrator's identity to our imaginations. In hindsight, we reckon it could be the alienated spirit of the mythic Negro suffering that seeks an objective recognition through a ritualistic blood letting. This may be cited as an example of O'Neill's innate flair for symbolism that would mature in his future plays.

On the *Glencairn,* it is the underlying primal alienation of life that the gay company of the evening is trying to mitigate, as sailors do, through their unassuming hedonism. But such actions cannot be sanctioned either officially (by the second mate) or mythically (the spirit of music); they can only lead to pain, bloodshed, and a return to the original condition, a short-circuiting of pipe dreams. Hence, the brief, intense expression of the pain of indulgent sailors seeking happiness foregrounds the primal pain of creation. Yet the connection, even within the limited scale of the one-act play, is dramatic rather than morally didactic, the two dimensions remaining separate as well as deeply integrated at the psychic level of the collective unconscious or the Dionysian oneness of being on which O'Neill, like FRIEDRICH NIETZSCHE (a powerful influence on him), had meditated.

In his desire to uphold the "big subject" in his plays, O'Neill significantly began with the metaphorical expansiveness of the sea, which is projected, in abstract terms, as the chief protagonist in this early play: "*The Moon of the Caribbees*—(my favourite)—is distinctly my own. The spirit of the sea—a big thing—is in this play the hero"; and the play is "an attempt to achieve a higher plane of bigger, finer values"(Clark 82–83). O'Neill does not hesitate to paternally acknowledge the pathbreaking relevance of this early work, for it was his "first real break with theatrical traditions" and once he had taken "this initial step, other plays followed logically" (Clark 84).

Bound East for Cardiff was O'Neill's first play to be staged; his debut with the PROVINCETOWN PLAYERS opened on July 28, 1916. O'Neill played a role in it as well—that of the second mate, with only one line of dialogue: "Isn't this your watch on deck, Driscoll?" (1:194). The play has been considered by many to be the "best" of the *Glencairn* quartet. The

principal characters are the same as in *The Moon of the Caribbees* and *The Long Voyage Home*. The focus is on the last stage of Yank's life following his accidental fall from a ladder in the ship during the voyage, which takes place between New York and Cardiff. Driscoll, sitting next to the dying Yank to distract him from his pain, recalls their long and consistent friendship ("we've stuck together iver since through good luck and bad" [1:189]), reminiscences which could be based on O'Neill's own reflections. The prospect of his comrade's premature death makes Driscoll "blubber loike an auld woman" (1:190), while a thick fog ominously envelops the ship and the latter recalls the drowning of the old ship *Dover* on "such a night as this" (1:191). Yank laments the warmth and life on the land that he has forfeited by sailing so long on the sea—"It must be great to have a home of your own, Drisc" (1:195). Finally death arrives to fetch him in the shape of "A pretty lady dressed in black" (1:198), whom Yank deliriously imagines standing before him; and with his passing, the fog also disappears. The critic Heywood Broun observes that it is in "the creation of mood and atmosphere" (14), rather than in revealing any interesting idea or twist of plot, that *Bound East for Cardiff* excels as a 'first' play by a fledgling playwright in the northeastern fishing village of Provincetown. In passing, it may be interesting to note the ironic fact that the character of Yank in *Bound East for Cardiff* was modeled on the real-life DRISCOLL, a powerful IRISH stoker and shipmate of O'Neill, who had committed suicide by jumping overboard. So the dialogue between Driscoll and Yank, between the stage character of the dying sailor wanting to belong and his real-life counterpart, may well represent O'Neill's meditation on death during the tumult of World War I.

In *The Long Voyage Home*, Olson, the Swedish sailor, with two years' savings in his pocket, is almost on the point of achieving the dream that Yank in *Cardiff* despairs about before his death—the chance of finally investing in and cherishing a life on the land and of farming, following many years of wasting his savings on drink. But ironically, once on shore during a break, though he avoids drinking with his friends at the bar, he is drugged by a gang of shanghaiers, robbed and kidnapped aboard another ship, the *Amindra,* which has a reputation for repression and cruelty. Far from earning his final freedom, Olson is forcibly bound for a two-year voyage around the Cape with the ominous probability of his never returning alive—the very fate he has been trying to avoid. His friends have no clue about his abduction as they reenter the saloon to look for him.

The fourth and "last" play of the quartet, *In the Zone,* takes place in fall 1915. The action centers on the sailor Smitty and misplaced suspicion regarding his possible identity as an enemy spy carrying a bomb onboard the munitions ship as it ventures through the German submarine zone. The cause of suspicion is the packet found in Smitty's bunk and the nature of whose contents he refrains from sharing. He is therefore caught, gagged, and tied with ropes as his colleagues open the mysterious and threatening box without his permission. But in an anticlimax, the contents turn out to be love letters from an erstwhile sweetheart who had rejected him for his uncontrolled inebriation. Abashed at their own mistake, the men release Smitty as he sobs with remorse and humiliation. The play's melodramatic effectiveness and popular appeal were the very reasons that made O'Neill criticize it as "facile" and "conventional." In tune with his lifelong antipathy to his father's melodramatic theater tradition, O'Neill skeptically commented on his own play: "it's long run as a successful headliner in vaudeville proves conclusively to my mind there must be something rotten in the state of Denmark" (quoted in Clark 78).

Bibliography

Berger, Jason. "Refiguring O'Neill's Early Sea Plays: Maritime Labor Enters the Age of Modernity." *Eugene O'Neill Review* 28 (2006): 13–31.

Bogard, Travis. *Contour in Time: The Plays of Eugene O'Neill.* New York: Oxford University Press, 1972.

Brietzke, Zander. "The Long Voyage Home: A Vicious Cycle at Sea." *Eugene O'Neill Review* 28 (2006): 32–49.

Broun, Heywood. "Down an Alley on Drama Trail." In *Playwright's Progress: O'Neill and the Critics,* edited by Jordan Y. Miller, 4–5. Chicago: Scott, Foresman, 1965.

Clark, Barrett. *Eugene O'Neill: The Man and His Plays.* New York: Robert M. McBride, 1929.

Kenton, Edna. *The Provincetown Players and the Playwright's Theatre 1915–1922.* Edited by Travis Bogard and Jackson Bryer. Jefferson, N.C.: McFarland, 2004.

Sarlós Robert Karoly. *Jig Cook and the Provincetown Players: The Theatre in Ferment.* Amherst: University of Massachusetts Press, 1982.

Rupendra Majumdar

Goldman, Emma (1869–1940)   Lithuanian immigrant Emma Goldman, frequently referred to as "Red Emma" and called "E.G." by her friends, is one of the most well known anarchists and feminists of her time. She was born in Kaunas, Lithuania, on June 27, 1869, and emigrated to the United States with her sister Helena who she was 16. After a brief marriage she moved to New York and began to gain notoriety around the time that O'Neill was born.

In 1919, just a year before O'Neill won the PULITZER PRIZE for BEYOND THE HORIZON, Goldman was deported from the United States for her opposition to mandatory conscription. She had been under constant surveillance in America, and authorities suspected her of instigating many subversive plots and violent activities, including the 1901 assassination of President William McKinley, accusing her of conspiracy because of her passing acquaintance with the killer. After being evicted from the country, Goldman continued to participate in social and political causes, including the Spanish Civil War and the Russian Revolution.

Although Goldman and O'Neill had several mutual friends, and while O'Neill was close to both a niece and a nephew of hers, there is no evidence that the two ever met. O'Neill reportedly first became aware of Goldman through BENJAMIN R. TUCKER, a well-known anarchist and owner of the Unique Book Shop in Manhattan. But given Goldman's constant presence in the news, the blossoming of radicalism in such places as GREENWICH VILLAGE and Provincetown, Massachusetts, and the anarchists among O'Neill's acquaintances, the playwright would inevitably have learned of her, perhaps even before Tucker introduced him to her work. O'Neill also purportedly published a poem in Goldman's leftist magazine *Mother Earth,* which was in print from 1905 to 1917, when police confiscated it.

Scholars and BIOGRAPHERS have no doubt that Goldman influenced O'Neill's work, even though his plays are not propaganda. Socialist ideas can be perceived in THE HAIRY APE and ALL GOD'S CHILLUN GOT WINGS, for instance, and in AH, WILDERNESS!, when the character of Richard criticizes American society, calling the Fourth of July "a farce," and his father says, "Son, if I didn't know it was you talking, I'd think we had Emma Goldman with us." The ICEMAN COMETH features the most overt influence of Goldman and political radicalism through its subplot as well as the characters of Larry Slade and Hugo Kalmar, modeled after anarchists O'Neill knew. The offstage character of Rosa Parritt is based at least partly on Emma Goldman, and her betrayal by her son Don alludes to an actual experience Goldman had with an informer. Even an early, unpublished play, The PERSONAL EQUATION (originally The Second Engineer), written for GEORGE PIERCE BAKER's playwriting workshop, reflects the principles of the infamous anarchist. The character of labor leader Olga Tarnoff in many ways parallels Goldman, including her speech, and the plot, while melodramatic, echoes anarchist beliefs.

Goldman carried on her anarchist activities to the end of her life. She died in Toronto, Canada, on May 14, 1940, after two debilitating strokes. Authorities allowed her to be buried in the United States at a cemetery in Forest Park, Illinois. Her tombstone reads, "Liberty will not descend to a people, a people must raise themselves to Liberty."

Bibliography

Frazer, Winifred L. *E.G. and E.G.O.: Emma Goldman and The Iceman Cometh.* Gainesville: University Presses of Florida, 1974.

Gelb, Barbara. "Concealing While Revealing: O'Neill's Way with Truth," *New York Times,* April 4, 1999, 2, 5.

Karen Charmaine Blansfield

Greek tragedy Eugene O'Neill's dissatisfaction with the hollowness of the modern stage was offset in his own mind and professional condition by his deep regard for the ancient theater of Periclean Greece as represented in the drama of Aeschylus, Sophocles, and Euripides. In emulating these classical play-wrights in contemporary terms, O'Neill endorsed the 20th-century attempt to revive the seriousness, depth, and range of Greek drama that was shared by other Western playwrights such as Hugo von Hofmannsthal, T. S. Eliot, Jean Giraudoux, Jean-Paul Sartre, and GEORGE BERNARD SHAW. Indeed, O'Neill can be said to be at the forefront of that endeavor of creating a new and lasting theater beyond ordinary realism to a state of "super NATURALISM."

O'Neill sought to follow his "Greek" objective at the fundamental level through a mythopoeic rendering of classical myths in modern dress. The legends of Jason, Medea, Theseus, Agamemnon, Oedipus, Orestes, and Electra found relevance in a modern setting. And O'Neill, like Eliot and Sartre, created the psychological, social, and historical parameters enabling those myths to find a local habitation and a name. Such a task was facilitated by the popularity of writers such as Sigmund Freud, Carl Jung (in the field of psychoanalysis), and Karl Marx in the 1920s and 1930s. Literary alignments had to be made sensitively to the best effect to present a Greek classical impulse in psychological or socialistic terms within a transitional age, moving from anxieties of the frontier, pristine ethos to an industrial and urban one.

O'Neill's use of the chorus, or the choric component in his drama, corresponds to his early interest in the theater of the Greeks, namely that of Aeschylus and Sophocles, during the 1920s. The function of the Greek chorus had been to underline the action of the plot, comment on the characters, and expose and synthesize the emotional and moral implications of the story at a heightened level through its use of song and dance of highly stylized nature. In O'Neill's drama, choric elements are at times expressed within the framework of the American folk culture (as in DESIRE UNDER THE ELMS) or through a simulation of the classical atomosphere (as in LAZARUS LAUGHED) or in his stage adaptation of a romanticed ballad such as Coleridge's *The Ancient Mariner.* In *Lazarus,* the chorus used masks in a fashion recalling the Greek practice, as well as pointing to modern psychoanalytical theories, changing them from time to time. What O'Neill sought in vain, was "a choric drama of celebration, extraordinary in its dimension, compelling in its intensity" (Travis Bogard, *Contour,* 283). Indeed O'Neill viewed the euphoria of the chorus of *Lazarus* in the perspective of Negro revival meetings.

Using his own innate resources, O'Neill succeeded in combining the Greek view of tragedy with the American dream of possession and personal aggrandizement. He did this through the dramatic weaving of American images (the western frontier, the Civil War), discourses, and anxieties in a language of narration and confession that recalled the 19th-century American novel as well as the Irish theater and AFRICAN-AMERICAN discourse. In giving his opinion about an "imaginative theatre," O'Neill had no hesitation in declaring that it was "the one true theatre" like that of the Greeks and Elizabethans and which could boast of being a "legitimate descendent of the first theatre that sprang by virtue of man's imaginative interpretation of life out of his worship of Dionysus" (quoted in Hinden 134). He considered the theater as a "temple" where the religion practiced was that of a symbolic celebration of life that is conveyed to a people who have forfeited its true essence and who are "starved in spirit by their soul stifling daily struggle to exist as masks among the masks of the living" (Hinden 134).

O'Neill's initiation into Greek tragedy had been through his exposure to the philosophy of FRIEDRICH NIETZSCHE at the age of 18. His fascination for the latter's *The Birth of Tragedy* (1872) and *Thus Spake Zarathustra* ensured, as he was to declare to Benjamin de Casseres in 1928, that his main literary idol was Nietzsche. *Zarathustra*—"It has influenced me more than any book I've ever read," he said (quoted in Sheaffer 123)—gave O'Neill a pioneering figure of enlightenment who embodied a need and a hope that neither the Church nor his immediate environment of the theater could provide. Primarily, O'Neill was impressed by Nietzsche's understanding of Greek tragedy as delineated in *The Birth of Tragedy* by his formulation of the dynamic synthesis of the Dionysian and Apollonian impulses in the Greek psyche.

The pair of terms was first used in a literary discourse in modern times by Nietzsche. In his seminal book *The Birth of Tragedy,* he coined the dual concept of the "Apollonian" and "Dionysian," based on the Greek gods Apollo and Dionysus, in relation to the evolution and susequent decline of Greek tragedy. "It is by those two art-sponsoring deities, Apollo and Dionysus," he said, "that we are made to recognize the tremendous split, as regards both origins and objectives, between the plastic, Apollonian arts and the non-visual art of music inspired by Dionysus." The two creative forces, we are told by Nietzsche, developed together in "fierce opposition."

The Birth of Tragedy directly influenced O'Neill's composition of *The* GREAT GOD BROWN (1925) and *Lazarus Laughed* (1926); and the same influence can be perceived more obliquely in other plays such as *The* HAIRY APE (1921), *Desire under the Elms* (1924), *The* ICEMAN COMETH (1939), and LONG DAY'S JOURNEY INTO NIGHT (1941). Yank, the ship's stoker in *The Hairy Ape,* embodies the threat of a Dionysian force to the white, capitalistic, upper class represented by Mildred. He is the "primordial one," all- encompassing and formidable: "I'm de end! I'm de start! . . . I'm de ting in coal that makes it boin; I'm steam and oil for de engines; . . . I'm de muscles in steel!" (1:128–129). As the play proceeds, Yank, however, attempts to move from the Dionysian to the Apollonian dimension but is not able to reconcile these two forces. In his venture, he makes the mistake of looking back in doubt, and the Dionysian impulse, in the shape of the gorilla in the cage, crushes him to death to punish and make him "belong" to one consistent truth. In *The Great God Brown* O'Neill makes the attempt of going a step beyond *The Hairy Ape* by pointing "the way towards his redemption and eternal transcendence" (Hinden 134). Mary Koutsoodaki concludes her discussion on *The Great God Brown* with praise for O'Neill's success in projecting to "the modern stage the Dionysiac paradox in the true spirit of the Greeks" (93).

According to Nietzsche, the synthesis between the Dionysian and the Apollonian could be achieved through music and the religious sensibility that was potentially latent in Greek society till Socratic rationality undermined it. But for O'Neill, contemporary Western society could not easily achieve this synthesis due to its own enervation of faith. Mildred's fainting in Yank's presence in the ship's stokehold signifies the natural antipathy of the elite toward the working class, which O'Neill tacitly identifies with Dionysian energy. Yet Yank, in his Dionysian bearing, is also attracted to the Apollonian world of speculation and individuality. This is shown in his adopting the posture of Auguste Rodin's sculpture *The Thinker*. This predilection proves fatal for him. His venture into the white capitalist world brings about his confinement in a cage in the zoo and the final rib-crushing embrace by the gorilla that makes him finally "belong."

In *Desire under the Elms*, O'Neill moves a little further into this conflict, showing old Cabot (as well as the overwhelming elm trees before the house) as the upholder of the Dionysian force that his youngest son, Eben, is trying to overcome. Eben succeeds, at a cost, by aligning interests with Abbie, Cabot's new and sensual third wife, "to complete the evolution" of the Dionysian urge through the acknowledgment of their incestuous desire for each other till the very end. It was through such "unnatural acts," such as incest, that Nietzsche believed nature from Greek times could be induced to give up her secrets. Abbie and Eben are thus enabled to reach a higher synthesis of the two forces in a ritualistic blood sacrifice that exorcises their mutual sin. They proceed to death with the tragic joy of life being "indestructibly joyful and powerful," as Nietzsche observed in *The Birth of Tragedy*. In *Desire*, O'Neill reached the pinnacle of his application of Nietzsche's concepts of Greek tragedy.

While O'Neill progressed as a playwright, his interest in Greek tragedy through Nietzsche was supplemented by his growing familiarity with such writers as AUGUST STRINDBERG (*Miss Julie, The Dance of Death*), Sigmund Freud (*Totem and Taboo, Beyond the Pleasure Principle, Analysis of the Ego*), and Jung (*Psychology of the Unconscious*). Yet there was no doubt in his mind what exercised the greater influence: "What has influenced my plays is my knowledge of the drama of all time—particularly Greek tragedy—and not any books on psychology" (quoted in Sheaffer 1973, 245). These two dimensions remained in his mind when he attempted one of his most ambitious ventures, his trilogy on the Orestes myth, MOURNING BECOMES ELECTRA (1931), set in New England at the end of the Civil War in the 1860s.

O'Neill observed in a letter to Manuel Komroff that *Mourning* had more complicated relationships than any Greek treatment and that it was "a psychological drama of lust" (quoted in Bogard 335). In his WORK DIARY for spring 1926, he questioned whether it was possible to get a "modern psychological appropriation of the Greek sense of fate" into a drama for a modern audience that cared little for divine retribution. He decided that there was potential in the plot of Electra's predicament and that it would be important to give her a tragic ending worthy of her, for she had "too much tragic fate within her soul" (quoted in Bogard 336) to slip into stage mediocrity. According to O'Neill the trilogy really belongs to Electra (Lavinia, the daughter of Christine/Clytemnestra, played brilliantly by the Russian actress Alla Nazimova in the production on October 26, 1931), for "it is she who dominates its action and fuses it" (69). As a play that employs a Greek legend as his model during the Great Depression, O'Neill achieves "a universal tragedy of tremendous stature" (Atkinson 65).

General Ezra Mannon/Agamemnon, returning to his home after the Civil War/Trojan War, dies in the presence of his wife Christine/Clytemnestra, who has poisoned him. Unlike the Aeschylian play, however, in which suffering leads to wisdom and tragic catharsis, O'Neill's adaptation of the Orestes myth points to confinement and despair.

In his later plays—*Long Day's Journey into Night, A MOON FOR THE MISBEGOTTEN*—O'Neill transmutes his understanding and embodiment of Greek tragedy from the doors of Atreus and Laius to those of James Tyrone and Josie Hogan, closer home.

King Atreus of Mycenae, was the son of Pelops, whose descendants were known as the Atreidae or Atreidi. His two sons, King Agamemnon and King Menelaus, were the main aggrieved instigators of the Trojan War. Agamemnon's tragic death on his return at the hands of his wife Clytemnestra and her lover Aegisthus, and the subsequent, macabre retribution that follows, forms the basis of Eugene O'Neill's play *Mourning Becomes Electra* (1930), set against the American Civil War.

King Laius of Thebes, was the father of Oedipus, who was fated to kill Laius and marry his mother, Iocasta. Oedipus was thus exposed in childhood to be killed before such a calamity could take place. But fate took its own inevitable course. The story provides the basis of Freud's psychoanalytical concept of the Oedipus Complex, which features in a number of O'Neill's plays.

The need for redemption is retained, only in terms of the modern American urban frontier—NEW LONDON, New York, engulfed in fog. This constitutes a point of synthesis in which O'Neill comes into his own arena of dramatic art in indigenous terms, as he had sworn he would from a young age in reaction against what he saw as the puerile 19th-century theater tradition of his father JAMES O'NEILL.

It is darkly ironic that Eugene O'Neill's sense of the tragic was reflected in his family, especially in the life of his eldest son, EUGENE O'NEILL, JR., who after establishing his credentials as a scholar and professor in Greek classical literature at Yale University, committed suicide in the manner of the Stoics by slashing his wrists. And it is this sense of the tragic waste of life, inspired by the Greek paradigm in modern American terms, that O'Neill is most effective in establishing in his contemporary, semiautobiographical final plays, especially *Long Day's Journey into Night*.

Bibliography

Atkinson, Brooks. "*Mourning Becomes Electra*" (review). *New York Times*, October 27, 1931, 65.

Black, Stephen A. "*Mourning Becomes Electra* as a Greek Tragedy." *Eugene O'Neill Review* 26 (2004): 166–188.

Bogard, Travis. *Contour in Time: The Plays of Eugene O'Neill*. Rev. ed. New York: Oxford University Press, 1988.

Brown, John Mason. Review of *Mourning Becomes Electra*." In *Playwright's Progress: O'Neill and the Critics*, edited by Jordan Y. Miller. Chicago: Scott, Foresman, 1965.

Falk, Doris V. *Eugene O'Neill and the Tragic Vision*. Brunswick, N.J.: Rutgers University Press, 1958.

Hermann-Miller, Eileen. "Staging O'Neill: Staging Greek Tragedy." *Eugene O'Neill Review* 25, no. 1 and 2 (Spring–Fall 2001): 70–75.

Hinden, Michael. "*The Birth of Tragedy* and *The Great God Brown*." *Modern Drama* 16, no. 2 (1973): 134.

Koutsoudaki, Mary. *The Greek Plays of Eugene O'Neill*. Athens: University of Athens, 2004.

Kushner, Eva. "Greek Myths in Modern Drama." In *Literary Criticism and Myth*, edited by J. P. Strelka. University Park: Pennsylvania State University Press, 1980.

Oates, Whitney, and Eugene O'Neill, Jr. *The Complete Greek Drama: All the Extant Tragedies of Aeschylus, Sophocles and Euripides, and the Comedies of Aristophanes and Menander*. New York: Modern Library, 1938.

———. *Seven Famous Greek Plays*. New York: Modern Library, 1950.

Sheaffer, Louis. *O'Neill: Son and Playwright*. Boston: Little, Brown, 1968.

———. *O'Neill: Son and Artist*. Boston: Little, Brown, 1973.

Rupendra Majumdar

Greenwich Village Greenwich Village is the name of the New York neighborhood in Lower Manhattan that has been home to many famous innovators in American culture, including leading writers, artists, composers, choreographers, and filmmakers. Just a partial list of the American vanguard in the arts associated with "the Village" in the early 20th century includes novelists Theodore Dreiser, Sinclair Lewis, and Willa Cather; playwrights Eugene O'Neill and SUSAN GLASPELL; poets E. E. Cummings and Edna St. Vincent Millay; artists Alfred Stieglitz, Georgia O'Keefe, and Charles Demuth; choreographer Martha Graham; and composer Cole Porter, among many others.

The traditional borders of Greenwich Village have always been Fourteenth Street on the north and Houston (pronounced How-ston) Street on the south. Today the area is said to run east from the Hudson River, through the original "West Village," to Washington Square Park at the center, and then past Broadway (once its original eastern border) to include an area of Manhattan's Lower East Side now called the "East Village."

Eugene O'Neill had many connections to the neighborhood. In 1913, after an unresolved debate about admitting AFRICAN AMERICANS and a scandal involving the unconventional marriage of the feminist schoolteacher Henrietta Rodman, a mild uptown forum called the LIBERAL CLUB suffered a split. Rodman led the club's more radical members to relocate to Macdougal Street, just south of Washington Square. The block where the reformed Liberal Club opened soon became the intellectual center of the village. The brothers Albert and Charles Boni opened a bookstore next door to the club to cater to its members' literary tastes. (Later the Boni Brothers would found an important literary series called the Modern Library.) Polly Holladay, the sister of Eugene O'Neill's friend Louis Holladay, opened Polly's Restaurant above the Liberal Club. The anarchist HIPPOLYTE HAVEL waited on tables, famously shouting "Bourgeois pigs!" at the customers; he was later immortalized in O'Neill's play *The ICEMAN COMETH*. One of America's new "little" theaters dedicated to artistic and literary rather than popular Broadway plays began in the Boni Brothers' Bookshop in 1913 and evolved into a group called the WASHINGTON SQUARE PLAYERS and later the THEATRE GUILD. However, the more daring PROVINCETOWN PLAYERS, who first produced O'Neill in 1916, soon opened the PLAYWRIGHTS THEATRE in an old brownstone next to the Liberal Club and then later moved into a converted stable in the same building.

Not far away on Greenwich Avenue, Max Eastman, who had resigned a philosophy professorship at Columbia University, revamped a dry socialist publication, *The MASSES*, to become the most daring, humorous, and rebellious publication of the new Village. *The Masses* advocated equal rights and the vote for women, socialism and anarchism, labor, Freudian psychoanalysis, modern art (with some reservations), and birth control. JOHN REED was a regular contributor and member of the editorial staff of the magazine. The assistant editor, Floyd Dell, produced some of the earliest plays in the Village at the Liberal Club, and along with Eastman and Reed, he joined a group centered on writers Susan Glaspell and GEORGE CRAM "JIG" COOK to found the Provincetown Players. Dell, famed for wearing a bohemian cape, was called by the historian Emily Hahn the "textbook case" bohemian (7). He also inaugurated the annual Greenwich Village balls, called "pagan routs," that became the center of Village social life. A more notorious institution was "Bruno's Garret," where Guido Bruno ran a combination newspaper office, boarding house, art gallery, and venue for poetry readings. Although Bruno used his weekly publications to bring to print some of the more experimental writers of the Village, including Djuna Barnes and Alfred Kreymborg, he also shamelessly commercialized the Village. Promoting Washington Square as America's Left Bank, he turned his garret into part tourist trap

and put up a bus terminal to profit from busloads of uptown "slummers" who came to get a glimpse of the wild artists in their native habitat.

Villagers could be found at any of these Village institutions, but they might just as often be found debating the new world of ideas, politics, poetry, painting, and the new theater in the Village's cafés, eateries, and watering holes. In addition to Polly's above the Liberal Club, there were also numerous Italian restaurants such as Mama Betolutti's on Third Street, and "theme" establishments that, for better or worse, helped create the Village's bohemian atmosphere, such as the Mad Hatter, with an *Alice in Wonderland* down-the-rabbit-hole décor; the Wigam, designed with an American Indian theme; the Samovar, famous for its location in a loft on Sixth Avenue near Fourth Street, which required entry up a ladder (a favorite of the Provincetown Players); the Pirate's Den with waitstaff in Buccaneer dress; and Romany Marie's, which was gypsy-inspired and featured Marie, a former anarchist, who would read palms and tell fortunes. For the hard drinkers, there were Irish saloons, the most famous of which, the Golden Swan, stood at the corner of Fourth Street and Sixth Avenue. Nicknamed the HELL HOLE, it was in this dive bar that Eugene O'Neill gained his introduction to Greenwich Village in 1915, and where he meet his second wife, AGNES BOULTON, in 1917.

Bibliography

Cowley, Malcolm. *Exile's Return: A Literary Odyssey of the 1920s*. New York: Penguin Books, 1976.

Hahn, Emily. *Romantic Rebels. An Informal History of Bohemianism in America*. Boston: Houghton Mifflin, 1967.

Heller, Adele, and Lois Rudnick. Introduction to *1915, The Cultural Moment: The New Politics, the New Woman, the New Psychology, the New Art, and the New Theatre in America*. New Brunswick, N.J.: Rutgers University Press, 1991, 1–14.

Lasch, Christopher. *The New Radicalism in America: The Intellectual as a Social Type*. New York: Vintage Books, 1965.

Richwine, Keith N. "The Liberal Club: Bohemia and the Resurgence in Greenwich Village, 1912–1918." Ph.D. diss., University of Pennsylvania, 1969.

Drew Eisenhower

H

Harkness, Edward Stephen (1874–1940) and
Hammond, Edward Crowninshield (1868–1940)
Their first names, social prominence, and friendship were not all that Edward Stephen Harkness and Edward Crowninshield Hammond had in common, for both were also, notably, targets of Eugene O'Neill's disparaging pen. In LONG DAY'S JOURNEY INTO NIGHT, aspects of Harkness and Hammond are combined to form the offstage character Harker, and in A MOON FOR THE MISBEGOTTEN, the two become the composite character T. Stedman Harder.

Edward Harkness was a scion of tycoon Stephen Vandenburgh Harkness, who built the family fortune as the silent partner of John D. Rockefeller, Sr. Born on January 22, 1874, in Cleveland, Ohio, Harkness was not, as O'Neill suggests in his characters Harder/Harker or in his poetry ("'Upon Our Beach'"), a self-absorbed plutocrat ("coddled from birth, everything arranged and made easy for him, deferred to because of his wealth") [A Moon for the Misbegotten; 3:884], but a lifelong philanthropist. He gave with abandon to a myriad of charities and civic organizations—to the New York Public Library, Columbia University's Medical Center, the Boy Scouts, Andover College, the College of William and Mary, Vassar College, Mount Holyoke College, Colgate University, Union Theological Seminary, Wellesley College, the Metropolitan Museum of Art, his alma mater Yale University, and countless others. His name appeared in the *New York Times* hundreds of times in the 1920s

and 1930s in reference to his generosity, though he preferred anonymity. A firm believer in institutionalized giving, Harkness was catholic in his vision, giving at home to the Democrat Alfred E. Smith's 1928 presidential campaign, though Harkness was Republican and Protestant, and abroad to British charities, Oxford University, and the Shakespeare Memorial Theatre in Stratford-on-Avon. Also at variance with O'Neill's depiction of the millionaire were Harkness's multifarious and eclectic interests. He enjoyed railroading (and invested heavily in Southern Pacific and New York Central lines), Egyptology, art, horticulture, travel, and the works of Shakespeare, in addition to the usual leisure pursuits of his class, golfing and yachting.

O'Neill asserts that the lives of his characters Harder and Harker were anticlimactic after their graduation from Ivy League schools, but such was not the case with Harkness, who went on to an audience with the king and queen of England and an honorary degree from Yale (a worthy achievement O'Neill had to admit); he also procured the Carnarvon Collection for the Metropolitan Museum of Art and the Pizarro manuscripts for the Library of Congress. And, of course, he spent his adult years building and managing one of the country's largest fortunes (and then giving it away). By the time Harkness died on January 29, 1940, at the age of 66, he had handed over $200,000,000 of his assets.

Like Harkness, Edward Hammond was from an established family, one that had owned the Walnut

Grove estate in Waterford, next to NEW LONDON, CONNECTICUT, since 1860. Affluent, though far less so than Harkness, Hammond was, like Harkness, a railroad enthusiast (president, in fact, of the New London Northern Railroad), an Ivy Leaguer (through Harvard), and a yachtsman. The two were, in fact, neighbors, Hammond having sold Harkness the property adjoining his, where the latter built a 42-room mansion. Because both were prominent and influential, an onlooker like young O'Neill, who was neither, may well have seen them as interchangeable, thereby conflating them later in his work. However, if the Hogan-Shaughnessy/Harder-Harker incident is more than apocryphal, the setting was certainly the Hammond estate since it was he who owned the ice pond as well as a strip of shore O'Neill's poem indicated in "'Upon Our Beach.'" Still, the millionaire's house mentioned in the poem, which can be glimpsed from "our" beach, recalls Harkness's house Eolia rather than Hammond's more modest residence.

It is difficult to determine what O'Neill knew of or drew from the local millionaires' lives when he "appropriated" them for his plays, whether to him a capitalist was a capitalist was a capitalist, but Hammond in temperament seems more akin to the snooty squire Harder than the shy, self-effacing, and altruistic Harkness. Whatever O'Neill borrowed and from whom, the mention of Standard Oil and the "Har" of Harker/Harder forever link Edward S. Harkness with O'Neill's supercilious and much derided characters.

Bibliography

Smith, Madeline C., and Richard Eaton. "The Truth about Hogan." *Eugene O'Neill Review* 18.1 and 2 (1994):163–170.

Wooster, James Willet. *Edward Stephen Harkness, 1874–1940.* Privately Printed, 1949.

Madeline C. Smith

Havel, Hippolyte (1871–1950)   Born in Burowski, Bohemia, and educated in Vienna, Hippolyte Havel was a prominent organizer, essayist, publisher, and raconteur within the international anarchist movement. Now a largely forgotten figure, even among

Hippolyte Havel *(Courtesy of the Labadie Collection, University of Michigan Library)*

anarchist circles, Havel was, during his time, at the center of the artistic and political avant-garde in GREENWICH VILLAGE.

A flamboyant character whose flowing hair and fondness for drink suggested the stereotypical bohemian, Havel was much more to his associates. Fluent in at least six languages, with an expansive knowledge of anarchist history, Havel had been expelled from Austria-Hungary, Germany, and FRANCE for his political activism.

In 1899, Havel met and began a relationship with EMMA GOLDMAN. The two traveled to Paris to organize the International Anarchist Congress, a nonauthoritarian alternative to the Socialist International, in 1900. His "Biographic Sketch" is still published as the introductory essay in Goldman's influential collection *Anarchism and Other Essays* (first published 1910).

Joining Goldman in New York, Havel quickly established himself a key contributor to anarchist publications, meetings, and public events. He became a tireless contributor to Goldman's journal *Mother Earth*, arguably the most important anarchist journal in America between 1906 and 1918, and the alternative educational institution, the Ferrer Center.

Among Havel's innovations was the development of venues in which ANARCHISM could be presented and discussed, outside the didactic form of political speeches. Influenced by the salons and cabarets he had experienced in Paris, Havel set about establishing such venues in New York, on an anarchist basis. He gave particular attention to nurturing performances of various types, viewing them as crucial to the creation of anarchist solidarity and community. Indeed, this emphasis on the development of a sense of anarchist community distinguished him from both individualist anarchists who stressed personal uniqueness and anarchist communists who focused on class struggle.

For Havel, cafés, salons, dinner parties, and theater were crucial for the development of solidarity among and between anarchists and artists. He viewed artists and anarchists as natural allies who challenged the boundaries of conventional thought and action, a challenge necessary for both creative development and social change. He advocated the idea that art was revolutionary, not strictly on a realist basis, as would be the case for the socialist realists who would follow, but through experimentation and abstraction as well.

Havel established three significant anarchist journals: *Social War*, *The Revolutionary Almanac*, and *Revolt*. These journals served as critical venues for the engagement of modernist art and radical politics and their dissemination across the boundaries separating art and politics.

O'Neill served a brief apprenticeship with Havel at *Revolt* before the paper was closed down after only three months for its opposition to U.S. involvement in World War I. This apprenticeship served to place O'Neill at the cultural center of anarchist activity in the United States, furthering his own intellectual and political development.

While it is conceivable that O'Neill and Havel crossed paths as early as 1909 when O'Neill shared a studio with anarchist painters at the Lincoln Arcade Building or certainly by 1915 when the playwright studied at the Ferrer Center, their friendship was cemented during the days at *Revolt*. Havel is portrayed as Hugo Kalmar in *The Iceman Cometh*, in what one commentator identifies as "a rather nasty caricature" (Porton 1999, 12). Kalmar (Havel) is given to jovial, inebriated rants, as in his "soapbox denunciations" ("Capitalist swine! Bourgeois stool pigeons! Have the slaves no right to sleep even?" *Iceman*, 3:570), which begin as wild declamations and wind down into sound and sudden sleep. He offers this view of the anarchist future. "Soon, leedle proletarians, ve vill have free picnic in the cool shade, ve vill eat hot dogs and drink free beer beneath the villow trees!" (*Iceman*, 3:623).

O'Neill draws attention to Kalmar's concern with maintaining a fashionable and neat appearance, *"even his flowing Windsor tie,"* and the actual poverty of his material existence as reflected in his *"threadbare black clothes"* and shirt *"frayed at collar and cuffs"* (3:566). Havel's life displayed the duality that has often characterized anarchist existence. In Havel, the aesthetic dreams of a new world reflected in the cafés and salons was juxtaposed with the reality of poverty and precarious work as a dishwasher and short-order cook. He died in 1950.

Bibliography

Alexander, Doris. 2005. *Eugene O'Neill's Last Plays: Separating Art from Autobiography*. Athens: University of Georgia Press

Antliff, Allan. *Anarchist Modernism: Art, Politics and the First American Avant Garde*. Chicago: University of Chicago Press, 2001.

Porton, Richard. *Film and the Anarchist Imagination*. London: Verso, 1999.

                                    J. Shantz

Hell Hole (The Golden Swan)   Today in GREENWICH VILLAGE, on the southeast corner of West Fourth Street and Sixth Avenue, there is a small "vest pocket" park featuring bluestone paths among dogwood, spuce, maple, and magnolia trees.

It is called Golden Swan Garden, in tribute to the bar and hotel that once stood there, the same Golden Swan frequented by Eugene O'Neill from shortly before he began working with the Prov-incetown Players until he moved to Cape Cod to set up housekeeping with second wife, Agnes Boulton.

The original Golden Swan, where Eugene O'Neill drank as a regular patron from 1915 to 1918–19, was an Irish bar owned and operated by Tom Wallace, a lugubrious gent who rarely left his rooms above until the late night patrons arrived. Ever proud of both his American connections and his Gaelic heritage, Wallace had decorated his establishment with photos of famous pugilists and

had created a veritable shrine to one-time Tam-many boss Dick Croker: Centered on the bar mirror was the politician's photo, ensconced by a pair of sturdy shillelaghs. The barroom itself was little dif-ferent from many other run-down bars in the run-down neighborhood around Washington Square: dark and dingy, smelling of stale beer and tobacco, the long bar across the back wall, assorted benches, tables, and chairs in the center. The main entrance was angled across the corner of Sixth and West Fourth; on West Fourth Street was the door to the back room, or "family entrance" (also accessible through the main bar), through which the amateur "tarts" and professional hookers had to arrive. This second room was made distinct by a large glass

The Hell Hole, 1917 *(Courtesy of the Smithsonian American Art Museum)*

case containing a stuffed white swan on a bed of gilded lily pads. The swan, like most of the habitués of "the Hell Hole" (as all the regulars called the saloon), had seen better days: It was moth-eaten and gray, and seemed not so much to float upon its lily bed as to lie recumbent, a tawdry taxidermic parody of the reclining painted odalisques so often seen in saloons of the day.

The back room of the Hell Hole has been preserved in an etching by Charles Demuth (O'Neill, who spent much of his time writing poetry at the Golden Swan, appears in the upper right corner) and in a watercolor by John Sloan. Both of these artists were regular customers, as were most of the Village's painters, writers, actors, anarchists, revolutionaries, and assorted nonconformists in the 1910s when O'Neill became a familiar figure in the taproom. The exterior of the building has also been captured, by photographer Robert L. Bracklow: Plate glass windows flank the main entrance of the three-story, partially plastered building. Above is a pub sign—a life-sized swan, in fairly good condition in the ca. 1900 photograph, but by the time O'Neill became a regular, weatherbeaten and decrepit.

The Sixth Avenue El careened alongside then away from the building toward Washington Square every few minutes, making conversation in the Hell Hole a vigorous vocal exercise. Mary Heaton Vorse, owner of the original warehouse and wharf where the Provincetowners first produced their plays and sometime patron of the bar, tried to explain the Hell Hole's activity: She recalled Tom Wallace and his "aged cronies" imbibing enough drink to become ill-tempered and quarrelsome, then "staggering off to bed. . . . with a knowledge that a pick-me-up was under [the] pillow." She saw the establishment's atmosphere as "at once alive and deadly. . . . [t]ruly . . . a hell hole and that was the fascination for O'Neill as well as the rest of us" (quoted in Gelb and Gelb 504 and elsewhere).

Among the fascinating elements of the Hell Hole for O'Neill was the gang of IRISH miscreants who called themselves the Hudson Dusters. Formerly the terror of the Village, by 1915 the remaining Dusters were drinkers, brawlers, truck drivers, and hijackers, or, if a Tammany Hall boss required it, dumpers of ballot boxes into the East River.

O'Neill treated the Dusters with enough respect not to put on the vernacular of the times with them; instead, he always spoke in the grammatical manner he'd been brought up to. In return, the Dusters respected O'Neill, and attended his plays with genuine interest. The Hell Hole was only one of several dives and flophouses that would fascinate Eugene O'Neill enough for him to render immortal in his plays. It was several steps above in gentility from the debased waterfront grogshop known as JIMMY THE PRIESTS, which Gene had quit in 1912, but several steps below the Garden Hotel (which, nevertheless, was disreputable in its own way, catering to ward heelers, boxing promoters, and circus folk) where O'Neill would later drink and sometimes sleep. It is the Hell Hole, however, that most strongly resembles Harry Hope's "No Chance Saloon" in *The* ICEMAN COMETH, and at the Hell Hole O'Neill met the majority of characters who, almost a quarter of a century later, would become the pathetic cast of pipe dreamers in one of his most celebrated dramas.

Louis Holladay, O'Neill's friend from his late teens when he began to explore the Village on his own, first brought him to the Hell Hole in the fall of 1915. At this point Gene had written a number of plays, al least two under the tutelage of GEORGE PIERCE BAKER in his famous "English 47" workshop at Harvard, but had not yet become involved with Provincetown. He was to make his first trip to Cape Cod in June 1916, and to join in the founding of the Players the following fall. In 1915–16, however, O'Neill was drinking heavily, and had no trouble immersing himself in the low life of Greenwich Village, which had been a bohemian haven for about 15 years, but which was still more impoverished than posh—the cheap, run-down rentals being sufficient for the impecunious artists who lived there. Holladay and his sister Polly were second-generation bohemians; their mother had left Evanston, Illinois, years earlier to become part of the early Village scene.

Through Louis and Polly, O'Neill met other Hell Hole regulars. Polly's lover, HIPPOLYTE HAVEL, an immigrant of inflammatory passions and flamboyant demeanor, would transmogrify into Hugo Kalmar, the "one-time editor of anarchist periodicals" who intermittently comes up for air at Harry Hope's to rage at capitalism and quote revolutionary poetry. Another friend of the Holladays, TERRY CARLIN, was in his early 60s when O'Neill met him at the Hell Hole: a true idealist and radical, he actually aspired to a personal life free of government. Not only did he preach a relatively odd admixture of Nietzcheism and Bakuninism, but he also did not work, lived in slums, slept in abandoned apartments, and survived on free lunches. He used this survival technique when he helped O'Neill through his period of drunken down-and-outness in the winter of 1915–16, and O'Neill never forgot his beneficence. By the time he and O'Neill had become friends, however, Carlin, while still charismatic and serene, was disillusioned about the possibilities of subverting the coercive state and had embraced a form of placid nihilism. He is the model for Larry Slade, the Last Chance Saloon's world-weary "old foolosopher" whose final philosophy is that "[A]ll things are the same meaningless joke . . . [grinning] from the one skull of death" (*Iceman* 636–637).

With the reclusive Hell Hole proprietor Tom Wallace as the self-cloistered Harry Hope, bartenders John Bull and Lefty Louie as Chuck Morello and Rocky Pioggi, respectively, and an African-American gambler named Joe Smith as Joe Mott, the "chorus of regulars" at Harry Hope's is almost complete. JAMES FINDLATER BYTH who is Jimmy Tomorrow, was a friend of O'Neill's from his earlier waterfront days, and had died a suicide before O'Neill began frequenting the Hell Hole; O'Neill's brother Jamie appears to be the model for Hickey, the seller of both dreams and nightmares, and O'Neill himself appears in the personas of the young mother obsessed traitor Don Parrit (who was also based on Donald Vose) and as the juvenile Harvard alumnus Willie Oban.

The real-life regulars at the Hell Hole also appear in plays other than *Iceman*. Havel is a minor figure in *The PERSONAL EQUATION*, and Joe Smith (whom O'Neill also credited with lifesaving aid during the winter of 1915–16) evolves partially into Jim Harris in ALL GOD'S CHILLUN GOT WINGS, primarily because Smith, like Harris, had a white wife. In addition, a story Smith told O'Neill seems to

have inspired another of O'Neill's "race" plays, *The DREAMY KID*.

Aside from those who appear in *The Iceman Cometh*, several of O'Neill's other friends from the Hell Hole and vicinity found their way into the plays: Christine Ell, a friend of Polly and former cook for Louis Holladay in his short-lived cellar café called "The Sixty," was a large, big-bosomed woman, beautiful in her own way but unaware of her appeal. Red-haired and green-eyed, she had been the subject of paintings by Charles Demuth and others; O'Neill would draw her portrait as big-hearted Josie Hogan in A MOON FOR THE MISBEGOTTEN and use her Earth-mother aura when he imagined the prostitute Cybele in *The GREAT GOD BROWN*. Christine's personal history of abuse also devolves into Anna Christie's background.

The Josie Hogan character was also claimed by another of O'Neill's hard-drinking pals (and a brief romantic interest), DOROTHY DAY. She believed she was a model for Josie because of her motherly concern for Gene, and pointed particularly to the scene in which Josie cradles the exhausted Jim Tyrone in her arms, forming the visual image of Mary holding the dead Christ (Black 205). Whether Day provided this iconic moment or not, she played a significant role in O'Neill's life at a crucial time. The radical 19-year-old journalist, and the inebriate budding playwright became table partners at the Hell Hole, and for a time were together constantly. O'Neill even stayed at Dorothy's apartment for several weeks, although it is fairly certain they did not have a sexual relationship. Religion (or spirituality) seems to have been a conduit for their mutual affection: Dorothy was drawn to the Catholic Church and would complete her conversion in the 1920s; O'Neill, although he'd stopped attending mass in his early teens (to the great ire of his father) would be called back to CATHOLICISM throughout his life by a combination of devotion, nostalgia, and guilt. The story of O'Neill's drunken recitations at the Hell Hole of Francis Thompson's poem about God's pursuit of the former believer, "The Hound of Heaven," with Dorothy as his rapt audience, is told by many of O'Neill's BIOGRAPHERS. Dorothy, however, would separate herself from the Hell Hole crowd as she became more religious;

in later life she would become a cofounder of the Catholic Worker Movement.

The Hell Hole was conveniently just one block over and east of the MacDougal Street location where the Provincetown Players staged O'Neill's BOUND EAST FOR CARDIFF and BEFORE BREAKFAST in the fall of 1916, so O'Neill continued his patronage, inviting along his new friends from Cape Cod who had mounted the first of his plays on Mary Heaton Vorse's WHARF THEATRE earlier that summer. Accompanying O'Neill in revelry were writers GEORGE "JIG" CRAM COOK and his wife SUSAN GLASPELL, who would remain the backbone of the Provincetown Players for years, the radical journalist JOHN REED and his lover LOUISE BRYANT, writer and sometime actress in O'Neill one-acts; and Hutchins Hapgood, another radical writer, and his wife Neith Boyce, both of whom would include O'Neill in memoirs. Joining the Provincetowners occasionally would be EMMA GOLDMAN, the fiery anarchist theoretician and journalist who had been admired by O'Neill since he was a teenager. Goldman's denunciation in. her journal *Mother Earth* of traitor-to-the-cause Donald Vose would form the backstory O'Neill would use for *Iceman's* Don Parritt, although O'Neill never personally knew Donald Vose.

A complication in the relationships O'Neill had formed was his own love affair with Louise Bryant; he had begun intimacies with her in the summer of 1916 and continued the affair after she married John Reed that November. "Free love" was, of course, the mantra for the unorthodox Greenwich Villagers, and Bryant had managed to convince O'Neill that Reed both knew about and approved of their relationship (see Barbara Gelb, *So Short a Time,* 1973). O'Neill, however, who although deeply infatuated with Bryant had come to be good friends with Reed, was wrought with guilt, and after Reed and Bryant left for Russia in 1917, O'Neill fell back into the bottle and drowned himself in longing for Bryant. This is perhaps why he clung so furiously to Dorothy Day that fall. But both Bryant and Day began to fade in Gene's mind when, drinking alone at the Hell Hole in late November, he encountered Agnes Boulton—24-year-old pulp-fiction writer—who, in the dark and from Eugene's boozy

perspective seemed to be a physical incarnation of Louise Bryant. Boulton was waiting for Christine Ell, who immediately and effusively introduced the two. Later JAMES "JAMIE" O'NEILL, JR. arrived and the four made an evening of it. When Boulton and O'Neill were finally alone, as Boulton remembered it, he declared his desire to spend every night with her for the rest of his life. There followed a brief and characteristically tempestuous courtship, and the two married the following April.

The year 1917 had been a good one for O'Neill professionally. The Provincetown Players had staged FOG in January. He had written IN THE ZONE, ILE, The LONG VOYAGE HOME, and MOON OF THE CARRIBEES that winter. His short story "TOMORROW" was published in *Seven Arts* magazine in June, and *The Long Voyage Home* appeared in *The Smart Set* in October. The WASHINGTON SQUARE PLAYERS had produced *In the Zone,* and Provincetown had produced *The Long Voyage Home* and *Ile* by November. Thus it was both a blessing and a curse for Boulton that she married O'Neill in 1918. The playwright was now becoming important, if not yet famous, while Boulton was making her living writing short stories and novelettes for romance magazines. Domestic life of the kind Agnes envisioned would never suit O'Neill as a writer at work; and although they were deeply in love for nearly all of the 10 years of their marriage, the strain was too much for O'Neill by the time he met Carlotta Monterey in 1926.

The marriage, Agnes's pregnancy, and Prohibition combined to estrange O'Neill from the Hell Hole in ensuing months, although he returned occasionally to catch up with his old friends the Hudson Dusters and especially Terry Carlin. But the death of Louis Holladay in January 1918 was probably the chief cause for O'Neill's withdrawal. In the early hours of January 23, Holladay, O'Neill, Day, Ell, Carlin, and Charles Demuth (O'Neill's wife had been around earlier but had returned home) ended up at Romany Marie's, another favorite haunt, and Holladay presented the group with a vial of heroine. Although the drug had the ordinary effect on others who took it, Holladay, who had a weak heart, slumped over on Dorothy Day's shoulder almost immediately after ingesting the powder, dead. "Within seconds," Louis Sheaffer explains in his biography of O'Neill, "the only ones in the place were Dorothy, Romany Marie and the dead man" (410). For a time O'Neill's response to the death of his good friend was to drink himself into a stupor at the Hell Hole, but. by April he'd seemed to come around, although Agnes believed them both still to be uncentered by the tragedy. At any rate, he and Agnes were married at Cape Cod, and by fall the couple had removed to the domestic realm of West Point Pleasant, New Jersey, and O'Neill had resumed writing.

Thereafter, O'Neill's marriage, his work, and his growing fame put him in a remission of sorts from ALCOHOLISM. He made one visit to the Hell Hole in November 1919, after his son SHANE RUDRAIGHE O'NEILL had been born, to find patrons toasting Prohibition with 20-cent sherry. O'Neill bought an expensive bottle of bootlegged whiskey, and in the company of Joe Smith, Lefty Louie, and others, celebrated his fatherhood. This was the first time he'd realized that "My Yosephine," the song he'd picked up at the Hell Hole and had given to Chris Christopherson to sing in "ANNA CHRISTIE," was claimed by Lefty Louie as his original composition. He later wrote to Agnes, "I think all the hours seemingly wasted at the HH would be justified if they had resulted in only this" (*Selected Letters* 100). That so much more came out of those hours at the Golden Swan is the fortune of O'Neill enthusiasts everywhere. The exquisite take on human nature that O'Neill developed as he observed and befriended the Hell Hole regulars informs his best plays, from *Anna Christie* to *The Iceman Cometh*, and the gaudy and vibrant bunch he encountered there both transfigured his dramas and enriched his life.

The Golden Swan continued as a Village venue until 1928, when it was targeted to make way for the Sixth Avenue subway, and in 1930 the *New York World* lamented, "Eugene O'Neill's Pet Saloon Is Gone." The New York Department of Parks and Recreation set up a playground on the Hell Hole site in 1935. By the 1980s the parcel was being used as a recycling center, and remained so until wholesale recycling was begun in the city in 1989, after which the half-acre space became a mere open area of weeds and concrete. In 1999, as part of the city's beautification project, the grounds were transformed into the lush little park it is today. In continuing tribute to O'Neill and to the real and fictive denizens of the Hell Hole / Harry Hope's, 21st-century devotees of O'Neill and his dramas continue to make the Golden Swan Park a regular stop on their literary pilgrimages.

Bibliography

Black, Stephen A. *Eugene O'Neill: Beyond Mourning and Tragedy*. New Haven, Conn., and London: Yale University Press, 1999.

Gelb, Arthur and Barbara Gelb. *O'Neill: Life with Monte Cristo*. New York: Applause Books, 2000.

O'Neill, Eugene. The Iceman Cometh. In *Collected Plays of Eugene O'Neill, 1932–1943*. Edited by Travis Bogard. New York: Library of America, 1988.

———. *Selected Letters of Eugene O'Neill*. Edited by Travis Bogard and Jackson Bryer. New Haven, Conn., and London: Yale University Press, 1988.

Scheaffer, Louis. *O'Neill Son and Playwright*. Boston: Little, Brown, 1968.

Further Reading

Diggins, John Patrick. *Eugene O'Neill's America: Desire under Democracy*. Chicago and London: University of Chicago Press, 2007.

Gelb, Barbara. *So Short a Time: A Biography of John Reed and Louise Bryant*. New York: W. W. Norton, 1973.

Cynthia McCowan

homosexuality Depictions of sexuality in any form on American stages have been fraught with controversy since the early 19th century, challenging playwrights, actors, producers, directors, and censors, as well as audiences. When Eugene O'Neill commenced work as a playwright, AMERICAN THEATER had not yet embraced modernist concepts inherent in the social- problem plays of HENRIK IBSEN and GEORGE BERNARD SHAW. In the mid-19th century, sexuality was almost entirely focused on revelation of the female physique or romanticized depictions of love, but the focus shifted as the century ended. O'Neill's challenging dramas—inspired by modernist innovations, classical GREEK

TRAGEDY, and the contemporary European plays of AUGUST STRINDBERG, Frank Wedekind, and the expressionist movement—brought concepts of modernism to Broadway, including the introduction of previously taboo topics.

Prior to World War I, a few American playwrights, including Edward Sheldon (to whom O'Neill once addressed an admiring letter), addressed sexuality. After the war, depictions of infidelity and immorality, out-of-wedlock pregnancies, and a somewhat more open awareness of sexuality in general appeared, although open homosexuality continued to be too controversial. Gay characters did occasionally appear, masked as sexually ambivalent bachelors and spinsters and in stereotypical portraits of "sissies." Played for comedy, such characters provided the only overt gay presence on American stages in that era. O'Neill's personal attitudes seem to reflect those of the mainstream in his time. A clue is present in an O'Neill letter to Benjamin De Casseres in which he writes, "Your article on the sissification of the stage handed me a large and satisfactory chuckle. I'll bet you'll have a large section of infuriated fairies crawling your frame for that one. Also the ladies are not due to be thrilled with joy" (O'Neill 1994, 317). Despite this, O'Neill continued to challenge moral boundaries, introducing incestuous themes in his classically inspired dramas DESIRE UNDER THE ELMS (1924) and MOURNING BECOMES ELECTRA (1931); and interracial marriage in ALL GOD'S CHILLUN GOT WINGS (1924).

In the PULITZER PRIZE–winning STRANGE INTERLUDE (1928), O'Neill rendered the only characterization that could be perceived unequivocally as gay in any of his plays—novelist Charles Marsden. Originally conceived as bisexual (according to O'Neill's initial notes for the play), the character emerged as a fully dimensional closeted gay man apparently based on two gay artists with whom the playwright was friends, Charles Demuth and Marsden Hartley.

O'Neill's Charles Marsden nonetheless reinforces some common stereotypes found in literature and life. His manner and mannerisms are feminine, and his dress and appearance are meticulous at all times to the point of dandyism. He is tied to a domineer-

ing mother and considered sexually unthreatening by the play's female protagonist, Nina Leeds. She and her lover, the virile Ned Darrell, regard Charles with the common responses of the homophobic heterosexual toward a gay person: at best, politely condescending, and at worst, cruelly insulting.

Nothing in O'Neill's depiction of Charles Marsden suggests any form of deviance from sexual norms of the period, however, though the drama's general atmosphere of amorality flouts all conventional notions. Charles confesses himself celibate (with the exception of one encounter with a prostitute in his youth), and he is asexually drawn to Nina. For her part, she considers Charles the perfect companion for middle age, a time when sexual desire diminishes. Charles is both attracted and repelled by Ned's aggressive masculinity, but never explicitly.

Like his contemporaries, O'Neill was well aware that inclusion of actively homosexual characters was impossible, and implied homosexuality needed to be carefully crafted within the constraints of the prevailing values (and cultural stereotypes) of the time. In its 1984–85 London and Broadway revival, critics pointed to the "camp appeal" of *Strange Interlude,* although it is doubtful that O'Neill—who took his work very seriously—intended it.

Although no overtly homosexual character appear in O'Neill's other plays, he explored the nature of masculinity and close relationships between men from his earliest plays to his last. The bonds established between the sailors of the four SS GLENCAIRN plays (1914–17) are stronger and deeper than they can articulate. The masochistic friendship between rival architects William Brown and Dion Anthony in *The GREAT GOD BROWN* (1926) depicts love at its most violent and jealously possessive, while the touching friendship between Erie Smith and the deceased desk clerk in HUGHIE (1939) suggests a curious, almost romantic courtship.

O'Neill's plays feature complex psychological characterizations of men in often solitary battles with the forces of fate or with each other in familial or social circumstances. The late plays focus on men and occasionally women in internalized conflicts with inner demons, and in relationships linking them as fellow sufferers in the absurd struggles of existence. Such characterizations lend themselves to a variety of interpretations, including gay-friendly readings. The Broadway revival in 2000 of A MOON FOR THE MISBEGOTTEN. (1943) presented a daring but effective reimagining of the character Josie Hogan as a closeted lesbian. How much (if any) of this sort of interpretation would have been intended or even approved by the playwright is impossible to know.

O'Neill's plays frequently challenged societal norms. However, more frank and direct explorations of homosexuality in American drama would begin with the works of TENNESSEE WILLIAMS in the late 1940s.

Bibliography

Alexander, Doris. *Eugene O'Neill's Last Plays: Separating Art from Autobiography.* Athens: University of Georgia Press, 2005.

———. "*Strange Interlude* and Schopenhauer." *American Literature* 25, no. 2 (May 1953): 213–228.

Black, Stephen: *Beyond Mourning and Tragedy.* New Haven, Conn.: Yale University Press, 1999.

Bogard, Travis. *Contour in Time.* Rev. ed. New York: Oxford University Press, 1988.

———. "The Wimp in the Shower." In *From the Silence of Tao House: Essays about Eugene and Carlotta O'Neill and the Tao House Plays.* Danville, Calif.: O'Neill Foundation, 1993, 163–170.

Dubost, Thierry. *Struggle, Defeat or Rebirth: Eugene O'Neill's Vision of Humanity.* Jefferson, N.C.: McFarland, 1997.

Floyd, Virginia. *The Plays of Eugene O'Neill: A New Assessment.* New York: Ungar, 1985.

Fone, Byrne R. S. *A Road to Stonewall: Male Homosexuality and Homophobia in English and American Literature, 1750–1969.* New York: Twayne, 1995.

Gelb, Arthur, and Barbara Gelb. *O'Neill: Life with Monte Cristo.* New York: Applause Books, 2000.

Gross, Robert F. "O'Neill's Queer Interlude: Epicene Excess and Camp Pleasures." *Journal of Dramatic Theory and Criticism* 12, no. 1 (Fall 1997): 3–22.

Lichtenberg, Joseph D., and Charlotte Lichtenberg. "Eugene O'Neill and Falling in Love." *Psychoanalytic Quarterly* 41 (1972): 63–89.

O'Neill, Eugene. *Eugene O'Neill at Work: Unpublished Work Diaries.* Edited by Virginia Floyd. New York: Ungar, 1991.

———. *Selected Letters of Eugene O'Neill.* Edited by Travis Bogard and Jackson R. Bryer. New York: Limelight Editions, 1994.

Sheaffer, Louis. *O'Neill: Son and Artist.* Boston: Little, Brown, 1973.

———. *O'Neill: Son and Playwright.* Boston: Little, Brown, 1968.

Simonson, Lee. *The Stage Is Set.* New York: Harcourt, Brace, Jovanovich, 1932.

Sinfield, Alan. *Out on Stage. Lesbian and Gay Theatre in the Twentieth Century.* New Haven, Conn.: Yale University Press, 1999.

James Fisher and Richard Compson Sater

I

Ibsen, Henrik (1828–1906) Henrik Ibsen, playwright and poet, was born in 1828 in Skien, Norway, and died in Kristiania (Oslo) in 1906. He wrote 26 plays and approximately 300 poems. Ibsen spent much of his professional career living outside Norway (1864–1891), in Italy and Germany. Though his oeuvre includes such important verse drama as *Peer Gynt* (1867) and symbolist plays such as *John Gabriel Borkman* (1896), he is especially identified with his realistic plays, including *The Pillars of Society* (1877), *A Dollhouse* (1879), *Ghosts* (1881), and *An Enemy of the People* (1882), in which he developed his signature approach of revealing the past's molding of the present. Versions of this approach may be detected in the work of many subsequent playwrights, including GEORGE BERNARD SHAW, O'Neill, and Arthur Miller.

The first play Eugene O'Neill saw on stage by the Norwegian playwright Henrik Ibsen was *Hedda Gabler* in 1907. He saw it at the Bijou Theatre in New York, where it starred Alla Nazimova, who was later to play Christine Mannon in MOURNING BECOMES ELECTRA. He went back to see the production 10 successive times because, "That experience discovered an entire new world of the drama for me. It gave me my first conception of a modern theatre where truth might live" (O'Neill 1994, 477).

The year previous to this experience, during his final semester at Betts Academy (Gelb 214), O'Neill had become obsessed by GEORGE BERNARD SHAW's book *The Quintessence of Ibsenism* (1890),

in which Shaw described Ibsen as the vanguard of a new radicalism in drama, a radicalism that could undermine conformist, pious bourgeois existence and unmask its life-lies.

In his play from 1916 NOW I ASK YOU, O'Neill explicitly uses references to *Hedda Gabler*, for example, in this conversation between Mrs. Ashleigh and her daughter, Lucy:

> LUCY—. . . But, Mother, it doesn't make any difference where I am, the conditions feel the same. I feel—cramped in. (*with an affected yawn, throwing herself into a chair*) And I'm mortally bored.
>
> MRS. ASHLEY—(*with a sigh*) Ever since you saw that play the other night you've done nothing but talk and act Hedda Gabler; so I suppose its no use trying to argue with her.
>
> LUCY—(*irritated at having her pose seen through*) I'm not talking Hedda Gabler. I'm simply telling you how I feel. (*somberly*) Though I confess there are times when General Gabler's pistols have their fascination.
>
> MRS. ASHLEY—(*with a smile*) Tut-tut, Lucy. You're too morbid today. You'll be longing next for someone to come "with vine leaves in his hair." (1:427)

Virginia Floyd has pointed out the similarities between Hickey in The ICEMAN COMETH and Gregers Werle in Ibsen's *The Wild Duck*. Both are "guilt-ridden destroyers" of other people's dreams, and both are responsible for the death of an innocent woman (518–519). In addition, both plays concern a conflict between the real and the ideal and the costs of losing the illusions Ibsen termed "life-lies."

Ibsen's influence on O'Neill may also be detected in "ANNA CHRISTIE." First, like Ellida Wangel in *Lady from the Sea,* who is called a mermaid by the townspeople, Anna, too, is likened to a mermaid by Mat Burke, and, indeed, the two women face similar problems: the desire to free themselves from imprisoning roles and to find a new identity. Second, the social problem at the heart of the play, the choices facing a poor farm woman, is progressively revealed to be located in past abuse as the play moves forward. The same may be said of the Tyrone family in LONG DAY'S JOURNEY INTO NIGHT, where James's background in immigrant poverty and his current status as an actor who "sold out" are progressively revealed to have had devastating and debilitating effects on his wife and children and, indeed, on himself.

An example of O'Neill recycling a gesture from Ibsen is Robert's last line in BEYOND THE HORIZON where he points to the sun, a reflection from the ending of *Ghosts.*

Travis Bogard has pointed out the similarities in plot between *Peer Gynt* and *The EMPEROR JONES:* "Both plays are about fugitives, running in desperation through the shards of their lives toward a dimly seen salvation whose discovery depends on their learning their essential identities."

The most profound influence Ibsen had on O'Neill probably came to him through GEORGE PIERCE BAKER, when he took Baker's English 47 playwriting class at Harvard University in 1914–15. This influence was not a matter of style or subject but concerned the writing process itself. In his book *Dramatic Technique* (1919), based on his classroom notes, Baker puts a great deal of emphasis on the playwright writing a scenario of the action of the play prior to developing its dialogue. To illustrate the usefulness of this approach, Barker quotes long sections from Ibsen's notebooks and letters. O'Neill cultivated this writing process to suit his own purposes and used it for most of his plays, barring those that

came to him in a flash of inspiration. Hence, O'Neill left behind detailed notebooks that have allowed scholars to come to at least some small understanding of his creative process (see WORK DIARY). As a late tribute, perhaps, the small bookcase in the Tyrones' summer home in LONG DAY'S JOURNEY INTO NIGHT contains "plays by Ibsen" (3:717).

Bibliography

Baker, George Pierce. *Dramatic Technique.* Boston: Houghton Mifflin, 1919.

Bogard, Travis. *Contour in Time.* New York: Oxford University Press, 1972. Available online. URL: http://www.eoneill.com/library/contour/amateursend/jones.htm.

Floyd, Virginia. *The Plays of Eugene O'Neill: A New Assessment.* New York: Frederick Ungar, 1985.

Gelb, Arthur, and Barbara Gelb. *O'Neill: Life with Monte Cristo.* New York: Applause Books, 2002.

O'Neill, Eugene. *Selected Letters of Eugene O'Neill.* Edited by Travis Bogard and Jackson R. Bryer. New York: Limelight Editions, 1994.

P. K. Brask

Ikala, **SS**   At the age of 22, while in BUENOS AIRES, ARGENTINA, Eugene O'Neill signed on the SS *Ikala,* a British tramp freighter bound for New York City. Freighters of this type had no specific route, and their itineraries were dictated by the destinations of the cargoes they secured. The vessel departed Buenos Aires on March 21, 1911, and arrived in New York on April 15. In route to New York the vessel stopped at Port of Spain, Trinidad, to take on ballast and coconuts. The vessel had to anchor off shore because the harbor was too shallow to accommodate it.

The *Ikala* was the first vessel O'Neill signed on as a member of the crew; he had the rank of an ordinary seaman. His rate of pay was far below the norm for an ordinary seaman of the time, from which it can be inferred that he did not have much experience as a sailor and that he was looking for an inexpensive way of returning to New York. The *Ikala* was not licensed to carry passengers, but it was not uncommon for vessels of this type to take on inexperienced men who were interested in the transportation from one place to the next. While

SS *Ikala* *(Courtesy of the Peabody Essex Museum)*

onboard, the men contributed to the workings of the ship. The work onboard a steamer, like the *Ikala*, was very different from that on a square-rigged sailing vessel like the CHARLES RACINE. Since the *Ikala* was a steamer, it was the stokers who were responsible for feeding the boilers to generate the steam power, which propelled the vessel; the seamen were relegated to the menial tasks of chipping rust and repainting the ship. In any event, O'Neill was living and learning the life of a seaman—living in the crew's quarters or forecastle, eating sailors' food, and trading stories with the other men.

O'Neill's experience aboard the *Ikala* added to his knowledge of the maritime world, which he used for numerous plays. The *Ikala* and its crew served as inspiration for the SS GLENCAIRN and its crew in BOUND EAST FOR CARDIFF, The LONG VOYAGE HOME, The MOON OF THE CARIBBEES, and IN THE ZONE.

Bibliography

Bisset, Sir James, with P. R. Stephensen. *Tramps and Ladies*. New York: Criterion Books 1959.

Richter, Robert A. *Eugene O'Neill and Dat Ole Davil Sea: Maritime Influences in the Life and Works of Eugene O'Neill*. Mystic, Conn.: Mystic Seaport, 2004.

Sheaffer, Louis. *O'Neill, Son and Playwright*. Boston: Little, Brown, 1968.

Robert A. Richter

Industrial Workers of the World (IWW, "Wobblies") The Industrial Workers of the World (IWW) is an international labor union founded in 1905 that censures class disparity, strives to unite workers within a single union, and aims to abolish capitalism and the wage system. The IWW flourished in the first two decades of the 20th century, and many of Eugene O'Neill's plays incorporate its ideals to varying degrees, although the playwright himself was skeptical about the organization's ability to render any real social change.

Two plays that most explicitly portray IWW principles are The HAIRY APE and The ICEMAN COMETH. *The Hairy Ape* literally illustrates the

CLASS divide, with the wealthy travelers on the upper deck of a transatlantic liner and the stokers in the cramped, grimy quarters below. The central character, Yank, most clearly delineates the IWW manifesto, especially after he has seen the white-gowned Mildred descend to the stokehold from above. He learns of the IWW in prison when a fellow inmate quotes a rabidly conservative senator who has denounced the IWW as a great national menace, a "devil's brew of rascals, jailbirds, murderers and cutthroats" and a "foul ulcer" on democracy. Ironically, after being released from prison, Yank attempts to join the IWW but is rejected under suspicion of being a spy. The character of Long also serves as a mouthpiece for the IWW, as, for example, when he says, "We wasn't born this rotten way. All men is born free and ekal. . . . [The upper class] dragged us down 'til we're on'y wage slaves in the bowels of a bloody ship, . . . Hit's them's ter blame—and damned Capitalist clarss!" (1:125).

In *The Iceman Cometh*, O'Neill makes few specific references to the IWW, but its activities are thinly veiled as something called the Movement, and many characters are ex-anarchists who have dismissed the Movement's manifesto. The most prominent, 60-year-old Larry Slade, dropped out after 30 years with the Movement because of greedy comrades and "the breed of swine called men in general" (3:580). Hugo Kalmar, a former editor for anarchist publications, spent 10 years in prison for his activities, including solitary confinement that ruined his eyesight. Finally, Don Parritt, an awkward 18-year-old whose mother Rosa has been arrested for orchestrating a bombing, has lost interest in the Movement, a shift in attitude that caused an angry parting with her. Don also tells Larry—who had once been Rosa's lover—that he decried an organization implanted with traitors. But in the end, Don confesses to being the spy who exposed his mother because he hated her. Imprisonment, he says, will "give her the chance to play the great incorruptible Mother of the Revolution, whose only child is the Proletariat. . . . She'll be able to say . . . 'Long live the Revolution!'" (3:704).

In *The Iceman Cometh*, disenchantment with the Movement parallels the pathetic pipe dreams of the saloon residents. As Larry says, "The tomorrow movement is a sad and beautiful thing, too!" (3:592).

O'Neill is also believed to have written two one-act comedies titled *The G.A.N.* (or *G.A.M.*, now lost) whose subjects were the IWW. While the IWW still exists, its membership and influence are significantly reduced from its heyday.

Bibliography

Alexander, Doris M., "Eugene O'Neill as Social Critic." *American Quarterly* 6, no. 4 (Winter 1954): 349–363.

Dugan, Lawrence. "O'Neill and the Wobblies: The IWW as a Model for Failure in *The Iceman Cometh*." *Comparative Drama* (Spring–Summer 2002): 109–125.

Karen Charmaine Blansfield

Irish/Irish Americans   *LONG DAY'S JOURNEY INTO NIGHT,* Eugene O'Neill's theatrical autobiography, is undoubtedly his most frequently performed play on American stages. Due to its autobiographical relevance, spectators often equate the Irish origins of the characters to a general decorum, failing to perceive how seriously O'Neill addressed the issue of Irish oppression in the play. The sparse echoes of Irish culture one finds in most of O'Neill's 50 published plays could also account for such an oversight. However, the ethnic discrimination Irish immigrants endured—together with various forms of social oppression O'Neill mentioned, which are almost comparable to a curse—was a serious matter for the playwright. In his social critique of the world around him, he posed basic questions regarding society as a whole, which included the painful integration of the Irish in a world that rejected them because of their ethnic origins. It follows that O'Neill's depiction of the living conditions of Irish people in the United States raises major social and existential issues. His outlook on this problem—because it corresponded to an essential feature of his life—proves very helpful for a general interpretation of some of his dramatic works. O'Neill linked social criticism to his philosophical meditations in an attempt to cure the wounds that resulted from a hurtful and continued discrimination against the Irish in America and Europe.

As an artist, O'Neill was wary of social criticism and, at one stage of his life, even admitted a complete change in his political attitude: "Time was when I was an active socialist, after that, a philosophical anarchist. But today, I can't feel that anything like that really matters" (quoted in Cargill et al. 107). Yet keeping at a distance from politics did not mean that he became indifferent to the lot of other people, especially those of Irish origins.

O'Neill's interest in the Irish is easily explained. Unlike some immigrants who hoped to start anew and create a different identity for themselves in the New World, his parents never rejected the culture of their forebears. Consequently, when Eugene became a "son and playwright," he retained in his mind some Irish history, both personal and communal. Edward Shaughnessy's accurate perception on this point deserves to be noted: "The playwright's roots are to be found in the poverty, sorrow and wrenching extirpations caused by the Great Famine of the late 1840s. JAMES O'NEILL and MARY ELLEN 'ELLA' O'NEILL, who were his parents, were products of that history whose significance was far greater than their own alone" (Shaughnessy 1988, 3). Comparable to the "several histories of Ireland" lining the bookcase mentioned in the opening stage direction of *Long Day's Journey into Night,* Ireland was part of his mental background. "With his father an emotional sounding board for the disturbances on the other side, Ireland was never far away throughout Eugene Gladstone O'Neill's formative years. 'One thing that explains more than anything about me,' he once said, 'is the fact that I'm Irish'" (Sheaffer 10). While he did not constantly put Ireland to the fore, his interest in the Irish did not wane as years went by, but his approach to the Irish question changed. A chronological study of O'Neill's vision of the Irish—and of their place in society—would show that he was more concerned about crude social issues at the beginning of his career than he was when he wrote his last plays.

Following the advice of Professor GEORGE PIERCE BAKER at Harvard University, O'Neill started from what he knew and depicted characters he considered his true countrymen. In his SEA plays, one finds Irish crew members who keep a specific Irish identity although—within the group—they are primarily defined as sailors. During the middle years of O'Neill's career, he granted less importance to this ethnic side because he may have found it difficult to link his realistic view of the Irish with the philosophical questions he was addressing.

In his first plays—The STRAW, for instance—O'Neill portrays Irish men or women in their daily struggle for survival. In his later works, not only in A TOUCH OF THE POET or MORE STATELY MANSIONS but also in A MOON FOR THE MISBEGOTTEN or even *Long Day's Journey into Night,* the issues were different. The change was due to an altered perspective. Financial hardship remained present—one cannot easily forget James Tyrone's poignant evocation of his poverty-stricken youth in *Long Day's Journey*—but if poverty reflected the characters' conflicts with society, their Irishness mainly posed the question of their general integration within the world, as is shown in *A Touch of the Poet.* Regarding that play, Travis Bogard rightly emphasizes that the connection was not merely ethnic, it also bore the influence of the visit of the Abbey Players: "A *Touch of the Poet* unexpectedly recalls the ABBEY THEATRE play O'Neill saw in 1911, *Birthright* by T. C. Murray. The Irish folk drama which provided him with the root situation for BEYOND THE HORIZON at the outset of his career and DESIRE UNDER THE ELMS at this mid-point served him yet one more time as he came to the end of his long life in the theatre" (395).

The Irishness of O'Neill's characters was deeply significant. One may even assume that his literary return to Ireland at the end of his career was due to no hazard, bearing in mind that the starting point of his career was linked to the work of the Irish Players. He may have wanted to be true to himself as a writer—to reacquaint himself with his origins—but this might not have been the sole motive for his choice. He may also have chosen to point an accusing finger at American society, while feeling that Irishness—being Irish in the United States especially—was both in its material and spiritual aspects representative of Man's daily combats with the world.

Such wide intellectual perspectives pose the question of the images he creates for his Irish characters. In *The HAIRY APE* or *The MOON OF THE*

CARIBBEES, for instance, O'Neill had to make his audience understand that they were faced with Irish characters living among sailors of other nationalities. The protagonists' Irish speech, their inadequate brogue, or cliché-like remarks about their physical traits found in STAGE DIRECTIONS—aimed at putting forward their Irish origins—may have partly resulted from specific dramatic restraints, but they had a deeper significance for the author. His requirements for A Moon for the Misbegotten (Fjelde 51) summarize his outlook on this matter. He wanted the actress to look Irish, or to be of Irish descent, so that she would spontaneously understand what was at stake in the play.

Today, one may have second thoughts about spontaneous understanding of a question because of a person's origins, or about physical and mental heredity. Still, these beliefs show that despite its faults, O'Neill's was no superficial illustration of what being Irish meant. Through various means, he was trying to illustrate what an Irish "soul" was. Therefore, he highlighted the ways in which people were identified as Irish. Through their speech modes, their brogue, their lilt, or even their physical appearance, he indicated they were classified as Irish. Consequently, they became social outcasts, as communities were willing to accept them only in terms of oppression. Proceeding in this manner—and one meets here with a paradox of art—through artificial portraits, O'Neill attempted to present spectators with what he felt was the truth of his characters' Irishness. Joel Pfister rightly underlines this aspect of his work: "O'Neill, influenced by Synge, Yeats, and Gregory (as well as by Ibsen, Strindberg, Shaw and Hauptmann), sought to redesign the figure of the nineteenth century American Irishman, popularized by playwrights like Dion Boucicault, John Brougham, James Pilgrim, William Macready, and Edward Harrigan (a stage Irishman undoubtedly well known to James O'Neill). It is the Irish tragic sense of determinism coupled with contemporary psychologists' pronouncements about familial determinism that partly sparks O'Neill's fascination with the 'can't help it' psychological resignation of the confessional Tyrones in Long Day's Journey" (Pfister 30).

Crossing the Atlantic in order to start a new life in the United States, Irish immigrants had hoped for significant changes in their living conditions. Unfortunately, their arrival in the New World proved less idyllic than expected. Exposing their illusions, O'Neill depicts the various hardships they endured in the United States. In the same way that, in MOURNING BECOMES ELECTRA, he showed how Lavinia was unable to start anew and had to accept that she was a Mannon, his Irish characters are the victims of a comparable fate and seem doomed to being poor or oppressed.

Despite the reservations one might have about O'Neill's views on ethnic identity, his pessimistic outlook on social perspectives seems true to life. What, in O'Neillian terms, could be defined as "the curse of the Irish," must be taken into account, since what he described reflected, at least partly, the social reality of the time. It does not correspond to a divine curse but is depicted in its material aspects—namely, social oppression.

> CREGAN—. . . To Ireland and the Irish and hell roast the soul of any damned Yank that wud kape thim down!
>
> SIMON—(*gravely*) Amen to that, Mr Cregan. And may they gain what they have longed for and fought for so long—liberty. (*More Stately Mansions* 3:297)

To a certain extent, O'Neill's particular position—he was American but defined himself as Irish—finds echoes in his works through the connections he established between Irish immigrants and their ancestors. Although the Irish only appear on American soil, memories stealthily invade characters' speeches and create a link between the two countries. Cregan drinks to the liberation of the Irish from American oppression, a grim reflection of their daily lives but also a sad remembrance of an Irish past. Simon Harford, who is American, sides with the Irish. He puts Cregan's remark in a wider historical perspective and includes the English in the list of oppressors.

Probably because of his own family history, O'Neill was partial to the Irish. His favorable outlook—perceptible in the plays—may also have sprung from his sympathy for a doomed people whom he perceived as forever oppressed. In this respect, Cregan and Simon's conversation illustrates the curse of the Irish: having got rid of the English, they have fallen prey to American harshness.

> TYRONE—My mother was left, a stranger in a strange land, with four small children, me and a sister a little older and two younger than me. My two older brothers had moved to other parts. They couldn't help. They were hard put to it to keep themselves alive. There was no damned romance in our poverty. Twice we were evicted from the miserable hovel we called home, with my mother's few sticks of furniture thrown out in the street, and my mother and sisters crying. I cried, too, though I tried hard not to, because I was the man of the family. At ten years old! There was no more school for me. I worked twelve hours a day in a machine shop, learning to make files. (*Long Day's Journey into Night*, 3:807)

Helplessness, oppression, and rejection: James Tyrone's youth in the United States leaves much to be desired. His remembrance is very moving as it corresponds to the sad story of many Irish immigrants. James does not darken his past living conditions, and his factual account, together with the short sentences he uses, add to the emotional impact of the scene. "Twice we were evicted": The mechanical, dehumanized aspect of the eviction is reinforced by the absence of any scapegoats. No contemptuous lawyers or greedy lodgers are accused, and the anonymity of the forces the Tyrone family had to face demonstrates of this latent idea of a cursed people, and of its battle against fate. In the circumstances, and this may account for the limited attention paid to social criticism by O'Neill's critics, oppression and rejection have the same impact on the characters as their fate, a common point already perceptible in some of O'Neill's early works.

Poverty had already surfaced in other plays. The question then is why (apart from the dramatist's growing skill) should we be so moved by James's account, and not by the destitution depicted in WARNINGS or *The Straw?* The answer may lie in the relationship between social oppression and fate. In the early plays, one sympathizes with the protagonists, but poverty is more exposed than felt, while James's memories find echoes in the spectators' minds. The eviction is, metaphorically, an inverted picture of immigration. The Irish family suddenly discovers the dark side of their American dream, and while they crave for integration, they are rejected. Then social oppression and the feeling of alienation, of not belonging, are no longer restricted to the eviction of the Tyrones but becomes an existential issue.

There is the rub—material or spiritual? Given the choice, many critics will study spiritual aspects rather than material circumstances and their links with ethnic issues, a choice that—if exclusive—might be the wrong one. The hypothesis being made here is that material and spiritual sides are *equally* important. Social tensions are more than a background in the plays, and the links between the two aspects give a wider meaning to O'Neill's works. To some extent, these two aspects correspond to Edward Shaughnessy's definitions of Irish-Americans:

> Essentially O'Neill presents two sorts of Irish-Americans. The first group, who accept the logic of the American dream, can be easily lampooned and stereotyped. Like other nineteenth-century immigrants, the Irish wished for success as defined in a brave new world. But O'Neill saw clearly that this surrender to mammon was certain to produce a sense of self-loathing. . . . The second and smaller group of Irish-Americans are O'Neill's "fog-people," a company of existential misfits who can never belong. (Shaughnessy 1998. 155)

James Tyrone's monologue about his childhood gives an epic dimension to his family's unfortunate American experience. Despite his future denial of Edmund's true knowledge of poverty, a link is established between the two generations, and the eviction becomes the focal point of a common Irish knowledge. His speech goes beyond the limits of his own time and contributes to connecting his past suffering with that of his son. Their ordeals are of a different nature, but they testify that social hardship keeps inflicting its bruises on the Irish. Whether one thinks of the main characters in *A Moon for the Misbegotten*, *The Straw*, or *A Touch of the Poet* or even of secondary characters in other plays (*The* ICEMAN COMETH, *The* LONG VOYAGE HOME, or *The Moon of the Caribbees*), all share common characteristics—poverty being one of them. The link between Irishness and poverty is so strong that in *More Stately Mansions*, Maloy believes that in becoming rich, Sara will eradicate her Irish identity. Far from weakening the idea of a permanent link with poverty, the famous actor James Tyrone brings a final proof to this idea in that even though he is rich, he never considers himself wealthy, as is shown by his miserliness regarding electricity.

The lack of money has direct consequences on the characters' daily lives, and not merely on their state of mind. O'Neill naturalistically depicted the result of financial straits in *The Straw*, where Eileen is sent to a sanatorium because she has tuberculosis. As for Edmund, one may guess that he caught his disease when he worked as a sailor on a tramp ship, or when he drifted away in the poor areas of BUENOS AIRES, ARGENTINA. *The Straw* and *Long Day's Journey into Night* concern different social classes, but male parental reaction to tuberculosis follows the same Irish pattern. In both plays, each father falls prey to the same frights—ending his days in the poorhouse—and is reluctant to pay for proper hospital treatment. Although coming from a very wealthy man, such a fear can hardly be understood in the case of James Tyrone. What matters is the trend—the knowledge that there will be no escaping the social curse of the Irish: being affected by poverty in some way. Consumption—which in Eileen's case will prove fatal—seems to be part of their Irishness. Jamie Tyrone asserts the need to fight tuberculosis, but his father's almost fatalistic acceptance of Edmund's disease indicates that despite his knowledge of modern treatment, he believes consumption to be one of the calamities that endlessly descend on the Irish. One needs to remember that consumption had already taken its toll through Mary's father, and the idea of an Irish curse gains in strength because, here again, it establishes an unbreakable link between past and present.

Can the curse of poverty be eluded? In *More Stately Mansions*, Sara could be seen as an exception, but her grand ownership is short-lived. She owns a huge house for a while but soon returns to her log cabin by the lake, where she and her family can be at one with the world again. Despite his rather important social position, James Tyrone is no exception to Irish geographical instability. The Tyrones spend most of their life in hotels, and Mary complains of James's inability to turn their house into a home.

Not being poor does not imply that one may belong to NEW LONDON society. James Tyrone—a famous actor—is excluded from the social network that Mary would like to join. The reasons for this exclusion are partly due to his Irishness and to the manner in which he puts forward his Irish identity. Through his behavior that shames his son—cutting hedges and wearing an old coat—he connects himself with other Irish citizens, unwittingly making a show of his poor origins.

> MARY—. . . Big frogs in a small puddle. It is stupid of Jamie. (*She pauses, looking out of the window—then with an undercurrent of lonely yearning.*) Still, the Chatfields and people like them stand for something. (3:738)

The reason for Mary Tyrone's loneliness, as Edmund justly points out, is not merely social discrimination against the Irish, and Mary is partly to blame for her solitude. Arthur and Barbara Gelb, however, give evidence that social discrimination against the Irish was no O'Neillian invention, as is shown by a New London resident named Edith Chappell Sheffield in her testimony to the biographers: "We considered the O'Neills shanty Irish," she said ruefully, "and we associated the Irish, almost automatically, with the servant class" (Gelb 95). Still, for James, trimming hedges may not be the best way of gaining access to higher social circles. Doing so, James breaks an unwritten communal law stating that landowners are not to do their own gardening. Oblivious to these rules, he keeps working while Jamie hides himself whenever important people drive by. Not that Jamie is socially blameless—his ALCOHOLISM, together with his regular presence at "Mamie's dump," also exclude him from New London Society. Cultural gaps appear between the WASPs (white Anglo-Saxon Protestants) and the Irish, and each member of the Tyrone household bears specific signs turning him or her into an unacceptable guest for other New London families. Ostracized and despised, the Irish are not wanted in some city circles but are accepted in other "zones," such as whorehouses for the young males, who pay little heed to religious precepts and meet their elders in bars or taverns. These repeated images of ostracized Irish people are close to a caricature in the plays. Still, beyond the cliché of whiskey-addicted people drinking their lives away in taverns lies the idea of homelessness, as Irish characters prove unable to find roots in the New World.

If one had doubts about the importance of bars, as opposed to homely places, one would only need to remember James Tyrone's unforgiven fault, when he left Mary alone during their honeymoon, got drunk, and was brought back to their room by fellow revelers. Inns, bars, or taverns become meeting points for Irishmen because they represent a place where they are no longer victims of communal and moral oppression against their ethnic group.

Confronted with forces of oppression, Irish men drift toward bars mechanically, hoping for some form of alcoholic salvation, which one could summarize as follows:

> Some say they drink to forget, but their ominous words betray a deeper desire. They are in fact methodically destroying themselves in a purification ritual whereby the curse that binds them is washed away by drinking whiskey, which bestows death and forgiveness upon them. Paradoxically, for these drinkers with Irish names, this resort to alcohol by way of extreme unction (a ritual often accompanied by a confession), is the ultimate sign of belonging, as though they wanted to return to a mythical Ireland, to the mother country where they might find a last resting place. (Dubost 30)

In *A Touch of the Poet,* using whiskey, Con Melody strives to put forward an image of the past so as to blur his vision of his present situation, which otherwise would be unbearable. Indeed, the con-

stant rebuffs of the Yankee community, which looks down on him for being both Irish and an innkeeper, are more than he can bear. When he decides to challenge Simon Harford's father for insulting his daughter, Sara warns him that because he is Irish, he will be perceived as "another drunken Mick" (as described in *A Touch of the Poet,* 3:249), as if in social terms, honor and Irishness were antithetical.

Social discrimination comes from the automatic association of the Irish with their drinking habits, but it is also due to their challenging communal values. In *A Touch of the Poet,* Deborah's experience—when she comes to see her son at the inn—reveals a danger that concerns family stability. She falls under the influence of Con Melody, can hardly resist the strength of his Irish charm, and is only saved by Melody's weak point.

> DEBORAH—. . . Is this—what the Irish call blarney, sir?
>
> MELODY—(*with a fierce, lustful sincerity*) No! I take my oath by the living God, I would charge a square of Napoleon's Old Guard singlehanded for one kiss of your lips. (*He bends lower, while his eyes hold hers. For a second it seems he will kiss her and she cannot help herself. Then abruptly the smell of whiskey on his breath brings her to herself, shaken with disgust and coldly angry.*). . . (3:218)

Melody's case could be characterized as one of self-exclusion since Deborah would probably have been kissed, had he not smelled of whiskey. Although he can only blame himself for his failure, the circumstances of his Don Juanesque defeat are emblematic of the way forces of exclusion act against the Irish. Drinking almost considered a "national" trait becomes a source of ethnic discrimination. Many fall victim to alcohol, but "going on the wagon," as O'Neill's characters would say, is no solution either. In a way, drama echoes society, and Irishmen are associated with an immoderate consumption of whiskey in the plays. Beyond the cliché—used as a weapon by the tenets of moral order—O'Neill draws his own portrait of *Homo Hibernicus,* whom he partly defines through his drinking habits.

Does it mean that Irishmen are always socially excluded? Not quite, and Mike Hogan in *A Moon for the Misbegotten* would not be the sole example of an Irishman joining the police force, but it remains that from an O'Neillian perspective, such a choice amounts to a loss of identity. Willingly or not, the Irish find themselves linked with or confronted by the police. Their unruly behavior might account for the clashes, but *A Touch of the Poet* exposes the delusion inherent in such presuppositions and reveals the gap between official explanations and reality. The fight that breaks out between Cregan, Con Melody, and policemen armed with clubs, is not—as officials would have it—solely motivated by the two men's misbehavior. The wealthy Harford family represents order, and consequently the police side with them, against the Irish, whatever Con Melody's motives may be. O'Neill's social critique gains in intensity as he shows that physical oppression directly results from a communal division based on social classes. Repression can also be read in terms of ethnic discrimination, an aspect that gives an even darker tinge to the betrayal of Irishmen who join a police force only too willing to victimize their fellow countrymen. It follows that reinforcing the power of WASPs—described in very critical terms both in *A Touch of the Poet* and *More Stately Mansions*—implies a rejection of one's community. It becomes the apex of persecution against the Irish because such a betrayal is self-destructive.

In O'Neill's theater, the Irish meet with various forms of oppression, and through their harsh existential struggle, the playwright draws a bleak portrait of American society. As personal stories are related, the American dream gives way to dystopia, but while oppressed, the Irish are not always portrayed as helpless victims. In many plays, they seem to be scapegoats, and yet, except for children, they are rarely innocent victims. In addition, communal distrust arises because in many respects they come out as challengers, a dangerous disturbing force for American society. Their drinking habits do not make model citizens of them, but their most serious offense is that their moral values differ from the expected ones.

O'Neill gives a more positive image of the Irish and their capacity to resist ethnic discrimination and oppression when he introduces another type of character. Servants or people who depend on a master bring a response to ethnic discrimination or social oppression, in that they illustrate what the power of the oppressed is. Compared to other Irish families, the Tyrones are wealthy people, but when they find themselves in a position to hire servants, they too suffer at their hands, hence Mary's complaints about her cook, her maid, and her chauffeur. James disagrees with her, but despite his attempts at convincing himself that he does not lose any money, facts prove him wrong. His lack of experience might explain his constant misfortune—as is the case for his land purchases—but the fault lies in his choice of Irish servants, who unfailingly prevail over their masters' wishes.

As a landlord, for example, Tyrone is unable to obtain his due when he asks Shaughnessy to pay his rent. He grumbles about it but does not take offense. The first reason for his willingness to accept financial defeat may result from his and Shaughnessy's common origins. The second reason for his surprising acceptance—when one remembers his statement that "life overdid the lesson for me, and made a dollar worth too much" (3:809)—equates with his passive attitude toward consumption. In the circumstances, he knows very well that social persecution against the Irish has resulted in their finding techniques of their own to fight oppression. Therefore, no matter how legitimate James's wish to be paid may be, it proves ineffective with regard to Shaughnessy's skill in diverting his attention, especially by appealing to their common Irishness.

The comedy scene between Harder and Hogan in *A Moon for the Misbegotten*—a soothing response to ethnic discrimination—illustrates the way in which a reversal of usual situations can occur. Following a dramatic tradition that consists of using humor as a weapon, O'Neill attacks American society through Harder, the millionaire. Once again, the playwright puts forward the pernicious nature of a world attractive to people because of its potential in terms of individual happiness, but which pays no heed to communal suffering engendered by social oppression and ethnic discrimination. O'Neill uses this comedy scene to reveal the power of the oppressed. He obviously relishes the description of Harder's defeat (acted out in *A Moon for the Misbegotten*, mentioned in *Long Day's Journey into Night*), and symbolically this episode enables him to avenge himself and his Irish ancestors for years of oppression undergone in the New World.

Showing how even in the lowest possible circumstances, the wealth and power of an American millionaire never beat a true Irishman, O'Neill puts forward an inverted image of submission. Hoping for the downfall of self-made millionaires, the dramatist pretends that these "heroes" have feet of clay. In fact, this comedy scene might be O'Neill's own version of a happy ending because Harder, the representative of the wealthy, cannot resist the power of the oppressed, which his own ancestors and their equals—through social oppression against the Irish—have generated for ages.

Revenge, even in the form of a humorous parody of American plutocrats, may have been necessary for O'Neill to reach a state of "understanding and forgiveness" (O'Neill 1984, 7) toward the United States. Regarding his interest in the Irish and what they meant in his works, one may devote more attention either to fate or to social oppression, but eventually one must take both factors into account. One could, for instance, praise the playwright for his skill since in his last plays, he attempted to draw a critical portrait of the United States and reached a universal scope through a very specific depiction of his Irish characters. The Irish and their conflicts with a society from which they are repeatedly rejected could then be read in expressionistic terms. In that case, the Irish, through their unending fight, become the epitome of people's existential struggle, whatever their origins might be, and bring an echo to individual feelings of exclusion.

Conversely, O'Neill's Irish plays also stand as a realistic expression of social strife as lived in the United States. O'Neill—especially through the moving episode of James Tyrone's recounting what he and his relatives had endured at the hands of American society—brings suffering to the fore and calls into question the very principles of a community that tolerates or accepts such inhuman treatments. His protagonists, often crushed by social oppression, try to resist—but very few succeed, and wealth makes them realize that their American dream is a delusion. When they retaliate against social oppression, O'Neill's Dionysian characters embody what he felt was the essence of Irishness, a boisterous attitude to life and a challenging spirit. While he does not depict his crude Irishmen as models, he may have felt that they represented the possibility of a more positive attitude to life. This brings to mind his intellectual convergence with FRIEDRICH NIETZSCHE, especially regarding man's attempt to go beyond the basic reality of his life, and shows the Irish's greatness in their daily battles, namely their fight against ethnic discrimination and social oppression. Despite this optimistic hint at a new definition of man, starting from the positive example of the Irish, the dark aspects of the past remained. Therefore, social oppression had to be represented, not as a mere background but as a remembrance of the cruel history of the Irish in the United States. For O'Neill, exposing oppression, ethnic discrimination, and rejection became a way of curing wounds that otherwise might never have healed.

Bibliography

Black, Stephen A. *Eugene O'Neill: Beyond Mourning and Tragedy.* New Haven, Conn.: Yale University Press, 1999.

Bogard, Travis. *Contour in Time: The Plays of Eugene O'Neill.* Rev. ed. New York: Oxford University Press, 1988.

Cargill, Oscar, N. Bryllion Fagin, and W. J. Fisher, eds. *O'Neill and His Plays: Four Decades of Criticism.* New York: New York University Press, 1961.

Dubost, Thierry. *Struggle, Defeat or Rebirth: Eugene O'Neill's Vision of Humanity.* Jefferson, N.C.: McFarland, 2005.

Fjelde, Rolf. "Structures of Forgiveness: The Endings of *A Moon for the Misbegotten* and Ibsen's *Peer Gynt.*" In *Eugene O'Neill in China,* edited by Liu Haiping and Lowell Swortzell, 51–57. New York: Greenwood Press, 1992.

Gelb, Arthur, and Barbara Gelb. *O'Neill.* Rev. ed. New York: Harper & Row, 1987.

O'Neill, Eugene. Preface to *Long Day's Journey into Night*. New Haven, Conn.: Yale University Press, 1984.

Pfister, Joel. *Staging Depth: Eugene O'Neill and the Politics of Psychological Discourse*. Chapel Hill: University of North Carolina Press, 1995.

Shaughnessy, Edward L. "O'Neill's African and Irish-Americans." In *The Cambridge Companion to Eugene O'Neill*, edited by Michael Manheim, 158–163. Cambridge: Cambridge University Press, 1998.

———. *Eugene O'Neill in Ireland: The Critical Reception*. Westport, Conn.: Greenwood Press, 1988.

Sheaffer, Louis. *O'Neill: Son and Playwright*. 1968. Reprint, Boston: Little, Brown, 1990.

Thierry Dubost

J

jazz Jazz is a particularly American construct, and like the inaccurate image of the United States as a melting pot for all nationalities, jazz is built from many diverse elements of melody, harmony, rhythm, and instrumentation.

Pianist Jelly Roll Morton (1890–1941), who came to prominence in the early years of the 20th century, claimed immodestly and without irony that he invented jazz. Although he was a key figure in its development, his pronouncement implies that jazz had no history prior to its birth—an absurd premise, even though the exact trajectory of its development may never be precisely plotted. Jazz borrowed elements from the blues, popular song, gospel, folk idioms, even the classical tradition, creating something entirely new and distinctly American in character.

Piano ragtime from the late 19th and early 20th centuries—as practiced by Scott Joplin and many others—was an early and important precursor of jazz, and the piano continued to be prominent as the new genre of music developed. Drums and bass gave jazz a rhythmic anchor, and brass or woodwinds provided vivid color, but there was no strict instrumentation and few rules. A solo performer or an ensemble of any size could make jazz.

Though the MUSIC had been simmering for some years previously, it first appeared on phonograph records in 1917, essayed by the Original Dixieland Jazz Band, but the influence of the music extended far beyond the grooves of a 78-rpm recording. New York, New Orleans, and Chicago quickly became hubs for distinct styles of jazz. In addition to Morton, adventurous soloists such as Buddy Bolden, King Creole, Louis Armstrong, Bix Biederbecke, and others pushed the music into new and exciting directions, while singers such as Bessie Smith skillfully blended jazz with the blues. At its best, jazz crackled with an energy and insistence that were contagious. Decried by priests and politicians, jazz was naturally embraced by the young men and women of the day. It was inescapable, and its force and influence were so strong that the decade of the 1920s took its name from it.

The Jazz Age would provide a unique and fertile soundtrack for Eugene O'Neill's most creative and experimental period. The "apprentice" plays were behind him, and he met the decade of the 1920s with an enthusiasm and fearlessness that reflected the times. His record collection—catalogued at his Danville, California, home TAO HOUSE—revealed how much he enjoyed listening to jazz, though his taste was broad. His library also included albums of blues, pop, folk, and light classics, spanning Rachmaninoff and West Indies chant to Al Jolson and the hillbilly swing of the Hoosier Hot Shots. The playwright's letters include a 1929 note from Le Plessis, FRANCE, to a friend who had sent him some recordings of Louis Armstrong, Bessie Smith, and others. O'Neill offers his thanks: "The records arrived—and they are some camellias! . . . Do you know Mr. Armstrong? If so, give him my fraternal benediction" (O'Neill 352).

O'Neill's appreciation for jazz and music in general was enthusiastic, but he was unskilled in its performance, theory, structure, or history. Nonetheless, he believed there were undeniable musical rhythms running through his plays. In an entry in his WORK DIARY from 1931, he recognizes "my unconscious use of musical structure in nearly all of my plays—impulsion and chief interest always an attempt to do what music does (to express an essentially poetic viewpoint of life) using rhythm of recurrent themes" (quoted in Floyd 228).

An examination of his entire body of work—aided immeasurably by Travis Bogard's well-compiled and annotated *Eugene O'Neill Songbook*—proves how regularly the playwright incorporated music into his plays. As Bogard points out in the *Songbook*, 37 of O'Neill's 50 plays include specified music. Examples include AH, WILDERNESS!, ALL GOD'S CHILLUN GOT WINGS, MOURNING BECOMES ELECTRA, the SS GLENCAIRN plays, and especially The ICEMAN COMETH, which have soundtracks that set the scene and develop character, while the lyrics frequently comment directly or indirectly on the action. Clearly, O'Neill's musical choices were not random but thoughtfully selected for maximum impact. Many of the playwright's best works are set in the years prior to the 1920s when jazz came into prominence—hence the preponderance of sentimental ballads, popular songs, and folk tunes that make up the *Songbook*.

Even in the contemporary-setting plays, however, O'Neill rarely incorporated jazz. One exception is his 1920 play DIFF'RENT, wherein spinster Emma Crosby attempts to woo Benny Rogers, 30 years her junior. Act 2 opens with the young man—recently returned from army service in France for World War I—enthusiastically listening to a record on Emma's Victrola. "Oh, baby!" he says to her when the song concludes. "Some jazz, I'll tell the world!" (2:28). Although Emma purchased the recordings only on his recommendation, she coyly pretends that she wanted them only for herself, that "them jazz tunes . . . put life and ginger in an old lady like me" (2:28). Benny, kidding, tells her she is not old if she likes jazz. He even suggests that she learn to dance to be truly up-to-date.

O'Neill does not specify the tune that blares from the phonograph, but his meaning is clear: The upbeat urgency of hot jazz underscores Emma's unsuitability as a partner for the younger man, a point further driven home by her too-youthful dress and garish makeup.

Aside from the reference in *Diff'rent*, O'Neill's plays (and the popular songs that embellish them) reveal little direct connection to the era in which they were written. Nonetheless, such works as The EMPEROR JONES, The HAIRY APE, STRANGE INTERLUDE, DYNAMO, and even LAZARUS LAUGHED are unquestionably a product of the Jazz Age, reflecting its modern nature, its nervous but excited rhythms, its element of risk, and even its lexicon of slang.

Dramatizing controversial subjects, O'Neill flouted convention. The plays he wrote during the 1920s—including three PULITZER PRIZE winners—cemented his reputation as the greatest contemporary playwright. In his restlessness to devise the right language to tell his tragic stories, he absorbed a variety of influences that certainly included the peculiarly American music known as jazz.

Bibliography

Bogard, Travis, ed. *The Eugene O'Neill Songbook.* Berkeley, Calif.: East Bay Books, 1993.

Floyd, Virginia, ed. *Eugene O'Neill at Work: Newly Released Ideas for Plays.* New York: Ungar, 1991.

O'Neill, Eugene. *Selected Letters of Eugene O'Neill.* Edited by Travis Bogard and Jackson R. Bryer. New Haven, Conn.: Yale University Press, 1988.

Richard C. Sater

Jenkins, Kathleen (Kathleen Jenkins O'Neill Pitt-Smith) (1888–1960)   The underlay to the meeting of Eugene O'Neill and Kathleen Jenkins, who would become his first wife, was sketched out by George Bellows, the Ashcan School artist with whom O'Neill had spent the winter of 1909 in a ramshackle farmhouse in Zion, New Jersey. Bellows had convinced his friend to attempt a move beyond the actresses and chorus girls who had been his companions under the tutelage of his brother JAMES O'NEILL, JR. (Jamie) and to aspire to associate with "nice" young women his own age. Kathleen was a child of gentility and privilege: Her father, although an alcoholic and divorced from his wife, traced his family to the pre-Revolutionary era; her mother's people were residents of the deluxe Gramercy Park area in Manhattan. Gene, uncomfortable around respectability but now eager for more refined company, was introduced to Kathleen at a party given by her mother at her residence on the Upper West Side.

Both young people were on an emotional cusp at age 20: Gene was ready for romance after a series of easy assignations; Kathleen was bored with propriety and sought out risk in the form of the aspiring artist who, by virtue of his father's fame, was something of a celebrity already. They were immediately taken with one another. Gene found Kathleen's Gibson Girl beauty and daring flirtatiousness beguiling, while Kathleen was drawn to Gene's brooding good looks and mercurial temperament. Both were headstrong and determined to keep company in spite of Mrs. Kate Jenkins's concerns about O'Neill's dependence on his family for income and his father JAMES O'NEILL's conviction that any woman interested in his son was motivated by the assumed O'Neill fortune.

The two saw one another throughout the summer of 1909. Eugene wrote Kathleen poetry, took

Kathleen Jenkins at the beach with Eugene O'Neill, Jr. *(Courtesy of the Sheaffer-O'Neill Collection, Charles E. Shain Library of Connecticut College)*

her for long walks, quoted HENRIK IBSEN, and talked about his radical notions of morality and class. She sympathized with his desire to be mothered, was enthralled by his sensitivity, and put up with (or never saw) his vanity, volatility, and self-pity. They drank together (Kathleen had been introduced to cocktails by her mother when she was 15) and socialized at George Bellows's studio. Kathleen was deeply in love and imagined Eugene's feelings mirrored her own. Gene, while he loved being loved, did not consider a future with Kathleen.

By fall, Kathleen was pregnant, and she expected Eugene to marry her. Panicked, Gene confessed to his father. James O'Neill acted immediately to get his son out of the country by arranging a SEA voyage and mining expedition to Honduras. But Kathleen, who must have been panicked herself, insisted on marriage; the two were secretly wed in Hoboken, New Jersey, on October 2, 1909, two weeks before Eugene O'Neill turned 21. When the birth of EUGENE O'NEILL, JR., on May 4, 1910, was revealed to the *New York World* by Kathleen's mother, the story reported that the marriage had taken place in July 1909, thus deflecting public suspicion that the child had been conceived out of wedlock. On all later documents, Kathleen would list their nuptial date as July 26, 1909.

Despite the regularization of the relationship, Eugene set sail for HONDURAS a week after the wedding and did not return to the United States for six and a half months. When he disembarked at the end of April 1910, he made no effort to see Kathleen; he read about his son's birth in the *World* article. On May 10, 1910, the *World* ran a picture of the young mother with the caption "Mrs. O'Neill, Who Is a Mother, Does Not Know Husband Is in City" (quoted in Gelb 1973, 139). These efforts at publicity were Kate Jenkins's attempts to shame the O'Neill family into acknowledging their daughter-in-law and her newborn. She could not have been more unsuccessful. O'Neill's mother MARY ELLEN "ELLA" O'NEILL had been instrumental in keeping the marriage secret while Gene was away and wanted nothing to do with her grandson. James responded to what he considered a form of blackmail on the part of Mrs. Jenkins by arranging for Eugene

Eugene O'Neill with Earl Stevens on a banana boat en route to Honduras, October 16, 1909, O'Neill's 21st birthday *(Courtesy of the Yale Collection of American Literature, Beinecke Rare Book and Manuscript Library)*

to go on the road as assistant stage manager in the company of the popular melodrama *The White Sister* and afterward to ship out again, this time to BUENOS AIRES, ARGENTINA. A divorce would be arranged on Gene's return.

After the hasty marriage and his one reported visit to see Eugene, Jr., after the Buenos Aires adventure, Eugene and Kathleen O'Neill did not see each other again. They were divorced on July 5, 1912, after a requisite trial and verdict of adultery (the only legal basis for divorce in New York State at the time). Kathleen asked for no alimony or child support and received full custody of her son. Although O'Neill established a relationship with Eugene, Jr., once the boy reached adolescence, the former husband and wife, as Kathleen would put it

in later years, "ignore[ed] one another's existence" (quoted in Schaeffer 145).

Although characteristically bitter at the "humiliation" of being accused of adultery (or perhaps merely because Kathleen had behaved so well during the whole affair), Eugene would use the experience of his first marriage again and again over the years. ABORTION, BREAD AND BUTTER, and SERVITUDE (all 1914); BEFORE BREAKFAST (1916); BEYOND THE HORIZON (1918); and even A TOUCH OF THE POET (1942) all concern unplanned pregnancies, entrapment in marriage, or futile lives played out against the background of domesticity. But O'Neill would eventually come to view Kathleen with respect and even to look at their failure with regret. As he famously remarked to his third wife, CARLOTTA MONTEREY O'NEILL, "The woman I gave most trouble to has given me the least" (quoted in Gelb 2000, 337, and elsewhere).

Kathleen Jenkins eventually remarried, and when Louis Scheaffer interviewed her in the late 1950s, she "seemed to her visitor to be holding her memories [of O'Neill] at arm's length" (Schaeffer 145). She referred to Eugene as "Mr. O'Neill," and Schaeffer recounts that her responses seemed to suggest "that he was someone she had known once but slightly, formally" (144). Kathleen was careful not to align herself with O'Neill the dramatist, saying that when she knew him, he wrote poetry, as all young suitors did at the time, but that she was "surprised" when he became famous as a playwright (145). She readily—perhaps graciously—admitted that she could never "have given him the understanding he needed" as a writer (Gelb 2000, 254). However, as Arthur and Barbara Gelb suppose, the now-widowed and elderly Mrs. Kathleen Jenkins O'Neill Pitt-Smith may have been thinking about the allowance she was receiving from O'Neill's estate, monitored by the woman who made her mark as O'Neill's muse—Carlotta Monterey O'Neill.

Bibliography

Gelb, Arthur, and Barbara Gelb. *O'Neill.* Enlarged ed. New York: Harper & Row, 1973.
———. *O'Neill: Life with Monte Cristo.* New York: Applause Books, 2000.
Schaeffer, Lewis. *O'Neill: Son and Playwright.* Boston: Little, Brown, 1968.

Cynthia McCowan

Jimmy "the Priest's"   Eugene O'Neill's main residence during his time of "great down-and-outness" ("Tomorrow," 3:947). The seven months in 1911–12 that O'Neill was and on-and-off roomer in the sailors' flophouse at 252 Fulton Street in lower Manhattan known as "Jimmy the Priest's"—from April to July 1911, and September 1911 to January 1912—were seminal in terms of his work as a playwright and critical in terms of the playwright's life. It was here that O'Neill met characters who would people his plays from *"ANNA CHRISTIE"* to *The ICEMAN COMETH,* including the pub's eponymous Jimmy, and it was here that the young man

would make a determined but unsuccessful attempt on his own life. Whether O'Neill learned of Jimmy's through his mates from the SS IKALA, with whom he'd shipped home from BUENOS AIRES in April 1911, or from his pal JAMES FINDLATER BYTH (James O'Neill's former press agent) who was already lodging there, or whether he stumbled upon the saloon on his own, is unknown. There was no name on the facade, only an illustration of a beer glass on the plate glass window and the legend "Schooners—five [cents]" to let customers know where to turn in. There were many clean and thrifty establishments for idle seamen along the south Manhattan waterfront, but although it was inexpensive, there was nothing clean or even decent about the bar and lodgings at 252 Fulton. O'Neill famously said that Jimmy's made the Russian playwright Maxim Gorky's set description for the sordid cellar saloon in *The Lower Depths* look like "an ice cream parlor in comparison" (Gelb and Gelb 294, and elsewhere).

Jimmy himself was James J. Condon, who became proprietor in 1908 after having run several other bars in the area. He was about 50 when O'Neill became a regular customer, and if not for O'Neill's presence and his later dramatic portraits of the ascetic saloon keeper and of the seedy estab-

Jimmy the Priest's, a waterfront flophouse located at 252 Fulton Street in New York City, where O'Neill attempted suicide in 1912 *(Courtesy of the Sheaffer-O'Neill Collection, Charles E. Shain Library of Connecticut College)*

lishment itself, Condon may have lived on only in the bleary memories of his less literary patrons. O'Neill's BIOGRAPHERS agree that the description of Johnny the Priest in "Anna Christie" is probably very close to the original: "With his pale, thin clean-shaven face, mild blue eyes and white hair, a cassock would seem more suited to him than the apron he wears. . . . . But beneath all his mildness one senses the man behind the mask—cynical, callous, hard as nails" (959). Condon himself did not drink, and, leaving the barman to stay open past midnight, went home soberly every evening to his respectable working-class neighborhood. On the job, however, he was both "hard as nails" and a soft touch. He'd brook no disturbances in his establishment, and at the first hint of a brewing battle, the combatants got the "bum's rush"—Jimmy's fists around collar and belt and a swift ejection onto the concrete steps. Condon would then return to his bar duties without so much as having raised his voice. Condon's impassive demeanor also hid his many generosities: No young sailor down on his luck was refused at least a back room table to rest his head, and carfare usually found its way into patrons' empty pockets at last call. Condon also never engaged in the practice of taking "blood money" from his boarders: Unlike most waterfront innkeepers, he would not impound the salary advances of sailors who still owed for their lodgings. Ethics seemed to have little to do with Jimmy's choices, however, since he also looked the other way when one of his regulars got up to shadow and then "rolled" a transient drunk.

O'Neill recalled the clientele of Jimmy's as "a hard lot . . . sailors, on shore leave or stranded, longshoremen, waterfront riffraff, gangsters, down and outers, drifters from the ends of the earth" (Gelb and Gelb 317), and in The Iceman Cometh Harry Hope's saloon is "the last harbor. No one here has to worry about where they're going next, because there is no farther they can go" (536). Yet O'Neill would consider the men he associated with at Jimmy's to be some of the best friends of his life. Besides James Condon was Byth, a writer turned hack by his alcoholism, who would save O'Neill's life several month's hence and who would become "Jimmy Tomorrow" in O'Neill's only short story as well as in

The Iceman Cometh; DRISCOLL, an Irish stoker much admired by O'Neill, who became a model for several SEA characters, chief among them Yank in The HAIRY APE; and Chris Christopherson, a lifelong sailor who had a love-hate relationship with the sea, and ended his career working on barges—as does the character he inspired, Anna Christie's father, Chris Christopherson. "The Lunger," who was so named for his racking cough, was assigned to the cell next door to O'Neill's; in later years O'Neill would posit that the Lunger had infected him with tuberculosis. A former telegraph operator, he served as a model for Knapp, the telegrapher in the one-act WARNINGS. Rounding out the roster was high spirited James Quigley; Quigley shared O'Neill's bent for womanizing and accompanied him on many a bender-and-bawdy-house adventure.

When O'Neill walked into Jimmy's place after a few disastrous weeks with his family in NEW LONDON, CONNECTICUT, following his return from Buenos Aires, he may very well have felt it to be his last harbor. At 22, O'Neill was no stranger to bar or bordello, had already prospected in HONDURAS, scrubbed decks and climbed riggings on the sailing vessel CHARLES RACINE, hauled and cleaned cattle hides for Swift & Company's South American Division, slept on the beaches and park benches of Buenos Aires, and had earned "ordinary seaman" status for work on his return trip aboard the Ikala. He had also married a wife and fathered a son—not in that order—which, in the elder O'Neills' eyes, was the most egregious of all his enterprises. Furious plans were afoot to excise KATHLEEN JENKINS and EUGENE O'NEILL, JR., from the O'Neill family, putting O'Neill on the worst of terms with his parents; only divorce proceedings late in 1911 would serve to plunge O'Neill deeper into that last harbor.

In April, however, O'Neill found himself at home with drifters and down-and-outers at Jimmy's and comfort in the nonjudgmental attitude of the proprietor. He rented a room with free lunch for three dollars a month, and with his father's support of a dollar a day as long as he showed up at James O'Neill's agent's office to collect, began a life of dissipation in earnest.

The block on which Jimmy's stood was in the dingy heart of the dockside trade and business district. The four and a half story red brick building that housed the bar and hotel faced Washington Market. Both market and building were about 100 years old in 1911, and both would remain downtown Manhattan landmarks until the mid-1960s. The Market, called "the Farm" by denizens of Jimmy's, was about 12 square blocks, where vendors hawked all varieties of produce, game, and livestock throughout the day and evening. A few doors from Jimmy's was the Hudson riverfront, where commercial and commuter traffic never ended; several blocks east was the South Street Seaport and the original Fulton Fish Market; the Lackawanna Railroad ran a half block away. The *Evening Globe* was printed and distributed on an adjoining block, and newsboys, printers, and pressman thronged to the bars after each edition. A noisier, smellier, busier arena would be hard to find; yet patrons daily made their way to the dark interior of the saloon, and many, like O'Neill, found shelter there where liquor was cheap, hours were late, and beds were available.

In both *"Anna Christie"* and *The Iceman Cometh,* O'Neill does some construction work on the historical Jimmy's by adding a "family entrance," so as to introduce female characters into the dramas. In reality, the saloon had no family entrance and allowed no women, thus making no concessions to the niceties even a dollar prostitute might require. Swinging doors led patrons to a mahogany bar, an older, plainer, more battered version of the late Victorian pieces that graced the better hotels and public houses of Manhattan: Massive and mirrored, it ran the length of one wall. Kegs of cheap whiskey and bottles of better liquor (O'Neill's set directions for *"Anna Christie"* mention that there is "evidently little call" for the showcase items) lined the back. The free lunch graced the bartop and sawdust covered the floor; aromas of greasy food, stale beer, and rank tobacco commingled with the smells from the produce, meat, and fish markets outside. In the rear area, set off by a curtain, were several round tables and a pot-bellied stove.

Upstairs, where O'Neill and pals lodged, were rows of cell-like rooms. His cell contained one chair, one chest of drawers, one bedbug-infested straw mattress, and one coverlet. Heat and light emanated from kerosene stoves and lanterns on each floor's hallway; each floor also offered a sink and a toilet. O'Neill was lucky enough to have a window to the outside. Most patrons got what air they could from mesh transoms above their flimsy "apartment" doors (Scheaffer 190–191).

O'Neill did take a break from this dismal environment in July, when the heat made lower Manhattan unbearable, to ship out aboard the SS NEW YORK bound for Cherbourg and Southampton with fellow lodgers Driscoll (whose first name has never been discovered) and Quigley. That he signed on as an "ordinary seaman" and returned aboard the SS PHILADELPHIA as an "able-bodied seaman" was a lifelong source of pride for the errant sailor. But by September, when he returned to Jimmy's, O'Neill was already spiraling into the depression that would culminate several months later in his suicide attempt. He spent the autumn drinking and whoring, the only deviation from deviance being his attendance at every one of Dublin's ABBEY THEATRE productions. He found himself fascinated with the Irish players' productions of JOHN MILLINGTON SYNGE, William Butler Yeats, and Augusta, Lady Gregory, both because they spoke to his own Irishness and because, as he would later confirm, they gave him "a glimpse of [his] opportunity" to bring the theater of his own country equally to life (Gelb and Gelb 314).

However, fast upon that spiritual respite came Kathleen Jenkins O'Neill's divorce proceedings and O'Neill's further contention with his family. Most humiliating to him must have been that to prove adultery, the only grounds for divorce in New York State, he was required to appear in what amounted to a dark bedroom farce. He was made to visit a Times Square brothel accompanied by his father's lawyer and an attorney friend of the Jenkins', take one of the girls upstairs, and be "discovered" by the two witnesses in flagrante delicto. This, compounded with O'Neill's abject self-hatred and guilt for having abandoned Kathleen and the baby and his shame at allowing his father to abet his treachery, must have sent him into the vortex of the downward spiral that had begun, as Stephen Black and others have surmised, when he discovered his mother's morphine addiction. Black believes O'Neill had been "heading toward the suicide attempt for a decade" (120) and that his cumulative act was his purchase of sufficient amounts of the barbiturate Veronal in late December and washing them down, locked in his room at Jimmy's in early January.

Fortunately, James Byth had noticed his growing despair as well as his uncharacteristic sobriety, and when hours (perhaps as much as a day) went by and O'Neill did not emerge from the upper floor, Byth broke down his door to find him comatose. Byth and the other regulars went immediately to work to walk the victim into consciousness, but it was James Condon who finally insisted he be checked into Bellevue Hospital, where reportedly he had his stomach pumped and was treated over a significant length of time (Black 119).

The question of how intentional or serious O'Neill's attempt at self-destruction was is a matter of considered opinion. Those who argue for O'Neill's sincerity point to his agonized memories of the event in correspondence with his second wife-to-be, AGNES BOULTON, as well as the subject matter of his one-act play EXORCISM. It is known only through contemporary reviews and actors' comments that the piece is a dark look at a young man's attempted suicide; significantly, after the first few productions, O'Neill destroyed all copies of the play.

Those who believe O'Neill's brush with death was a charade gone wrong also point to the Agnes letters, in which they see some humor, and to O'Neill's own public recollections. In later years, he would by turns refuse to discuss his dark night, treat it as a Keystone Komedy of errors (with pals stopping at watering holes along the route to the hospital to fortify themselves), or imply that he had merely meant to make a "gesture" of despair. Whatever the case, in late January he experienced some sort of turnabout, because he packed up and left Jimmy the Priest's for good.

Clearly, O'Neill's experiences at Jimmy's and the friendships forged there never left him. Late in his life, recalled his widow CARLOTTA MONTEREY O'NEILL, after they had lived and traveled in Europe, visited parts of Asia, and had owned fine homes on both coasts, he was fondest of recalling his days in the seedy waterfront saloon. "I liked [the rest]" he told Carlotta, "but they weren't very exciting" (Sheaffer 191 and others). As for his comrades in dissolution, although they would live

on in O'Neill's best plays, Byth, Driscoll, and Christopherson were dead within five years of O'Neill's leaving. Byth, ever the pipe-dreaming hopeful, would throw himself from his cell at Jimmy's the next year, when he'd become convinced of his own hopelessness. Driscoll, too, always so "strong and confident" to Eugene, would take his own life, jumping overboard while serving on the SS *St. Louis* in 1914. And Christopherson would die by accident and alcohol, stumbling into the dark waters as he boarded his barge in 1917 (Richter 75, 79). Jimmy the Priest's establishment would also go to ground in 1919, when Condon was arrested on murder charges for serving poisoned drink. The probable truth is that a bootlegger with whom Condon had refused to cooperate tainted his stock. Condon was acquitted, but his business was ruined, and Jimmy the Priest's closed for good the day after the trial.

The Fulton Street area remained energetically commercial until late mid-20th century. The brick building at 252 Fulton continued into its old age as a maritime warehouse. Washington Market remained an open-air bazaar until 1940, when it was enclosed for shopper comfort, and continued to thrive. In the mid-1960s, however, developers were closing in on the vicinity as the venue for a huge construction scheme, and in 1966 the entire area was demolished to make way for the project. Considering the tragic history of Jimmy the Priest's, it is disturbing to note that the structure built upon its grave was the World Trade Center.

Bibliography

Black, Stephen A. *Eugene O'Neill: Beyond Mourning and Tragedy.* New Haven, Conn., and London: Yale University Press, 1999.

Gelb, Arthur and Barbara Gelb. *O'Neill: Life with Monte Cristo.* New York: Applause Books, 2000.

O'Neill, Eugene. *"Anna Christie."* In *Collected Plays of Eugene O'Neill, 1913–1920.* Edited by Travis Bogard. New York: Library of America, 1988.

———. *The Iceman Cometh.* In *Collected Plays of Eugene O'Neill, 1932–1943.* Edited by Travis Bogard. New York: Library of America, 1988.

———. *"Tomorrow."* In *Collected Plays of Eugene O'Neill, 1913–1914.* Edited by Travis Bogard. New York: Library of America, 1988.

Richter, Robert. *Eugene O'Neill and Dat Ole Davil Sea: Maritime Influences in the Life and Works of Eugene O'Neill.* Mystic, Conn.: Mystic Seaport Press, 2004.

Scheaffer, Louis. *O'Neill, Son and Playwright.* Boston: Little, Brown, 1968.

Cynthia McCowan

Jones, Robert Edmond (1887–1954)   Known as "Bobby" to his friends, Robert Edmond Jones was one of the most prominent and influential scene designers in AMERICAN THEATER history. He was born on December 12, 1887, in Milton, New Hampshire. Between 1912 and 1915, he traveled around Europe and was highly influenced by theatrical trends there and by his time studying at Max Reinhardt's Deutsches Theater. Bringing many European innovations back to America, Jones is credited with introducing what was called a "New Stagecraft," which was a rebellion against the clutter and detail of current drama in favor of simplicity, sparseness, and EXPRESSIONISM. Jones's design for a 1915 production of Anatole France's *The Man Who Married a Dumb Wife*, directed by Harley Granville Barker, is generally considered to herald the inauguration of this new stagecraft.

Jones was an early member of the PROVINCE-TOWN PLAYERS, developing a close personal and professional relationship with Eugene O'Neill, who was a year younger; the two exchanged numerous letters during their lives. Jones worked on more productions with the playwright than any other scenic designer, and he also designed O'Neill plays for the THEATRE GUILD. His stagings included the Broadway debut of "ANNA CHRISTIE" in 1921 as well as the premieres of DESIRE UNDER THE ELMS (1924); *The* FOUNTAIN (1925); *The* GREAT GOD BROWN (1926); and, 20 years later, *The* ICEMAN COMETH, which marked O'Neill's return to the stage after more than a decade away. As a member of the TRI-UMVIRATE, Jones—along with O'Neill and Jones's former Harvard classmate KENNETH MACGOWAN—was instrumental in reshaping the Provincetown Players into the EXPERIMENTAL THEATRE, INC.

While Jones gained international renown as a stage designer, he also served as a director, taking on some of O'Neill's early one-act plays. After helping to found the Experimental Theatre, Jones directed

Robert Edmund Jones *(Courtesy of the Sheaffer-O'Neill Collection, Charles E. Shain Library of Connecticut College)*

several plays for the new organization, including *Desire under the Elms*, *The Fountain*, and *The Great God Brown*. His role as director, while sporadic, reached outside the O'Neill sphere, such as his work with Lillian Gish in 1932 on a production of *Camille*. Jones died on November 26, 1954, one year after O'Neill, in the home in which he had been born.

Bibliography

Jones, Robert Edmond. *The Dramatic Imagination: Reflections and Speculations on the Art of the Theatre.* New York: Methuen, 1969.

———. *Drawings for the Theatre.* New York: Theatre Arts Books, 1970.

Pendleton, Ralph, ed. *The Theatre of Robert Edmond Jones.* Middletown, Conn.: Wesleyan University Press: 1958.

Karen Charmaine Blansfield

L

Liberal Club In 1913, the Liberal Club, which was originally a rather earnest society devoted to political reform, suffered a revolt and a schism led by the feminist Henrietta Rodman. Objecting to the club's refusal to admit either AFRICAN AMERICANS or the anarchist EMMA GOLDMAN as members, Rodman and a splinter group of self-styled radicals started a new chapter of the club in GREENWICH VILLAGE, the center of the artistic, social, and political revolt between 1912 and 1918 that is referred to by historians as the Little Renaissance. Located at 137 Macdougal Street, the new Liberal Club became a physical as well as a philosophical focal point for the bohemian rebels of the Village. It was connected by a passageway to the Boni brothers' bookstore and was next door to the future home of the PROVINCETOWN PLAYERS, both vital meeting places for the artists, writers, intellectuals, journalists and activists who were drawn to the Village during the 1910s in search of the new and the modern, and who naturally became members of the Liberal Club. Eugene O'Neill was a member, as were his friends Polly Holladay, HIPPOLYTE HAVEL, and people who were also active in the Provincetown Players, including SUSAN GLASPELL, JOHN REED, LOUISE BRYANT, Charles Demuth, GEORGE CRAM "JIG" COOK, and O'Neill's future lawyer, Harry Weinberger. Other members included Theodore Dreiser, Marsden Hartley, Sinclair Lewis, Upton Sinclair, and Lincoln Steffens.

The Greenwich Village Liberal Club was nothing like its earnest progenitor. Far more of its members' energy was devoted to social gatherings than to intellectual programs. It was famous for its annual fund-raising balls, called "Pagan Routs," at which revelers dressed in Greek and Roman costumes and partied until dawn. Of particular importance to O'Neill's career was the group known as the Players or the Dell Players, after Floyd Dell, the associate editor of *The Masses* magazine, who was its director, playwright, and general moving spirit. Dell's inaugural play, "St. George in Greenwich Village," satirized many of the modern ideas that the Villagers held dear, and its humorous self-satire set the tone for a number of productions to follow. Most important for O'Neill, some of the Dell Players, desiring a more serious and professional approach to theater, split off from the group and founded their own theater, the WASHINGTON SQUARE PLAYERS, which, in turn, was the source for the Provincetown Players, among whose founders were many amateur playwrights whose work had been rejected by the Washington Square Players. Like many Little Renaissance institutions, the Liberal Club ended with World War I. It became increasingly difficult to maintain the building as the young radicals began to scatter from the Village. After one final fund-raising dance failed to solve its financial problems, it closed its doors in November 1918.

Bibliography

Murphy, Brenda. *The Provincetown Players and the Culture of Modernity.* Cambridge: Cambridge University Press, 2005.

Stansell, Christine. *American Moderns: Bohemian New York and the Creation of a New Century*. New York: Metropolitan Books, 2000.

Brenda Murphy

Light, James (1895–1964) A member of the PROVINCETOWN PLAYERS James Light served in various roles as producer, performer, designer, and, most notably, director. He became close friends with Eugene O'Neill, whom he meet in 1917, and he was integral in helping the playwright to move AMERICAN THEATER away from MELODRAMA to a more stylistic and innovative art form. Although Light was considered an intelligent director, he could also apparently be erratic and uneven, which resulted in his being behind some of the best and the worst of O'Neill's productions.

James "Jimmie" Light *(Courtesy of the Sheaffer-O'Neill Collection, Charles E. Shain Library of Connecticut College)*

Among the O'Neill plays Light directed are *The HAIRY APE* and *ALL GOD'S CHILLUN GOT WINGS*, and he also took on works by other playwrights, including AUGUST STRINDBERG's *Spook Sonata* (codirected with ROBERT E. JONES) and *The Dream Play*, as well as E. E. Cummings's *Him*. Light's strong personality often conflicted with that of GEORGE CRAM COOK, director of the Provincetown Players, and when Cook took a sabbatical, Light stepped in as his replacement. In 1920, during an enormously successful production of *The EMPEROR JONES*—which cast a black actor, CHARLES S. GILPIN, in the main role—both Cook and Light were charged with violating a law against Sunday performances, a case they eventually won.

In 1923, in the wake of creative differences among various members, the Provincetown Players was reshaped into the EXPERIMENTAL THEATRE, INC., under the guidance of O'Neill, Jones, and KENNETH MACGOWAN (known informally as the TRIUMVIRATE). In this group—for which Light eventually became president and director—Light was involved with some of the most radical and experimental of O'Neill's works. One was the playwright's adaptation of Samuel Taylor Coleridge's poem "The RIME OF THE ANCIENT MARINER," which Light codirected with Jones. The production, though not very successful, made extensive use of masks, designed by Light, and it also incorporated a chorus. In the program notes, Light emphasized that the masks were not intended to imitate life but rather to convey ideas through a spiritual atmosphere.

Perhaps the most controversial situation Light encountered was the 1924 production of *All God's Chillun Got Wings*, in which the renowned black actor PAUL ROBESON (whom Light often coached) was cast as a character married to a white woman, played by Mary Blair. The interracial nature of the play brought poison pen letters and threats from the Ku Klux Klan and other groups against Light as well as O'Neill. Ironically, despite the firestorm, the play opened to mixed reviews.

In 1928, Light was appointed coach of the Yale Dramatic Association, and the following year, he received a Guggenheim fellowship, with which he traveled abroad. During the next decade, Light was affiliated with New York's New School for Social

Reseach, serving as dean of its drama faculty from 1939 to 1942.

Bibliography

"Blue Law Agitators Lose First Court Case," *New York Times*, December 11, 1920.

"James Light Dies: O'Neill Associate," *New York Times*, February 12, 1964.

"To Close Sunday Theatre." *New York Times*, December 10, 1920.

Wainscott, Ronald H. *Staging O'Neill: The Experimental Years, 1920–1934.* New Haven, Conn.: Yale University Press, 1988.

Karen Charmaine Blansfield

M

Macgowan, Kenneth (1888–1963) Producer, critic, and professor, Kenneth Macgowan exerted a vital influence on the theatrical growth of Eugene O'Neill, encouraging the playwright's move away from traditional REALISM and toward Macgowan's own aesthetic of the stage. Both men deemed it important that playwrights, directors, and designers work in mutual harmony to create a professional and spiritual theater. Macgowan and O'Neill developed not only a professional relationship but a close personal one as well; upon their first meeting, O'Neill immediately felt a kinship with both Macgowan and his wife. The two men exchanged dozens of letters throughout their lives, many of them now lost.

Macgowan was born on November 30, 1888, in Winthrop, Massachusetts. After graduating from Harvard in 1911, he served as assistant drama critic for the *Boston Evening Transcript* and then as entertainment editor for the *Philadelphia Evening Ledger*. In 1913, he married Edna Behre, an aspiring artist, and four years later they moved to New York. There, Macgowan was elected executive director of the New York Drama League, and from 1918 to 1919 he served as publicity director for Goldwyn Pictures Corporation. In 1919, Macgowan began a four-year stint as theater critic for the *New York Globe*, a position he held simultaneously for *Vogue* magazine, and, that same year, he was appointed associate editor for *Theatre Arts Magazine*. Nearly a decade later, he was a producer and director with the Actors' Theatre (1927–29).

A quiet, private man, Macgowan was fundamental in reshaping the PROVINCETOWN PLAYERS into the EXPERIMENTAL THEATRE, INC., in 1923. Together with O'Neill and stage designer ROBERT EDMOND JONES—Macgowan's Harvard classmate— this TRIUMVIRATE articulated the vision of a new theater, for which O'Neill appointed Macgowan director, with Jones and the playwright himself acting as associate directors.

In the mid-1920s, primarily for financial reasons, Macgowan moved beyond the Experimental Theatre to produce plays on Broadway, and a few years later, he moved to Hollywood to become a story editor for RKO Pictures, soon advancing to the role of producer. After leaving RKO in 1935, he went on to work for Twentieth Century-Fox, Paramount, and other studios. In the course of his 15-year film career, Macgowan produced some 50 works, including *Little Women* (1933) with Katharine Hepburn (who stated in her autobiography that she had lost her virginity to Macgowan); the Oscar-winning *La Cucaracha* (1934), the first film produced in modern Technicolor; *Becky Sharp* (1935); *Young Mr. Lincoln* (1939); Alfred Hitchcock's *Lifeboat* (1944); and *Jane Eyre* (1944). He also became something of an expert in historical biographies and produced films in this genre as well.

In 1946, Macgowan retired from the film industry to head the newly founded Department of Theatre Arts at the University of California, Los Angeles (UCLA), a position he held until 1958. He received an honorary doctorate from UCLA and was designated professor emeritus. The theater arts building there is named in his honor.

While Macgowan clearly achieved eminence in the dramatic field, his interest in other fields reflected his eclectic, creative mind. He actively engaged in scholarly studies in sociology, detective fiction, and archaeology, becoming a member of the Archaeological Institute of America. He coauthored the book *What Is Wrong with Marriage* (1929), wrote a study of prehistoric American cultures, *Early Man in the New World* (1950), and edited *Sleuths* (1931), an anthology of detective stories. Kenneth Macgowan died on April 27, 1963, in Los Angeles.

Bibliography

Bloom, Thomas. *Kenneth Macgowan and the Aesthetic Paradigm for the New Stagecraft in America.* New York: P. Lang, 1994.

Macgowan, Kenneth. *The Theater of Tomorrow.* New York, 1921.

The Theater We Worked For: The Letters of Eugene O'Neill to Kenneth Macgowan. Edited by Jackson Bryer. New Haven, Conn.: Yale University Press, 1982.

Karen Charmaine Blansfield

Marblehead, Massachusetts   Before Eugene and CARLOTTA MONTEREY O'NEILL returned to New York City from California in 1945, they considered building another house at SEA ISLAND, GEORGIA, the elite enclave where they spent four years following their 1929–31 sojourn in FRANCE at Le Plessis, near Tours. They soon thought better of it, but BIOGRAPHERS record that they were no happier in New York than while living there in earlier years. In 1928, they fled the city for Europe, in 1931 for the Georgia coast. Now, in 1948, they headed for New England, the region where O'Neill said he felt "closest to the battle of moral forces" (quoted in Sheaffer 1973, 612). There they bought an 1880 shingled house at Marblehead, Massachusetts, that reminded Eugene of his boyhood summer home, MONTE CRISTO COTTAGE in NEW LONDON, CONNECTICUT. Situated directly on the Atlantic, the house needed to be winterized and remodeled at greater cost than expected, making the novelty of setting up housekeeping in an unfamiliar place

Marblehead house *(Courtesy of the Yale Collection of American Literature, Beinecke Rare Book and Manuscript Library)*

rather more subdued than the exhilarating "fresh starts" at Le Plessis, Sea Island, and TAO HOUSE.

Carlotta told Louis Sheaffer that her husband "wanted a place by the sea where the water wouldn't be warm in the summer or cold in the winter, and it would be sunny the year around. He was looking for Paradise, that's what he wanted. I was continually picking homes because Mr. O'Neill, not being well . . . [felt] the weather, the climate [was to blame]: it is too damp or too dry, or it's too this or too that . . . so we would sell and go to the next place and make a home" (quoted in Sheaffer papers). Arthur and Barbara Gelb relate that O'Neill once copied into his notebook these words from FRIEDRICH NIETZSCHE's *Thus Spake Zarathustra*: "I am a wanderer and a mountain climber. . . . I like not the plains, and it seemeth I cannot long sit still. And whatever may become of my fate and experience—a wandering and a mountain climbing will be part of it. In the end one experienceth nothing but one's self" (quoted in Gelb 680).

In September 1950, two years after the O'Neills moved to Marblehead, EUGENE O'NEILL, JR., committed suicide, a crisis for the playwright made even more painful because he had come to realize that he would never write again because of the tremor in his hands. The physical and emotional problems suffered by both Eugene and Carlotta led to violent arguments followed by periods of relative calm. Sheaffer writes that O'Neill's contacts with the outside world came to consist largely of visits

Eugene O'Neill at Marblehead, circa 1948 *(Courtesy of the Yale Collection of American Literature, Beinecke Rare Book and Manuscript Library)*

from his barber and doctor and brief reunions with a few old friends (1973, 626). When a frail Eugene took a hard fall outside the house on a snowy February night in 1951, perhaps after a particularly violent argument with Carlotta, a broken leg led to hospitalization, first in Salem and later in New York, where close friends tried to legally separate the couple. But the effort was in vain, and in May, when Eugene could travel, he returned to Boston, accompanied by a nurse, and to a reconciliation with his wife.

From South Station, O'Neill's Boston doctor drove him to the Shelton, a small residential hotel near Boston University where the final chapter of O'Neill's life ended with his death on November 27, 1953, two and a half years later. During that time, Eugene designated Carlotta his sole heir, disinherited his son SHANE RUDRAIGHE O'NEILL and daughter OONA O'NEILL, gave his papers to the Yale University Library, destroyed a large cache

of notes and drafts for the unfinished play cycle A TALE OF POSSESSORS SELF-DISPOSSESSED, and made plans for his funeral. It has been reported that shortly before his death, by now an invalid, he rose part way up in bed and exclaimed, "I knew it, I knew it! Born in a goddam hotel room and dying in a hotel room!" (quote in Sheaffer 1973, 670).

There was no conventional funeral, and only his wife, doctor, nurse, and a priest were present at the committal in Boston's Forest Hills Cemetery, where the simple gravestone reads "Rest in Peace." Louis Sheaffer concluded his biography of O'Neill by suggesting that the playwright's "true epitaph" may be found in LONG DAY'S JOURNEY INTO NIGHT, when he says through Edmund, the son who represents Eugene, "It was a great mistake, my being born a man—I would have been much more successful as a sea gull or a fish. As it is, I will always be a stranger who never feels at home, who does not really want and is not really wanted, who can never belong, who must always be a little in love with death" (quoted in Sheaffer 1973, 673).

Bibliography

Gelb, Arthur and Barbara Gelb. *O'Neill.* Enlarged ed. New York: Harper & Row, 1973.

Sheaffer, Louis. *O'Neill: Son and Artist.* Boston: Little, Brown, 1973.

———. Papers, Sheaffer-O'Neill Collection, Department of Special Collections and Archives, Charles E. Shain Library. Connecticut College, New London.

Brian Rogers

melodrama   The dominant dramatic genre of the AMERICAN THEATER throughout the 19th century, melodrama declined as psychologically realistic plays that focused on contemporary social problems increasingly relegated the superficial appeal of melodrama to silent movies. As early as 1800, plays by August Kotzebue and Guilbert de Pixérécourt introduced and popularized melodrama, which typically featured gripping plots and visceral excitement leavened by sentimentality and humor. In America, after the Civil War and the enduring example of the unprecedented popularity of the melodramatic stage adaptation of Harriet Beecher Stowe's novel *Uncle Tom's Cabin* (1852), melodrama and its techniques were occasionally co-opted by social reformers (particularly in support of temperance); more traditionally, it featured visual spectacle, including onstage fires, shipwrecks, all manner of natural disasters, riots, and war scenes. *Mazeppa* (1831), *The Octoroon* (1859), *The Heart of Maryland* (1895), and *Ben-Hur* (1899) were among the most popular and enduring melodramas on U.S. stages, continuing to attract audiences well into the modernist era.

With the rise of REALISM in European drama, inspired by the social-problem plays of HENRIK IBSEN in the 1870s, American melodrama abandoned historical settings to depict contemporary life. Steele MacKaye's *Hazel Kirke* (1880), Bronson Howard's *Shenandoah* (1888), William Gillette's *Secret Service* (1895), and Clyde Fitch's *The City* (1909) followed this formula, paving the way for early 20th-century dramatists to abandon melodra-matic trappings in favor of more psychologically complex characters and significant themes drawn from present-day realities.

American playwrights, including those mentioned above (as well as Augustin Daly, Dion Boucicault, and David Belasco) won approval with their original melodramas, while lesser talents adapted popular literary works to melodramatic form, as in the case of Alexandre Dumas's 1844 novel *The Count of Monte Cristo,* adapted for the stage around 1870 by Charles Fechter. Eugene O'Neill's father JAMES O'NEILL scored a major success as Edmond Dantès in the Fechter adaptation in 1883, encouraging him to purchase the stage rights in 1885. Despite his preference for acting in the plays of Shakespeare or in religious drama, James O'Neill subsequently played Dantès more than 6,000 times since his audience demanded to see him in that role.

Clear distinctions between good and evil, suspenseful situations, tight and logically (and linearly) structured action—all melodramatic devices present in *The Count of Monte Cristo*—endure in many forms of drama, but as a distinct genre, it gradually fell out of fashion as cinema adopted many of its conventions. By the early 20th century, the grand manner of acting admired in melodramatic scenes of pathos or terror (typical of James O'Neill and his contemporaries) appeared outsized and overwrought when compared with more natural acting techniques inspired by plays in a more realistic approach.

Growing up in the household of an exemplar of the melodramatic tradition, Eugene O'Neill was both drawn to and repelled by its conventions. His own plays, particularly the earliest, employed melodramatic elements and simultaneously mocked them as outmoded and superficial. O'Neill's attitude on melodrama is expressed in LONG DAY'S JOURNEY INTO NIGHT (1939), in which he presents a fictionalized portrait of his father as James Tyrone, an aging matinee idol convinced he has squandered his promise as a serious actor for the financial rewards of a popular melodramatic vehicle. Tyrone's sons Jamie and Edmund (O'Neill's stage alter-ego) savagely ridicule their father's profession and the play in which he has made his

James O'Neill as Edmund Dantès in the 1912 film adaptation of *The Count of Monte Cristo* *(Courtesy of Culver Pictures)*

fortune, while sympathizing with their father's frustrated artistic dreams.

Melodramatic elements were replaced by a sparseness of style in O'Neill's plays that led to comparisons with classical tragedy, as seen in the PULITZER PRIZE–winning BEYOND THE HORIZON (1920) and DESIRE UNDER THE ELMS (1924). Yet these and others were often identified as melodramas by contemporary drama critics, despite the fact that the psychological depth of O'Neill's characters and themes, and his avoidance of the easy satisfactions supplied by a typically melodramatic play—from homey sentiments on traditional values to romantic and sentimental attitudes (including the inevitable triumph of good over evil)—underscores that his mission was far different from that of audience-pleasing melodrama.

The difficulty of classifying O'Neill's dramatic style in any particular way results from the experimental nature of his work prior to the mid-1930s and the stripping away of obvious dramatic techniques in his last works. For example, his final play, A MOON FOR THE MISBEGOTTEN (1943), which improbably mixes elements of farce with tragedy, was described by some critics as melodrama, although little in this elegiac work conforms to traditional definitions of the form. Yet melodramatic theater was deeply ingrained in O'Neill from childhood, a heritage he both disdained and made use of as one of many influences on his development as a dramatist.

Bibliography

Diamond, George Saul, "The Ironic Use of Melodramatic Conventions and the Conventions of *The Count of Monte Cristo* in the Plays of Eugene O'Neill." *Dissertation Abstracts International* 38 (1977): 2,123A–2,124A.

Manheim, Michael, ed. *The Cambridge Companion to Eugene O'Neill.* Cambridge: Cambridge University Press, 1998.

———. "O'Neill's Transcendence of Melodrama in *A Touch of the Poet* and *A Moon for the Misbegotten.*" *Comparative Drama* 16, no. 3 (Fall 1982): 238–250.

Ryba, Mary Miceli. "Melodrama as a Figure of Mysticism in Eugene O'Neill's Plays." *Dissertation Abstracts International* 38 (1977): 2,794A.

Singer, Ben. *Melodrama and Modernity.* New York: Columbia University Press, 2001.

James Fisher

merchant marine   The merchant service is the area of shipping related to the transport of goods and people. An individual working in that service is referred to as a merchant marine or merchant sailor.

Eugene O'Neill was actively engaged in the maritime world for about two years, a brief time in the life of a man who lived to be 65, but his days at SEA reverberated throughout his life and marked his work in unpredictable ways. Of the 45 plays O'Neill authorized for publication, significantly, 19 of those deal with the maritime world.

O'Neill BIOGRAPHERS, dramatic literature scholars, and theater practitioners acknowledge the importance of his maritime experience on O'Neill, but few have an in-depth understanding of the maritime world and the culture that shaped the playwright's work. The culture of the sea has its own rules and its own vocabulary. Life at sea gives rise to a camaraderie that comes from shared experiences, under extreme pressure, unimaginable to the outsider. O'Neill's connection to the sea and the profound effect it had on his sea plays offers a fuller understanding of the man and the work.

In his autobiographical play LONG DAY'S JOURNEY INTO NIGHT, O'Neill gives voice to his maritime experience through the character Edmund, as he speaks to his father, James Tyrone.

You've just told me some high spots in your memories. Want to hear mine? They're all connected with the sea. Here's one. When I was on the Squarehead square rigger, bound for Buenos Aires. Full moon in the Trades. The old hooker driving fourteen knots. I lay on the bowsprit, facing astern, with the water foaming into spume under me, the masts with every sail white in the moonlight, towering high above me. I became drunk with the beauty and singing rhythm of it, and for a moment I lost myself—actually lost my life. I was set free! I dissolved in the sea, became white sails and flying spray, became beauty and rhythm, became moonlight and the ship and the high dim-starred sky! I belonged, without past or future, within peace and unity and a wild joy, within something greater than my own life, or the life of Man,

Eugene O'Neill wearing his "American Line" sweater, one of his most prized possessions *(Courtesy of the Yale Collection of American Literature, Beinecke Rare Book and Manuscript Library)*

to Life itself! To God, if you want to put it that way. Then another time on the American Line, when I was lookout on the crow's nest in the dawn watch. A calm sea, that time. Only a lazy ground swell and a slow drowsy roll of the ship. The passengers asleep and none of the crew in sight. No sound of man. Black smoke pouring from the funnels behind and beneath me. Dreaming, not keeping lookout, feeling alone, and above, and apart, watching the dawn creep like a painted dream over the sky and sea which slept together. Then the moment of ecstatic freedom came. The peace, the end of the quest, the last harbor, the joy of belonging to a fulfillment beyond men's lousy, pitiful, greedy fears and hopes and dreams. (3:811–812)

The "Squarehead square rigger" O'Neill refers to was the Norwegian bark the CHARLES RACINE, on which he sailed in 1910. He also mentions the American Line, a passenger steamship line, for which he worked as a seaman. O'Neill's time aboard the *Charles Racine* was his entry into the "brotherhood" of seafarers, and he exited that community shortly after his release from service with the American Line.

O'Neill's first contact with the sea came at an early age in NEW LONDON, CONNECTICUT. His father, JAMES O'NEILL, had bought property there in 1884, four years before Eugene was born. The seaport town would become the O'Neill family's summer home for some 30 years; they had no other permanent residence. An actor of significant celebrity, James O'Neill was often on tour, which meant that Eugene and his older brother Jamie (JAMES O'NEILL, JR.) were either in boarding school or living in theatrical hotels with their parents, with the exception of their summers in New London.

New London is on the easternmost edge of Long Island Sound at the mouth of the Thames River, and it has one of the best natural deepwater harbors on the eastern seaboard. From its founding in the 17th century until the early 20th century, New Londoners made their living from the sea and related industries. During O'Neill's youth, New London was a maritime community in transition. The last vestiges of a significant whaling indus-

try were dying out, but stories and a rich whaling history remained. Even though whaling was at its end, New London harbor was still active with fishing vessels, steamers, barges, yachts, and revenue cutters providing a constant flow of traffic on the Thames River. The great maritime heritage was also evident in the town itself, with palatial homes built from whaling money, social clubs and other establishments that catered to seafaring men, and industries that supported shipping.

New London's busy harbor was just a stone's throw from where the O'Neills lived; every vessel that entered or exited New London passed by their home. Eugene O'Neill had the chance to observe and absorb the ways of the maritime world, laying a foundation of knowledge for his later firsthand experience.

O'Neill biographer Louis Sheaffer has written that New London made O'Neill feel at home on land and on the water, with the city sitting on the Thames and close to the Atlantic Ocean. It sparked dreams of far-off places and gave O'Neill the opportunity to experience bars, seamen's dives, and whorehouses, a preview of what he would later find in New York City, BUENOS AIRES, and Southampton.

In 1910, at age 21, O'Neill began his stint of living and working with sailors at sea and on shore. The age of sail had almost faded into history, but O'Neill was lucky in his timing. He spent two months aboard the *Charles Racine,* one of the last square-riggers, and then transitioned to voyages on three steamers, the SS IKALA, the SS NEW YORK, and the SS PHILADELPHIA. These were extraordinary experiences for a novice. In 1920, O'Neill said to Olin Downes, who wrote for the *Boston Sunday Post,* "My real start as a dramatist was when I got out of an academy and among men, on the sea" (quoted in Estrin 10).

The *Charles Racine* was a unique vessel under the command of a well-respected and experienced captain, Gustav Waage. Captain Waage had a reputation for efficiency in delivering cargo without loss or damage. He was known for fast passages, and he never spared anything to achieve his goals, demanding a great deal from his officers and crew, and also himself. He loved to sail and had little respect for steamers, which "boiled themselves

Crew of the SS *Charles Racine* *(Courtesy of the Peabody Essex Museum)*

across oceans" (letter from Severin Waage to Louis Sheaffer, 25 June 1958, Sheaffer-O'Neill Collection). Captain Waage had convinced the owners of the *Charles Racine* to build the vessel for him in the early 1890s. The *Racine* was the only square-rigger the company owned; all of their other vessels were steamers. By the turn of the 20th century, most of the ships in service were steamers; the time of the great age of sail and square-rigged ships had passed. But there were a few trades where square-riggers were still viable, and one of those was carrying lumber from Boston and Portland, Maine, to Buenos Aires, Argentina. Buenos Aires was undergoing a great economic boom, and it was in need of lumber for building.

O'Neill's decision to go to sea was spurred by the bad publicity his father was receiving due to Eugene's recent marriage to KATHLEEN JENKINS, the birth of EUGENE O'NEILL, JR., and Eugene's estrangement from his young family. In hopes that the negative publicity in New York would subside, James O'Neill took Eugene on tour with him to Boston. While in Boston, O'Neill met sailors from the *Charles Racine* and learned that the ship occasionally took on passengers. O'Neill convinced his father that it would be a good idea for him to go to sea. After James O'Neill met Captain Waage, he felt confident that his son would be taken care of, and an agreement was made that Eugene would board the *Racine* as a passenger for the trip from

Boston to Buenos Aires. It was not uncommon in New London for fathers to send their wayward sons to sea in hopes that they would find direction and purpose in their lives. In addition, arrangements were made for a friend to accompany O'Neill on the trip. The friend has not been definitely identified, but there is speculation that it was Louis Holladay, O'Neill's friend from GREENWICH VILLAGE, New York.

Captain Waage was paid $75 for O'Neill's fare (Sheaffer 1968, 161). In a letter to the ship's owners on June 7, 1910 Captain Waage wrote: "The passengers are two boys, who I have been asked to take care of, and it is understood that they are going to work on the voyage" (letter from Gustav Waage to Sigval Bergesen, Sheaffer-O'Neill Collection). Having two sets of extra hands would have been a welcome addition for the ship's crew. It was difficult at the time for a Norwegian ship to acquire adequate crew in American ports; they were unable to compete with American and British ships, which paid higher wages. Also, men were more interested in working on steamships, which provided more comfortable living conditions and an easier work routine. O'Neill was fortunate to have found passage on the *Charles Racine*. It provided him with a rare challenge and a romantic view of a disappearing world.

Not only were the *Charles Racine* and its captain unusual for their time, but the passage from Boston to Buenos Aires in summer 1910 was also an unusual one. The passage began in early June and ended in early August after 57 days at sea. It was one of the slowest and most difficult passages that Captain Waage had ever experienced. By contrast, during another passage that year, the *Racine* sailed from Nova Scotia to Buenos Aires in 37 days (Sheaffer 1968, 169).

Upon the ship's arrival in Buenos Aires, Captain Waage wrote to the owners to report that for the first 16 days of the passage, they experienced wonderful sailing weather and expected that they would arrive in Buenos Aires in record time. Their luck changed dramatically, and Waage reported that they "ran into calms, gales and headwinds," which meant the ship was at a standstill or maybe even being blown backwards. During the final portion of the passage, said Waage, "we experienced three full storms, one of which was a full hurricane. The sails were tied with extra seizings, and we consequently lost no sails. On the other hand, we unfortunately lost some deck cargo when the vessel heeled" (transcription Log of *Charles Racine*, Sheaffer-O'Neill Collection).

O'Neill had a full range of experiences aboard the *Charles Racine*. He witnessed the full beauty and romance of a square-rigger under sail, with the wind at its back, driving the ship through the sea. He could look up and see the sails billowing high above him. He also experienced the opposite extreme when the ship was becalmed and there was no wind to move it forward. The ship just lolled on the open sea under the equatorial sun, the men wishing for the slightest breeze. And finally, O'Neill experienced the ferocity of the sea as the *Racine* rode out a hurricane; no matter its size, a ship can seem insignificant in a storm-tossed sea. Not only was O'Neill introduced to the impact of the environment on shipboard life, but he was introduced to the culture of the community of men who had their own traditions, social hierarchy, superstitions, and folklore. Aboard the *Racine,* he learned the ways of a ship and sailors that he put to practice on other vessels.

Every large and medium-sized port had a sailortown, a neighborhood with a high concentration of businesses that catered to sailors: bars, brothels, boarding houses, shipping agents, chandlers, and seaman's aide societies. Some of the establishments were reputable; many were not. Upon arrival in port, a ship's crew was descended on by runners, whose establishments were ready to cater to each sailor's whim, need, and desire. Sailors had money to spend when they arrived in port, having been paid for the passage they had just completed. By the early 1900s, Buenos Aires had developed as the most popular eastern South American port among the seafaring community. Severin Waage, son of Captain Waage and a captain himself, spoke of the docks of Buenos Aires in 1910 as full of nightclubs and the sounds of many languages. He recalled the agents from different bordellos coming aboard the ship and leaving their cards. One card read, "Come up to my house, plenty fun, perty girls, plenty dance, three men killed last night" (letter from Osmund Christophersen to Louis Sheaffer, Sheaffer-O'Neill Collection).

O'Neill was familiar with sailortowns from living in New London and visiting Boston, but his arrival in Buenos Aires's sailortown was different—this time he was arriving as a sailor. He was experiencing the extremes of a sailor's life—the loneliness and isolation that comes from extended periods at sea and the indulgences and excesses available ashore. At the age of 21, O'Neill disembarked in Buenos Aires with money to spend, which had been provided by his father before he left Boston.

Buenos Aires was not a safe place for sailors or any transient men. Many disreputable elements preyed on sailors, who had no one to look out for them or notice they were missing. The abuses were many, and the authorities often ignored them. Some bars and boardinghouses engaged in crimping or shanghaiing. This method of providing crews for vessels involved either trickery or kidnapping. Some sailors passed out from too much drink or were knocked out by a blow to the head or by a narcotic slipped in their drink. They would wake up onboard ship, stripped of whatever money they had and indebted to the ship for their first month's wages, which had been paid to the crimp who had delivered them. One of the most notorious crimps in Buenos Aires was Tommy Moore, who ran a sailors' boardinghouse and pub. He became known for shipping corpses. He would splash a corpse with alcohol and sew a rat into the clothing so the body had some movement, then deliver it to a ship, claiming the man was passed out from drinking.

During the beginning of his stay in Buenos Aires, O'Neill slept aboard the *Charles Racine* and spent the occasional night at the Continental Hotel, but he returned to the ship for meals. The *Racine* did not stay in port for long, and O'Neill began sharing a room with Frederick Hettman, an American working in Argentina whom O'Neill had met at the hotel. In an effort to save money, O'Neill moved out of the hotel into a less-expensive boardinghouse. While in Buenos Aires, O'Neill took on menial jobs, one of which was for Singer Sewing Machine, breaking up old sewing machines, and another loading hides on to a ship. He did not stay with any of the jobs for very long.

The majority of O'Neill's time was spent frequenting the bars near the docks. One in particular was the Sailor's Opera, patronized by sailors of many nationalities. One of the main attractions was an all-female ensemble of violinists, whose violins were stringless. The actual music was provided by an all-male ensemble or a solo pianist hidden behind a curtain. An added appeal was that the girls wore no underwear beneath their short skirts (Sheaffer 1968, 173).

Buenos Aires had more than just bars and brothels for a sailor's entertainment. The waterfront district of Barracas had theaters that showed pornographic films made in FRANCE and Spain. The main rooms of the theaters were lined with small curtained alcoves just big enough for a bed. Prostitutes were available between films. O'Neill said to an interviewer, "Those moving pictures in Barracas were mighty rough stuff. Nothin' was left to the imagination. Every form of perversity was enacted, and, of course, sailors flocked to them" (quoted in Estrin 67).

O'Neill refers to Buenos Aires and his experiences there in a number of his plays, particularly in the one-act BOUND EAST FOR CARDIFF, in which he refers to Tommy Moore, the Sailor's Opera, and the moving pictures in Barracas.

Eventually O'Neill left the boardinghouse and lived "on the beach," which was not uncommon among the transient population in Buenos Aires. He used what little money he had to buy alcohol. In 1920, O'Neill told Olin Downes of the *Boston Sunday Post,* "I hadn't any job at all, and was down on the beach—'down,' if not precisely 'out'" (quoted in Estrin 9). He fell into a deep depression, sinking so low that he could fall no further, and he either had to pick himself back up again or just disappear. Fortunately, he chose the former and pulled himself together enough to secure a position on a British tramp steamer bound for New York City.

On March 21, 1911, O'Neill departed Buenos Aires aboard the SS *Ikala.* The word *tramp* means that the vessel did not have a regular route; its itinerary was determined by the cargoes it secured and their destinations. In Buenos Aires, the *Ikala* was not able to acquire a full crew, so Captain Carruthers was willing take on "scenery bums"—

transients who joined the ship to get from one place to another. O'Neill came on in this capacity; as a working passenger.

Compared to the *Charles Racine*, the *Ikala* was more typical of the type of ships plying the oceans at the time, and the differences in the life onboard and the work that needed to be done was tremendous. The *Racine* relied on its sails and the wind for power, whereas the *Ikala* relied on coal to heat the boilers that generated steam for the engines. The crew making up the two vessels was also dramatically different. Aboard the *Racine*, the sailors worked together to handle the sails to propel the vessel forward. On the *Ikala*, the crew was divided into the seamen, who were responsible for all the operation and maintenance above decks, and the stokers and trimmers, who were responsible for keeping the fires in the furnaces burning. The *Ikala* was part of the modern age, and the *Racine* was a remnant from a time gone by. Aboard the *Ikala*, O'Neill lived in the crew's quarters, but on the *Racine* he lived apart from the crew.

It was aboard the *Ikala* that O'Neill probably experienced firsthand the camaraderie that exists between sailors and the trust and respect that they have for each other. O'Neill demonstrated his understanding of shipboard life in his one-act SS GLENCAIRN plays, which were inspired by his time aboard the *Ikala*. O'Neill also witnessed the division and animosity that existed between sailors and stokers. The most essential crew aboard steamships were the stokers. They actually generated the power to make the ship move by feeding the furnaces, taking away from the seamen what little prestige they had. O'Neill used the animosity between seamen and stokers to strengthen the dramatic tension in a number of his plays, particularly The HAIRY APE and "ANNA CHRISTIE."

The passage from Buenos Aires to New York took less than a month, including a stop in Trinidad, where the vessel anchored off shore. On returning to New York O'Neill rented a room for $3 a month at JIMMY "THE PRIEST'S," a bar and flophouse in the heart of sailortown. O'Neill was attracted to Jimmy's for its inexpensive liquor of relatively good quality and its free lunch. He described the clientele at Jimmy's as a "hard lot, at first glance. Every

type; sailors on shore leave or stranded; longshoremen, waterfront riffraff, gangsters, down and outers, drifters from the ends of the earth. . . . They were sincere, loyal and generous. In some queer way they carried on. I learned at Jimmy the Priest's not to sit in judgment on people" (quoted in Sheaffer 1968, 192). Jimmy had a reputation of being protective of his regular clientele and not willing to put up with troublemakers. As a result, the bar and flophouse were a refuge for many men. The opening scene of "Anna Christie" takes place at Tommy the Priest's and O'Neill provides an accurate description of the actual bar.

After three months in New York, O'Neill went to sea again, this time not as a passenger: He signed on the American Line's SS *New York* as an ordinary seaman. O'Neill was proud of the fact that he was able to sign on officially as a sailor. It proved that he had gained experience and expertise to be able to do the job. The American Line ships provided regular passenger service between New York and Southampton, England. The *New York* was larger than the other vessels he had been on previously, and the crew was significantly larger. The ship carried 1,290 passengers, and the crew totaled nearly 400.

According to O'Neill, "there was about as much 'sea glamour' in working aboard a passenger steamship as there would have been in working in a summer hotel! I washed enough deck area to cover a good-sized town" (quoted in Mulett 30). He did not mind the work on the *New York*, but he resented the passengers who lounged and promenaded around the decks while he was on his hands and knees scrubbing. The extremity of the contrast between O'Neill's place aboard ship and that of the passengers destroyed his image of the heroic sailor whom he had come to know and admire.

The friction between the stokers and sailors was also more pronounced than O'Neill had seen aboard the *Ikala*. The "black gang"—the name given to the firemen, or stokers and trimmers, who tended the furnaces—looked down on the seamen as weaklings and part of the past. The work of the black gang was mechanical. To produce the superheated steam to drive the engines, the ship's boilers consumed about 13 tons of coal per hour. Trimmers trundled the coal from storage bunkers in wheelbarrows and carried away the ashes. Despite the physical requirements of their job, stokers were skilled practitioners of fire, able to gauge its quality by the color and sound of the burning coal. They fed the furnaces and took instructions from engineers, who ran the engines, while communicating with the officers on the bridge by way of bells and whistles. O'Neill later would use his insights into life on a passenger steamer, the conflict between stokers and sailors, and give vent to some of his resentments regarding the social CLASSES in the play *The Hairy Ape*.

When the *New York* arrived in Southampton, it needed to go into dry dock for repairs. O'Neill stayed in Southampton and had the opportunity to get the feel of the British port. At the time, England was in the throes of the Great Labor Strike of 1911. At the center of the strike were the dock laborers and transportation workers, joined by the stokers and seamen who put aside their differences and pledged their support. The railroads stopped running, and ships were stuck in port. It was during this time that O'Neill met DRISCOLL, a stoker from the American Line's SS *Philadelphia*. They became strong friends, and Driscoll would later become the inspiration for a number of characters in many of O'Neill's plays.

Once the strike ended, O'Neill was able to secure a position as an able-bodied seaman (now simply able seaman) aboard the *Philadelphia*. He was extremely proud of achieving the rank, which was a step up from what he had been on the *New York*. The designation of able-bodied seaman proved that he had the skills and experience of a sailor, and he cherished that thought throughout his life.

O'Neill arrived back in New York in late August 1911, having been gone only approximately five weeks. Upon his return he took up residency again at Jimmy "the Priest's," where he stayed through the end of the year. In December, he heard from his wife Kathleen that she wanted a divorce. The only grounds for divorce at the time were adultery, so a scenario was created where O'Neill was found in a hotel room with a woman. O'Neill was so demoralized by the experience that he fell into a deep depression and attempted suicide by taking a narcotic. He was revived by his friends at Jimmy's,

but the experience was a turning point for him. Once again he had hit rock bottom, and he had two choices: either perish or pick himself up and continue on with life. He left New York and joined his parents on tour, then returned to New London.

Leaving New York at that time marked the end of O'Neill's life as a sailor, a period that lasted only two years. But during that time, he had had a full range of experiences—from the beauty of squared-rigged sailing to the mechanization and drudgery of steamships and the pleasures and depravities of life in sailortowns on three continents. O'Neill cherished those times and would recall them again and again in conversation and letters with friends and family. He drew upon that period in his life continually as he developed as a playwright, and the plays related to the sea launched his career and a new AMERICAN THEATER.

Bibliography

Bisset, Sir James, with P. R. Stephensen. *Tramps and Ladies*. New York: Criterion Books, 1959.

Black, Stephen A. *Eugene O'Neill: Beyond Mourning and Tragedy*. New Haven, Conn., and London: Yale University Press, 1999.

Bonsor, N. R. P. *North Atlantic Seaway*. Vol. 3. Jersey, Channel Islands: Brookside Publications, 1979.

Bunting, W. H. *Portrait of a Port: Boston 1852–1914*. Cambridge, Mass.: Belknap Press of Harvard University Press, 1971.

Colby, Barnard L. *For Oil and Buggy Whips: Whaling Captains of New London County, Connecticut*. Mystic, Conn.: Mystic Seaport Museum, 1992.

Decker, Robert Owen. *The Whaling City*. Chester, Conn.: Pequot Press, 1976.

Downes, Olin. "Playwright Finds His Inspiration on Lonely Sand Dunes by the Sea." In *Conversations with Eugene O'Neill*, edited by Mark W. Estrin, 10. Jackson: University Press of Mississippi, 1990.

Estrin, Mark W., ed. *Conversations with Eugene O'Neill*. Jackson and London: University Press of Mississippi, 1990.

Flayhart, William Henry, III. *The American Line (1871–1902)*. New York and London: W. W. Norton, 2000.

Gelb, Arthur, and Barbara Gelb. *O'Neill*. Enlarged ed. New York: Harper & Row, 1973.

————. *O'Neill: Life with Monte Cristo.* New York: Applause Books, 2000.

Hawthorne, Hildegarde. *Old Seaport Towns of New England.* New York: Dodd, Mead & Company, 1916.

Hugill, Stan. *Sailortown.* London: Routledge & Kegan Paul, 1967.

Kalonyme, Louis. "O'Neill Lifts Curtain on His Early Days." In *Conversations with Eugene O'Neill,* edited by Mark W. Estrin, 67. Jackson: University Press of Mississippi, 1990.

Lloyd's Register of British and Foreign Shipping 1907/1908, 1909/1910 & 1910/1911. London: Lloyd's Register of British and Foreign Shipping, 1908, 1909, and 1910.

Lubbock, Basil. *The Last of the Windjammers.* 2 vols. Glasgow: Brown, Son & Ferguson, Ltd., 1953–54.

Maddocks, Melvin. *The Seafarers: The Great Liners.* Alexandria, Va.: Time-Life Books, 1978.

Miller, William H., Jr. *The First Great Ocean Liners.* New York: Dover Publications, 1984.

Mullett, Mary B. "The Extraordinary Story of Eugene O'Neill." In *Conversations with Eugene O'Neill,* edited by Mark W. Estrin, 30. Jackson: University Press of Mississippi, 1990.

Record of American and Foreign Shipping. New York: American Bureau of Shipping, 1910 and 1917.

Richter, Robert A. *Eugene O'Neill and Dat Ole Davil Sea.* Mystic, Conn.: Mystic Seaport Museum, 2004.

————. *Touring Eugene O'Neill's New London.* New London: Connecticut College, 2001.

Shay, Frank. *A Sailor's Treasury.* New York: W. W. Norton, 1951.

Sheaffer, Louis. *O'Neill: Son and Artist.* Boston: Little, Brown, 1973.

————. *O'Neill: Son and Playwright.* Boston: Little, Brown, 1968.

Shaeffer-O'Neill Collection. Department of Special Collections and Archives, Charles E. Shain Library, Connecticut College, New London.

Villiers, Alan. *The Way of the Ship.* New York: Charles Scribner's Sons, 1970.

Weibust, Knut. *Deep Sea Sailors: A Study in Maritime Ethnology.* 2nd ed. Stockholm: Kungl. Boktryckeriet P. A. Norstedt & Soner, 1976.

Robert A. Richter

Monte Cristo Cottage Eugene O'Neill's boyhood home in NEW LONDON, CONNECTICUT, was named for his actor father JAMES O'NEILL's famous role in a stage adaptation of Alexandre Dumas's novel, *The Count of Monte Cristo.* The O'Neill family was usually in residence only from June to early September, an annual respite from James's acting schedule, which filled the other nine months of the year. Coming to New London for the first time in 1884, over the years the family occupied at least two other houses and a hotel before moving into the eight-room Victorian dwelling at 325 Pequot Avenue for the summer of 1900 (Gelb 102–105, 159), when Eugene was 11. James had created the house by combining a store and a schoolhouse that stood on the land. Monte Cristo Cottage was pleasantly situated only steps from the banks of the Thames River, its wide porch almost literally a stage looking out across the broad estuary at its confluence with Long Island Sound. Having been turned into a museum and study center in the 1970s, it stands there today an icon of AMERICAN THEATER history.

The two lighthouses marking the entrance to New London harbor were visible from the front lawn, the slow, incessant rhythm of their horns breaking the stillness when fog descended. Fishers Island lay just offshore, and the shores of distant Long Island could be discerned on a clear day. The maritime activity of the historic port was particularly lively in the summer: The yachts of the wealthy dropped anchor, the frequency of the New York passenger boats increased, and the annual Harvard-Yale rowing regatta attracted thousands of spectators. The Fourth of July, with its carnival aspect and fireworks reflecting on the river, was another summer highlight. Young O'Neill was often in the harbor with his own rowboat, swam in its relatively clean waters, and made acquaintance with the characters who worked at the docks and other waterfront enterprises within walking distance of his home.

In sharp contrast to the idyllic and colorful nature of its setting, Monte Cristo Cottage was also the stage on which the chronic dysfunction of the O'Neill family played out. LONG DAY'S JOURNEY INTO NIGHT, the intensely autobiographical play

Monte Cristo Cottage at 325 Pequot Avenue in New London, Connecticut *(Courtesy of the Sheaffer-O'Neill Collection, Charles E. Shain Library of Connecticut College)*

that penetrates to the heart of this dysfunctionality, is set in the living room of the house, which looks today much as it did when the O'Neills lived there. The house is also part of the setting for AH, WILDERNESS!, the gentle 1933 comedy that depicts a boy's coming of age within the embrace of settled family life. The parlors of both plays are clearly patterned after that of the O'Neill home. One of the eight rooms under the family roof was O'Neill's own: small, simple, and private, in contrast to the impersonal hotels and boarding schools where he spent most of the year. To be sure, the house and its environs are inseparable in their physical characteristics from the galaxy of individuals O'Neill knew and observed during the parts of 19 years he spent there, above all his own family members, and it is the totality of this experience from which he

later drew so much over the course of his playwriting career. It would be difficult to overestimate the influence of Monte Cristo Cottage and all it represented on the playwright's emotional development and his lifetime achievement. It has been characterized as no less than the crucible of O'Neill's genius, an analogy made by George White, founder of the EUGENE O'NEILL THEATER CENTER in nearby Waterford.

It is worth noting that during his summers in New London, O'Neill also gained valuable perspective on the dynamics of more "normal" family life by observing at close range those played out in the homes of his good friend Arthur McGinley and of the Rippin family, at whose boarding house a few doors away the O'Neills often took their meals. Writing his first plays, the 25-year-old Eugene had a good taste of conventional family life while actually living at the Rippin home for several months in the winter of 1913–14, continuing his recovery from tuberculosis while the rest of the family went on tour.

Life at Monte Cristo Cottage, on the other hand, was anything but normal, due in large part to the chronic unhappiness of Eugene's mother, MARY ELLEN "ELLA" O'NEILL. Among many other things, Ella O'Neill complained about what she perceived to be her husband's unwillingness to spend the money required to bring the house up to her expectations. Despite its waterfront site in an attractive neighborhood, Ella found it gloomy and ill-designed, which to a large extent it was, having been cobbled together from existing buildings not originally designed as houses. The upstairs rooms were both small and low, the first-floor ceiling having been raised to well over 11 feet when the house was being put together.

Visiting in the 1950s to gather material for his O'Neill biography, Louis Sheaffer observed that the house had a Jekyll-and-Hyde personality: the parlor and sun porch cheerful in the early morning hours, when the rising sun cast a warm glow through the stained-glass transom and parlor windows; increasingly dark as the day progressed; and particularly gloomy in the evening, when the disproportionately high ceilings detracted from any feeling of warmth. He also saw that it reflected James O'Neill's varying "fiscal moods"—the fine parquet flooring, well-built stair balustrade and handsome fireplace tile work offset by cheap construction elsewhere (Louis Sheaffer papers, Sheaffer-O'Neill Collection). Like many houses in summer resort neighborhoods— and for a time this part of New London had such pretensions—it was not insulated, lacked central heating until 1912, and could be chilly in unseasonable weather.

Ella's complaints about the physical shortcomings of the cottage were, however, only one manifestation of her pervasive sense of homelessness and loneliness, and O'Neill's later comments on his family's lack of a real home are expressed as much as an echo of his mother's complaints as of his own. In letters and conversations, he would refer to Ella's spiritual homelessness, recollections that reached

their highest sustained pitch in the lines of Mary Tyrone, the mother figure in *Long Day's Journey into Night,* who repeatedly assails her husband for failing to provide her with a proper home, a litany harshly embellished by Edmund Tyrone (the Eugene character) when he refers to the house as "a summer dump in a place she hates." In 1944, in a conversation with a visiting friend while living unhappily in a San Francisco hotel, O'Neill most forcefully articulated the early sense of homelessness he as well as his mother had felt, a recollection almost certainly prompted by having recently given up TAO HOUSE, the California house that had come closest to being a real home in his lifetime. It was Tao House that somehow enabled him to write his undisputed masterpiece, *Long Day's Journey into Night,* as well as the elegy for his brother Jamie, A MOON FOR THE MISBEGOTTEN, set also in New London and vividly drawn from his painful family history.

Many years before that time, when O'Neill began to taste success, belatedly weaning himself from financial dependence on his father, he also began to contemplate a new home that would supplant the only one he had ever known. As his BIOGRAPHERS report, and as his and CARLOTTA MONTEREY O'NEILL's letters and conversations make plain, he spent a lifetime searching for it. It could be argued that the ingrained pattern of his family's peripatetic life in his formative years, when he was "at home" for only three months of the year, was reenacted in painfully protracted fashion right up to the moment of his death in a Boston hotel room in 1953. For nearly a quarter of a century, he and his second and third wives occupied a series of dwellings that turned out to be no more satisfactory, for many and various reasons, than Monte Cristo Cottage had been to his mother.

The novelty of the first house O'Neill could call his own, PEAKED HILL BAR, situated directly on the Atlantic near Provincetown, Massachusetts, wore off after a couple of years, as did the allure of BROOK FARM, a large, wooded estate in affluent Ridgefield, Connecticut. SPITHEAD, a unique waterfront house in Bermuda seemed to be the answer, but the marriage to AGNES BOULTON foundered there, and he abandoned it almost overnight. A rented château near Tours, France, occupied with Carlotta Monterey both before and after their marriage in Paris, ceased to please a full year before their three-year lease was to expire. An eight-room Manhattan duplex did not suit, and they shortly retreated to the isolation of Casa Gerotta, a beachfront house in SEA ISLAND, GEORGIA, built to their exact specifications, only to depart within five years. After a brief, false start in the damp Pacific Northwest, they built Tao House, the most successful of their homes by far, on a mountainside in Danville, California, but occupied it for only six years. Growing health problems and wartime restrictions rendered mountainside living impossible for them, and after a year in San Francisco hotels, they returned to the East and decided, while living in a small New York hotel suite, that they would undertake their last "fresh start" in an old-fashioned New England cottage in MARBLEHEAD, MASSACHUSETTS, north of Boston. The cottage reminded the playwright of the Monte Cristo Cottage, its property lapped by the same waters that washed the rocks along Pequot Avenue in New London.

Travis Bogard has described Monte Cristo Cottage as the "fixed foot" of Eugene O'Neill's travels through the world, the succession of houses he occupied throughout his adult life forming an "encompassing circle" around that house. Commenting on the brief visit Eugene and Carlotta made to the cottage in June 1931, after six years of luxurious living abroad, Bogard suggested that the dismay O'Neill felt upon seeing it again is difficult to name, being not only regret and pain, but reflecting "a sense of debts unpaid and benefits forgot" (Bogard 356). Without even entering the house that day, he was profoundly aware that it "contained his truth"—the truth he would distill in *Long Day's Journey* 10 years later, 3,000 miles away. In an article published in the *Chicago Tribune* in 1988 entitled "O'Neill's Haunted House," David McCracken wrote that as O'Neill's first home, Monte Cristo Cottage lingered in the playwright's mind all his life, citing the assertion of the French philosopher Gaston Bachelard—a near contemporary of O'Neill—that our first home is our "first universe" (10).

In 1919, a year before James O'Neill death, he and Ella O'Neill sold Monte Cristo Cottage, and Ella subsequently sold the furniture. In 1971, it was designated a National Historic Landmark, and the Eugene O'Neill Theater Center in neighboring Waterford, Connecticut, was able to take possession of it in 1974. After the death of the cottage's last occupant in 1975, the center took it over with the intention of turning it into a museum and study center. Through the ensuing three decades, it has been gradually repaired, restored, and furnished under the care of its two longtime curators. In 2005, a small annex, similar in architectural outline to a kitchen "lean-to" that had been removed decades before, was attached to the rear to provide additional museum support space. Open seasonally for tours and at other times by appointment, the cottage attracts several hundred visitors annually: school groups, theater studies students, conference and seminar participants, and interested individuals, including occasional travelers from abroad. For actors and directors, the house is something of a shrine; among those who have made the pilgrimage, usually in preparation for an O'Neill role or production, are Zoe Caldwell, COLLEEN DEWHURST, Brian Dennehy, Geraldine Fitzgerald, Julie Harris, Helen Hayes, David Hays (designer of the first American production of *Long Day's Journey into Night*, who lived in the house for several months), Salome Jens, Theodore Mann, Siobhan McKenna, JOSÉ QUINTERO, JASON ROBARDS, Kevin Spacey, Robert Redford, Liv Ullmann, and Teresa Wright.

Bibliography

Black, Stephen A. *Eugene O'Neill: Beyond Mourning and Tragedy.* New Haven, Conn., and London: Yale University Press, 1999.

Bogard, Travis. *Contour in Time: The Plays of Eugene O'Neill.* Rev. ed. New York: Oxford University Press, 1988.

Gelb, Arthur, and Barbara Gelb. *O'Neill: Life with Monte Cristo.* New York: Applause Books, 2000.

McCracken, David. "O'Neill's Haunted House," *Chicago Tribune*, October 16, 1988, Sect. 10.

O'Neill, Eugene. *Selected Letters of Eugene O'Neill.* Edited by Travis Bogard and Jackson R. Bryer. New Haven, Conn.: Yale University Press, 1988.

Richter, Robert A. *Eugene O'Neill and Dat Ole Davil Sea: Maritime Influences in the Life and Works of*

Eugene O'Neill. Mystic, Conn.: Mystic Seaport, 2004.

Sheaffer, Louis. *O'Neill: Son and Artist.* Boston: Little, Brown, 1973.

———. *O'Neill: Son and Playwright.* Boston: Little, Brown, 1968.

Sheaffer-O'Neill Collection. Department of Special Collections and Archives, Charles E. Shain Library, Connecticut College, New London.

Brian Rogers

music   In the early years of the 20th century, a revolution in the philosophy of American stage-craft occurred—a revolution that had its roots in a European theater increasingly disinterested with spectacle and MELODRAMA on the one hand and with stark REALISM on the other. When it crossed the Atlantic, this revolution was christened "art theater" by one of its greatest proponents, art critic and dramaturge Sheldon Cheney (Bogard 1972, 172). According to Cheney, art theater was a revolution of both dramatic content and dramatic form. It consisted of the dramatization of inner essences rather than superficial realities, and its form required the creation of a structural unity between the various arts that comprised theatrical production. Thus, set design, lighting design, costume design, and props design were acknowledged to be significant parts of the whole, and, as such, expected to aid in the communication of inner essences.

Absent from the list of the various theater arts to be dramatically and structurally united was the art of music, though this did not correspond to any such absence of music on the stage. In fact, music was a common component of the early modern theater: Musical acts were frequently featured on the still-popular vaudeville stage, formulaic musical comedies abounded, and commercial melodramas often utilized accompaniment to enhance the thrill of climactic scenes (Bogard 1993, Foreword). While those who followed the precepts of art theater recognized music as an art form theoretically suited to a dramatization of inner spiritual truths, in practice little was done to reclaim music from the territory of melodramatic embellishment and

Eugene O'Neill at his player piano "Rosie" at Tao House *(Courtesy of the Yale Collection of American Literature, Beinecke Rare Book and Manuscript Library)*

comic underscore. Music, it appeared, was tainted by its association with purportedly inferior forms of theater.

Eugene O'Neill was perhaps the first American playwright to seriously attempt to create a place for music within the dramatic unification of the theater arts (Bogard 1993, Foreword). A participant in the art theater movement, he openly explored experimental forms of theater and staging and was for a few years (1916–1922) the in-house playwright of a "little theater" group—the PROVINCETOWN PLAYERS. But while most of O'Neill's contemporaries within the art theater movement simply did without music, O'Neill seemed capable of intuitively creating a revolution of orchestration in the theater. Although he did not set out to appropriate the program of art theater as a guideline for his use of music, his employment of it did, in fact, parallel the revolution taking place in other areas of the theater. O'Neill intuitively took the precepts that the new art theater applied to dramatic content and stagecraft and applied them to music in his work: He used music to emotionally express the inner essences of individuals and groups of people, and he integrated music into the very structure of his plays.

Evidence of this can be found in O'Neill's earliest works. In BOUND EAST FOR CARDIFF, his first produced work and one of a number of plays referred to collectively as the SEA plays, O'Neill utilized music and musical elements in a manner that was to reappear in numerous works throughout the course of his career. The opening STAGE DIRECTIONS state, "*At regular intervals of a minute or so the blast of the steamer's whistle can be heard above all the other sounds*" (1:187). The repetition of the whistle is used to situate the play within the context of a journey, and multiple journeys are at the core of the play itself. There is the physical journey of the steamer on its way from New York to Cardiff, the emotional journey of the crew as they anxiously monitor the condition of the wounded Yank, and the biological and spiritual journey of Yank as he passes from life to death. The relentless nature of the whistle is used to accentuate the inability of the sailors to cease their journeys or to change course. As he struggles to come to terms with approaching death, Yank notes to his friend Driscoll, "We shouldn'ta made this trip" (1:196). Yet in spite of regret, the whistle continues to sound inexorably, moving the characters and the audience toward the play's conclusion. O'Neill thus transforms the properties of the whistle—its innate symbolization of journeying and its relentless sounding—into an audible and musical manifestation of the play's deeper psychological and spiritual realities. At the same time, the simple realism of the presence of a whistle aboard a steamer creates a structural integration of sound and setting.

The MOON OF THE CARIBBEES, another of the sea plays written and produced shortly after *Bound East for Cardiff*, contains a similar use of continuous music. Here the recurring sound is that of a negro chant, heard drifting across the water for the duration of the play (1:527). In his closing stage directions, O'Neill provides a description of the music:

it is "*like the mood of the moonlight made audible*" (1:544). The chant is intended as an audible manifestation of nature, its duration creating a sense of infinity in keeping with the scope of nature, and its relentlessness reflecting the indifference of nature in the face of human existence. The chant is at the structural center of the play as well, for it can be argued that "the chant is the central agent of conflict in the play, the protagonist against whom the men react" (Bogard 1972, 87). A brief consideration of the play affirms this argument: The sailors are driven to song, drink, dance, women, and fighting as they strive to drown out the music surrounding them and overcome nature's insistence on their insignificance. It should be noted that these two plays, though products of O'Neill's earliest days as a writer, were accurate indicators of what was to come; LONG DAY'S JOURNEY INTO NIGHT, often considered O'Neill's greatest work, features the continuous music of a foghorn functioning in a similar manner to the whistle and the chant of these early sea plays.

While the sea plays contain music that dramatizes the essence of nature in one form or another, later plays contain music that illustrates the psychological states of various characters. *The* EMPEROR JONES, produced in 1920, utilizes sound as an expression of personal psychological reality. The dominant sound of this play is not a gentle chant or a shrill whistle, but the predatory beat of the tom-tom, which O'Neill informs us "*starts at a rate exactly corresponding to normal pulse beat—72 to the minute—and continues at a gradually accelerating rate from this point uninterruptedly to the very end of the play*" (1:1,041). This suggested pulse is associated with the character of Jones, the self-proclaimed emperor turned fugitive. Once Jones is out in the woods on his own, the tom-tom becomes the key to his true mental and emotional state. Jones fights to remain calm, but the beat the audience inevitably associates with his heart accelerates and expresses the actual level of his fears. This is demonstrated in a few lines from scene three: "(*Jones stands trembling—then with a certain reassurance*) He's gone, anyway. Ha'nt or not ha'nt, dat shot fix him. (*The beat of the far-off tom-tom is perceptibly louder and more rapid*)" (1:1,048). His veneer is one of reassurance, but the music of the drum expresses his true state. Of course, the tom-tom is also associated with the subject negro population of the play. It is an element of their culture and a constant audible reminder to the audience of all that Jones is running away from—not just his pursuers, but his own people and his own heritage. O'Neill cleverly unites the representation of Jones's heartbeat with the representation of his racial tradition to express the complexity of black psychology that must be navigated by AFRICAN AMERICANS in life and in death. At the same time, the tom-tom of *The Emperor Jones* provides the play's structural momentum in a very practical sense. Once Jones is lost in the woods, the only thing that spurs him on in his physical, emotional, and subconscious journey is the noise of the drum. The tom-tom reminds Jones that he is now the prey, not the predator, and propels him forward through eight scenes to the end of the play and his death. To remove the music would be to remove much of the work's growing tension.

O'Neill experimented further with the use of music as an expression of psychological states in ALL GOD'S CHILLUN GOT WINGS. In the opening stage directions, O'Neill writes that the quality of the black and white laughter should be markedly different, should *"express the difference in race"* (2:279). This expression of racial difference also occurs in the outbreak of contrasting songs three times in the first act. The contrast of the different races' laughter and song creates a dialogue that continues throughout the play and serves structurally as a form of scenery, setting the stage in a racial and psychological sense for the audience. When the blacks in the opening scene are heard to be *"participants in the spirit of Spring"* (2:279), the groundwork for the character of Hattie Harris is laid. And when the whites are portrayed in song as *"awkward in natural emotion"* (2:279), the groundwork for Ella Harris's twisted relations with men in general and Jim in particular is laid. The songs of this play are not merely a part of the supporting structure, however, for they also relate to and expose the play's dramatic content in a unique way. Of particular note is the song sung at Ella and Jim's wedding. The first stanza utilizes the symbolism of the mourning dove to evoke the innocence and peace of a child unaware of racial or socioeconomic divides. The second stanza, like the first, references the play's title through the symbolism of the eagle. The young man, chasing his freedom and his future, and the young couple, soaring through their courtship on the wings of illusion, are both represented by the eagle. The final stanza states simply, "Sometimes I wish that I'd never been born" (2:295). In this piece of foreshadowing, O'Neill traces the growth and launching of his characters and then outlines their coming fall to earth. The song does not function as a melodic monologue—the form preferred in musical theater—but instead serves as thematic exposition, revealing the social and psychological forces that will eventually dictate the outcome of the characters' lives.

In the 1928 production of MARCO MILLIONS, O'Neill continued to explore the application of music along the structural and dramatic lines of *All God's Chillun Got Wings*. The play's many settings were brought to life through complex orchestration: A team of composers created pieces in "imitative Venetian, Middle Eastern, Indian, and Chinese styles, ranging from sentimental love songs to oriental dances to military marches to funeral dirges" (Wainscott 206). In addition, music was used to mark the passage of time, the change of setting, the opening and closing of every scene, and the transitions between each scene (Wainscott 206). This was a significant departure from the common use of music as mere decoration or embellishment; O'Neill relied on his music to create a coherent structural framework for the play's dramatic action. And as with *All God's Chillun Got Wings*, O'Neill employed songs with heavily symbolic lyrics to expound on the play's thematic and emotional concerns. The audience is introduced to the character of Marco, and to the central conflict of that character and of the play, through song. The simple poem that Marco composes for his love in act 1, scene 2 (2:397) reveals the conflict between idealism and realism, between spirituality and materiality, which runs throughout the course of the play. The Princess Kukachin—the counterpart to the Marco character in many ways—also engages in song as an act of self-revelation. It is through song that she unburdens her heart and, albeit unknowingly, engages in the play's central conflict as she voices first despair, then an understanding of the religious thought that is both her heritage and her ultimate release:

> I am not.
> Life is.
> A cloud hides the sun.
> A life is lived.
> The sun shines again.
> Nothing has changed.
> Centuries wither into tired dust.
> A new dew freshens the grass.
> Somewhere this dream is being dreamed. (2:448)

A chorus of sailors and female attendants mediates between the juxtaposed musical voices of Marco and Kukachin. Like the instrumental music used to establish the setting, these choric pieces establish the world as it is—the parameters that Marco and Kukachin cannot escape from. This was not the only play where O'Neill experimented with the use of a chorus: The HAIRY APE contains choric elements, and LAZARUS LAUGHED contains no less than eight distinct choruses.

The art theater movement played a central role in the development of American drama. It provided a crucial contrast to the melodramatic theater of the 19th century and helped shape the trajectory of early modern theater. O'Neill, as a participant in that movement, was similarly influential. His pioneering use of music, guided by the precepts of art theater, opened the door for many playwrights to come; TENNESSEE WILLIAMS's *The Glass Menagerie* and Arthur Miller's *Playing for Time* would not have been possible without O'Neill's early sea plays and later experiments in EXPRESSIONISM. In the works of O'Neill, America witnessed a structural and dramatic integration of music and theater that it had not known was possible. And AMERICAN THEATER was the richer for it.

See also JAZZ.

Bibliography

Bogard, Travis. *Contour in Time: The Plays of Eugene O'Neill.* New York: Oxford University Press, 1972.

Bogard, Travis, ed. *The Eugene O'Neill Songbook.* Berkeley: East Bay Books, 1993. Available online. URL: http://www.eOneill.com/library/songbook/contents.htm. Accessed October 24, 2005.

Cheney, Sheldon. *The Theatre: Three Thousand Years of Drama, Acting, and Stagecraft.* New York: Tudor Publishing Company, 1935.

Wainscott, Ronald H. *Staging O'Neill: The Experimental Years, 1920–1934.* New Haven, Conn.: Yale University Press, 1988.

Jane Harris

N

Nathan, George Jean (1882–1958) One of the leading drama critics of his time, George Jean Nathan wrote acerbic, erudite reviews for over half a century. Born on February 14, 1882, in Fort Wayne, Indiana, Nathan graduated from Cornell University in 1904 and entered the field of journalism. He contributed to the *New York Herald*, leaving that post to edit the magazine *Smart Set* with H. L. Mencken from 1914 to 1923. In 1924, also with Mencken, Nathan helped to found the intellectual, avant-garde *American Mercury* magazine, for which he was a writer and editor as well. In addition, Nathan was one of the founding editors of the literary newspaper the *American Spectator* and, after 1943, a columnist for the *New York Journal-American*. Author of more than 40 books, most of them collections of his criticism, Nathan has been more widely translated than any of his contemporary critics.

Nathan was quite the socialite, holding court at such locales as the 21 Club and the Stork Club. Like his fellow critic ALEXANDER WOOLLCOTT, Nathan provided the inspiration for a dramatic character—in this case, the savage, witty critic Addison DeWitt in the film *All About Eve*.

Some scholars consider Nathan to be the father of American drama criticism as well as a key contributor to AMERICAN THEATER development. His scathing attacks on American drama in the first decade or two of the 20th century denounced what he considered shallow plays that pandered to popular taste. Broadway, he argued, should foster high artistic standards, while dramatic criticism should do the same, a philosophy he articulated in *The Autobiography of an Attitude* (1925).

Nathan recognized the genius of Eugene O'Neill early on, and he remained a staunch champion of the playwright throughout his life. He used his considerable influence to get O'Neill's work produced

George Jean Nathan *(Courtesy of Culver Pictures)*

on Broadway, efforts that helped bring about the 1920 New York production of BEYOND THE HORIZON. Nathan and O'Neill also developed a close personal relationship, exchanging numerous letters. (Nathan had a similar relationship with and admiration of GEORGE BERNARD SHAW.)

Nathan died in New York City on April 8, 1958. In his will, he established the annual George Jean Nathan Award to encourage the art and development of quality drama criticism through articles, essays, and books. The first award went to Harold Clurman in 1958–59 for his collection of reviews and essays, *Lies Like Truth: Theatre Reviews and Essays.*

Bibliography

Connolly, Thomas F. "Biography of George Jean Nathan." Available online. URL: http://www.arts.cornell.edu/english/awards/nathan/bio.html. Accessed March 15, 2007.

———. *George Jean Nathan and the Making of Modern American Drama Criticism.* Madison, N.J.: Fairleigh Dickinson University Press, 2000.

Nathan, George Jean. *The Autobiography of an Attitude.* 1925. Reprint, St. Clair Shores, Mich.: Scholarly Press, 1971.

Karen Charmaine Blansfield

naturalism   Naturalism is a literary genre closely related to REALISM, though in the theater world the distinction between the two remains ill-defined. O'Neill once fumed, "I would to God some genius were gigantic enough to define clearly the separateness of these terms once and for all!" ("Strindberg" 108). "Realism" broadly refers to a 19th-century revolt against MELODRAMA and romanticism, toward an art form that reflects the everyday life of unheroic and unexceptional individuals. "Naturalism" in drama connotes a grittier, darker form of realism while adhering to the definition of naturalism we find in general literary studies—a genre in which characters' fates are dictated by the caprices of historical, environmental, and biological forces beyond their control. Characters in naturalism, as opposed to those in realism, have little to no "agency," or control over their environments. In a typical melodrama, virtue

(good) triumphs over vice (evil), while the naturalistic plot generally follows the opposite trajectory, with the endings either fatalistic and gloomy or left unresolved. Theater critics and European literary scholars are more likely to apply realism and naturalism interchangeably. It is also important not to confuse literature's use of the terms to those found in the field of philosophy, though some connections do exist.

The term "naturalism" derives in part from Victor Hugo's preface to his historical play *Cromwell* (1827), in which Hugo denounces the dramatic unity of classical GREEK TRAGEDY in favor of a new kind of theater that reflects truer laws of "nature" (Styan 2, Törnqvist 29). Naturalism was strongly influenced by the evolutionary theory of Charles Darwin and popularized as a distinctive literary movement near the end of the 19th century by the French writer Émile Zola. Zola believed that literature should act as a scientific laboratory in which social experiments might be performed with plot and character to reveal discoveries as remarkable as those made in the field of science. O'Neill himself equated the traditional concepts of Fate and God with what he called "man's biological past creating the present" ("Neglected Poet" 125).

On the significance of the genre to O'Neill's plays, Egil Törnqvist writes, "From naturalism O'Neill overtook the modern, 'scientific' view of heredity and environment as the powers determining man's fate. With Darwin and Zola he revealed the beast in man, seeing him as a victim of his own biological past, of his own animal instincts or of a corrupt society" (29; see also Rundle). One prominent critic of literary naturalism observes that the thematic "core" of all naturalist texts "appears to rest on the relationship between a restrictive social and intellectual environment and the consequent impoverishment both of social opportunity and of the inner life" (Pizer 13). Naturalism is therefore a highly democratic genre, celebrating social difference and individual freedom while at the same time representing their destruction by forces of social intolerance, biological necessity, and self-doubt. As such, every O'Neill play contains some elements of naturalism, though more often than not he combines several approaches in the same work.

O'Neill began as a serious playwright by taking his cue from naturalist authors such as Joseph Conrad, Jack London, and Stephen Crane for whom the open SEA served as a potently symbolic naturalistic force. The idea of the sea as an inescapable, often lethal trap for sailors, PROSTITUTES, and waterfront wastrels appears in O'Neill's four SS GLENCAIRN one-acts, as well as his full-length plays BEYOND THE HORIZON and "ANNA CHRISTIE." O'Neill appeared to believe, wrote one reviewer of the latter play, that it is "useless" for human beings "to patch together makeshift shelters in any futile attempt to shut out the ruthless universe; useless, even cowardly, not to measure one's strength against these stern realities. . . . For Eugene O'Neill the sea is usually the constant symbol of these eternal realities, the inhuman powers of nature against which men and women must measure their puny strength" (Parker 29).

O'Neill also understood, as Zola had before him, that only through authentic dialogue could the hackneyed conventions of melodrama be destroyed, and thus his "vulgar tongue" led audiences to associate the playwright with other naturalist authors (Törnqvist 29). When Chris Christopherson, for instance, attempts to apologize to his daughter Anna in "Anna Christie" for abandoning her at an early age and thus allowing her to fall into a life of prostitution, she retorts in a streetwise Swedish-American dialect, "Don't bawl about it. There ain't nothing to forgive, anyway. It ain't your fault, and it ain't mine. . . . We're all poor nuts, and things happen, and we yust get mixed in wrong, that's all," "You say right tang, Anna, py golly!" Chris agrees, "It ain't nobody's fault! [Shaking his fist.] It's dat ole davil, sea!" (1,015).

Similarly, in LONG DAY'S JOURNEY INTO NIGHT, Mary Tyrone, the close portrait of O'Neill's mother MARY "ELLA" QUINLAN O'NEILL, echoes Anna's absolution to her father by also insisting that the Tyrone family's self-destructive pathologies are not their fault: "None of us can help the things life has done to us. They're done before you realize it, and once they're done they make you do other things until at last everything comes between you and what you'd like to be, and you've lost your true self forever" (749). When taken to its extreme,

Anna and Mary's sentiment, repeated throughout the O'Neill canon by a host of varied characters in diverse milieus, manifests what early O'Neill critic Sophus Winther describes as a "naturalistic ethics": If no one is to blame, then moral certainty cannot exist. Such an ethics is not restricted to preconceived notions of good and evil; rather, it is relativistic and conscious of the ever-changing nature of moral standards. Winther maintains that O'Neill "goes even further in that he condemns a fixed standard as destructive of life, holding that in the last analysis it will lead to false pride, arrogant and cruel behavior, hypocrisy and a destructive fanaticism" (123).

Throughout the 1920s, O'Neill's most experimental decade, the evolving playwright rejected naturalism outright in spite of the fact that the genre had won him the PULITZER PRIZE for both *Beyond the Horizon* and "*Anna Christie*." "Naturalism is too easy," he remarked in a 1924 *New York Times* interview. "It would, for instance, be a perfect cinch to go on writing *Anna Christies* all my life. I could always be sure of the rent then . . . shoving a lot of human beings on a stage and letting them say the identical things in a theatre they would say in a drawing room or a saloon does not necessarily make for naturalness. It's what those men and women do not say that usually is most interesting" (quoted in Kantor 48). Over this period, he looked to the Swedish playwright AUGUST STRINDBERG to provide a model for what O'Neill called "supernaturalism," which constitutes "behind-life" plays that penetrate naturalism's "banality of surfaces" ("Strindberg" 108, 109), such as ALL GOD'S CHILLUN GOT WINGS, The GREAT GOD BROWN, and STRANGE INTERLUDE.

O'Neill's most celebrated plays, however, are written in the naturalistic tradition, with strong expressionistic undertones, including his later masterpieces of the 1930s and 1940s, MOURNING BECOMES ELECTRA, *Long Day's Journey Into Night*, The ICEMAN COMETH, and A MOON FOR THE MISBEGOTTEN. Other early 20th-century American dramatists such as Edward Sheldon, Elmer Rice, and Sophie Treadwell also applied naturalistic elements in their dramas while at the same time rejecting the pure realism of late-19th-century naturalist texts.

This conflation of techniques, particularly when combined with EXPRESSIONISM, has come to characterize an American style of drama over the last century. Younger American dramatists—Clifford Odets, TENNESSEE WILLIAMS, Zoë Akins, William Saroyan, Lillian Hellman, Thornton Wilder, and others—unleashed fresh perspectives on the changing genre of naturalism, and in their own right set the stage for the next gifted generation—Arthur Miller, Lorraine Hansberry, Edward Albee, August Wilson, Sam Shepard, et al.—each of whom, in his or her own unique way, carried on O'Neill's naturalistic exploration of what he called the "inscrutable forces behind life" ("Inscrutable" 99).

Bibliography

Kantor, Louis. "O'Neill Defends His Play of the Negro." In *Conversations with Eugene O'Neill*, edited by Mark W. Estrin, 40. Jackson: University Press of Mississippi, 1990.

O'Neill, Eugene. *"Anna Christie." Collected Plays of Eugene O'Neill, 1913–1920*, edited by Travis Bogard, 957–1,027. New York: Library of America, 1988.

———. "Neglected Poet." Letter to Arthur Hobson Quinn. In *O'Neill and His Plays: Four Decades of Criticism*, edited by Oscar Cargill, N. Bryllion Fagin, and William J. Fisher, 125–126. New York: New York University Press, 1961.

———. "Inscrutable Forces." A letter to Barret Clark, 1919. In *O'Neill and His Plays: Four Decades of Criticism*, edited by Oscar Cargill, N. Bryllion Fagin, and William J. Fisher, 99–100. New York: New York University Press, 1960.

———. *Long Day's Journey into Night. Collected Plays of Eugene O'Neill, 1932–1943*. Vol. 3. Edited by Travis Bogard. New York: Library of America, 1988, 713–828.

———. "Strindberg and Our Theatre." 1924. In *O'Neill and His Plays: Four Decades of Criticism*, edited by Oscar Cargill, N. Bryllion Fagin, and William J. Fisher, 108–109. New York: New York University Press, 1961.

Parker, Robert Allerton. "An American Dramatist Developing." In *Playwright's Progress: O'Neill and the Critics*, edited by Jordan Yale Miller, 28–31. Chicago: Scott, Foresman & Company, 1965.

Pizer, Donald. Introduction to *The Cambridge Companion to American Realism and Naturalism: Howells to London*, edited by Donald Pizer, 1–18. Cambridge: Cambridge University Press, 1995.

Rundle, Erika. "The Hairy Ape's Humanist Hell: Theatricality and Evolution in O'Neill's 'Comedy of Ancient and Modern Life.'" *The Eugene O'Neill Review* 30 (2008): 48–144.

Törnqvist, Egil. *A Drama of Souls: Studies in O'Neill's Super-Naturalistic Technique*. New Haven, Conn.: Yale University Press, 1969.

Winther, Sophus Keith. *Eugene O'Neill: A Critical Study*. New York: Random House, 1934.

New London, Connecticut New London, Connecticut, is located at the mouth of the Thames River at the eastern end of Long Island Sound and is situated on one of the deepest and most sheltered natural harbors on North America's Atlantic coast. From its founding in 1646 and into the 20th century, the city has turned to the SEA for its livelihood. For more than a century, New Londoners were engaged in trade with the West Indies, transporting local produce and livestock and returning with sugar, molasses, and rum. The trade was disrupted by the Revolutionary War and never really recovered. By the end of the War of 1812, New London was no longer engaged in trade with the West Indies. At that time, the city turned its attention to whaling, which proved to be very profitable. New London evolved into the second largest whaling port in North America, and whalers continued to sail from the city into the early 20th century.

The whaling industry peaked in the mid-19th century, and toward the end of the century, New London was beginning to diversify. The city was developing as a summer resort community, and it was during this period that the O'Neill family came to New London. JAMES O'NEILL's friend John McGinley was a reporter for the *New London Day* and encouraged James to come to New London. MARY ELLEN "ELLA" O'NEILL had family connections in the city; her mother had recently moved to New London to be near her sister. James's acting career was going very well, and in 1883 he stepped into the role of Edmond Dantès in *The Count of Monte Cristo*.

Whaler's Row in New London, Connecticut, probable influence for the Mannon home in *Mourning Becomes Electra* *(Courtesy of the Sheaffer-O'Neill Collection, Charles E. Shain Library of Connecticut College)*

In 1884, James and Ella purchased two adjacent properties on Pequot Avenue. One property contained a small house, which the neighbors referred to as "the Pink House" due to its color, and the other property contained a store and barn. James made arrangements for work to be done on the Pink House so that it would be more comfortable as a summer residence for the family. He intended to rent the other property (Gelb 98). The O'Neills did not take up residence in the Pink House until the end of summer 1887, a year prior to Eugene O'Neill's birth. James purchased a third piece of land on Pequot Avenue in 1886, which was adjacent to the other properties. The third property included a two-story structure that at one time had been a store with living quarters on the second floor, a barn, and a structure that at one time had been a school. The family moved to the third prop-

erty in 1900 after it had undergone significant renovations and they had outgrown the smaller Pink House (Gelb 104–105). The house on the third property is referred to as the MONTE CRISTO COTTAGE, and it is the setting for LONG DAY'S JOURNEY INTO NIGHT and AH, WILDERNESS! Eugene O'Neill spent almost every summer of his youth in New London until 1915.

The O'Neill family often had their meals at the Packard, a boarding house on Pequot Avenue run by the Rippin family; it was a short walk from Monte Cristo Cottage. Eugene O'Neill also lived with the Rippins during the winter of 1913–14. It was during this period that he wrote his one-act plays The WEB, THIRST, RECKLESSNESS, WARNINGS, and FOG. He also wrote an early draft of BOUND EAST FOR CARDIFF, which at the time he called *Children of the Sea.*

Monte Cristo Cottage and the Packard were located on the outskirts of an exclusive resort community, the Pequot Colony. At the center of the Pequot Colony was the Pequot House, a summer hotel that opened in 1853. As the popularity of the Pequot House grew, the hotel built summer rental cottages to accommodate more guests. The resort drew an elite clientele from New York City and Washington, D.C. Private individuals began building summer cottages in the neighborhood as well, and it became known as the Pequot Colony. Some of the owners of the private cottages joined together to form the Pequot Casino Association. In 1894, the association purchased a waterfront property and built a casino—a social club that had dining rooms, a ballroom, a billiard room, and tennis courts. In back of the building was a pier that went over the water to a gazebo built on the rocks. The pier serves as the setting for the prologue and epilogue of O'Neill's play The GREAT GOD BROWN. The O'Neill family was not of the same social CLASS as members of the Pequot Casino, which was reserved for the more well-to-do.

Farther down Pequot Avenue and along the shore at the mouth of the Thames River is New London Lighthouse, and offshore at the mouth of the harbor is the newer Ledge Lighthouse, which was built in 1909. The foghorn from New London Light, later replaced by the foghorn at Ledge Light, could be heard throughout the community during a foggy day or night. It is this horn that torments Mary Tyrone in Long Day's Journey into Night. O'Neill also refers to New London Light in a happier context when Nat Miller, the newspaper publisher in Ah, Wilderness!, suggests that he take the family for a drive to the lighthouse on the Fourth of July.

Eugene O'Neill loved the water, both swimming and boating, and the water was accessible to him directly across the street from Monte Cristo Cottage. A neighbor, Margaret Kiley, recalled O'Neill as a "fish, a regular water rat, forever playing around in the water" (quoted in Sheaffer 59). O'Neill also frequented Ocean Beach, which was beyond the Pequot Colony from the O'Neill home. The New London trolley was extended in 1892 from downtown to Ocean Beach, which made it an easy-to-reach and popular destination. O'Neill and his friends frequented the site and enjoyed the boardwalk, dancing by the bandstand, and fireworks displays during festivals. Another significant summer attraction was "boat day," which centered on the annual Harvard-Yale boat race. Spectators in all manner of watercraft, from large yachts to small rowboats, would line both sides of the Thames River to watch the university rowing teams compete in a four-mile race. O'Neill used "boat day" as the setting for the final scene in STRANGE INTERLUDE.

Given New London's proximity to New York City and Boston, it was often a stop for touring theater companies. The Lyceum Theatre opened in 1890 and became a popular venue for touring productions and pre-Broadway tryouts. Companies headed by William Gillette, David Belasco, and James O'Neill made the Lyceum part of their New England tours. James O'Neill's company often opened the Lyceum's season with The Count of Monte Cristo or another play in their repertoire. James O'Neill provided his son with tickets so that he and his friends could attend many of the productions.

New London also had a less wholesome side. At the turn of the last century, traveling salesmen reported New London as having one of the liveliest red-light districts between New York and Boston (Sheaffer 59). The center of the red-light district was Bradley Street, which coincidently was the location of the New London police headquarters. Eugene O'Neill was introduced to the brothels and bars of Bradley Street by his elder brother, JAMES O'NEILL, JR. One of their favorite establishments was a brothel on Bradley Street run by Addie Burns, who was immortalized in Long Day's Journey into Night as Mamie Burns. Another New London PROSTITUTE named Violet, who was known for playing the piano, is referenced in the play. Some of O'Neill's New London friends recognized the description of Cybel's parlor in act 1, scene 3 of The Great God Brown as one of the Bradley Street brothels that they frequented (Gelb 200).

O'Neill had a group of friends who were referred to as the Second Story Club. Their name is derived from the fact that they would meet in Dr. Joseph Ganey's apartment on Main Street in New London,

Eugene O'Neill with a cohort of friends at Ocean Beach in New London, Connecticut. O'Neill is second from right, Edward Keefe third, and Arthur McGinley fourth. *(Courtesy of the Sheaffer-O'Neill Collection, Charles E. Shain Library of Connecticut College)*

above his first-floor office. The Second Story Club was seen as New London's bohemian center. Members of the group included "Doc" Ganey, Ed Keefe, "Ice" Casey, "Hutch" Collins, Scott Linsley, and Art and Tom McGinley. The McGinley family served as inspiration for the family in O'Neill's only comedy, *Ah, Wilderness!* Many of the club members remained friends of O'Neill's throughout his life.

The club members would gather at "Doc" Ganey's residence to play cards, drink, and read from his extensive personal library. Ganey, 10 years O'Neill's senior, had acquired many avant-garde works banned in the United States during his travels abroad. O'Neill was a voracious reader and availed himself of Ganey's library. During this period in New London, he read the poems of Ernest Dowson, Edward FitzGerald, Algernon

Swinburne, Charles Baudelaire, and Oscar Wilde and also read GEORGE BERNARD SHAW, Karl Marx, Friedrich Engels, Fyodor Dostoyevsky, Lev Tolstoy, Maksim Gorky, Joseph Conrad, and Jack London (Black 87).

During the summer of 1912, at his son's request, James O'Neill made arrangements for O'Neill to have a job as a reporter at the *New London Telegraph*, one of the two newspapers in town. Frederick P. Latimer, editor in chief and part owner of the paper, was willing to take O'Neill on, but the paper had not budgeted for an additional reporter, so James O'Neill paid Eugene's $10-a-week salary. O'Neill had great respect for Latimer and shared some of his early plays with the editor. Latimer recognized O'Neill's ability as a playwright and shared that with James O'Neill. But O'Neill was not considered to be a good reporter. He lacked a reporter's instinct and the ability to capture the facts of a story succinctly. In addition to covering news stories, he contributed verse for the paper's "Laconics" column, where he had more freedom to express himself. He only worked for the newspaper for a few months, but his relationship with Latimer continued while O'Neill remained in New London. The playwright continued to share his plays with Latimer, and O'Neill once said, "He's the first one who really thought I had something to say, and believed I could say it" (quoted in Sheaffer 228). O'Neill played tribute to Latimer by partially basing the character of Nat Miller in *Ah, Wilderness!* on the editor.

New London and its residents inspired settings and characters for many of O'Neill's plays. Still standing today are four Greek revival style houses in downtown New London that served as the inspiration for the Mannon residence in MOURNING BECOMES ELECTRA. The houses were built between 1835 and 1845 and were nicknamed Whale Oil Row due to the fact that the wealth of the original owners came from the whaling industry. *Mourning Becomes Electra* contains many references to New London residents and places. A MOON FOR THE MISBEGOTTEN is also set in New London's environs, and the character T. Stedman Harder is inspired by Edward Crowninshield Hammond, who had an estate in the neighboring town of Waterford (see HARKNESS, EDWARD STEPHEN, AND HAMMOND, EDWARD CROWNINSHIELD). O'Neill had a great deal of disdain for Hammond and the wealthy class that he represented. There are reports that O'Neill was chased off Hammond's private beach on numerous occasions. O'Neill explored his relationship and feelings towards the well-to-do in his one-act play *Fog*, which he wrote in New London. In the one-act, O'Neill himself served as the inspiration for the character the Poet, and Hammond could have inspired the Man of Business. Ironically, the EUGENE O'NEILL THEATER CENTER is located on the old Hammond estate.

One of the New Londoners who played a role in O'Neill's life in New London was Adam Scott, an AFRICAN-AMERICAN man who was an elder of a local Baptist church and a bartender at one of the establishments frequented by O'Neill and his friends. O'Neill was intrigued by the contradictions of a religious man with an ungodly profession, and he based Brutus Jones in *The EMPEROR JONES* on Scott. In addition to the plays mentioned above, other plays that are inspired by New London people and places include BREAD AND BUTTER, *The FIRST MAN*, and DESIRE UNDER THE ELMS.

Bibliography

Black, Stephen A. *Eugene O'Neill—Beyond Mourning and Tragedy.* New Haven, Conn., and London: Yale University Press, 1999.

Gelb, Arthur, and Barbara Gelb. *O'Neill: Life with Monte Cristo.* New York: Applause Books, 2000.

Richter, Robert A. *Eugene O'Neill and Dat Ole Davil Sea: Maritime Influences in the Life and Works of Eugene O'Neill.* Mystic, Conn.: Mystic Seaport, 2004.

————. *Touring Eugene O'Neill's New London.* New London: Connecticut College, 2001.

Sheaffer, Louis. *O'Neill: Son and Playwright.* Boston: Little, Brown, 1968.

Robert A. Richter

New York, SS The American Line vessels SS *New York* and SS *PHILADELPHIA* provided regular passenger service between New York and Southampton, England. Both vessels were built in 1888 and at their launching were at the height of luxury for transatlantic passenger steamers. By the time Eugene O'Neill signed on the *New York* in July 1911, the American Line vessels had been surpassed in size and luxury by newer ships operated by other transatlantic steamship companies. But for O'Neill, the experience and his rank of ordinary seaman were significant and differed greatly from his time on the square-rigged sailing vessel the *CHARLES RACINE* and the tramp steamer the SS *IKALA*. The *New York* was much larger than the other two vessels O'Neill had sailed on, and it was the first that carried passengers; it could carry 1,290 passengers and had a crew of almost 400. The *New York* was also the first ship O'Neill sailed on where indisputably he was a fully fledged member of the crew.

The trip from New York to Southampton normally took a week, but during the O'Neill's voyage, the *New York* developed engine trouble and arrived in Southampton a day late. O'Neill's duties as an ordinary seaman included washing the decks and shifting baggage and mail. He did not mind the work, but he resented the passengers who lived in luxury as he was on his hands and knees scrubbing the decks. He also was struck by the animosity that existed between the seamen and the firemen or stokers, who were responsible for feeding the furnaces with coal to generate the steam for the ship's engines. Onboard steamers, the role of the seamen was devoid of creativity and skill, reducing them to menial labor, whereas the abilities and skill of the stokers directly impacted the ship's capacity for speed and maintaining its schedule, which was vital to company's success.

O'Neill gave voice to the CLASS differences between the passengers and crew in his play *The* HAIRY APE, and the animosity between seamen and stokers figures prominently in *The Hairy Ape*, CHRIS CHRISTOPHERSEN, and "ANNA CHRISTIE." O'Neill also drew on experiences from the American Line ships in his early play *The* PERSONAL EQUATION.

See also MERCHANT MARINE.

Bibliography

Flayhart, William Henry, III. *The American Line (1871–1902)*. New York and London: W. W. Norton, 2000.

Richter, Robert A. *Eugene O'Neill and Dat Ole Davil Sea: Maritime Influences in the Life and Works of Eugene O'Neill*. Mystic, Conn.: Mystic Seaport, 2004.

Sheaffer, Louis. *O'Neill, Son and Playwright*. Boston: Little, Brown, 1968.

Robert A. Richter

Nietzsche, Friedrich (1844–1900)   Friedrich Nietzsche is regarded as one of the most significant figures in Western philosophy. He lived at a time of extremes, and extremes were reflected in his work. Born in 1844, Nietzsche grew up during the turbulent years of the 1848 revolutions in western Europe, the time also of the publication of Karl Marx's *Communist Manifesto*. It was an era of revolutionary socialist egalitarianism and of the radical reactionary elitism of the nationalist right

that would spur the horrors of World War I and its aftermath.

Nietzsche's philosophy greatly influenced O'Neill, who claimed both to have read Nietzsche's book *Thus Spake Zarathustra* at least once each year and that it influenced him more than any written work. Nietzsche is given a special place, alongside Peter Kropotkin and Max Stirner, on the Tyrone bookshelves, according to the stage directions of LONG DAY'S JOURNEY INTO NIGHT.

Nietzsche's works have long inspired those seeking to develop their individuality more fully and break free from received ideas and accepted values. In particular, his challenge to create a free work of art of oneself has held great appeal for artists, anarchists, bohemians, and other free-thinkers.

The Apollonian and Dionysian were, according to Nietzsche, the two forces of Greek tragedy, and he presents these terms in his book *The Birth of Tragedy*. The Apollonian, named for Apollo, the sun god, represented the light of human analytic capabilities. All forms and structures were Apollonian, including rational thought. This represented human individuality. The Dionysian, named for Dionysus, the god of wine, on the other hand, represented the ecstatic, the Dionysian principle being an aspect of individual will. Thriving on instincts and desires it represents the abandonment of rationality and the embrace of chaos, including the irrationalism of the mass. For Nietzsche, real tragedy only resulted from the tension between the two forces.

In Nietzche's philosophy, there is no rational pattern or moral purpose to be discovered in history or nature. Humans are a thoughtless accident of history. Those philosophies and religions that try to expunge the passions are decadent. Humans are driven by will, and it, not reason, determines thought and action. The *Ubermensch* (superman) is the artist, the one in whom the will for power is sublimated in courageous creativity.

Nietzsche attacked traditional Christianity as the leading example of the slave morality for its focus on humility, pity, and forgiveness. He undoubtedly struck a chord with O'Neill given the playwright's own conflictual relationship with CATHOLICISM.

O'Neill also shared Nietzsche's disdain for state socialist politics, inasmuch as its collective forms expressed the resentment of the herd. Nietzsche disparaged the anarchists and socialists of his day who were motivated by a spirit of revenge or personal weakness and fear. Speaking with indignation at their lack of rights, such anarchists and socialists were, in his view, too lazy or fearful to see that a right is a power that must be exercised, and their suffering rested in a failure to create new lives for themselves. Socialism stood as a new religion—a new slave morality, in Nietzsche's phrase. As in the case of Christianity, Nietzsche opposed the self-limiting, self-sacrificing characteristics of socialism that marked it as a new religion.

These criticisms are themes that appear in O'Neill's writings and statements on socialism and anarchist communism, and they are also reflected in his portrayals of these political movements in works such as The ICEMAN COMETH and The HAIRY APE. The slave mentality or sense that the powerless are more virtuous and thus must wait for an imagined salvation is reflected starkly in the hopeless longing of the characters in Harry Hope's bar in The Iceman Cometh. O'Neill was also inspired by Nietzsche's views on art and theater and influenced by Nietzsche's theory of GREEK TRAGEDY as Apollo's struggle with Dionysus, the emotional element in life and art.

Friedrich Nietzsche died on August 25, 1900, in Weimar, Germany, age 55.

Bibliography

Alexander, Doris. *Eugene O'Neill's Creative Struggle: The Decisive Decade, 1924–1933.* University Park: Pennsylvania State University Press, 1992.

Diggins, John Patrick. *Eugene O'Neill's America: Desire under Democracy.* Chicago: University of Chicago Press, 2007.

Nietzsche, Friedrich. *Thus Spake Zarathustra.* Translated and with a preface by Walter Kaufmann. 1883–92. Reprint, New York: Penguin Books, 1978.

J. Shantz

Nobel Prize in literature   The Nobel Prize in literature was made possible by a bequest from the Swedish industrialist and inventor of dynamite, Alfred Nobel. Nobel's will established a fund that was to be distributed annually in the form of prizes to those who had conferred the greatest benefit on mankind in the previous year in the fields of physics, chemistry, medicine, literature, and "fraternity between nations." The prize in literature was to go to "the most outstanding work in an ideal direction." The first Nobel Prize in literature was awarded in 1901. Eugene O'Neill won the prize in 1936, the second American to win, following Sinclair Lewis in 1930. O'Neill did not attend the award ceremony, held in Stockholm on December 10, 1936. His acceptance speech was read by James E. Brown, Jr., the American chargé d'affaires. Brown alluded to O'Neill's letter to him noting that it was his hope that "all those connected with the festival will accept in good faith his statement of the impossibility of his attending, and not put it down to arbitrary temperament, or anything of the sort" (Nobelprize.org "Banquet Speech"). In fact, O'Neill had no intention of attending the ceremony, telling reporters on November 12, 1936, the day he was informed about the prize, that he would not be able to arrange his affairs in order to come to Sweden.

In his presentation speech, Per Hallström, permanent secretary of the Swedish Academy, said that O'Neill's work "is based on an exceedingly intense, one might say, heart-rent, realization of the austerity of life, side by side with a kind of rapture at the beauty of human destinies shaped in the struggle against odds" (Nobelprize.org "Presentation Speech"). In his acceptance speech, O'Neill said that the award was "a symbol of the recognition by Europe of the coming-of-age of the American theatre," noting that his plays were simply the most widely known of the work done by American playwrights since the war (Nobelprize.org "Banquet Speech"). He felt that this statement was appropriate but somewhat disingenuous, or "phonus balonus," as he wrote to playwright Russell Crouse (O'Neill 456), because he was bitter that his fellow playwrights had failed to acknowledge what he had done for them in opening the AMERICAN THEATER to serious plays. O'Neill also acknowledged his debt to AUGUST STRINDBERG in his speech, a sincere tribute that was meant to be a gracious tribute to

Sweden as well, but his intention backfired somewhat because of the Swedes' perennial embarrassment that they had never given the Nobel Prize to their greatest writer.

In late December 1936, O'Neill became very ill with appendicitis and subsequently a postoperative infection, which meant that he had to receive his Nobel Prize in his hospital room. It was given to him by the Swedish consul general of San Francisco on February 17, 1937, in a brief ceremony at the Merritt Hospital in Oakland, California.

Bibliography

O'Neill, Eugene. *Selected Letters of Eugene O'Neill.* Edited by Travis Bogard and Jackson R. Bryer. New Haven, Conn.: Yale University Press, 1988.

Nobelprize.org. "Banquet Speech." Eugene O'Neill: The Nobel Prize in Literature. Available online. URL: http://nobelprize.org/nobel_prizes/literature/laureates/1936/oneill-speech.html. Accessed December 1, 2007.

———. "Presentation Speech." The Nobel Prize in Literature 1936. Available online. URL: http://nobelprize.org/nobel_prizes/literature/laureates/1936/press.html. Accessed December 1, 2007.

Brenda Murphy

O

O'Neill, Carlotta Monterey (Hazel Neilson Tharsing) (1888–1970) Eugene O'Neill's third wife, Carlotta Monterey was born Hazel Neilson Tharsing in Oakland, California, on December 28, 1888. She was the daughter of French/Dutch and Danish parents, Neillie Gotchett Tharsing and Christian Nielsen Tharsing. Her parents' marriage ended in 1892 when Nellie left Christian and moved to San Francisco, California, to manage and operate rooming houses. She left Hazel in the care of her sister, Mrs. John Shay, who brought her up as a daughter in Oakland, California, for 10 years (1892–1902).

Hazel attended St. Gertrude's, a Catholic boarding school in Rio Vista, California, where she was later remembered as a loner with a flair for the dramatic. Beginning in 1906, she spent five years in Europe furthering her education. In Paris, she took French, ballet, and fencing lessons. In London, she studied singing and acting at Sir Herbert Beerbohm Tree's Academy of Dramatic Arts (later the Royal Academy of Dramatic Art) and appeared in a revival of *The Geisha.*

In 1907, Hazel was named Miss California and was a runner-up in the national finals. In 1911, she married John Moffat, a Scottish lawyer and speculator in mining stocks, nine years her senior; they divorced in 1914. In March 1915, she made her Broadway debut in *Taking Chances,* a sex farce, and the following season she toured the country as Luana in *The Bird of Paradise.* She also changed her name to Carlotta Monterey—"Carlotta"

being more suited to her Latin-like good looks and "Monterey" being the name of a dramatically beautiful California peninsula. Dramatic-looking, with glossy jet hair and a pale complexion, one of the great beauties of her age, Carlotta had a bent for self-dramatization and great drive but little acting talent.

In October 1916, Carlotta, married Melvin C. Chapman, a 20-year-old law student. In 1917, a daughter, Cynthia Chapman, was born. Less than one year later, so that she might return to the stage, Carlotta left Cynthia Jane to be reared by her grandmother, Nellie. Carlotta and Chapman divorced in 1923, and Carlotta entered into relationships with two men: James Speyer, an elderly Wall Street banker who established a trust fund in her name that provided her with an annual income of $14,000 until the end of her life, and Ralph Barton, a famous *New Yorker* illustrator and caricaturist, whom she hastily married and divorced in 1926. Charlie Chaplin, a friend of Barton, felt that Carlotta wanted "to be all sufficient to a man of genius, to cut him off from everybody and minister to his genius, while she herself shone in reflected glory" (Shaeffer 1968, 217). Barton committed suicide in 1931.

In 1922, Carlotta met Eugene O'Neill when she played Mildred Douglas in The HAIRY APE; at the time, she thought him ill-mannered, and O'Neill reportedly was unimpressed by her acting in the play. The pair met by chance again in the summer of 1926 at Belgrade Lakes, Maine, when

Eugene O'Neill with Carlotta *(Courtesy of the estate of Ben Pinchot)*

Carlotta was in the company of Elizabeth (Bess) Marbury, partner to Richard Madden, O'Neill's literary agent. At the time, O'Neill was married to AGNES BOULTON, his second wife. After a series of furtive meetings with Carlotta, O'Neill left Agnes for Carlotta in February 1928. Setting sail for England, O'Neill and Carlotta fled the scandal of their relationship, hoping to avoid publicity while urging Agnes to grant O'Neill a speedy divorce—Agnes would not capitulate for one and one-half years.

The couple could not avoid becoming front-page news, but they were able to maintain some degree of privacy by using a forwarding address and persuading a small circle of confidants to keep their destination secret. Stopping briefly in London, they moved on to Paris. For the next three years, France

would be their country and villas in Guéthary, Cap d'Ail, and Saint-Antoine du Rocher their subsequent homes.

During this period, Carlotta proved to be sensitive to publicity and prone to quarreling with O'Neill, exacerbated by his drinking. In October 1928, the two set sail for Asia with Mrs. Tuve Drew, a combination maid, masseuse, and companion. The pair engaged separate cabins—Gene working in his, Carlotta fretting in hers. When O'Neill wasn't drinking or gambling, he swam in waters Carlotta considered filthy—indeed, she regarded most of Asia as "filthy, noisy, crowded, and flagrant in immorality, the two suffered from bouts of the flu" (Black 364).

While in Shanghai seeking medical attention for O'Neill, the two were recognized, and their quarreling continued: Carlotta moved out of their hotel after O'Neill struck her. En route to Manila, the press caught up with them, though O'Neill had disguised himself as a priest. O'Neill's drinking continued unabated, and Carlotta left the ship on New Year's Day, 1929, leaving O'Neill in the care of Mrs. Drew. For the next two weeks, the pair sailed apart on two separate ships following a similar course; Carlotta kept apprised of O'Neill's sobriety and state of mind via radio message. Eventually, Carlotta allowed O'Neill to join her on her ship, and they sailed into Genoa together. The two were married on July 22, 1929, in Paris, 20 days after O'Neill's divorce became final. From then until his death on November 27, 1953, O'Neill was to be Carlotta's fourth—and final—husband.

During their 24 years of marriage, Carlotta served as her husband's gatekeeper, limiting and cutting off O'Neill's contact with his former friends, and nurse, muse, and manager. Carlotta sometimes said that with O'Neill her maternal instincts came out, and O'Neill testified in sundry ways to his "need" for her. He credited her with facilitating the creation of MOURNING BECOMES ELECTRA, and as his health deteriorated, Carlotta transcribed his faltering handwriting. Carlotta nursed O'Neill through the agony of recounting his childhood in writing LONG DAY'S JOURNEY INTO NIGHT. In the 1941 inscription to that play, written on their 12th wedding anniversary, O'Neill thanked his wife for giving him "the faith in love that enabled me to face my dead at last and write this play—write it with deep pity and understanding and forgiveness for all the four haunted Tyrones" (3:714).

While there were a series of separations and reconciliations throughout their marriage, their union prospered as long as O'Neill could continue to write. When his deteriorating health prevented him from writing, however, the level of discord between then intensified. On one occasion in 1951, when O'Neill tried to escape a fight, falling in snow and breaking a leg, Carlotta left him lying in the snow. The next evening, Carlotta was found in a hallucinatory state, diagnosed with bromide psychosis. O'Neill signed a petition alleging her insane and incapable of caring for herself; one month later, he withdrew his petition, and the pair reunited. Shortly thereafter, O'Neill moved with Carlotta to the Shelton Hotel in Boston, Massa-

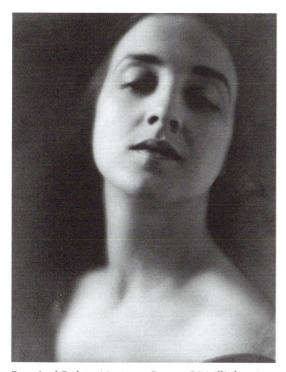

Portrait of Carlotta Monterey, Eugene O'Neill's favorite of her. Photo by Marcia Stein *(Courtesy of the Sheaffer-O'Neill Collection, Charles E. Shain Library of Connecticut College)*

chusetts. Carlotta was at O'Neill's side when he died there on November 27, 1953.

After his death, Carlotta told O'Neill's BIOGRAPHERS that their marriage was not a love affair, but that she appreciated O'Neill as an artist and provided him with a protective environment in which he could work. She intimated that O'Neill never loved any woman—he loved only his work, but he respected her. To temper the criticism that she believed would be leveled at her after his death, Carlotta privately published a volume of O'Neill's letters, inscriptions, and poetry, in which he expressed his passionate love for her.

In her remaining years, Carlotta worked to promote the Eugene O'Neill legacy. Less than 18 months after his death, she defied O'Neill's wish that LONG DAY'S JOURNEY INTO NIGHT not be published until 25 years after his death and never produced for the stage. Over the objection of O'Neill's publisher, Bennet Cerf of Random House, she allowed the Swedish Royal Dramatic Theatre to stage the play and for Yale University Press to publish it, in February 1956. In the United States, *Long Day's Journey into Night* was produced for the first time on Broadway in 1956 under the direction of JOSÉ QUINTERO, winning O'Neill a posthumous PULITZER PRIZE and cementing his legacy as America's preeminent playwright.

In 1958, Carlotta moved from the Lowell Hotel to the Carlton House in New York City. In 1968, she entered St. Luke's Hospital; in 1969, she was transferred to the DeWitt Nursing Home (both in New York City). She died at the Valley Nursing Home in Westwood, New Jersey, on November 18, 1970, and is buried beside her husband at Forest Hills Cemetery in Boston, Massachusetts. Her revised diaries for the years 1928–43 as well as her correspondence are housed in the Beinecke Library at Yale University.

Bibliography

Black, Stephen A. *Eugene O'Neill: Beyond Mourning and Tragedy.* New Haven, Conn.: Yale University Press, 1999.

Gelb, Arthur, and Barbara Gelb. *O'Neill.* New York: Harper & Row, 1962.

———. *O'Neill: Life with Monte Cristo.* New York: Applause Books, 2000.

Monteiro, George. "Sabato Magaldi, Carlotta O'Neill's Man in Brazil." *Eugene O'Neill Review* 26 (2004): 199–214.

Quintero, José. *If You Don't Dance They Beat You.* Boston: Little, Brown, 1974.

Ranald, Margaret Loftus. *The Eugene O'Neill Companion.* Westport, Conn.: Greenwood Press, 1984.

Sheaffer, Louis. *O'Neill: Son and Artist.* Boston: Little, Brown, 1973.

———. *O'Neill, Son and Playwright.* Boston: Little, Brown, 1968.

Eileen Herrmann

O'Neill, Edmund Burke (1883–1885)   The second son of JAMES O'NEILL and his wife MARY ELLEN "ELLA" O'NEILL, Edmund Burke O'Neill was born in St. Louis, Missouri, just as his father was beginning to tour in the melodrama that would make him rich, *The Count of Monte Cristo.* James's role as Edmond Dantès would shape and define his identity as an actor, as well as entrap him for life.

Edmund O'Neill was named for the 18th-century IRISH statesman and philosopher Edmund Burke, whom James greatly admired. But he would not live long enough to see whether he emulated his namesake. In winter 1885, Ella O'Neill left her son and his older brother James in the care of her mother, BRIDGET QUINLAN, so that she could join her husband in Colorado, where he was currently performing. During her absence, JAMES O'NEILL, JR.—who was five years older than Edmund—contracted the measles. Edmund subsequently caught the disease, and he died in early March, just a year and a half old. Presumably James had gone into the baby's room, and Ella accused him of doing so deliberately, in an attempt to kill his baby brother. Her resentment of James haunted both mother and son for the rest of their lives.

Ella never recovered from Edmund's death, which tortured her because she felt she had deserted him. So even as she charged James with the terrible occurrence, she felt herself responsible for having been away at the time. Ella greatly feared having another child, yet she also wanted one to compensate for the loss of Edmund. When Eugene O'Neill was born, she was given morphine to cope with

the pain. That medicinal use soon spiraled into addiction, and the wrenching combination of guilt, drug dependence, and mother-son relationships is played out in Eugene O'Neill's intensely autobiographical work, LONG DAY'S JOURNEY INTO NIGHT. The play portrays Edmund's death as a critical and defining episode in the Tyrone family—as it probably was for the playwright in his own family as well. However, the character of Edmund in *Long Day's Journey into Night* represents Eugene himself, while the dead baby, named Eugene, haunts the play like a ghost.

Bibliography

Gelb, Arthur, and Barbara Gelb. *O'Neill.* New York: Harper & Brothers, 1962.

Karen Charmaine Blansfield

O'Neill, Edward (Edmund O'Neill, Edmond O'Neill) (fl. 1833) **and O'Neill, Mary** (fl. 1833)   Eugene O'Neill's grandfather used several versions of his name, starting with Edmund, the name his descendants call him (Mallett). Evidence indicates he later used the spelling "Edmond" but settled finally on Edward (Schaefer, Gelb). Whether he is referred to as Edmund, Edmond, or Edward, James's father—Eugene's grandfather—played a crucial role in the tragedy of this immigrant family.

Mary O'Neill, Eugene's grandmother, was a distant cousin of her husband. They married around 1833 in the IRISH town of Tinneranny, Rosbercon, County Kilkenny. In 1851 during the potato famine, they embarked with their eight children on a ship they called "The Great India" (Kunckel letter). After six weeks, they disembarked in Quebec, eventually establishing themselves in Buffalo, New York. The O'Neills' final child, Margaret, was born in Buffalo on December 31, 1851 (Mallett). Their eldest son, Richard (Dick), died in Buffalo, possibly sending James's father into depression. Edward declared he must see his homeland again and returned to Ireland, either abandoning his family or simply going for what stretched into a very long "visit" (Kunckel letter). Most family members, including Eugene's father James, then age 10, took menial jobs to support their fatherless family. After six years back in Ireland, Edward died somewhat mysteriously of what police proclaimed was accidental poisoning (Gelb 42).

The family's fortune turned, however, when James's older sister, Josephine, married a saloon-keeper and moved to the prosperous city of Cincinnati, Ohio. Mary and the rest of her children soon followed. In Cincinnati, Mary O'Neill's married daughters each took in a younger sibling. This resulted in James living in relative affluence with Josephine. It is with Josephine that James was introduced to Shakespeare and the theater (Gelb 45).

Mary O'Neill continued to struggle on but was helped eventually by receiving the Civil War pension of her young, battle-killed son, Edward. When Mary passed away at age 68, James provided his mother with a burial plot and substantial headstone in Cincinnati's St. Joseph's Cemetery. Ironically, the many tragic events that befell the family of Edward and Mary O'Neill helped forge the award-winning plays of their grandson Eugene.

Bibliography

Gelb, Arthur, and Barbara Gelb. *O'Neill: Life with Monte Cristo.* New York: Applause Books, 2000.

Kunckel, Frank A. Family history letter to nephew Manley W. Mallett, 1937. Sheaffer-O'Neill Collection, Department of Special Collections and Archives, Connecticut College, Charles E. Shain Library.

Mallett, Manley W. *My Eighty-Four Ancestral Families.* Largo, Fla.: Mallett, 1979.

Sheaffer, Louis. *O'Neill: Son and Playwright.* Boston: Little, Brown, 1968.

Mary Mallett

O'Neill, Eugene Gladstone, Jr. (1910–1950)

Born on May 14, 1910, the son of Eugene O'Neill and his first wife, KATHLEEN JENKINS, Eugene O'Neill, Jr., became an accomplished classics scholar and professor of Greek studies. His birth was an unwelcome event to his father, who had already separated from Kathleen after only a few months of marriage. O'Neill felt entrapped by the marriage, and he and Jenkins divorced in 1912. Initially he had no interest in his son, whom he saw

Eugene O'Neill, Jr., and his father *(Courtesy of the Sheaffer-O'Neill Collection, Charles E. Shain Library of Connecticut College)*

briefly, according to Jenkins, in 1912 but not again until 1921. Subsequently, though their relationship generally remained distant, O'Neill did take pride in his namesake, encouraging and financing many of his intellectual pursuits.

Educated in New York public institutions and at the exclusive Horace Mann School, Eugene O'Neill, Jr., went on to earn a Ph.D. in classics at Yale, the university that had awarded his father his only degree—an honorary doctorate. In the course of his undergraduate studies, O'Neill, Jr., won a number of awards in ancient Greek poetry, philosophy, translation, and research. In 1932, he initiated his graduate work at the University of Freiburg, Germany, returning to Yale to earn his doctorate, which was awarded in 1936. He then taught at Yale for several years, ending his affiliation in 1947, due in large part to his increasing psychological and drinking problems.

During his career at Yale, O'Neill, Jr., also pursued his interest in radio and worked as an announcer at WTIC in Hartford, Connecticut. He continued with radio work as well as public lectures throughout his life. Both during and after his tenure at Yale, O'Neill, Jr., also taught part-time at other institutions, including Sarah Lawrence College, Princeton University, the New School for Social Research, and Fairleigh Dickinson College.

Like his father, O'Neill, Jr., had a disastrous record in romantic affairs. When he was only 21, he married Elizabeth Green. They divorced in April 1937, and the following month he entered into an ill-fated second marriage to Janet Hunter Longley, daughter of a Yale math professor. That union ended the following summer, and in July 1939, O'Neill, Jr., took his third and last wife, Sally Hayward, who left him in 1944. His last relationship, tumultuous and abusive, was with Ruth Lander, an art agent, with whom he moved to Woodstock, New York, in 1948. She too left O'Neill, Jr., though she finally agreed to return to what was to be a short-lived reunion.

In his final years, O'Neill, Jr., flirted briefly with communism (although he had attempted to enlist in the military in his youth). He grew increasingly despondent, speaking frequently of suicide, and on September 13, 1950, at the age of 40, he took his own life. Eugene O'Neill did not attend his son's funeral.

Critics and scholars have perceived representations of O'Neill's eldest son in plays including DESIRE UNDER THE ELMS, The ICEMAN COMETH, and MOURNING BECOMES ELECTRA, as well as in early short works such as ABORTION. The major scholarly contribution O'Neill, Jr., made was the well-received two-volume edition of The Complete Greek Drama, which he coedited with Whitney J. Oates. Perhaps ironically, Oates authored the introductory section on GREEK TRAGEDY, while O'Neill, Jr., wrote the one on Greek comedy.

Bibliography

Gelb, Arthur, and Barbara Gelb. O'Neill. New York: Harper & Row, 1962.

Oates, Whitney, and Eugene O'Neill, Jr. The Complete Greek Drama All the Extant Tragedies of Aeschylus, Sophocles and Euripides, and the Comedies of Aristophanes and Menander. New York: Modern Library, 1988.

Karen Charmaine Blansfield

O'Neill, James (James O'Neill, Sr.) (1845–1920) Born in County Kilkenny, Ireland (some sources give the date as November 15 and the year as any between 1845 and 1849), to EDWARD O'NEILL and MARY O'NEILL, James O'Neill was the seventh of nine children. He came to the United States in 1850 with his parents and siblings, part of the massive IRISH immigration of the mid-19th century. Settling in Buffalo, New York, where 60-year-old Edward worked as a laborer, the family faced abject poverty, which was severely worsened five years after their arrival when Edward deserted his wife and children to return to Ireland, where he died. The hunger and deprivation experienced during his childhood remained with James O'Neill for the remainder of his life, as did the harsh conditions he experienced working 12 hour days for 50 cents a week as an apprentice file maker. In 1858, O'Neill's elder sister, Josephine, married a saloonkeeper named Sears who brought the entire family to Cincinnati, Ohio, where James found work as

Eugene O'Neill, Jr., at his father's old desk (at which he wrote The Emperor Jones and The Hairy Ape, among others) in the summer of 1950. Probably the last photograph taken of Eugene, Jr., before his suicide. Photo by Harry Teichlaut (Courtesy of the Sheaffer-O'Neill Collection, Charles E. Shain Library of Connecticut College)

a machinist. With the outbreak of the Civil War, he worked for another brother-in-law in a military uniform store in Norfolk, Virginia, returning to Cincinnati at war's end.

In 1865, when he was paid to go on as an extra at Cincinnati's National Theatre, O'Neill discovered an inclination for the stage and what seemed a comparatively easy way to make a living. O'Neill decided to pursue a theatrical career, which paid 25 cents per performance. O'Neill spent his first months in the company playing small roles in sentimental melodramas, and by all accounts, he took this newfound opportunity seriously, learning all aspects of stagecraft and making valuable professional acquaintances through his charm and native intelligence. A strong voice and handsome appearance brought continued employment in stock companies in St. Louis and Baltimore as well as encouraging words from leaders of the profession, including Edwin Forrest, Edwin Booth, and Joseph Jefferson. In 1870, O'Neill accepted an engagement as leading man of John Ellsler's Academy of Music in Cleveland, Ohio, where he acted with visiting stars including Forrest and Jefferson.

One of the most prestigious theaters in the Midwest, McVicker's in Chicago, Illinois, hired O'Neill as a leading man in 1872. He appeared there in a range of classical roles, mostly Shakespearean, before shifting his allegiance to Hooley's Opera House in 1874. There he alternated the roles of Othello and Iago with Edwin Booth, an experience O'Neill regarded as a career highlight (he also played Macduff to Booth's Macbeth). His pride in this achievement is recounted by James Tyrone, his dramatic alter ego, in his son's semiautobiographical drama of O'Neill family tensions, LONG DAY'S JOURNEY INTO NIGHT (1941). Remembering Booth's statement professing, "'That young man is playing Othello better than I ever did!' That from Booth, the greatest actor of his day or any other! And it was true!" (Gelb 57). Tyrone (like O'Neill) realizes that the artistic promise represented by this anecdote was not ultimately fulfilled.

In this period, O'Neill's theatrical success was momentarily overshadowed by personal scandal when his leading lady, Louise Hawthorne, died in an accident many believed was actually a suicide

James O'Neill at 22, 1869 *(Courtesy of the Harvard College Library Theatre Collection)*

resulting from an unhappy love affair with O'Neill. Another relationship with a Chicago woman, Nettie Walsh, led to a child she claimed to be O'Neill's. An attempt to extort money from O'Neill failed when he offered to raise the child as his own. In the midst of all this, O'Neill became attracted to Mary Ellen "Ella" Quinlan, daughter of his friend Thomas Quinlan (see O'NEILL, MARY ELLEN "ELLA"). When Hooley's Opera House moved its operations to San Francisco, California, O'Neill went along, playing opposite Clara Morris, who arranged for him to appear at Palmer's Union Square Theatre in New York in 1876. By this time, Thomas Quinlan had died, and Ella and her mother moved to New York, where O'Neill proposed marriage. They wed on June 14, 1877, despite the fact that the courtship and first months of their marriage were marred by a lawsuit brought by Walsh. Ella stood by O'Neill during the ordeal, and the suit was ultimately dismissed. O'Neill's long union with Ella, a delicate woman raised in a convent, was otherwise free of public scandal and the marriage endured, producing three sons: JAMES O'NEILL, JR. (Jamie), EDMUND BURKE O'NEILL, and Eugene Gladstone O'Neill. Edmund's death from measles in 1885 is considered by scholars to be a seminal event igniting decades of family tragedy, from Ella's solitary battle with morphine addiction (exacerbated by the difficult birth of Eugene) to the ALCOHOLISM of both Jamie and Eugene. Many details of the O'Neill family difficulties are referenced in *Long Day's Journey into Night*, and Eugene added elements from the experiences of his third wife, CARLOTTA MONTEREY O'NEILL, yet the play captures the essence of each family member through its merging of fact and fiction. Jamie's ultimate death resulting from alcoholism and despair over Ella's 1922 death is examined in O'Neill's final play, A MOON FOR THE MISBEGOTTEN (1943), in which the character of James Tyrone, Jr., Jamie's alter ego, is continued.

James O'Neill's acting success continued in San Francisco after his marriage to Ella, including an opportunity to play Jesus Christ in Salmi Morse's *The Passion*, a lavish David Belasco–produced spectacle modeled on the Oberammergau Passion Play. O'Neill was effective in the production, and as a devout Catholic he was deeply committed to the role, although controversy erupted when some vocal opponents pointed out that the production violated a local ordinance prohibiting impersonation of the Deity. Local authorities closed *The Passion* and arrested its cast, including O'Neill, and further attempts to produce the play failed, leaving O'Neill in fear that his career was in jeopardy.

O'Neill's fortunes changed almost immediately when he was summoned to New York's Booth Theatre to take over Charles Thorne's leading roles when the actor unexpectedly died. Thorne had been preparing to play Edmond Dantès in Charles Fechter's adaptation of Alexandre Dumas's 1844 novel *The Count of Monte Cristo*, but it was O'Neill who took the role when the play opened on February 12, 1883. Despite mixed reviews, the MELODRAMA became popular with audiences, so much so that it was held over until contractual obligations finally required vacating the Booth Theatre. This development allowed O'Neill to buy the rights to the play, which he shrewdly took on tour. Even more successful on the road than it had been in New York, *The Count of Monte Cristo* became a financial bonanza for O'Neill, who kept it in his repertoire and became permanently identified with the role. Considering himself first and foremost a Shakespearean actor, however, O'Neill found this enormous success both a financial blessing and a curse since audiences seemed to want him only as Dantès. He came to feel trapped by the part, which he played more than 6,000 times (including Broadway revivals in 1900 and 1907 and a 1913 silent film version) during the last 35 years of his career.

James O'Neill *(Courtesy of the Yale Collection of American Literature, Beinecke Rare Book and Manuscript Library)*

In 1884, O'Neill purchased two properties in NEW LONDON, CONNECTICUT, while visiting Ella's mother there. For the next 35 years, the O'Neills spent most summers in New London, 19 of them at the house they named the MONTE CRISTO COTTAGE, located on Connecticut's Thames River. It also provided the setting for Eugene's *Long Day's Journey into Night* and a more fictionalized (and romanticized) treatment of New London environs in his *AH, WILDERNESS!* (1933). During the rest of the year, O'Neill, usually with Ella and their sons in tow, barnstormed the country with *The Count of Monte Cristo.* He also appeared on Broadway and toured in Europe and across the United States in other plays, although rarely achieving the success accompanying revivals of *The Count of Monte Cristo.* These plays included an all-star revival of Adolphe D'Ennery and Eugene Cormon's *The Two Orphans* (1904), which O'Neill produced, as well as *The Dead Heart* (1890), *The Envoy* (1891), *The New South* (1891), *Fontenelle* (1892), *Richelieu* (1893), *Virginius* (1893), *The Courier of Lyons* (1894, a revision of *The Lady of Lyons*), *Hamlet* (1895), *The Dream of Matthew Wayne* (1895), *When Greek Meets Greek* (1898), *The Musketeers* (1899), *The Honor of the Humble* (1902), *The Manxman* (1902), *Audrey* (1902), *Romeo and Juliet* (1903), *The Adventures of Gerard* (1903), *The Sacrament of Judah* (1903), *The Voice of the Mighty* (1905), *The Abbi Bonaparte* (1908), *The White Sister* (1909), *Joseph and His Brethren* (1913), *The Melody of Youth* (1916), and *The Wanderer* (1917).

O'Neill also appeared in vaudeville in abridged versions of *Virginius* beginning in 1904 and *The Count of Monte Cristo* in 1911 and 1912 on the Orpheum circuit. He began giving "farewell" tours as early as 1906 but acted until near the end of his life. Popular with fellow members of the theatrical profession, O'Neill belonged to the Lambs' and Friars' clubs and was a significant participant in founding the Actors' Fund and in opposing the ruthless managerial tactics of the monopolizing Theatrical Syndicate during the 1890s.

Family life improved for the O'Neills with Ella's final defeat of her morphine addiction in 1914 (although some BIOGRAPHERS believe she suffered a brief relapse in 1917 when she endured a mastectomy), although Jamie's continued descent into alcoholism caused distress, as did Eugene's

rebellions until he found a new sense of purpose following months in GAYLORD FARM SANATORIUM in 1913 to cure tuberculosis. In this period, the senior O'Neill's career was nearing its end. Praised by contemporary critics for an acting style more natural than that of many of his late 19th-century peers, his brand of romantic theater was rapidly superseded by a more realistic and serious drama, of which his son became the driving force in the late 1910s. The senior O'Neill expressed reservations about the modernist themes of his son's early dramas, feeling the theater's central purpose was escapism. He found Eugene's one-act plays depressing, yet despite his final illness, James O'Neill was in proud attendance at the 1920 Broadway opening of *BEYOND THE HORIZON,* for which his son won the first of four PULITZER PRIZES for drama.

O'Neill was struck by a car in New York City in December 1918. Although the injuries sustained were not serious, a precipitous decline in his health began leading to a stroke suffered in 1920, followed by a diagnosis of intestinal cancer. Moved from New York to a New London hospital, he died there on August 10, 1920.

James O'Neill was immortalized by his son in the character of James Tyrone in *Long Day's Journey into Night,* but the character does him a disservice. O'Neill was not the miser his son depicts; in fact, he was well known for generosity within his profession, and there is no evidence that he compelled his family to live in second-rate hotels while he was touring. Although the melodramatic stage he represented was certainly in decline in 1912, the year in which *Long Day's Journey into Night* is set, James O'Neill was one of a small group of major theatrical stars of the early modernist period. Although frustrated in his desire to fully realize his potential, he attained remarkable success, particularly considering his humble origins, lack of formal education, and the troubles suffered by all members of his family.

Bibliography

Alexander, Doris. *Eugene O'Neill's Last Plays: Separating Art from Autobiography.* Athens: University of Georgia Press, 2005.

Black, Stephen A. "O'Neill and the Old Ham." *Eugene O'Neill Review* 17, nos. 1–2 (Spring–Fall 1993): 77–81.

Gelb, Arthur, and Barbara Gelb. *O'Neill: Life with Monte Cristo*. New York: Applause Books, 2000.

Matlaw, Myron. "Robins Hits the Road: Trouping with O'Neill in the 1880s." *Theatre Survey* 29, no. 2 (November 1988): 175–192.

Sheaffer, Louis. *Eugene O'Neill: Son and Artist*. Boston: Little, Brown, 1973.

———. *Eugene O'Neill: Son and Playwright*. Boston: Little, Brown, 1968.

James Fisher

O'Neill, James, Jr. (Jamie O'Neill) (1878–1923)

In the final assessment, Jamie O'Neill was one who, living hedonistically, squandered his talents. But for the first-born son of actor JAMES O'NEILL and his wife MARY ELLEN "ELLA" O'NEILL, things might have been otherwise. Like his younger brother Eugene, Jamie had the potential for success, for his natural gifts were considerable and his education first-rate.

Born on September 10, 1878, in San Francisco, California, where his parents resided for two years, Jamie was adored by his parents from birth, and with good reason, as the child was both handsome and intelligent. But a family tragedy that occurred in Jamie's early years was to profoundly shape his future. It concerned the arrival of a baby brother, EDMUND O'NEILL, born in 1885, and Jamie's unwitting culpability in the baby's death, a death that would haunt the sensitive child. Sick with measles and in the custody of his maternal grandmother BRIDGET LUNDIGAN QUINLAN while Ella traveled with her husband, Jamie inadvertently transmitted the disease to 18-month-old Edmund. Mary Tyrone recalls the loss of her child in LONG DAY'S JOURNEY INTO NIGHT, and if art imitates life, Ella must have imparted blame, as Mary clearly does to her elder son for the younger child's death (765–766).

Some months after this event, at age seven, Jamie was sent to Notre Dame in South Bend, Indiana, where he would pursue a rigorous course of study until his departure in 1894. At Notre Dame, he wrote POETRY, appeared in productions, and won awards for "elocution, rhetoric, grammar, arithmetic, Christian doctrine and penmanship" (Shaughnessy 45). His time at parochial school was time well spent, and the outgoing and popular Jamie, bolstered by periodic visits from his parents, thrived. But toward the end of his stay, his work fell off, and thinking a change was indicated, the O'Neills enrolled their son in Georgetown Preparatory (1894–95) and soon thereafter in St. John's Preparatory School (fall 1895). From there Jamie headed, in 1896, to St. John's College, later Fordham University, for his freshman year. An excellent student, he won numerous prizes—in English composition, Greek, Latin, chemistry, trigonometry, elocution, English literature, calculus, and (remarkably) religious instruction (Shaughnessy 56–58). He also earned accolades for his prose and verse submissions, and he served as editor of the prestigious *Fordham Monthly*.

But another family crisis was developing that would affect Jamie adversely. In October 1888, Ella, having endured the painful delivery of her third and last child, Eugene, became addicted to morphine as a consequence of her travail. Discovering his mother's addiction (having caught her in flagrante delicto), the adolescent Jamie, attached as he was to his saintly mother and incapable of attributing her with any weakness, turned his resentment on his unwitting brother. It was an anger that would fester and intensify in later years with the budding playwright's successes (in the face of Jamie's own failures), though hostility was always tempered by a kind of fraternal love. In act 4 of *Long Day's Journey into Night* (3:821), a drunken Jamie Tyrone (Jamie O'Neill) confesses this ambivalence to his brother, Edmund (Eugene). As a youth, Jamie also began to see his mother as a victim of his father's insensitivity and selfishness and turned oedipally, predictably, and implacably against James.

During his senior year at Fordham, Jamie, conspiring with his chums, conceived of a practical joke designed to "shock and awe" the Jesuit priests—one that would have unfortunate and long-term consequences for the perpetrator. Recounted in *A MOON FOR THE MISBEGOTTEN* for its entertainment value (3:876), the incident resulted in the prankster's permanent dismissal. For his nearly successful attempt to pawn off a prostitute as his sister to the Jesuits, Jamie was sent down in 1899. While he would live another two dozen years, Jamie (Jim as he was known at school) would never again evince or reclaim the promise of those early years.

Though he had indulged in womanizing and drinking at college and had helped initiate his brother into the same habits, Jamie, once dismissed, was unrestrained and unbridled in pursuit of vice. He worked at various jobs—as a traveling salesman for a lumber company and as an actor of minor roles in *The Musketeers* and *The Count of Monte Cristo,* the play his father starred in. While he evinced some thespian talent, blessed as he was with a resonant voice and a retentive memory, Jamie lacked James's work ethic. Moreover, his performances were uneven, due in good measure to bacchanalian pursuits. Still, his father had influence in the theater, and in 1902 Jamie picked up roles in *Audrey* and later *The Adventures of Gerard* and *The Two Orphans.* In 1905 he appeared in *Virginius,* a one-act vaudeville production, with James, who was then hoping to escape Château d'If for good and form his own acting company (Ranald 570). Breaking with his signature role of Edmond Dantès, James launched a full-length production of Sheridan Knowles's *Virginius,* but the reviews proved unkind, the play folded, and it was back to the château for James and his son.

Jamie's life fell into a predictable pattern of summers at MONTE CRISTO COTTAGE, which the O'Neills moved into in 1900 in NEW LONDON, CONNECTICUT, and itinerant acting during the season. Periodically living apart from his family, the elder son was still emotionally dependent on his mother and financially dependent on his father. It was largely through his father's good offices that Jamie found work, acting in the failed 1908 production of *Abbé Bonaparte* (with his father), and in *The Travelling Salesman* in 1909. In 1911, Jamie and his father were on tour in *Monte Cristo,* and in 1912, following Eugene's suicide attempt, they were joined on the vaudeville circuit in New Orleans by the youngest O'Neill. After completing a film version of *The Count of Monte Cristo* with his father in that same year, one not destined to be released commercially, Jamie met and fell in love with

Pauline Frederick, while father, son, and actress were rehearsing *Joseph and His Brethren.* Alcohol, according to Jamie, ended the romance, for, as he could not forego his real passion, Pauline declined his marriage proposal (Boulton 192–193). Apocryphal or not, the story of his rejection, as related by Jamie to Eugene's second wife, AGNES BOULTON, may have served as inspiration for Lily and Sid's static and star-crossed romance AH, WILDERNESS! (Gelb 560). Increasingly drunk and at odds with his father, a disillusioned and embittered Jamie saw his "star" set just as his brother's was ascending.

By 1917, Jamie was haggard, unemployed, and reduced to living on the $15-a-week "allowance" that James provided (Boulton 17). When Eugene met and, in 1918, married Boulton, inaptly referenced as "the Wild Irish Rose" by her brother-in-law, Jamie joined the couple for a summer in Provincetown, Massachusetts. Returning to New York in the fall, he continued to imbibe unabated, drunk even as his father died in August 1920.

One redeeming, if unforeseen, consequence of James's death was that Jamie, having discovered his life's purpose (to attend his mother), stopped drinking. For a two-year period, he maintained his sobriety, visiting his brother at PEAKED HILL BAR and escorting his mother to California in 1922. But the bliss of having his mother to himself was not to last: Ella, suffering from what probably was a brain tumor, died of a stroke. Just before her death a desperate Jamie had sent a telegram urging his brother to hurry to the West Coast, but the playwright claimed he was in no condition to travel. Jamie, unable to cope with the stress of his mother's illness and death, resumed drinking and whoring with abandon, In *A Moon for the Misbegotten,* Jim Tyrone reveals to Josie Hogan his shameful tryst with the prostitute aboard the train that carried his mother's body on its final journey. Jamie O'Neill's dissolute conduct following his mother's death would prompt the dramatic confession and absolution scene in his brother's last play. Devastated by the death of, arguably, the only woman he ever loved, Jamie was too inebriated to retrieve the coffin at Grand Central and too drunk to attend the funeral.

Ella might have been her son's salvation, but once she was gone, Jamie drank his way through his share of the estate, staying with friends Helen and HAROLD DEPOLO for a time in Darien, Connecticut (the DePolos' home not the best place to learn abstinence). In the year that remained to him, Jamie declined further as he engaged in drunken brawls, squandered his inheritance, and kept company with derelicts. In February 1923, Jamie, attending a production of *"ANNA CHRISTIE,"* disrupted the performance with a shout of "Why shouldn't my brother, the author, know all about whores?" (Sheaffer 1973, 107). Later that year, he was taken forcibly to a sanatorium in Norwich, Connecticut, and then to Riverlawn Sanatorium in Paterson, New Jersey. Completely debilitated, suffering from delirium tremens, virtually blind, he died of arteriosclerosis and cerebral apoplexy on November 8, 1923 (Ranald 572). In keeping with the shabbiness of his final days, Jamie was dressed for burial in a cheap undertaker's half-suit and placed in a plain pine box. It was Agnes Boulton, the woman he had once approved of and later maligned, who delayed the funeral to arrange for a better send-off for her brother-in-law (Sheaffer 1973, 117). Following the funeral at St. Stephen's Church on East Twenty-eighth Street, Jamie joined his father, the man he had warred with for most of his life, and his mother, the woman he adored, in the family plot in St. Mary's Cemetery, New London.

Jamie O'Neill remains vital in the pathetic but engaging character of Jamie/Jim Tyrone, while echoes of his life and times resound in other O'Neill characters—Sid Davis of *Ah, Wilderness!*; Willie Oban, Don Parritt, and Theodore "Hickey" Hickman of *The ICEMAN COMETH* (Gelb 509, Boulton 17); Dion Anthony of *The GREAT GOD BROWN* (Sheaffer 1973, 169); and the masked doppelgänger Loving in *DAYS WITHOUT END* (Sheaffer 1973, 411).

Bibliography

Alexander. Doris. *The Tempering of Eugene O'Neill.* New York: Harcourt, 1962.

Boulton. Agnes. *Part of a Long Story.* London: Peter Davies, 1958.

Gelb, Arthur, and Barbara Gelb. *O'Neill: Life with Monte Cristo.* New York: Applause Books, 2000.

Ranald, Margaret Loftus. *The Eugene O'Neill Companion.* Westport, Conn.: Greenwood, 1984.

Shaughnessy. Edward L. "Ella, James, and Jamie O'Neill." *Eugene O'Neill Review* 15, no. 2 (1991): 5–92.

Sheaffer, Louis. *O'Neill: Son and Playwright.* Boston: Little, Brown, 1968.

———. *O'Neill: Son and Artist.* Boston: Little, Brown, 1973.

Madeline Smith

O'Neill, Mary Ellen "Ella" (1857–1922)   Born at New Haven, Connecticut, on August 13, 1857, Mary Ellen Quinlan, the mother of Eugene O'Neill, was the daughter of IRISH immigrants THOMAS JOSEPH QUINLAN and BRIDGET LUNDIGAN QUINLAN. When she was still an infant, her businessman father moved the family to Cleveland, Ohio, where he achieved financial and social success. He raised his daughter to appreciate the finer things, providing for her education in music, literature, and the social graces. Born a Roman Catholic, Mary Ellen became devout in her faith, which would provide comfort in difficult times. She was generally sheltered from the harsh economic and social conditions faced by many IRISH AMERICANS in those times, the very forces that shaped the man she would eventually marry.

Well-educated, religious, and dignified, Mary Ellen was known to friends and family as "Ella" when she enrolled at St. Mary's Academy at Notre Dame, Indiana, in fall 1872. When she considered entering the convent there, the presiding mother superior encouraged her to experience the world for at least a year before making a definite decision. Ella's musical background led her to consider a career as a pianist before she made the acquaintance of a friend of her father. In 1872, Ella met actor JAMES O'NEILL in Cleveland as he was achieving his first theatrical successes. When Ella's father died in 1874, she moved with her mother to New York, where O'Neill was becoming an established fixture on the rough-and-tumble American stage. O'Neill courted her and, despite the objections of Ella's mother, who did not approve of James's profession, they married on June 14, 1877, at St. Ann's Roman Catholic Church in New York.

Mary "Ella" Quinlan O'Neill about the time she met James O'Neill. *(Courtesy of the Yale Collection of American Literature, Beinecke Rare Book and Manuscript Library)*

Following their marriage, the O'Neills traveled to a theatrical engagement in Chicago, Illinois, where O'Neill was slapped with a paternity suit by a former lover, Nettie Walsh, who claimed he had fathered her son (the suit was ultimately dismissed). Although Ella supported O'Neill throughout the incident, the revelation of his previous relationships and hard drinking shattered her romantic illusions. She avoided socializing with stage personnel and kept out of O'Neill's public life when possible, remaining in hotel rooms while he carried out his professional duties. However, she traveled on tour with O'Neill as he moved on to San Francisco, California, where their first child, JAMES O'NEILL, JR. (Jamie) was born on September 10, 1878. While on tour with O'Neill in St. Louis in fall 1883, Ella was again pregnant, and she returned to New York

in time for the birth of EDMUND BURKE O'NEILL on September 16. With two children, Ella toured with O'Neill less frequently. He met with great success playing Edmond Dantès in *The Count of Monte Cristo,* a role that provided a handsome income for the family for decades, despite the fact that its enduring popularity ultimately frustrated O'Neill's artistic aspirations.

Ella took up residence with her children in an apartment at the Richfield Hotel in New York, but because she missed O'Neill, she toured with him on the West Coast in early 1885, leaving the children with her mother. While she was gone, Jamie contracted measles and exposed baby Edmund, who became dangerously ill. Contacted in Denver, Colorado, where O'Neill was playing in *The Count of Monte Cristo,* Ella rushed back to New York, arriving too late to be with Edmund before he died. This tragedy, and the guilt she felt about her absence, haunted her for the remainder of her life. Despite this, in fall 1885, the O'Neills sent Jamie to a boarding school at St. Mary's Academy in Notre Dame so they could continue to tour together. Reuniting in summer 1886 at a house in NEW LONDON, CONNECTICUT, where they had purchased property in 1884 and 1886 with earnings from O'Neill's success in *The Count of Monte Cristo,* the family attempted to create a stable home life. O'Neill purchased the rights to *The Count of Monte Cristo* and toured in it successfully every season for decades. While on tour in Europe in 1887, Ella's mother died, and Ella was unable to return for the burial.

On October 16, 1888, while in residence at New York City's BARRETT HOUSE hotel by Longacre Square (now Times Square), Ella gave birth to Eugene Gladstone O'Neill. The difficult birth led a doctor to prescribe morphine to relieve Ella's pain, and she became addicted, although some scholars suggest that she had previously taken the drug to relieve her distress in the aftermath of Edmund's death. In any event, over the ensuing years, Ella sought various cures for her addiction, all unsuccessful until 1914, when she took matters into her own hands by entering a Brooklyn convent where she finally overcame her morphine habit. Some O'Neill BIOGRAPHERS suggest she relapsed briefly in 1917. Few people outside the family were aware of Ella's struggle with morphine, and most regarded her as a gracious, quietly dignified woman.

Despite Ella's resistance to stage life, her marriage to O'Neill endured, continuing for 43 years until his death in 1920. As their sons grew to adolescence, the O'Neills were distressed by their rebellion and restlessness as well as the overindulgence in liquor that led to ALCOHOLISM in both. Ella generally deferred to her husband in dealing with the problems caused by their sons, who were dismissed from schools and various odd jobs, including with O'Neill's theatrical troupe. James O'Neill encouraged Jamie's attempts to become an actor, although the younger O'Neill found little success and descended further into alcoholism.

Neither James nor Ella O'Neill could have been happy about the sort of plays Eugene began writing around 1913, after spending several months in a sanatorium recovering from tuberculosis exacerbated by excessive drinking, yet they were relieved that he seemed to be finding a profession as a writer. Both attended the first production of his full-length drama BEYOND THE HORIZON in 1920, shortly before James O'Neill's death. Ella, who had endured a mastectomy a few years before, with a recurrence of her cancer in 1919, attempted to assist Jamie, whose alcoholism had spun out of control. He quit drinking and lived with Ella in California until she suffered a stroke and died in Los Angeles, California, on February 28, 1922. Jamie escorted Ella's body east by train, falling into a completely alcoholic state to the point that he was unable to attend her funeral service at St. Leo's Church in New York City, followed by burial in New London, Connecticut. After Ella's death, Jamie returned to his old ways and drank himself to death a year later. His experiences following his mother's death were sadly dramatized in Eugene's final play, A MOON FOR THE MISBEGOTTEN (1943).

Aspects of Ella's persona are evident in her son's plays, but none more so than LONG DAY'S JOURNEY INTO NIGHT (1939), a semiautobiographical work set in 1912, the year in which Eugene attempted suicide, suffered tuberculosis, and was reborn as a dramatist. Taking the name of his dead brother, Edmund, for his dramatic alter ego, O'Neill gave Ella back her first name, Mary, in what most schol-

ars consider the greatest female character in his oeuvre, Mary Tyrone. Guilt-ridden, drug-addicted, and deeply religious, Mary is haunted by her loss of faith, disoriented, and mired in a futile search for her lost dreams. "What is it I'm looking for?" Mary wonders in the play's last moments, "I remember when I had it I was never lonely nor afraid. I can't have lost it forever, I would die if I thought that. Because then there would be no hope" (3:825, 826). Morphine provides Mary's escape, yet it is not a peaceful one as she searches restlessly through the fog of addiction for her lost self. Unable to articulate that which she seeks, Mary represents O'Neill's career-long exploration of modernist man's search for connection, a futile search for the roots that his characters believe they once had through faith, love, or family, and cannot rediscover.

Bibliography

Alexander, Doris. *Eugene O'Neill's Last Plays: Separating Art from Autobiography.* Athens: University of Georgia Press, 2005.

Black, Stephen A. "Ella O'Neill's Addiction." *Eugene O'Neill Newsletter* 9, no. 1 (Spring 1985): 24–26.

———. *Eugene O'Neill: Beyond Mourning and Tragedy.* New Haven, Conn.: Yale University Press, 1999.

Gelb, Arthur, and Barbara Gelb. *O'Neill: Life with Monte Cristo.* New York: Applause Books, 2000.

Shaughnessy, Edward L. "Ella O'Neill and the Imprint of Faith." *Eugene O'Neill Review* 16, no. 2 (Fall 1992): 29–43.

Sheaffer, Louis. *Eugene O'Neill: Son and Artist.* Boston: Little, Brown, 1973.

———. *Eugene O'Neill: Son and Playwright.* Boston: Little, Brown, 1968.

James Fisher

O'Neill, Oona (Oona O'Neill Chaplin) (1925–1991)

Oona O'Neill, daughter of AGNES BOULTON and Eugene O'Neill, was born on May 14, 1925, in Bermuda. Her father had recently finished revising The GREAT GOD BROWN, and her mother had just completed The Guilty One when the baby arrived, and Eugene immediately began a period of hard drinking. He had been struggling to control his ALCOHOLISM, but it would be half a year more before he would have lasting success. In the second summer of Oona's life, O'Neill became reacquainted with the actress Carlotta Monterey (later CARLOTTA MONTEREY O"NEILL,) and long before Oona was three, her father abandoned his marriage to Agnes and went off to France with Carlotta. Oona would not see her father again until she was six, and she would see him on only a few occasions afterward, never for more than a week.

Nevertheless, Oona remembered having had a happy childhood, living mainly in New Jersey after O'Neill's departure. Two years in a Virginia boarding school proved difficult. After that, her mother moved to Manhattan, where Oona completed her education at the Brearley School. Her friends included Gloria Vanderbilt and Carol Marcus (who married the playwright William Saroyan and later the actor Walter Matthau). Aram Saroyan's *Trio* gives a vivid portrayal of Oona's friendship with these two women and their life in the social spotlight. On April 12, 1942, Gene wrote in his WORK DIARY: "News comes that Oona has become Stork Club publicity racket Glamour Girl—at this of all times!—I am not amused!" (433). She also briefly captured the attention of the young writer J. D. Salinger.

A notion that she might become an actress led Oona to Hollywood. She auditioned for Charlie Chaplin, who had had some acquaintance with her father in the late 1910s, in the milieu of the PROVINCETOWN PLAYERS in GREENWICH VILLAGE. Rather than cast her in his film, Chaplin proposed marriage, and on June 16, 1943, she became his wife. Gene was furious with her for making such a match—she had just turned 18, and Chaplin was 54—and refused all contact or communication with her for the rest of his life.

Agnes had less trouble accepting this new turn in her daughter's life, though she must have wondered about its prospects. Chaplin was served with a paternity suit by another woman at the time of

Eugene and Oona O'Neill *(Courtesy of the Hageman Collection, The Eugene O'Neill Foundation)*

Oona and Agnes Boulton *(Courtesy of Culver Pictures)*

the marriage. However, the union proved enduring and deep, with eight children. Chaplin's clashes with U.S. federal authorities in the "Red Scare" period led to their moving to Switzerland in 1952. After Eugene O'Neill's death in 1953, Oona and her brother SHANE RUDRAIGHE discovered that they were specifically excluded from his will. They continued to share an interest in certain royalties from O'Neill's plays, by the terms of earlier agreements; Oona consistently turned over her share to her brother. She also ceded her share of the proceeds from the sale of the Bermuda property, SPITHEAD, in 1961.

Agnes visited Oona in Switzerland in 1959, and Oona visited her mother in 1967, when Agnes was in the hospital, suffering from an intestinal ailment. She returned the following year, following her mother's death, to take care of the estate, and in the process she removed untold manuscripts and other items to Switzerland. Many other things, including a lot of the ephemera associated with her mother's marriage to O'Neill, which Agnes had collected, Oona ordered destroyed. In so doing, she took the advice of O'Neill biographer Louis Sheaffer, who had known her mother and

had surveyed the vast quantity of documents in Agnes's possession, which included receipts and notes to the gardener and letters from old friends, but which might also have included such things as correspondence between her father and the painter Thomas Eakins, and perhaps a draft of the sequel Agnes had intended to her memoir, *Part of a Long Story.*

Around this same time, Oona began a lively correspondence with Sheaffer, who was just publishing the first volume of his biography. They would write to each other on remarkably intimate terms about O'Neill and other matters until Sheaffer's death in 1993. This is a fascinating and moving correspondence, which merits publication, if the Chaplin family would allow it; their letters are now located in the Sheaffer-O'Neill COLLECTION at Connecticut College. Meanwhile, during the years following her mother's death, Oona was completely occupied tending to the failing health of her husband, who died at the age of 88 in 1977. Jane Scovell's 1998 biography of Oona reveals that these years were very difficult for Oona, with constant attention to her ailing husband, and in the process she became a heavy drinker.

Scovell characterizes the remaining years of Oona's life as a series of desperate attempts to recapture her youth and freedom. She had relationships with younger men, paradoxically seeking some replacement for the father figure she had now lost twice. Her health deteriorated rapidly from her drinking, and pancreatic cancer finally brought her life to a painful end on September 27, 1991.

Oona does not clearly figure in any of Gene's plays, though possibly she might be glimpsed in Sara Melody in *A TOUCH OF THE POET*, who is described as "an exceedingly pretty girl with a mass of black hair, fair skin with rosy cheeks, and beautiful, deep-blue eyes." She has certain fine features, but "her jaw is too heavy," like an O'Neill jaw. Her manners are a combination of aristocratic (like a Brearley School girl) and peasant (Boulton? or O'Neill?). Sara has the self-assertion of the entitled, but the caution of one who knows her "title" does not count for much, in some eyes, and she boldly defies her father's will. This play was revised as late as 1942, coinciding with the time when Gene's opinion of Oona was changing for the worse, as revealed in his WORK DIARY (II, 412, 448).

Bibliography

O'Neill, Eugene. *Work Diary 1924–1943*. Preliminary edition transcribed by Donald Gallup. 2 vols. New Haven, Conn.: Yale University Library, 1981.

Saroyan, Aram. *Trio: Portrait of an Intimate Friendship*. New York: Linden Press, 1985.

Scovell, Jane. *Oona: Living in the Shadows*. New York: Warner Books, 1998.

William Davies King

O'Neill, Shane Rudraighe (1919–1977)   Shane Rudraighe O'Neill, the son of AGNES BOULTON and Eugene O'Neill, was born on October 30, 1919, in Provincetown, Massachusetts. In *Part of a Long Story* (1958), Boulton recounts how, in the second year of their marriage, she became aware of her pregnancy and dreaded telling Eugene because he had made it clear that he wanted nothing to interrupt the solitude of their existence. However, his writing had been going well, his drinking compulsion had abated, and so he surprised her by welcoming the birth of a son. Nonetheless, the first few months of the boy's life were marked by the almost complete absence of O'Neill, who was in New York overseeing the production of BEYOND THE HORIZON, and even when Gene returned, he took only a distant interest in his son, assigning the work of child care initially to Agnes and later to Fifine Clark, a nurse who became known to Shane as Gaga. The distance between father and son never significantly closed.

Shane knew many homes as a boy, mainly Provincetown; BROOK FARM in Ridgefield, Connecticut; and SPITHEAD in Bermuda, where he began his schooling. After Eugene left Agnes in 1928, Shane saw his father on only a few occasions, and their correspondence was sporadic. This separation nearly coincided with the death of his beloved Gaga. Shane attended many boarding schools, where he took interest in little except for art, but both his parents pushed him to prepare himself for college. Ultimately, he failed to earn a high school diploma, and his various impulses to become a veterinarian, an artist, or even a ranch hand came to nothing.

During the early 1940s, Shane underwent periods of heavy drinking, suicide attempts, an unsuccessful relationship, and drug addiction, mostly living in Greenwich Village and occasionally working odd jobs as a carpenter and on charter boats. In 1944, he married Catherine Givens, and the following year she gave birth to EUGENE O'NEILL III. Eugene and his third wife, CARLOTTA MONTEREY O'NEILL, who had not seen Shane for some five years, visited this grandchild, Eugene's first; however, the baby died before it reached three months of age, probably of sudden infant death syndrome. This incident led to the end of all communication between the playwright and his son.

By the late 1940s, Shane had developed an addiction to heroin, which he would never overcome. After living in Spithead for some years, he and his family (his fifth child was born in 1955) settled in New Jersey, near his mother Agnes. During these years, he had several encounters with the police, and finally he and Cathy divorced in the early 1960s. In the early 1950s, meanwhile, he was befriended by Croswell Bowen, one of the early O'Neill BIOGRAPHERS, who would state, on the title page of *The Curse of the Misbegotten*, that his book was written "with the assistance of Shane O'Neill." Many saw creative promise in Shane, including Bowen, who

Shane O'Neill in 1957 *(Courtesy of the Sheaffer-O'Neill Collection, Charles E. Shain Library of Connecticut College)*

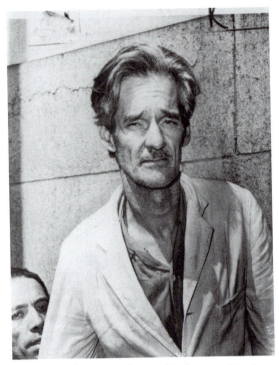

Shane O'Neill in 1962 after a police line-up. *(Courtesy of the Sheaffer-O'Neill Collection, Charles E. Shain Library of Connecticut College)*

saw something "Christlike" in Shane. His half sister Barbara Burton remembered him as unusual and fine; his children remember him as a loving man. Nevertheless, addiction and an unbroken record of failure, disappointment, and despair, which Bowen attributed to "the curse of the misbegotten," drove him to suicide in 1977, when he jumped from a fourth-floor apartment window in New York.

Sons figure in many of the plays Eugene O'Neill wrote after Shane's birth, but many of those son characters seem to reflect O'Neill's relation to his own father, JAMES O'NEILL. The one character who has been analyzed as possibly being, in some ways, a representation of Shane is Don Parritt in The ICEMAN COMETH. An anxious young man, deeply unsure of himself, certain that he has betrayed his libertine mother, Don comes to Larry Slade, whom he identifies as a virtual father figure, asking for guidance. Larry initially wants nothing to do with this young man, who only reminds him of his own unsuccessful relationship with the boy's

mother, a decade earlier. Eventually, because of the intersecting saga of Hickey, with its tragic trajectory, Larry comes to the point of giving Don some (ambiguous) "push," which enables or permits or drives Don to jump to his death from an upper-story window of Harry Hope's saloon and flophouse. O'Neill was writing this play in 1939 at the time Shane turned up, following his failure to graduate from high school, to seek advice and guidance from his father, roughly a decade after Eugene had left Agnes. Unfortunately, Shane eventually found himself in freefall from that upper story, with no literary trope to preserve him.

Bibliography

Boulton, Agnes. *Part of a Long Story.* New York: Doubleday & Company, 1958.

Bowen, Croswell, with the assistance of Shane O'Neill. *The Curse of the Misbegotten: A Tale of the House of O'Neill.* New York: McGraw-Hill Book Company, 1959.

King, William Davies. "Oresteian Structures in *The Iceman Cometh.*" *Eugene O'Neill Review* 27 (2005): 126–134.

William Davies King

O'Neill, Silverdene Emblem (Blemie) (1927–1940)

Eugene O'Neill's Dalmatian Silverdene Emblem "Blemie" O'Neill was not the only non-human member of the O'Neill family during the years CARLOTTA MONTEREY O'NEILL shared with Eugene—their menagerie also included turtles (Baltimore and Ohio), chickens, other dogs and cats, and a pond of goldfish. But Blemie held a privileged place in his master's and mistress's heart. Carlotta described him as "the most pleasant and amusing child," as well as the "most grateful" of all the O'Neill children (Gelb, 1960, 827). "He is *sweet!*," wrote Carlotta on the day he arrived (December 11, 1928), "and beautifully bred—& looks healthy—English bred dogs are best—! Gene likes him! I love him! He weeps a little the first morning—he is lonely & things are strange! *I know!*" (quoted in Bogard 431).

Born in England in 1927, Blemie was shipped to Eugene and Carlotta while they lived in Le Plessis, near Tours, FRANCE. A distinguished Dalmatian who lived for 13 years, Blemie moved with the family to New York City, SEA ISLAND, and ultimately TAO HOUSE in Danville, California, where he died of natural causes. Blemie attended rehearsals, took his master for long walks, and, as the actress Lillian Gish reminisced, "acted as host" to visitors (Gelb, 1960, 714). His headstone at Tao House reads, "Sleep In Peace, Faithful Friend."

O'Neill wrote a lasting testament to Blemie's significance in the family for Carlotta on December 26, 1940, entitled "The Last Will and Testament of Silverdene Emblem O'Neill" just after the dog's death on December 17th. Written as a consolation for the grieving mistress, O'Neill wrote the piece in Blemie's voice, one buried in the mind of his master, and it is filled with a generous tenderness, which, if familiar-sounding from much of the author's work, is seldom if ever so purely and lovingly expressed. With a gentle condescension, the superior (and self-admiring) dog urges his human companions not to mourn him, but rather to recognize that, delivered from worldly cares, he will rest eternally with the satisfaction of knowing he has loved and been loved. Reflecting on human acquisitiveness and its attendant anxieties—contentedly free of them himself—he offers his canine perspective as a pure vision of life, where the greatest rewards come from sharing love, offering consolation and joy to one's loved ones, and accepting with grace and optimism the inevitable end to life while those left behind find further companionship in the earthly vale.

Now read as an author's own essay on mortality, and written as the process of writing itself became more difficult for O'Neill due to a debilitating hand tremor, the "Last Will and Testament" captures an ironic amusement with worldly vanities (Blemie cannot resist appraising his own virtues) and a lusty enthusiasm for life's unfettered appetites. The dog's vision of paradise includes multitudes of bitches, full bowls of food, and warm fires to curl up before, along with a frank consideration of the degradations imposed by time and a willingness to embrace the inevitable decay of those qualities that stoke one's self-importance. Most striking may be the replacement of earthly pride and longings—so much the material of O'Neill's oeuvre and torment of his characters—with the satisfactions of loyalty and lasting love. However elusive, these ideals are captured beautifully in Blemie, as seen through his master's eyes, and wittily, movingly articulated in his "Last Will and Testament."

Bibliography

Bogard, Travis. *The Unknown O'Neill: Unpublished and Unfamiliar Writings of Eugene O'Neill.* New Haven, Conn.: Yale University Press, 1988.

Gelb, Arthur, and Barbara Gelb. *O'Neill.* New York: Harper and Brothers, 1960.

O'Neil, Eugene. Foreword to *The Unknown O'Neill: Unpublished and Unfamiliar Writings of Eugene O'Neill.* New Haven, Conn.: Yale University Press, 1988, 433–434.

Alex Roe

P

Peaked Hill Bar Provincetown, Massachusett's quiet location within the sheltering crook of the tip of Cape Cod stands in dramatic contrast to the remote dune lands just behind the town. When he first came to Provincetown in 1916, Eugene O'Neill was attracted to this empty, windswept terrain, and three years later, he acquired the abandoned lifesaving station there that became his summer residence for a time. Taking its name from the treacherous sand bars offshore, Peaked Hill Bar had been one of the rescue stations built on the Cape's ocean side in the 19th century. When erosion threatened it, a replacement station was built on safer ground in 1915. But the erosion reversed itself, and the spectacularly sited structure, no longer needed by the U.S. Life-Saving Service (later the Coast Guard), was bought by copper magnate Sam Lewisohn and converted to a residence by the wealthy arts patron and prominent social rebel, Mabel Dodge.

In 1919, Lewisohn sold the property to JAMES O'NEILL, Eugene's father, who bought it as a wedding present for his son and Eugene's second wife, AGNES BOULTON. In its remoteness, Peaked Hill Bar offered total freedom from the distractions of society, and O'Neill wrote each morning in a second-floor room facing the ocean, climbing to the rooftop lookout now and then to take in the vast panorama. Dodge had brought in white wooden furniture, divans, and large pieces of decorative Italian pottery, which, together with a floor painted in a rich blue and the many fittings of a former life-saving station, created an interior progressive for its time. It was described in detail by Agnes Boulton in her 1958 memoir *Part of a Long Story*.

During the couple's four summers there, or in rented winter quarters in town, O'Neill completed BEYOND THE HORIZON and CHRIS CHRISTOPHERSEN; worked on The FOUNTAIN; and saw *Beyond the Horizon*, The EMPEROR JONES, GOLD, "ANNA CHRISTIE," The STRAW, DIFF'RENT, and The HAIRY APE produced in New York City. But for all the productivity encouraged by the house and its setting, it took determination to live there. There was no road, and the trudge through the sand to town was arduous; provisions had to be brought by horse and wagon. Friends and family often came to stay, and when SHANE RUDRAIGHE O'NEILL was born in 1919, a governess, Fifine Clark, joined the household. Complications involving new productions in New York, the death of O'Neill's father and mother (in 1920 and 1922, respectively), and the decline of his brother Jamie, generated tensions played out in drinking binges and marital strife. Where once the windy isolation of Peaked Hill Bar had acted as a tonic, its inconvenience came to outweigh its psychological and aesthetic advantages and, in autumn 1922, the family moved to BROOK FARM in Ridgefield, Connecticut, relatively close to New York, the locus of O'Neill's widening fame.

The weathered, shingled building finally succumbed to the SEA in 1931, but not before its literary history was extended briefly by the author

Peaked Hill Bar in Provincetown, Massachusetts *(Courtesy of the Sheaffer-O'Neill Collection, Charles E. Shain Library of Connecticut College)*

Edmund Wilson. He rented the house in 1927, joining the circle of the remaining keepers of the PROVINCETOWN PLAYERS' flame, among them SUSAN GLASPELL, Mary Heaton Vorse, and Harry Kemp. John Dos Passos and E. E. Cummings and their wives were visitors, and Hazel Hawthorne made it the atmospheric setting for her novel *Salt House.*

Bibliography

Black, Stephen A. *Eugene O'Neill: Beyond Mourning and Tragedy.* New Haven, Conn., and London: Yale University Press, 1999.

Boulton, Agnes. *Part of a Long Story.* Garden City, N.Y.: Doubleday, 1958.

Hawthorne, Hazel. *Salt House.* New York: Frederick A. Stokes Co., 1934.

O'Neill, Eugene. *Selected Letters of Eugene O'Neill.* Edited by Travis Bogard and Jackson R. Bryer. New Haven, Conn.: Yale University Press, 1988.

Richter, Robert A. *Eugene O'Neill and Dat Ole Davil Sea: Maritime Influences in the Life and Works of Eugene O'Neill.* Mystic, Conn.: Mystic Seaport, 2004.

Sheaffer, Louis. *O'Neill: Son and Playwright.* Boston: Little, Brown, 1968.

Brian Rogers

Philadelphia, **SS** Eugene O'Neill arrived in Southampton, England, in July 1911 aboard the SS *NEW YORK,* a sister ship of the SS PHILADELPHIA. Shortly after O'Neill's arrival, England was hit by the Great Labor Strike of 1911. The strike revolved around the rights of dock laborers and transportation workers. Stokers and seamen, who normally did not fraternize with each other, put aside their differences and joined together to show their solidarity for the transportation and dock workers. During the strike, the railroads stopped running, and ships were stuck in port. It was during this period that O'Neill became friends with DRISCOLL, a stoker from the SS *Philadelphia.*

Once the strike was over, O'Neill joined the crew of the *Philadelphia.* He advanced in rank from ordinary seaman aboard the *New York* to able-bodied seaman (now simply able seaman) on the *Philadelphia.* This was a milestone in O'Neill's life: The advance in rank demonstrated that he had gained skill and expertise during his other experiences at sea.

The securing of the position on the *Philadelphia* might have been instigated by Driscoll, or O'Neill could have simply been transferred from the SS *New York* since both ships were owned by the American Line. The duties of an able seaman were very similar to those of an ordinary seaman with the exception of the added duty of standing an occasional two-hour watch on the crow's nest, a significant task. The route to and from New York and Southampton was through the North Atlantic, which is known for rough seas, severe weather, and heavy traffic. The crew had to keep a watchful eye for other vessels, including fishing vessels that might be anchored on the fishing grounds and icebergs. Just eight months later, traveling the same route as the *Philadelphia,* the "unsinkable" *Titanic* went down after hitting an iceberg. In *LONG DAY'S JOURNEY INTO NIGHT,* the autobiographical character Edmund Tyrone recalls standing watch on the crow's nest and remarks that it was a high point in his life (3:811–812).

O'Neill's time aboard the *Philadelphia* was relatively short. The vessel departed Southampton on August 19, 1911, and O'Neill signed off the *Philadelphia* in New York on August 26. His arrival in New York marked the end of his career as a sailor. But he cherished his time at SEA, and the American Line sweater that was part of his uniform remained a prized possession.

Driscoll and the *Philadelphia* provided O'Neill with the inspiration for *The HAIRY APE.* He also drew on his experiences from the American Line for his early plays *WARNINGS* and *FOG* and his unpublished play *The PERSONAL EQUATION.*

See also MERCHANT MARINE.

Bibliography

Flayhart, William Henry, III. *The American Line (1871–1902).* New York and London: W. W. Norton, 2000.

Richter, Robert A. *Eugene O'Neill and Dat Ole Davil Sea: Maritime Influences in the Life and Works of Eugene O'Neill.* Mystic, Conn.: Mystic Seaport, 2004.

Sheaffer, Louis. *O'Neill: Son and Playwright.* Boston: Little, Brown, 1968.

Robert A. Richter

philosophical anarchism   Eugene O'Neill derived "philosophical anarchism" (also known as "individualist anarchism" or "egoism") from numerous sources: the Unique Book Shop in New York City, which O'Neill first visited in 1906; the "Ash Can" painters Robert Henri and George Bellow's Ferrer School, where he studied informally in 1915; HIPPOLYTE HAVEL's *Revolt* magazine, where he served a brief apprenticeship in the same year; and the many friends and radical associates of his early GREENWICH VILLAGE days. At age 18, when O'Neill first began frequenting the Unique Book Shop, its proprietor, BENJAMIN R. TUCKER, an acolyte of Thomas Jefferson, Walt Whitman, and Henry David Thoreau, was obsessing over a book he was preparing to publish for his own imprint. The book was Max Stirner's founding manifesto of philosophical anarchism, *The Ego and His Own* (1844), which is listed on Edmund Tyrone's (O'Neill's closest autobiographical avatar) bookshelf in the STAGE DIRECTIONS of *LONG DAY'S JOURNEY INTO NIGHT.* O'Neill's NEW LONDON friend and Manhattan roommate Ed Keefe, who appears in the playwright's earliest full-length drama, *BREAD AND BUTTER,* recalled that when O'Neill first brought him to Tucker's store, "I remember one book he made me buy: Max Stirner's *Ego and His Own*" (quoted in Gelb 243).

Contrary to EMMA GOLDMAN's "communist anarchism," philosophical anarchism espoused three main principles: unconditional nonviolence; one-on-one instruction in the ways of the philosophy rather than mass propaganda; and the complete dismissal of all socially constructed institutions—government, military, press, organized religion, etc—as "phantoms," "ghosts," or "spooks" to be exorcised completely from one's thoughts. Throughout *The Ego and His Own,* Stirner also rails against all "fixed ideas," such as "morality, legality, Christianity, and so forth" (55) in much the same way that Ralph Waldo Emerson denounced "foolish consistency." The expression "fixed idea" appears in many of O'Neill's plays. O'Neill biographer Louis Sheaffer catalogs Stirner's views in the broadest sense: "With Germanic thoroughness Stirner took on the State, the Press, Parents, Family Life, Morality, Education, Liberalism, Socialism, Communism, Christianity, all religions, in fact, all schools of thought, and demolished just about everything in sight and ever known in civilization in favor of individualism inviolate, anarchism in its ultimate form" (122).

O'Neill pronounced himself a philosophical anarchist at least as early as 1914 while studying playwriting with GEORGE PIERCE BAKER at Harvard University. One of his classmates there remembered that the 26-year-old O'Neill was "intellectually . . . a philosophical anarchist; politically, a philosophical socialist" (quoted in Pfister 107). But as late as 1946, while overseeing a rehearsal for THE ICEMAN COMETH, O'Neill remarked to his future biographer Croswell Bowen, "I am a philosophical anarchist, which means, 'Go to it, but leave me out of it'" (quoted in Bowen 82). Along with Baker, O'Neill's two most significant mentors in philosophical anarchism were TERRY CARLIN and Hutchins Hapgood. Carlin, the model for the "philosophical drunken bum" Larry Slade in *The Iceman Cometh* (3:581), was an anarchist "hobo hero" tortured into ALCOHOLISM and vagabondage by the effects his philosphy had on friends and lovers. Hapgood, a founding member of the PROVINCETOWN PLAYERS, was a journalist and author who wrote countless articles exposing the lives of vaudeville stage performers, Bowery bums, pickpockets, PROSTITUTES, immigrant laborers, and anarchists; Hapgood's books include *An Anarchist Woman* (1909), in part

a portrait of Carlin's hyper-individualistic lifestyle, and *The Spirit of Labor* (1907), which deals with Chicago's anarchist-syndicalist movement.

Philosophical anarchism thus lends itself to artistic openness, particularly with regard to subject matter. Doris Alexander describes Carlin, though not a writer himself, as believing "in the hidden poetry of lost souls" (*Eugene* 88); and Hapgood, in his glance backward on his life of rebellion entitled *A Victorian in the Modern World* (1939), defined his uncompromising belief in philosophical anarchism as "a willingness to receive hospitably whatever dawning forces there may be in the submerged; a refusal to deny their possible validity in a more complex society. . . . It is deeply sympathetic with the psychology of the underdog" (277). Hapgood and Carlin were dyed-in-the-wool "master of the misbegotten" well before the turn of the 20th century; but by the 1920s, O'Neill's reputation for this surpassed his friends' easily.

Philosophical anarchism's central tenets permeate the full canon of O'Neill's plays, including, but not limited to, The PERSONAL EQUATION, The EMPEROR JONES, The HAIRY APE, The GREAT GOD BROWN, STRANGE INTERLUDE, AH, WILDERNESS!, DAYS WITHOUT END, The Iceman Cometh, and Long Day's Journey into Night. But perhaps the most resonant is Stirner's idea of social institutions as "spooks" to be dismissed from one's consciousness outright. William O. Reichert, a scholar of political philosophy, explains that the philosophical anarchist considers the state a malignant abstraction rather than a palpable threat to fight against: "The state, rather than being a real structure or entity, is nothing more than a conception. To destroy the state then, is to remove this conception from the mind of the individual. . . . [to the philosophical anarchist] revolution is not political at all" (859). According to Stirner, and later Tucker and the rest of the philosophical anarchists, the most effective means to rebel against state-sponsored outrages is simply to accept the fact that the state and the business interests and religious hypocrites that support it and even the notion of "mankind" (as in "the betterment of") exist merely as "phantoms," "ghosts," or "spooks" that invidiously haunt our minds but have no basis in reality.

The character Hartmann in O'Neill's *The Personal Equation* (written for Baker's seminar in 1915) refers to the American notion of "fatherland or motherland" as a "sentimental phantom" (1:320) and goes on to say that "the soul of man is an uninhabited house haunted by the ghosts of old ideals. And man in those ghosts still believes!" (1:321). Over a decade later, O'Neill's spiritually lost character Nina Leeds in *Strange Interlude* snarls a Stirnerian line at her moralizing companion, Charles Marsden, when she describes her conscious attempt, following the death of her lover, Gordon Shaw, in World War I, to "believe in any god at any price—a heap of stones, a mud image, a drawing on a wall, a bird, a fish, a snake, a baboon—or even a good man preaching the simple platitudes of truth, those Gospel words we love the sound of but whose meaning we pass on to spooks to live by!" (2:669). And later still, in O'Neill's failed morality play *Days Without End* (1933), the demon Loving scorns the faith of a priest and his alter-ego John in the "old ghostly comforts" of religion and even the "equally futile ghost" of believing in a "pseudo-Nietzschean savior" (3:161,159). Here is Stirner applying the phantom-ghost-spook metaphor in a passage that could well provide the basis for a complete essay on O'Neill's soul-searching play *The Great God Brown* (1925):

> The ghost has put on a body, God has become man, but now man is himself the gruesome spook which he seeks to get behind, to exorcise, to fathom, to bring to reality and speech; man is—*spirit*. . . . Man has become to himself a ghost, an uncanny spook, to which there is even assigned a distinct seat in the body. . . . (52)

Bibliography

Alexander, Doris. *Eugene O'Neill's Last Plays: Separating Art from Autobiography.* Athens: University of Georgia Press, 2005.

Bowen, Croswell. "The Black Irishman." In *O'Neill and His Plays: Four Decades of Criticism,* edited by Oscar Cargill, N. Bryllion Fagin, and William J. Fisher, 64–84. New York: New York University Press, 1961.

Dowling, Robert M. "On Eugene O'Neill's 'Philosophical Anarchism.'" *The Eugene O'Neill Review* 29 (Spring 2007): 50–72.

Hapgood, Hutchins. *A Victorian in the Modern World.* New York: Harcourt, Brace, 1939.

Pfister, Joel. *Staging Depth: Eugene O'Neill and the Politics of Psychological Discourse.* Cultural Studies of the United States. Chapel Hill: University of North Carolina Press, 1995.

Reichert, William O. "Toward a New Understanding of Anarchism." *The Western Political Quarterly* 20, no. 4. (December 1967): 856–865.

Sheaffer, Louis. *O'Neill: Son and Playwright.* Boston: Little, Brown, 1968.

Stirner, Max. *The Ego and His Own: The Case of the Individual Against Authority.* 1844. Reprint, translated by Steven T. Byington, with an introduction by J. L. Walker. New York: Benj. R. Tucker, 1907.

plagiarism   Accusations of imitation are not, for most writers, the sincerest form of flattery, and that went double for Eugene O'Neill. He endured, after all, two bouts of plagiarism charges, the most troublesome being the suit pressed by Georges Lewys (Gladys Adelina Lewis), who alleged that her novel *The Temple of Pallas-Athenae* (1924) was the unacknowledged source for STRANGE INTERLUDE (1928). And while such litigation is unwelcome at any time, what O'Neill saw as a nuisance suit was particularly niggling at this juncture when he was shedding one wife for another and moving from one country to another. To date his most lucrative effort (the play sold 100,000 copies and earned O'Neill $275,000), *Strange Interlude* was a likely target for a down-on-her-luck writer who needed a little recognition (O'Neill had already netted three PULITZER PRIZES) or cash or both. It was not surprising, then, that in 1929 Lewys initiated the suit, which, predictably, she lost in 1931. Judge John Munro Woolsey fined her court costs and also charged her $17,500 for pressing a frivolous lawsuit; of this, $10,000 was equally divided between the THEATRE GUILD and the publisher Boni & Liveright, also named in the suit, and the remainder went to O'Neill. These awards made the decision a classic: For the first time, a charge of plagiarism was penalized monetarily, and it brought to an end (according to Lawrence Langner) the frequent claims of plagiarism made against successful play productions. When Lewys declared bankruptcy in 1933, however, the playwright was left with $7,500 in unpaid legal fees to brood over.

The basis of Lewy's suit was the eugenic theme at the heart of her work and in evidence, tangentially, in O'Neill's play. Both works also center on women who find fathers for their children outside of marriage, choosing adultery as a means of perpetuating family name, fortune, or title, rather than bearing children by weak or degenerate husbands. In both works, a blonde, healthy, and athletic mother of a eugenic child is jealous of her prospective daughter-in-law, and in both the husband of the heroine suffers a sudden stroke, which leads to his death on the eve of his putative son's marriage. Furthering Lewys's claim against O'Neill was the fact that she had sent copies of her work in 1924 to O'Neill's publisher, Boni & Liveright, which rejected the manuscript, and to the Theatre Guild, which ultimately produced *Strange Interlude*. But the zeal with which Lewys assailed her "Bill of Particulars," listing not only similarities in plot, character, and purpose but asserting the common vocabulary as well, was her undoing, as Woolsey found that neither ideas nor the dictionary could be plagiarized or appropriated. Weighing in on his side, O'Neill had capable representation, Harry Weinberger (O'Neill, living in FRANCE, chose not to appear); a convincing expert witness, critic GEORGE JEAN NATHAN, who recalled precisely when O'Neill first mentioned his idea for the play, a date that conveniently antedated *The Temple*; and a reputation that eclipsed Lewys's modest literary achievements. She was just 19 when she wrote her litigious work in 1917, but by the time Woolsey gave his opinion, she had published two novels, *The Charmed American* (1919) and *The Merry-Go-Round* (1922), and a volume of poetry, *The Epic of Verdun and Ballads* (a copy of the 1928 anthology was placed in the ossuary at Verdun). In her post-O'Neill days, she added to her canon *The House of Love* (1935) and *Call House Madam* (1942). But after her encounter with the literary giant, Lewys faded from view, her two lawsuits and the resulting publicity (the other against Universal Studios over film rights to *Merry-Go-Round*, netting her $10,750) serving as her fleeting moments in the sun.

Though Lewys's suit found its way to federal court before ultimately failing, Alice E. Parsons's allegations of plagiarism against O'Neill met with far less success. Insisting to O'Neill's publisher, Horace Liveright, that the playwright had been influenced by her trilogy (unpublished and title unknown) when he wrote *The GREAT GOD BROWN* and *The FOUNTAIN*, the would-be writer attempted to extort publication from the firm, a coup that her plays had failed to achieve on their own merit (she had bearded the publisher unsuccessfully in 1919 on this subject). In renewing her efforts, she argued that O'Neill's new plays (1925–26) marked a departure from his earlier work and that they were, in fact, more reminiscent of her own plays in style, thought, and phrasing. When Liveright ignored her, she bided her time until the release of *Strange Interlude*, and then she pounced, dashing off another missive to Liveright in which she noted that publication of her work would be "the simplest step toward compensation" for her injuries and might serve as a response (of sorts) to the playwright's latest effort. This time Liveright responded, unequivocally rejecting her and her trilogy and leaving the manipulative Miss Parsons to her well-deserved anonymity.

Bibliography

Gilmer, Walker. *Horace Liveright: Publisher of the Twenties*. New York: David Lewis, 1970, 177–184.

Langner, Lawrence. *The Magic Curtain: The Story of a Life in Two Fields, Theatre and Invention, by the Founder of the Theatre Guild*. New York: Dutton, 1951, 275–287.

Smith, Madeline C., and Richard Eaton. *Eugene O'Neill in Court: Documents in the Case of Georges Lewys v. Eugene O'Neill, et al*. New York: Peter Lang, 1993.

———. "Lewys v. O'Neill Again—or, Who Was That Lady?" *Eugene O'Neill Review* 13, no. 2 (1989): 45–54.

Madeline C. Smith

Playwrights' Theatre See PROVINCETOWN PLAY-HOUSE.

poetry Eugene O'Neill's sketchy indulgence in the writing of verse, according to Barrett H. Clark, began around the year 1909 (Clark 61). It was a lighthearted, callow, jocund sort of verse, at times quite crude, imitative, and even vulgar, yet appealing to the popular, journalistic readership of a small-town American newspaper, the *New London Telegraph.* For O'Neill at this time, many events—pleasant, unpleasant, and pathbreaking—took place in the wake of his initiation into the art of creative writing: his marriage to and separation from KATHLEEN JENKINS, his first wife; the birth of his first son, EUGENE O'NEILL, JR.; his gold-prospecting voyage to Honduras; and his recuperation at a tuberculosis sanatorium, during which period, as Clark observes, the urge to write first came to him, for it was there that O'Neill's mind "got the chance to establish itself, to digest and evaluate . . ." (O'Neill quoted in Clark 28).

Most of O'Neill's poems published in the *New London Telegraph* under the heading "Laconics" in 1912, were imitations of famous poets such as Baudelaire, Villon, Burns, Longfellow, Kipling, Whitman, and others, and they made no pretense of being highbrow. Indeed they ought to be regarded, as Barrett Clark observes, O'Neill's "artistic wild oats" (65) rather than mature versification. But there was a deeper need as well, as Louis Sheaffer asserts, "more crucial to his survival was his poetry" (201). To a large extent, O'Neill's nascent poetic effusions provided the groundwork for the dissemination of ideas and forms that would develop further in his plays. The stream of poetical images that embody his conflicting ideas of success and failure or the dreams of transcendence beyond known horizons—these parturient facets of his poetry are often traceable in the familiar domain of his drama.

It is worrying to note, however, that in the 70-odd years between the first publication of O'Neill's fledgling poetry in the *New London Telegraph* in 1912 and his collected volume of verse edited by Donald Gallup and published by the Yale University Library in 1979, there has hardly been any scholarly interest in his poetry, leaving aside the occasional article, such as William H. Davenport's "The Published and Unpublished Poems of Eugene O'Neill" in the *Yale University Gazette,* October 1963. Richard Dana Skinner's *Eugene O'Neill: A Poet's Quest* (1935) provides one more tenuous lead.

O'Neill's two major muses were "Woman" and the "SEA," in all their colorful as well as dark variations of mood and spirit. The poems addressed to or concerning women may be seen to reflect the mindset of a range of female characters in his plays. In "Ballad of Old Girls" (1912), he remembers Cora, Edith, Bettie, Maude, Mabel, May—those "chorus ladies / That cared for wine" and who had passed away with the "snows of yesteryear." They would be reborn as the merry bar-girls of The ICEMAN COMETH and the scarlet woman Min in DESIRE UNDER THE ELMS. O'Neill's adolescent lyricism was directed to girlfriends such as Maibelle Scott ("Only You") and particularly his "Bee," or BEATRICE ASHE ("Just a Little Love," "Full Many a Cup of the Forbidden Wine," "Ballade of the Two of Us," "Roundelau to Her Nose," "Troilet of My Flowers"). In his later poems to Bee, O'Neill reaches a poignant maturity of emotion as he foresees separation and a paradise lost—"A Dream of Last Week," "Beyond the Great Divide," "The Woman Who Understands"—the image of a love reborn from the ashes, the idea of an archetypal beloved who "understands" the lapses of her man and, "strong in belief," waits for him like HENRIK IBSEN's Solveig did for Peer Gynt. O'Neill balances an overwhelmingly sensual love ("I shall come to you in the delirium of noon" poem no 47, O'Neill 81) recalling the passions of Eben and Abbie in *Desire under the Elms* with the more bonhomie kind of affection toward women like Mary Clark ("Ballad of the Birthday of the Most Gracious of Ladyes") and Katherine Murray ("Ye Disconsolate Poet to His Kitten"), both of whom nursed him at the GAYLORD FARM SANATORIUM in 1913 and are warmly portrayed in the character of Eileen Carmody in the play *The Straw.*

The sea for O'Neill often constitutes a composite metaphor suggesting myriad facets of nature—the moonlight, the surf, the fog, a seagull's cry, the distant roar, the keening of a Negro chant across the bay, the spirits of drowned sailors singing in the chorus of Samuel Taylor Coleridge's *Rime of the Ancient Mariner,* which O'Neill adapted for the stage in 1922 as The ANCIENT MARINER. In "Nocturne," a sense of tragedy is evoked through a seagull's scream that reverberates till his late masterpiece, LONG DAY'S JOURNEY INTO NIGHT. In

"The Glints of Them," O'Neill is in a Yeatsian mode as he incorporates the ugly and bleak within the "golden" aura of life:

> "The sullen vessel straining at the chain/the
>   pungent smell of oily pitch and tow
> A vista of strange lands seen once again
> A breath of memory from the long ago
> The longing song of fortune's castaways—
> Gold summer days"

The sailor cannot resist the grim summons of the sea in "The Call" for he keeps "pining once more to roam"; he is restless with past memories of "fronds of nipa palms" and the impressionistic image of a black lagoon sleeping like "an ebony eunuch indifferent to the sun." But indifference is sometimes converted to belligerence when the enemies of beauty and peace—materialism and capitalism—have to be destroyed at any cost. The poet becomes a sinister submarine biding his time. He will destroy the sluggish merchant ships because "the sea is beautiful" and "that is why / I lurk menacingly / In green depths."

O'Neill often records the decadence of life in his poetry ("Ballad of the Seamy Side," "To Winter," "Revolutions") that he witnessed on merchant navy ships and in dumps like the HELL HOLE. At such times he would bolster his flagging spirits by invoking ancestral voices—Shakespeare (*King Lear*), Coleridge (*The Ancient Mariner*), Francis Thompson (*The Hound of Heaven*)—who also were compelled to explore the equations of man and god at critical moments. The pressing theme of "The Hound of Heaven" parallels O'Neill's alleged return to CATHOLICISM's fold after 1930, dramatized in the career of John Loving of DAYS WITHOUT END (1934), and his adaptation of *The Ancient Mariner* likewise affirm the confessional mode along similar lines of anxiety even earlier in 1922.

In "The Lay of the Singer's Fall," the poet contends against the devil's wry advocacy of suicide (*The Iceman Cometh*) with his own values of the drama:

> The singer became a man and he fought
> With the might of his pen and hand
> To show for evil that cure long sought
> And spread truth over the land.

But despair is prevalent in a monochromatic, sterile wasteland where buildings "scrape the sky" with an antipathy to color, and resemble "frozen grey phalluses" amid the apelike chatter of unbelief. God "snickers like a Methodist preacher" who cashes in on the evolutionary theory of DARWINISM ("make moonshine out of worms").

The future perhaps belongs to Frankenstein and his dubious progeny who, rather than the poet, project the truths of life in a vainglorious attempt of heroic revelation:

> But who shall say this ?
> Not I—one, perhaps a son of Frankenstein
> One who can sing the fire
> With the lips of furnaces
> One who can be a Phoenix
> Disdaining rebirth
> For the greater meaning of living.
>
> ("'Tis of Thee")

Like T. S. Eliot's J. Alfred Prufrock, who knew he was not Prince Hamlet, O'Neill's poet too confesses the futility of heroic affirmation in a grand Miltonic quest. He would rather sing a "masochistic song" (poem no 61, O'Neill 103) recording the pain endured by a fallen Adam.

O'Neill's apparent parody of mainstream poets ironically incorporates, to an extent, their poetic influence as well, just as his utter disillusionment with his father's brand of 19th-century MELODRAMA sustained aspects of the genre in his drama. We find impressionistic images of a lost paradise ("parrots of the past in forgotten orange trees") or an urban, Edward Hopper–like landscape ("Underdrawers / On the lines / Between fire-escapes / Loose their / Evanescent / Charm"). A Whitmanesque universe endorses an elemental vitality and innocence of being at the dawn of a new era: "O Sea which is myself! How I love to reveal my nakedness to the sun on solitary beaches!" (poem no. 62 O'Neill 105).

Bibliography

Clark, Barrett. *Eugene O'Neill: The Man and His Plays.* New York: Robert McBride & Co., 1929.

O'Neill, Eugene. *Poems, 1912–1942.* New Haven, Conn.: Yale University Library, 1979.

Davenport, William H. "The Published and Unpublished Poems of Eugene O'Neill. *Yale University Gazette* 38, no. 2 (1963): 51–66.

Sheaffer, Louis. *O'Neill: Son and Playwright*. Boston: Little, Brown, 1968.

Skinner, Richard Dana. *Eugene O'Neill: A Poet's Quest*. New York and Toronto: Longmans, 1935.

Rupendra Majumdar

prostitution/prostitutes   If Eugene O'Neill's female characters earn their own living, they are likely to do so on their backs. Practitioners of the oldest profession figure (onstage or off) in at least a dozen of the dramatist's works. Many of O'Neill's ladies of the night are versions of one favorite literary cliché—whores with hearts of gold—but he had little use for such other stage standards as the doomed fallen woman and the repentant prostitute. Given the cultural condemnation of "working girls," especially in the early 20th century, O'Neill paints remarkably varied and often sympathetic portraits of women who choose or are forced to sell themselves.

While O'Neill was no GEORGE BERNARD SHAW, dedicated to exposing how capitalism made prostitution one of the few jobs available to uneducated women, he was aware that female bodies are a commodity exchanged among men. The pathetic Rose Thomas of *The WEB* (1913) is the victim of her pimp as well as the customers who use her—not to mention the self-righteous "good people" who scorn her attempts to break free of her profession. For the sailors in *The MOON OF THE CARIBBEES* (1918), the price for a pint of rum is three shillings while sex with the island women costs four.

O'Neill's most fully realized prostitute is the title character of "ANNA CHRISTIE" (1920). Raped by her cousin when she was a teenager, Anna left the farm where she was raised and escaped to the city only to find that working in a brothel provided her best means of survival. At first glance, the plot of "*Anna Christie*" seems to mimic one of the oldest melodramatic formulas: the fallen woman redeemed by love of a good man, stoker Mat Burke. Rather than being immediately repentant, however, Anna is a feisty individual who indicts men like Mat who

Eileen Ryan and Patricia Brooks as prostitutes in the 1946 production of *The Iceman Cometh* (*Courtesy of the Sheaffer-O'Neill Collection, Charles E. Shain Library of Connecticut College*)

patronize (in all senses) women like her. Critics continue to debate the conclusion of the play and to lament Anna's abject oath of loyalty to Mat, but not even the questionably "happy" ending undermines the complexity and originality of O'Neill's portrayal of a woman driven to prostitution.

The "college tart" Belle in *AH, WILDERNESS!* (1932) succeeds in shocking young Richard Miller rather than seducing him, while Michael Cape gets spiritual—not carnal—solace from the tired "Woman" he picks up in *WELDED* (1922–23). Despite the number of prostitutes in O'Neill's plays, there is markedly little commercial sex. Male characters like Dion Anthony, Michael Cape, Richard Miller, and Jamie Tyrone would rather talk with tarts than sleep with them, and the playwright himself was less interested in the business of prostitution than he was in what the individual women could provide for men. More often than not, this proves to be a ready ear, sympathy, and soft breasts. The compassionate earth mother Cybel, pursued by both Dion Anthony and Billy Brown in *The GREAT GOD BROWN* (1925), is the epitome of the comforting whore: She cannot save these troubled men, but she can help ease them into death.

Even as O'Neill's career drew toward its close, prostitutes continued to play an important role in his dramas. Most obvious is the trio of streetwalkers in the otherwise all-male The ICEMAN COMETH (1939). Wrapping their fantasies in semantics, these three insist on being called "tarts" rather than "whores," and they provide as much comic relief as serious social commentary. Only the four family members and a maid appear in LONG DAY'S JOURNEY INTO NIGHT (1941), but Jamie Tyrone's alcoholic account of his evening in a brothel with Fat Violet is revealing. Although he does eventually have sex with Violet, Jamie went to the whore house to have "a weep on any old womanly bosom" (3:816). As numerous critics have pointed out, the inebriated piano-playing Violet is clearly a surrogate for Jamie's mother, who has descended so deeply into her drug-induced fog that she cannot even recognize her own family.

O'Neill's last completed play, A MOON FOR THE MISBEGOTTEN (1943), is both the culmination of, and in some ways a rejection of, all that precedes it. As Moon progresses, Jim Tyrone reveals to Josie Hogan that he spent 50 dollars every night to share his train berth with "a blonde pig" while bringing his mother's body home for burial (3:931). Wracked by anguish over his mother's abandonment of him and by guilt over his response, Jim begs Josie to stop pretending that she is sexually promiscuous. His last tormented hero demands a *virgin* with a heart of gold.

Bibliography

Hall, Ann C. "'Gawd, you'd think I was a piece of furniture': O'Neill's *Anna Christie*." In *Staging the Rage: The Web of Misogyny in Modern Drama,* edited by Katherine H. Burkman and Judith Roof, 171–182. Madison, N.J.: Fairleigh Dickinson University Press, 1998.

Johnson, Katie N. "'*Anna Christie*': The Repentant Courtesan, Made Respectable." *Eugene O'Neill Review* 26 (2004): 87–104.

Westgate, J. Chris. "Staging the 'Poor, Wicked Lot'": O'Neill's Rebuttal to Fallen Woman Plays." *Eugene O'Neill Review* 28 (2006): 62–79.

Judith Barlow

Provincetown Players   Eugene O'Neill owes much of his discovery and early success to the PROV-INCETOWN PLAYERS, a theater company formed by a colony of artists and writers in Provincetown, Massachusetts, in 1915. In fact, O'Neill's first production, BOUND EAST FOR CARDIFF, was produced by the company in Provincetown in 1916. The Players flourished in both Provincetown and later at the PROVINCETOWN PLAYHOUSE (initially called the Playwrights' Theatre) in New York City's GREENWICH VILLAGE neighborhood. Between 1916 and 1922, the Players produced more than 90 plays by American playwrights, including 15 plays by O'Neill: BOUND EAST FOR CARDIFF (1916), THIRST (1916), BEFORE BREAKFAST (1916), FOG (1917), The SPINER (1917), The LONG VOYAGE HOME (1917), ILE (1917), The ROPE (1918), WHERE THE CROSS IS MADE (1918), MOON OF THE CARIBBEES (1918), The DREAMY KID (1919), EXORCISM (1920), The EMPEROR JONES (1920), DIFF'RENT (1920), and The HAIRY APE (1922). In 1923, the company was reorganized as the EXPERIMENTAL THEATRE, INC. While achieving commercial success on Broadway throughout the 1920s, O'Neill continued to produce his experimental plays Off-Broadway through the Experimental Theatre, Inc., at the Provincetown Playhouse.

On the eastern side of Massachusetts, a strangely shaped peninsula juts out about 90 miles into the Atlantic Ocean. Curving upward like an arm ending in a fist, Cape Cod is a region rich in natural beauty and dotted with historic towns. Provincetown, where the Pilgrims first landed before sailing across Cape Cod Bay to the area that is now Plymouth, is located on the far tip of the Cape. Initially developed as a whaling port in the mid-19th century, Provincetown then became a fishing village for a wave of Portuguese immigrants. By the beginning of the 20th century, the town witnessed the arrival of a new group—the "summer people." Fleeing the summer heat, city dwellers began to arrive not only from nearby Boston but also New York, and because it was located so far out to SEA, artists were attracted to Provincetown's unique unobstructed northern sunlight that allowed for exceptional painting outdoors. As early as the 1890s, a summer painting school conducted classes on the beach, and by 1907, novelists, journalists, and political activists from New York joined the painters forming a small "Bohemia"—a place where artists and writers can live freely, rebelling against conventional social behavior and artistic rules.

The artistic rebels who came to Provincetown were part of a cultural and political awakening that took place in the United States in the years preceding World War I, often called the "Little Renaissance." This generation rejected the Victorian world's strict codes of behavior, stuffy tastes, and reactionary politics and embraced a host of new intellectual movements promising greater personal, creative, and social freedom. In POETRY, free verse dispensed with the rules of meter and rhyme; modern art, popularized by a 1913 exhibit at the New York Armory, freed the artist from making perfect copies of reality; and Freudian psychology and psychoanalysis, promised to liberate the individual from psychological repression. Meanwhile, cultural radicals debated the political philosophies of ANARCHISM (advocating the abolishment of all government authority in favor of voluntary cooperation between individuals and communities) and socialism (an economic and political theory advocating the abolition of private property and communal ownership of the means of production), and they participated in labor strikes to improve the appalling living and working conditions of industrial workers and immigrants. Many in this generation also campaigned for civil rights for AFRICAN AMERICANS and fought for the right of women to the vote in the woman's suffrage movement, culminating in 1920 with the ratification of the Nineteenth Amendment to the U.S. Constitution.

Against this background, young people migrated to the cities to experiment with personal freedom and to become active in the new movements. They found safe havens in the bohemian neighborhoods in America's cities such as New York's Greenwich Village, Chicago's 57th Street District, and Provincetown, all of which became centers of the new beliefs and home to like-minded rebels.

It was to this world that a young Eugene O'Neill came seeking to revolutionize AMERICAN THEATER. O'Neill became a frequent visitor to Greenwich Village, and characters based on the radicals he knew in his days in the Village appear in his plays throughout his career. These include *The Hairy Ape*, which portrays the leftist labor union the

IWW (INDUSTRIAL WORKERS OF THE WORLD); *The Iceman Cometh*, which has several anarchist characters; and A *Long Day's Journey into Night*, in which the youngest son, Edmund Tyrone, is castigated by his father for associating with anarchists.

In summer 1915, an eclectic mix of American writers and artists from Greenwich Village were vacationing in Provincetown. These included Mary Heaton Vorse, a journalist who spearheaded the New York exodus to Provincetown. SUSAN GLASPELL, a short-story writer who would become, next to O'Neill, the second most prolific playwright of the Provincetown Players; Glaspell's husband, a writer and devotee of Greek philosophy, GEORGE CRAM "JIG" COOK, who emerged as the group's leader; Neith Boyce, a renowned journalist; and Boyce's husband Hutchins Hapgood, an anarchist and critic. Wilbur Daniel Steele, a popular short-story writer was there, as were the modernist artists Charles Demuth (famous for the painting *The Number Five in Gold*); B. J. O. Nordfelt; and ROBERT EDMOND JONES, who would later design settings for a number of O'Neill productions. Joining this company was Max Eastman, editor of *The Masses*, the famous magazine that proclaimed art and revolution, and his wife Ida Rauh, who would become the most dedicated actress of the group, among others.

According to Hutchins Hapgood, the cultural rebels in Provincetown were frustrated that all of their social efforts had been unable to stop the violence of World War I, and the group sought a "positive response to these negative forces" finding a "creative urge" (Hapgood 394). They decided to present two plays in one of the rented cottages: *Constancy* by Neith Boyce, which is a look at the consequences of a couple's open relationship; and *Suppressed Desires* by Susan Glaspell and George Cram Cook, a satire of a bohemian couple's trendy adoption of Freudian psychoanalysis. The performances were so successful that the group cleaned out a fish house on an old rickety wharf in town that Mary Vorse bought in July 1915, and installed a stage. Two large doors could be rolled away to use Cape Cod Bay as a natural backdrop. This became the WHARF THEATRE. On the wharf, the group performed two more plays: Cook's *Change Your Style*, a satire of the conflict between traditional painting and modern art; and Wilbur Daniel Steele's *Contemporaries*, about the arrest of an activist who had led a group of freezing homeless men into a church for shelter.

The group returned the following year, and several new members appeared, including JOHN REED, a poet, journalist, and labor activist. Reed was later a founding member of the American Communist Party and became the only American buried next to the Kremlin in Moscow. Reed's girlfriend and later his wife, the journalist LOUISE BRYANT, also came along, and both wrote plays. Reed and Bryant's time with the Players as well as Bryant's

relationship with Eugene O'Neill were popularized in the feature film *Reds*. Bryant worked with two other new members, the modern artists William and Marguerite Zorach, to create one of the first American plays to use modern art for the sets, acting, scenery of the play and called *The Game*.

One day the group was visited by TERRY CARLIN, who was staying in a shack in Truro, one town down the Cape from Provincetown. When asked if he would submit a script, Carlin made the legendary reply, "I don't write. . . . But Mr. O'Neill has got a whole trunk full of plays" (quoted in Glaspell 204). The next evening, Carlin brought his shack mate, the shy 28-year-old Eugene O'Neill, over to the cot-

Setting up for *Bound East for Cardiff* at the Wharf Theatre in Provincetown, Massachusetts. O'Neill is on the step ladder, Hippolyte Havel is seated at center, and George Cram "Jig" Cook is at far right. *(Courtesy of the Museum of the City of New York)*

tage rented by Glaspell and Cook. O'Neill remained outside the room as the group read *Bound East for Cardiff.* Afterward, according to Susan Glaspell, "we knew what we were for." *Bound East for Cardiff,* the story of a dying sailor and his shipmate, was staged at the Wharf Theatre later that summer and was, according to Glaspell, accompanied by the sea O'Neill had written "so feelingly about." The water literally "rolled under the flooring and shook the piles" of the old wharf (204).

The summer of 1916 proved to be a remarkably creative time for the group. After the premiere of *Bound East for Cardiff,* Cook told Glaspell that he had announced their next production would include a new play of hers. When Glaspell gasped, "But I have no play!" Cook replied "Nonsense . . . you've got a stage, haven't you?" (Glaspell 205). Staring at the empty stage, Glaspell recalled envisioning characters entering and exiting. Before the next bill, she wrote *Trifles,* a landmark feminist play about a lonely farmwife accused of murdering her husband. By the end of the summer, the participants in the wharf productions formed an official company, voting to call themselves The Provincetown Players, agreeing on a constitution, and making plans to move their operations to New York. In November, the Players opened their doors in a brownstone at 139 Macdougal Street, just south of Washington Square Park in the center of Greenwich Village. In 1918, they moved down the street to number 133, a converted stable. The Provincetown Playhouse is still at 133 Macdougal Street today, now owned by New York University.

Broadway theater in the early 20th century was dominated by plays designed to promote individual stars following formulas of plot and characterization. The plays the Provincetown Players and Eugene O'Neill created freed the playwright and the audience to explore many different issues in whatever style seemed appropriate. Their plays explored personal experience, often relating this experience to the larger social and political questions facing America and the world. They also delved deeply into human psychological and spiritual nature. The Provincetown Players produced plays that would never have been produced in commercial Broadway theaters. To promote their first New York season, the group distributed a flyer that stated their artistic ideals:

> The present organization is the outcome of a group of people interested in the theater, who gathered spontaneously during two summers at Provincetown, Mass. for the purpose of writing, producing and acting their own plays. . . . The impelling desire of the group was to establish a stage where playwrights of sincere, poetic, literary and dramatic purpose could see their plays in action and superintend their production without submitting to the commercial manager's interpretation of public taste. (quoted in Deutsch 17)

There were other companies in America dedicated to artistic theater productions at this time, but most focused on European playwrights. The Provincetown Players made a major contribution to forming a modern American drama by dedicating themselves to producing exclusively new work by American dramatists. Further, participation in their productions was open to a more diverse group of individuals than in any theater of the era. Women comprised about half of the company's founding members and were thus allowed unprecedented involvement in all aspects of productions—as playwrights, actors, and directors. Ida Rauh, the Players' hardest-working actress, insisted on finding actors from Harlem when directing O'Neill's *The Dreamy Kid* (1919), a choice of casting that was instrumental in ending the Broadway convention of having white actors perform African-American characters in black face make up (Sarlos 110). This led later to the casting of CHARLES S. GILPIN in O'Neill's *The Emperor Jones* (1920). Gilpin became the first African-American actor in the 20th century to perform in a major New York (later Broadway) role.

In 1922, George Cram Cook and Susan Glaspell sailed for Greece, where Cook's devotion to GREEK TRAGEDY led him. After a struggle for control of the theater, the Provincetown Playhouse in MacDougal Street passed to a new organization, the Experimental Theatre, Inc., which was run by O'Neill, the theater critic KENNETH MACGOWAN, and the scenic designer Robert Edmond Jones. During the 1920s, O'Neill continued to have his more controversial and experimental plays produced at the Provincetown Playhouse, including *All God's Chillun Got Wings*, *THE GREAT GOD BROWN*, and *LAZARUS LAUGHED*.

Opinions differ as to how or when O'Neill may have succeeded in the theater if he had not found Provincetown and the Provincetown Players. Despite one good review of his self-published 1914 book *"THIRST" AND OTHER ONE-ACT PLAYS*, his plays were ignored by all theater producers. With the production of *Bound East for Cardiff*, O'Neill had discovered a company that shared his vision for remaking American theater in the name of art rather than commerce. The Provincetown Players produced every play O'Neill contributed, and their collaboration afforded him the freedom, without the pressure of box-office sales, to create new and challenging forms of theater.

Provincetown itself provided an artistic community for O'Neill, and the sand dunes and shoreline around the town gave him the solitude he required for his writing. He often returned to Provincetown after joining the Players to write and to take long walks and solitary swims. When O'Neill was married to his second wife, AGNES BOULTON, his father JAMES O'NEILL bought the couple a renovated life saving station on the Atlantic side of the Cape called PEAKED HILL BAR. O'Neill left when Provincetown began to become crowded in the summer, but today the spirit of rebellion continues in Provincetown's importance as a destination for writers and artists and a thriving gay and lesbian community.

Bibliography

Black, Cheryl. *The Women of Provincetown, 1915–1922.* Tuscaloosa: University of Alabama Press, 2002.

Deutsch, Helen, and Stella Hanau. *The Provincetown: A Story of the Theatre.* New York: Farrar & Rinehart, 1931.

Egan, Leona Rust. *Provincetown as a Stage: Provincetown, the Provincetown Players, and the Discovery of Eugene O'Neill.* Orleans, Mass.: Parnassus Imprints, 1994.

Glaspell, Susan. *The Road to the Temple: A Biography of George Cram Cook.* Edited and with new introduction and bibliography by Linda Ben-Zvi. Jefferson, N.C.: McFarland, 2005.

Hapgood, Hutchins. *A Victorian in the Modern World.* New York: Harcourt Brace, 1939.

Heller, Adele, and Lois Rudnick. *1915, The Cultural Moment: The New Politics, the New Woman, the New Psychology, the New Art, and the New Theatre in America.* New Brunswick, N.J.: Rutgers University Press, 1991.

Kenton, Edna. *The Provincetown Players and the Playwrights' Theatre, 1915–1922.* Edited by Travis Bogard and Jackson R. Bryer. Jefferson, N.C.: McFarland, 2004.

Murphy, Brenda. *The Provincetown Players and the Culture of Modernity.* New York: Cambridge University Press, 2005.

Sárlos, Robert Karoly. *Theatre in Ferment: Jig Cook and the Provincetown Players.* Amherst: University of Massachusetts Press, 1982.

Vorse, Mary Heaton. *A Footnote to Folly: Reminiscences of Mary Heaton Vorse.* New York: Arno Press, 1980.

Drew Eisenhauer

Provincetown Playhouse, The (Playwrights' Theatre)   Located at 133 MacDougal Street in the Greenwich Village neighborhood of New York City, this was the permanent home of the amateur theater company the PROVINCETOWN PLAYERS. The Players, led by GEORGE CRAM COOK, introduced the world to the plays of Eugene O'Neill, SUSAN GLASPELL, Djuna Barnes, and Edna St. Vincent Millay and was instrumental in ushering modern theater into America. The Provincetown Players formally organized in Provincetown, Massachussetts, in September 1916, and member Floyd Dell was sent to the Village to locate a suitable space the group could rent to begin their first season in New York City. Dell headed first to the block where the heart of activity in the Village seemed to beat the loudest: MacDougal Street between Third and Fourth Streets, just one block south of Washington Square. At 137 MacDougal was the Liberal Club, with the popular restaurant Polly's below it; at 135 was the Washington Square Bookshop; and around the corner on Fourth Street were some of the Villagers' favorite tearooms and bars. Dell's first choice was actually 133 MacDougal, which housed bottling works whose lease was

Provincetown Playhouse at 133 MacDougal Street, New York City *(Copyright Berenice Abbot/Commerce Graphics)*

expiring in mid-October, but he let it go because it meant either a delay in starting their season or an additional payment to cover the broken lease. Once Cook arrived in the city, he visited the same block and secured from owner Mrs. Jenny Belardi the first floor of 139 MacDougal Street, the parlor of an 1840 brownstone row house, for $50 a month. The Players refurbished the first floor of 139 into a theater, though not without many run-ins with the City Tenement Commission and court appearances over their refurbishments. Encouraged by O'Neill's suggestion, the theater was called The Playwright's Theatre to underscore its mission of encouraging the creation of new American plays. It was here the Players first received national notice for the ama-

teur productions of their unique plays, performed on a small 14-by-10-and-a-half-foot-deep stage, with their audiences seated in uncomfortable slat wood benches that sat up to 150 patrons. Cook and the Players knew almost immediately that they would soon need a larger space if they were to continue.

Two years later, the 1918–19 season began with the Players moving to a new site, albeit three doors south, that allowed them to create a relatively larger space to work. Though also leasing this new building from Mrs. Belardi, the new location at 133 MacDougal Street would feel more like a home to the group, allowing for offices, their first box office, more dressing rooms, a restaurant on the second floor, and an expanded work space. Another important Village theater group, the WASHINGTON SQUARE PLAYERS, had once seriously considered turning the same space into a theater but gave up on it when potential complications arose with building codes and refurbishment needs. Ironically, the Provincetown group was forced to move when on September 19, 1918, the city's Tenement House and Building Department ruled that they could not continue running a theater at 139; that same day, however, the inspectors approved their proposal for the conversion of 133. Once the group received a sizeable donation from Dr. Albert C. Barnes, the work to renovate 133 began. Cook, who decided to donate one month's rent to the theater fund and moved his bedroom onto the new stage, commandeered the transformation of 133 into a theater.

The Bromley and Company Manhattan Land Book of 1911 lists the dimensions of the four-story pre-Victorian building at 133 as 24 feet, six inches wide by 89 feet nine inches deep, with the main building occupying about 48-feet toward the front, with a one-story extension covering the rest (Bromley). The building's double doors and sloped ramp had once welcomed horses as they were brought in from Washington Square Park. Journalist and political activist JOHN REED, a cofounder of the Players, forbade the group to remove a hitching ring in the right wall on the ground floor, suggesting the Players should never forget the "significance of the humble origins of their Playhouse," so the ring was polished, and painted around it was "Here Pegasus Was Hitched" (Ozieblo 131). Village historian Allan Churchill wrote that the former stable never lost the "faint, pungent aroma of horses and manure," which journalist Frank Hanley later confirmed, having attended plays there as a young reporter for *The Quill* (Churchill 210, Hanley). The Players turned a section of the ramp off the street into a small box office, and the rest was used as a lobby, where during future intermissions "the audience balanced precariously on the slope" (Deutsch 41). The large front door was purported to swing open on its own with loud squeaks and "yowls," particularly during the colder and windier times of the year. Rather than find a way to fix this, the Players hired two boys, Albert and Henry (ages

eight and 10), at 25 cents a night, to stand against the door and keep it closed during performances (Deutsch 46).

The basement was converted into a set-construction shop and storeroom, and a corner below the stage was sectioned off to create dressing rooms for the actors, meaning that the actors would have to walk up a flight of stairs to the stage. The ground (level-with-the-street) floor became the stage and auditorium. Benches were installed on a sloped floor they built in the hope that every seat would have an unencumbered view of the stage. The Players circular of fall 1918 proclaimed that the theater was equipped with "new seats with cushions" and "solid backs that have six inches more space from back to back," as compared to the seating at 139 (Sarlos, *Provincetown* 204). A Federal Theatre Technical Survey (the theater was later used by the Federal Theatre Project) from May 1937 diagrams the stage at 22 feet with a "small passage way" at the back and a "three feet nine-and-a-half inches apron in front of the curtain line" (Sarlos, *Jig* 204). The walls of the theater were painted "a rich tawny orange, the ceilings were deep indigo blue and the plain proscenium rectangle was painted deep smoke gray" (Kenton 81, Boulton 240). Houselights were installed, veiled and controlled by a dimmer, and an "extraordinarily large" stage lighting control board was installed (Kenton 81). The stage had a curtain that opened smoothly, a luxury after the ragtag self-built curtains they had endured at 139. The mechanics of performing in the still-cramped stage space of the new Provincetown Playhouse was the inspiration for technical experimentation in their stagecraft. Because there was no fly loft, the scenery was kept downstairs in the basement, and in the stage floor there was a slot. When a scene needed to be changed, the old set was "shoved . . . down the slot" and the new scenery sent up through the same slot, all of this done manually by stagehands without the help of pulleys or any other kind of mechanical device. Because the slots were cut in the stage floor where footlights would typically be located, ceiling lights were hung arid proscenium lights were also used. A row of 12 250-watt "baby spots" were also used at "the teaser and tormentor positions." Only for special effects did they ever use footlights (Vilhauer 277, 283). The Players were one of the first to place their lights above the actors and were a major player in initiating a shift in stagecraft that affected all theater productions from this time forward.

Christine Ell, who had started a restaurant a year before on the second floor of 139, moved everything from 139 to the second floor of 133 and reopened in the new location. Malcolm Cowley remembered the room as "huge" and the "same size as the Playhouse." He described the walls painted a reddish-brown, all the furniture painted black, with a dining room to the right of the rear end of the room. Hutchins Hapgood wrote that Christine's was where "Greenwich Village had its best expression at that time" and tells that many wild scenes took place at Christine's after the shows, filled with members of the Players and other Villagers (Hapgood 422).

Cook began talking of installing a plaster dome cyclorama, like those featured in European art theater, almost as soon as they moved into 139, but this did not take place for two more years. In 1920, after reading O'Neill's play The EMPEROR JONES, Cook declared the necessity of finally completing the dome in the theater he had sworn from the beginning they would erect. Though the executive committee of the Players told Cook the company could not afford it, Cook defied their decision and started building the structure on his own. Cook's interest in the dome can be traced back to conversations with New Stagecraft designer ROBERT EDMOND JONES in 1914 and seeing models of a *Kuppelhorizont*, as it was known in Germany, in stagecraft exhibitions of the time. Cook consulted with a local contractor and then he and company member and architect Donald Corley drew up plans to alter the Provincetown Players' building, with the ultimate sacrifice being eight feet of stage floor. A newspaper article by company member JAMES LIGHT describes the dome, for which the Players had mixed concrete, plaster, and "removed old lath and beams":

> It is of rigid iron and concrete construction; it eradicates all the failings of the cloth cyclorama. It will not wrinkle, it will not move when touched. It radiates light where a cloth cyclo-

rama absorbs light. The cloth cyclorama has a curve in only one direction; the dome has a constant curve in every direction. It requires, as we have installed it, no masking or very little, and because of the peculiarities of our stage it is never in the way. The constant rate of change in direction of the surface of the dome is what gives the sense of infinity. The light rays strike along this curve and are reflected in millions of directions. Every light ray, as it strikes the small particles of sand finish, casts its shadow as a complementary color. The mingling of a colored light with the complementary shadow produces, with the constant curve of surface, the effect of distance, and makes the dome appear what in reality it is—a source of light. It changes all our ideas of setting plays. (Deutsch 61–62)

First, Cook and Corley installed a series of uprights that were then covered with iron netting. They carefully measured the elliptical and circular shape they wanted to create, and then plaster was applied, though its ability to set was slowed with crushed ice so they could apply clear-washed sand; the desired reflection would be better if the surface was not actually smooth. The last phase was to apply crushed ice again to remove any sand that did not lie smoothly on the reflecting surface. Even with the labor being done by group members, the dome cost the Players the entire balance of their bank account to create, which some in the group thought insanity. An advanced lighting board was also said to be installed, though there is no discussion of where it came from or how it was paid for. The dome became a major advancement in the scenic effects possible at the theater and the Players had the distinction of having the first ever in America.

A few years later Cook began exploring the possibility of creating a "Dome Theatre," which would boast a unique design that had the ability to change its stage areas in multiple ways, including the proscenium arch and curtain, and wouldn't require "a single inch of scenery," having all domes and no walls (Kenton 141–142). On the possibility of making this a reality, the Players consulted their lawyers, who recommended incorporating. The resulting incorporation was the first time there was a formal or legal naming of a theater called the "Provinc-etown Playhouse," even though the name had been written outside the theater from early on upon their move to 133 Macdougal Street and the name "The Playwright's Theatre" was rarely used once the group left 139. When Cook and Glaspell decided to leave the Players after the fourth bill of the 1921–22 season, the executive committee of the Players met and decided to also incorporate the name "Prov-incetown Players" as a legal entity before Cook and Glaspell left to travel to Greece. After the season that year ended, the company announced a year's hiatus, but the company never returned. Prevented from calling themselves the Provincetown Players by a number of the directors of the corporation, a new group headed by O'Neill, KENNETH MACGOWAN, and Robert Edmond Jones incorporated themselves as the EXPERIMENTAL THEATRE, INC., but they con-tinued to call the theater at 133 MacDougal the Provincetown Playhouse. A remnant group of the Players, headed by James Light and the Players' longtime business manager, Mary Eleanor Fitzger-ald, returned to use the Playhouse from 1924 until 1929, but the group ended after financial difficulties as a result of the stock market crash.

Belardi owned the property until 1940 when the Drydock Savings Bank, who held the first mortgage, and Mr. Hyman Boris, who held the second mort-gage, foreclosed. Different organizations had rented the theater from Belardi until that time, including the Federal Theater Project, which primarily used it to train theater practitioners from the five bor-oughs of New York City. The buildings that housed 133–139 MacDougal were auctioned to Province-town Playhouse Apartments, Inc., in 1941, but an amateur group called the Light Opera Theatre that performed Gilbert and Sullivan comic operas con-trolled the Playhouse for many years, renting it out to theater companies for single productions and to companies for short seasons. New York Uni-versity's law school eventually bought the building and theater producer Arthur Cantor administrated the use of the theater until 1992, when the the-ater was closed by the city because it wasn't up to building code. Productions during this time included the American premiere of Edward Albee's first New York production, *The Zoo Story* (1960),

plays by Lanford Wilson, David Mamet, and John Guare and the long-running production of Charles Busch's *Vampire Lesbians of Sodom* (1985–1990). The Playhouse remained closed until May 1998 after New York University refurbished the theater and reopened it for use by the university's Edu-cational Theatre program and for special events. During this renovation, the original walls, floor-ing, and stage were replaced and, unfortunately, the dome cyclorama was destroyed after its delicate state caused it to collapse as crews prepared for the stage's demolition. In 2008, New York University announced its plans to tear down the structures at 133–139 MacDougal in order to replace the build-ing's foundation and build offices for its law school. While their plans always included renovating the theater, in response to protests by Village preserva-tionists, NYU has stated that the walls and facade will be preserved in the process.

Bibliography

Boulton, Agnes. *Part of a Long Story; Eugene O'Neill as a Young Man in Love.* London: P. Davies, 1958.

Bromley Map 1911, Maps Division, New York Public Research Library.

Churchill, Allan. *The Improper Bohemians: A Re-cre-ation of Greenwich Village in Its Heyday.* New York: Dutton, 1959.

Deutsch, Helen, and Stella Hanau. *The Provincetown: A Story of the Theatre.* New York: Farrar and Rine-hart, 1931.

Hanley, Frank. "Two Off-Broadway Houses." *The Quill* (April 8, 1968), Provincetown Players Scrapbook, Billy Rose Theatre Collection, New York Public Library.

Hapgood, Hutchins. *A Victorian in the Modern World.* New York: Harcourt, Brace and Co., 1939.

Kenton, Edna. In *The Provincetown Players and the Playwright's Theatre, 1915–1922.* Edited by Tra-vis Bogard and Jackson R. Bryer, Jefferson, N.C.: McFarland, 2004.

Ozieblo, Barbara. *Susan Glaspell, a Critical Biography.* Chapel Hill: University of North Carolina Press, 2000.

Sarlos, Robert Karoly. *Jig Cook and the Provincetown Players, Theatre in Ferment.* Amherst: University of Massachusetts Press, 1982.

———. "The Provincetown Players: Experiments in Style." Ph.D. diss., Yale University Ann Arbor: UMI, 1966.

Vilhauer, William Warren. "A History and Evaluation of the Provincetown Players." Ph.D. diss., State University of Iowa, Ann Arbor: UMI, 1965.

Jeff Kennedy

publishers Eugene O'Neill's earliest publication (1914) was the privately printed *"THIRST" AND OTHER ONE-ACT PLAYS* (paid for by JAMES O'NEILL). Except for giving O'Neill bragging rights in his playwriting class at Harvard (he was the only published playwright), it created little stir. Subsequently (1916), Frank Shay, who had bought out the Washington Square Bookshop from the Boni brothers, issued a series of pamphlets of PROVINCE-TOWN PLAYERS productions, including *BOUND EAST FOR CARDIFF* and *BEFORE BREAKFAST*, and GEORGE JEAN NATHAN and H. L. Mencken published *The LONG VOYAGE HOME, ILE,* and *The MOON OF THE CARIBBEES* in two issues of their magazine *The Smart Set* (1917 and 1918).

However, O'Neill still had no publisher to look after his interests—until, that is, Horace Liveright of the firm of Boni and Liveright (B&L) took a chance on the fledgling playwright and produced a volume of O'Neill's one-act plays *The Moon of the Caribbees and Six Other Plays of the Sea* in April 1919 (*Moon of the Caribbees, Voyage Home, Bound East, IN THE ZONE, ROPE, Ile,* and *WHERE THE CROSS IS MADE*) and even gave O'Neill a $125 advance. This was a lucky investment since O'Neill's winning of a PULITZER PRIZE for *BEYOND THE HORIZON* (his first Broadway play) in 1920 brought an almost immediate profit.

Energetic, unconventional, flamboyant, Liveright was willing to gamble on such unknown or up-and-coming writers as JOHN REED, Max Eastman, Upton Sinclair, Djuna Barnes, Lewis Mumford, Ernest Hemingway, and William Faulkner; he and Albert Boni had already succeeded immensely in their first gamble—the start of the Modern Library series. During the next decade, Liveright came to represent not only O'Neill but also Theodore Dreiser, Sinclair Lewis, Sherwood Anderson, Robinson Jeffers, Hart Crane, Ernest Boyd, and others. And as a partygoer, party thrower, and heavy drinker—with an enthusiasm for theater (even though it helped to bring about his ruin)—he must have appealed to O'Neill. Through him and the B&L office parties, O'Neill met some of the future literary greats of America and such B&L employees and partners as Lillian Hellman, SAXE COMMINS, Manuel Komroff, and Bennett Cerf, some of whom were to stand him in good stead in the future. In addition to publishing his authors, Liveright (Albert Boni had separated from Liveright in 1918) fought for them in the courts in Boston and New York against various attempts at CENSORSHIP and charges of PLAGIARISM, of indecency and immorality in their books.

As his popularity grew, O'Neill profited—unusual for a playwright—with publications of his stage successes as they occurred: limited editions of the more popular plays, a one-volume edition of the complete plays, a complete set uniformly bound

Saxe Commins and Bennet Cerf *(Courtesy of the Sheaffer-O'Neill Collection, Charles E. Shain Library of Connecticut College)*

of the plays as they were produced, and generous allowance made for his altering and revising of manuscripts and proofs in his concern for the perfect published text. O'Neill's royalties started at 10 percent, advanced to 15 percent, and after the success of STRANGE INTERLUDE, moved to 17.5 percent. In sum, the relationship between O'Neill and his publisher was (despite occasional bumps) unusually good and rewarding to both. However, by 1930 Liveright's expenditures outweighed his intake. He had earlier (1925) been forced to sell the flagship of his company, the Modern Library, to Bennett Cerf; shortly afterward, he was out of the company. In 1933, the company declared bankruptcy.

Almost immediately there was what Bennett Cerf called a "raid" by many hungry publishers on the company's assets—its important authors. Cerf himself circumvented O'Neill's agent, Richard Madden, contacted O'Neill directly, and visited him at Casa Genotta, his home on SEA ISLAND, GEORGIA. Random House (founded 1927), Cerf's company, became O'Neill's publishers and remained so for the rest of his life. With the change, all of the stock that Liveright had amassed—manuscripts, papers, plates—went to Random House. Now, by way of Random House, Cerf could offer O'Neill a trade edition, deluxe editions, Modern Library reprints, and more, not counting the original first publications of AH, WILDERNESS! (1933), DAYS WITHOUT END (1934), The ICEMAN COMETH (1946), and A MOON FOR THE MISBEGOTTEN (1952). Saxe Commins, who had been working for Liveright and acting as O'Neill's special liaison for the last three years, also went to Random House (at O'Neill's request and as part of the deal), where he played the same role, as far as O'Neill was concerned. O'Neill's royalties advanced to 20 percent.

In 1950, New Fathoms Press brought out an unauthorized edition of some O'Neill plays no longer in copyright, Lost Plays, containing ABORTION, The MOVIE MAN, The SNIPER, A WIFE FOR A LIFE, and SERVITUDE. O'Neill considered taking legal action but dropped the matter. In 1964 Random House published Ten "Lost" Plays of Eugene O'Neill, which included the Lost Plays of 1950 and the originally privately printed "Thirst" and Other One-Act Plays of 1914.

Two years after O'Neill's death, feeling himself committed to O'Neill's desire that LONG DAY'S JOURNEY INTO NIGHT not be published until 25 years after his death and never produced, Bennett Cerf refused CARLOTTA MONTEREY O'NEILL's request that it be published anyway. Carlotta, with the law on her side as O'Neill's heir, gave publication rights to the less-scrupulous Yale University Library, which, through the Yale University Press, brought out Long Day's Journey into Night (1956) and later A TOUCH OF THE POET (1957), HUGHIE (1959), and MORE STATELY MANSIONS (1964).

Bibliography

Cerf, Bennett. *At Random: The Reminiscences of Bennett Cerf.* Edited by Phyllis Cerf Wagner and Albert Erskine. New York: Random House, 1977, 29–67; 81–89.

Dardis, Tom. *Firebrand: The Life of Horace Liveright.* New York: Random House, 1995.

Egleston, Charles, ed. *The House of Boni & Liveright, 1917–1933: A Documentary Volume.* Detroit: Gale, 2004, 163–187.

Gallup, Donald C. *Pigeons on the Granite: Memories of a Yale Librarian.* New Haven, Conn.: Yale University Press, 1988, 282–310.

Gilmer, Walker. *Horace Liveright: Publisher of the Twenties.* New York: David Lewis, 1970.

Hellman, Lillian. *An Unfinished Woman.* In *Three.* Boston: Little, Brown, 1979, 40–61.

Satterfield, Jay. *The World's Best Books: Taste, Culture and the Modern Library.* Boston and Amherst: University of Massachusetts Press, 2002.

Richard Eaton

Pulitzer Prize The Pulitzer Prize was established in 1903 by millionaire journalist Joseph Pulitzer, who specified in his will that "The trustees of Columbia [University] were to be ultimately responsible for bestowing the prizes, but they were to be guided by the recommendations of an Advisory Board" composed of "the President of Columbia and a dozen assorted editors and publishers, drawn from newspapers across the nation" (Toohey vii). By the terms of the Pulitzer plan of award for drama, which began in 1917, the drama prize was

Eugene O'Neill runs in triumph on the beach at Provincetown, Massachusetts, after learning that he has been awarded the Pulitzer Prize. *(Courtesy of the Sheaffer-O'Neill Collection, Charles E. Shain Library of Connecticut College)*

to be awarded annually "for the original American play, performed in New York, which shall best represent the educational value and power of the stage in raising the standard of good morals, good taste, and good manners" (quoted in Hohenberg 19). The winning playwright would receive $1,000 in prize money. In the event that no suitable play could be found for that year, the prize was not to be awarded. In its first year, the jury decided that no play merited the prize.

Eugene O'Neill received Pulitzer Prizes for four of his plays: BEYOND THE HORIZON (1920), "ANNA CHRISTIE" (1922), STRANGE INTERLUDE (1928), and (posthumously) LONG DAY'S JOURNEY INTO NIGHT (1957). His prize for *Beyond the Horizon* was the second Pulitzer awarded; the first went to Jesse Lynch Williams's *Why Marry?* (1918). However, O'Neill's Pulitzer awards were steeped in controversy. Hamlin Garland, an author who served on the jury

between 1918 and 1922, repeatedly discouraged the other members from honoring O'Neill. Appalled by O'Neill's modernism, and especially his frank depiction of sex, Garland argued that it would be inappropriate to "vote a prize to the morbid kind of play that O'Neill writes" (Garland 299). For this reason, he voted against *Beyond the Horizon* and "*Anna Christie,*" as well as DESIRE UNDER THE ELMS when it was suggested for the honor.

Despite Garland's reservations, the critical reception of *Beyond the Horizon,* O'Neill's first prize-winning play, was overwhelmingly positive. The production, starring Richard Bennett as Robert Mayo, opened at the Morosco Theatre on February 3, 1920, and ran for 111 performances. The success of *Beyond the Horizon* was particularly impressive because it was produced "[w]ith makeshift settings that were cheap and tawdry, a patchwork cast, and [a] daunting matinee schedule" (Toohey 13). Even though the play was a popular and critical success, it was not an easy choice for the 1920 Pulitzer Prize. Garland, who was chair of the drama jury, campaigned for his friend Percy MacKaye's *Washington,* which he called "the only [play of the season] that has dignity and beauty of appeal" (quoted in Hohenberg 46). Later, when his fellow jurors lobbied for O'Neill's play, he wrote to the president of Columbia University to see whether the jury could award the prize to *Abraham Lincoln,* by the British playwright John Drinkwater. In the end, he grudgingly accepted the jury's recommendation but complained to the president of Columbia University, "I can not regard O'Neill's play as 'Noble' or 'Uplifting' which are I believe the expressed terms of the bequest. Nevertheless as it is the outstanding play of the season thus far, I will join in the award" (Garland 278). However, when *Beyond the Horizon* was announced as the winner, the following remark was included: "The Advisory Board recorded their high appreciation of *Abraham Lincoln,* by John Drinkwater, and regretted that by reason of its foreign authorship, this play was not eligible for consideration with the award" (quoted in Hohenberg 48).

In 1922, O'Neill won his second Pulitzer Prize for "*Anna Christie.*" The play opened at the Vanderbilt Theater on November 2, 1921, and ran for

177 performances. O'Neill's initial version of this play, entitled CHRIS CHRISTOPHERSEN, portrayed Anna as a beautiful and innocent young woman, but that play was a decided failure. After substantial revisions, O'Neill chose to characterize Anna as a young, haggard PROSTITUTE and retitled the play. Theater critics disagreed about whether *"Anna Christie"* represented Eugene O'Neill's full artistic capabilities, but most reviewers joined in praising Pauline Lord's stellar performance as the title character. Garland, who at first refused even to see the play, complained that "to give him another [prize] would be to emphasize a kind of thing which is essentially unwholesome . . . essentially unAmerican" (Garland 299).

O'Neill received his third Pulitzer in 1928 for *Strange Interlude.* It opened on January 30, 1928, at the John Golden Theatre and ran for 426 performances—more than *Beyond the Horizon* and *"Anna Christie"* combined. In addition to its innovative staging of character's thoughts, the play is notable for being the first play to require a dinner break during the performance. It was the longest play "ever presented professionally in America, comparable in length only to O'Neill's other Giant, MOURNING BECOMES ELECTRA" (Toohey 60). Even though the critical reception of *Strange Interlude* varied dramatically, ranging from unqualified praise to harsh censure, the Pulitzer Prize jury immediately and unanimously selected *Strange Interlude* for the 1928 honor.

The Pulitzer committee awarded O'Neill his fourth prize for *Long Day's Journey into Night* in 1957, four years after his death. Opening at the Helen Hayes Theatre on November 7, 1956, it ran for 390 performances. Critics immediately praised the play as an admirably intimate piece of theater, with BROOKS ATKINSON observing that it "restores the drama to literature and the theatre to art" (quoted in Toohey 290). Richard Watts, Jr., of the *New York Evening Post* called it "a magnificent and shattering play . . . with unsparing candor over some of the most pitiful and terrible personal concerns that a playwright ever tore out of his youthful memories" (quoted in Toohey 288). Jury member Professor Campbell explained, "We believe that the Pulitzer award has seldom gone to so great a play" (quoted in Hohenberg 262).

Two of Eugene O'Neill's other plays were considered for, but did not win, the Pulitzer Prize. In the controversy over the 1925 Pulitzer Prize, which caused Hamlin Garland to withdraw from the jury, *Desire under the Elms* was briefly considered but not selected because it was deemed "inferior to [O'Neill's] two previous prize-winning plays" (quoted in Hohenberg 99). The award instead went to Sidney Howard's *They Knew What They Wanted.* And in 1932, *Mourning Becomes Electra,* which was considered a "conventional Pulitzer Prize candidate" (Hohenberg 106), lost to *Of Thee I Sing,* by George S. Kaufman and Morrie Ryskind. According to John L. Toohey, "Had O'Neill not already won the prize on three previous occasions, it almost surely would have gone to him" (98). In 1947, the year that *The* ICEMAN COMETH would have been up for the award, no prize was given.

Bibliography

Garland, Hamlin. *Selected Letters of Hamlin Garland.* Edited by Keith Newlin and Joseph B. McCullough. Lincoln: University of Nebraska Press, 1998.

Hohenberg, John. *The Pulitzer Prizes: A History of the Awards in Books, Drama, Music, and Journalism, Based on the Private Files over Six Decades.* New York: Columbia University Press, 1974.

Toohey, John L. *A History of the Pulitzer Prize Plays.* New York: Citadel, 1967.

Shawna Lesseur-Blas

Q

Quinlan, Bridget Lundigan (unknown–unknown) and **Thomas Quinlan, Joseph** (unknown–unknown) Like the O'Neills (see O'NEILL, EDWARD and O'NEILL, MARY), Eugene O'Neill's maternal grandparents left their home in Tipperary, Ireland, because of the potato famine. In 1857, soon after Thomas, Bridget, and their young son William arrived in New Haven, Connecticut, Mary Ellen Quinlan was born. They soon moved to Cleveland, Ohio, where Thomas Quinlan established himself as a successful merchant of everything from fancy cakes to cigars and liquor.

Now affluent, the Quinlans sent their daughter Mary Ellen, called "Ella," to a convent school, where she excelled at playing the piano. Bridget Quinlan was very strict with young Ella, while Thomas pampered his daughter. When Ella was just 14 years old, her father introduced her to his customer and friend, the young actor JAMES O'NEILL. Despite Bridget's displeasure, Ella developed a crush on James. When Thomas Quinlan died from the effects of overdrinking and tuberculosis, Ella was one year shy of graduation. Thomas Quinlan's will endowed Ella with a substantial amount of money. Despite Bridget's misgivings, Ella went to New York to continue her musical studies. She and James met again and were married.

James urged Ella, then a young mother, to go on tour with him. Despite Ella's conflicts with her mother, she arranged for Bridget to come to New York to care for Ella's young son JAMES O'NEILL, JR. (Jamie), and baby EDMUND O'NEILL. While Ella was on tour, first Jamie and then Edmund became sick with measles. Edmund died before Ella could return to New York. Ella's grief was so profound that she blamed everyone—James, Bridget, and even young Jamie—for the loss of her infant. A great sadness closed in on the family, leading eventually to Ella's addiction to morphine—prescribed to her after the unplanned birth of Eugene. As with the tragedies of the O'Neill family, the immense grief of the Quinlans helped forge the plays of their grandson.

Bibliography

Gelb, Arthur, and Barbara Gelb. *O'Neill: Life with Monte Cristo.* New York: Applause Books, 2000.

Kunckel, Frank A. Family history letter to nephew Manley W. Mallett, 1937. Sheaffer O'Neill Collection, Department of Special Collections and Archives, Charles E. Shain Library, Connecticut College, New London.

Mallett, Manley W. My *Eighty-Four Ancestral Families.* Largo, Fla.: Mallett, 1979.

Sheaffer, Louis. *O'Neill: Son and Playwright.* Boston: Little, Brown, 1968.

Mary Mallett

Quintero, José (José Benjamin Quintero) (1924–1999) José Benjamin Quintero was born on October 15, 1924, in Panama City, Panama. Though he came to the United States to study medicine, he instead became involved in theater work. In time he became a celebrated director and founder of the Circle in the Square Theatre in New York City.

In the early 1970s, as Quintero approached the age of 50, he made the commitment to stop drinking alcohol. His therapist at the time advised him to write a personal journal to use as a tool for self-reflection. In 1973, Quintero chose to edit his personal journal and publish it in the form of a book entitled *If You Don't Dance They Beat You*. In this book, Quintero's only official autobiography, he wove a fabric of enticing and magical tales about his childhood, his friendships, and the theatrical post–World War II era during which he became a professional director and cofounder of the Off-Broadway Circle in the Square Theatre. Through his narration, Quintero highlighted significant moments in his youth, his reasons for leaving his family, and his native country of Panama. The book included portions of its author's bohemian life during the seven years that preceded his first return visit home. Quintero also alluded to his ongoing search to understand the Spanish cultural influences of his childhood and the profound impact upon him of the mysticism inherent in his family's way of practicing CATHOLICISM. It also laid bare the humiliation he and his family had suffered as a result of his father's philandering and rejection. *If You Don't Dance They Beat You* is a cautionary tale, which Quintero used to express his humanity by describing aspects of the emotional cost of his evolution from being a self-proclaimed prodigal son to internationally revered artist.

In the years following the book's 1973 publication, incidents that were artistically sketched came to be considered accurate facts and were often used by journalists and historians as the basis to make comparisons between Quintero's life and that of Eugene O'Neill's. But Quintero's autobiography was a book that, in private, many of his friends and colleagues affectionately referred to as "José's first novel." As with many an autobiography, Quintero's reflections on his past were personal interpretations and perceptions. The book's stream-of-consciousness manner of presentation was more indicative of its author's quixotic and romantic personal style of communicating rather than the text's serving as an accurate historical resource. This latter aspect of the book is one on which historians and intimates of Quintero might certainly agree; the great director's autobiography serves as an ideal document to assess his mesmerizing and elegiac story-telling skills. Quintero's way of expressing his thoughts on life and art were perhaps the defining characteristic of his inimitable directorial method.

Quintero developed a strong band with the plays of Eugene O'Neill, and the mythology that emerged during his career about that bond often took on almost mystical qualities, which suited his personality and emotional inclinations and converged ideally with O'Neill's predilection to write about destiny and to question the nobility inherent in tragedy. The similarities between Quintero and O'Neill's family histories and personal journeys, ones that seemed to connect them beyond death itself, were interpretations of facts and circumstances in both men's lives that Quintero fostered. Certainly both men faced down a similar addiction (ALCOHOLISM) and thereupon evolved spiritually, following the call of their inspirational muses to the end. The self-knowledge that resulted from surviving and surmounting such obstacles resulted in Quintero's gifted artistic and directorial abilities, including his intuitive feel for how to best cast O'Neill's most baffling characters. This, combined with his ability to inspire his casts to illuminate the darkest secrets of O'Neill's spiritually damned souls, secured O'Neill and Quintero's artistic immortality.

Four major factors attributable to José Quintero can be cited as pivotal in what is known as the EUGENE O'NEILL RENAISSANCE: (1) Quintero's impulse to find the parallels between his own life and O'Neill's, combined with his inexhaustible drive to uncover psychological truths; (2) Quintero's intuitive feel for good casting, an ability that led him to cast JASON ROBARDS and COLLEEN DEWHURST in what became their career-defining and signature O'Neill roles; (3) CARLOTTA MONTEREY O'NEILL's decision to entrust Quintero with the rights to produce the American premiere of LONG DAY'S JOURNEY INTO NIGHT, O'Neill's most autobiographical play and the key play in the playwright's formidable canon; and (4) Quintero's determination to stage the largest number ever of professional productions of O'Neill's plays despite the outcome in positive or negative reviews and to do so in theatrical venues with the highest profile possible. These four major factors prompted theater scholars to undertake what has become an ongoing process of reexamining O'Neill's entire body of works. Because of Quintero's breakthrough O'Neill productions, an indefinable barrier holding O'Neill back from taking his rightful place in the annals of classical tragedy was finally knocked down.

José Quintero's Broadway productions of Eugene O'Neill's plays include *Long Day's Journey into Night* (1956), *STRANGE INTERLUDE* (1963), *MARCO MILLIONS* (1964), *HUGHIE* (1964), *MORE STATELY MANSIONS* (1967), *A MOON FOR THE MISBEGOTTEN* (1973), *"ANNA CHRISTIE"* (1977), *A TOUCH OF THE POET* (1977–78), *The ICEMAN COMETH* (1985), and again *Long Day's Journey into Night* (1988).

Quintero's Off-Broadway and regional theater productions of O'Neill plays include *The Iceman Cometh*, Circle in the Square Theatre (1956); *A Moon for the Misbegotten*, Spoleto Festival (1958); *DESIRE UNDER THE ELMS*, Circle in the Square (1963); and *WELDED*, Columbia University (1981). Quintero also produced but did not direct a production of *AH, WILDERNESS!* at the Philadelphia Academy of Art in 1953. José Quintero won the Tony Award and Drama Desk Award for his direction of *A Moon for the Misbegotten* in 1974 and the Vernon Rice Award for his direction of *The Iceman Cometh* in 1956. In 1988, he was awarded the Eugene O'Neill Medallion by the Theatre Committee for Eugene O'Neill and the EUGENE O'NEILL SOCIETY. He died on February 26, 1999.

José Quintero's compellingly human, truthful and psychologically realistic process of approaching the text analysis of Eugene O'Neill's plays, one befitting a 21st-century, scientifically matured era, enabled ancient concepts of drama to be illuminated and to live on in the present. In essence, the nature of Eugene O'Neill's canon has proven to be timeless. The latter observation is one Eugene O'Neill himself voiced in *Long Day's Journey into Night* through Mary Tyrone, the character representing O'Neill's mother MARY ELLEN "ELLA" O'NEILL, who says, "The past is the present, isn't it? It's the future, too. We all try to lie out of that but life won't let us" (3:765).

Further Reading

Garvey, Sheila Hickey. *Not for Profit: A History of New York's Circle in the Square Theatre*. Ann Arbor, Mich.: University Microfilms International, 1985.

Gelb, Arthur, and Barbara Gelb. *O'Neill: Life with Monte Cristo*. New York: Applause Books, 2000.

Little, Stuart W. *Off-Broadway: The Prophetic Theater*. New York: Coward, McCann & Geoghegan, 1972.

Mann, Theodore. *Journeys in the Night: Creating a New American Theatre with Circle in the Square*. New York: Applause Books, 2007.

McDonough, Edwin J. *Quintero Directs O'Neill*. Chicago: A Capella Books, 1991.

Quintero, José. *If You Don't Dance They Beat You*. Boston: Little, Brown, 1974.

Sheila Hickey Garvey

R

realism The true-to-life depiction of people and events has recurred in the arts throughout history, but realism as an artistic movement is said to have originated in France during the mid-19th century with the literature of authors such as Honoré de Balzac, Gustave Flaubert, and Guy de Maupassant. The movement, thought to be a reaction to notions of idealism and romanticism that were prevalent at the time, spread globally, influencing not only literature but visual arts, music, and drama as well. While France had experienced revolution with subsequent failed social reform, many other countries experienced similar social problems, heightened by war, unemployment, and immigration/emigration issues. These circumstances, in combination with such developments as Karl Marx's ideas on the distribution of wealth; Charles Darwin's theories on heredity, environment, and progress in nature; August Comte's philosophy of cause and effect in nature; and the advent of popular journalism and photography were influential factors in the public's acceptance of more realistic forms of art, which would come closer to resembling their own lives and struggles.

While melodramas, vaudeville, and comic operas were prevalent forms of drama during the 19th century, playwrights such as HENRIK IBSEN of Norway, AUGUST STRINDBERG of Sweden, and Anton Chekhov of Russia were opting for less sensationalism and greater accuracy in representations of the human experience in their plays. Constantin Stanislavsky and Vladimir Nemirovich-Danchenko,

founders of the Moscow Art Theatre in 1898, were instrumental in supporting new work of this kind, providing a venue for new, realistic dramas that utilized contemporary settings, limited the use of symbolism and special effects, and put an emphasis on ordinary people and events while addressing broader issues of social class and morality. Dramatic soliloquies and monologues were often omitted or minimized in favor of realistic dialogues and more natural patterns of speech akin to everyday communication. In turn, audiences had a more direct connection to the characters and events, rather than being left to interpret the situation portrayed on stage. Further contributions to the realist movement included Constantin Stanislavsky's development of a process now known as method acting, whereby actors channeled genuine emotions in order to portray the emotions called for in plays. This provided for closer proximity to real-life emotion and put further emphasis on the importance of audience *believing* actors, rather than just understanding or interpreting them. In these ways, it was thought that drama might have a greater social and personal impact, rather than serving as simple entertainment.

In the early 20th century, following World War I, and with immigration and employment issues prevailing, American audiences were ready for more truthful depictions of life in art. Realism had already begun appearing in American literature in the writings of authors such as Henry James and Mark Twain. However, it had not yet surfaced in the nation's theater. Eugene O'Neill changed the course of American drama by introducing American audiences to the kind of realism that European audiences had been experiencing, which had been strangely absent from American drama of the past.

Since O'Neill's father, JAMES O'NEILL, was a well-known actor, Eugene had traveled with his father's touring company and had grown up experiencing the common MELODRAMA of the day. He began to establish his opinions on such styles of showy drama early on in life, expressing contempt for commercial theater, which was infused with romantic ideals and little philosophical or spiritual substance. His own father had given up performances of Shakespeare for higher-paying roles in popular dramas, including the work for which he was best known, *The Count of Monte Cristo*. To Eugene, these dramas with their romantic ideals had little to do with real life. He made plain his belief that the popular styles of American theater were trite, full of shortcomings, and without the truth and power that literature and drama should possess. O'Neill turned to the European pioneers of realism—Ibsen, Strindberg, and Chekhov—for inspiration. His early one-act plays exhibited characteristics of realism, focusing on his own experiences. He employed nonlinear plots and unpredictable outcomes, which he thought more closely resembled the experience of everyday life. His characters were commonly outsiders not typically portrayed in AMERICAN THEATER. They were often inarticulate, speaking in slang, subsequently revealing aspects of themselves, such as their education, CLASS, and their past, that could not be detected simply from traditional dialogue. These characters were influenced by the environment and forces beyond themselves, not always triumphing over such forces as they had in romantic works.

Though sufficiently, influenced by the work of Sigmund Freud, Carl Jung, and FRIEDRICH NIETZSCHE to experiment with EXPRESSIONISM in the 1920s, O'Neill returned to a more obvious and pronounced use of realism in his later, best-known plays. Works such as *A TOUCH OF THE POET*, *The ICEMAN COMETH*, *LONG DAY'S JOURNEY INTO NIGHT*, and *A MOON FOR THE MISBEGOTTEN* sought to employ realism in character, form, and structure.

O'Neill found inspiration in his own experience during this time. His plays, while not completely imitating his life, became increasingly autobiographical, focusing on the complex relationships of his own family and their many struggles. O'Neill was preoccupied with shattering the illusions common to romanticism throughout his career, and this meant portraying those most difficult parts of the human experience—addiction, failure, death, and all those struggles that comprise human tragedy. Indeed, the shattering of illusions is one of the great themes of what is commonly considered O'Neill's best play, *Long Day's Journey into Night*.

Although scholarly examination of O'Neill's plays certainly provides evidence of the influence of a diverse range of styles, including but not limited to expressionism, classicism, romanticism, and NATURALISM (often considered to be an offshoot of realism), O'Neill is best known for his employment of brutal realism, which many believe runs as an undercurrent beneath the surface of his plays that are clearly infused with other styles. This infusion of realism elevated American drama, paving the way for later, more serious exploration in the works of such playwrights as Tony Kushner, David Momet, and TENNESSEE WILLIAMS.

Bibliography

Bloom, Harold. *Eugene O'Neill*. New York: Chelsea House Publishers, 1987.

Carpenter, Frederic I. *Eugene O'Neill*. Rev. ed. Boston: Twayne Publishers, 1979.

Frenz, Horst. *Eugene O'Neill*. New York: Frederick Ungar Publishing Company, 1971.

Murphy, Brenda. *American Realism and American Drama 1880–1940*. Cambridge: Cambridge University Press, 1987.

Schiach, Don. *American Drama 1900–1990*. Cambridge: Cambridge University Press, 2000.

Jennifer Palladino

Reed, John Silas (Jack Reed) (1887–1920)   Best known perhaps for his firsthand account of the Bolshevik Revolution entitled *Ten Days That Shook the World* (1919), John "Jack" Reed was a political activist, journalist, playwright, and poet and one of the founding members of the PROVINCETOWN PLAY-ERS, the cohort of experimental dramatists that discovered Eugene O'Neill and thus helped usher in a new kind of AMERICAN THEATER.

John Silas Reed was born on October 22, 1887, in Portland, Oregon, the son of Charles Jerome and Margaret Green Reed. He was raised in upper-class comfort and educated at Morristown Preparatory School in New Jersey and Harvard University. At Harvard, he was published regularly in the *Harvard Monthly* and the *Lampoon* and was a contributor to Hasty Pudding drama productions before graduating in 1909. Two years later, Reed went to GREENWICH VILLAGE, where he became an editor of *The Masses* and interacted with prominent socialists and activists such as EMMA GOLDMAN, Hutchins Hapgood, Margaret Sanger, and Mabel Dodge.

One night, Reed heard "Big" Bill Haywood, head of the INDUSTRIAL WORKERS OF THE WORLD (IWW), speak about a silk strike in Paterson, New Jersey, where thousands of workers had left the mill and were subsequently assaulted by police. The story was not being covered in the press, so Dodge and Reed devised a plan to make this happen: a pageant in which the workers themselves would perform the history and hardships of the strike. The pageant, directed by Reed, was performed at Madison Square Garden in 1913 and marked one of the most significant moments in the history of American political theater.

After a trip to Europe in 1913, Reed was offered an assignment from the *Metropolitan* to cover the Mexican Revolution. His book *Insurgent Mexico* (1914) details his experiences with revolutionaries and his close relationship with Pancho Villa. A trip to eastern Europe in 1915 first sparked Reed's hatred for the czarist regime in Russia and his sympathy for the Russian people. On a visit home to Oregon in 1915, he met and fell in love with LOUISE BRYANT, a married writer. Bryant eventually left her husband and joined Reed in New York in January 1916.

Reed had probably known Eugene O'Neill peripherally in the Village, and in 1916 O'Neill joined Reed's experimental theater group in Provincetown, Massachusetts, headed by GEORGE CRAM "JIG" COOK and his wife SUSAN GLASPELL, which

Eugene O'Neill and John Reed in Provincetown, Massachusetts *(Courtesy of the Sheaffer-O'Neill Collection, Charles E. Shain Library of Connecticut College)*

began the previous summer and would eventually be called the Provincetown Players. Reed contributed *Freedom* to the first bill of plays in summer 1916, and he performed in O'Neill's *BOUND EAST FOR CARDIFF*. Reed also helped draft the Provincetown Players manifesto. Although O'Neill was living in an abandoned fisherman's shack that summer, he took many meals at Reed and Bryant's rented home. Meals were not the only thing O'Neill and Reed shared; O'Neill fell in love with Louise Bryant, and the two began an affair that continued long after the summer ended. Louise eventually left O'Neill heartbroken when she finally married Reed in November 1916 and left with him for Russia in 1917.

In Russia, Reed became immersed in the revolution and met both Vladimir Lenin and Leon Trotsky. He documented his experiences in dozens of articles and in *Ten Days That Shook the World.* Upon returning to the United States in 1918, Reed, along with his fellow editors at *The Masses,* stood trial in federal court for conspiracy and interference with the recruitment of armed forces: the trial resulted in a hung jury (see the "America" chapter in Rosenstone). Reed was instrumental in forming the Communist Labor Party (CLP) and was sent back to Moscow in late 1919 to gain recognition of the CLP. While in Russia, he learned that he and other leaders of the CLP were charged in the United States with criminal ANARCHISM. In trying to return to America, Reed was jailed in Finland for smuggling false documents, currency, and diamonds. He was released in June 1920 and reunited with Bryant in Moscow. In fall 1920, Reed contracted typhus; he died on October 19, 1920. He received a hero's funeral in Moscow and is buried in the Kremlin.

Bibliography

Baskin, Alex. *John Reed: The Early Years in Greenwich Village.* New York: Archives of Social History, 1990.

Gelb, Arthur, and Barbara Gelb. *O'Neill: Life with Monte Cristo.* New York: Applause Books, 2000.

Homberger, Eric. *John Reed.* New York: Manchester University Press, 1990.

Rosenstone, Robert A. *Romantic Revolutionary: A Biography of John Reed.* New York: Alfred A. Knopf, 1975.

Beth Wynstra

Robards, Jason (Jason Nelson Robards, Jr.) (1922–2000)

Jason Nelson Robards, Jr., was born in Chicago on July 26. 1922. He was the son of the Broadway actor and film matinee idol Jason Robards, Sr., and Hope Glanville Robards. Robards, Jr., watched as his father's career suffered a steady decline after the advent of talking pictures. His parents divorced while he was in grade school, and after this he rarely saw his mother, whom he considered a cold and distant woman. After graduating from Hollywood High School, Robards, Jr., joined the U.S. Navy and was stationed in Pearl Harbor at the time of the Japanese attack. While serving on the USS *Nashville* in 1944, he found a copy of *STRANGE INTERLUDE*—this was his first introduction to the works of Eugene O'Neill. Following the war, he decided to become an actor.

After studying for one year with the highly regarded acting teacher Charles Jehlinger at the American Academy of Dramatic Arts, Robards left his formal training, largely because he needed money to support his wife and children. In 1953, he was cast in the Off-Broadway Circle in the Square theater's production of *American Gothic.* The show's director, a young Panamanian American named JOSÉ QUINTERO, would become Robards's life-long friend and most significant artistic collaborator.

Over a remarkable career that spanned six decades. Robards received a Tony for his role in Budd Shulberg's *The Disenchanted* (1958), two Oscar Awards for his roles in *All the President's Men* (1976) and *Julia* (1977), an Oscar nomination for his role as Howard Hughes in *Melvin and Howard* (1980). and an Emmy Award for the televised version of *Inherit the Wind* (1988). His final screen appearance was in 1999's *Magnolia,* where he played a negligent father dying of cancer (which Robards himself was battling at the time) to Tom Cruise's unapologetically resentful son.

Jason Robards did not write an autobiography, but he was always available for interviews. When asked, he would freely express his political beliefs. With characteristic boyish charm, Robards would provide his uncensored thoughts about people he liked and people he did not like. He candidly discussed the aspects of his life that were unpleasant, such as his four marriages, his struggle with ALCOHOLISM, and a life-threatening 1972 car accident, one of his several near-death experiences. In fact, Jason Robards made self-examination a lifelong endeavor and the source of his art. His search for truth led him to the plays of Eugene O'Neill.

After this first great success and subsequent roles in some of the playwright's later masterpieces, Robards embraced O'Neill's plays as if they were his personal guides for living. As he aged, he used his evolving knowledge of Eugene O'Neill's canon to improve his craft and even his life. But in 1956, at the time of his first landmark acting performance as the charismatic, manipulative, and murderous salesman Theodore "Hickey" Hickman in *Iceman,* the then 34-year-old Robards had no idea how profoundly his future would be tied to O'Neill's legacy.

Robards's performance in *Iceman* at the Off-Broadway Circle in the Square Theatre brought him critical acclaim in New York City. Six months later, his next O'Neill performance, this time on Broadway in the American premiere of LONG DAY'S JOURNEY INTO NIGHT, brought him international stardom. Robards's brilliant interpretation of Jamie Tyrone, the stage representation of Eugene O'Neill's alcoholic older brother, is widely regarded as definitive. The production played on Broadway for two years. During this record-breaking run, *Long Day's Journey* was invited to be the American entry at the Paris Festival. In July 1957, it transferred to FRANCE for one week, where it played in repertory with the British entry, *Titus Andronicus,* starring Sir

Jason Robards, Jr., as James Tyrone (left), with Bradford Dillman as Edmund, in *Long Day's Journey into Night.* Photo by Gjon Mili *(Courtesy of the Sheaffer-O'Neill Collection, Charles E. Shain Library of Connecticut College)*

Laurence Olivier and Vivien Leigh. José Quintero directed the former; Olivier directed the latter.

Robards had the good fortune to leave his indelible mark on the roles of both Hickey Hickman and Jamie Tyrone when he was asked to re-create his performances, first in the Sydney Lumet–directed and condensed television version of *The Iceman Cometh* in 1960 and then in the 1962 Lumet-directed film version of *Long Day's Journey into Night,* with Katharine Hepburn and Sir Ralph Richardson.

Robards's next great O'Neill performance on Broadway was in 1964 when he played the gambler Erie Smith in the American premiere of O'Neill's one-act play HUGHIE. The production and Robards's performance in it were slow to achieve acceptance as the play was not favorably reviewed. However, admiration for the production grew when it toured nationally. Eventually, and largely because of Robards's faith in the quality of the play, *Hughie* came to be accepted as a gem in O'Neill's canon, and its protagonist, the grieving derelict Erie Smith, became another of Jason Robards's signature O'Neill roles.

Despite the fact that Robards's breakthrough career successes occurred when he performed O'Neill, the meaningful impact of his connection to O'Neill did not become clear to him until he created the role of the dying Jim Tyrone for the 1973 Broadway run of A MOON FOR THE MISBEGOTTEN. While preparing to play James Tyrone, Jr., in O'Neill's autobiographical masterpiece *Long Day's Journey into Night* in 1956, Robards read *A Moon for the Misbegotten.* He knew that he was perfectly cast for the character he portrayed in *Journey,* a younger version of the middle-aged and physically ailing alcoholic Jim Tyrone in *Moon.* Yet the gifted actor had not fully grasped that the older Jamie's certain death from alcoholism might also be mirrored in his destiny, nor that his ability to evoke the souls of O'Neill's doomed wastrels was due to the fact that he was in danger of becoming one himself. In 1972, 16 years after his first performance as Jamie Tyrone, Robards survived a drinking-related car accident so horrific that he finally accepted the fact that if he did not give up drinking alcohol, he would share Tyrone's fate.

Robards approached all of his post-1972 O'Neill productions in an entirely different way then he did prior to his accident. He focused on the improvement of his already formidable craft by using his performances in each new or revisited O'Neill play to hone his technical acting skills, broaden his emotional range, and restore order and sanity to his personal life. In the second, resurrected phase of his career, Robards reexamined O'Neill's canon with the belief that it offered as important a method of training for American actors as other cultures' respected classical plays.

After the successful 1973 Broadway run of *A Moon for the Misbegotten*, Robards committed himself to again performing in three O'Neill plays that had helped make his name: *Hughie* (1976), *The Iceman Cometh* (1984), and *Long Day's Journey into Night* (1988). He also added to his distinguished O'Neill résumé by playing Con Melody in A TOUCH OF THE POET (1977) and Nat Miller in AH, WILDERNESS! (1988). José Quintero directed Robards in all but one of these productions. During the planning stages of *Ah, Wilderness!*, Quintero developed cancer, and the Long Wharf Theatre's artistic director Arvin Brown took over.

Jason Robards's bond to Eugene O'Neill was like José Quintero's in that it was often mystical and mythic. It also resembled the actress COLLEEN DEWHURST's bond to O'Neill in that the tie was apparently inescapable. In the first half of his career, Robards proved that he had the intuitive ability to portray some of O'Neill's darkest and most disenfranchised souls. In the second half, he portrayed a broader range of O'Neill's characters to expand the range of his acting technique. Robards's commitment to improve his craft, as demonstrated through his O'Neill work, was so admired by his artistic peers that he became known within his profession as "the actor's actor."

Jason Robards died on December 26, 2000, in Bridgeport, Connecticut. His widow Lois asked the great Canadian classical actor Christopher Plummer to deliver her husband's eulogy. Robards and Plummer had been friends for nearly 50 years, having acted together at Canada's Stratford Festival and on Broadway, having been neighbors of long standing in Connecticut, and having been youthful drinking companions. The privately held funeral mass occurred on a bitterly cold and snowy New Year's Day at the start of the 21st century. When it was Plummer's time to speak, he saluted Robards's intermingling of life and art: "It seems I have known Jason since time began. We started out as young actors working together on Broadway, back in those sunny prehistoric days when there was little difference between the stage and real life—in fact, to Jason they always remained one and the same" (quoted in Black et al. 182). Throughout their individual and distinguished careers, their mutual regard for each other's artistic strengths was total. Robards marveled at Plummer's towering technical abilities when acting in classical plays, while Plummer admired Robards's prowess in REALISM with similar awe. It was Christopher Plummer who would receive the first Jason Robards Award, an honor established in Robards's memory by New York's Roundabout Theatre, a venue both actors considered an artistic home.

There are moments in live theater that are timeless. One such magical moment occurred as the act-end lights dimmed during performances of José Quintero's production of *Hughie*. This was when Jason Robards flashed a cocky grin at the hotel night clerk while delivering Erie Smith's final line, "Easy when you got my luck—and know how" (3:851).

Bibliography

Black, Stephen A., Zander Brietzke, Jackson R. Bryer, and Sheila Hickey Garvey, eds. *Jason Robards Remembered*. Jefferson, N.C.: McFarland, 2002.

McDonough, Edwin J. *Quintero Directs O'Neill*. Chicago: A. Capella Books, 1991.

Sheila Hickey Garvey

Robeson, Paul (Paul Leroy Bustill Robeson) (1898–1976) Actor, singer, linguist, civil rights and left-wing political activist, Paul Robeson was born on April 9, 1898, in Princeton, New Jersey, the son of a former slave. A formidable scholar and athlete, he graduated from Rutgers University and became a basketball player before turning to action. He met Eugene O'Neill in 1923 when O'Neill chose him as CHARLES S. GILPIN's replacement for the title role in *The EMPEROR JONES*. Unlike Gilpin, whom O'Neill considered a "ham" largely because of his arrogance and frequent drunkenness, Robeson was an actor "with considerable experience, wonderful presence & voice, full of ambition and a damn fine man personally with real brains" (O'Neill 177). Robeson began with the PROVINCE-TOWN PLAYERS' 1924 revival of *The Emperor Jones* and continued to successfully play Brutus in the 1925 London revival, the 1925 performances at the Punch and Judy Theater, and the 1930 shows in Berlin. In 1933, he also starred in the FILM ADAPTA-TION of *The Emperor Jones.* According to Robeson, "This is undoubtedly one of '*the* greatest plays'—a true classic of the drama, American or otherwise" (quoted in Lewis 58). In addition to his work in *Jones,* Robeson also played Jim Harris in the controversial ALL GOD'S CHILLUN GOT WINGS in 1924, 1925, and 1933.

Robeson passionately respected O'Neill, referring to the playwright as "a broad, liberal-minded man . . . [who] has had Negro friends and appreciated them for their true worth. He would be the last to cast any slur on the colored people" (quoted in Lewis 59–60). He also boldly asserted, "I honestly believe that perhaps never will I portray a nobler type than 'Jim Harris' or a more heroically tragic figure than 'Brutus Jones, Emperor,' not excepting 'Othello'" (quoted in Lewis 59). In fact, he did play the title role of *Othello* in Europe and the United States; in 1943, he became the first black man ever to play the part on Broadway.

In addition to Robeson's active stage career, other highlights of his professional life include five British films about Africa, numerous tours as a black spiritual, folk, and concert singer, and controversial political activism in support of black rights and world peace. In 1945, he was awarded the NAACP's Spingarn Medal in recognition of his achievements. Although he never played the part, it is interesting to note that O'Neill considered Robeson for the title role in LAZARUS LAUGHED—a white man—because of Robeson's powerful voice, ideal laugh, and his undeniable strength as an actor (O'Neill 365).

Paul Robeson died on January 23, 1976, age 77; he was interred in the Ferncliff Cemetery in Hartsdale, New York.

Bibliography

O'Neill, Eugene. *Selected Letters of Eugene O'Neill.* Edited by Travis Bogard and Jackson R. Bryer. New Haven, Conn.: Yale University Press, 1988.

Lewis, David Levering, ed. *The Portable Harlem Renaissance.* New York: Viking Penguin, 1994.

Shawna Lesseur-Blas

S

sea, the At SEA ISLAND, GEORGIA, where Eugene O'Neill built a house with his third wife, CARLOTTA MONTEREY O'NEILL, named Casa Genotta, his study with a view of the sea was "fitted as a ship's cabin" (Gelb 759), attesting to his fondness of the ocean and its people. That O'Neill at one point planned a cycle of autobiographical plays under the heading of the "Sea-Mother's Son" is further testimony that he considered himself one of "the everlasting children of the mysterious sea," in Joseph Conrad's phrase (which gave O'Neill the original title for BOUND EAST FOR CARDIFF, "Children of the Sea"). That is, he was someone with a special affinity for the godlike powers represented by this primal force. As he stated in one of his early poems (see POETRY), "Weary am I of the tumult, sick of the staring crowd, / Pining for wild sea places where the soul may think aloud" (O"Neill 1). In Travis Bogard's view, O'Neill absorbed "the concept of men moving in the pattern established by an elemental force to which they belong and by which they are controlled in spite of the pressure of their individual wills" (39) from his reading of Conrad's novels.

This force is at work in many of O'Neill's plays. Arthur and Barbara Gelb state that of his published plays, "no less than 13 are set entirely on or in part aboard ship, and in six more the sea figures as an integral part of the action" (157). To this must be added such well-known speeches as Edmund's in LONG DAY'S JOURNEY INTO NIGHT, when he tells his father of the freedom he felt on the "Squarehead square rigger, bound for BUENOS AIRES," feeling at

one with the sea (3:811–812). This oceanic feeling, as Sigmund Freud termed it, has its counterpoint in *The* ICEMAN COMETH when Larry Slade likens Harry Hope's bar to a "Bottom of the Sea Rathskeller" (3:577)—that is, as a grungy reverse Valhalla where dead sailors continue to drink in oblivion. The sea, then, is not a figure of singular or simple meaning in O'Neill's work. It stands for freedom, a mother-god, nature as a living force, nature as indifferent to human fate, nature as controlling human fate, transformation, life, pain, the unconscious, the mysterious life force, love, and death.

O'Neill uses the sea dramatically to suggest that something greater lies behind what we see and experience as human will, and that human will can work in concert with this and experience joy or work against it. It should be mentioned that water is a symbol in EAST ASIAN THOUGHT, specifically Taoism (an Eastern wisdom tradition O'Neill studied, prompting him to name his home in Danville, California, TAO HOUSE), that represents how to follow the Way: One can either go with the flow, so to speak, or fight, at one's peril, against it.

In O'Neill's earliest short plays, the dark side is in evidence. In THIRST, written in 1913, the sea claims all three shipwrecked survivors in punishment, it seems, for their turning against each other, while *"The sun glares down like a great angry eye of God"* (1:51)—though, of course, punishment for the characters' cruel behavior could be seen as a positive aspect of the sea. In WARNINGS, also written in 1913, James Knapp, a wireless operator, does not take a doctor's warning of his hearing loss seriously because his wife nags him to go back to the sea to provide for his family. While at sea, Knapp cannot hear warning alerts, and his ship collides with a derelict. He commits suicide rather than face the shame.

The code of the sea does not tolerate cowardice or carelessness. In FOG, from 1914, the sea sets the eerie mood for the passengers on a lifeboat: "*A dense fog lies heavily upon the still sea. There is no wind and the long swells of the ocean are barely perceptible. The surface of the water is shadowy and unreal in its perfect calmness. A menacing silence, like the genius of the fog, broods over everything*" (1:97). This description of the sea as somehow animate and having a will deeper and greater than human will, a will that diminishes the status of the human in the scheme of things, at times takes O'Neill close to the "inhumanist" position of Robinson Jeffers and to an extent Hart Crane. In this position, humanity is part of the cosmos but not its most important part or its purpose and measure.

In the SS GLENCAIRN cycle of plays, the sea, or its code, forges a unique and intimate bond, a special camaraderie among sailors, which fashions their lives (*Bound East for Cardiff*, 1914); it produces fear and paranoia (IN THE ZONE, 1917); it becomes the enforcer of a sailor's fate (The LONG VOYAGE HOME, 1917); and it is a vehicle for exotic experiences (The MOON OF THE CARIBBEES, 1917), while maintaining a strict CLASS distinction between the crew and officers.

In ILE (1917), the frozen sea inspires rebellion and mad pride and shows its remoteness from land-based domesticity, as the crew is driven to near-mutiny and Mrs. Keeney into actual madness by Captain Keeney's relentless drive for whale oil. In *The ROPE* (1918), on the other hand, the ocean, heard in the background and seen as reflected light, becomes a kind of equalizer as it passively swallows the 20-dollar gold pieces the innocent child, Mary, throws into it, the very gold that has caused the play's conflict.

Longing is a significant theme in the full-length play BEYOND THE HORIZON, written in 1918 and awarded the PULITZER PRIZE in 1920. "Supposing I was to tell you that it's just Beauty calling me, the beauty of the far off and unknown, the mystery and the spell of the East which lures me in the books I've read, the need of the freedom of great wide spaces, the joy of wandering on and on—in quest of the secret which is hidden over there, beyond the horizon?" Robert Mayo says this to his older brother Andrew. "Suppose I told you that was the one and only reason for my going?" (1:577.) His questions undoubtedly echo O'Neill's own sense of the lure of the sea and a hunger for what lies beyond the horizon.

In "ANNA CHRISTIE," completed in 1920, Chris Christopherson, captain of the barge *Simon Winthrop*, famously views the sea as "dat ole davil" (1:964), a malevolent force that destroys and twists people's lives and keeps them away from a sensible, safe life on land—not that he could live on land. His daughter Anna, however—whom, at the beginning of the play, Chris has not seen for 15 years, having left her with her mother to be raised on a farm in Minnesota—is drawn to the sea. In fact, she is so much identified with the sea that it seems to her, on the barge in the fog, that she has been living "a long, long time—out here in the fog. (*frowning perplexedly*) I don't know how to tell you yust what I mean. It's like I'd come home after a long visit away some place. It all seems like I'd been here before lots of times—on boats—in this same fog. (*with a short laugh*) You must think I'm off my base." Her father answers gruffly, "Anybody feel funny dat vay in fog." Anna persists: "But why d'you s'pose I feel so—so—like I'd found something I'd missed and been looking for—'s if this was the right place for me to fit in? And I seem to have forgot—everything that's happened—like it didn't matter no more. And I can feel somehow—like you feel yust after you took a bath. And I feel happy for once—yes, honest!—happier than I ever been before!" (1:982). Indeed, so identified with the sea is Anna that Mat Burke, a shipwrecked sailor who comes aboard the barge, can say, "I thought you was some mermaid out of the sea . . ." (1:984).

These two identifications of the sea—one as the tormenter of human life, the other as home, a place of belonging—seem to be a matter of choice. If one chooses to fight with the sea, struggle will indeed be one's life, and like Chris, a person will spend a lot of time blaming the sea for his or her troubles. If one chooses to give in to the mystery of the sea, then for at least those moments, one will feel at home and connected with the life force. Each choice, though, overlooks the reality of the other. The sea is the source of both life and death, sorrow and bliss.

The sense of belonging to the sea that Anna expresses, and the similar feeling voiced in Edmund Tyrone's speech in *Long Day's Journey into Night* is the "oceanic feeling" described by Sigmund Freud in *Civilization and Its Discontents* (1930). "This state gives the individual a 'feeling of an indissoluble bond, of being one with the external world as a whole.' Freud speculates that this feeling derives from the primary narcissism of infancy, where the child cannot distinguish between internal and external sensations: only later does the ego learn to differentiate itself from the world outside" (Brewster). For Freud this state in an adult is a sign of regression, but for O'Neill it seems to be a sensation of true connection with the world. Indeed, as David Copland Morris has argued in an article about the psychology of Robinson Jeffers's "inhumanist" perspective, this sense of belonging in and to the world does not only, and maybe not at all, contain regressive dreams of returning to the womb, it may well be the spur of a mature ecological understanding of the human in a wider context, as an interactive part of an ecology and not its ruler, its reason for being not the top of its hierarchy (Morris).

Hierarchies were always part of the MERCHANT MARINE, in which O'Neill had served, but on ships using wind power, the crew could still feel a worthy part of an organization. In *The HAIRY APE*, written in 1921, we encounter the brutality of life allotted to firemen and stokers belowdecks, as if incarcerated there. The firemen's forecastle, writes O'Neill, should give the effect of *"a cramped space in the bowels of a ship, imprisoned by white steel. The lines of bunks, the uprights supporting them, cross each other like the steel framework of a cage. The ceiling crushes down upon the men's heads. They cannot stand upright. This accentuates the natural stooping posture which shoveling coal and the resultant over-development of back and shoulder muscles have given them. The men themselves should resemble those pictures in* which the appearance of Neanderthal Man is guessed at" (2:121). This powerful stage image of people broken down and turned into beasts by their allotted place on the sea is starkly contrasted by Paddy's speech, in this very setting of days gone by, when work in the open air demanded "skill and daring" and sailors were "sons of the sea as it 'twas the mother that bore them. . . . 'Twas them days men belonged to ships, not now. 'Twas them days a ship was part of the sea and a man was part of a ship, and the sea joined all together and made it one" (2:126–127). Now, however, the stokers must become part of the machinery and rejoice in that role if they want to belong, according to Yank.

MARCO MILLIONS, completed in 1925, presents us with a chant of the sea when, in act 2, scene 3, Princess Kukachin's royal junk gets ready to lie at anchor. As they work, the boatswain, the sailors, and eventually the princess sing a chant to accompany their work. The sailors' part of the chant includes such lines as, "There is peace deep in the sea / But the surface is sorrow. . . . Death lives in a silent sea, / Gray and cold under cold gray sky, / Where there is neither sun nor wind / Nor joy nor sorrow! . . . There are harbors at every voyage-end / Where we rest from the sorrows of the sea" (2:440–441).

Quiet followed by *"lapping of ripples against the piles [of the pier] and their swishing on the beach"* (2:473) and *"the lapping of waves"* (2:475) announce the entrances of recent high school grads and friends Billy Brown and Dion Anthony in the prologue to *The GREAT GOD BROWN*, written in 1925. They will, of course, become future ideological competitors as, respectively, materialistic architect-businessman Billy and idealistic artist Dion. Margaret, to whom both men are attracted but who will marry Dion, is also preceded by *"the sound of lapping waves"* (2:477). Soon enough, the metaphorical seas will be much less calm and gentle for these three characters as their relationship grows tempestuous. In the epilogue, the play returns to the setting of the prologue. Dion is long dead, and Margaret is at the pier with their three grown sons. Left alone, Margaret exclaims, "I want to feel the moon at peace in the sea! I want Dion to leave the sky for me! I want him to sleep in the tides of my heart!" (2:535).

In DYNAMO, completed in 1928, a gaunt and pale Reuben, leaning against Mrs. Fife, grateful of her offer to be his mother, expounds on his new god and on how life originated in the sea and lives in us:

> Did I tell you that our blood plasm is the same right now as the sea was when life came out of it? We've got the sea in our blood still! It's what makes our hearts live! And it's the sea rising up in the clouds, falling on the earth in rain that drives the turbines that drive Dynamo! The sea makes her heart beat, too!—but the sea is only hydrogen and oxygen and minerals, and they're only atoms, and atoms are only protons and electrons—even our blood and the sea are only electricity in the end! And think of the stars! Driving through space, round and round, just like the electrons of the atom! But there must be a center around which all this moves, mustn't there? There is in everything else! And that center must be the Great Mother of Eternal Life, Electricity, and the Dynamo is her Divine Image on earth! (2:874)

Here O'Neill may be warning against a materialist interpretation of universal interconnectedness of the "oceanic feeling."

In the first part of MOURNING BECOMES ELECTRA, completed in 1931, we reencounter an image of life on the sea as one of exotic adventure when Captain Brant comes courting Lavinia. When Brant observes, "Women are jealous of ships. They always suspect the sea" (2:909) and recalls Lavinia's interest when he told her of being shipwrecked in the South Seas, she retorts, "(in a dry, brittle tone) I remember your admiration for the naked native women. You said they had found the secret of happiness because they had never heard that love can be a sin" (2:909).

Thus, it is safe to say that the sea, as an image and as life, figures prominently in O'Neill's plays, from early to late in his career. He used it as a figure of longing, of difference, as an elemental force, as a shaper and a destroyer of life, and as a hint that behind the lives of humans lies something greater, something unknown with which we can work in concert or against which we can struggle endlessly and futilely. In other words, the sea is a figure of life, and it is as complex as life, which in O'Neill's view means that it is hard indeed, albeit sprinkled with moments of bliss and joy; it causes rage and it may have a deeper meaning. Indeed, it is a figure of truth, as in the poem "To Alice," written "probably in 1925 in Bermuda, to a young woman with whom Eugene O'Neill used to swim," writes Donald Gallup (in O'Neill 95).

> The sun
> And you
> Two things in life
> Are true.
>
> Two things are true.
> You are one.
> Your hair
> And the sun.
>
> Your eyes
> And the sea
> Innocence
> And liberty.
>
> Rusty chains
> Eat the soul
> We are wise
> But you are whole.
>
> You, the sun, & sea,
> Trinity!
> Sweet spirit, pass on
> Keep the dream
> Beauty
> Into infinity.

(O'Neill 95)

Bibliography

Bogard, Travis. Contours in Time: The Plays of Eugene O'Neill. New York: Oxford University Press, 1972.

Brewster, Scott. "Das Unbehangen in der Kultur (Civilization and Its Discontents)." In The Literary Encyclopedia (November 1, 2002). Available online. URL: http://litencyc.com/php/sworks.php?rec=true&UID=5736. Accessed February 1, 2007.

Gelb, Arthur, and Barbara Gelb. O'Neill. London: Jonathan Cape. 1962.

Morris, David Copland. "Courtesy in the Universe: Jeffers, Santayana and the 'Adult Habit of

Thought.'" *Jeffers Studies* 1, no. 3 (2005). Available online. URL: http://www.jeffers.org/archive/pastissues/v1n3.html. Accessed May 5, 2007.

O'Neill, Eugene. *Poems, 1912–1944.* Edited by Donald Gallup. New Haven, Conn.: Ticknor & Fields, 1980.

P. K. Brask

Sea Island, Georgia (Casa Genotta)   In spring 1931, six months after the O'Neills left the Château du Plessis (Le Plessis) in Tours, FRANCE, where Eugene had completed MOURNING BECOMES ELECTRA, the play's premiere by the THEATRE GUILD elicited the most favorable critical response he would enjoy in his lifetime. Worn out from monitoring weeks of rehearsal for the long trilogy, the couple then went to Sea Island, Georgia, for a rest and soon decided to build a house there that would provide the privacy they craved.

Christened Casa Genotta from a blend of their names, the 22-room villa was designed by Francis Abreu in the Mediterranean Revival style then in vogue. Abreu adeptly supplied the combination of nautical and ecclesiastical features specified by CARLOTTA MONTEREY O'NEILL, the former theme reaching fullest expression in Eugene's writing room, made to resemble the broad-windowed stern cabin of a galleon. Surrounded by a high wall and lush plantings, the beachfront hacienda featured a terra-cotta roof, tile floors, exposed cypress beams, medieval-style wrought iron handles, hinges and other fixtures, and white walls setting off the owners' eclectic collection of masks, prints, and objets d'art. The servants wore rubber-soled shoes, and houseguests, among them Somerset Maugham, were impressed by the monastic stillness of the place.

While Sea Island may have evoked the "blessed isles" of *Mourning Becomes Electra,* during the four years the O'Neills lived there, from 1932 to 1936, they found that it was not as blessed as expected. At odds with the hot summer climate and tropical fauna, they were also upset by noisy parties next door and attempts by reporters to intrude on their privacy. Unlike the geographical and cultural isolation of the French château, which helped Eugene commit *Mourning Becomes Electra* to paper, much more than isolation was required to resolve the inherent problems of DAYS WITHOUT END, with which he struggled for months.

These problems were suddenly set aside in fall 1932, when an epiphany prompted O'Neill to compose AH, WILDERNESS!, the gently comedic depiction of a young man's coming of age in the kind of settled home O'Neill wished he had had at that age. He wrote to KENNETH MACGOWAN that the play proved "emotionally we still deeply hanker after the old solidarity of the family unit" (O'Neill 423).

Architectural drawing of Casa Genotta, Sea Island, Georgia *(Courtesy of the Sheaffer-O'Neill Collection, Charles E. Shain Library of Connecticut College)*

A year later, after a long respite from writing that ended with a late-summer stay in the Adirondacks, O'Neill returned to the galleon room with something new in mind: a cycle of plays demonstrating the "iniquity" of American materialism as manifested in successive generations of a single family. But this ambitious concept again led to struggle, and although he eventually finished A TOUCH OF THE POET, he later destroyed the drafts of all but one of the other cycle plays.

O'Neill's writing struggles from 1932 to 1936—the "comedy of recollection" excepted—were almost certainly exacerbated by the unsuccessful efforts of the couple to put down roots at Sea Island. Enthusiastic at first, ultimately the O'Neills felt no more at home on the Georgia coast than they had in France, or than Eugene and AGNES BOULTON had been in Bermuda or Connecticut. The experience negated all that Carlotta had done to create the perfect sanctuary for her husband. After Sophus and Eline Winther came for a visit from the Pacific Northwest and described that region in seductive terms, the O'Neills left for Seattle in October 1936 to resume their quest for a permanent home. But privacy eluded them there as well when, soon after their move, the world learned that the judges in Stockholm had awarded O'Neill the NOBEL PRIZE IN LITERATURE.

Bibliography

Black, Stephen A. *Eugene O'Neill: Beyond Mourning and Tragedy.* New Haven, Conn.: Yale University Press, 1999.

Bowen, Croswell. *The Curse of the Misbegotten.* New York: McGraw-Hill, 1959.

Gelb, Arthur, and Barbara Gelb. *O'Neill.* Enlarged ed. New York: Harper & Row, 1973.

O'Neill, Eugene. *Selected Letters of Eugene O'Neill.* Edited by Travis Bogard and Jackson R. Bryer. New Haven, Conn.: Yale University Press, 1988.

Sheaffer, Louis. *O'Neill: Son and Artist.* Boston: Little, Brown, 1973.

Brian Rogers

Shaw, George Bernard (1856–1950)   Irish-born playwright, critic, and essayist George Bernard Shaw was a central force in modernist drama, promoting the social problem dramas of HENRIK IBSEN as a model. Born in Dublin on July 26, 1856, Shaw was 20 when he moved to England, where he lived for the rest of his life. His plays were first performed in the 1890s, and by the turn of the century, he had become an established playwright. For Shaw, the realistic drama pioneered by Ibsen provided a political platform on which the ills of contemporary society could be debated. His influence was widespread after 1900 and inspired America's first internationally significant dramatist, Eugene O'Neill.

Shaw's first plays—*Widower's House* (1892), *Mrs. Warren's Profession* (1893), and *The Philanderer* (1893)—were obviously indebted to Ibsen's style, although these and his later works are enlivened by his perverse humor and scalding social criticism. In *Candida* (1894), *You Never Can Tell* (1895), *The Devil's Disciple* (1897), *Caesar and Cleopatra* (1898), *Man and Superman* (1902), *Major Barbara* (1905), *Misalliance* (1910), *Androcles and the Lion* (1912), *Pygmalion* (1912), *Heartbreak House* (1919), *Back to Methuselah* (1919), *Saint Joan* (1923), and *The Apple Cart* (1929), Shaw demonstrated that modern drama could transcend the superficial plays that had dominated European stages prior to the 20th century and provided a model for like-minded innovators such as O'Neill.

Traveling with his father's various theatrical tours during his childhood and adolescence, O'Neill was undoubtedly aware of the occasional American productions of Shaw's plays, which typically generated controversy, most particularly the 1905 production of *Mrs. Warren's Profession*, which resulted in the arrest of the play's producer and star. Few American actors or managers dared stage Shaw's work in this period, including O'Neill's father, celebrated romantic actor JAMES O'NEILL, who resisted the new wave of realistic drama and modernist innovations that his son would bring to the fore on U.S. stages within a decade, often inspiring the same sort of controversy surrounding Shaw's plays. The most obvious parallel between Shaw and O'Neill is in their individual skill at challenging audiences and shattering accepted conventional thematic boundaries. Although most American producers continued to resist Shaw's plays until the mid-1910s, his influence on U.S.

dramatists is evident in the works of Clyde Fitch, Langdon Mitchell, Edward Sheldon, Rachel Crothers, Robert E. Sherwood, Philip Barry, S. N. Behrman, and O'Neill.

During his student days, O'Neill read the classics as well as a range of contemporary literature, including Ibsen, AUGUST STRINDBERG, and Shaw. While at school, he also read Shaw's *The Quintessence of Ibsenism* (1891), a critical study of Ibsen's drama, which BIOGRAPHERS Arthur and Barbara Gelb assert "opened Eugene's eyes to what the theatre could be in the hands of an uncompromising visionary." The book became O'Neill's "gospel" when he entered Princeton University, beginning a lifelong admiration for Shaw's achievement. Recognizing their shared desire to transform modern drama and to confront audiences with social and personal realities, O'Neill also wanted to move beyond Shaw's innovations, and this conflict is apparent in his early plays. In one, SERVITUDE (1913–14), O'Neill satirizes the Shavian "new woman" (and Nora of Ibsen's *A Doll's House*) in the character of Ethel Frazer, both mocking her idealism and seriously exploring it, suggesting that liberation for women may not necessarily bring them fulfillment. In a similar satiric vein, O'Neill lampooned new movements in theater in *Now I Ask You*, an unproduced play written in 1917. For this play, O'Neill makes use of the basic plot and thematic structure of Shaw's *Candida*, also weaving in aspects of Ibsen's women characters, flashes of Chekhovian melancholia, the image of FRIEDRICH NIETZSCHE's superman, and various progressive social attitudes. These satiric plays are rare among O'Neill's dramatic works, as is his only comedy, the bittersweet AH, WILDERNESS! (1933), in which Shaw is again referenced when young Richard Miller (a humorous self-portrait of O'Neill as a passionately radical adolescent) is chastised by his narrow-minded mother for reading Shaw's plays and the works of other "scandalous" writers, while Richard's more enlightened father admits to reading and liking the plays, describing Shaw as "a damned comical cuss" (3:98).

Scholars point to the influence of Shaw's *Heartbreak House* (1912–14) on O'Neill's characters and themes in STRANGE INTERLUDE (1928) and consider the title character of Shaw's *Captain Brassbound's Conversion* (1899) as a model for Captain Adam Brant of MOURNING BECOMES ELECTRA (1931). In 1915, O'Neill attended a performance of Shaw's *Pygmalion* starring Mrs. Patrick Campbell and later saw THEATRE GUILD productions of other Shaw plays in the 1920s. All told, the Guild, which became O'Neill's producer with MARCO MILLIONS (1928), staged American premieres of seven Shavian works and revivals of others.

When invited by William Butler Yeats to join the Irish Academy in 1932, O'Neill wrote that "Anything with Yeats, Shaw, A. E. [Houseman], O'Casey, Flaherty, Robinson in it is good enough for me." When he was awarded the NOBEL PRIZE IN LITERATURE in 1936, O'Neill expressed in a letter to Russel Crouse his pleasure at being in the company of Shaw and Yeats, noting that these awards were a "credit to old Ireland." In 1946, while reluctantly giving interviews at the time of the Broadway production of The ICEMAN COMETH (1939), O'Neill told interviewer Kyle Crichton that he regretted the fact that he had never met Shaw, a playwright whose work had significantly influenced him.

George Bernard Shaw died on November 2, 1950, in Hertfordshire, age 94. By the time of his death, he had become a legend in his time.

Bibliography

Alexander, Doris M. "Captain Brant and Captain Brassbound." *Modern Language Notes* 74, no. 4 (April 1959): 306–310.

Brashear, William R. "O'Neill and Shaw: The Play as Will and Idea." *Criticism: A Quarterly for Literature and the Arts* 8 (1966): 155–169.

Gelb, Arthur, and Barbara Gelb. *O'Neill: Life with Monte Cristo.* New York: Applause Books, 2005.

Manheim, Michael, ed. *The Cambridge Companion to Eugene O'Neill.* Cambridge: Cambridge University Press, 1998.

O'Neill, Eugene. *Selected Letters of Eugene O'Neill.* Edited by Travis Bogard and Jackson R. Bryer. New York: Limelight Editions, 1994.

Weintraub, Stanley. "Eugene O'Neill: The Shavian Dimension." *Shaw: The Annual of Bernard Shaw Studies* 18 (1998): 45–61.

James Fisher

Spithead   When Eugene O'Neill and his second wife, AGNES BOULTON, went to Bermuda late in 1924 to escape the Connecticut winter, they also wanted to leave behind the sources and scenes of their personal and professional problems. Visiting the British Crown colony at the suggestion of friends, they rented two cottages high above the pink sands of the south shore and were soon extolling the climate and rejoicing in the absence of distractions. By the time they returned to the island in February 1926, O'Neill seemed interested in putting down roots there. Settling into a spacious villa offering the requisite ocean views, and with their governess, Fifine Clark to care for the children, the productive playwright finished LAZARUS LAUGHED and immediately began STRANGE INTERLUDE. Learning of an 18th-century stone house for sale, lapped by the calm waters of the bay side of Warwick Parish, the couple bought the historic building, intending to renovate it with proceeds from the sale of their Connecticut estate, BROOK FARM.

"Bermuda is really a start on a new tack," Eugene wrote to KENNETH MACGOWAN. According to W. Davies King, the O'Neills wanted to believe that Spithead "would become . . . the conducive place . . . for their marriage, a home for all their desires and a source for that long-sought sense of belonging" (King, 2001, 61). In an April 1927 letter to Agnes, who had returned to Connecticut to be with her ailing father, Eugene wrote that Spithead "is in some strange symbolical fashion our reward, that it is the permanent seat of our family—like some old English family estate" (O'Neill 239), and that they had finally won "this ultimate island where we may rest and live toward our dreams with a sense of permanence and security that here we do belong." Once painted by Winslow Homer, Spithead had been built by the privateer Hezekiah Frith, who, according to Louis Sheaffer, used it both as a dwelling and as a storehouse for booty seized from French and Spanish ships (Sheaffer 238).

Ultimately, a romantic waterfront setting in an island paradise was no more satisfactory for the questing O'Neills than a gracious country estate in Connecticut. Ill with the flu during a summer heat wave, Eugene longed for temperate New England. To a friend he complained that "the solitude gets damned oppressive at times. But it's a fine place to get work done" (O'Neill 245). And work he did, though still unable to confront the roiling sources of his marital discontent. In New York on his own that fall, working on productions and reveling in an uncharacteristically active social life, he acknowledged at last his incompatibility with his wife, and his accelerating affair with Carlotta Monterey (later CARLOTTA MONTEREY O'NEILL)—who told BIOGRAPHERS Arthur and Barbara Gelb that Eugene wanted her to create a "properly run" home for him—swept the troubled marriage to its end (Gelbs 656).

Agnes Boulton continued to occupy Spithead for a time after the divorce, and it was inherited by the children, SHANE RUDRAIGHE O'NEILL and OONA O'NEILL. Looking today much as it did in the late 1920s, the restored house is owned by the Waters family. It was the site of a reception for the EUGENE O'NEILL SOCIETY, hosted by the late Joy Bluck Waters on the occasion of the society's 1999 conference.

Bibliography

Bowen, Croswell. *The Curse of the Misbegotten*. New York: McGraw-Hill, 1959.

Gelb, Arthur, and Barbara Gelb. *O'Neill*. Enlarged ed. New York: Harper & Row, 1973.

King, W. Davies, ed. *"A Wind Is Rising": The Correspondence of Agnes Boulton and Eugene O'Neill*. Madison, N.J.: Fairleigh Dickinson University Press, 2000.

———. "'Our Home, Our Home:' Eugene O'Neill and Agnes Boulton at Spithead." *Eugene O'Neill Review*, nos. 1–2 (Spring–Fall 2001): 60–69.

O'Neill, Eugene. *Selected Letters of Eugene O'Neill*. Edited by Travis Bogard and Jackson R. Bryer. New Haven, Conn.: Yale University Press, 1988.

Sheaffer, Louis. *O'Neill: Son and Artist*. Boston: Little, Brown, 1973.

Waters, Joy Bluck. *Eugene O'Neill and Family: The Bermuda Interlude*. Warwick, Bermuda: Granaway Books, 1992.

Brian Rogers

stage directions   Eugene O'Neill offered extremely detailed stage directions in his plays, not only to convey what he intended to actors and directors but also to make his intentions apparent to the plays' readers, regardless of what was achieved onstage. According to BIOGRAPHERS Arthur and Barbara Gelb, "Casting was inevitably a horror to him, for he felt he was yielding, inch by inch, the characters he had created" (418). He complained in 1926 that "I am certainly getting God damn tired of . . . *approximations* to what I've written. . . . It makes me feel hopeless about writing except for my own satisfaction in a book" (O'Neill 1988, 213–214). Of his use in STRANGE INTERLUDE of the "aside" (which, like the stage direction, was a means by which to delineate a character's thought process), he bitterly explained: "If the actors weren't so dumb, they wouldn't need asides; they'd be able to express the meaning without them" (quoted in Gelb 650).

O'Neill used stage directions—that is, text other than that spoken by the characters—to comment in minute detail on a character's physical appearance, behavior, and state of mind; to lay out the settings and action, at times beyond what could be easily achieved on stage; and sometimes even to describe how a scene should be played and how it should be perceived by the audience. To find examples of this, one need only look at his earliest plays. The Older Man in *A WIFE FOR A LIFE* (1913) is described this way: "*His face is the face of one who has wandered far, lived hard, seen life in the rough, and is a little weary of it all*" (1:3). The stage directions for *The WEB* (1913) reveal what is *not* apparent about a character: "*Rose Thomas, a dark-haired young woman looking thirty but really only twenty-two . . . has . . . a quantity of rings, none of them genuine*" (1:15). Even at the start of his career, O'Neill describes characters as having conflicting aspects in their physiognomy. We are told of *The Web*'s Tim Moran that "*although distinctly a criminal type his face is in part redeemed by its look of manliness*" (19). And in the same play can be found an example of O'Neill's use of stage directions to allude to the metaphysical: "*She seems to be aware of something in the room which none of the others can see—perhaps the personification of the ironic life force that has crushed her*" (27–28). This is seen again in *THIRST* (1913), in which "*The sun glares down from straight overhead like a great angry eye of God. The eerie heat waves float upward in the still air like the souls of the drowned*" (1:51).

One finds in *Thirst* an early instance of O'Neill's description of characters' mental states: "*In the eyes of all three [characters] the light of a dawning madness is shining*" (1:32). He begins to describe aspects, or presumed aspects, of characters' personalities and backgrounds that are not apparent. We learn in *BREAD AND BUTTER* (1914) that Harry is "*A bit of a sport, given to beer drinking, poker parties and kelly pool, if the foppish mode of his light check clothes be any criterion*" (1:118); and Lucy in *NOW I ASK YOU* (1916) "*is an intelligent, healthy American girl suffering from an overdose of undigested reading, and has mistaken herself for the heroine of a Russian novel*" (1:414).

Several of O'Neill's works from this period have the mostly silent action at the beginning of the play spelled out. We are told in *BEFORE BREAKFAST* (1916) that Mrs. Rowland enters, yawning; sticks pins in her hair; comes to the middle of the room; yawns again; stretches her arms; stares about the room; goes wearily to the clothes hanging on the right; takes an apron from the hook and ties it about her waist; says "damn" in exasperation when it doesn't tie; finally ties it; slowly goes to the stove and lights a burner; fills the coffee pot; sets it over the flame; slumps into a chair by the table; and puts a hand over her forehead "*as if she were suffering from headache. Suddenly her face brightens as though she had remembered something, and she casts a quick glance at the dish closet; then looks sharply at the bedroom door and listens intently for a moment or so*" (1:391–392). The stage directions for *The MOON OF THE CARIBBEES* (1917) detail in an almost choreographed manner the simultaneous actions of multiple characters (1:542).

The stage directions of O'Neill's subsequent plays would show an increasingly literary bent. At the beginning of act 1 of *BEYOND THE HORIZON* (1918), "*an old gnarled apple tree, just budding into leaf, strains its twisted branches heavenwards, black against the pallor of distance*" (1:573). At the end of the play, Ruth "*remains silent, gazing . . . dully with the sad humility of exhaustion, her mind already sinking back into the spent calm beyond the further troubling of any hope*" (1:653). At the outset of *WHERE THE CROSS IS MADE* (1918), "*Moonlight, winnowed by the wind which moans in the stubborn angles of the old* house, creeps wearily in through the portholes and rests like tired dust in circular patches upon the floor and table" (1:695). Stage directions also became more expansive, taking up about two pages at the start of act 3, scene 2 of the 1919 CHRIS CHRISTOPHERSEN (1:876–878).

O'Neill's description of Smithers in The EMPEROR JONES (1920) shows a painterly quality: "The tropics have tanned his naturally pasty face with its small, sharp features to a sickly yellow, and native rum has painted his pointed nose to a startling red. His little, washy-blue eyes are red-rimmed" (1:1,031). His description of Jones goes beyond physical details: "His features are typically negroid, yet there is something decidedly distinctive about his face—an underlying strength of will, a hardy, self-reliant confidence in himself that inspires respect" (1:1,033). And he describes the setting in scene 2 from the viewpoint of an audience's changing perspective: "In the rear the forest is a wall of darkness dividing the world. Only when the eye becomes accustomed to the gloom can the outlines of the separate trunks of the nearest trees be made out, enormous pillars of deeper blackness" (1:1,044).

As was mentioned earlier, in several of O'Neill's plays, he describes the characters as having contradictory facial characteristics. In GOLD (1920), for example, Bartlett's "jaw and tight-lipped mouth express defiant determination, as if he were fighting back some weakness inside himself, a weakness found in his eyes" (1:908). Harriet's face in DIFF'RENT (1920) "is plainly homely and yet attracts the eye by a certain boldly-appealing vitality of self-confident youth" (2:14). Similarly, Michael's face in WELDED (1923) has "features at war with one another—the forehead of a thinker, the eyes of a dreamer, the nose and mouth of a sensualist" (2:235). Characters' complex relationships are often suggested though their physical resemblances and differences. In MOURNING BECOMES ELECTRA (1931), "The moonlight, falling full on them" [Christine and Lavinia] accentuates strangely the resemblance between their faces and at the same time the hostile dissimilarity in body and dress" (2:930); and Orin's "mouth and chin have the same general characteristics as his father's had, but the expression of his mouth gives an impression of tense oversensitiveness quite foreign to the General's"

(2:956–957). In MORE STATELY MANSIONS (1939), Sara's "manner has taken on a lot of Deborah's self-assured poise, and her way of speaking copies Deborah, although the rhythm of Irish speech still underlies it" (3:395). Jamie Tyrone in LONG DAY'S JOURNEY INTO NIGHT (1941) "has fine brown eyes, their color midway between his father's lighter and his mother's darker ones" (3:722).

The epilogue of MARCO MILLIONS (1924), consisting entirely of descriptive text, shows O'Neill at his most fanciful. We are told that the play is over. Marco Polo rises from an aisle seat in the first row and, still dressed in 13th-century clothes, leaves the theater with the rest of the audience. "His car, a luxurious limousine, draws up at the curb. He gets in briskly, the door is slammed, the car edges away into the traffic, and Marco Polo, with a satisfying sigh at the sheer comfort of it all, resumes his life" (2:467). In The GREAT GOD BROWN (1925) and LAZARUS LAUGHED (1926), which O'Neill subtitled "A Play for an Imaginative Theatre," he used stage directions to explain his complex plans for employing masks. For instance, in Lazarus Laughed, "There are seven periods of life shown . . . and each of these periods is represented by seven different masks. . . . Thus in each crowd . . . there are forty-nine different combinations of period and type" (2:541).

In 1941, O'Neill wrote a detailed outline for seven short plays with the overall title By Way of Obit. According to O'Neill,

> In each [play] the main character talks about a person who has died to a person who does little but listen. Via this monologue you can get a complete picture of the person who has died—his or her whole life story—but just as complete a picture of the life and character of the narrator. And you also get, by another means—a use of stage directions, mostly—an insight into the whole life of the person who does little but listen. (O'Neill 1987, 218)

He added that "these plays are written more to be read than staged" (218). HUGHIE (1941), the only completed play of the series, contains descriptions of the silent character that seem meant to be read: "The Clerk's face would express despair, but the last time he was able to feel despair was back around World

War days" (3:837), and *"Beatific vision swoons on the empty pools of the Night Clerk's eyes"* (3:848). O'Neill felt that the play should be produced with the stage directions and interior monologue heard on a sound track that would accompany the live dialogue, along with a background film of the city (Sheaffer 523). Interviewed in 1922, O'Neill stated that he could not imagine staging a production of his own work, since

> I am sure the inner spiritual and psychological unity of the written play as a thing in itself would be destroyed.... After all, is not the written play a thing? Is not *Hamlet,* seen in the dream theatre of the imagination as one reads, a greater play than *Hamlet* interpreted even by a perfect production? (quoted in Estrin 22)

In 1929, O'Neill stated: "Hereafter I write plays primarily as literature to be read" (O'Neill 1982, 191). He felt that both productions and performers were incapable of realizing his plays as written. That same year, he wrote:

> My interest in the production steadily decreases as my interest in plays as written increases. They always—with the exceptions you know— fall so far below or beside my intent that I'm a bit weary and disillusioned with scenery and actors. . . . And where there is genuine inspiration and spirit, as in P'town [Provincetown], there is nothing for it to work with (money, I mean). . . . I think I will end up writing plays to be published with "No Productions Allowed" in red letters on the first page. (O'Neill 1988, 338—339)

Most of the time, O'Neill wrote his plays knowing that the public would have the opportunity to read them. His father paid for the publication of five of his early plays in 1914, and the magazine *The Smart Set* printed *The* LONG VOYAGE HOME in 1917 and *The Moon of the Caribbees* in 1918. Boni & Liveright, Inc. was the publisher of *The Moon of the Caribbees and Six Other Plays of the Sea* in 1919 and continued to publish his plays—even issuing *Marco Millions* in 1927 before it had been produced. They also published a two-volume limited edition of *The Complete Works of Eugene O'Neill* (1924). *Strange*

Interlude, published four years later, sold extremely well. In 1930, the *New York Times* reported that in America, "Shaw, Barrie, Galsworthy and O'Neill [are] the quartet whose work sells with a faithful consistency. . . ." Preeminent PUBLISHERS Horace Liveright, Inc. and Random House published his plays successfully in later years.

Bibliography

Estrin, Mark W., ed. *Conversations with Eugene O'Neill.* Jackson and London: University Press of Mississippi, 1990.

Gelb, Barbara, and Arthur Gelb. *O'Neill.* New York: Harper & Brothers, 1962.

O'Neill, Eugene. *"As Ever, Gene": The Letters of Eugene O'Neill to George Jean Nathan.* Edited by Nancy L. Roberts and Arthur W. Roberts. Rutherford, N.J.: Fairleigh Dickinson University Press, 1987.

————. *Selected Letters of Eugene O'Neill.* Edited by Travis Bogard and Jackson R, Bryer. New Haven, Conn.: Yale University Press, 1988.

————. *"The Theatre We Worked For": The Letters of Eugene O'Neill to Kenneth Macgowan.* Edited by Jackson R. Bryer, with the assistance of Ruth M. Alvarez. New Haven, Conn.: Yale University Press, 1982.

Sheaffer, Louis. *O'Neill: Son And Artist.* Boston: Little, Brown, 1973.

"The Plays That Are Put into Print, and Why," *New York Times,* March 23, 1930, sec. 9, p. 1.

John Hagan

Strindberg, August (1849–1912) August Strindberg was a Swedish playwright, novelist, short story writer, essayist, poet, painter, and experimental photographer. During his career, he spent considerable time in Denmark, Germany, France, and Italy. His collected works fill 72 volumes and include approximately 60 plays. In addition, his collected letters fill 22 volumes. On the stage he was a pioneer of both NATURALISM in such plays as *The Father* (1887) and *Miss Julie* (1888) and of EXPRESSIONISM in his later plays such as *The Dance of Death* (1900) and *A Dream Play* (1901), and in his chamber plays that included *The Pelican* (1907) and *Ghost Sonata* (1907). His work is usually divided into two periods, pre and post Inferno. This Inferno (also the title of an autobiographical novel, 1897), a breakdown he suffered in the years 1894–1896, moved him toward a more mystical worldview. Prior to this period, Strindberg was influenced by such thinkers as Schopenhauer and FRIEDRICH NIETZSCHE. Afterward, he was greatly inspired by the 18th-century mystical thinker Swedenborg. During his last productive years, he was intensely involved with *Intima teatern* [the Intimate Theater], 1907–10, a small theater (161 seats) in Stockholm dedicated to his own work, which he started with the actor August Falck.

Strindberg's dramaturgical palette was often intense and visionary. In *A Dream Play* and *To Damascus,* he explored the quest for meaning; in *The Burned Site* and *The Ghost Sonata* he depicted people trapped in a web of deceit; and in *The Father, Miss Julie, The Dance of Death* and *The Storm,* he delved deeply into the battle of the sexes. Unmasking hypocrisy lies as a subtext in much of his work.

When Eugene O'Neill won the NOBEL PRIZE IN LITERATURE, ill health prevented him from attending the awards banquet at Stockholm's City Hall on December 10, 1936. He therefore sent a speech to be read on his behalf by the American chargé d'affaires in Sweden, James E. Brown, Jr. In that speech, O'Neill pays homage to the Swedish dramatist August Strindberg, acknowledging Strindberg's influence on his writing. "It was reading his plays when I first started to write back in the winter of 1913–14 that, above all else, first gave me the vision of what modern drama could be, and first inspired me with the urge to write for the theatre myself," he wrote, adding, "I am only too proud of my debt to Strindberg. . . . For me, he remains . . . the master, still to this day more modern than any of us, still our leader" (Nobelprize.org). In the cover letter O'Neill sent to Brown, he was careful to point out "that I have never written anything truer or more sincere than the acknowledgement therein of my debt to Strindberg. It is no mere artful gesture to please a Swedish audience. It's a plain statement of fact and my exact feeling, and I am glad of the opportunity to get it said on record" (O'Neill 455).

As a playwright, Strindberg wrote historical plays, plays in the style of NATURALISM, and plays that tended toward EXPRESSIONISM, or what O'Neill called super-naturalism—plays that revealed the souls of their characters.

Both Travis Bogard and Virgina Floyd suggest a deep connection between Strindberg's work and O'Neill's first full-length play, *BREAD AND BUTTER,* especially "the definite influence on O'Neill of Strindberg's *The Dance of Death*" (Floyd 65). Floyd also sees a connection between the expressionistic scenes in O'Neill's *The HAIRY APE* and Strindberg's *A Dream Play,* "which also depicts a quest for the meaning of life. Yank is Strindberg's dreamer" (Floyd 242–243). Yank's fixation on Mildred as his nemesis can be read as echoing Strindberg's recurring theme of woman despoiling manly ambition and vision. Both Strindberg and O'Neill, of course, also depicted many self-deluded ambitious and visionary men such as Strindberg's Jakob Hummel in *The Ghost Sonata* and the Captain in *The Dance of Death.* O'Neill's above-mentioned Yank can hardly be seen as a role model, nor can a delusional striver like Cornelius Melody in *A TOUCH OF THE POET,* who shares many nasty qualities with Strindberg's Jean in *Miss Julie.* Strindberg's disdain of marriage, in such plays as *The Father* and *The Pelican,* may be seen as reincarnated in as late a play as O'Neill's *LONG DAY'S JOURNEY INTO NIGHT.* And Travis Bogard has pointed out the structural similarity between a play such as *MARCO MILLIONS* and Strindberg's journey plays, such as *To Damascus, A Dream Play,* and *The Great Highway.*

It was not only Strindberg's plays that were meaningful to O'Neill. In a letter to BEATRICE ASHE from 1914, he mentions that he has been reading the stories in Strindberg's collection *Married.* The stories that caught O'Neill "harp on the fact of an insufficient income ruining so many lives by compelling them against the dictates of nature to waste their youth in waiting for each other." The stories made him "full of gloom for I could not help finding a personal application in all of them" (O'Neill 33).

The early O'Neill play *BEFORE BREAKFAST* is clearly derivative of Strindberg's *The Stronger.* However, despite the fact that the two writers share a number of concerns as well as similarities in their ways of representing these concerns on stage, it would be a mistake to see O'Neill as some literary prolongation of Strindberg's work. Strindberg is fascinating because of the intensity with which he was able to stage his view of life without making his characters mere puppets and to do so in a variety of styles. The same can be said for O'Neill, but what makes him fascinating is that however much or little he "owes" to Strindberg, it is *his* view of life we see on the stage and not Strindberg's. In the end, the greatest influence Strindberg had on O'Neill was to make him realize what was possible on the stage, that what he disliked about his father JAMES O'NEILL's theater was not theater itself. This aesthetic conflict with his father about the nature of the theater may itself be seen as Strindbergian.

Bibliography

Bogard, Travis. *Contours in Time: The Plays of Eugene O'Neill.* New York: Oxford University Press, 1972.

Floyd, Virginia. *The Plays of Eugene O'Neill: A New Assessment.* New York: Frederick Ungar Publishing, 1985.

Nobelprize.org. "Banquet Speech." Eugene O'Neill: The Nobel Prize in Literature. Available online. URL: http://nobelprize.org/nobel_prizes/literature/laureates/1936/oneill-speech.html. Accessed December 1, 2007.

O'Neill, Eugene. *Selected Letters of Eugene O'Neill.* Edited by Travis Bogard and Jackson R. Bryer. New York: Limelight Editions, 1994.

P. K. Brask

Synge, John Millington (1871–1909) John Millington Synge was born to a Protestant Anglo-Irish family in Rathfarnham, a suburb of Dublin, Ireland. Synge's early education was frequently interrupted by illness, and he found little comfort in the religious strictness of his family of staunch anti-Catholics. At age 14 he read the works of Charles Darwin, which led him to reject Christianity two years later. In 1889, he entered Trinity College, Dublin, to study Gaelic. While studying at Trinity, Synge became a student at the Royal Irish Academy of Music and, after graduating, he moved to Germany

to study music. After only six months, however, he decided to dedicate his life to literature.

Synge's first play, *Riders to the Sea* (1902), embodies the symbols and archetypes of the Gaelic culture almost mystically, while detailing the common, everyday lives of villagers. *The Playboy of the Western World* (1907), considered his best and the most controversial play, explores Oedipal themes of patricide and incest, which infuriated many people in Ireland.

In his final major play, *Deirdre of the Sorrows* (1910), Synge dramatizes a folktale of a young woman promised as a bride to an old, senile king. The play dramatizes such conflicts as society versus nature, youthfulness versus age, and power versus love. The lovers' passion forces them to make heroic sacrifices for each other. Synge's talent as a playwright was widely recognized throughout his lifetime. He found supporters for his work among the remote villages of Ireland and the sophisticated literary circles.

Eugene O'Neill first encountered plays by Synge in 1911 when Dublin's ABBEY THEATRE undertook its first U.S. tour. By 1907, Synge had emerged as the Abbey's most important dramatist even though his early death in 1909, one month short of his 39th birthday, limited his dramatic canon to only six plays. Recognizing Synge's importance, the Abbey Theatre's director, poet and playwright William Butler Yeats, structured the 1911 tour to feature Synge's work. He believed that Synge's international reputation would "consolidate" the Abbey Theatre's international standing (McCormack 393). Of seven Abbey Theatre playwrights represented in the tour, only Synge had four plays performed: *In the Shadow of the Glen* (1903), *Riders to the Sea*, *The Well of Saints*, and *The Playboy of the Western World*. The tour's emphasis on Synge purposefully coincided with the first U.S. commercial publications of Synge's plays and his nonfiction work *The Aran Islands*.

The impression made by Synge's plays in performance and their availability in print led to his being included among the "foreign dramatists" Eugene O'Neill read while recovering from tuberculosis—the time in O'Neill's life that ended his "protracted period of self-destructive behavior," and he began to write (Shaughnessy 23). O'Neill's early exposure to Synge was furthered even more when he took GEORGE PIERCE BAKER's playwriting class at Harvard University in 1914, as Baker "could explain very precisely how . . . Synge used the speech rhythms of the Irish counties to create a character" (Black 174). The result of this exposure is the intense and prominent presence of John Millington Synge in Eugene O'Neill's plays.

Synge's first performed play, *In the Shadow of the Glen,* was premiered in 1903 in Dublin by the Irish National Theatre Society (the company that opened the Abbey Theatre in 1904). When first performed in Dublin, Synge's plays often provoked protests, ranging from various audience disruptions to attacks in the Dublin press. These protests were leveled by morally and socially conservative (mostly Catholic) Dubliners, even from those who claimed to be nationalists seeking political independence for Ireland from Britain. The attacks exploded into a riot during the third performance of Synge's masterwork *The Playboy of the Western World* in January 1907. When the Abbey brought *Playboy* to America in 1911, various conservative IRISH-AMERICAN Catholic groups organized protests against Synge's plays—especially against *Playboy*—in an effort to repeat the Dublin disturbances. Like all contemporary protests against Synge's plays, at heart the protests had to do with the fact that Synge portrayed modern, assertive, and independent women who define men rather than allow men to define them. In essence, Synge's assertive women characters undermined the colonial paternalism of Britain and CATHOLICISM. Of course, the protests against *Playboy* in Philadelphia and New York during the Abbey's 1911 tour led directly to great fascination for the Dublin theater. O'Neill, in turn, found the protests to be amusing (Black 116).

Synge's *Riders to the Sea,* set among fishing folk on Ireland's remote Aran Islands, follows a mother, Maurya, as she experiences the death of her sixth and last son, all having died on the sea. In every respect, the sea shapes the play's characters and actions. O'Neill was immediately struck by the all-encompassing tragedy of *Riders to the Sea.* O'Neill biographer Stephen Black notes that O'Neill "long remembered the old woman in *Riders* and once . . . compared himself to her feeling he had 'gotten to

that stage now where nothing can hurt or anger me'" (116). This sentiment is directly voiced in O'Neill's late great masterwork LONG DAY'S JOURNEY INTO NIGHT by Mary Tyrone in act 3 when, distracted by her failing hands, she states, "But even they can't touch me now" (3:777). This is almost a direct echo of Synge's Maurya near the end of *Riders:* "There isn't anything more the sea can do to me" (11). Of course, on a basic level, *Riders*'s presence is in all of O'Neill's early SEA plays, from their short one-act forms that follow *Riders*'s example to the thematic sense of the sea representing all that the characters cannot control, hence beginning O'Neill's exploration of "life's meaning without God" (Shaughnessy 66). Maurya's prayers to God are not answered in *Riders,* and O'Neill's characters, like those in the early sea play THIRST, struggle and suffer a seemingly meaningless existence in God's absence.

In addition to exploring life in terms of an empty religion, *Riders to the Sea* specifically portrays Ireland's 1904 reality, which Synge witnessed firsthand among the folk he lived with on the Aran Islands:

> The maternal feeling is so powerful on these islands that it gives a life of torment to the women. Their sons grow up to be banished as soon as they are of age, or live here in continual danger on the sea; their daughters go away also, or are worn out in their youth with bearing children. (Synge *The Aran Islands* 1911, 113)

Synge portrays this maternal reality in Ireland through Maurya watching her children vanish, which is specifically presented only through Maurya's suffering. It is this example that O'Neill embraced in much of his work. Through the suffering of his characters, like Synge's Maurya, O'Neill portrays his portrait of America.

Maurya's last speeches in *Riders to the Sea* become part of a pagan Gaelic keening (mourning) song that is sung by the island women. These speeches ring of Maurya's lamentations for not only her last son, Bartley, but also for the death of who she thought she had been:

> It isn't that I haven't prayed for you, Bartley, to the Almighty God. It isn't that I haven't said

prayers in the dark night till you wouldn't know what I'd be saying; but it's a great rest I'll have now, and great sleeping in the long nights after Samhain [autumn], if it's only a bit of wet flour we do have to eat, and maybe a fish that would be stinking. (11)

This idea of self-lamentation, or self-keening is used by O'Neill in a number of his plays, as in the late play A TOUCH OF THE POET. In act 4, the play's Con Melody, after shooting his beloved mare, laments in a keening fashion for the death of the man he had thought he was:

Wasn't she the livin' reminder, so to spake, av all his lyin' boasts and dreams? He meant to kill her wid one pistol, and then himself wid the other. But faix, he saw the shot that killed her had finished him, too. . . . and seeing her die made an end av him." (3:273)

As mentioned above, Synge lived on the Aran Islands for various periods (1898–1901), and there he observed among the mothers he met the behavior he ascribes to Maurya—her self-keening, or conscious suffering of the loss of self-identity. In fact, Synge based his plays on his direct observations of Irish country life on Aran and other remote rural sections of the country. This process was detailed in the prefaces to the published editions of Synge's work. O'Neill undoubtedly read these prefaces and while doing so came to appreciate the process of turning observations and experiences into plays. Suddenly, O'Neill's experiences at sea, in bars, within his own family, and so on, could all resonate as play material. The initial result of this encounter is that O'Neill embraced Synge's method of writing through observation and experience and filled his plays with common people struggling for meaning in their lives. A mature O'Neill would later build on Synge's writing method to make it his own. He would also come to recognize precedents in Synge's plays and draw on them for his own powerful works that reveal Synge's profound presence in O'Neill's canon.

When O'Neill began writing, he recognized a precedent established in Synge's The Playboy of the Western World, which portrays ordinary folk in a barroom setting—an unusual development when Synge's play premiered in 1907, and it remained so when O'Neill wrote the first act of "ANNA CHRISTIE" in 1921. In his late great plays, O'Neill set A Touch of the Poet and The ICEMAN COMETH in barrooms and focused on their inhabitants. A Touch of the Poet portrays a braggart in Con Melody, just as Synge's Playboy presents a braggart in its character Christy Mahon. O'Neill borrows Christy's vanity of playing to a mirror for Con. Christy sees himself and comments, "Didn't I know rightly I was handsome" (Synge 1911, 44). Con flatters himself before his mirror image prior to reciting Byron's heroic verse, "I still bear the unmistakable stamp of an officer and a gentleman" (3:202–203). Even Con's former service in the British military, made especially absurd given his Irish birth, echoes Synge's Old Mahon who mimics British army officers: ". . . he a man'd be raging all times . . . like a gaudy officer you'd hear cursing and damning and swearing oaths" (Synge 1911, 34). Synge's Playboy is likewise a strong presence in O'Neill's The Iceman Cometh, far beyond the barroom setting.

Both Playboy and Iceman present visitors who are celebrated and welcomed by the regulars of each bar as Christ-like saviors offering some form of desired redemption. Harry Hope's patrons in O'Neill's play await Hickey's visit that pays for their drinks and encourages their hopeless pipe dreams. Synge's Christy is welcomed for his tale of killing his oppressive, brutish father. Christy proves a failed savior when his tale is proven false, and Hickey fails to live up to his old myth. Instead of buoying the pipe dreams of Harry Hope's patrons and leading them into a drinking frenzy, Hickey tries to persuade them to abandon their dreams as he confesses to murdering his wife. Both plays thematically present the failure of false saviors in a world where religion has failed its people.

Even O'Neill's fascination with fog, with characters being lost in it if they fight it or find peace if they embrace it, is similar to Synge's use of mist, as with Nora in In the Shadow of the Glen. This notion of an enveloping aspect of nature is philosophically reached by both Synge and O'Neill repeatedly. In *The Aran Islands,* Synge writes of an evening when he sat on a pier on Inishmaan (one of the Aran Islands) and sensed himself becoming one with nature: "The sense of solitude was immense. I could not see or realize my own body, and I seemed to exist merely in my perception of the waves and the crying birds, and of the smell of seaweed" (*Aran Islands* 1911, 148). In *Long Day's Journey into Night,* Edmund Tyrone, the character based on O'Neill himself, talks of being at sea on a square-rigger ship: "I dissolved in the sea, became white sails and flying spray, became beauty and rhythm, became moonlight . . . and the high dim-starred sky!" (3:811–812). In this, too, Synge provides a precedent or, rather, is a presence in O'Neill's masterpiece.

In many respects, all of Eugene O'Neill's characters return to Synge's *Riders to the Sea* and its closing sentiment voiced by Maurya: "What more can we want than that? . . . No man at all can be living for ever, and we must be satisfied" (Synge 1995, 12). Arguably, O'Neill's characters struggle to be satisfied—whether they are capable of it or not.

Bibliography

Black, Stephen A. *Eugene O'Neill: Beyond Mourning and Tragedy.* New Haven, Conn.: Yale University Press, 1999.

McCormack, W. J. *Fool of the Family: A Life of J. M. Synge.* London: Weidenfield & Nicolson, 2000.

Ritschel, Nelson O'Ceallaigh. *Performance and Textual Imaging of Women on the Irish Stage, 1820–1920: M. A. Kelly to J. M. Synge and the Allgoods.* Lewiston, N.Y.: Edwin Mellen Press, 2007.

———. *Synge and Irish Nationalism: The Precursor to Revolution.* Westport, Conn.: Greenwood Press, 2002.

Shaughnessy, Edward. *Down the Nights and Down the Days: Eugene O'Neill's Catholic Sensibility.* Notre Dame, Ind.: University of Notre Dame Press, 2000.

Synge, John Millington. *The Aran Islands.* Boston: John W. Luce, 1911.

———. *Riders to the Sea.* In *The Playboy of the Western World and Other Plays.* Oxford: Oxford University Press, 1995, 1–12.

———. *The Playboy of the Western World.* Boston: John W. Luce, 1911.

Nelson O'Ceallaigh Ritschel

T

Tale of Possessors Self-Dispossessed, A

That's right! A hair of the dog that bit you! That's the ticket! We Harfords have been bitten by 111 dogs—and they're all the same dog, and his name is Greed of Living and when he bites you there's a fever comes and a great thirst and a great drinking to kill it, and a grand drunk, and a terrible hangover and headache and remorse of conscience—and a sick empty stomach without greed or appetite. But take a hair of the dog and the sun will rise again for you—and the appetite and the thirst will come back, and you can forget—and begin all over! (quoted in Gallup 190)

At one point, this was the speech that would close the last play, *The Hair of the Dog,* in Eugene O'Neill's largely finished 11-play cycle *A Tale of Possessors Self-Dispossessed.* In a later draft of the outline, the closing speech, by a different character, reads:

What solution do you offer? Beautiful solutions, but no evasion over consciousness. We had every chance, brains education, great teacher (Christ, Buddha, etc.)—have had them always with us. But greed checked us. Let us try ourselves, find ourselves guilty, condemn ourselves. And let us make the noble effort of our senses be to build a better character big enough to hold all the world, rid this earth of ourselves, give the insects a chance. They may prove as greedy and as brainless as we. They may prove no better, but certainly, oh very certainly, the cannot be worse! (quoted in Gallup 191)

Though these dark, nihilistic, statements on human nature are said by characters in a play and not by O'Neill himself, they are drafts of the last ideas he wanted to leave with the audience at the end of 11 plays on American history from 1754 to 1932 as lived through by one family, the Harfords. In an interview in *Time* on October 21, 1946, he expressed his sense of loss of values, saying, "I feel . . . that America is the greatest failure in history. It was given everything, more than any other country in history, but we've squandered our soul by trying to possess something outside of it, and we'll end as that game usually does, by losing our soul and the thing outside it too. But why go on—the Bible said it much better: 'For what shall it profit a man if he gain the whole world, and lose his own soul?'" (quoted in Gallup 260).

This biblical verse, Matthew 16:26, became the underlying theme of the cycle, and its title, *A Tale of Possessors Self-Dispossessed,* may be seen as a restatement of its insight that by possessing something and identifying oneself with this possession, one may lose oneself—that is, one may be self-dispossessed. In this way, all the notes for the cycle describe characters attempting to become someone by possessing things, ideas, or other people and in the process losing a sense of who they are, mainly expressed as bad conscience (followed by anger at feeling badly) or, equally unsuccessfully, attempting to become someone by being possessed by—living for—others, ideas, and so on. In the outline for *The Man on Iron Horseback,* play 10 in the cycle, an old eunuch in Shanghai in 1892 or 1893 says to Jonathan Harford, the railroad magnate, "One should look with the quiet eyes of peace at everything and see that it is nothing." Jonathan: "Even at oneself?" The eunuch: "Above all at oneself." Jonathan says: "You must possess everything in order to be free of it. It is easy to give up things you have not, but I expect the desire is still there. To possess desire, then you can be free of it" (quoted in Gallup 139). Later on in the same outline, Jonathan has a conversation with his main competitor, Goddard. Says Jonathan, "I can travel on my own line now from New York to Yokahoma. You can congratulate me on that, can't you?" Goddard: "No. I'm afraid I can't: for when you get to Yokahoma you will still be you" (quoted in Gallup 141).

The intended cycle, of which only one play was completed by O'Neill, A TOUCH OF THE POET, was a huge undertaking, and conceptualizing it and outlining it took up a substantial part of O'Neill's creative energies in the 1930s and early 1940s, during a time when his health was not very good.

The evolution of ideas that eventually led to O'Neill's cycle went through a number of stages involving first five, then seven, then eight, then nine, and finally 11 plays, and as the numbers grew the cycle extended both forwards and backwards in time. The final cycle consisted of the following titles, in order: *Give Me Liberty and—, The Rebellion of the Humble, Greed of the Meek, And Give Me Death, A Touch of the Poet,* MORE STATELY MANSIONS, *The Calms of Capricorn, The Earth is the Limit, Nothing is Lost but Honor, The Man on Iron Horseback,* and *The Hair of the Dog.* Since only one of the plays was completed (*More Stately Mansions* was near completion when the playwright died), and O'Neill rewrote significantly between outlines and various drafts, there is no way of knowing what the final outcome of the cycle would have been or whether, once he had drafted all the plays, it would still consist of these 11 plays.

Nevertheless, Donald Gallup, the curator of Yale University's Collection of American Literature,

adapted the notes for O'Neill's planned four-act installment *The Calms of Capricorn* into a performable play. O'Neill worked on the scenario intermittently from 1931 to 1935, and in 1982 Gallup published his adaptation in addition to a transcription of the scenario. O'Neill planned *Calms* to be the seventh (originally the fifth) installment to *A Tale of Possessors,* and the action takes place from 1857 to 1858; it was meant as a sequel to *More Stately Mansions,* with Simon and Sara Harford's son Ethan, now a clipper-ship captain, as the protagonist. Gallup's adaptation has never been produced, and he admitted in his introductory remarks that "to some it will be a violation, pure and simple, of O'Neill's expressed wishes, and therefore indefensible. To others, it may be welcomed as giving additional invaluable details of the vast project to which America's foremost dramatist devoted most of his time, thought, and creative energies from 1934 to 1939—a period that should have been his most productive and mature . . . Its 'development' into a more accessible form is designed merely to increase its readability; while adhering as closely as possible and with a minimum of elaboration to O'Neill's original text" (xii, xiii).

Travis Bogard observes that "The plays appear to have been connected to the development of transportation facilities throughout the nineteenth century, from coaches and the canal boats Con Melody [in *A Touch of the Poet*] inveighs against, to clipper ships, railroads and, finally, automobiles. In each plan, the developing lines of transportation are the routes for possession of the country, moving through the land like the greedy fingers of the Sisters [Ethan Harford's half-sisters, appearing in *Give Me Liberty and—, The Rebellion of the Humble, Greed of the Meek,* and in *And Give Me Death*], bringing power to the possessors" (381). O'Neill wished all notes and outlines destroyed, apart from *A Touch of the Poet,* insisting, "Nobody must be allowed to finish my plays" (quoted in Gelbs 938).

The scope of the projected cyle attests to the vastness and inventiveness of O'Neill's dramatic vision. Says Travis Bogard: "That O'Neill could not complete the historical cycle as it was designed is one of the greatest loses the drama in any time has sustained. . . . Nothing in the drama, except

Shakespeare's two cycles on British history, could have been set beside it. The two plays that have survived [*A Touch of the Poet* and the uncompleted *More Stately Mansions*] reveal something of the power of life that beat in it, but they show only vestiges of what its full plan realized would have provided: a prophetic epitome for the course of American destiny" (Bogard 369).

Eugene O'Neill at his desk at Tao House *(Courtesy of the Yale Collection of American Literature, Beinecke Rare Book and Manuscript Library)*

Bibliography

Bogard, Travis. *Contures in Time: The Plays of Eugene O'Neill.* New York: Oxford University Press, 1972.

Bower, Martha. "The Cycle Women and Carlotta Monterey O'Neill." *Eugene O'Neill Newsletter* 10, no. 2 (Summer–Fall 1986).

Gallup Donald C. *Eugene O'Neill and His Eleven-Play Cycle, "A Tale of Possessors Self-Dispossessed."* New Haven, Conn.: Yale University Press, 1998.

———. Introductory note to *The Calms of Capricorn: A Play Developed from O'Neill's Scenario. With a Transcription of the Scenario.* Edited, adapted, and with an introduction by Donald Gallup. New Haven: Ticknor & Fields, 1982, vii–xiii.

Gelb, Arthur. "O'Neill's Hopeless Hope for a Giant Cycle," *New York Times,* September 28, 1958.

Gelb, Arthur, and Barbara Gelb. *O'Neill.* London: Jonathan Cape, 1962.

Barbara Gelb. "The 'Child' O'Neill Tore Up," *New York Times,* October 29, 1967.

O'Neill, Eugene. *The Calms of Capricorn: A Play Developed from O'Neill's Scenario: With a Transcription of the Scenario.* Edited, adapted, and with an introductory note by Donald Gallup. New Haven, Conn.: Ticknor & Fields, 1982.

P. K. Brask

Tao House In 1936, displeased with the tropical climate and unexpected lack of privacy at SEA ISLAND, and only four years after moving into their oceanfront villa on the Georgia coast, Eugene and CARLOTTA MONTEREY O'NEILL decided to relocate to the Pacific Northwest, 3,000 miles from the unhappy memories that colored their attitude toward the East. But almost immediately, problems of climate and privacy intruded there as well: The autumn rains and fog of Puget Sound reminded them of the wet winters endured at Le (du) Plessis, the rented château in France, while O'Neill's NOBEL PRIZE IN LITERATURE, announced soon after their arrival, brought the hated limelight to their doorstep. Decamping for San Francisco's Fairmont Hotel, the O'Neills began searching for a secluded homesite in sunnier California. Not for the first time, Carlotta complained to friends that they had no roots, no home, but they soon found 158 acres for sale on a high slope overlooking the San Ramon Valley at Danville, California, and there the couple built a house they would occupy for six years and two months, the longest they would spend at any of their many places of residence.

As at Sea Island, Carlotta oversaw the design and construction of a dwelling tailored to her husband's needs. She filled it with Chinese furniture and accessories, and they called it Tao House, perhaps in the hope that there they might experience the inner harmony to be gained through the ancient Chinese belief. For a time it seemed to work, for on this semiarid hillside, far from the sound of the SEA where he claimed he felt most at home, Eugene O'Neill wrote the two masterpieces that would consolidate his status as America's greatest dramatist: *The ICEMAN COMETH* (1940) and *LONG DAY'S JOURNEY INTO NIGHT* (1941). Here he also wrote A *MOON FOR THE MISBEGOTTEN, HUGHIE,* and A *TOUCH OF THE POET,* the latter being the only completed part of an ambitious cycle of plays, *A Tale of Possessors Self-Dispossessed*, begun at Sea Island.

Simpler in design and detail than the Sea Island house, Tao House was to become the most settled and satisfactory of the numerous places occupied by the O'Neills during their long quest for a home, and it may be argued that the success of this mountainside retreat was a major factor enabling Eugene to write his greatest plays. Biographer Stephen Black has pointed out that the layout of the house was designed to allow its strong-willed occupants a sufficient degree of separation to allow them to live together in harmony, "coming together by choice rather than jostling by constant necessity" (471). Eugene felt at home here, perhaps for the first time in his life. Coming to terms with his family history and able at last to move beyond mourning and tragedy (Black 447), he could now respond fully and fluently to the inspiration that resulted in his late masterworks.

The psychological and physical conditions enabling those masterworks could not last, however. O'Neill's health problems were intensifying, chief among them a debilitating tremor in his hands, and wartime shortages and disruptions also made life on the isolated mountainside increasingly difficult. He was frustrated by the inability of his son SHANE RUDRAIGH O'NEILL to find his way in life, and happy memories of two brief visits from daughter OONA O'NEILL turned sour when in 1943, at age 18, she married 54-year-old Charlie Chaplin, so angering her 55-year-old father that he never communicated with her again. With Eugene unable to write, Carlotta coping with health problems of her own, and their sometimes shaky relationship aggravated by their inability to find the domestic staff they depended on, Tao House and its furnishings

Tao House in Danville, California *(Courtesy of the Hageman Collection, The Eugene O'Neill Foundation)*

were sold, and early in 1944 the couple moved to San Francisco, eventually settling into a suite at the Huntington, where they stayed for 20 months.

Once again, O'Neill had abandoned a home, resuming the nomadic pattern begun during his early years as a boarding-school student and son of a traveling actor whose only real home was the summer cottage in NEW LONDON, CONNECTICUT. The pattern continued through his young adulthood and three marriages, and despite repeated talk about putting down roots with Carlotta, the closest they came to doing so was at Tao House. In the 24 years of their marriage, they occupied at least 16 different mansions, apartments, penthouses, and hotel suites, some for a matter of weeks while a new residence was being built or remodeled, some for months, Sea Island for four years, and Tao House for just over six. Of their precipitous departure from the French château in 1931, BIOGRAPHERS Arthur and Barbara Gelb noted that O'Neill had "the remarkable capacity of being able to walk away from a country estate as casually as he had once moved his orange crates out of an unpaid-for GREENWICH VILLAGE flat. He seemed unable to regard any house as a home, however much he had craved it at first and however elaborately it was appointed for him" (734).

But Tao House was different. O'Neill called it his "final harbor," and it probably would have been had wartime exigencies and chronic health problems not forced them to leave a place they had come to love but felt "crushed" by, as Eugene wrote to GEORGE JEAN NATHAN and others (O'Neill 550). It did become the final harbor for their beloved Dalmatian Blemie, who died after a long, sad decline and was buried on the property. As his end approached, Carlotta was prompted to remark that Blemie was "the only one of our children who has not disillusioned us" (quoted in Sheaffer 518). O'Neill's extraordinarily poignant tribute to their pet, "The Last Will and Testament of Silverdene Emblem O'Neill," echoes the ailing playwright's growing awareness of his own mortality and figurative homelessness.

In San Francisco, gazing at the magnificent view from the Huntington, O'Neill told a visitor, "I have never had a home, never had a chance to establish roots. I grew up in hotels. My mother never had

a home . . . It's strange, but the time I spent at sea on a sailing ship was the only time I ever felt I had roots in any place" (quoted in Sheaffer 553). Despite the convenience of hotel living and ready access to medical care, both missed their friends in the East and were desperate for change, so in October 1945 the O'Neill's returned to New York City, where reconnection with the theater world acted as a tonic for a time. But the flawed premieres of *The Iceman Cometh* and *A Moon for the Misbegotten* signaled the decline of their author's reputation, and the comforts of a luxurious East Side penthouse did nothing to alleviate their disappointment or ease the simmering tension between husband and wife borne out of Carlotta's growing hostility to many of Eugene's friends. Reconciling after a brief estrangement, in 1948 they once again put the city behind them, heading this time for MARBLEHEAD, MASSACHUSETTS. Buoyed up by the prospect of again living day and night with the sound of waves, gulls, and foghorns, O'Neill wrote to SAXE COMMINS that he felt he might be able to write again, "and again have some roots—of seaweed—with my feet in a New England sea" (O'Neill 580).

Bibliography

Black, Stephen A. *Eugene O'Neill: Beyond Mourning and Tragedy.* New Haven, Conn.: Yale University Press, 1999.

Gelb, Arthur, and Barbara Gelb. *O'Neill.* Enlarged ed. New York: Harper & Row, 1973.

O'Neill, Eugene. *Selected Letters of Eugene O'Neill.* Edited by Travis Bogard and Jackson R. Bryer. New Haven, Conn.: Yale University Press, 1988.

Sheaffer, Louis. *O'Neill: Son and Artist.* Boston: Little, Brown, 1973.

Brian Rogers

Theatre Guild   A major New York theatrical producing organization, the Theatre Guild was founded at the end of World War I as a replacement for the defunct WASHINGTON SQUARE PLAYERS, which had closed in spring 1918. Guild board members, most of whom had been founders of the Washington Square Players, included Lawrence Langner, Philip Moeller, Rollo Peters, Lee Simonson, Maurice Wertheim, and Helen Westley, with Theresa Helburn and Dudley Digges emerging as important forces when they joined shortly after the organization's establishment. The Theatre Guild aimed to raise the quality of plays and productions on the Broadway stage, inspired by the rise of the "Little Theatre" movement in the preceding decade and the "new stagecraft" techniques arising from modernist Europe. The guild's first production, Jacinto Benavente's *The Bonds of Interest* (1919), was a succès d'estime, but the critical acclaim and popular success accorded their second production, St. John Ervine's *John Ferguson* (1919), initiated a prolific era of producing that continued for decades and encompassed some of the most important American and international plays of the period.

In the early 1920s, Theatre Guild productions were often of European plays, including acclaimed stagings of seven of GEORGE BERNARD SHAW's plays—among them, *Heartbreak House* (1920) and *Saint Joan* (1923)—and the work of other modernists, including Ferenc Molnar's *Liliom* (1921) and *The Guardsman* (1924), Leonid Andreyev's *He Who Gets Slapped* (1922), and Karel Capek's *R.U.R.* (1922). Within a few years, the guild shifted its energies toward the works of new American dramatists, staging the first productions of Elmer Rice's *The Adding Machine* (1923), Sidney Howard's PULITZER PRIZE–winning *They Knew What They Wanted* (1924), S. N. Behrman's *The Second Man* (1927) and *Biography* (1932), Dubose and Dorothy Heyward's *Porgy* (1927) and its musicalized version *Porgy and Bess* (1935), Maxwell Anderson's *Elizabeth the Queen* (1930) and *Mary of Scotland* (1933), Robert E. Sherwood's Pulitzer Prize–winning *Idiot's Delight* (1936) and *There Shall Be No Night* (1940), Philip Barry's *The Philadelphia Story* (1939), William Saroyan's Pulitzer Prize–winning *The Time of Your Life* (1939), the acclaimed PAUL ROBESON in *Othello* (1943), Rodgers and Hammerstein's *Oklahoma!* (1943) and *Carousel* (1945), and William Inge's *Come Back Little Sheba* (1950), among many others.

Not surprisingly, the Theatre Guild also produced O'Neill plays, although early on they turned down several, including *The* STRAW (1918–19), GOLD (1920), *The* FIRST MAN (1920–21), the Pulitzer Prize–winning "ANNA CHRISTIE" (1921), *The* FOUNTAIN (1921–22), and WELDED (1922–23). O'Neill wrote to critic GEORGE JEAN NATHAN in 1919 in the aftermath of the guild's rejection of *The Straw*, lamenting the "virus of popular success" he believed had infected the Guild after the lucrative outcomes of *John Ferguson* earlier that year. O'Neill opined that "the Guild is doomed to fail through the same timid endeavor to please 'their public'" as he believed had infected the Washington Square Players. Despite this, O'Neill continued to submit new works to the guild.

The Theatre Guild's shift toward new American plays in the mid-1920s paralleled O'Neill's rise to prominence and, regretting rejections of earlier O'Neill works, most particularly *"Anna Christie,"* the guild sought opportunities to produce his subsequent plays. Many of O'Neill's earliest works had been staged by the PROVINCETOWN PLAYERS before his partnership with TRIUMVIRATE KENNETH MACGOWAN and ROBERT EDMOND JONES, but beginning with MARCO MILLIONS (1928) and continuing through a failed 1947 pre-Broadway tour of O'Neill's final play, A MOON FOR THE MISBEGOTTEN (1943), the Theatre Guild staged virtually all of O'Neill's plays, including the Pulitzer Prize–winning STRANGE INTERLUDE (1928), DYNAMO (1929), MOURNING BECOMES ELECTRA (1931), AH, WILDERNESS! (1933), DAYS WITHOUT END (1933), and *The* ICEMAN COMETH (written in 1939 and produced in 1946).

O'Neill's collaboration with the Theatre Guild was a mixed blessing, which he himself noted in a 1928 letter to AGNES BOULTON, his second wife, noting that both *Marco Millions* and *Strange Interlude* were hits, but that the latter was playing to "practically subscribers only (at 2.50 a seat). There will be hardly anyone able to see it but subscribers—the Golden [Theatre] is so small—for six weeks yet. So out of my two successes I'm not liable to become rich. Working with the Guild has its advantages—but also its financial disadvantages. When you get a real hit you can't realize on it" (O'Neill 275). The balance of successes and failures were tipped slightly toward hits, with O'Neill winning critical acclaim for *Strange Interlude* and *Mourning Becomes Electra* and particular financial rewards with the long run (and subsequent tours) of his only comedy, *Ah, Wilderness!*, starring Broadway legend George M. Cohan. However, Theatre Guild productions of O'Neill's plays also brought bitter failure with the flops of *Dynamo* and *Days Without End*, the last encouraging O'Neill's withdrawal from active production of new plays for more than a decade. Speculation in the press that O'Neill had broken with the guild over his disappointment in these failures roused him to take pains to deny a rift and he expressed gratitude for the guild's support of his work. When he finally agreed to a production of *The Iceman Cometh*, he allowed the Theatre Guild to stage it in 1946. Received apathetically by critics and audiences, this disappointment, coupled with the 1947 out-of-town closing of the Theatre Guild–produced *A Moon for the Misbegotten*, O'Neill's last play written in 1943, and mounting health problems, led him to turn away from stage production of his works for the remainder of his life.

Bibliography

Eaton, Walter Prichard. *The Theatre Guild: The First Ten Years*. New York: Scholarly Press, 1971.

Langner, Lawrence, and Teresa Helburn. *The Story of the Theatre Guild: 1919–1947*. New York: Theatre Guild, 1947.

Nadel, Norman. *A Pictorial History of the Theatre Guild*. Special Material by Lawrence Langner and Armina Marshall. New York: Crown, 1969.

O'Neill, Eugene. *Selected Letters of Eugene O'Neill*. Edited by Travis Bogard and Jackson R. Bryer. New York: Limelight Editions, 1994.

Shea, Laura. "O'Neill, the Theatre Guild, and *A Moon for the Misbegotten*." *Eugene O'Neill Review* 27 (2005): 76–97.

Vena, Gary. "Chipping at the Iceman: The Text and the 1946 Theatre Guild Production." *Eugene O'Neill Newsletter* 9, no. 3 (Winter 1985): 11–17.

Wainscott, Ronald H. "Exploring the Religion of the Dead: Philip Moeller Directs O'Neill's *Mourning Becomes Electra*." *Theatre History Studies* 7 (1987): 28–39.

Waldau, Roy S. *Vintage Years of the Theatre Guild, 1928–1939*. Cleveland, Ohio, and London: The Press of Case Western Reserve University, 1972.

James Fisher

"Thirst" and Other One-Act Plays (1914)   The first volume O'Neill ever published, *"Thirst" and Other One-Act Plays* includes The WEB, THIRST, WARNINGS, FOG, and RECKLESSNESS. It appeared in 1914 through Gorham Press of Boston with the financial help of $450 from O'Neill's father, JAMES O'NEILL. Some time after, O'Neill called these early plays the "first five Stations of the Cross in my plod up Parnassus" (quoted in Sheaffer 273). The book's sales were negligible, and O'Neill admitted late in life to the critic Mark Van Doren (in a letter dated April 27, 1944) the irony that "the A-1 collector's item of all my stuff and has sold as much as $150 a copy . . . the publisher at one time offered me all the remainder of the edition (and that was practically all the edition, for few copies were sold) at 30 cents a copy! With the usual financial acumen of an author, I scorned his offer as a waste of good money on my lousy drama!" (quoted in Sheaffer 291; with its dust jacket intact, the book now sells for upward of $2,000).

In summer 1913, family friend Clayton Hamilton, a playwright and critic, stayed with the O'Neills for several weeks at MONTE CRISTO COTTAGE in NEW LONDON, CONNECTICUT, and strongly encouraged the budding playwright. After the volume came out, Hamilton wrote a short *Bookman* review (1915) that deserves quoting in its entirety:

> Another playwright of promise is Mr. Eugene G. O'Neill—a son of the noted actor, Mr. James O'Neill—who has recently published five one-act plays under the title of *Thirst*. This writer's favorite mood is that of horror. *He deals with grim and ghastly situations that would become intolerable if they were protracted beyond the limits of a single sudden act.* He seems to be familiar with the sea; for three of these five plays deal with terrors that attend the tragedy of a ship-wreck. He shows a keen sense of the reactions of character under stress of violent emotion; and his dialogue is almost brutal in its power. More than one of these plays should be available for such an institution as the Princess Theatre in New York. (emphasis mine, Hamilton 229)

The line in italics above might be read as the germ for O'Neill's ideas for BEFORE BREAKFAST and WHERE

Provincetown Players performing *Thirst* at the Wharf Theatre in 1916. From left: Louise Bryant, George Cram "Jig" Cook, and Eugene O'Neill as the "Mulatto Sailor" *(Courtesy of the Yale Collection of American Literature, Beinecke Rare Book and Manuscript Library)*

THE CROSS IS MADE, both written in the years immediately following Hamilton's review and both dealing with "grim and ghastly situations" expressly designed to "become intolerable" to the audience, though the plays were one-acters. O'Neill thanked Hamilton in a letter five years later (1920, the year he won his first PULITZER PRIZE for BEYOND THE HORIZON), writing, "Do you know that your review was the only one that poor volume ever received? And, if brief, it was favorable! You can't imagine what it meant, coming from you. It held out a hope at a very hopeless time. It *did* send me to the hatters. It made me believe I was arriving with a bang; and at that period I very much needed someone whose authority I respected to admit I was getting somewhere" (O'Neill 125). But following the triumphant reception of *Beyond the Horizon,* for which Hamilton also wrote a "fine tribute" in *Vogue* (O'Neill 124), the "hopeless hope" he describes of his early years continued to haunt the author and stood as one of the most significant themes in his plays, no matter what his professional accomplishments, to the end of his life.

Bibliography

Hamilton, Clayton. "O'Neill's First Book: A Review of *Thirst, and Other One-Act Plays.*" In *O'Neill and His Plays: Four Decades of Criticism,* edited by Oscar Cargill, N. Bryllion Fagin, and William J. Fisher, 229. New York: New York University Press, 1961.

O'Neill, Eugene. *Selected Letters of Eugene O'Neill.* Edited by Travis Bogard and Jackson R. Bryer. New York: Limelight Editions, 1994.

Sheaffer, Louis. *O'Neill: Son and Playwright.* Boston: Little, Brown, 1968.

Triumvirate, the   See EXPERIMENTAL THEATRE, INC.

Tucker, Benjamin Ricketson (1854–1939)   Born on April 17, 1854, into a wealthy, liberal family in New Bedford, Massachusetts, and raised in a climate of radical Protestantism and Paineite individualism, Benjamin Tucker's personal experiences convinced him that people, following their own reason in a community of fellowship, could govern themselves without recourse to instituted authorities such as the state. Tucker was the first prominent American thinker to identify himself as an anarchist. He would become the central figure in the emergence and development of PHILOSOPHICAL ANARCHISM (also known as individualist anarchism) in the United States, introducing the works of Pierre-Joseph Proudhon and Max Stirner, among others, to North American audiences. He was well-rounded, and in addition to ANARCHISM, Tucker advocated egoism, atheism, and free love. Influenced by his radical upbringing, he refused to sanction violence in the cause of anarchy. Indeed, he would eventually break with the anarchist communist organizer EMMA GOLDMAN over her support for the attempted assassination of the industrialist Henry Clay Frick by Goldman's partner, Alexander Berkman.

Tucker's bookstore, the Unique Book Shop in New York City, proved an important social venue for anarchists and other freethinkers of various stripes. Eugene O'Neill was introduced to Tucker by his friend Louis Holladay during his time at Princeton in 1906–07 and soon became a regular at the Unique Book Shop. The eclectic collection at Tucker's bookstore exposed O'Neill to experimental and provocative works of philosophy, politics, and art that were not available anywhere else in the United States. Many of the works had been translated or published by Tucker himself, who was the first North American publisher to print Max Stirner's 1844 individualist classic *The Ego and Its Own* (1907), a book that was quite influential in the development of O'Neill's political consciousness. Tucker also published the important libertarian journals *Radical Review* and the highly influential *Liberty,* which became regarded as the best English-language anarchist journal. He was admired by writers including GEORGE BERNARD SHAW and Walt Whitman.

Tucker's anarchism, unlike that of his anarchist communist contemporaries Goldman and Berkman, was based on gradual, nonviolent rather than revolutionary social and cultural change. In place of force, Tucker advocated the liberation of the individual's creative capacities. He looked to gradual enlightenment through alternative institutions, schools, cooperative banks, and workers' associations as practical means to enact change. Social change, for Tucker, required personal transformation first and foremost, a perspective that

O'Neill himself claimed as a great influence on his own outlook. At the same time, while rejecting force, which he termed domination, Tucker did assert the right of individuals and groups to defend themselves.

Tucker spent the last years of his life in seclusion, choosing to live an anarchist life quietly with his lover Pearl Johnson and daughter Oriole Tucker in FRANCE. He died in Monaco on June 22, 1939, age 85.

Bibliography

Diggins, John Patrick. *Eugene O'Neill's America: Desire under Democracy.* Chicago: University of Chicago Press, 2007.

Dowling, Robert M. "On Eugene O'Neill's 'Philosophical Anarchism'" 29 (Spring 2007): 50–72.

Pfister, Joel. *Staging Depth: Eugene O'Neill and the Politics of Psychological Discourse.* Chapel Hill: University of North Carolina Press, 1995.

J. Shantz

W

Washington Square Players (1915–1918)   The Washington Square Players, along with the PROVINCETOWN PLAYERS, advanced the tradition of Off-Broadway theater and fostered the creativity of native playwrights like Eugene O'Neill by giving them an outlet for their artistic exploration free from the commercial constraints of Broadway. Specifically, they were a group of bohemian artists that offered "the amateur actor, appearing in a small theatre [an opportunity] to perform plays whose purpose seemed to lie in poetic truth or psychological reality" (Bigsby and Wilmeth 10). According to the group's manifesto, the Washington Square Players hoped to establish "a higher standard" in AMERICAN THEATER through "experiment and initiative," with the stipulation that for a play to be produced, it "must have artistic merit," and "[p]reference [would] be given to American plays" (Langner 94). However, the group was criticized by some, including O'Neill, because they focused more energy on competing with Broadway and courting the press and less on nurturing American talent and creativity. While the Washington Square Players and the Provincetown Players contributed in much the same way to the development of Off-Broadway drama, the Washington Square Players were generally less committed to O'Neill's work.

Inspired in part by dissatisfaction with the LIBERAL CLUB's attempt to begin a dramatic branch, Lawrence Langner, Albert Boni, and Ida Rauh formed the Washington Square Players in December 1914. Only two months later, on February 19, 1915, the Washington Square Players opened at the New York Bandbox Theatre on East 57th Street with three one-act plays and a pantomime. Two of the plays, *Licensed* by Lawrence Langer and *Eugenically Speaking* by Edward Goodman, were original works by members of the organization. They also paired *Interior,* by the Belgian Maurice Maeterlinck, with an anonymous pantomime entitled *Another Interior,* in which the hero is a stomach's gastric juice and the antagonists are food entering the digestive tract. This opening program typified the Washington Square Players' performances in that the majority of their productions were satirical one-act plays.

Some of the more noteworthy American plays produced by the Washington Square Players were *Moondown* by JOHN REED (March 1915), *Overtones* by Alice Gerstenberg (November 1915), *Trifles* by SUSAN GLASPELL (November 1916), *The Girl in the Coffin* by Theodore Dreiser (December 1917), *Suppressed Desires* by Susan Glaspell and GEORGE CRAM "JIG" COOK (January 1918), *The Home of the Free* by Elmer Rice (April 1918), and *Close the Book* by Susan Glaspell. Although the group rejected several of O'Neill's plays, including THIRST and BOUND EAST FOR CARDIFF, the Washington Square Players did perform O'Neill's IN THE ZONE (October 1917) and *The ROPE* (May 1918) at the Comedy Theatre, the larger venue where the organization moved after gaining popularity.

The Rope was on the Washington Square Players' final playbill. They disbanded in spring 1918 due to growing financial tension and a decline in membership as Americans were drawn further into World War I. Before separating, the group produced 62 one-act plays as well as six full-length plays. In 1919, Lawrence Langner and several other Washington Square Players reunited to form the THEATRE GUILD.

Bibliography

Bigsby, Christopher, and Don B. Wilmeth, eds. Introduction to *The Cambridge History of American Theater,* vol. 2. 3 vols. Cambridge: Cambridge University Press, 1999.

Langner, Lawrence. *The Magic Curtain: The Story of Life in Two Fields, Theatre and Invention.* New York: E. P. Dutton, 1951.

Shawna Lesseur-Blas

Wharf Theatre　The Wharf Theatre in Provincetown, Massachusetts, has become legendary as the venue where Eugene O'Neill's plays were first performed. Situated at the end of a dilapidated pier known as Lewis Wharf, the theater was actually a gray, weathered fish house that had been spruced up by the PROVINCETOWN PLAYERS for their summer productions. With its dramatic ocean backdrop, this "theater-on-the-wharf" proved an ideal setting for O'Neill's early SEA-inspired plays.

No official records of the Wharf Theatre remain, but memoirs, correspondence, drawings, and other materials provide a fairly accurate picture of its design and appearance. The building was not large, measuring just 25 by 35 feet wide and 15 feet high, and seating about 100 people. Lingering odors of smoke, salt, and tar permeated the building, as did the sounds and smells of the ocean, whose waters slapped the weathered floor planks that hugged the worn pilings on which the wharf stood.

Like many other Provincetown piers, Lewis Wharf had fallen into disrepair by the early 1900s, a relic of the Cape's codfishing heyday. Situated below Commercial Street, it originally stretched over 300 feet into the harbor but had been whittled down by weather to about 100 feet. In 1915, novelist and labor journalist Mary Heaton Vorse and her second husband, Joseph O'Brien, bought the rick-

The Wharf Theatre　*(© Leona Rust Egan)*

ety structure, which had a couple of small shacks on it along with the larger building.

That summer, Vorse rented the first floor of the fish house to artist Margaret Steele (wife of writer Wilbur Daniel Steele) and leased out the second floor to the New York City Modern Art School. In July, Steele turned her space over to the burgeoning Provincetown Players, who wanted to stage plays there, despite the building's sad shape. That summer's fare included *Constancy* by Neith Boyce as well as *Suppressed Desires* by GEORGE CRAM "JIG" COOK and his wife SUSAN GLASPELL. A second bill in September featured Cook's *Change Your Style* and Wilbur Steele's *Contemporaries.* Buoyed by the season's success, the Players began planning an encore for the following summer. Meanwhile, they labored to refurbish the ramshackle performance space, hauling out nets, tackle, anchors, and other debris left by the fishermen. Jig Cook arranged the erection of a sectional stage measuring 10 by 12 feet near the back wall, where wide doors, through which fish had once been hauled, could be opened to expose the ocean, with its mesmerizing horizon of sea and sky.

A near disaster came close to squelching the 1916 season. Two days before the scheduled July 13 opening, a fire ripped through the Wharf Theatre, destroying the stage curtain and scorching the walls. But the Players' concerted efforts to make hasty repairs allowed the first bill to open on time, a trio of one-act plays: Boyce's *Winter's Night,* Steele's *Not Smart,* and JOHN REED's *Freedom.* However, it was the season's second bill that was to prove the most memorable and would establish Provincetown as a major site in AMERICAN THEATER history. On July 28, a suitably foggy night, the second bill opened with Eugene O'Neill's *BOUND EAST FOR CARDIFF,* followed by Steele's *Not Smart* and Louise Bryant's *The Game.* Other plays staged at the Wharf Theatre that summer included Boyce's *Enemies,* Glaspell's landmark work *Trifles,* Reed's *Eternal Triangle,* and a children's play by Henry Marion Hall titled *Mother Carey's Chickens.*

In total, the theater hosted 16 productions during this second and last season. The final productions of the Provincetown Players at the Wharf Theatre took place on September 1 and 2, 1916, with *THIRST*—O'Neill's first sea play—as well as reprisals of *The Game* and *Suppressed Desires.* Two days later, on September 4, the Players met in the theater to officially outline their mission statement and to formally adopt the name of the Provincetown Players. Not long afterward, the troupe moved its headquarters to a brownstone on Macdougal Street in GREENWICH VILLAGE, but leaving an indelible identity and legacy in Provincetown.

After the departure of the Provincetown Players, the Wharf Theatre and the pier on which it stood endured for another six years before finally collapsing into the sea during a winter storm in 1922. During these intervening years, Lewis Wharf continued to attract a crowd of bohemians, some of whom, in 1920, opened a coffee house in the old theater, called the Sixes and Sevens. One of those artists was Courtney Allen, who would later construct a model of the Wharf Theatre based primarily upon his own recollections. That replica, commissioned by the Provincetown Museum and measuring six feet long, 32 inches wide, and 27 inches high, was

officially unveiled in a small ceremony on July 24, 1963. Speakers at that event included Vorse, who was then in her 80s, as well as Charles Hapgood, the son of Neith Boyce and her husband Hutchins Hapgood.

Bibliography

Egan, Leona Rust. *Provincetown as a Stage.* Orleans, Mass.: Parnassus Imprints, 1994.

Gelb, Arthur. "Wharf-Theater Era Takes a Curtain Call," *New York Times,* July 24, 1963.

Sarlos, Robert Karoly. *Jig Cook and the Provincetown Players.* Boston: University of Massachusetts Press, 1982.

Vorse, Mary Heaton. *Time and the Town.* New York: Dial, 1942.

Karen Charamaine Blansfield

Williams, Tennessee (Thomas Lanier Williams III) (1911–1983)

Born on March 26, 1911, in Columbus, Mississippi, Thomas Lanier Williams III—better known as Tennessee Williams—became one of the best-known American playwrights of the 20th century. He is, in fact, generally regarded as the foremost post–World War II American dramatist, a theatrical innovator surpassed only by Eugene O'Neill in the realization of his ambitious goals. Williams's opinion of O'Neill varied from dismissive to admiring, but he was quoted near the end of his life as acknowledging that "O'Neill gave birth to the American theatre and died for it." Honored with PULITZER PRIZEs for *A Streetcar Named Desire* (1947) and *Cat on a Hot Tin Roof* (1955), Williams wrote poetic, impressionistic, character-driven dramas in the southern Gothic style, probing repressed tensions and sexual confusions and shocking mid-20th century audiences unaccustomed to the frank intimacies and intense emotionalism of his works. Williams initiated a period of renewed energy and excitement in AMERICAN THEATER just as O'Neill had done in the decade following World War I, inspiring contemporaries toward innovation in form and content.

A prolific writer frequently praised for the lyricism of his language and for recurring themes examining the difficulty of the artistic, emotionally fragile, or fugitive outsider to negotiate life's realities, Williams shared with O'Neill a desire to expand the boundaries of realistic drama (laced with symbolic and poetic imagery) in such works as *The Glass Menagerie* (1944), *Summer and Smoke* (1948), and *The Rose Tattoo* (1951), along with *A Streetcar Named Desire*. And also like O'Neill, Williams's work grew more experimental over time, including controversial plays such as *Camino Real* (1953), a bold plunge into surreal theatrical illusionism; *Cat on a Hot Tin Roof*; and subsequent plays such as *Orpheus Descending* (1957), *Suddenly Last Summer* (1958), and *The Night of the Iguana* (1961), in which increasingly grotesque symbolic elements depicted an increasingly predatory universe. Problems with alcohol and drugs resulting from personal difficulties, including the death of his longtime lover Frank Merlo, did not slow Williams's writing, but after the early 1960s, his plays won scant approval from critics despite continued experimentation.

Williams's first success, *The Glass Menagerie*, a semiautobiographical "memory play," featured legendary stage star Laurette Taylor as Amanda Wingfield, a character modeled on Williams's domineering mother. The play included a Williams alter ego, Tom Wingfield, the narrator. This part-true, part-fictional account of his family's pained relationships closely parallels O'Neill's LONG DAY'S JOURNEY INTO NIGHT (1939), itself a "memory play" containing entwined elements of truth and fiction to illuminate the universal qualities of familial dysfunction, a central theme firmly linking the plays of O'Neill and Williams.

As with O'Neill, Williams's addictions inform his plays, much as they surely made the task of writing more difficult. Williams's HOMOSEXUALITY also informs his work: His conflicted acceptance of his sexual proclivities evolved over the course of his 40 years of dramatic accomplishment, mirroring changing American attitudes on homosexuality. Literary influences on Williams are many, including Hart Crane, D. H. Lawrence, and Anton Chekhov; and scholars Allean Hale and Lyle Leverich stress the influence of O'Neill's early one-acts BEFORE BREAKFAST (1916) and *The* DREAMY KID (1918) on Williams's *Moony's Kid Don't Cry* (1946), which also borrows imagery of a caged animal suggested by O'Neill's *The* HAIRY APE (1922).

Critics compare depictions of masculinity, GENDER, and sexual desire, as well as the use of irony, humor, and symbolism in the plays of O'Neill and Williams. A little-known 1930s Williams play, *Hello Moon*, concerns the sexual awakening of a young man by a more experienced woman and seems indebted to DESIRE UNDER THE ELMS (1924), but only fragments of *Hello Moon* survive; curiously, Williams acknowledges in his notebook in 1942 that he was reading *Desire under the Elms* apparently for the first time, calling it "incredibly bad writing," although as a student at the University of Missouri, where he took a course on O'Neill's plays, it seems likely that Williams encountered *Desire* at that time. While writing a term paper, "Some Representative Plays of O'Neill and a Discussion of His Art," Williams expressed mixed feelings regarding O'Neill's achievement, noting that O'Neill was "first, last, and always the born showman." In a school newspaper, he derided O'Neill's use of spoken asides in STRANGE INTERLUDE (1928) as an obvious device, yet his own early work echoes the play's colloquial language and sexual confusions.

Early in his career, Williams considered writing a southern trilogy of plays inspired by O'Neill's New England trilogy, MOURNING BECOMES ELECTRA (1931). In 1940, he spent time writing in Provincetown, Massachusetts, the site of the beginnings of O'Neill's playwriting success, and while there he saw a revival of O'Neill's DIFF'RENT (1920). Williams biographer Lyle Leverich suggests that Emma Crosby, the play's central female character, is "an hysterical precursor" to the quintessential Williams heroines, Alma Winemiller of *Summer and Smoke* and Blanche DuBois of *A Streetcar Named Desire*.

Williams told an interviewer that he had written a letter to O'Neill in the aftermath of the disappointing critical reception to the Broadway premiere of *The* ICEMAN COMETH (1939) in 1946, stating that although he initially found the play too long, "I gradually realized that its length, and the ponderosity of it, are what gave it a lot of power. I was deeply moved by it, finally." Some scholars note that the Broadway appearance of O'Neill's *The Iceman Cometh* may have influenced imagery in Williams's *A Streetcar Named Desire.* According to Williams, O'Neill wrote a grateful reply to his letter. In a 1957 interview, Williams mentioned that he found the original 1956 Broadway production of *Long Day's Journey into Night* to be a "gloomy" affair, yet the interviewer noted that Williams was at the same time reading AGNES BOULTON's memoir of her marriage to O'Neill.

Although Williams scarcely mentions O'Neill in letters and his notebooks (and does not mention O'Neill at all in his *Memoirs*), he painted a portrait called "Homage to Eugene O'Neill." Late in his life in an interview, Williams made rueful comparisons between his own decline in popularity and that which O'Neill suffered during the last two decades of his life. In 1981, Williams told Dotson Rader that he thought Edward Albee and Lanford Wilson were better dramatists than O'Neill, but added, "I liked O'Neill's writing. He had a great spirit, and a great sense of drama, yes. But most of all it was his spirit, his *passion,* that moved me."

Tennessee Williams died on February 25, 1983, in New York City, age 71.

Bibliography

Devlin, Albert, ed. *Conversations with Tennessee Williams.* Jackson: University Press of Mississippi, 1986.

Isaac, Dan. "O'Neill's Correspondence with Arthur Miller and Tennessee Williams." *Eugene O'Neill Review* 17, nos. 1–2 (Spring–Fall 1993): 124–133.

Leverich, Lyle. *Tom: The Unknown Tennessee Williams.* New York: Crown, 1995.

Maufort, Marc. "'Sometimes—There's God—So Quickly!': Imprints of Eugene O'Neill in *A Streetcar Named Desire.*" *Tennessee Williams Literary Journal* 3, no. 1 (Winter 1993–94): 23–30.

Sofer, Andrew. "Something Cloudy, Something Queer: Eugene O'Neill's *Ah, Wilderness!* and Tennessee Williams's *Period of Adjustment* as Problem Comedies." *Journal of Dramatic Theory and Criticism* 19, no. 1 (Fall 2004): 35–56.

Williams, Tennessee. *Notebooks.* Edited by Margaret Bradham Thornton. New Haven, Conn.: Yale University Press, 2006.

James Fisher

Woollcott, Alexander (1887–1943) Well known as the inspiration for the character of Sheridan Whiteside in George S. Kaufman and Moss Hart's play *The Man Who Came to Dinner,* Alexander Woollcott was a prominent, prolific, and provocative drama critic for the *New York Times* as well as the *New York Herald* and the *World.* He also created the "Shouts and Murmurs" page for the *New Yorker* magazine and hosted a radio program called "Town Crier," in which he skewered friends and offered commentary on plays and books. Woollcott belonged to the prestigious Algonquin Round Table, whose membership included Tallulah Bankhead, Dorothy Parker, Harpo Marx, and Robert Benchley among its luminaries.

Born on January 19, 1887, in Phalanx, New Jersey, Woollcott graduated from Hamlin College in 1909. His family was filled with avid readers, which gave him his love of literature. He was renowned for his witty, loquacious, even sentimental style, as well as for his enthusiasm for a good play. As a critic, he favored REALISM and economy in drama and believed it crucial that a playwright fully understand the nature of the theater space. Prominent as he was, Woollcott gained a different kind of notoriety when he wrote a negative review of *Taking Chances,* a French farce produced by the Shuberts. Inflamed by this assessment, the Schuberts banned Woollcott from all their theaters, leading to a high-profile law case that ended in victory for the critic along with, ironically, a new and broader fame.

Woollcott was an early and prophetic advocate for Eugene O'Neill, ranking him among the best living playwrights, one whose works would last, and lavished on him more praise than any other critic of the time. He particularly commended O'Neill for the force and vitality of his plays, his mastery of dialogue, and especially his acute imagination. At the same time, however, Woollcott could criticize O'Neill for his verbosity and his often crude language. By the late 1920s, Woollcott was becoming increasingly disenchanted with O'Neill, censuring him for pretentiousness, implausibility, and weak characterization in such plays as ALL GOD'S CHILLUN GOT WINGS, MARCO MILLIONS, and DESIRE UNDER THE ELMS. His criticisms of O'Neill equaled his once profuse praise and exceeded those of any other critic. In 1928, Woollcott committed a theatrical blunder when, having obtained a script of STRANGE INTERLUDE, he wrote a scathing article about it for *Vanity Fair* that was published before the play even opened. Woollcott's editor sent another writer to review the opening night, and that critic's review was quite favorable.

Throughout his theatrical relationship with O'Neill, however, Woollcott never ceased to acknowledge the playwright's preeminent stature and the durability of his work. Woollcott himself did not live to see the production of two O'Neill masterpieces, The ICEMAN COMETH and his crowning achievement, LONG DAY'S JOURNEY INTO NIGHT. The critic died of a heart attack suffered as he was making a radio broadcast on January 23, 1943.

Bibliography

Burns, Morris U. *The Dramatic Criticism of Alexander Woollcott*. Metuchen, N.J.: Scarecrow Press, 1980.

Karen Charmaine Blansfield

Work Diary Beginning in 1924, Eugene O'Neill kept a daily record of his activities, jotting notes into what he called "scribbling diaries." When he received a leather-bound five-year diary as a gift from his wife Carlotta in 1931, he began transcribing key information from the first five of his scribbling diaries into the larger volume, destroying the originals afterward.

Ultimately, he filled four of the five-year diaries through mid-1943 when he ceased writing, apparently following the same procedure of transcribing key data from the separate scribbling diaries. The four volumes—labeled the WORK DIARY by the playwright—were consigned to the O'Neill COLLECTION at the Yale University Library after his death.

American literature curator Donald Gallup transcribed the diaries initially in 1968–69, although the contents were not to be made public until 1978, 25 years after the playwright's death, as directed by his widow. A two-volume preliminary edition of the Work Diary was published by Yale University Library in 1981 with a plain blue paper binding; no formal, final edition has yet been issued.

In his introductory note to the preliminary edition, Gallup outlines the challenges of deciphering O'Neill's painstakingly cramped script and cryptic, abbreviated entries and translating them into a readable text. O'Neill frequently used initials only or other shorthand to identify plays, people, locations, and so on. Gallup made few changes except to clarify, presenting the information as closely as possible to O'Neill's originals.

The Work Diary offers a concise, unadorned, day-by-day record of a playwright at work—what, when, and where he was writing. From the first entry to the last, the diary chronicles the familiar plays that established O'Neill's reputation, from DESIRE UNDER THE ELMS in 1924 to A MOON FOR THE MISBEGOTTEN in 1943. He reflects little on his successes and just as tersely on the failures.

Mostly abbreviated entries also catalogue visits by friends, family birthdays, and health problems. Other milestones in O'Neill's career and personal life merit notes as well, such as the move into Casa Genotta on SEA ISLAND, GEORGIA, in June 1932, and the award of the NOBEL PRIZE IN LITERATURE with its attendant media interest in November 1936. A memorandum at the end of each month lists how many "c.w.d."s ("creative work days") were devoted to the plays on which he worked during that particular month.

The Work Diary also offers some insight into the difficulties O'Neill encountered, inferred from the number of days devoted to particular manuscripts. DAYS WITHOUT END, for example, went through an exhaustive process of writing and revision (including several title changes) before he considered it complete in 1934, almost eight years after he had begun it.

Additionally, the diary provides glimpses of plays uncompleted—including *The 13th Apostle* (also known as *The Last Conquest*), *The Life of Bessie Bowen*, and *Blind Alley Guy*—and ideas never fully developed, such as his "astronomer-astrologer idea" from 1927 or his "Haunted House" and "Symphony form" ideas (both from 1931). Historical figures interested O'Neill as possible source material as well; he mentions Rabelais, Robespierre, Aeschylus, and Benedict Arnold for potential dramatic treatment.

Some of O'Neill's ideas proved more fruitful; the "Clipper Ship-around-Horn play" noted on June 20, 1931, ultimately became *The Calms of Capricorn*. In December 1934, O'Neill conceived a series of four or five plays under that same title. By the following month, he refers to it as a "cycle . . . grand ideas for this Opus Magnus if [I] can ever do it" (*Diary*, 206). Numerous diary entries spread over the next nine years track the development of this cycle, which became A TALE OF POSSESSORS SELF-DISPOSSESSED as well as his great final plays.

Later entries are comprised primarily of abbreviations and ongoing medical problems, including one annotation that appears with disturbing regularity in 1942 and 1943: "Park[inson's] bad." A heartbreaking observation from January 28, 1943, records his destruction of drafts and notes for plays "I know I will never write now" (O'Neill 457). O'Neill's Work Diary concludes on May 4 of that year.

In addition to the complete text of the Work Diary, the preliminary edition includes a remarkable addendum: the full text of the only known extant scribbling diary, which provides a fascinating glimpse at the sort of detail contained in O'Neill's originals. It is a diary in the traditional sense, wherein the playwright records his thoughts and feelings in addition to his daily activities.

O'Neill believed that his 1925 diary had been "stolen & sold by former wife" AGNES BOULTON, as he annotates on page 1 of the first five-year diary (O'Neill 1). In fact, the manuscript was discovered among her possessions after her death in 1968; it too was acquired by the Yale Library and was thus available for Donald Gallup's use when he prepared the Work Diary for publication.

In the 1925 diary, O'Neill the playwright details the progress of his plays under construction or in production, while O'Neill the man chronicles his emotional highs and lows along with his theatrical successes and failures and the growing marital discord between himself and Agnes. He documents his physical fitness regimen and his attempts to control his alcohol consumption and quit smoking. He comments about books he was reading, friends' visits, even the weather. Altogether, the 1925 almanac is richly detailed enough to make one wish that O'Neill had not destroyed the other scribbling diaries.

An invaluable companion to the preliminary edition of the Work Diary is *Eugene O'Neill at Work: Newly Released Ideas for Plays*, edited and annotated by Virginia Floyd, which appeared in 1981, transcribed from a series of notebooks kept by the playwright, separate from the diary. In the notebooks, he fleshed out many of the ideas or titles mentioned in the Work Diary. As such, *Eugene O'Neill at Work* is perhaps a richer source of material for scholars—but the Work Diary itself is nonetheless a valuable if abbreviated tour guide of O'Neill's life from 1924 to 1943.

Bibliography

Floyd, Virginia, ed. *Eugene O'Neill at Work: Newly Released Ideas for Plays*. New York: Ungar, 1981.

O'Neill, Eugene. *Work Diary 1924–1943*. 2 vols. Preliminary edition transcribed by Donald Gallup. New Haven, Conn.: Yale University Library, 1981.

Richard Compson Sater

PART IV

Appendices

CHRONOLOGY OF O'NEILL'S LIFE

1888

Eugene Gladstone O'Neill is born on October 16 in a hotel room at the Barrett House in New York City. Two days after O'Neill's birth, the family, including his mother Mary Ellen "Ella" Quinlan O'Neill and older brother James O'Neill, Jr. (Jamie), joins his actor father James O'Neill on his tour for *The Count of Monte Cristo*. His mother is administered morphine for pain during childbirth and becomes an addict. For the next seven years, O'Neill travels with his parents under the care of his nurse, Sarah Sandy, and spends his summers in New London, Connecticut, with his father, mother, and brother.

1895

On October 18, O'Neill, age seven, matriculates into St. Aloysius Academy at Mount St. Vincent, a Catholic boarding school in the Bronx, New York City.

1899

Eugene's final year at St. Aloysius Academy.

1900

On May 24, O'Neill receives his first Holy Communion. On October 16, O'Neill arrives at the De La Salle Institute in New York City, on West 58th Street off Fourth Avenue, and he lives in his family's hotel apartment 10 blocks north of Central Park West.

1901

On October 4, Eugene returns to the De La Salle Institute for his second year and begins boarding at the school.

1902

O'Neill matriculates into the Betts Academy in Stamford, Connecticut.

1903

O'Neill realizes the truth of his mother's morphine addiction while visiting Monte Cristo Cottage during his summer break, when she attempts suicide by drowning in New London's Thames River. Denouncing his Catholic faith, O'Neill, with encouragement from his brother Jamie, begins drinking heavily and patronizes the saloons and brothels of New London and New York.

1906

O'Neill graduates from Betts Academy in the spring and matriculates into Princeton University on September 20. That year, his bohemian friend Louis Holladay introduces him to Benjamin R. Tucker's Unique Book Shop. O'Neill begins reading anarchist and socialist literature, along with the writings of Friedrich Nietzsche, Max Stirner, George Bernard Shaw, Henrik Ibsen, Maxim Gorky, and other selections of what Tucker called "advanced literature."

1907

O'Neill attends 10 performances of Henrik Ibsen's *Hedda Gabler*. He is expelled from Princeton University in June and takes a job as a clerk for the New York–Chicago Supply Company. Living with his family at the Hotel Lucerne on Amsterdam Avenue and 79th Street, O'Neill wanders the saloons and brothels of Manhattan's Tenderloin district with Louis Holladay and others. He befriends his father's publicity agent James Findlater Byth, who later appears as the character "Jimmy Tomorrow" in his late masterpiece *The Iceman Cometh*.

1909

Having quit his job and living on a seven dollar a week allowance from his father, O'Neill marries Kathleen Jenkins on October 2 in New Jersey while she is two months pregnant with his first son. With encouragement from his father, who disapproves of his marrying a Protestant, O'Neill flees to Honduras with a gold prospector about a week after the marriage. On October 16, he celebrates his 21st birthday on a banana boat off the west coast of Mexico. While in Honduras, he contracts malaria, and no gold is found.

1910

O'Neill separates from Kathleen Jenkins. Eugene Gladstone O'Neill, Jr., is born on May 5 in New York City; he will apparently see him once in fall 1912 but not again until 1921. On June 4, O'Neill sails from Boston to Buenos Aires, Argentina, on the Norwegian barque *Charles Racine*. Two months later, he arrives in Buenos Aires, where he works odd jobs, lives hand-to-mouth, and tours the city's brothels and low waterfront dives.

1911

O'Neill returns to New York in March as a seaman on the British steamship *Ikala*. On April 15, he leaves the *Ikala* after they dock in New York and spends several months as a boarder at Jimmy "the Priest's," a waterfront flophouse. He joins the crew of the SS *New York* on July 22. On August 26, he arrives back in New York on the SS *Philadelphia*, having achieved the rank of able-bodied seaman. He arranges a liaison with a prostitute as a legal pretext for divorcing Kathleen Jenkins. He visits his family in New London briefly, returns to Jimmy "the Priest's," and attends Ireland's famed Abbey Players' six-week engagement in New York.

1912

In early January, at the age of 23, O'Neill attempts suicide at Jimmy "the Priest's" with an overdose of the sleeping drug Veronal. His roommate James Findlater Byth and other boarders at Jimmy's save his life, an event he later dramatizes in his 1919 play *Exorcism* (destroyed by O'Neill). He joins his father on the vaudeville circuit, playing a small part in a vaudeville adaptation of *The Count of Monte Cristo*. He returns to New London in April; his divorce with Jenkins is official in July; and in August he gets a job as a staff writer for the *New London Telegraph*. That summer is portrayed in his late autobiographical masterpiece *Long Day's Journey into Night*. O'Neill is diagnosed with tuberculosis in November. After spending two days at a state sanatorium in early December, on Christmas Eve he enters Gaylord Farm Sanatorium in Connecticut.

1913

Having read the plays of August Strindberg, John Millington Synge, and Gerhart Hauptmann, among others, while at Gaylord Farm, O'Neill makes a conscious decision to become a playwright. After his release in June, he writes *A Wife for a Life*, *The Web*, *Thirst*, *Recklessness*, and *Warnings* in New London and copyrights them all at the Library of Congress.

1914

O'Neill writes his first full-length plays, *Bread and Butter* and *Servitude*, along with the one-acts *Fog*, *Bound East for Cardiff*, *The Movie Man*, and *Abortion*. In August, his father pays the printing costs for Gorham Press to publish his first book, *"Thirst" and Other One-Act Plays*, which includes *Thirst*, *The Web*, *Recklessness*, *Fog*, and *Warnings*. That fall, O'Neill participates in Professor George Pierce Baker's playwriting workshop, English 47, at Harvard University, where he writes the one-act play *Dear Doctor* and the full-length *Belshazzar* (both destroyed by O'Neill).

1915

O'Neill writes the one-act play *The Sniper* and the full-length *The Personal Equation,* which was not produced in his lifetime, for Baker's seminar. Worried about his financial situation, his father no longer pays for O'Neill's class at Harvard, and O'Neill moves back to New York. He resides at the Garden Hotel at Madison Avenue and 27th Street and begins to frequent the Golden Swan in Greenwich Village, otherwise known as the Hell Hole. During this time he befriends the West Side gang the Hudson Dusters and the philosophical anarchist Terry Carlin.

1916

In June, Terry Carlin convinces O'Neill to join him on a trip to Provincetown, Massachusetts. There he meets the experimental theater group the Provincetown Players, including George Cram "Jig" Cook, Susan Glaspell, Hutchins Hapgood and his wife Neith Boyce, John Reed, Louise Bryant, and others. He reads them a revised version of *The Movie Man,* which they reject, then *Bound East for Cardiff,* which they instantly accept for production that summer. O'Neill enjoys a successful premiere as a playwright on July 28 with *Bound East.* That summer, he writes the one-act plays *Before Breakfast* and *The G.A.N.* (destroyed by O'Neill), the full-length play *Now I Ask You,* and the short story "Tomorrow." O'Neill and Louise Bryant, John Reed's lover and later wife, conduct an open affair. At a brief visit to New London in late September and early October, he probably writes his short story "The Screenews of War." On November 3, in New York, the Provincetown Players hold their debut at the Provincetown Playhouse, located at 139 Macdougal Street in Greenwich Village. Their first bill includes *Bound East for Cardiff,* and they produce *Before Breakfast* on December 1.

1917

O'Neill moves to Provincetown in early March, stays through the summer, and writes his "sea plays" *The Long Voyage Home, The Moon of the Carribees, In the Zone,* and *Ile.* In June, "Tomorrow" is published in the journal *The Seven Arts,* which also publishes *The Long Voyage Home* that October. He moves back to New York City in the fall. Over the course of 1917, a triumphant year for O'Neill, the Provincetown Players produce *Fog* on January 5, *The Sniper* on February 16, *The Long Voyage Home* on November 2, and *Ile* on November 30. The Washington Square Players produce *In the Zone* on October 31. That fall, he meets his wife-to-be Agnes Boulton at the Golden Swan (better known as the Hell Hole).

1918

O'Neill moves to Provincetown in late winter with Agnes Boulton, whom he marries on April 12. He completes his short story "S.O.S." and his one-act play *The Rope,* produced by the Provincetown Players on April 26, *The Dreamy Kid*; *Where the Cross Is Made*; *Shell Shock*; and *Beyond the Horizon,* which is optioned by the Broadway producer J. D. Williams. In the fall, O'Neill and Agnes Boulton move to West Point Pleasant, New Jersey. *Where the Cross Is Made* is produced by the Provincetown Players, now at 133 Macdougal Street, on November 22, and *The Moon of the Caribbees* is produced on December 20.

1919

In May, O'Neill and Agnes Boulton move to Peaked Hill Bar in Provincetown; the former Coast Guard station is a wedding present from James O'Neill. Boni & Liveright publishes *The Moon of the Caribbees and Six Other Plays of the Sea.* He completes *The Straw, Chris Christophersen* (optioned by producer George C. Tyler). He writes the one-act plays *Exorcism,* based on his 1912 attempted suicide at Jimmy "the Priest's," *Honor among the Bradleys,* and *The Trumpet,* each of which he later destroys (the last two are never produced). When Boulton becomes too pregnant to live in the barren isolation of Peaked Hill Bar, they rent a house in Provincetown. O'Neill's second child, Shane Rudraighe O'Neill is born on October 30. *The Dreamy Kid,* the first American play by a white production company to have an all-black cast, is produced on October 31.

1920

On February 3, *Beyond the Horizon* is produced at the Morosco Theatre on Broadway. In March, O'Neill writes *Gold* in Provincetown. *Chris Christophersen* opens in Atlantic City on March 8 and *Exorcism* at the Provincetown Playhouse on March 26. In June, O'Neill wins his first Pulitzer Prize for *Beyond the Horizon.* James O'Neill dies of intestinal cancer on August 10 in New London, and Eugene's brother Jamie quits drinking and joins their mother in the management of James's estate. O'Neill returns to Peaked Hill Bar and completes *"Anna Christie," The Emperor Jones,* and *Diff'rent. The Emperor Jones* premieres at the Provincetown Playhouse on November 1 to great critical acclaim and moves to Broadway. *Diff'rent* opens on December 27.

1921

O'Neill writes *The First Man* in March. *Gold* is produced on Broadway on June 1 and closes after only 13 performances. *"Anna Christie"* opens on November 2 to wide critical acclaim. On November 10, *The Straw* appears and receives mediocre reviews. The first prolonged meeting with his son Eugene O'Neill, Jr., takes place in New York. In December, he completes *The Hairy Ape.*

1922

O'Neill's mother Ella O'Neill dies on February 28 in Los Angeles, California, due to a brain tumor. *The First Man* opens on March 4 and *The Hairy Ape* on March 9, the same day his mother's body arrives in New York. His brother Jamie accompanies her remains, but his alcoholism has relapsed (recounted in *A Moon for the Misbegotten*), and O'Neill refuses to meet them at the train. O'Neill is awarded his second Pulit-

zer Prize for *"Anna Christie"* on May 21. He completes *The Fountain* in Provincetown that summer, then moves his family to Brook Farm in Ridgefield, Connecticut, in autumn.

1923

O'Neill, Kenneth Macgowan, and Robert Edmund Jones replace the defunct Provincetown Players with the Experimental Theatre, Inc. O'Neill receives a gold medal from the National Institute of Arts and Letters. O'Neill completes *Welded* in the spring and *All God's Chillun Got Wings* that fall. Jamie O'Neill dies at a sanatorium in Paterson, New Jersey, of complications from alcoholism on November 8.

1924

O'Neill moves his family to Bermuda, where he writes *Desire under the Elms.* The Experimental Theatre, Inc., produces *Welded* on March 17, *The Ancient Mariner* on April 6, and *All God's Chillun Got Wings* on May 15. O'Neill and the Provincetown Playhouse receive threats from the Ku Klux Klan and other racists because the lead for *All God's Chillun,* played by the African-American actor Paul Robeson, is kissed on the hand onstage by a white woman, the actress Mary Blair. O'Neill ignores the threats, and nothing comes of it. On November 11, *Desire under the Elms* opens at the Greenwich Village Theatre.

1925

O'Neill's third child, Oona O'Neill, is born on May 14 in Bermuda. O'Neill moves to Nantucket with his family in July, then back to Brook Farm in October. *Marco Millions* and *The Great God Brown* are completed. *The Fountain* is produced on December 10. His alcoholism, which worsens over the course of the year, reaches a head, and Kenneth Macgowan persuades him to consult the psychoanalyst G. V. Hamilton.

1926

The Great God Brown is produced on January 23. The O'Neills travel to Bermuda in February and buy Spithead. O'Neill undergoes therapy with G. V. Hamilton and, after several setbacks, successfully quits drinking. In May he completes *Lazarus Laughed*. On June 23, Yale University awards O'Neill an honorary doctorate. During that summer, he rents a cottage at Belgrade Lakes, Maine. In October, he begins a love affair in New York with the actress Carlotta Monterey, whom he knows from her work as Mildred Douglas in *The Hairy Ape,* then returns to Bermuda in November. He writes film treatments of *The Hairy Ape* and *Desire under the Elms* (unproduced).

1927

O'Neill completes *Lazarus Laughed* and *Strange Interlude*. The Theatre Guild accepts *Marco Millions* and options *Strange Interlude*. O'Neill visits Carlotta in New York in August, returns to Bermuda in October, and goes back to New York in November.

1928

Marco Millions is produced on January 9, *Strange Interlude* on January 30, and *Lazarus Laughed* on April 9 at the Pasadena Community Playhouse. O'Neill is awarded his third Pulitzer Prize for *Strange Interlude*. O'Neill and Carlotta travel together to Europe on February 10. In March, they rent a villa in Guéthary, France; he completes *Dynamo* while in Europe and initiates divorce negotiations with Agnes Boulton. He and Carlotta visit China in October, and he travels to Manila in December; while in Asia, he contracts influenza, and his drinking temporarily relapses.

1929

Carlotta and O'Neill separate on January 1 in Ceylon and reunite in Egypt on January 15. *Dynamo* is produced by the Theatre Guild on February 11 and receives poor reviews. O'Neill and Agnes Boulton finalize their divorce on July 2. In June, O'Neill and Carlotta move to Château du Plessis (Le Plessis) in the Loire Valley; they are married in Paris on July 22.

1930

O'Neill travels in Spain and Morocco during October and returns to France in November. He composes several drafts of *Mourning Becomes Electra.*

1931

O'Neill completes *Mourning Becomes Electra*. He visits Las Palmas in the Canary Islands in March; on May 17, he returns to New York and oversees rehearsals for the Theatre Guild's production of *Mourning Becomes Electra,* which opens on October 26 to great critical acclaim (most probably the play that wins him the Nobel Prize in 1936). O'Neill and Carlotta visit Sea Island, Georgia, and decide to build a house there.

1932

Struggling through many drafts of his "God play" *Days Without End*, O'Neill writes a complete draft of *Ah, Wilderness!* in three weeks. He and Carlotta move to Casa Genotta ("Gene" + "Carlotta") on Sea Island.

1933

Ah, Wilderness! is produced by the Guild Theatre and opens on October 2 on Broadway; the play, O'Neill's only mature comedy, enjoys terrific popular success. O'Neill completes *Days Without End* and vacations that summer at Wolf Lake in New York.

1934

Days Without End is produced on January 8; the play receives disastrous reviews, and, after nearly suffering a nervous breakdown, he returns to Wolf Lake for two months in August and September.

1936

Dividing his time between New York and Sea Island and suffering from gastritis and prostate problems, O'Neill begins work on scenarios and drafts for a planned American history cycle, *A Tale of Possessors Self-Dispossessed,* including a draft of *A Touch of the Poet*. On November 12, he becomes the first American dramatist awarded the Nobel Prize in literature. He does not attend the ceremony due to poor health, but sends a statement acknowledging the great influence of the Swedish playwright August

Strindberg on his work and modern theater. During the ensuing winter, he rents a house in Seattle, Washington, and has his appendix removed that December in Oakland, California. He and Carlotta then move to San Francisco.

1937

O'Neill almost dies of an infection in California, though he continues work on his cycle. He and Carlotta rent houses in Berkeley in April and Lafayette in June. In December, they move into Tao House in Danville, California, where they reside from 1937 to 1944.

1939

As a result of worsening hand tremor and neuritis, O'Neill shelves his historical cycle, including drafts of *A Touch of the Poet* and *More Stately Mansions*, in favor of writing *The Iceman Cometh*, which he completes in December.

1940

O'Neill expresses agitation over the onset of World War II but nevertheless works on *Long Day's Journey into Night*. His Dalmatian "Blemie," whom he and Carlotta had bought in France, dies; O'Neill memorializes the dog with "The Last Will and Testament of Silverdene Emblem O'Neill."

1941

O'Neill completes *Long Day's Journey into Night;* he and later critics consider this play his greatest achievement, arguably the finest play ever written by an American.

1942

O'Neill begins work on *A Moon for the Misbegotten* and writes the last draft of *A Touch of the Poet,* the only finished play of his historical cycle. He also completes *Hughie,* a one-act play begun in 1941 and the only surviving installation of a planned series entitled *By Way of Obit.*

1943

On June 16, O'Neill's daughter Oona, at 18 years of age, marries Charlie Chaplin, who is 54. O'Neill does not accept the marriage and refuses to see his daughter. Oona and Chaplin have eight children (whom O'Neill never sees), and by all accounts they enjoy a very happy marriage. O'Neill completes his final play *A Moon for the Misbegotten.*

1944

O'Neill is diagnosed with cortical cerebellar atrophy; he and Carlotta sell Tao House in February and move into a hotel in San Francisco.

1945

O'Neill moves to New York in October, where he stays in a hotel. On November 29, he sends the script of *Long Day's Journey into Night* to Random House, his publisher in New York, insisting that the manuscript be locked in their safe, not published until 25 years after his death, and never produced.

1946

O'Neill and Carlotta move into a New York penthouse on East 84th Street in the spring. On October 9, the Theatre Guild produces *The Iceman Cometh* on Broadway to lackluster reviews; after its successful revival at Circle in the Square in 1956, however, it comes to be considered one of American drama's highest achievements.

1947

A Moon for the Misbegotten opens in Columbus, Ohio, on February 20.

1948

O'Neill and Carlotta separate on January 18 and reconcile in March. In August, Eugene's son Shane, who had attempted suicide multiple times and had become a chronic drug and alcohol abuser, is arrested and receives a two-year suspended sentence for heroin possession. O'Neill refuses to help him through the legalities or provide money for legal expenses and fines. O'Neill and Carlotta move to a cottage in Marblehead, Massachusetts, in the fall. O'Neill's tremor grows so severe he is incapable of writing.

1950

On September 25, Eugene O'Neill Jr., who once had a successful career as a classics scholar and professor at Yale University, commits suicide at a friend's house in Woodstock, New York.

1951

O'Neill is hospitalized at Salem Hospital on February 5 after breaking his leg. Carlotta is hospitalized as a psychiatric patient, her mental condition caused by bromide poisoning. O'Neill, encouraged by friends, signs a statement that Carlotta is mentally deranged. O'Neill and Carlotta reconcile on May 17, then sell their cottage in Massachusetts and move into the Shelton Hotel in Boston. O'Neill bequeaths his papers and manuscripts to Yale University.

1952

O'Neill makes Carlotta the executrix of his literary and financial estate. He destroys many drafts of unfinished plays but forgets that *More Stately Mansions*, which he considered unfinished and most likely would have destroyed, is included among the papers left to Yale University.

1953

On November 27, age 65, Eugene Gladstone O'Neill dies of pneumonia in his hotel room. He is buried on December 2, at Forest Hills Cemetery in Boston, Massachusetts.

1956

Yale University Press publishes *Long Days Journey into Night* after Carlotta disregards Eugene's wishes and, as literary executrix, approves its publication by Yale University Press. On February 10, *Long Day's Journey into Night* premieres at the Royal Dramatic Theatre in Sweden; it opens in the United States at the Wilbur Theatre, Boston, on October 22 and on Broadway at the Helen Hayes Theatre in New York on November 7. This same year, *The Iceman Cometh* is revived at the Circle in the Square Theatre. O'Neill is awarded his fourth Pulitzer Prize for *Long Day's Journey into Night*. The combination of these two remarkable productions, both directed by José Quintero and starring Jason Robards (as James Tyrone, Jr., in *Long Day's Journey* and Theodore "Hickey" Hickman in *Iceman*), ignites a Eugene O'Neill renaissance that establishes O'Neill's reputation as America's greatest dramatist.

CHRONOLOGICAL BIBLIOGRAPHY
OF O'NEILL'S WORKS

All of the plays listed below have been published in *Complete Plays* (3 vols., edited by Travis Bogard, New York: Library of America, 1988).

In addition, the following short story has recently been published:

"'The Screenews of War': A Previously Unpublished Short Story by Eugene O'Neill." Edited with an introduction by Robert M. Dowling. *Resources for American Literary Study*. Vol. 31. New York: AMS Press, Inc. (2007): 169–98.

1913
A Wife for a Life
The Web
Thirst
Recklessness
Warnings

1914
Fog
Bread and Butter
Bound East for Cardiff
Abortion
The Movie Man
Servitude

1915
The Sniper
The Personal Equation

1916
Before Breakfast
Now I Ask You

"Tomorrow"
"The Screenews of War"

1917
In the Zone
Ile
The Long Voyage Home
The Moon of the Caribbees

1918
The Rope
"S.O.S."
Beyond the Horizon
Shell Shock
The Dreamy Kid
Where the Cross Is Made

1919
The Straw
Chris Christophersen
Exorcism (destroyed by O'Neill)

1920
Gold
"Anna Christie"
The Emperor Jones
Diff'rent

1921
The First Man
The Hairy Ape

1922

The Fountain

1923

Welded
All God's Chillun Got Wings

1924

Desire under the Elms

1925

Marco Millions
The Great God Brown

1926

Lazarus Laughed

1927

Strange Interlude

1928

Dynamo

1931

Mournings Becomes Electra

1932

Ah, Wilderness!

1933

Days Without End

1939

More Stately Mansions
The Iceman Cometh

1941

Long Day's Journey into Night

1942

A Touch of the Poet
Hughie

1943

A Moon for the Misbegotten

SELECTED BIBLIOGRAPHY OF
SECONDARY SOURCES

Alexander, Doris M. "Captain Brant and Captain Brassbound." *Modern Language Notes* 74, no. 4 (April 1959): 306–310.

———. "Eugene O'Neill as Social Critic." In *O'Neill and His Plays: Four Decades of Criticism,* edited by Oscar Cargill, N. Bryllion Fagin, and William J. Fisher, 390–407. New York: New York University Press, 1961.

———. *Eugene O'Neill's Creative Struggle: The Decisive Decade, 1924–1933.* University Park: Pennsylvania State University Press, 1992.

———. *Eugene O'Neill's Last Plays: Separating Art from Autobiography.* Athens: University of Georgia Press, 2005.

———. "Hugo of *The Iceman Cometh:* Realism and O'Neill." *American Quarterly* 5 (1953): 357–366.

———. "The Missing Half of Hughie." *Drama Review* 1967.

———. "*Strange Interlude* and Schopenhauer." *American Literature* 25 (1953): 213–228. Reprinted in Houchin, John H., ed. *The Critical Response to Eugene O'Neill,* edited by John H. Houchin, 105–117. Westport, Conn.: Greenwood Press, 1993.

———. *The Tempering of Eugene O'Neill.* New York: Harcourt, Brace & World, 1962.

Allen, Kelcey. "'Marco Millions' Is Poignant O'Neill Satire." In Miller, Jordan Y. *Playwright's Progress: O'Neill and the Critics,* by Jordan Y. Miller, 55–57. Chicago: Scott, Foresman & Company, 1965.

Antliff, Allan. *Anarchist Modernism: Art, Politics and the First American Avant Garde.* Chicago: University of Chicago Press, 2001.

Atkinson, Brooks. *Broadway.* New York: Macmillan Company, 1970.

———. "O'Neill Tragedy Revived," *New York Times,* May 9, 1956. Reprinted in *Twentieth Century Interpretations of* The Iceman Cometh: *A Collection of Critical Essays,* edited by John H. Raleigh, 33–34. Englewood Cliffs, N.J.: Prentice Hall, 1968.

———. "Tragedy Becomes Electra," *New York Times,* November 1, 1931. Reprinted in *The Critical Response to Eugene O'Neill,* edited by John H. Houchin, 105–117, 126–129. Westport, Conn.: Greenwood Press, 1993.

Atkinson, Jennifer McCabe. *Eugene O'Neill: A Descriptive Bibliography.* Pittsburgh: University of Pittsburgh Press, 1974.

Baker, George Pierce. *Dramatic Technique.* Boston: Houghton Mifflin, 1919.

Barlow, Judith. *Final Acts: The Creation of Three Late O'Neill Plays.* Athens: University of Georgia Press, 1985.

———. "O'Neill's Female Characters." In *The Cambridge Companion to Eugene O'Neill,* edited by Michael Manheim, 164–177. New York: Cambridge University Press, 1998.

Baskin, Alex. *John Reed: The Early Years in Greenwich Village.* New York: Archives of Social History, 1990.

Basso, Hamilton. "The Tragic Sense." *New Yorker* (February 28, 1948): 24–34; (March 6, 1948): 24–34; (March 13, 1948): 24–37.

Bentley, Eric. "Trying to like O'Neill." *Kenyon Review* 14 (1952): 476–492. Reprinted in *Twentieth Century Interpretations of* The Iceman Cometh: *A Collection of Critical Essays,* edited by John H. Raleigh, 331–345. Englewood Cliffs, N.J.: Prentice Hall, 1968.

Ben Zvi, Linda. *Susan Glaspell: Her Life and Times.* New York: Oxford University Press, 2005.

Berger, Jason. "Refiguring O'Neill's Early Sea Plays: Maritime Labor Enters the Age of Modernity." *Eugene O'Neill Review* 28 (2006): 13–31.

Berlin, Normand. "Endings." In *Modern Critical Interpretations: Eugene O'Neill's The Iceman Cometh,* edited with an introduction by Harold Bloom, 95–106. New York: Chelsea House Publishers, 1987.

———. *Eugene O'Neill.* New York: Grove Press, 1982.

Bernstein, Samuel. *The Strands Entwined: A New Direction in American Drama.* Boston: Northeastern University Press, 1980.

Bigsby, Christopher, ed. *The Cambridge Companion to David Mamet.* Cambridge: Cambridge University Press, 2006.

Bigsby, Christopher, and Don B. Wilmeth, eds. Introduction to *The Cambridge History of American Theater.* Vol. 2. Cambridge: Cambridge University Press, 1999.

Bisset, Sir James, with P. R. Stephensen. *Tramps and Ladies.* New York: Criterion Books, 1959.

Black, Stephen A. *Eugene O'Neill: Beyond Mourning and Tragedy.* New Haven, Conn.: Yale University Press, 1999.

———. "*Mourning Becomes Electra* as a Greek Tragedy." *Eugene O'Neill Review* 26 (2004): 167–188.

———. "O'Neill and the Old Ham." *Eugene O'Neill Review* 17, nos. 1–2 (Spring–Fall 1993): 77–81.

Black, Stephen A., Zander Brietzke, Jackson R. Bryer, and Sheila Hickey Garvey, eds. *Jason Robards Remembered, Essays and Recollections.* Jefferson, N.C.: McFarland, 2002.

Bloom, Harold. *Eugene O'Neill.* New York: Chelsea House Publishers, 1987.

Bloom, Harold, ed. *Tony Kushner.* New York: Chelsea House, 2005.

Bloom, Steven F. "Drinking and Drunkenness in *The Iceman Cometh*: A Response to Mary McCarthy." *Eugene O'Neill Newsletter* 9, no. 1 (Spring 1985): 3–12.

———. "'The Mad Scene: Enter Ophelia!': O'Neill's Use of the Delayed Entrance in *Long Day's Journey into Night.*" *Eugene O'Neill Review* 26 (2004): 226–238.

Blumberg, Marcia. "Eloquent Stammering in the Fog: O'Neill's Heritage in Mamet." In *Perspectives on O'Neill: New Essays,* edited by Shayamal Bagchee, 97–111. Victoria, B.C.: University of Victoria, 1988.

Bogard, Travis. *Contour in Time: The Plays of Eugene O'Neill.* Rev. ed. New York: Oxford University Press, 1988.

Bogard, Travis, ed. *The Unknown O'Neill: Unpublished and Unfamiliar Writings of Eugene O'Neill.* New Haven, Conn.: Yale University Press, 1988.

Bonsor, N. R. P. *North Atlantic Seaway.* Vol. 3. Jersey, Channel Islands: Brookside Publications, 1979.

Boulton, Agnes. *Part of a Long Story: Eugene O'Neill as a Young Man in Love.* Garden City, N.Y.: Doubleday & Company, 1958.

Bowen, Croswell. "The Black Irishman." In *O'Neill and His Plays: Four Decades of Criticism,* edited by Oscar Cargill, N. Bryllion Fagin, and William J. Fisher, 64–84. New York: New York University Press, 1961.

———. *The Curse of the Misbegotten: A Tale of the House of O'Neill.* New York: McGraw-Hill, 1959.

Bower, Martha Gilman. "The Cycle Women and Carlotta Monterey O'Neill." *Eugene O'Neill Newsletter* 10, no. 2 (Summer–Fall, 1986). Available online. URL: www.eoneill.com/library/newsletter/x-2/x-2f. htm. Accessed April 3, 2009.

———. *Eugene O'Neill's Unfinished Threnody and Process of Invention in Four Cycle Plays.* Lewiston, N.Y.: Edwin Mellen Press, 1992.

———. Introduction: Eugene O'Neill in *More Stately Mansions. A Touch of the Poet and More Stately Mansions.* Edited by Martha Gilman Bower. New Haven, Conn.: Yale University Press, 2004, vii–xiv.

———. "*More Stately Mansions* Redux: Straightening Out the 'Twisted Path.'" *Eugene O'Neill Review* 26 (2004): 239–247.

Bradley, Gerald. "Goodbye Mr. Bones: The Emergence of Negro Themes and Characters in American Drama." *Drama Critique* 7 (Spring 1964): 79–85.

Brashear, William R. "O'Neill and Shaw: The Play as Will and Idea." *Criticism: A Quarterly for Literature and the Art* 8 (1966): 155–169.

Brewster, Scott. "Das Unbehangen in der Kultur (Civilization and Its Discontents)." *The Literary Encyclopedia* (November 1, 2002). Available online.

URL: http://litencyc.com/php/sworks.php?rec=true&UID=5736. Accessed February 1, 2007.

Brietzke, Zander. *The Aesthetics of Failure: Dynamic Structure in the Plays of Eugene O'Neill.* Jefferson, N.C.: McFarland, 2001.

———. *American Drama in the Age of Film.* Tuscaloosa: University of Alabama Press, 2007.

———. "The Gift of Ric Burns." *Eugene O'Neill Review* 28 (2006): 113–130.

———. "*The Long Voyage Home*: A Vicious Cycle at Sea." *Eugene O'Neill Review* 28 (2006): 32–49.

Brown, John Mason. "*Marco Millions.*" In *O'Neill and His Plays: Four Decades of Criticism,* edited by Oscar Cargil, N. Bryllion Fagin, and William J. Fisher, 181–183. New York: New York University Press, 1961.

———. "*Mourning Becomes Electra.* Eugene O'Neill's Exciting Trilogy, Is Given Excellent Production at the Guild," *NY Post* 10/27/3. In *Playwright's Progress: O'Neill and the Critics,* edited by Jordan Y. Miller, 67–71. Chicago: Scott, Foresman & Co., 1965.

Brustein, Robert. *The Theatre of Revolt.* Boston: Little, Brown, 1964.

Bryant, Louise. *Six Red Months in Russia.* London: William Heinemann, 1919.

Bunting, W. H. *Portrait of a Port: Boston 1852–1914.* Cambridge, Mass.: Belknap Press of Harvard University Press, 1971.

Burns, Morris U. *The Dramatic Criticism of Alexander Woollcott.* Metuchen, N.J.: Scarecrow Press, 1980.

Burns, Ric, Arthur Gelb, and Barbara Gelb. *Eugene O'Neill: A Documentary Film.* PBS: *American Experience.* Premiered March 27, 2006.

"Cadillac Hotel to Be Torn Down," *New York Times,* March 19, 1940, 25.

Callens, Johan. "'Black is white, I yells it out louder 'n deir loudest': Unraveling the Wooster Group's *The Emperor Jones.*" *Eugene O'Neill Review* 26 (2004): 43–69.

Cargill, Oscar. Introduction to *O'Neill and His Plays: Four Decades of Criticism,* edited by Oscar Cargill, N. Bryllion Fagin, and William J. Fisher, 1–16. New York: New York University Press, 1961.

Cargill, Oscar, N. Bryllion Fagin, and William J. Fisher, eds. *O'Neill and His Plays: Four Decades of Criticism.* New York: New York University Press, 1961.

Carpenter, Frederic I. *Eugene O'Neill.* Rev. ed. Boston: Twayne Publishers, 1979.

Cerf, Bennett. *At Random: The Reminiscences of Bennett Cerf.* Edited by Phyllis Cerf Wagner and Albert Erskine. New York: Random House, 1977.

Cheney, Sheldon. *The Theatre: Three Thousand Years of Drama, Acting, and Stagecraft.* New York: Tudor Publishing Company, 1935.

Chothia, Jean. *Forging a Language: A Study of the Plays of Eugene O'Neill.* New York: Cambridge University Press, 1979.

Chuang Tzu. "The Chuang Tzu." In *A Source Book in Chinese Philosophy,* edited and translated by Wing-Tsit Chan, 177–210. Princeton, N.J.: Princeton University Press, 1963.

Chura, Patrick. "'Vital Contact': Eugene O'Neill and the Working Class." *Twentieth Century Literature* 49, no. 4 (Winter 2003): 520–546.

Clark, Barrett H. *Eugene O'Neill: The Man and His Plays.* Rev. ed. New York: Dover, 1947.

Colburn, Steven E. "The Long Voyage Home: Illusion and the Tragic Pattern of Fate in O'Neill's SS *Glencairn* Cycle." In *Critical Essays on Eugene O'Neill,* edited by James J. Martine, 55–65. Boston: G.K. Hall & Co., 1984.

Colby, Barnard L. *For Oil and Buggy Whips: Whaling Captains of New London County, Connecticut.* Mystic, Conn.: Mystic Seaport Museum, 1992.

Connolly, Thomas F. "Biography of George Jean Nathan." Available online. URL: http://www.arts.cornell.edu/english/awards/nathan/bio.html. Accessed March 15, 2007.

———. *George Jean Nathan and the Making of Modern American Drama Criticism.* Madison, N.J.: Fairleigh Dickinson University Press, 2000.

Cooper, Burton. "Some Problems in Adapting O'Neill for Film." In *Eugene O'Neill's Century: Centennial Views on America's Foremost Tragic Dramatist,* edited by Richard F. Morton, Jr., 73–86. New York: Greenwood Press, 1991.

Costello, Donald. "Sidney Lumet's *Long Day's Journey into Night.*" *Literature Film Quarterly* 22 (1994): 78–92.

Cowley, Malcolm. "A Weekend with Eugene O'Neill." In *O'Neill and His Plays: Four Decades of Criticism,* edited by Oscar Cargill, N. Bryllion Fagin, and William J. Fisher, 1–16, 41–49. New York: New York University Press, 1961.

Crane, Stephen. "Maggie: A Girl of the Streets." In *Crane: Prose and Poetry*. Edited by J. C. Levenson. New York: Library of America, 1984, 5–78.

Crichton, Kyle. "Mr. O'Neill and the Iceman." In *Conversations with Eugene O'Neill*, edited by Mark W. Estrin, 188–202. Jackson and London: University Press of Mississippi, 1990.

Cunningham, Frank R. "The Ancient Mariner and the Genesis of O'Neill's Romanticism." *Eugene O'Neill Newsletter* 3, no. 1 (1979): 6–9.

———. "A Newly Discovered Fourth Production of *Lazarus Laughed*." *Eugene O'Neill Review* 22 (1998): 114–122.

Dardis, Tom. *Firebrand: The Life of Horace Liveright*. New York: Random House, 1995.

———. *The Thirsty Muse: Alcohol and the American Writer*. New York: Houghton Mifflin, 1991.

Day, Cyrus. "The Iceman and the Bridegroom: Some Observations on the Death of O'Neill's Salesman." In *Twentieth Century Interpretations of* The Iceman Cometh, edited by John Henry Raleigh, 79–86. Englewood Cliffs, N.J.: Prentice Hall, 1968.

Dearborn, Mary V. *Queen of Bohemia: The Life of Louise Bryant*. Boston and New York: Houghton Mifflin, 1996.

De Casseres, Benjamin. "'Denial without End': Benjamin De Casseres' Parody of Eugene O'Neill's 'God Play' *Days Without End*." Edited by Robert M. Dowling. *Eugene O'Neill Review* 30 (Fall 2008).

Decker, Robert Owen. *The Whaling City*. Chester, Conn.: Pequot Press, 1976.

DePolo, Harold. Typescript of memo dated 1/30/60. New London: Sheaffer-O'Neill Collection, Connecticut College.

Dewhurst, Colleen, and Campbell Scott. 1988. Interview by Sheila Hickey Garvey. Yale University, New Haven, Conn.

Diamond, George Saul. "The Ironic Use of Melodramatic Conventions and the Conventions of *The Count of Monte Cristo* in the Plays of Eugene O'Neill." *Dissertation Abstracts International* 38 (1977): 2,123A–2,124A.

Diggins, John Patrick. *Eugene O'Neill's America: Desire under Democracy*. Chicago: University of Chicago Press, 2007.

———. "'The Secret of the Soul': Eugene O'Neill's *The Iceman Cometh*." *Raritan* 19, no. 1 (1999): 63–76.

Dowling, Robert M. "On Eugene O'Neill's 'Philosophical Anarchism.'" *Eugene O'Neill Review* 29 (Spring 2007): 50–72.

———. Review of *Marco Millions (based on lies)*. Waterwell, The Lion at Theatre Row, 410 West 42nd Street, New York City. August 4–2, 200. *The Eugene O'Neill Review* 29 (2007): 83–87.

———. *Slumming in New York: From the Waterfront to Mythic Harlem*. Champaign: University of Illinois Press, 2007.

Downes, Olin. "Playwright Finds His Inspiration on Lonely Sand Dunes by the Sea." In *Conversations with Eugene O'Neill*, edited by Mark Estrin, 6–12. Jackson: University Press of Mississippi, 1990.

Dubost, Thierry. *Struggle, Defeat or Rebirth: Eugene O'Neill's Vision of Humanity*. Jefferson, N.C.: McFarland, 1997.

Dugan, Lawrence. "O'Neill and the Wobblies: The IWW as a Model for Failure." *The Iceman Cometh. Comparative Drama* (Spring–Summer 2002): 109–125.

Dunbar, Paul Laurence. "The Negroes of the Tenderloin." In *The Sport of the Gods and Other Essential Writings*, edited by Shelley Fisher Fishkin and David Bradley, 264–267. New York: Modern Library, 2005.

Eaton, Walter Pritchard. *The Theatre Guild: The First Ten Years*. New York: Brentano's, 1929.

Egan, Leona Rust. *Provincetown as a Stage: Provincetown, the Provincetown Players, and the Discovery of Eugene O'Neill*. Orleans, Mass.: Parnassus, 1994.

Egleston, Charles, ed. *The House of Boni & Liveright, 1917–1933: A Documentary Volume*. Detroit: Gale, 2004, 163–187.

Egri, Peter. "'Belonging' Lost: Alienation and Dramatic Form in Eugene O'Neill's *The Hairy Ape*." In *Critical Essays on Eugene O'Neill*, edited by James J. Martine, 77–111. Boston, Mass.: G. K. Hall & Co., 1984.

———. "The Use of the Short Story in O'Neill's and Chekhov's One-Act Plays." In *Eugene O'Neill: A World View*, edited by Virginia Floyd, 115–144. New York: Frederick Ungar Publishing, 1979.

Eisen, Kurt. *The Inner Strength of Opposites: O'Neill's Novelistic Drama and the Melodramatic Imagination*. Athens: University of Georgia Press, 1994.

Engel, Edwin A. *The Haunted Heroes of Eugene O'Neill.* Cambridge, Mass.: Harvard University Press, 1953.

Estrin, Mark W., ed. *Conversations with Eugene O'Neill.* Jackson: University Press of Mississippi, 1990.

Falk, Doris V. *Eugene O'Neill and the Tragic Tension: An Interpretive Study of the Plays.* New Brunswick, N.J.: Rutgers University Press, 1958.

———. "The Many Endings of *Days Without End.*" In *O'Neill and His Plays: Four Decades of Criticism,* edited by Oscar Cargill, N. Bryllion Fagin, and William J. Fisher, 415–423. New York: New York University Press, 1961.

Feingold, Michael. "Orderly Anarchisms: *The Personal Equation.*" *Village Voice* (August 8, 2002). Available online. URL: http://www.villagevoice.com/2008-08-15/theater/orderly-anarchisms/. Accessed February 8, 2008.

Fisher, James. *The Theatre of Tony Kushner: Living Past Hope.* New York: Routledge, 2001.

Fjelde, Rolf. "Structures of Forgiveness: The Endings of *A Moon for the Misbegotten* and Ibsen's *Peer Gynt.*" In *Eugene O'Neill in China,* edited by Liu Haiping and Lowell Swortzell, 51–57. New York: Greenwood Press, 1992.

Flanagan, Thomas. "Master of the Misbegotten." In *There You Are: Writings on Irish and American Literature and History,* edited by Christopher Cahill, 41–61. New York: New York Review of Books, 2004.

Flayhart, William Henry, III. *The American Line (1871–1902).* New York and London: W. W. Norton, 2000

Floyd, Virginia. *The Plays of Eugene O'Neill: A New Assessment.* New York: Ungar, 1985.

Floyd, Virginia, ed. *Eugene O'Neill at Work: Newly Released Ideas for His Plays.* New York: Ungar, 1981.

Fone, Byrne R. S. *A Road to Stonewall: Male Homosexuality and Homophobia in English and American Literature, 1750–1969.* New York: Twayne, 1995.

Frank, Glenda. "Tempest in Black and White: The 1924 Premiere of Eugene O'Neill's *All God's Chillun Got Wings.*" *Resources for American Literary Studies* 26, no. 1 (2000): 75–89.

Frazer, Winifred L. *E.G. and E.G.O.: Emma Goldman and* The Iceman Cometh. University of Florida Humanities Monograph No. 43. Gainesville: University Presses of Florida, 1974.

"A Free Magazine." *The Masses* 4 (February 1913): 1.

Frenz, Horst. *Eugene O'Neill.* New York: Frederick Ungar Publishing Company, 1971.

Gallup, Donald C. *Eugene O'Neill and His Eleven-Play Cycle, "A Tale of Possessors Self-Dispossessed."* New Haven, Conn.: Yale University Press, 1998.

———. *Pigeons on the Granite: Memories of a Yale Librarian.* New Haven, Conn.: Yale University Press, 1988.

Gardner, Virginia. *"Friend and Lover": The Life of Louise Bryant.* New York: Horizon Press, 1982.

Garland, Hamlin. *Selected Letters of Hamlin Garland.* Edited by Keith Newlin and Joseph B. McCullough. Lincoln: University of Nebraska Press, 1998.

Gelb, Arthur. "Wharf-Theater Era Takes a Curtain Call," *New York Times,* July 24, 1963.

Gelb, Arthur, and Barbara Gelb. *O'Neill.* Enlarged ed. New York: Harper & Row, 1973.

———. *O'Neill: Life with Monte Cristo.* New York: Applause Books, 2000.

———. "The Twisted Path to *More Stately Mansions.*" *Eugene O'Neill Review* (November 6, 1988).

Gelb, Barbara. "To O'Neill, She Was Wife, Mistress, Mother, Nurse," *New York Times,* October 21, 1973. Available online. URL: http://www.eoneill.com/library/on/gelbs/times10.21.1973.htm. Accessed December 12, 2007.

Gilfoyle, Timothy J. *City of Eros: New York City, Prostitution, and the Commercialization of Sex, 1790–1920.* New York: W. W. Norton, 1992.

Gilmer, Walker. *Horace Liveright: Publisher of the Twenties.* New York: David Lewis, 1970, 177–184.

Glaspell, Susan. *The Road to the Temple: A Biography of George Cram Cook.* Edited and with a new introduction and bibliography by Linda Ben-Zui. Jefferson, N.C.: McFarland, 2005.

Glover, Christopher S. "Female Characters in (and not in) Eugene O'Neill's *The Iceman Cometh*: Tracing Twentieth-Century Feminist Response into a New Era." *Eugene O'Neill Review* 25 (2001): 12–23.

Goldberg, Isaac. "At the Beginning of a Career." In *O'Neill and His Plays: Four Decades of Criticism,* edited by Oscar Cargill, N. Bryllion Fagin, and William J. Fisher, 234–243. New York: New York University Press, 1961.

Goodall, Jane R. *Performance and Evolution in the Age of Darwin: Out of the Natural Order.* London and New York: Routledge, 2002.

Gottfried, Martin. *"Mourning Becomes Electra,"* Women"s Wear Daily, New York Theater Critics Reviews, November 12, 1972.

Gramm, Julie M. "'Tomorrow': From Whence the Iceman Cometh." *Eugene O'Neill Review* 15, no. 1 (1991): 78–92.

Grecco, Stephen R. "High Hopes: Eugene O'Neill and Alcohol." *Yale French Studies* 50 (1974): 142–149.

Greeley-Smith, Nixola. "'No Money in Milk Cows' Says Woman Dairy Farmer Who's Made a Brave Fight," *Evening World*, October 7, 1916.

Gross, Robert F. "O'Neill's Queer Interlude: Epicene Excess and Camp Pleasures." *Journal of Dramatic Theory and Criticism* 12, no. 1 (Fall 1997): 3–22.

Haiping, Liu. "Taoism in O'Neill's Tao House Plays." *Eugene O'Neill Newsletter* 12, no. 2 (1988): 28–33.

Hall, Ann C. *"A Kind of Alaska": Women in the Plays of O'Neill, Pinter, and Shepard.* Carbondale: Southern Illinois University Press, 1993.

———. "'Gawd, you'd think I was a piece of furniture': O'Neill's *Anna Christie*." In *Staging the Rage: The Web of Misogyny in Modern Drama*, edited by Katherine H. Burkman and Judith Roof, 171–182. Madison, N.J.: Fairleigh Dickinson University Press, 1998.

Hamilton, Clayton. "O'Neill's First Book: A Review of *Thirst, and Other One-Act Plays*." In *O'Neill and His Plays: Four Decades of Criticism*, edited by Oscar Cargill, N. Bryllion Fagin, and William J. Fisher, 229. New York: New York University Press, 1961.

Hamilton, Gilbert V. *A Research on Marriage.* New York: Albert & Charles Boni, 1929.

Hamilton, Gilbert V., and Kenneth Macgowan. *What Is Wrong with Marriage.* New York: Albert & Charles Boni, 1929.

Hammond, Percy. "Desire under the Elms," *New York Herald Tribune*, November 12, 1924. In *O'Neill and His Plays: Four Decades of Criticism*, edited by Oscar Cargill, N. Bryllion Fagin, and William J. Fisher, 170–171. New York: New York University Press, 1961.

Handlin, Oscar. "Yankees." In *Harvard Encyclopedia of American Ethnic Groups*, edited by Stephen Thernstrom, 1,028–1,030. Cambridge, Mass.: Belknap Press of Harvard University Press, 1980.

Hapgood, Hutchins. *A Victorian in the Modern World.* New York: Harcourt Brace & Company, 1939.

Harrington, John P. "The Abbey in America: The Real Thing." In *Irish Theatre on Tour*, edited by Nicholas Grene and Christopher Morash, 35–50. Dublin: Carysfort Press, 2005.

Hawthorne, Hazel. *Salt House.* New York: Frederick A. Stokes Co., 1934.

Hawthorne, Hildegarde. *Old Seaport Towns of New England.* New York: Dodd, Mead & Company, 1916.

Helburn, Theresa. "O'Neill: An Impression." In *Conversations with Eugene O'Neill*, edited by Mark W. Estrin, 148–151. Jackson and London: University Press of Mississippi, 1990.

Hellman, Lillian. *An Unfinished Woman.* In *Three.* Boston: Little, Brown, 1979, 40–61.

Hinden, Michael. "*The Birth of Tragedy* and *The Great God Brown*." *Modern Drama* 16, no. 2 (1973): 129–140.

Hartnoll, Phyllis. *The Oxford Companion to the Theatre.* 3rd ed. London: Oxford University Press, 1967.

Hays, Peter. "Child Murder and Incest in American Drama." *Twentieth Century Literature* 36, no. 4 (Winter 1990): 434–448.

Hewes, Henry. "Hughie." In *O'Neill and His Plays: Four Decades of Criticism*, edited by Oscar Cargill, N. Bryllion Fagin, and William J. Fisher, 224–226. New York: New York University Press, 1961.

Homberger, Eric. *John Reed.* New York: Manchester University Press, 1990.

Houchin, John H. *Censorship of the American Theatre in the Twentieth Century.* Cambridge: Cambridge University Press, 1997.

Houchin, John H., ed. *The Critical Response to Eugene O'Neill.* Westport, Conn.: Greenwood Press, 1993.

Hugill, Stan. *Sailortown.* London: Routledge & Kegan Paul, 1967.

Humphrey, Robert E. *Children of Fantasy: The First Rebels of Greenwich Village.* New York: John Wiley & Sons, 1978.

Isaac, Dan. "O'Neill's Correspondence with Arthur Miller and Tennessee Williams." *Eugene O'Neill Review* 17, nos. 1–2 (Spring–Fall 1993): 124–133.

Isaacs, Edith. *The Negro in American Theatre.* New York: Theatre Arts, 1947.

Johnson, James Weldon. *Black Manhattan.* 1930. Reprint, New York: Da Capo Press, 1991.

Johnson, Katie N. "'*Anna Christie*': The Repentant Courtesan, Made Respectable." *Eugene O'Neill Review* 26 (2004): 87–104.

Jones, Robert Edmond. *The Dramatic Imagination: Reflections and Speculations on the Art of the Theatre.* New York: Methuen, 1969.

———. *Drawings for the Theatre.* New York: Theatre Arts Books, 1970.

Kalem, T. E. "Theatre: Dream Addict." *Time* (January 9, 1978). Reprinted in *The Critical Response to Eugene O'Neill,* edited by John H. Houchin, 236–238. Westport, Conn.: Greenwood Press, 1993.

Kane, Leslie, ed. *David Mamet in Conversation.* Ann Arbor: University of Michigan Press, 2001.

Kantor, Louis. "O'Neill Defends His Play of the Negro." In *Conversations with Eugene O'Neill,* edited by Mark W. Estrin, 44–49. Jackson: University Press of Mississippi, 1990.

Kemp, Harry. "Out of Provincetown: A Memoir of Eugene O'Neill." *Theatre Magazine* 51 (April 1930): 22–23. Reprinted in *Conversations with Eugene O'Neill,* edited by Mark W. Estrin, 95–102. Jackson: University Press of Mississippi, 1990.

Kenton, Edna. *The Provincetown Players and the Playwrights' Theatre, 1915–1922.* Edited by Travis Bogard and Jackson R. Bryer. Jefferson, N.C.: McFarland, 2004.

Kimbel, Ellen. "Eugene O'Neill as Social Historian: Manners and Morals in *Ah Wilderness!*" *Critical Essays on Eugene O'Neill,* edited by James J. Martine, 137–144. Boston: G. K. Hall & Co., 1984.

King, William Davies. "Oresteian Structures in *The Iceman Cometh.*" *Eugene O'Neill Review* 27 (2005): 126–134.

———. "'Our Home, Our Home:' Eugene O'Neill and Agnes Boulton at Spithead." *Eugene O'Neill Review* nos. 1–2 (Spring–Fall 2001): 60–69.

King, William Davies, ed. *"A Wind Is Rising": The Correspondence of Agnes Boulton and Eugene O'Neill.* Madison, N.J.: Fairleigh Dickinson University Press, 2000.

Kinne, Wisner Payne. *George Pierce Baker and the American Theatre.* Cambridge, Mass.: Harvard University Press, 1954.

Koutsoudaki, Mary. *The Greek Plays of Eugene O'Neill.* Athens: University of Athens, 2004.

Krutch, Joseph Wood. "Strange Interlude." 1928 review. In *O'Neill and His Plays: Four Decades of Criticism,* edited by Oscar Cargill, N. Bryllion Fagin, and William J. Fisher, 184–186. New York: New York University Press, 1961.

Kunckel, Frank A. Family history letter to nephew Manley W. Mallett, 1937. Sheaffer-O'Neill Collection, Department of Special Collections and Archives, Charles E. Shain Library, Connecticut College, New London.

Kushner, Tony. "The Genius of O'Neill." *Eugene O'Neill Review* 26 (2004): 248–256.

Labaree, Benjamin W. *America and the Sea: A Maritime History.* Mystic, Conn.: Mystic Seaport, 1998.

Langner, Lawrence. *The Magic Curtain: The Story of Life in Two Fields, Theatre and Invention.* New York: E. P. Dutton, 1951.

Langner, Lawrence, and Teresa Helburn. *The Story of the Theatre Guild: 1919–1947.* New York: Theatre Guild, 1947.

Lao Tzu. "Tao Te Ching." In *A Source Book in Chinese Philosophy,* compiled and translated by Wing-tsit Chan, 139–176. Princeton, N.J.: Princeton University Press, 1963.

LaPlanche, J., and J.-B. Pontalis. *The Language of Psycho-Analysis.* Translated by Donald Nicholson-Smith. New York: Norton, 1973.

Laufe, Abe. *The Wicked Stage: A History of Theatre Censorship and Harassment in the United States.* New York: F. Ungar, 1978.

Lawson, Hilda J. "The Negro in American Drama." Ph.D. diss., Urbana-Champaign University of Illinois (University Microfilm, 1939).

Leonard, Linda Schierse. *Witness to the Fire: Creativity and the Veil of Addiction.* Boston: Shambhala, 2001.

Lewis, David Levering, ed. *The Portable Harlem Renaissance.* New York: Viking Penguin, 1994.

Lewisohn, Ludwig. "*Gold.*" Review (1921). In *The Critical Response to Eugene O'Neill,* edited by John H. Houchin, 26–27. Westport, Conn.: Greenwood Press, 1993.

———. "Welded." Review (1922). In *O'Neill and His Plays: Four Decades of Criticism,* edited by Oscar Cargill, N. Bryllion Fagin, and William J. Fisher, 163–165. New York: New York University Press, 1961.

Library of the Performing Arts, Lincoln Center, Theodore Mann, Transcript for "O'Neill," Channel 13 Television.

———, Norman Nadel, reprinted in *Firstnite,* Week of January 21, 1963, p. 8.

Lichtenberg, Joseph D., and Charlotte Lichtenberg, "Eugene O'Neill and Falling in Love," *Psychoanalytic Quarterly* 41 (1972): 63–89.

Lloyd's Register of British and Foreign Shipping 1907/1908, 1909/1910 & 1910/1911. London: Lloyd's Register of British and Foreign Shipping, 1908, 1909, and 1910.

Long, Chester C. *The Role of Nemesis in the Structure of Selected Plays by Eugene O'Neill.* The Hague: Mouton, 1968.

Lubbock, Basil. *The Last of the Windjammers.* 2 vols. Glasgow: Brown, Son & Ferguson, 1953–54.

Macgowan, Kenneth. "More Tosh." *Provincetown Playbill*, season 1924–25, no. 1:4.

———. "The O'Neill Soliloquy." In *O'Neill and His Plays: Four Decades of Criticism*, edited by Oscar Cargill, N. Bryllion Fagin, and William J. Fisher, 449–435. New York: New York University Press, 1961.

———. Review of *Diff'rent*. In *O'Neill and His Plays: Four Decades of Criticism*, edited by Oscar Cargill, N. Bryllion Fagin, and William J. Fisher, 147–149. New York: New York University Press, 1961.

———. *The Theatre of Tomorrow.* New York: Boni & Liveright, 1921.

Macgowan, Kenneth, and Robert Edmond Jones. *Continental Stagecraft.* New York: Harcourt Brace, 1922.

Macgowan, Kenneth, and Herman Rosse. *Masks and Demons.* New York: Harcourt Brace, 1923.

Maddocks, Melvin. *The Seafarers: The Great Liners.* Alexandria, Va.: Time-Life Books, 1978.

Mailer, Norman. "The White Negro: Superficial Reflections on the Hipster." *Dissent* 3, no. 4 (Summer 1956): 276–293.

Majumdar, Rupendra Guha. "O'Neill's American Precursors." *Laconics* 1 (2006). Available online. URL: http://www.eoneill.com/library/laconics/1/1d.htm. Accessed June 8, 2007.

———. *The Paradox of Heroism in Modern American Drama.* Brussels: Peter Lang, 2003, 214–228.

Mallett, Manley W. *My Eighty-Four Ancestral Families.* Largo, Fla.: Mallett, 1979.

Mandl, Bette. "Absence as Presence: The Second Sex in *The Iceman Cometh*." *Eugene O'Neill Newsletter* 6, no. 2 (1982): 10–15. Reprinted in *The Critical Response to Eugene O'Neill*, edited by John H.

Houchin, 184–190. Westport, Conn.: Greenwood Press, 1993.

———. "'Thinking Aloud' in Eugene O'Neill's *Strange Interlude*." *Eugene O'Neill Review* 26 (2004). Available online. URL: http:/www.eoneill.com/library/review/26/26d.htm. Accessed September 8, 2007.

Manheim, Michael, ed. *The Cambridge Companion to Eugene O'Neill.* New York: Cambridge University Press, 1998.

———. *Eugene O'Neill's New Language of Kinship.* Syracuse, N.Y.: Syracuse University Press, 1982.

———. "Remnants of a Cycle: *A Touch of the Poet* and *More Stately Mansions*." In *Eugene O'Neill*, edited by Harold Bloom, 145–164. New York: Chelsea House Publishers, 1987.

———. "The Stature of *Long Day's Journey into Night*." In *The Cambridge Companion to Eugene O'Neill*, edited by Michael Manheim, 206–216. New York: Cambridge University Press, 1998.

———. "The Transcendence of Melodrama in O'Neill's *The Iceman Cometh*." In *Critical Essays on Eugene O'Neill*, edited by James J. Martine, 145–158. Boston: G. K. Hall & Co., 1984.

Martine, James J. *Critical Essays on Eugene O'Neill.* Boston: G. K. Hall & Co., 1984.

Matlaw, Myron. "James O'Neill's Launching of *Monte Cristo*." In *When They Weren't Doing Shakespeare*, edited by Judith L. Fisher and Stephen Watt, 88–105. Athens: University of Georgia Press, 1989.

———. "Robins Hits the Road: Trouping with O'Neill in the 1880s." *Theatre Survey* 29, no. 2 (November 1988): 175–192.

May, Henry F. *The End of American Innocence: A Study of the First Years of Our Own Time.* 1959. Reprint, New York: Knopf, 1969.

Mayfield, Sara. *The Constant Circle: H. L. Mencken and His Friends.* New York: Delacorte Press, 1968.

McCarthy, Mary. "Eugene O'Neill—Dry Ice." *Partisan Review* 13 (1946): 577–579. Reprinted in *Twentieth Century Interpretations of* The Iceman Cometh: *A Collection of Critical Essays*, edited by John H. Raleigh, 50–53. Englewood Cliffs, N.J.: Prentice Hall, 1968.

McCormack, W. J. *Fool of the Family: A Life of J. M. Synge.* London: Weidenfeld & Nicolson, 2000.

McCown, Cynthia. "All the Wrong Dreams: *Marco Millions* and the Acquisitive Instinct." *Eugene*

O'Neill Review 27 (2005). Available online. URL: http://www.eoneill.com/library/review/27/27m.htm. Accessed May 25, 2007.

McCracken, David. "O'Neill's Haunted House," *Chicago Tribune*, October 16, 1988, Sect. 13.

McDonough, Edwin J. *Quintero Directs O'Neill*. Pennington, N.J.: Cappella Books, 1991.

McMombie, J., trans. "Black Orpheus." *Massachusetts Review* 6 (Autumn 1964).

Merrill, Flora. "Fierce Oaths and Blushing Complexes Find No Place in Eugene O'Neill's Talk." In *Conversations with Eugene O'Neill*, edited by Mark W. Estrin, 70–74. Jackson and London: University Press of Mississippi, 1990.

Miller, Jordan Y. *Playwright's Progress: O'Neill and the Critics*. Chicago: Scott, Foresman & Company, 1965.

Miller, William D. *Dorothy Day: A Biography*. New York: Harper & Row, 1982.

Miller, William H., Jr. *The First Great Ocean Liners*. New York: Dover Publications, 1984.

Mitchell, Loften. *Black Drama: The Story of the American Negro in the Theatre*. New York: Hawthorne, 1967.

Monteiro, George. "Sabato Magaldi, Carlotta O'Neill's Man in Brazil." *Eugene O'Neill Review* 26 (2004): 199–214.

Morris, David Copland. "Courtesy in the Universe: Jeffers, Santayana and the 'Adult Habit of Thought.'" *Jeffers Studies* 1, no. 3 (2005). Available online. URL: http://www.jeffers.org/archive/pastissues/v1n3.html. Accessed May 5, 2007.

Muchnic, Helen. "The Irrelevancy of Belief: *The Iceman Cometh* and *The Lower Depths*." In *O'Neill and His Plays: Four Decades of Criticism*, edited by Oscar Cargill, N. Bryllion Fagin, and William J. Fisher, 431–442. New York: New York University Press, 1961.

Mukerji, Dahn Gopal. *Caste and Outcast*. 1923. Reprint, Stanford, Calif.: Stanford University Press, 2002.

Mullett, Mary B. "The Extraordinary Story of Eugene O'Neill." In *Conversations with Eugene O'Neill*, edited by Mark W. Estrin, 26–37. Jackson and London: University Press of Mississippi, 1990.

Murphy, Brenda. *American Realism and American Drama, 1880–1940*. New York: Cambridge University Press, 1987.

———. "Fetishizing the Dynamo: Henry Adams and Eugene O'Neill." *Eugene O'Neill Review* 16, no. 1 (1992): 85–90.

———. *The Iceman Cometh* in Context: An American Saloon Trilogy." *Eugene O'Neill Review* 26 (2004): 214–225.

———. *O'Neill: Long Day's Journey into Night*. New York: Cambridge University Press, 2001.

———. "O Neill's America: The Strange Interlude between the Wars." In *The Cambridge Companion to Eugene O'Neill*, edited by Michael Manheim, 135–147. New York: Cambridge University Press, 1998.

———. *The Provincetown Players and the Culture of Modernity*. Cambridge: Cambridge University Press, 2005.

Nadel, Norman. *A Pictorial History of the Theatre Guild*. Special Material by Lawrence Langner and Armina Marshall. New York: Crown, 1969.

Nathan, George Jean. "Eugene O'Neill (1888–1953)." In *A George Jean Nathan Reader*. Edited by A. L. Lazarus. Madison, N.J.: Fairleigh Dickinson University Press, 1990, 133–144.

Nelson, Doris. "O'Neill's Women." *Eugene O'Neill Newsletter* 6, no. 2 (Summer–Fall 1982): 3–7.

Neuberger, Richard L. "O'Neill Turns West toward New Horizons," *New York Times*, November 22, 1936.

Nietzsche, Friedrich. *Thus Spake Zarathustra*. Translated and with a preface by Walter Kaufmann. 1883–92. Reprint, New York: Penguin Books, 1978.

Nobelprize.org. "Banquet Speech." Eugene O'Neill: The Nobel Prize in Literature. Available online. URL: http://nobelprize.org/nobel_prizes/literature/laureates/1936/oneill-speech.html. Accessed December 1, 2007.

———. "Presentation Speech." The Nobel Prize in Literature 1936. Available online. URL: http://nobelprize.org/nobel_prizes/literature/laureates/1936/press.html. Accessed December 1, 2007.

O'Neill, Eugene. *Eugene O'Neill: Complete Plays*. 3 vols. Edited by Travis Bogard. New York: Library of America, 1988.

———. "Damn the Optimists!" In *O'Neill and His Plays: Four Decades of Criticism*, edited by Oscar Cargill, N. Bryllion Fagin, and William J. Fisher, 104–106. New York: New York University Press, 1961.

————. "Inscrutable Forces." (Letter to Barrett Clark, 1919). In *O'Neill and His Plays: Four Decades of Criticism*, edited by Oscar Cargill, N. Bryllion Fagin, and William J. Fisher, 99–100. New York: New York University Press, 1961.

————. Letter to George Pierce Baker, July 16, 1914. In *O'Neill and His Plays: Four Decades of Criticism*, edited by Oscar Cargill, N. Bryllion Fagin, and William J. Fisher, 19–20. New York: New York University Press, 1961.

————. "Memoranda on Masks." *American Spectator* (December 1937). Reprinted in *O'Neill and His Plays: Four Decades of Criticism*, edited by Oscar Cargill, N. Bryllion Fagin, and William J. Fisher, 116–122. New York: New York University Press, 1961.

————. *Poems 1912–1942*. New Haven, Conn.: Yale University Library, 1979.

————. "'The Screenews of War': A Previously Unpublished Short Story by Eugene O'Neill." Edited with an introduction by Robert M. Dowling. *Resources for American Literary Study* 31 (Fall 2007): 169–198.

————. *Selected Letters of Eugene O'Neill*. Edited by Travis Bogard and Jackson R. Bryer. New York: Limelight Editions, 1994.

————. *"The Theatre We Worked For": The Letters of Eugene O'Neill to Kenneth Macgowan*. Edited by Jackson R. Bryer, with the assistance of Ruth M. Alvarez. New Haven, Conn.: Yale University Press, 1982.

————. *The Unknown O'Neill: Unpublished and Unfamiliar Writings of Eugene O'Neill*. Edited by Travis Bogard. New Haven, Conn.: Yale University Press, 1988.

————. *Work Diary, 1924–1943*. 2 vols. Preliminary edition edited by Donald Gallup. New Haven, Conn.: Yale University Library, 1981.

Orlandello, John. *O'Neill on Film*. Rutherford, N.J.: Fairleigh Dickinson University Press, 1982.

Osofsky, Gilbert. *Harlem: The Making of a Ghetto, Negro New York, 1890–1930*. 1963. Reprint, New York: Harper Torchbooks, 1968.

Ozieblo, Bárbara. *Susan Glaspell: A Critical Biography*. Chapel Hill: University of North Carolina Press, 2000.

Parkes, Adam. *Modernism and the Theatre of Censorship*. Oxford: Oxford University Press, 2002.

Pendleton, Ralph, ed. *The Theatre of Robert Edmond Jones*. Middletown, Conn.: Wesleyan University Press, 1958.

Peters, R. S., and C. A. Mace. "Psychoanalysis and Derivative Schools" and "Psychology." In *Encyclopedia of Philosophy*, vol. 7, editor in chief Paul Edwards, 23–25. New York: Macmillan and Free Press, 1967.

Pfister, Joel. *Staging Depth: Eugene O'Neill and the Politics of Psychological Discourse*. Chapel Hill: University of North Carolina Press, 1995.

Playgoer. "Eugene O'Neill's *The Straw* Is Gruesome Clinical Tale," *New York Sun*, November 11, 1921. In *The Critical Response to Eugene O'Neill*, edited by John H. Houchin, 37–38. Westport, Conn.: Greenwood Press, 1993.

Porter, Laurin. "*Hughie*: Pipe Dream for Two." In *Critical Essays on Eugene O'Neill*, edited by James J. Martine, 78–88. Boston: G. K. Hall & Co., 1984.

————. "*A Touch of the Poet*: Memory and the Creative Imagination." In *The Critical Response to Eugene O'Neill*, edited by John H. Houchin, 238–250. Westport, Conn.: Greenwood Press, 1993.

Porton, Richard. *Film and the Anarchist Imagination*. London: Verso, 1999.

Quinn, Arthur Hobson. "Eugene O'Neill, Poet and Mystic." *Scribner's Magazine* (December 1926): 369–381.

————. *History of the American Drama from the Civil War to the Present Day*. New York: Harper & Brothers, 1927.

Quintero, José. *If You Don't Dance They Beat You*. Boston: Little, Brown, 1974.

————. Interview by Sheila Hickey Garvey "Eugene O'Neill: The Later Years" conference, Suffolk University, Boston, May 31, 1986.

Raleigh, John H., "The Historical Background of *The Iceman Cometh*." In *Twentieth Century Interpretations of* The Iceman Cometh: *A Collection of Critical Essays*, edited by John H. Raleigh, 54–62. Englewood Cliffs, N.J.: Prentice Hall, 1968.

Ranald, Margaret Loftus. *The Eugene O'Neill Companion*. Westport, Conn.: Greenwood Press, 1984.

————. "From Trial to Triumph (1913–1924): The Early Plays." In *The Cambridge Companion to Eugene O'Neill*, edited by Michael Manheim, 51–68. New York: Cambridge University Press, 1998.

Reaver, J. Russell. *An O'Neill Concordance.* Detroit: Gale Group, 1969.

Reds, 194 min., Paramount Pictures, Hollywood, 1981. Paramount DVD re-release, 2006.

Richter, Robert A. *Eugene O'Neill and Dat Ole Davil Sea: Maritime Influences in the Life and Works of Eugene O'Neill.* Mystic, Conn.: Mystic Seaport, 2004.

Ritschel, Nelson O'Ceallaigh. *Performance and Textual Imaging of Women on the Irish Stage, 1820–1920: M. A. Kelly to J. M. Synge and the Allgoods.* Lewiston, N.Y.: Edwin Mellen Press, 2007.

Roazen, Paul. "Eugene O'Neill and Louise Bryant: New Documents." *Eugene O'Neill Review* 27 (2005): 29–40.

Robards, Jason. Interview by Sheila Hickey Garvey. John F. Kennedy Center for the Performing Arts, Washington, D.C., August 12, 1985.

Robinson, James A. *Eugene O'Neill and Oriental Thought: A Divided Vision.* Carbondale: Southern Illinois University Press, 1982.

Rosenstone, Robert A. *Romantic Revolutionary: A Biography of John Reed.* New York: Alfred A. Knopf, 1975.

Rothstein, Mervyn. "Everybody Attends O'Neill Party," *New York Times,* October 18, 1988. Available online as "O'Neill Lauded in His Own Words." URL: http://tinyurl.com/6326yo. Accessed January 5, 2008.

Russett, Cynthia Eagle. *Darwin in America: The Intellectual Response, 1865–1912.* San Francisco: W. H. Freeman & Company, 1976.

Ryba, Mary Miceli. "Melodrama as a Figure of Mysticism in Eugene O'Neill's Plays." *Dissertation Abstracts International* 38 (1977): 2,794A.

Sarlós, Robert Karoly. *Jig Cook and the Provincetown Players.* Amherst: University of Massachusetts Press, 1982.

Saroyan, Aram. *Trio: Portrait of an Intimate Friendship.* New York: Linden Press, 1985.

Satterfield, Jay. *The World's Best Books: Taste, Culture and the Modern Library.* Boston and Amherst: University of Massachusetts Press, 2002, 114–116.

Sauer, David K., and Janice A. Sauer. *David Mamet: A Research and Production Sourcebook.* Westport, Conn.: Praeger, 2003.

Schiach, Don. *American Drama 1900–1990.* Cambridge: Cambridge University Press, 2000.

Schlueter, June, ed. *Feminist Rereadings of Modern American Drama.* Rutherford, N.J.: Fairleigh Dickinson University Press, 1989.

Scovell, Jane. *Oona: Living in the Shadows.* New York: Warner Books, 1998.

Shaughnessy, Edward L. *Down the Nights and Down the Days: Eugene O'Neill's Catholic Sensibility.* Notre Dame, Ind.: University of Notre Dame Press, 2000.

———. "Ella O'Neill and the Imprint of Faith." *Eugene O'Neill Review* 16, no. 2 (Fall 1992): 29–43.

———. *Eugene O'Neill in Ireland: The Critical Reception.* Westport, Conn.: Greenwood Press, 1988.

———. "O'Neill's African and Irish-Americans." In *The Cambridge Companion to Eugene O'Neill,* edited by Michael Manheim, 158–163. Cambridge: Cambridge University Press, 1998.

———. "O'Neill's Catholic Dilemma in *Days Without End.*" *Eugene O'Neill Review* (1991). Available online. URL: http://www.eoneill.com/library/on/shaughnessy/review91.htm. Accessed November 3, 2002.

Shaw, George Bernard. *The Quintessence of Ibsenism.* 1891. Reprint, New York: Dover Publications, 1994.

Shay, Frank. *A Sailor's Treasury.* New York: W. W. Norton, 1951.

Shea, Laura. "O'Neill, the Theatre Guild, and *A Moon for the Misbegotten.*" *Eugene O'Neill Review* 27 (2005): 76–97.

Sheaffer, Louis. Notes in the Sheaffer-O'Neill Collection. Department of Special Collections and Archives, Charles E. Shain Library, Connecticut College, New London.

———. *O'Neill: Son and Playwright.* Boston: Little, Brown, 1968.

———. *O'Neill: Son and Artist.* Boston: Little, Brown, 1973.

Sheaffer-O'Neill Collection. Department of Special Collections and Archives, Charles E. Shain Library, Connecticut College, New London.

Sheehan, Paul. *Modernism, Narrative and Humanism.* Cambridge: Cambridge University Press, 2002.

Simonson, Lee. *The Stage Is Set.* New York: Harcourt, Brace, Jovanovich, 1932.

Sinfield, Alan. *Out on Stage: Lesbian and Gay Theatre in the Twentieth Century.* New Haven, Conn.: Yale University Press, 1999.

Singer, Ben. *Melodrama and Modernity.* New York: Columbia University Press, 2001.

Sipple, William. "From Stage to Screen: *The Long Voyage Home* and *Long Day's Journey into Night.*" *Eugene O'Neill Newsletter* 7 (Spring 1983): 10–14.

Skinner, Richard Dana. *Eugene O'Neill: A Poet's Quest.* New York: Longmans, Green & Co., 1935.

Slochower, Harry. "Eugene O'Neill's Lost Moderns." In *O'Neill and His Plays: Four Decades of Criticism,* edited by Oscar Cargill, N. Bryllion Fagin, and William J. Fisher, 383–389. New York: New York University Press, 1961.

Smith, Madeline C., and Richard Eaton. "And Thou Bee-side Me . . . Beatrice Ashe and Eugene O'Neill." *Philological Papers* 44 (1998): 80–85.

———. "Harold DePolo: Pulp Fiction's Dark Horse." *Eugene O'Neill Review* 20, nos. 1–2 (Spring–Fall 1996): 80–87.

———. "The Truth about Hogan." *Eugene O'Neill Review* 18, nos. 1–2 (Spring–Fall 1994): 163–170.

Smith, Madeline C., and Richard Eaton, eds. *Eugene O'Neill: An Annotated International Bibliography, 1973 through 1999.* Jefferson, N.C.: McFarland, 2001.

Smith, Susan Harris. "Inscribing the Body: Lavinia Mannon as the Site of Struggle." *Eugene O'Neill Review* 19, nos. 1–2 (Spring–Fall 1995): 45–54.

Sova, Dawn B. *Banned Plays: Censorship Histories of 125 Stage Dramas.* New York: Facts On File, 2004.

Stansell, Christine. *American Moderns: Bohemian New York and the Creation of a New Century.* New York: Metropolitan Books, 2000.

Stirner, Max. *The Ego and His Own: The Case of the Individual against Authority.* Translated by Steven T. Byington with an introduction by J. L. Walker. 1844. Reprint, New York: Benjamin R. Tucker, 1907.

Susan Glaspell Society, The. Web site. Available online. URL: http://academic.shu.edu/glaspell/. Updated March 9, 2008.

Sweeney, Charles P. "Back to the Source of Plays." In *Conversations with Eugene O'Neill,* edited by Mark W. Estrin, 56–59. Jackson and London: University Press of Mississippi, 1990.

Synge, John Millington. *The Aran Islands.* Boston: John W. Luce, 1911.

Tanaka, Koji. "The Limit of Language in Daoism." *Asian Philosophy* 14, no. 2 (July 2004): 191–205.

Thompson, Francis. *The Complete Poetical Works of Francis Thompson.* New York: Modern Library, 1918.

Timár, Esther. "Possible Sources for Two O'Neill One-Acts." *Eugene O'Neill Newsletter* 6, no. 3 (1982): 20–23.

"Times Sq. Edifice Linked to History," *New York Times,* March 1935, pp. RE1–2.

Tiusanen, Timo. *O'Neill's Scenic Images.* Princeton, N.J.: Princeton University Press, 1968.

———. "Composition for Solos and a Chorus: *The Iceman Cometh.*" In *Modern Critical Interpretations: Eugene O'Neill's* The Iceman Cometh, edited with an Introduction by Harold Bloom, 23–24. New York: Chelsea House Publishers, 1987.

Toohey, John L. *A History of the Pulitzer Prize Plays.* New York: Citadel, 1967.

Törtqvist, Egil. *A Drama of Souls: Studies in O'Neill's Super-Naturalistic Technique.* New Haven, Conn.: Yale University Press, 1969.

———. *Eugene O'Neill: A Playwright's Theatre.* Jefferson, N.C.: McFarland, 2004.

———. "Philosophical and Literary Paragons." In *The Cambridge Companion to Eugene O'Neill,* edited by Michael Manheim, 18–32. New York: Cambridge University Press, 1998.

Tuten, Frederic. "Writing the Playwright: Tony Kushner in Conversation with Frederic Tuten," *Guernica Magazine* (June 2005). Available online. URL: http://www.guernicamag.com/interviews/71/writing_the_playwright_1/. Accessed January 22, 2008.

U.S. Bureau of the Census. Censuses for 1900 and 1920. Washington, D.C., 1900, 1920.

Van Laan, Thomas F. "Singing in the Wilderness: The Dark Vision in Eugene O'Neill's Only Mature Comedy." In *The Critical Response to Eugene O'Neill,* edited by John H. Houchin, 52–60. Westport, Conn.: Greenwood Press, 1993.

Vena, Gary. "Chipping at the Iceman: The Text and the 1946 Theatre Guild Production." *Eugene O'Neill Newsletter* 9, no. 3 (Winter 1985): 11–17.

Vidal, Gore. "Theatre." *Nation* (October 25, 1958). Reprinted in *The Critical Response to Eugene O'Neill,* edited by John H. Houchin, 234–236. Westport, Conn.: Greenwood Press, 1993.

Villiers, Alan. *The Way of a Ship.* New York: Charles Scribner's Sons, 1953.

Voelker, Paul D. "Eugene O'Neill and George Pierce Baker: A Reconsideration." *American Literature* 49, no. 2 (May 1977): 206–220.

———. "Politics, but Literature: The Example of Eugene O'Neill's Apprenticeship." *Eugene O'Neill Newsletter* 8, no. 2 (Summer–Fall 1984). Available online. URL: http://eoneill.com/library/newsletter/

vii_2/vii-2b.htm. Accessed December 15, 2007. Originally a paper presented at the Twelfth Annual Twentieth-Century Literature Conference: Politics of Literature, held at the University of Louisville in February 1984.

Voglino, Barbara. *"Perverse Mind": Eugene O'Neill's Struggle with Closure.* London: Associated University Presses, 1999.

Vorlicky, Robert H., ed. *Tony Kushner in Conversation.* Ann Arbor: University of Michigan Press, 1997.

Vorse, Mary Heaton. *Time and the Town.* New York: Dial, 1942.

Wainscott, Ronald H. "Exploring the Religion of the Dead: Philip Moeller Directs O'Neill's *Mourning Becomes Electra.*" *Theatre History Studies* 7 (1987): 28–39.

———. *Staging O'Neill: The Experimental Years, 1920–1934.* New Haven, Conn.: Yale University Press, 1988.

Waldau, Roy S. *Vintage Years of the Theatre Guild, 1928–1939.* Cleveland, Ohio, and London: The Press of Case Western Reserve University, 1972.

Warren, George C. "Lazarus Laughed." In *O'Neill and His Plays: Four Decades of Criticism,* edited by Oscar Cargill, N. Bryllion Fagin, and William J. Fisher, 178–180. New York: New York University Press, 1961.

Wasserstrom, William. "Notes on Electricity: Henry Adams and Eugene O'Neill." *Psychocultural Review* 1 (1977): 161–178.

Waterman, Arthur E. *Susan Glaspell.* New York: Twayne, 1966.

Waters, Joy Bluck. *Eugene O'Neill and Family: The Bermuda Interlude.* Warwick, Bermuda: Granaway Books, 1992.

Weegmann, Martin. "Eugene O'Neill's *Hughie* and the Grandiose Addict." *Psychodynamic Practice* 9, no. 1 (February 1, 2002): 21–32.

Weibust, Knut. *Deep Sea Sailors: A Study in Maritime Ethnology.* 2nd ed. Stockholm: Kungl. Boktryckeriet P.A. Norstedt & Soner, 1976.

Weintraub, Stanley. "Eugene O'Neill: The Shavian Dimensions." *Shaw: The Annual of Bernard Shaw Studies* 18 (1998): 45–61.

Wertheim, Albert. "Eugene O'Neill's *Days Without End* and the Tradition of the Split Character in Modern American and British Drama." *Eugene O'Neill Newsletter* 6, no. 3 (Winter 1982).

Westgate, J. Chris. "Staging the 'Poor, Wicked Lot'": O'Neill's Rebuttal to Fallen Woman Plays." *Eugene O'Neill Review* 28 (2006): 62–79.

Wetzsteon, Ross. *Republic of Dreams, Greenwich Village: The American Bohemia, 1910–1960.* New York: Simon & Schuster, 2002.

Wilkins, Frederick C. "Editor's Foreword: Something Old, Something Borrowed." *Eugene O'Neill Newsletter* 7, no. 3 (Winter 1983). Available online. URL: http://www.eoneill.com/library/newsletter/vii_3/vii-3a.htm. Accessed October 8, 2007.

———. "Three Lost Plays of Eugene O'Neill." *Eugene O'Neill Society Newsletter* (Winter 1982). Available online. URL: http://www.eoneill.com/library/newsletter/vi_3/vi-31.htm. Accessed June 30, 2007.

Wilmer, Steve E. "Censorship and Ideology: Eugene O'Neill (*The Hairy Ape*)." *Cycnos* 9 (1992): 53–60.

Wilson, Garff, B. *A History of American Acting.* Bloomington: Indiana University Press, 1966.

Winther, Sophus Keith. *Eugene O'Neill: A Critical Study.* New York: Random House, 1934.

Woolf, S. J. "Eugene O'Neill Returns after Twelve Years." In *Conversations with Eugene O'Neill,* edited by Mark W. Estrin, 167–173. Jackson and London: University Press of Mississippi, 1990.

Woollcott, Alexander. "Second Thoughts on First Nights," *New York Times,* November 13, 1921. Reprinted in *The Critical Response to Eugene O'Neill,* edited by John H. Houchin, 29–30. Westport, Conn.: Greenwood Press, 1993.

Wooster, James Willet. *Edward Stephen Harkness, 1874–1940.* Privately Printed, 1949.

Wyatt, Euphemia Van Rensselaer. "A Great American Comedy." In *The Critical Response to Eugene O'Neill,* edited by John H. Houchin, 149–150. Westport, Conn.: Greenwood Press, 1993.

LIST OF CONTRIBUTORS

Judith E. Barlow is a professor of English with a joint appointment in women's studies at the University at Albany, State University of New York. She is the author of *Final Acts: The Creation of Three Late O'Neill Plays* and editor of *Plays by American Women, 1900–1930* and *Plays by American Women, 1930–1960*. Prof. Barlow has taught in Bulgaria and China and has published numerous essays on American dramatists, including Eugene O'Neill, Sophie Treadwell, Lillian Hellman, and Tina Howe. Next year, S.U.N.Y. Press will publish her newest book, a critical anthology of short works by women produced by the Provincetown Players.

Karen C. Blansfield has contributed numerous essays to books and encyclopedias, including *Western Drama through the Ages*, *Literature and Law*, *Understanding Plays as Texts for Performance*, *Contemporary Gay American Poets and Playwrights: A Bio-Bibliographical Critical Sourcebook*, *Woody Allen: A Casebook*, *Gender and Genre: Essays on David Mamet*, *British Playwrights 1956–1995: A Research and Production Sourcebook*, *The Columbia Encyclopedia of Modern Drama*, *Southern Writers: A Biographical Dictionary*, *The Greenwood Encyclopedia of Multiethnic American Literature*, *The Gay and Lesbian Theatrical Legacy: A Biographical Dictionary of Major Figures in American Stage History in the Pre-Stonewall Era*, *Facts On File Companion to American Drama*, and *American Dramatists: A Bio-Bibliographical Critical Sourcebook*. She has also published articles in *South Atlantic Review*, *Journal of American Drama & Theatre*, *Studies in American Humor*, and other journals. Dr. Blansfield is the author of *Cheap Rooms and Restless Hearts* (1988), a study of the works of O. Henry, and she edited the British edition of David Mamet's *Glengarry Glen Ross* (2004). She has also served as dramaturge on numerous professional stage productions.

P. K. Brask is a professor at the University of Winnipeg's Department of Theatre and Film. He has published essays, poetry, short stories, translations, and interviews in a variety of journals. His books include *Aboriginal Voices: Amerindian, Inuit, and Sami Theatre* (coeditor), *Contemporary Issues in Canadian Theatre and Drama* (editor), *Essays on Kushner's Angels* (editor), *Seven Canons* (coeditor), *A Sudden Sky: Selected Poems by Ulrikka S. Gernes* (coeditor, cotranslator), and *We Are Here: Poems by Niels Hav* (cotranslator). He has also written plays and libretti.

Zander Brietzke teaches modern and American drama at Columbia University, and since 2004 is the editor of the *Eugene O'Neill Review* at Suffolk University in Boston. He has also taught at Lehigh University, the College of Wooster, and Montclair State University. An ex-president of the Eugene O'Neill Society, he is the author of *The Aesthetics of Failure: Dynamic Structure in the Plays of Eugene O'Neill* (McFarland, 2001) and *American Drama in the Age of Film* (Alabama, 2007).

Tom Cerasulo holds the Shaughness Family Chair for the Study of the Humanities at Elms College in Chicopee, Massachusetts. He has published on film adaptations and on the cultural history of American authorship. Recent work appears in *Arizona Quarterly*, *MELUS*, the *Litchfield Review*, and *Studies in American Culture*. His book *Writers Like Me: Fitzgerald, West, Parker, Schulberg, and Hollywood*, which reconsiders Hollywood's effect on American literary authors, is forthcoming from the University of South Carolina Press.

Patrick Chura is assistant professor of American literature at the University of Akron. He is the author of *Vital Contact: Downclassing Journeys in American Literature from Herman Melville to Richard Wright* (Routledge, 2005) and has written articles on Abraham Cahan, Eugene O'Neill, Harper Lee, Henry David Thoreau, and William Shakespeare.

John Curry is the Assistant Director of the Student Support Services Program at the College at Brockport, State University of New York, where he also teaches literature and writing courses. He earned a master's degree in English literature from the College at Brockport upon completion of his thesis entitled "A Historical Study of Occupations and Work in Selected Plays of Eugene O'Neill." He has presented essays on O'Neill at conferences, including "O'Neill's People," at the International Conference in 1995. He lives in Brockport, N.Y., with his wife and two daughters.

Laurie M. Deredita is the Ruth Rusch Sheppe '40 Director of Special Collections and Archives in the Charles E. Shain Library at Connecticut College, and she has been the curator of the Sheaffer-O'Neill Collection since 1999. Her undergraduate degree is from Skidmore College, and she has an M.Phil. from Yale University in Spanish literature and an M.S.L.S. from the School of Library Service at Columbia University.

Thierry Dubost is a professor at the Université de Caen, Basse-Normandie, France. He is the author of *Struggle, Defeat or Rebirth: Eugene O'Neill's Vision of Humanity* (MacFarland, 1997, Reprint 2005); *The Plays of Thomas Kilroy* (McFarland, 2007); and the coeditor of *La femme noire américaine: Aspects d'une crise d'identité* (Presses Universitaires de Caen, 1997), *George Bernard Shaw, un dramaturge*

engagé (PUC, 1998), and *Du dire à l'être: Tensions identitaires dans la littérature nord-américaine* (PUC, 2000). His research interests include Irish, American, and African drama. His translation of Wole Soyinka's *Death and the King's Horseman* was published in 1986 by Hatier (Collection Monde Noir).

Richard Eaton is professor emeritus of English at West Virginia University and the author of articles and book reviews in a number of fields. As coauthor, he has produced some 20 articles and four books about Eugene O'Neill, including *Eugene O'Neill in Court* (1993), *Eugene O'Neill: An Annotated International Bibliography, 1973 through 1999* (2001), and *Eugene O'Neill: Production Personnel* (2005).

Drew Eisenhauer is completing a dissertation entitled "The Provincetown Players and the Two Modernisms," at the University of Maryland, College Park. The dissertation seeks to explore the relationship between the dramatic experiments of the original Provincetown Players (1915–22) and the international currents of modernism and the avant-garde of their era. Drew's particular focus is on the contexts of the early Provincetown and New York productions, which were largely undertaken by and performed for an audience of American writers, radicals, and cultural bohemians. His analysis recovers the vision of the American modernist artist as a figure socially committed and politically engaged, qualities later marginalized in American modernism. Drew teaches at the University of Maryland and has delivered a series of papers at international conferences on individual members of the Provincetown Players, including Eugene O'Neill, Susan Glaspell, Alfred Kreymborg, and Floyd Dell, and has published an article on Glaspell in the collection *Disclosing Intertextualities: The Stories, Plays, and Novels of Susan Glaspell*. He has also directed Eugene O'Neill's *Bound East for Cardiff* for the Provincetown Theatre Company and been active in community theater in Baltimore, Maryland.

James Fisher, professor of theater and head of the Department of Theatre at the University of North Carolina at Greensboro, is the author of *Understanding Tony Kushner* (University of South Carolina Press, 2008), *The Historical Dictionary of the American Theater: Modernism* (with Felicia Hardison Londré; Scarecrow Press, 2007), *The Theater of Tony Kushner: Living Past Hope* (Routledge, 2001), *The Theatre of Yesterday and Tomorrow: Commedia dell'arte on the Modern Stage* (Mellen, 1992), and bio-bibliographies for Greenwood Press of Al Jolson (1994), Spencer Tracy (1994), and Eddie Cantor (1997). He has edited several volumes, including *"We Will Be Citizens": New Essays on Gay and Lesbian Theatre* (McFarland, 2008), *Tony Kushner: New Essays on the Art and Politics of the Plays* (McFarland, 2006), and six volumes of *The Puppetry Yearbook* (Mellen). He has published essays and reviews in numerous journals and collections, and he is also a director and actor, has held several research fellowships, and is book review editor for *Broadside*, the publication of the Theatre Library Association. In 2007, Fisher received the Betty Jean Jones Award for Excellence in the Teaching of American Theatre from the American Theatre and Drama Society.

Brian Folker is an assistant professor at Central Connecticut State University. A specialist in British romanticism, he is interested in poetry, literary and political theory, and in the tension between concepts of order and large-scale conflict. His essays have appeared in *ELH* and *Studies in Romanticism*.

Sheila Hickey Garvey, Ph.D., is a professor of theater at Southern Connecticut State University, where she teaches acting and directing and stages productions in SCSU's John Lyman Center for the Performing Arts. She is a former president of the International Eugene O'Neill Society. Her O'Neill writings are based largely on interviews with the major artists who contributed to the Eugene O'Neill Renaissance. Dr. Garvey is a coeditor and contributor to the book *Jason Robards Remembered* (McFarland, 2000) and is a Moss Hart Award winner and an elected life member of the New England Theatre Conference's College of Fellows.

John Hagan is an actor and writer. He has contributed to several journals, including *Artforum, October, Millennium Film Journal, Cinefantastique,* *Filmjournal, Thousand Eyes, Segno Cinema* and *Les Cahiers de la Cinémathèque,* and to the books *Film Makers Speak: Voices of Film Experience, Film before Griffith,* and *Dictionary of Literary Biography: Screenwriters.* He has taught courses on O'Neill and Shakespeare at Hunter College in New York City.

Jane Harris is an actress, theater teaching artist, and playwright. She has worked to create and support youth theater in central Connecticut for the past five years as an arts administrator and as an educator, partnering with Oddfellows Playhouse, Hartford Children's Theatre, and numerous after-school organizations. She trained professionally with the Hartford Ballet and graduated summa cum laude from Central Connecticut State University with a B.A. in English and theater.

Linda L. Herr is a professor of theater at Connecticut College and has been chair of that department for the better part of 30 years. She has served on the board of trustees of The O'Neill Center, representing Connecticut College, which accredits the O'Neill's college program, The National Theater Institute, and its summer program, Theatermakers. She has taught undergraduate courses in acting, directing, theater and culture, and American drama, as well as a senior seminar on O'Neill at the Monte Cristo Cottage in New London. She has published on O'Neill; her last article, "Stillborn Future: Dead and Dying Infants and Children in the Plays of Eugene O'Neill" in *Art, Glitter, and Glitz: Mainstream Playwrights and Popular Theatre in 1920 America,* was published in 2004. Prof. Herr received an M.A. from Hofstra University and was the recipient of a Danforth Fellowship for Women.

Eileen Herrmann, a two-time Fulbright recipient, is associate adjunct professor at Dominican University of California. She has lectured at the Universities of California at Davis and Santa Cruz, San Francisco State University, and Johannes Gutenberg University, Mainz, in Germany. She has written and lectured on Eugene O'Neill in the United States and abroad. She has authored several papers on the art of Eugene O'Neill, and serves on the boards of the Eugene O'Neill Foundation and the

Eugene O'Neill Society. She is currently editing a book of essays addressing the political dimensions of the drama of Eugene O'Neill.

Jeff Kennedy is a clinical associate professor at Arizona State University in the interdisciplinary arts and performance program. While a teaching fellow in the program in educational theater at New York University, with his Ph.D. dissertation on the history of the Provincetown Playhouse, he was part of the refurbishment and reopening of the Playhouse in 1998, designing the historical gallery inside the theater and writing a monograph on the history of the playhouse.

William Davies King is professor of theater at the University of California, Santa Barbara. He is the author of *Henry Irving's "Waterloo": Theatrical Engagements with Late-Victorian Culture and History* (University of California Press, 1993; winner of the 1993 Joe A. Calloway Prize), *Writing Wrongs: The Work of Wallace Shawn* (Temple, 1997), and *"A Wind Is Rising": The Correspondence of Agnes Boulton and Eugene O'Neill* (Fairleigh Dickinson, 2000). He has recently published a book about his own collecting, *Collections of Nothing* (University of Chicago Press), and *Another Part of a Long Story: Literary Traces of Eugene O'Neill and Agnes Boulton* is forthcoming from the University of Michigan Press.

Shawna Lesseur-Blas wrote her honor's thesis on O'Neill at the University of North Carolina Wilmington, from which she graduated in spring 2008. She is now a graduate teaching assistant in the English department at the University of Connecticut.

Rupendra Guha Majumdar is a Reader in English literature at Delhi University. He is also a poet and an artist. He was a Visiting Fulbright Fellow in the English department at Yale University in 1981 and 1992. His publications include *Central Man: The Paradox of Heroism in Modern American Drama* (Peter Lang, 2003); four books of poetry in English—*Blunderbuss* (1971); *Apu's Initiation* (1975); *Tomcat* (1980) and *The Hiroshima Clock* (1990)—and his poems have featured in various anthologies, such as *Modern English Poetry in India*

(edited by P. Lal, 1971); *The Oxford Book of Animal Poems* (edited by Michael Harrison and Christopher Stuart-Clark, Oxford University Press, 1992); and *Spotlight on Poetry: Poems around the World 3* (edited by Brian Moses and David Orme, HarperCollins, 1999). He has contributed to *The Columbia Encyclopedia of Modern Drama* (edited by Evert Sprinchorn and Gabrielle H. Cody, Columbia University Press, 2007) and *The Facts On File Companion to World Poetry: 1900 to the Present* (edited by R. Victoria Arana, Facts On File, 2007).

Mary K. Mallett is a computer engineer and genealogist. Her great-grandmother, Anastasia O'Neill Kunkle, was Eugene O'Neill's aunt. Many of Anastasia's memories of the O'Neill family immigration were recorded by her son, Frank, and were subsequently passed down to Ms. Mallett. Ms. Mallett publishes the Rosbercon O'Neill family newsletter and serves as head of the U.S. Rosbercon O'Neill family organization. She has organized several O'Neill family reunions, including a weekend-long gathering of Eugene's cousins and grandchildren in New London, Connecticut.

Cynthia McCown is associate professor of American literature and chair of the English department at Beloit College in Wisconsin. Also a member of the theater arts department, she teaches theater history and modern drama as well. She has published in *The Eugene O'Neill Review* on Elmer Rice and Sidney Howard (in *Art, Glitter, and Glitz: Mainstream Playwrights and Popular Theatre in 1920s America*) and on American arts and entertainment 1900–10. She has a chapter on O'Neill forthcoming in a collection from McFarland.

Brenda Murphy is Board of Trustees Distinguished Professor of English at the University of Connecticut, where she has taught since 1989. Her scholarly work reflects her interest in placing American drama, theater, and performance in the broader context of American literature and culture. Among her books are *The Provincetown Players and the Culture of Modernity* (2005), *O'Neill: Long Day's Journey Into Night* (2001), *Congressional Theatre: Dramatizing McCarthyism on Stage, Film, and Tele-*

vision (1999), *Miller: Death of a Salesman* (1995), *Tennessee Williams and Elia Kazan: A Collaboration in the Theatre* (1992), *American Realism and American Drama, 1880–1940* (1987), and, as editor, *The Cambridge Companion to American Women Playwrights* (1999).

Jennifer Banach Palladino is a writer from Connecticut. She has written for literary critic Harold Bloom in conjunction with his literary series for Facts On File, and for Random House's Academic Resources division.

Robert A. Richter is director of Arts Programming at Connecticut College. He received a B.A. in anthropology and theater from Connecticut College and an M.A. in liberal studies from Wesleyan University. His book, *Eugene O'Neill and Dat Ole Davil Sea*, which explores the maritime influences on O'Neill and his work, was published in 2004, and he was a finalist for the 2005 Connecticut Book Award. In 2000 he directed *Eugene O'Neill's New London: The Influence of Time & Place*, a sixth-month celebration and exploration of Eugene O'Neill and New London County in the late 19th and early 20th centuries.

Nelson O'Ceallaigh Ritschel's latest book, *Performative and Textual Imaging of Women on the Irish Stage, 1820–1920: M. A. Kelly to J. M. Synge and the Allgoods*, was published in January 2007. Previous books include *Synge and Irish Nationalism: The Precursor to Revolution* (2002) and *Productions of the Irish Theatre Movement, 1899–1916* (2001). Dr. Ritschel's most recent essays, "Shaw, Connolly, and the Irish Citizen Army" and "Synge and the Influence of the Abbey Theatre on Eugene O'Neill," appeared in 2007 in *Shaw: The Annual of Bernard Shaw Studies 27* and the *Eugene O'Neill Review*, respectively. He has previously published numerous articles on Synge and Irish theater in journals such as *New Hibernia Review, Lit: Literature, Interpretation, Theory*, and *The New England Theatre Journal*. He is currently working on a book on Shaw, Synge, James Connolly, and Irish socialism. Most recently, he was invited to contribute an article for *Shaw: The Annual of Bernard Shaw Studies 30*, which will

exclusively focus on Shaw and Ireland. Dr. Ritschel received a Ph.D. from Brown University and is currently an associate professor at Massachusetts Maritime Academy on Cape Cod, where he will serve on the editorial board of a new venture, *The Nautilus: A Journal of Maritime Literature, History, and Culture*.

Alex Roe is a theater director, actor, and playwright who has presented work across the United States and Europe. In 2001, he became the producing artistic director of Metropolitan Playhouse, a resident theater in New York City devoted to the exploration and celebration of America's theatrical heritage. Mr. Roe performed the role of "Blemie" in Metropolitan's staging of *The Last Will and Testament of Silverdene Emblem O'Neill* in 2007.

Brian Rogers spent most of his career as director of the Connecticut College library in O'Neill's hometown of New London. He continued to develop the O'Neill collection begun by former librarian Hazel Johnson, and in the early 1990s was able to enlarge it significantly with the papers of author Louis Sheaffer, who had first come to New London more than 30 years before to begin work on his biography of the playwright.

Erika Rundle is assistant professor of theater arts at Mount Holyoke College, where she teaches performance history and dramatic theory. She is working on a book entitled *Primate Dramas: Evolution, Theatricality, and the Performance of Species*, which traces the influence of Darwinism on dramatic structure in 20th-century American theater and film. Her work has been published in *TDR: The Drama Review, PAJ: A Journal of Performance and Art, The Eugene O'Neill Review*, and *Theater*. Rundle also works as a freelance translator and dramaturge; her translation of Marie NDiaye's *Hilda* premiered in San Francisco and New York in 2005.

Richard Compson Sater is a freelance writer and scholar with a long-standing interest in the life and works of Eugene O'Neill. Sater earned his doctorate in fine arts from Ohio University, in Athens, writing a dissertation about O'Neill's use of music and musical elements in his SS *Glencairn* plays. Dr. Sater has accumulated 10 years of teaching fine arts and writing at four universities. He has also served in the Air Force Reserve for 22 years and was promoted to the rank of lieutenant colonel in 2008. He resides in Seattle, Washington.

J. Shantz is a professor at Kwantlen Polytechnic University in Vancouver, British Columbia. He has also held classes on literature and revolution and activist theater at community centers and free schools. His writings have appeared in numerous journals and anthologies.

Troy Sheffield, a former professional competitor in international extreme in-line skating events, graduated summa cum laude from Central Connecticut State University with a B.A. in English with a minor in philosophy. Troy went on to receive his master's in education and a teaching certificate through the University of Connecticut. Troy now teaches seventh grade integrated language arts at McGee Middle School in Berlin, Connecticut.

Madeline C. Smith is professor of English at California University of Pennsylvania and the author of articles and book reviews in a number of fields. As coauthor she has produced some 20 articles and four books about Eugene O'Neill, including *Eugene*

O'Neill in Court (1993), *Eugene O'Neill: An Annotated International Bibliography, 1973 through 1999* (2001), and *Eugene O'Neill: Production Personnel* (2005).

David White served for three seasons as the literary manager and director of educational outreach at the Eugene O'Neill Theatre Center. He is currently the artistic director of WordBRIDGE Playwrights Laboratory and an assistant professor in the department of theater at Towson University in Baltimore.

Beth Wynstra is a doctoral candidate in theater at the University of California, Santa Barbara. Her dissertation, "Rhetoric and the Birth of the Modern American Political Theater," applies Aristotelian notions of rhetoric to 20th-century political performance. Ms. Wynstra authored *Always, Gene,* a one-act play produced at the 2002 Eugene O'Neill Festival that explores the connections between the women in Eugene O'Neill's life and the female characters in his plays. Beth holds an M.A. in English and comparative literature from the University of California, Irvine, and has taught acting, directing, theater history, playwriting, and public speaking. In 2008 Wynstra won the Outstanding Teaching Assistant Award from the Academic Senate at the University of California, Santa Barbara.

INDEX